Psychotherapist's Casebook

Theory and Technique
in the Practice
of Modern Therapies

Irwin L. Kutash

Alexander Wolf

Editors

Foreword by Jerome Frank

Psychotherapist's Casebook

Jossey-Bass Publishers

San Francisco • London • 1986

PSYCHOTHERAPIST'S CASEBOOK
Theory and Technique in the Practice of Modern Therapies
by Irwin L. Kutash and Alexander Wolf, Editors

Copyright © 1986 by: Jossey-Bass Inc., Publishers
433 California Street
San Francisco, California 94104
&
Jossey-Bass Limited
28 Banner Street
London EC1Y 8QE

Library of Congress Cataloging-in-Publication Data

Psychotherapist's casebook.

(The Jossey-Bass social and behavioral science series)
Bibliography: p. 509
Includes indexes.
1. Psychotherapy. 2. Psychoanalysis. I. Kutash,
Irwin L. II. Wolf, Alexander (date). [DNLM: 1. Psy-
choanalysis—methods. 2. Psychotherapy—methods.
WM 420 P9749]
RC480.P823 1986   616.89′14   85-45907
ISBN 0-87589-685-5 (alk. paper)

Manufactured in the United States of America

The paper in this book meets the guidelines for
permanence and durability of the Committee on
Production Guidelines for Book Longevity of the
Council on Library Resources.

JACKET DESIGN BY WILLI BAUM

FIRST EDITION

Code 8601

The Jossey-Bass
Social and Behavioral Science Series

Foreword ❧

Irwin L. Kutash and Alexander Wolf have done a monumental job of securing so many excellent contributions with such a high level of clarity. This compendium well conveys the state of the art of psychotherapy in the United States toward the end of the twentieth century. Almost all major current forms of psychotherapy are represented. Each presentation consists primarily of an example of the therapy in question introduced by or interwoven with a brief exposition of its underlying theoretical orientation. All the presentations are competent and many are outstanding. The overall impression conveyed by this collection is that psychotherapy is a lively, variegated enterprise conducted by persons with a wide range of training and personalities, who all are enthusiastic about their work.

At first glance the differences between the various therapies are wide and, in some cases, apparently unbridgeable. These differences may be exaggerated by the way in which the therapies and patients are presented. Each therapist emphasizes those concepts and procedures that distinguish his or her form of therapy from the others. Since patients consciously or unconsciously comply with the therapist's expectations, they produce case histories that accentuate these distinctions. Thus some therapists see themselves as investigators helping patients to unearth past traumatic events and relate them to current difficulties, and the case histories of their patients are essentially life stories. Other therapists see themselves as teachers or trainers providing methods by means of which patients can learn to overcome certain specific symptoms, such as bulimia or sexual impotence. Accordingly, their case histories explore cause-and-effect ties between immediate environmental influences and behavior, with especial emphasis on monitoring the patient's ability to carry out certain therapeutic assignments. Other therapists seek to develop a totally open, nondefensive personal encounter with the patient, and their case histories focus on detailed accounts of the emotional vicissitudes of the therapeutic relationship.

The range of criteria for outcome of therapy is almost as wide as the range of therapeutic procedures. Behaviorally oriented therapists judge outcome in terms of objective, quantifiable criteria such as patients' reports of having solved certain problems or overcome certain maladaptive behaviors. At the other extreme, therapists who regard the therapeutic encounter itself as the essence of therapy evaluate outcome in terms of unquantifiable subjective criteria such as increased access to internal states or enhanced sense of self-fulfillment. In any case, despite these apparent side differences in methods of therapy and criteria of success, there is no reason to doubt that all the therapies and therapists represented in this volume are effective with some patients.

What is one to make of this? No medical illness would respond to such a wide range of therapies. Is psychotherapy a cure for which there is no disease?

A plausible explanation for this strange state of affairs is that patients who come to psychotherapy, regardless of their specific complaints, all suffer from the negative meanings they attach to their life experiences and their symptoms, and that all forms of psychotherapy share certain components that enable their patients to alter these meanings in a favorable direction. All help patients to counteract feelings of despair, fear, guilt, and the like with hope, heightened self-confidence, and similar positive emotions and attitudes.

All therapies facilitate these transformations of meanings through certain features that all share. One of these features is the patients' perception of the therapist both as an expert and as a prestigious member of the larger society. As a result, the therapist's acceptance of the patient for treatment in itself inspires the patient's hopes for relief and combats demoralizing feelings of isolation.

Another therapeutic feature that one can surmise to be shared by all therapies, even though it may not be explicitly stated, is that all arouse patients emotionally. Emotional arousal, which seems to be prerequisite to changes in behavior and attitudes, is most apparent in some of the group therapies, but it is implicit in even the most task-oriented objective therapies. Since the therapist's prescriptions inevitably require the patient to abandon old ways of thinking, behaving, and feeling for new untried ones, these therapies also are bound to arouse patients emotionally.

The therapeutic tool of all therapies is symbolic communication, conveyed primarily by words but in some therapies also involving meaningful activities or exercises. So in the last analysis the effectiveness of all therapies rests on the therapist's communication skills. Basic to the success of all therapies is the therapist's ability to convey his or her understanding of the patient's problems or feelings as well as total commitment to the patient's welfare. These are the essential components of the therapeutic alliance, on which the success of all therapeutic encounters ultimately depends.

This book reveals the current state of the art of psychotherapy by what it omits as much as by what it includes. Although they do not make unwarranted claims for their particular methods, all therapists report only successes; nor do they describe, except by implication, which patients are most suitable or unsuitable for their particular procedures. The criteria of outcome for all are stated in terms of the theory of that particular therapy so that the outcomes reported by one school cannot be compared with those of another. All therapists emphasize those aspects of their treatments that distinguish them from others, leaving open the question of what unstated features of each might also account for some of their successes. Issues like these are objects of continuing research, and some encouraging progress is being made in elucidating them. The task now is to develop information about interactions between the patient's personality and symptoms and the therapist's personality and mode of therapy that will eventually enable informed choices for matching patients with therapists and therapeutic procedures.

This book is highly recommended to experienced clinicians and beginners alike, as well as all others who seek to familiarize themselves with the current state of the art of psychotherapy in the United States today. It is an authoritative, well-presented overview of representative psychotherapies. It will be especially helpful to persons thinking of becoming psychotherapists. Everyone will find some of the therapies congenial and others unacceptable. The therapist can freely choose the approach or combination of approaches that is most personally congenial, confident that whatever the procedure—if through it the therapist conveys serious interest in the patient's welfare, enhances the patient's hopes of benefit, and strengthens the sense of self-efficacy—the procedure in all probability will be beneficial. This skillfully edited compilation of accounts by leading practitioners of the major schools of psychotherapy is a truly outstanding contribution to the field, and I hope this book receives the wide level of attention it deserves.

March 1986

Jerome D. Frank
*Professor Emeritus
of Psychiatry
Johns Hopkins University
Medical School*

To James S. Simkin,
who died while completing his chapter
on Gestalt therapy. Simkin was a pioneer
in the Gestalt therapy field. His book,
Gestalt Therapy Mini Lectures, *is part*
of his legacy as an author, teacher,
and practitioner.

Preface ✤

Extensive reflection and knowledge without much experience resembles
one of those editions with two lines of text on a page and forty lines
of commentary. Extensive experience without much reflection and
knowledge is like an edition without notes which is often unintelligible.

Schopenhauer, ''Councils and Maxims''
Paraga and Paralipomena, 1851

    The array of theories and techniques of psychotherapy in use today is vast
indeed, but the entire spectrum is rarely accessible to practitioners. Instead, most
psychotherapists are trained in one particular school of thought and have just a
smattering of knowledge (usually of a theoretical nature) about a few others. Traditionally, psychotherapy practitioners doggedly hold on to their own orientations,
even though they have little basis for comparing them with other approaches. This
book is a step toward broadening the therapist's knowledge of what is being done
by reputable clinicians from all major schools of thought. *Psychotherapist's Casebook*
is intended to demonstrate, through annotated case histories, the major therapy
techniques in present use.

    In the literature of psychotherapy, descriptions of the theoretical underpin-
nings of most major therapy systems as well as discussions of technique are plen-
tiful. What has been missing has been a clear presentation of how these theories
and techniques translate into actual practice. The resulting gap between thoughts
on why therapy should be done a certain way or how a certain technique should
be applied and what actually happens in a therapeutic session leaves many practitioners, teachers, and researchers of psychotherapy at a loss. *Psychotherapist's Casebook*
is intended to bridge this gap. It is a unique view through the keyhole into the offices
of therapists of every stripe and persuasion, and we believe it provides a true view
of what goes on in those offices. We hope the cases in this book will serve to show
therapists the variety of approaches in use, demonstrate how they work, and stimulate
all of us to expand constricted ways of practicing, to increase enlightened evaluation of ourselves and others, and generally to become more open-minded in our
appraisals of what works or does not work in practice.

    We have followed a loosely prescribed format in presenting the therapies described in this book. For each approach, theory and technique are presented in terms of how they translate into practice. We asked each contributor to devote approximately 25 percent of his or her chapter to theory and technique and 75 percent to translation; that is, to a description of the theory or technique in use with a real patient, whose anonymity is protected but whose essence is captured in a case presentation.

The casebook is intended as a resource that psychotherapists of every school can use to explore the field. We hope it will raise questions, such as: Is my form of therapy applicable to all clients or should clients be matched to techniques that might be more effective with their personalities or types of problems or disorders? Does my systems approach take all the systems into account? Does my approach take the personality of the therapist into account? Do clients need to "live through" as well as "work through" their conflicts?

Specifically, we intend this book for psychotherapists of every school— psychologists, psychiatrists, social workers, counselors, and nurse practitioners— as well as students and teachers.

In order to make this book as comprehensive as possible yet keep it manageable in scope, we have tried to select the most widely accepted and applied forms of therapy in use today. We divided them into six categories: psychoanalytic/psychodynamic therapies, neo-Freudian and non-Freudian analytic therapies, humanistic psychology, behavioral/directive therapies, group therapies, and family system/marital therapies. Our aim was to portray the major forms of therapy that are representative of each of these general categories. For example, it was obviously impossible to include every individual group, family, or marital approach practiced, but we hope the examples we have selected cover the range of therapies in that category. While the inclusion of some additional techniques could hardly be argued, space limitations caused us to be extremely selective. We believe that the examples we have included are essential to achieving our goal of creating a handbook that would allow readers to compare and contrast and come to their own conclusions about schools of therapy and how effective they are, as well as help provide an answer to the question "which technique will work for me?"

The contributors to this book were selected because they are experts who either originated or helped to develop the techniques they describe and demonstrate. Among the innovators who have contributed to this work are Carl Rogers (client-centered psychotherapy), Albert Ellis (rational-emotive psychotherapy), and Alexander Wolf (psychoanalysis in groups). All are individuals with years of experience in the techniques they illustrate. This close association of the authors with their topics means that the cases in this book are truly representative of forms of therapy; it may also explain the zeal and faith these authors express about their methods. All of them firmly believe in what they do and would like the reader to believe it, too. Thus readers need to consider each presentation, make comparisons, and draw conclusions as to questions such as: Who is right? Are they all right? All wrong? Are they right for certain clients only? Can any of those techniques be integrated? Should some be discarded? Can some be expanded on or further evolved? Are any antiquated? And so on. In a sense, this book opens a curtain that is rarely drawn. We hope that what readers find here will serve to further them as therapists who know not just one school but the breadth of the field.

One crucial question that arose from our reading the manuscript is are there common curative factors across therapy techniques? Reading through the divergent orientations led us to these conclusions: (1) In all approaches, the psychological issues of the client constitute, in one way or another, the main focus. (2) In each, an interaction occurs between people. (3) Each therapist of whatever school has special skills in listening, responding, or communicating. (4) The therapists from each orientation have professional status (that is, a diploma). And (5) each specific technique is based on a theory. Another question that we asked is are there unique curative factors? The analytic techniques and derivatives bring the psychosphere into the therapy office with their utilization of transference, and distinction between and utilization of both reality and fantasy. The humanistic techniques search for meaning in each individual. The family and some group approaches deal with curing systems, not problems based on individual dynamics. The behavioral approaches have a clarity of focus and goals, with experimentally validated procedures, and they work on the assumption that behavior is learned. We hope that readers will pose many more questions and find their answers as well as add to our conclusions in the course of using this book.

By way of acknowledgments, we would like to commend the contributors for their courage and conviction in being willing and able to "put their work where their theory was": to open the curtain, to reveal what really occurs behind their closed doors, and to let others peruse their sessions.

We are moved and stimulated by the diversity of therapeutic means we have been able to assemble. We are convinced that each contributor sees his treatment approach as his most valuable method up to the present. We admire, respect, and are inspired by their dedicated commitment to showing us their ways. We enjoy the challenge they present to our own views of treatment. They are breaking barriers, and this volume is our attempt to let their messages reach broader audiences.

We believe that there is no merit in maintaining a dignified abstention in which we proclaim the highest efficacy only for our own brand of psychotherapy. We do not believe anything is furthered by a claim of the purity of one set of interventions. We have not asked our contributors to agree among themselves or with us, but to earnestly, directly, and earthily tell us what they do and why. We praise their views, their changing means, and the liveliness of what they tell us. For these are the methods that surely play a part in helping their patients toward recovery.

The contributors to this book have focused creatively on the new, relied on the traditional yet departed from it, and given us powerful models and styles to emulate and build upon. In their cumulative work they can make an impact on our intellect and professional growth. In the variety of their theories and techniques they have opened new paths for us to follow. We wish to express our gratitude to them for their courage and for their persistence in finding new ways to attain success for themselves and their clients.

As in two earlier volumes we have been associated with, *Violence: Perspectives on Murder and Aggression* and *Handbook on Stress and Anxiety: Contemporary Knowledge, Theory, and Treatment*, we endorse controversy over premature eclecticism. We hope that if this book makes clearer what each technique is and what its practitioners do, readers will be able to form their own opinions, develop their own techniques, and research their ideas in their own work. This is our ultimate hope because of the benefit it would undoubtedly provide to the millions of people who are in therapy now and who will begin in the near future.

March 1986   Irwin L. Kutash
                                                    Livingston, New Jersey

                                                    Alexander Wolf
                                                    New York City

Contents ❦

Contents

The Editors ℰ𝓈

IRWIN L. KUTASH is in the private practice of psychotherapy and psychoanalysis in Livingston and Maplewood, New Jersey. He is a clinical associate professor of mental health sciences at the New Jersey College of Medicine and Dentistry. He is a senior supervisor, training psychoanalyst, and a faculty member of the New York Center for Psychoanalytic Training and the Institute for Psychoanalysis and Psychotherapy of New Jersey. He is also a field supervisor at the Graduate School of Applied and Professional Psychology of Rutgers University and a psychological consultant to the New Jersey Department of Institutions and Agencies. Kutash received his Ph.D. degree (1972) in clinical psychology from the Institute of Advanced Psychological Studies of Adelphi University and holds a postdoctoral certificate in psychotherapy and psychoanalysis from the postgraduate Center for Mental Health, where he received a ten-year service award (1982). He also holds a diplomate in clinical psychology from the American Board of Professional Psychology.

Kutash has served as president of the Society of Psychologists in Private Practice in New Jersey and as a board member of the New Jersey Association for the Advancement of Psychology. He is past chairman of the Mental Health Advisory Council to the Regional Mental Health Board and was a member of a presidential task force on employee assistance programs under the Carter administration.

Kutash is currently president of the New Jersey Academy of Psychology and serves on the board of the New Jersey Psychological Association.

Kutash has written extensively on the topics of violence and victimology and anxiety. He originated the equilibrium-disequilibrium theory of stress-induced anxiety and, with L. B. Schlesinger, co-developed the criminal fantasy technique, a psychological test of criminal psychopathology. He is the author of many book chapters and articles on psychoanalysis in groups and on di-egophrenia, including the section on anxiety and victimology in the *Encyclopedia of Psychology*, edited by Raymond Corsini, and collaborated with Alexander Wolf and Irving Goldberg on the book *Psychoanalysis in Groups: The Primacy of the Individual*. Kutash is editor and contributing author of the books *Violence: Perspectives on Murder and Aggression*, with S. B. Kutash and L. B. Schlesinger, and the *Handbook on Stress and Anxiety: Contemporary Knowledge, Theory, and Treatment*, with L. B. Schlesinger. In the spring of 1981, the latter was the main selection of the Behavioral Science Book Club.

ALEXANDER WOLF is in the private practice of psychotherapy and psycho-analysis in New York City. He is a senior supervisor, training psychoanalyst, and a faculty member of the Postgraduate Center for Mental Health and the New York Center for Psychoanalytic Training. He was for twenty-five years an associate clinical professor of psychiatry at the New York Medical College and a training analyst, supervisor, and faculty member in the psychoanalytic division there. He received his M.D. degree (1932) from Cornell University Medical College.

Wolf and E. K. Schwartz were awarded the First Annual Mildred Burgum Award by the Professional Association of the Postgraduate Center for Mental Health for their publication of "The Quest for Certainty" in 1956.

Wolf received the Adolph Meyer Award in 1957 from the Association for Improvement in Mental Health "for his contributions to psychoanalysis in groups" and in 1963, the first Wilfred C. Hulse Memorial Award for outstanding contribu-tions to group therapy from the Eastern Group Psychotherapy Society. He delivered the twenty-eighth annual Karen Horney Lecture in 1980 on di-egophrenia and genius, on behalf of the Association for the Advancement of Psychoanalysis. He was awarded Distinguished Fellowship in the American Group Psychotherapy Association in 1983 and received the Distinguished Writers Award of the New York Center for Psychoanalytic Training in 1985.

Wolf instituted the practice of psychoanalysis in groups in 1938. In 1956 he originated the concept of di-egophrenia, the name he gave to a disorder that he discovered many persons of genius suffer from. As a result, he has been study-ing di-egophrenics and genius for some years.

In 1975, Wolf was honored by his professional colleagues in the publication *The Leader in the Group* (edited by Z. A. Liff) for his thirty-five years of teaching, supervising, writing, and clinical practice (a series of chapters containing selected writings of Wolf's on the leader in the group as well as contributions by distinguished psychoanalysts are included in the book).

Wolf has published 113 papers in neurology, psychiatry, psychoanalysis, and psychoanalysis in groups, and he is at present engaged in writing a volume on di-egophrenia with Irwin L. Kutash.

Wolf is the author of *Psychoanalysis in Groups*, with E. K. Schwartz; *Beyond the Couch*, with E. K. Schwartz, I. Goldberg, and G. McCarty; and *Psychoanalysis in Groups: The Primacy of the Individual*, with I. L. Kutash and I. Goldberg.

Contributors ❧

HAROLD P. BLUM is clinical professor of psychiatry at New York University where he is a training and supervising analyst at the Psychoanalytic Institute. He is also the director of the Sigmund Freud Archives. Blum received his M.D. degree (1953) from the Boston University School of Medicine. He is a former editor of the *Journal of the American Psychoanalytic Association*, author of *Psychoanalytic Explorations of Technical Discourse on the Theory of Therapy*, and editor of *Female Psychology*.

LOIS BRIEN is a Gestalt therapist in private practice in the San Diego area and is adjunct faculty at both San Diego State University and National University. She received her Ph.D. degree (1959) in speech and hearing pathology from the University of Iowa. She is a founding and training member of the Institute for the Study and Practice of Gestalt Therapy, San Diego. Brien is a former member of the Gestalt Institute of San Francisco and was a long-time faculty member of the California School of Professional Psychology in Berkeley, California. She is coauthor of several chapters on Gestalt therapy (with C. Sheldon and E. Kepner) and was an early student of Frederick S. Perls and James S. Simkin.

JACQUELINE S. BROCKWAY maintains a private practice in clinical and counseling psychology in Portland, Oregon, having recently retired from the Veterans Administration Medical Center in White City, Oregon. She received her Ph.D. degree (1974) in counseling psychology from the University of Oregon. She formerly served as a clinical psychologist and chief of the day treatment program at the Veterans Administration out-patient clinic in Honolulu.

JAMES F. T. BUGENTAL is director of Inter/Logue, a training and service center for existential-humanistic psychotherapy in Santa Rosa, California. He is a member of the Adjunct Faculty of the Saybrook Institute and the Clinical Faculty of the Stanford Medical School. Bugental is a past president of the (American) Association for Humanistic Psychology (1962–1963), and of the California State Psychological Association (1960–1961). He received his Ph.D. degree (1948) from Ohio State University in psychology. He is author of the books *The Search for Authenticity: An Existential-Analytic Approach to Psychotherapy*, *The Search for Existential Identity: Patient-Therapist Dialogues in Humanistic Psychotherapy*, and *Psychotherapy and Process: The Fundamentals of an Existential-Humanistic Approach*.

JOHN M. DUSAY is an associate clinical professor at the University of California School of Medicine in San Francisco. He also maintains a psychiatric private practice in San Francisco. He received his M.D. degree (1961) from the University of Kansas School of Medicine. Dusay is a cofounder and the past president (1972–1975) of the International Transactional Analysis Association and is the recipient of the Eric Berne Scientific Award (1973) for "Egograms and the Constancy Hypothesis." Dusay's publications include *Egograms: How I See You and You See Me*, "Transactional Analysis in Groups" in the *Comprehensive Group Psychotherapy*, "Eric Berne" in *Comprehensive Textbook of Psychiatry* (2nd and 3rd eds.), "Transactional Analysis in Counseling" in *Counseling and Psychotherapy*, and "Transactional Analysis" in *Current Psychotherapies*.

ALBERT ELLIS is executive director of the Institute for Rational-Emotive Therapy in New York. He has received the 1985 American Psychological Association Award for Distinguished Professional Contributions to Knowledge. Ellis received his Ph.D. degree (1947) in clinical psychology from Columbia University. He has published over 500 articles and 49 books and monographs, including *Reason and Emotion in Psychotherapy*, *A New Guide to Rational Living*, and *Overcoming Resistance: Rational-Emotive Therapy with Difficult Clients*.

JAMES L. FRAMO is Distinguished Professor in the School of Human Behavior at the United States International University in San Diego, California. He received his Ph.D. Degree (1953) from the University of Texas. He is the founding member and past president of the American Family Therapy Association (AFTA). In 1984 he was the recipient of AFTA's Distinguished Achievement in Family Therapy Award. His books include *Intensive Family Therapy*, *Family Interaction: A Dialogue Between Family Researchers and Family Therapists*; *Family Therapy: Major Contributions*, and *Explorations in Marital and Family Therapy: Selected Papers of James L. Framo*.

GEORGE FULLER-VON BOZZAY is a founder and clinical director of the Biofeedback Institute of San Francisco; associate clinical professor in the Department of Biological Dysfunction, University of California Medical Center, San Francisco; clinical instructor in psychiatry and behavioral sciences at the Stanford University School of Medicine (1978–1984); and on the psychology faculty in the Behavioral Sciences Department of City College of San Francisco. He received his Ph.D. degree (1967) in clinical psychology from the University of Massachusetts. Fuller-von Bozzay's publications include *Biofeedback: Methods and Procedures in Clinical Practice*, *Behavioral Medicine*, *Stress Management and Biofeedback: A Clinician's Desk Reference*, and *Projects in Biofeedback: A Text/Workbook*.

IRA A. GREENBERG is a clinical psychologist and hypnotherapist in private practice in West Los Angeles and is employed part-time at Camarillo State Hospital, where he directs weekly televised psychodrama sessions and leads hypnotherapy groups. He is founder and executive director of the Behavioral Studies Institute, which conducts management consultations, the Psychodrama Center for Los Angeles, and the Group Hypnosis Center in Los Angeles. He received his Ph.D. degree (1967) from Claremont Graduate School in psychology. Among the books Greenberg has written are *Psychodrama and Audience Attitude Change*, *Psychodrama: Theory and Therapy*, and *Group Hypnotherapy and Hypnodrama*.

JEFFREY C. GREENBERG maintains a private practice in psychotherapy and psychoanalysis in Livingston, New Jersey. He is a trustee and member of the Executive Board of the New Jersey Academy of Psychology. He received his Ph.D. degree (1982) in school psychology from the University of Georgia. Currently, he is furthering his training through the New York Center for Psychoanalytic Training. Formerly, Greenberg was staff psychologist at the Essex County Guidance Center in New Jersey. He has completed research on organization and its application to cognition/emotion and personality and is currently working in the area of object relations theory and development processes and their application to diagnosis and clinical practice as well as di-egophrenia.

HERBERT HOLT is the dean of the Westchester Institute, director of the New York Institute of Existential Analysis, and medical director of the Cathedral Counseling Service, Cathedral Church of Saint John the Divine in New York City. He is the founding president of the Association for Applied Psychoanalysis and president of the American Society for Existential Psychiatry. He is author of *Free to Be Good or Bad*, a contributing author to *Comprehensive Handbook of Psychiatry* (2nd ed.), and editor of *Journal of Modern Psychotherapy*.

LEONARD HORWITZ is chief of clinical psychology at the Menninger Foundation and is a training and supervising analyst with the Topeka Institute for Psychoanalysis. He received his Ph.D. degree (1951) in psychology from New York University. He was graduated from the Topeka Institute for Psychoanalysis in 1970. Horwitz was among the founders of the group psychotherapy program at the Menninger Foundation and served as the director of that service between 1969 and 1978. He has been active nationally with the American Group Psychotherapy Association (AGPA) and has served as program chairman, treasurer, and member of the board of directors. Currently he is president of AGPA. He is the author of *Clinical Predictions in Psychotherapy*.

DOUGLAS H. INGRAM is training and supervising psychoanalyst at the Psychoanalytic Division, Department of Psychiatry, New York Medical College and at the American Institute for Psychoanalysis of the Karen Horney Psychoanalytic Institute and Center. He received his M.D. degree (1968) from New York University School of Medicine. Ingram completed his analytic training at the Karen Horney Institute in New York City. From 1979 to 1983 he served as medical director of the Karen Horney Clinic. Ingram's writings are mainly concerned with the clinical application of Karen Horney's theory of personality and psychoanalytic treatment.

DAVID S. JANOWSKY has been an associate professor of psychiatry at Vanderbilt University, a professor of psychiatry at the University of California, San Diego, and also the director of that department's Affective Disorders Mental Health Clinical Research Center, which is sponsored by the National Institute of Mental Health. Beginning in 1986, he assumes the Chairmanship of Psychiatry at the University of North Carolina in Chapel Hill. He received his M.D. degree (1964) from the University of California at San Francisco. In 1981, he was cited in Pekkanem's *Best Doctors in the U.S.* He is a member of the editorial board of the *Journal of Clinical Psychopharmacology* and the *Journal of Clinical Psychiatry* and is the author of more than 200 articles and more than 100 book chapters on affective disorders and psychopharmacology.

JULIE M. KUEHNEL is a clinical psychologist in Camarillo, California, an assistant professor of psychology at California Lutheran College, and an assistant research psychologist with the University of California at Los Angeles. She received her Ph.D. degree (1975) in counseling psychology from the University of Texas at Austin. She is coauthor of the *Handbook of Marital Therapy* (with R. P. Liberman).

ROBERT PAUL LIBERMAN is a professor of psychiatry in the University of California at Los Angeles School of Medicine. He is chief of the Rehabilitation Medicine Service at the Brentwood Medical Center and is director of the Clinical Research Unit at Camarillo State Hospital. Liberman received his M.D. degree (1963) from the Johns Hopkins University School of Medicine. Among the books he has written are *Personal Effectiveness: Guiding People to Assert Their Feelings and Improve Their Social Skills* and *Handbook of Marital Therapy*.

GRETCHEN K. LOBITZ is a clinical and consulting psychologist in private practice in Denver, Colorado. She received her Ph.D. degree (1974) from the University of Oregon in clinical psychology. Prior to establishing her own practice, she taught at the University of Denver and Colorado Women's College. Her primary professional activities have been in the treatment of marital and sexual disorders and in women's issues, particularly infertility. In 1985, she received the Ellis Graham Colorado Distinguished Psychologist Award.

W. CHARLES LOBITZ is a clinical and consulting psychologist in private practice in Denver, Colorado, and is a clinical associate professor of psychology at the University of Colorado Medical School. He received his Ph.D. degree (1974) from the University of Oregon in clinical psychology. He is past president of the Colorado Association for Sex Therapy, and in 1985, he received the Ellis Graham Colorado Distinguished Psychologist Award. He has done research and published in the area of marital and sexual therapy, stress management, and sports psychology. His most recent book is *Skiing Out of Your Mind: The Psychology of Peak Performance*.

JOSEPH LOPICCOLO is professor of psychology and psychiatry at Texas A&M University, where he is also director of the Program for Clinical Studies. He established and directed the Sex Therapy Center at the State University of New York at Stony Brook from 1974 to 1984. LoPiccolo received his Ph.D. degree (1969) in clinical psychology from Yale University. LoPiccolo has published more than fifty journal articles in the area of sexual dysfunction. He is also the author of two books: *Becoming Orgasmic: A Sexual Growth Program for Women* (with J. Heiman and L. LoPiccolo), and the *Handbook of Sex Therapy*.

MALCOLM J. MARKS is a member of the Professional Advisory Board of the New York School for Psychoanalytic Psychotherapy and a faculty member and training analyst at the New Jersey Division of the New York Center for Psychoanalytic Training. He received his Ed.D. degree (1957) from the Department of Psychological Foundations at Columbia University. He is author of "Normal and Pathological Narcissism in Relation to the Vicissitudes of Identity Formation: A Clinical Application of the Work of Edith Jacobson," in *Current Issues in Psychoanalytic Practice* (edited by H. Strean).

MARY ANN MATTOON is a Jungian analyst in private practice in Minneapolis, Minnesota. She received her Ph.D. degree (1970) from the University of Minnesota in psychology. She is also a diplomate (1965) of the C. G. Jung Institute, Zurich, Switzerland. Mattoon teaches courses in Jungian psychology at the University of Minnesota. Her published works include two books, *Understanding Dreams* and *Jungian Psychology in Perspective*.

ELIZABETH E. MINTZ is in private practice in Westchester and Manhattan, New York. She received her Ph.D. degree (1956) in clinical psychology from New York University and trained as a psychoanalyst at the National Psychological Association for Psychoanalysis. Mintz's books include *Marathon Groups: Reality and Symbol* and *The Psychic Thread: Paranormal and Transpersonal Aspects of Psychotherapy*.

STEPHEN A. MITCHELL is a supervising analyst and on the faculties at the William Alanson White Institute and the New York University Postdoctoral Program in Psychoanalysis and Psychotherapy. He received his Ph.D. degree (1972) from New York University in clinical psychology and his psychoanalytic certificate (1977) from the William Alanson White Institute. He is coauthor (with Jay Greenberg) of *Object Relations in Psychoanalytic Theory*.

JOHN J. O'CONNOR is supervising psychologist at Unified Services for Children and Adolescents in Troy, New York. He is also assistant clinical professor in the Department of Pediatrics at Albany Medical College and child psychologist on the staff at Saint Mary's Hospital in Troy, New York. He maintains a private practice in Delmar, New York. He also provides family therapy consultation to Berkshire Mental Health Center in Pittsfield, Massachusetts. He received his Ph.D. degree (1974) in counseling psychology from the State University of New York at Albany. He has published a number of papers on the topic of brief strategic treatment.

LOUIS R. ORMONT is clinical professor of psychology at the Postgraduate Institute for Psychotherapy, Department of Psychology, Adelphi University. He received his Ph.D. degree (1960) from Columbia University in psychology. He has written extensively on the resistance phenomenon in group psychoanalysis and conjoint treatment. His books include *The Practice of Conjoint Treatment* and *The Talking Cure*.

M. JOAN ORMONT is on the faculties of the Philadelphia School of Psychoanalysis and the Mid Manhattan Institute for Psychoanalysis. She has been a conjoint therapist with her husband, Louis R. Ormont, for eighteen years. She received her Ph.D. degree (1978) in psychoanalysis from Heed University in Florida. An article she wrote on the family life of psychoanalysts was published by the New York Times Magazine.

DOROTHY E. PEVEN is a clinical social worker in private practice in the Chicago area and a member of the faculty of the Alfred Adler Institute of Chicago, where she serves as lecturer, training analyst, and practicum supervisor. She received her M.S.W. degree (1969) from Jane Addams Graduate School of Social Work, University of Illinois, and her certification in psychotherapy (1972) from the Alfred

Adler Institute of Chicago. Peven's publications include "Current Role Confusion Among Young Women from the Viewpoint of Adler's Psychology," (with B. H. Shulman), and "Adlerian Psychotherapy," in *Psychotherapy Handbook* (edited by R. Herink).

CARL R. ROGERS is a resident fellow at the Center for Studies of the Person in La Jolla, California. He received his Ph.D. degree (1931) in clinical psychology from Columbia University. He has been president of the American Psychological Association and the American Academy of Psychotherapists. He has received both the Distinguished Scientific Contribution Award and the First Distinguished Professional Contribution Award from the American Psychological Association, and is the only psychologist to be thus doubly honored. He is the originator of the form of psychotherapy that has been known as nondirective, client-centered, and, more recently, person-centered. He has written a dozen books—the best known being *On Becoming a Person*—and scores of articles. His three most recent books are *Carl Rogers on Personal Power*, *A Way of Being*, and *Freedom to Learn*.

CLIFFORD J. SAGER is clinical professor of psychiatry at New York Hospital-Cornell Medical College (Payne Whitney Clinic) and director of family psychiatry at New York's Jewish Board of Family and Children's Services, where he also directs the Sex Therapy and Remarried Consultation Services. Sager received his M.D. degree (1941) from The New York University School of Medicine. He is past president of the Society for Sex Therapy and Research, American Group Psychotherapy Association, and the Society of Medical Psychoanalysts. Sager has been the recipient of awards from both the American Association for Marriage and Family Therapy and the American Family Therapy Association for distinguished contributions to family therapy. He is author of several books, including *Treating the Remarried Family*, *Intimate Partners*, *Marriage Contracts and Couple Therapy*, and coeditor of *Progress in Group and Family Therapy* (with H. S. Kaplan) and *Black Ghetto Family in Therapy* (with T. Brayboy and B. Waxenberg). He is also coeditor of the *Journal of Sex and Marital Therapy* (with H. S. Kaplan and R. Schiavi).

WILL SCHUTZ is president of Will Schutz Associates, an organization that does organizational consulting and produces psychological and organizational instruments. Schutz received his Ph.D. degree (1951) from UCLA in psychology. He has been a central figure in the human potential movement for twenty years. Schutz's books include *FIRO (The Interpersonal Underworld)*, *Joy*, *Here Comes Everybody*, *Elements of Encounter*, *Body Fantasy*, *Leaders of Schools*, *Profound Simplicity*, and *The Truth Option*.

CYNTHIA SHELDON is cofounder and current president of the Gestalt Institute of San Francisco. She received her MSW degree (1962) from the University of California at Berkeley in clinical social work. Sheldon's articles include "Women and Gestalt Awareness" (with L. Brien in *Gestalt Awareness* (edited by T. Downing), and "Gestalt Therapy and Women" (with L. Brien) in *Psychotherapy for Women* (edited by E. Rawling and D. Carter).

BERNARD H. SHULMAN is chairman of the Department of Psychiatry at Saint Joseph's Hospital in Chicago and clinical professor of psychiatry at North-western University Medical School. He was president of the International Association for Individual Psychology from 1970 to 1982. Schulman received his M.D. degree (1946) from the Chicago Medical School, University of Health Sciences, and completed psychoanalytic training at the Alfred Adler Institute, Chicago (1951). He is the author of *Essays on Schizophrenia* and coauthor (with R. Forgus) of *Personality, A Cognitive View*.

ANNE NECHAMA SIMKIN was wife of and psychological assistant to the late James S. Simkin of the Simkin Training Center in Gestalt Therapy at Big Sur, California. She received her M.A. degree (1979) from Antioch University West in psychology, and received certificates of completion in training programs in the principles and methods of Gestalt therapy at the Gestalt Training Center, San Diego (1977), and at the Simkin Training Center in Gestalt Therapy (1984). She is author of the articles "I Sang My Mother a Lullaby" and "The Simkin Training Center in Gestalt Therapy: How It Was for Me" in *Voices: The Journal of the American Academy of Psychoanalysis*.

JAMES S. SIMKIN was coleader with Frederick S. Perls of Gestalt therapy training workshops for professional psychotherapists at the Esalen Institute from 1964 to 1969. He received his Ph.D. degree (1951) in clinical psychology from the University of Michigan. He took his postdoctoral training in Gestalt therapy at the New York Institute of Gestalt Therapy between 1952 and 1955. In 1956 he began his private practice of psychotherapy, and from 1972 until his death in 1985 he trained licensed psychotherapists at the Simkin Training Center in Gestalt Therapy in Big Sur, California. In addition to many articles and chapters on Gestalt therapy, he produced a Gestalt therapy training film, "In the Now," and the book *Gestalt Therapy Mini Lectures*.

DAPHNE D. SOCARIDES is a postdoctoral fellow in clinical psychology at Cedars-Sinai Medical Center in Los Angeles, California. She received her Ph.D. degree (1985) in clinical psychology from the Graduate School of Psychology, Albert Einstein College of Medicine, Yeshiva University, in New York City. She is coauthor, with Robert D. Stolorow, of "Affects and Selfobjects," published in the 1984/1985 edition of the *Annual of Psychoanalysis*.

ROBERT D. STOLOROW is a psychoanalyst in private practice in Los Angeles, California, and member of the Southern California Psychoanalytic Society. He received his Ph.D. degree (1970) in clinical psychology from Harvard University. He is coauthor of three books: *Faces in a Cloud: Subjectivity in Personality Theory* (with George Atwood), *Psychoanalysis of Developmental Arrests: Theory and Treatment* (with Frank Lachmann), and *Structures of Subjectivity: Explorations in Psychoanalytic Phenomenology* (with George Atwood).

JOAN K. TAYLOR is cofounder and former director of the New Jersey Center for Family Studies, a training institute for family therapists. She continues to be active in teaching at the Center and maintains a private practice in Chatham, New Jersey. She received her Ph.D. degree (1958) in clinical psychology from Teachers College, Columbia University.

MANUEL TRUJILLO is director of research in the Department of Psychiatry at Beth Israel Medical Center and the principal investigator in an ongoing research project on short-term dynamic psychotherapy. He received his M.D. degree (1968) from Sevilla University in Spain. Trujillo has held administrative and research positions at the Columbia University College of Physicians and Surgeons (1977–1978), Downstate Medical Center (1980–1981), and Mount Sinai School of Medicine (since 1981). He has contributed material to *Treating the Oedipal Patients in Brief Psychotherapy* (edited by A. J. Horner).

LEWIS R. WOLBERG is clinical professor of psychiatry at New York University School of Medicine and the founder of the Postgraduate Center for Mental Health in New York City. He received his M.D. degree (1930) from Tufts University School of Medicine. He is a founding fellow of the American Academy of Psychoanalysis. Wolberg has been especially active in the field of hypnosis and has received many awards for his original work on its therapeutic uses. He is the author of a number of textbooks, including *The Technique of Psychotherapy*, *Medical Hypnosis*, *Hypnoanalysis*, *Psychotherapy and the Behavioral Sciences*, *Short-Term Psychotherapy*, *The Handbook of Short-Term Psychotherapy*, *The Dynamics of Personality*, and *The Practice of Psychotherapy*.

Psychotherapist's Casebook

Theory and Technique
in the Practice
of Modern Therapies

Part One ✺

Psychoanalytic and Psychodynamic Therapies

Psychoanalysis is based on Sigmund Freud's discovery that a level of consciousness exists that is not accessible to immediate awareness but can affect one's experiences and behavior. Treatment in psychoanalysis consists of techniques for making the unconscious conscious. Psychoanalysts use interpretations of transference and resistance, relating of the past history to present behaviors, free association by the patient, and analysis of dreams and of slips of the tongue to advance the aim of resolving unconscious conflicts and allowing the person autonomy from unconscious influences. Introspection and self-observation are fostered.

"Classical" psychoanalysis has given rise to many derivative forms of psychoanalytic psychotherapy, perhaps because the treatment of mental disorders requires constant modification of the practitioner's systematic method, based on the needs and dynamics of the individual patient. These derivative techniques include those based on object relations theory, psychoanalytic developmental psychology (ego psychology), self psychology, psychoanalytic phenomenology, and the drive/relational model. These techniques, along with "classical" psychoanalysis and short-term psychoanalytically based dynamic psychotherapy, make up Part One.

In Chapter One, "Psychoanalysis," Harold P. Blum illustrates and reviews the nature of analytic evidence derived from the analytic process. Psychoanalysis is presented as an intertwined therapy and scientific study, as well as a body of knowledge and a theory. The author presents classical psychoanalytical process as organized around free association and interpretation of all verbal and nonverbal data, with a central focus on transference and countertransference. As results of this process, unconscious infantile conflicts and functions are traced to their genetic roots, neurotic symptoms and behaviors are revealed as repetitions of the past, connections between past and present are restored, and the domain of the ego is expanded with structural change. Blum illustrates the technique with a case that included the analysis of a lie about object loss.

In Chapter Two, "Psychoanalytic Psychotherapy," Irwin L. Kutash and

1

Jeffrey Greenberg present psychoanalytic psychotherapy and differentiate it from psychoanalysis. The authors describe some forms of psychoanalytic psychotherapy as tailored to patient groups formerly excluded as untreatable by psychoanalysts and others as differing in the inclusiveness of their goals for personality reorganization. They describe contemporary forms of psychoanalytic psychotherapy and present a case of a di-egophrenic patient treated within a drive/relational model, a model that combines aspects of Freudian instinctual drive theory, Sullivanian relational theory, and object relations theory into a cohesive approach.

In Chapter Three, "Self Psychology and Psychoanalytic Phenomenology," Daphne D. Socarides and Robert D. Stolorow focus on two fundamental contributions of self psychology to psychoanalytic therapy: (1) delineation of the empathic-introspective mode of inquiry as defining the therapeutic stance and (2) the concept of selfobject transferences, wherein the analyst is experienced as a functional part of the patient's own self-organization. The authors expand and refine Kohut's selfobject concept, proposing that selfobject functions pertain fundamentally to the integration of affect into the organization of self-experience and that the need for selfobject ties pertains most centrally to the need for attuned responsiveness to affect states in all stages of the life cycle. They place particular emphasis on the developmental importance of integrating depressive affect and present a clinical case exemplifying the principles of treating severe developmental derailments in this area.

In Chapter Four, "Ego Psychology," Malcolm J. Marks identifies the essential contributions of ego psychology as its attitude toward the human condition and its respect for the autonomous functioning of the individual. He traces the theory and technique of psychoanalytic developmental psychology to Freud's structural theory, which encompasses instinctual life and its psychic development, the development of the reality-testing, organizing ego function, and the internalization of values and standards that serve drive regulation and the establishment of self-esteem and object constancy. The work of Heinz Hartmann, Anna Freud, Jacobson, Spitz, Mahler, and Gertrude and Rubin Blanck is presented as an extension of Freud's theory and enables the psychotherapist to address the goal of ego strengthening and structure building by using the therapeutic dyadic relationship to further internalization processes. The focus of ego psychology, according to Marks, has moved from extracting primary-process material to strengthening the capacity for repression, particularly in those with lower-level structures for whom there is not simply "the return of the repressed" but an incapacity for repression. The effort in this chapter is to highlight the profound contributions of the heirs of Freud and their significance for psychotherapeutic technique. Marks offers verbatim transcription of a demonstration interview with a schizophrenic in remission as an example of the application of ego psychology in the initial structuring of the treatment relationship.

In Chapter Five, "Short-Term Dynamic Psychotherapy," Manuel Trujillo briefly reviews the history of psychoanalytically based short-term dynamic psychotherapy, especially the clinical contributions of Sifneos, Malan, and Davanloo. After dispelling some myths about short-term dynamic psychotherapy, the author concentrates on techniques developed by Davanloo. He illustrates issues such as evaluation for suitability, use of transference, and handling termination with extensive patient material from video-recorded psychotherapy sessions.

1

Psychoanalysis

Harold P. Blum

The major route toward solving analytic problems and resolving controversies within the field has been clinical study: we return to analytic data, we suggest new formulations deriving from clinical evidence, we enlarge analytic knowledge from clinical experience, and we test new hypotheses in the crucible of the analytic process. This chapter represents clinical psychoanalysis as an intertwined therapy and scientific study, inseparable from analysis as a body of knowledge and a theory. I shall give an example of a unique analytic process that began with an extraordinary deception and shall draw inferences from the analysis of a lie about object loss. The analytic process will illustrate the nature of analytic inference. Psychoanalytic observation, hypothesis, and theory are interdependent and reciprocal. Clinical psychoanalysis remains the main research method and laboratory of psychoanalysis (although nonclinical observations have also informed and expanded psychoanalytic knowledge). Differences in the analytic process may produce different analytic data and evidence, and the analytic process itself may color the evidence obtained and subsequent inferences. Because implicit assumptions and points of view underlie any effort at analytic interpretation, it is neither possible nor desirable to propose hypothesis and inference entirely without any theoretical framework. "The full meaning of clinical findings can only be developed in the framework of theory . . . . All attempts at simplification, of which there are many, at a concentration on only one aspect at the expense of others, [must] be paid for by a severe limitation on the explanatory reach and the predictive value of analysis" (Hartmann, 1958b, pp. 134, 141). Psychoanalytic theory is a determinant of clinical experience. Problems and pitfalls ensue when there are gaps and inconsistencies between observations, hypotheses, and formulations; when description is confused with explanation; when different theoretical frameworks are combined without concern for compatibility; and when the selection of data and alternative inferences is skewed.

The classical psychoanalytic process is organized around free association and

This chapter appeared in an earlier version entitled "The Psychoanalytic Process and Analytic Inference: A Clinical Study of a Lie and a Loss," *International Journal of Psychoanalysis,* 1983, *64,* 17–33.

interpretation of all possible verbal and nonverbal data, with a center field of transference and countertransference. In this process, unconscious infantile conflicts and fixations are traced to their genetic roots, with evidence of various forms of compromise formations and developmental transformations. Neurotic symptoms and behavior are revealed as childish repetitions of the past in the present, based on persistent unconscious pathogenic conflicts. Connections between past and present are restored and the domain of the ego vastly expanded with progressive structural change. This is the essential core of the process and goals of psychoanalytic therapy.

Success depends on the analyst's insight into transference and resistance and considerations of the totality of the analytic situation and process in making appropriate interventions. Work proceeds from the psychic surface, which is ascertained from a consideration of all the available analytic data, the phase of analysis, and the patient's readiness for interpretation. An interpretation itself is an inference drawn from analytic evidence. Based on understanding and conveying insight, it should be tactful and timely, flexible in application, and appropriately on target. The analyst should be aware of the effects, particularly on the transference, of interpretations and of all interventions and communications. The complex network of bilateral unconscious cues and communication in the analytic process means that evidence must be examined for artifacts and distortions of the process itself (Rangell, 1968; Arlow, 1979).

The analytic attitude should be one of neutrality, with impartial objectivity toward the analytic data, with equidistance from id, ego, superego (A. Freud, [1936] 1946), and reality. A neutral analytic attitude will be associated with coexistent attitudes of candor and therapeutic commitment and "sympathetic understanding" in the face of intense provocations of all sorts (Freud, [1913a] 1958, p. 140). Neutrality does not mean alienation or animosity. It actually fosters transference investment while avoiding transference contamination and gratification, transference/countertransference confusion, and constraints on the patient's free association and individuality. Neutrality is specifically related to the analyst's nondirective stance and the nonintrusion of the analyst's own problems and values into the treatment; "we ought not to give up the neutrality towards the patient, which we have acquired through keeping the countertransference in check" (Freud, [1913b] 1958, p. 164).

Concerned with an impartial, objective analytic attitude in the selection of evidence, Freud stated, "In making the selection, if [the analyst] follows his expectations he is in danger of never finding anything but what he already knows; and if he follows his inclinations, he will certainly falsify what he may perceive" ([1912] 1958, p. 112). Freud further underscored the importance to the analyst of understanding the transference/countertransference field when he stated, "The doctor must put himself in the position to make use of everything he is told for the purposes of interpretation and of recognizing the concealed unconscious material without substituting a censorship of his own for the selection that the patient has foregone" ([1912] 1958, p. 115). Whereas this is relevant to all patients, it stands in bold relief when a patient deliberately seeks to deceive the analyst.

Integrated analytic function and work depend on analyzing countertransference as an impediment. The analyst uses countertransference signals in conjunction with all other cues and clues as a guide to comprehending the analytic material.

There is no guarantee of the validity of countertransference reactions or of the analyst's empathy, and these responses have to be subject to critical examination (Beres and Arlow, 1974). The countertransference itself is a very broad topic related to the analyst's other reactions to the patient and the particular analytic situation (Kernberg, 1965). In the case to be described, countertransference analysis contributed to the illumination of the patient's unconscious denial and derision in his lie. The impact of the patient's deliberate deception of the analyst and the potential for the analyst to feel "fooled" and the victim of a fraud had significant countertransferential reverberations.

The circular transference/countertransference reactions and the interwoven fantasies and realities of the analytic situation are understood with both macroscopic and microscopic, intrapsychic and external, transference and reality considerations (Rangell, 1979; Sandler, Dare, and Holder, 1973). Analytic work and "the work of interpretation which transforms what is unconscious into what is conscious" (Freud, [1917a] 1963, p. 455) can then gradually and carefully extend from phenomenological patterns to metapsychological models.

As the analytic process gets underway with an analytic pact, an alliance develops beween patient and analyst for cooperation and joint participation in the analytic work (Kanzer, 1981). This alliance arises from the correct attitude, position, empathy, and interpretive work of the analyst, from maintenance of the analytic framework, and from the patient's personality resources; it does not need special technical nurturance and is maintained and restored through appropriate interpretation. Such an alliance develops with difficulty, however, where mutual trust is lacking and where prevarication provokes countertransference. The acquisition of insight, the experience of new and affectively meaningful understanding, has a powerful impact on the patient's continuing interest and investment in the analytic process. Despite the negative transferences and inevitable resistance, there is a stimulation and excitement to beginning the discovery of the meaning of symptoms and understanding why, how, and under what circumstances the patient has fallen ill. It is an "eye opener" for patients to discover their modes of self-deception, the ways in which they have defended against their anxieties, disguised their own motives, misunderstood their loved ones, and unwittingly contributed to their own difficulties. The pace of uncovering and discovery, its scope and depth, vary in each individual analysis, but such discovery is one of the valuable effects of analysis; it stimulates further curiosity and strengthens analytic inquiry.

The patient identifies with the analytic attitude and with the functions and goals of analysis. Both analyst and patient must have the capacity for a "therapeutic split" between observation and experience (Sterba, 1934) and for controlled regression in the service of the analysis. While providing a reliable, stable "holding environment" (Winnicott, 1965a), analysis fosters a controlled regression. Analysis, however, is not a supportive psychotherapy and is in many respects a demanding, difficult, regressive, and reorganizing experience.

Research issues concerning the analytic process and analytic evidence should be periodically reevaluated in light of developments in psychoanalysis. Although it has been sadly said that psychoanalysts remain better friends if they do not read and respond to each other's papers, it is apparent that an awakening of interest and a greater sharing of ideas occur when clinical material is presented and discussed at meetings. The evocation of real character and conflict, the challenge of organizing analytic data, the presentation of evidence that becomes coherent and convincing, and the shared search for understanding tend to diminish doctrinal differences and break down barriers to analytic thought and inference. Moreover, we need a continuing commitment to and investment in clinical analytic research by psychoanalysts in collecting and assessing analytic evidence and in reporting and publishing our analytic findings.

It is in this spirit that I turn now to the presentation of clinical material, material that complements my previous reconstruction of object loss (Blum, 1980). This case presentation, of necessity compressed, is an overview of an analysis. It will enable us to contemplate further the nature of analytic evidence and inferences.

Clinical Presentation

The following quote from Freud ([1915b] 1961, p. 290) and the question "Where does the truth lie?" should be kept in mind as I present this case: "Consideration for the dead, who, after all, no longer need it, is more important to us than the truth, and certainly, for most of us, than consideration for the living."

The case that I shall present invited a serious question from the outset—namely, the question of analyzability. Always a concern, analyzability is dubious, at best, when a patient starts with fabrication. The patient was in his thirties, married, a relatively successful engineer, who was extremely anxious in his initial consultation. He was more or less depressed, discontent, excessively concerned about being liked; he felt he couldn't get close to his family and too often wondered and worried about death. His father had died before the patient was ten years old. The initial evaluation suggested that he could benefit from analysis and that analysis offered the possibility of a major exploration and reorganization of his personality with attenuation of his deep-seated conflicts and depressive tendencies. He seemed to accept the recommendation. Just before he was to begin analysis, he telephoned the analyst, saying, "My mother died, and I will be in touch with you after the funeral." I told him that I was very sorry and expressed condolence and said I would wait to hear from him. He did not contact me for more than a year and a half. I later learned that during that time he had seen another therapist, who had also advised psychoanalysis. The patient then telephoned, asking for consultation to continue analytic treatment. He now really wanted to start analysis with me, and he had something to tell me at the outset.

He confessed that he had fled from analysis by invoking a completely false alibi: the story that his mother had died was not true; it was a fabrication, a "big lie." Could such a patient, who begins analysis with dishonesty and with an "outrageous lie," really be analysed? Was he a sociopath? Could he free-associate and not be delinquent toward the fundamental rule? Would he lie throughout the analysis? Many patients initially withhold material such as an affair, an abortion, or perverse tendencies, but they do not start with a deliberate lie. In short, the question of selection and suitability was paramount. I was intrigued and perplexed by this remarkable behavior. The patient seemed somewhat ashamed and expressed mild feelings of humiliation and guilt over having deceived the analyst. He could not explain the rather bizarre behavior but asserted that he was not a habitual liar and he respected the truth.

What was interesting was not only his verbal communication but his nonverbal behavior. The patient was so tremulous, so visibly agitated that the chair shook along with his head and torso. He looked as if he might "jump out of his skin," and he seemed to make the room vibrate. His mother had been ill with a possible malignancy at the time of the fabricated report of her death. Although he had wept when he learned of this news, the report of her death was entirely premature, and she was very much alive at the time the patient returned to me for possible analysis. It was prognostically positive that there was a feeling of relatedness and affective communication of his desire for help. The patient presented a kind of childlike pseudo innocence, a plea to be accepted despite his delinquency, a fear of rejection coupled with a pathetic and almost desperate look that sought pity and protection.

I wondered about the lie in the service of denial and repression, the problems of acting out and other regressive potential, and the nature of the underlying superego pathology. His blatant lie, condoned and yet condemned meekly and after the fact, was a form of acting out through subversion of verbalization (Blum, 1976). Did he have to leave before he was left, and would he sustain analysis without interruption and repeated flight? What might be predicted about major resistances, transference constellations, and the ultimate explanation for such a fantastic fabrication? It seemed likely that the falsification and flight served an initial transference resistance and were probably part of an unconscious fantasy. I conjectured that the patient had committed a symbolic oedipal crime and had an unconscious need for punishment and atonement. Simultaneously it was useful to ponder the limits of manifest content, first impressions, and initial explanation. "It is not in the least our business to 'understand' a case at once: this is only possible at a later stage, when we have received enough impressions of it. For the present we will suspend our judgment and give our impartial attention to everything that there is to observe" (Freud, [1909] 1955, pp. 22–23).

Other analytic considerations also influenced my assessment. The patient had, indeed, returned, had come back to "the scene of the crime," having fled punishment with his "alibi." He came not only to confess but to understand behavior that he considered alien and irrational. He knew he could have fled from analysis without any excuse, but he had been compelled to invent the pathetic pseudology. The other factor was the nature of the fabrication itself, a truly outrageous lie. And it was a lie about the death of his mother; one of the most forbidden childhood wishes was nakedly expressed. It was so extreme and egregious that it had to have a prominent defensive function and could not simply be the primary expression of his undisguised matricidal wish. If the patient could be taken seriously when he said that he was not given to chronic lying in his adolescent or adult life, then when he told one, it was a whopper. Such a lie might testify to denial in fantasy and in action and to the return from repression of some overwhelming traumatic experience. The lie was clearly related to the anticipated loss of his mother, and he had told me in our initial interview that his father had died when he was nine to ten years of age.

The presence of many areas of well-integrated functioning held out hope for his ego strength and analyzability. He showed appreciation and concern for his family and had honestly advanced his career and work. Having a trial of analysis in mind, I told the patient that I would accept him for treatment and that if he and the treatment proved suitable for each other, we would hope to learn the reasons for his strange and unreasonable behavior and to work out the conflicts and problems

behind his anxiety and depression. He seemed relieved. He promptly and regularly
continued the analytic work. He initially associated to the analysis as a safety net
and security blanket, at first seeking approval, affection, and absolution. Whereas
some patients with parent loss in childhood, fixated to the traumatic past, resist
change and new relationships, his initial attachment to analysis involved a transference fantasy of reunion by magical return of the lost parent. The analytic work
was expectably difficult, but it was also productive and rewarding, producing interpretation of his pathogenic conflicts and defenses and working through of childhood
traumata leading toward a mutually acceptable termination after approximately
six years of analysis.

The leitmotif of the lie and loss ran like a red thread through the analysis
and was gradually understood from many points of view and on different developmental levels, with major additional meanings gleaned in the final phase of treatment. Only certain salient features of the patient's analysis and of the life history
that was reassembled from it will be presented here.

Appropriate and informal in manner and dress, he smiled readily, and had
a quick wit and sense of humor. He liked to joke when he wasn't too anxious or
depressed, and he needed to joke when he wanted to alleviate his depression. He
was fun-loving but a potential "killjoy," excitable and readily rejected and dejected.
At the time we started treatment he had a devoted, worrisome wife of approximately
his age and two small children. He had been born into an immigrant Jewish family
and had grown up in another city. There were two siblings, a brother eight years
older and a sister two years older than the brother. He was often left in solitary
play. His mother was remembered as chronically depressed, often tearful. She tended
to equate good mothering with feeding and physical care; retiring and withdrawn,
she was often emotionally unavailable or insensitive. She was unable to inquire
about the patient's feelings or to be very responsive to his conversations and questions. He was very close to his father, who was much more cheerful and, though
very hardworking, given to jocular play and friendly, affectionate banter with the
patient. The death of his father in the boy's tenth year was a terrible experience
and followed a painful downhill course in which the father's vitality and vigor were
lost in the advance of his malignant illness. Since there was a rather large age difference between the patient and his siblings, he had restricted contact with them
but was very pleased to have whatever attention was offered to him. Of great importance to his later development was his brother's interest in him during his late
adolescence. The patient had not done well in school and was not prepared for work
or a career until guided by his brother. The family had always been poor, and after
the father's death their life was a literal struggle for socioeconomic survival. His
mother had trained for new work and again spent long hours away from home.
His life was filled with loneliness, longing, sadness, and wish-fulfilling self-aggrandizing daydreams in which he achieved fame and fortune, admiration and esteem,
and the conquest of attractive women.

A crucial question was whether the patient's initial fabrication was a symptom or part of a character defect. He did not lie in general, although he was given
to bragging, particularly during the latency period. As a group phenomenon, his
peer group had told tall stories, and he had been given to presenting himself as
a far better athlete than he was in reality. He had wanted to be the biggest and
the best, with the mightiest bat and balls. His parents had told little white lies to

their relatives to hide their humiliating poverty. He disclaimed other dishonesty on the part of his parents or siblings. The patient had, on occasion, stolen little items from the dimestore until he was caught and reprimanded by his brother. As a little boy, he had also once taken coins from his mother's purse and had lost the money, for which he was soundly spanked. The deprivations and punishments contributed to his feeling inadequate, disillusioned, and intimidated. Punishment and poverty unconsciously strengthened his self-denigration, his homosexual submissive impulses toward his father, and his unconscious rage and identifications with castrated, humiliated parents.

The patient recalled his mother's compassionate attempts to help his father after the father developed cancer. His mother became more depressed. Her intermittent feelings of helplessness and hopelessness intensified; and yet she made episodic efforts to provide tender care and offer comfort. These efforts often miscarried because of the mother's misery and her bouts of colitis with cramps and diarrhea, often so severe that the patient remembered with disgust her excrement on the floor when she couldn't reach the bathroom in time. This was an area of familial silence and shame. He also emphasized the efforts at family closeness and warmth, the good times, particularly among himself, his father, and his brother, with shared laughter and games, occasionally playing tricks on one another.

He had, of course, "tricked" me in the first session, and there was no question that there was an aggressive, derisive quality in making a fool of the father figure. In its sadomasochistic provocation, the fabrication also represented a pathetic plea for sympathy; he thought he wanted to be pitied as a poor orphan and to avoid antagonizing a figure of authority. He invited punishment and humiliation and ran from pain and punishment. His anxiety and depression could be contagious, as could his efforts at humor and joking. He had been the class comic and had tried to disguise being a poor student by being the funny one, the wise guy. His curiosity and learning were clearly impaired by his neurotic problems, and his curiosity and motivation to learn rapidly were mobilized in the analysis. Although he lied to other people a few times during the analysis, mostly in the form of self-aggrandizing, bragging about his accomplishments, or mentioning powerful people with whom he was associated, there were no further deliberate falsifications in the analysis. There were omissions and secretive reactions, such as delay in telling the analyst about masturbation, watching pornography, and temper responses to his family. The analyst was tested for sincerity and integrity, for his capacity to bear the patient's demands and depression, and for an analytic attitude rather than moral indignation or exoneration—for example, concerning his initial lie.

The loss of his father, with all its implications and ramifications, rapidly emerged as a central psychological configuration early in the analysis. The patient had fantasies of "playing dead," with humorous revivals (like his fabrication of his mother's death). Far more worrisome were obsessive thoughts that he would return home to his wife and children, whom he felt he loved so much, and find them massacred. This thought filled him with dread; he would want either to avoid going home or to rush home to make sure everyone was all right. In a recurring dream his father fell off the roof, and the little boy, standing behind him or at his side, reached down, caught him, and magically pulled him back. The patient's playfulness had a childlike quality, although he could be described as adolescent in terms of many other features. He often thought about death, and his many "sick"

jokes lightly dismissed the dangers of severe illness, injury, and death. When he
initially consulted me, he had been worried about the failing health of his mother
and of his former therapist; they might die, but he would live. He felt assured and
yet not entirely free of worry about his analyst's health and longevity (typical of
patients with childhood object loss). He had not been permanently lost but had
come back to analysis. I interpreted that his leaving and returning were a form
of enactment of his repetitive dream of his father falling from a height and being
rescued by the patient.

One of the most significant meanings of the consultation drama of the lie,
leaving analysis, and then returning now emerged. The patient killed me off symbolically when he left the treatment and then resurrected me again! He too died
and was rescued and resurrected while unconsciously killing the previous therapist
in treatment. The theme of death, resurrection, and rebirth recurred throughout
the analysis. The trauma of his father's death was reenacted with an effort at mastery
alongside the denial of the death. The denial concerned the meaning of death and
included denial of irreversible loss. The dramatization of the denial indicated the
obligatory need to repeat the trauma in an episodic form of verbal and nonverbal
enactment. The lie was a concentration of a fantasy and a magical alteration of
reality. The patient confirmed Weinshel's (1979) formulation of fabrication as a
means of not dealing with painful or traumatic material. There were early indications that the fabrication had a screen function for pivotal traumatic events and
important unconscious fantasies. The fantastic fabrication would serve as a vehicle
for reconstruction and would be fitted into the nexus of the patient's particular life
history as described by Deutsch ([1922] 1982). Much of the material was condensed
and telescoped, so that what is sketched in some sequence here was reorganized
in the analytic process. Freud ([1900] 1953) very early grappled with this problem
in reconstruction: "If, during a child's prehistoric epoch, his nurse has been dismissed, and if soon afterwards his mother has died, the two events are superimposed
on each other in a single series in his memory as revealed in analysis" (p. 255).

Cycles of death, resurrection, and subsequent loss appear throughout the
analytic material. In a slip of the tongue, when the patient remarked on where the
analyst was born and bred, he said, "born and dead." He fantasied himself in
a recurrent daydream as a girl floating on a leaf set adrift in the currents. This
highly condensed image included his identifications with both parents, particularly
his mother, and his fantasy of being born as the girl she wanted. It also referred
to identification with Moses and the Egyptian princess who bore him in a family
romance. His father's and his own identification with the Jewish mythical hero and
lawgiver was a factor in his superego development. In this family romance, a narcissistic and oedipal creation, he was reborn as a great leader and savior, along
the lines of the myth of the birth of the hero.

Associations to falling off the roof were again symbolic, representative of
both birth and death. He thought of movies of assassins, murders, and mayhem.
He had actually seen death at first hand, which reminded him of his father and
of his uncle. This brought to mind a terrible, vivid memory from his adolescence.
His uncle had killed himself by jumping out a window (note the themes of birth,
death, and falling). The patient had been due to visit his uncle and was obsessed
with thoughts that he could have saved his uncle's life if he had indeed visited.
Here again were birth and death, the fantasy of rescue, being rescued, and undoing

the murderous deed. He developed suicidal ideation and insomnia and had visual images of his uncle's face in the coffin. After a single psychiatric consultation, the patient and his family were reassured that everything would be all right, that he was in effect just a nervous kid who would recover from the shock of the suicide. He thought of the crushed bodies of war victims and the dashed skull of a girl he had seen who had died as a result of a suicidal jump from a building. At the same time he thought of the assassination of President Kennedy and dreamed of operating on the bashed head of the president, reconstructing the brain (compare analytic reconstruction). He was gradually able to understand the revival of the loss of his father at the time of his uncle's death and his guilt over their deaths. He was the assassin who had unconsciously achieved an oedipal but pyrrhic victory over the father he ambivalently loved so very much. Bringing his father back from the dead was simultaneously an expression of his love and longing and of his need to undo his fantasied destruction. He was like Freud's patient ([1900] 1953, p. 260) who felt he was capable of wanting to push his father off a mountain top and later developed obsessive self-reproaches after his father's painful illness and death.

At the time his father died, the patient had had a cognitive grasp of death. Unlike Freud's ten-year-old who stated, "I know father's dead, but what I can't understand is why he doesn't come home to supper" ([1900] 1953, p. 254),[1] my patient had consciously regarded his father as irreversibly lost. At the same time, in the kind of split of the ego that Freud ([1937b] 1964) noted in connection with denial, he continued to daydream and dream that his father would be back. He preferred his father to his mother, and another unconscious meaning of the "big lie" emerged. He had recognized intellectually that he probably harbored matricidal wishes, but they had no meaning to him at the beginning of the analysis. He later understood that the fabrication of her death served the double denial of his mother's illness and his father's death. He also would have preferred that his father had lived and his mother had died. If it was possible to make me believe that what was false was true, then the patient could also disregard the truth and believe in what was false (Fenichel, ([1939] 1954). I reminded him of children's games of "let's pretend." The family shared suppression and denial concerning the father's cancer. He was not told the diagnosis, and the physician and family cooperated in the deception and the father's self-deception. In his deliberate falsification with me, the patient repeated and reversed what the doctor and family had done to his father as a patient. There was a conspiracy of silence over the illness, as there had always been over money and sexual matters. The question of birth and death was connected with infantile sexual curiosity and theories. There was ample evidence of primal-scene exposure and probably thinly disguised homosexual longing for his father and brother.

Although maternal transference was intermittently present, the predominant transference object was the father, and the predominant developmental phase was the Oedipus complex. Preoedipal material appeared more frequently in oral regressive form and associated with maternal transference than in any other preoedipal form. He had caring thoughts about his mother; he remembered moments of warmth, her devoted efforts to feed and nurture, the tragic unhappiness of her life, and his

---

[1]Freud ([1900] 1953, p. 255), beginning developmental considerations of the child's concept of death, also described a four-year-old girl's realistic idea of death as never coming back again.

wishes that she could have been far more nurturant and sensitive. The sights and sounds of the bathroom were associated with her colitis. His mother was prone to give herself enemas; she would also give him enemas, despite his protests, if there were any signs of constipation or illness. Hidden behind the anger and discomfort, the excitement and mutual seduction, was another aspect of his negative oedipal position as well as his castration at the hands of a phallic woman. The falling in his dreams was, therefore, also the loss of feces, representing the loss of potency, the penis, and both parents; falling also had the opposite symbolic meanings of birth and rebirth. He had lost his father through death and was afraid of losing his mother and of his own castration and death. Paradoxically, he sometimes felt better when discussing an actual death that proved to be related to circumstances that reassured him that he was not responsible and was not a murderer. "And death once dead, there's no more dying then" (Shakespeare, Sonnet 146). His great lie meant he was innocent, exonerated by his "bullshit." As a fecal object, the lie was "living shit" and dead loss. His fleeing from homosexual submission protected against anal rape and robbery, and the revival of trauma, incontinence, crying, and expressive sadness was equated with a feared femininity.

As the analysis deepened, his disappointment, injury, and rage with his mother came more clearly to the surface. He remembered her sad, mournful face, her depression, her lamenting her hard life that had so much pain and grief. Again, she did not hesitate to inflict this on her child, who was, in many respects, an only child because of the great age difference between himself and his siblings. He was often reminded of his naughtiness, of his shortcomings. When he upset her, which was not difficult to do, or when she had an attack of colitis, he was told that she would die—he was giving her a cancer. In short, he was not only making her miserable, he was to be her executioner. This realization clarified some of his tormenting guilt and the sadomasochistic mother/son relationship. He was the youngest; he was more delicate, very special; and she loved him dearly. At the same time, he was her potential enemy. She felt bereaved, and he, in turn, felt bereaved and bewildered. What had he done to her, who was being cruel to whom? How could he cheer her up; how could he get rid of her contagious misery? His mother's inconsistent discipline, the loss of parental authority after his father's death, the many deprivations and nonbenign neglect, the feeling that he was an orphan who had to take matters into his own hands, had all contributed to a peculiarly harsh, brittle, and inconsistent superego. His deception was related to the psychology of the exception. An instability of regulation and control permitted the episodic enactments that intensified his guilt. His "many superegos" permitted many truths (Ferenczi, ([1927] 1980). The enactments were paradoxically the result of his unconscious entitlement and overpermissiveness, as well as his unconscious guilt and self-punishment. He unconsciously feared and wished for castration and death.

Although the oedipal organization and the superego were the most important analytic considerations in this case, the preoedipal determinants were also significant. The patient's mother's depression compromised her caretaking and nurturance. Separation anxiety in childhood and the insomnia of adolescence were only partly mastered as an adult, and he had to guard his independence and autonomy. Analytic separations would result either in greater closeness and clinging to the analyst and to his wife or in provoking fights with his wife and then giving her the "silent treatment." He appeared to have earlier transferred his affection from the depressed mother to the more responsive father, who was, in some respects, both a father and a mother. This insight was a further contribution to the understanding of the transferred ambivalence to the father as well as of the developmental insult caused by the loss of the father. However, a pervasive arrest at the level of development attained just before the father's death did not occur. The arrested mourning and reactivated conflicts did contribute to subsequent developmental disturbance and disharmony, but there was antecedent disturbance as well as later progressive gains along some developmental lines (see Altschul, 1968; Furman, 1974; Pollock, 1961).

The transference conflicts had concentrated in the father transference, which was related to the unconscious resurrection of the lost father, the activation of and struggle against mourning, and a defensive/adaptive shift from maternal transference and tendencies toward preoedipal regression. The father transference defended against maternal and preoedipal transference issues. Because of defense and developmental reorganization, the transference does not recapitulate the development of the neurosis, and it cannot be the sole guide to reconstruction. Following his exposition of the encompassing importance of the transference neurosis, Freud ([1917a] 1963) contemplated the analytic process and cautioned:

> It will not be out of place to give a warning that we can draw no direct conclusion from the distribution of the libido during and resulting from the treatment as to how it was distributed during the illness. Suppose we succeeded in bringing a case to a favorable conclusion by setting up and then resolving a strong father-transference to the doctor. It would not be correct to conclude that the patient had suffered previously from a similar unconscious attachment of his libido to his father. His father-transference was merely the battlefield on which we gained control of his libido; the patient's libido was directed to it from other positions. A battlefield need not necessarily coincide with one of the enemy's key fortresses. The defense of a hostile capital need not take place just in front of its gates. Not until after the transference has once more been resolved can we reconstruct in our thoughts the distribution of libido which had prevailed during the illness [pp. 455–456].

Both regressive alteration and progressive transformation complicate oedipal and preoedipal issues and relationships. The reconstruction of the infantile neurosis and its changes in life in the formation of the adult neurosis restores the complicated connections between past and present but proceeds on a higher level of synthesis and abstraction and at a greater distance from immediate analytic observation than transference analysis. But transference alone does not depict development or pathogenesis. Evidence for pathogenesis derives from the totality of the analytic process, and final reconstruction may be remodeled during termination or left to the analyst alone after the analysis is over.

As we shall see, the father transference in this case screened the underlying powerful developmental impact of the mother's depression. Her depression was a major pathogenic influence. The patient's tendency toward global identifications with her, his narcissistic fragility, and his compensatory narcissistic fantasies were based on a preoedipal disturbance. Torn between dependent and autonomous strivings, he manifested oscillating clinging, coercive tantrums, and intense separation conflicts with modulated repetition in transference regression. His object relations and narcissism were particularly vulnerable to regression, with unstable self-esteem. A basic depressive mood and predisposition to depression were assumed to have developed prior to, and then in parallel with, the oedipal phase. The impression was that his primarily oedipal disorder had significant and detectable determinants arising from earlier psychosexual phases and the process of separation/individuation (Mahler, 1975, 1979a). The depressive mood of his mother also contributed to his depressive tendencies and to an early proclivity toward denial, splitting of the ego to protect the narcissistic love object from rage, and fantasies of fusion (later reunion) with the idealized object. In connection with maternal depression, A. Freud (1965) noted, ''What happens is that such infants achieve their sense of unity and harmony with the depressed mother not by means of their developmental achievements but by producing the mother's mood in themselves'' (p. 87). In some respects, he had remained an infant who had wanted immediate gratification and did not want to acknowledge the reality of what was unpleasurable. However, except in his dreams, there was never a manifest loss of object constancy, so that some adequate structuralization, ego strengths, and resilient recovery from traumatization could be postulated for the infantile period. The multiple childhood traumata were nevertheless incompletely understood and mastered by the mature ego, and ego synthesis of traumatic states and consequences had not been accomplished.

His guilt was intensified after his father's death by the close, intimate, and unconsciously incestuous relationship with his mother. This was reproduced in fantasies about the analyst and the analyst's wife and in fears of retaliation for his incestuous wishes and for his aggression against the mother on whom he was even more dependent as the only surviving parent. He wanted to possess and control her for both sexual and dependent gratifications and was afraid of his own anger toward her. The problems were also reflected in his marriage and his many problems with intimacy, closeness, and distance recapitulated in the transference. Afraid to be dependent, he was angry when dependent needs were not gratified inside and outside the analysis. He found that it was difficult for him to discuss death and explain it to his children. He compared his physical, emotional, and mental attributes with those of his mother and father. His resemblance to his father was emphasized as an assertion of his manhood, as his father's unconscious resurrection and reincarnation. He would then be entitled to his mother which again aroused the specter of death and the unconscious fear of his father's vengeance in the form of a similar malevolent fate.

In his closeness to his mother, his psychological attunement to her attitudes and moods, a new dimension of shared fantasy and affect appeared. His mother, forlorn and bereaved, had left many of her relatives behind in Europe. World War II had started at the time the patient entered the oedipal phase, and he recalled that his mother's grieving at that time continued into his later childhood and adolescence. She knew that her loved ones were in mortal danger and correctly suspected that these Jewish relatives had been murdered. The mother's intense bereavement preceded the onset of the father's malignancy. She was faced with multiple losses followed by the loss of her husband. The trauma of the father's death was, therefore, complicated by the mother's antecedent deep depression and mourning and her

impotent rage about the massacre of her family.[2] Her determination and hope for
the patient's future also emerged.

New meanings of the patient's fantasy of the massacre of his own family
surfaced toward the end of analysis. The patient was identified with his bereaved
mother, whose family had been massacred. At the same time, he was identified
with the Nazis, who were responsible for the massacre and who would eventually
kill his mother (and him). After all, she also regarded him as the enemy who would
destroy her with colitis and cancer. Behind the identification with the Nazis was
his infantile identification with the aggressor and infantile death wishes for his mother.
His mother's mourning hung like a pall over the family, an atmosphere that became
ever more doleful with the illness and death of his father and the intensification
of the family's psychological and economic impoverishment.

The central theme of death and resurrection, massacre and rescue appeared
in a new light. His mother had occasionally lamented that she would be better off
dead, which the patient experienced as a reproach and rejection. He recovered a
vague memory, dating from age three or four, of an incident with gas fumes at
night. She might well have made a suicide attempt or even more than one attempt.
His vague thoughts were entirely disconnected from the issue of the familial massacre.
The timing of the suicidal attempt would have coincided with his mother's surmise
that her loved ones in Europe were in grave danger or already killed. Her suicidal
behavior could have resulted in the massacre of her own family here, jeopardizing
the patient's life. He had survived his father but had earlier survivor guilt in identification with, and in relation to, his mother, who survived her murdered relatives.
In addition, he was identified with his mother as suicidal victim and homicidal executioner. He might massacre his family, as his mother almost massacred her spouse
and children and as the Nazis massacred his maternal relatives. The murderer
represented his despised self and the object images of his suicidal mother and vengeful
father.

His mother had never been able to complete mourning because of her own
inner problems and because of the murder of her love objects. She had needed so
much to be mothered and to be consoled for her multiple and cumulative losses.
Her fragility and depression and his increased dependence on her as the surviving
parent made it particularly difficult for him to express aggression or criticism of
her. His self-accusation represented her accusations, which he internalized, as well
as self-reproach for his hostility and his disappointing his mother and himself in
his inability to comfort her, to redeem her deprivations, and to compensate for the
familial suffering and sacrifices. He struggled against his identification with her
and was unaware of their shared psychic reality and reciprocal fantasies. Fearful
of failure, he had a special need to succeed. His hidden ambition was rooted in
competitive wishes to outdo his father and siblings and, even more poignantly, to

---

[2]"The complement to this cultural and conventional attitude towards death is provided
by our complete collapse when death has struck down someone whom we love—a parent or a
partner in marriage, a brother or sister, a child or a close friend. Our hopes, our desires, and
our pleasures lie in the grave with him, we will not be consoled, we will not fill the lost one's
place. We behave as if we were a kind of Asra, who die when those they love die" (Freud, ([1915b]
1961, p. 290).

justify his survival. He and his mother were both survivors of each other's hostile fantasies, of his father, and of murdered relatives. His ambivalence toward his mother was heightened by her depressive withdrawal and by her threat to destroy him with herself.

The initial fabrication, therefore, screened multiple traumata from infancy to adolescence (Deutsch, ([1922] 1982; Weinshel, 1979) and simultaneously revealed a crucial dimension of the patient's history. His mother was in fact ill at the time he was first moved to undertake analytic consultation. Her possible demise threatened to reactivate the trauma of her suicide attempt and her (and his) rescue and survival. The patient shared the guilt of survival through his mother. Her suicidal behavior intensified his primitive violent fantasies, fear of his aggression, and guilt over her suffering and self-destructiveness; but he also responded to unconscious expectations and hopes. There were mixed maternal messages—she wished him to passively withdraw or die; to deny; to count blessings; and actively to compensate her for her missing objects, phallus, and self-regard. He would, with his siblings, achieve redemption and the rebirth of a new and far better life. It was fortunate that he did not feel these demands as an actual only child.

As a child, he was identified with his mother as a remote victim and survivor of the Holocaust (Bergmann and Jucovy, 1982). The incomplete mourning and life-and-death issues shared with his mother, the living with a "mater dolorosa" who was both "alive and dead" in her feelings, attitudes, and withdrawal resulted in the far-reaching effects, transmission of trauma, and the confirmation of primitive conflicts and fantasies. The paradoxical desire to kill or cure the parent permeated his early life and contributed to later adolescent attitudes of passive rebellion and social consciousness (Kestenberg, 1980). He wanted to deny and master the shock and strain trauma (Kris, 1956) that he and his parents had experienced.

The Holocaust themes are interwoven with the deception and self-deception of the victims (as with his father's cancer). The cultural and psychohistorical facets of fabrication in general are significant in their impact on particular individuals but are beyond the scope of this chapter. The collusive silence specifically applied to his mother's suicidal behavior. There was no meaningful discussion of suicidal feelings or intent but an implicit cue not to question or report. Suspicion of concealment and fabrication of the attempt as an "accident" was analytically inferred but not definitely confirmed. There was no effort to enlighten the confused, frightened child, to confront the threat of abandonment and his overwhelming affective reactions. The family could not effectively cope with either the mother's anguished cry for help or feelings of betrayal, manipulation, and masochistic provocation. The boy felt his mother's rejection, the symbolic murder of self and love objects, in her suicidal/homicidal behavior, and this contributed to his own "worthless" and self-punitive attitudes (Warren, 1966).

The adolescent experience of the uncle's death screened the infantile traumata, which were repeated in transference derivatives. Reconstruction of the early experience of the uncle's death was necessary to deal with the denial and fragmented memories and to reassemble the experiences and reactions in a cohesive picture (Rosen, 1955; Wallerstein, 1967). The sources of the transference and a causal, chronological, and developmental sequence for the legacy of his losses and the meanings of his symptomatic lie could then be understood.

The terminal phase of analysis reactivated all the feelings of abandonment and loss, with further mourning in the transference and revived fantasies of death and resurrection as the oedipal victor. This terminal phase of therapy broadened the patient's understanding of feelings of desertion and rage and his identification with his fallen father. After the fall and the escape from analysis, he would be launched like an astronaut or athlete to new heights of phallic conquest and independent achievement. Working through on new developmental levels, he could find replacement and restitution in his current family and work. His imagery was replete with symbols of birth and death, sleep and walking, travel and homecoming. He anticipated termination with a peculiar bittersweet mixture of grief and relief. Never lost, the termination of the analysis unmasked again the "great lie" of humanity, the denial of death. His lie was a "living lie," a lie that gave life to his parents and to his lost relatives. The desire to fabricate may give rise to immortal works of art and fiction in creative individuals, and many writers have suffered parental loss in childhood (Kanzer, 1953).

Discussion

The analytic process resembles a scientific experiment. Within a relatively constant, reliable, and stable framework, interaction occurs between the patient's varying communications and the analyst's variable interventions. Any session or sequence of sessions may be studied for its form and content, for the patient's language, affect, and gesture style, for particular subject preferences and personal linguistic forms of grammar and syntax. Dreams and daydreams, metaphor, imagery, objects, symbolism, the manner of opening and closing the session, and so forth may be followed in each session and over the course of the analysis.

The myriad of derivatives of unconscious conflicts and fantasies are clarified and subject to analysis once working through and working to the underlying determinants have occurred. What appears to be rambling talk and jumbled images is actually dynamically and genetically determined. In the case described, as in all analytic cases, an enormous number of observations and patterns can be followed through the treatment. Although one session may be misleading in its implications, the course of the analysis is then corrective (Freud, [1937b] 1964). Examining what transforms disconnected associations, thoughts, and affects into supportable hypotheses, Arlow (1979) noted the importance of the context of particular data. Form and sequence, repetitions, similarities and opposites, allusions, silences, and nonverbal communication lead to connections and the gradual emergence of themes within the associations. In turn, these themes lead to an organization of the material into configurations. Frequently, derivatives of a core conflict and central fantasy system become the leitmotif of treatment, like the Wolf Man's primal-scene schema and the theme of death and its denial and undoing in this case.

Organization of analytic data into a meaningful integration is essential to analytic methodology and later inference. Prototypical for analytic interpretation, Freud ([1923b] 1961) described the convergence of evidence: "The analyst, too, may himself retain a doubt of the same kind in some particular instances. What makes him certain in the end is precisely the complication of the problem before him which is like the solution of a jigsaw puzzle. . . . If one succeeds in arranging the confused heap of fragments . . . so that the picture acquires a meaning, so that there is no gap anywhere in the design and so that the whole fits into the frame—if all these conditions are fulfilled, then one knows that one has solved the puzzle and that there is no alternative solution'' (p. 116).

This ideal solution applies to a central interpretive focus, and often alternative interpretations and inferences have to be evaluated for accuracy, priority, overdetermination, and level of explanation. New data may extend or amend earlier hypotheses. Insight itself is a circular, creative process that permits interpretation. It advances, and derives from, the analytic process and analytic evidence (Blum, 1979).

As the analyst listens and responds to the patient and reads and responds to the literature, new analytic data resonate with his or her previous analytic education and experience. The analyst subjects the evidence to scrutiny and evaluation before forming an explanatory hypothesis. The analysis of the transference is enlarged with other perspectives, including consideration of the noninterpretive influence of the analyst (for example, education, suggestion) (Stone, 1981), the phase and length of analysis, the phase and life situation of the patient, and the effects of subtle unconscious adaptations by analyst and patient to each other's personality during a protracted analysis. Every psychoanalytic situation has its own unique realities that need to be defined by analyst and patient (think, for example, of the special situation of clinic and didactic analysis). To gather analytic data and determine what is valid evidence, the analyst scrutinizes the structure of the analytic situation, his or her own modes of participation and observation, and the patient's use of the analyst and the process.

Attention to the nature of analytic evidence and inference—that is, to our epistemology—should lead to more precise investigation and formulation and closer correlation between clinical inference and metapsychology (Kris, 1947). Waelder (1962) demonstrated six levels of increasing abstraction, from the clinical discourse in the analytic process to the discourse of metapsychology. Analytic data are first observed, ordered, organized, abstracted, and generalized. At the level of clinical theory, inferences are drawn concerning defense, unconscious guilt, regression, and the like.

Many inferences can be drawn from this one case concerning the psychology of lying or deliberate falsification, the trauma of parent loss in childhood, the effects of maternal depression, the effects on the child of parental suicidal behavior, and so on. The material lends itself to confirmation of many pertinent formulations. Freud ([1917b] 1957) made major contributions in ''Mourning and Melancholia'' and in other papers and letters to our understanding of object loss. A large and valuable literature on object loss has been added to Freud's pioneering formulations and will not be reviewed in detail here.

From the manifold inferences in this case, I shall select a few that I found of particular interest for further analytic reflection and investigation. The inferences move, as in analysis, from the more concrete clinical to the more abstract theoretical, from the specific to the general, and from the immediate present to the more remote past.

1. Because of the initial lie and flight from analysis, a negative assessment of analyzability might be assumed. In this instance, the correct assessment would have to be based on additional evidence. Although we can predict definite nonanalyzability in some cases and have learned to predict analyzability with greater understanding and reliability than in the past, a trial of analysis is still indicated in borderline situations.

2. The lie did not prove to be a manifestation of sociopathy. In its extremely childish character, it was analogous to Freud's ([1913b] 1958) description of lies told

by children. The case confirmed Freud's explanation that such lies are instigated by powerful unconscious motives that may give notice of disposition to future neurosis but should not be regarded as prognostic for bad character.

3. The lie was simultaneously an unconscious confession. The truth was that the patient's father was dead and his mother alive. The inner truths, akin to the truth in delusion, unknown to the patient, were his representation of his mother as already dead in her depressive withdrawal and her perpetual mourning. The lie expressed the patient's matricidal wishes and protected him against her suicidal/homicidal threats. In fabricating his mother's death, he denied the meaning and finality of his father's death as well as his unresolved oedipal guilt. The lie itself could be understood as a resurrection of a lost object, a narcissistic triumph, and a disturbance of reality associated with trauma and denial.

4. The clinical inferences, beginning with the assessment of analyzability, are drawn within a framework of analytic knowledge and theory. The clinical study of a dramatic, deliberate initial deception raised questions about the patient's superego, and the structural hypothesis was used in organizing the analytic data. In the course of analytic work, the patient's inconsistent and infantile superego was amenable to structural change. The patient's conflicts over loyalty, justice, and responsibility were significantly related to contradictory parental identifications (for example, loyalty versus betrayal).

5. Parent loss in childhood may result in developmental arrest, deviation, or disharmony but may also spur various forms of mastery and sublimation. The developmental disturbance in this case was highly selective, as in the continued use of denial and undoing while other areas showed progressive mastery as in the development of wit and humor. Much depends on antecedent personality maturity and strengths, surviving object relationships, and the capacity to mourn. Mourning is not completed in childhood, and a child's partial mourning will be impeded by the unresolved mourning of the surviving parent.

6. The transference neurosis is ego-edited and does not literally recapitulate the development of the infantile neurosis. Developmental sequence and consequence are inferred and then organized into coherent patterns with more or less priority and precision. Inferences of pathogenesis transcend the transference and encompass the modifications and complexities of development. In this case, the source of the intense father transference in adult analysis could not be fully understood without taking into account the mother's disturbance and her and the patient's coadaptation to the father's death.

7. The importance of reconstructing both shock and strain traumata—that is, both nodal events and enduring patterns—as well as the interaction of external and psychic reality is emphasized. The traumatic experience of a parent's suicidal behavior or the death of a parent in childhood is not simply revived in a transference pattern, and the lifting of denial and confusion, the restoration of cause and effect, depends on both transference analysis in the here and now and reconstruction of the past. Case histories are not "short stories" because an analytic autobiography is constantly revised. Patients have real experience, real families, and an authentic, unique life with the most individual events, patterns, and meanings. Freud ([1926b] 1959) reaffirmed his earlier views: "The correct reconstruction, you must know, of such forgotten experiences of childhood always has great therapeutic effect whether they permit objective confirmation or not" (p. 276).

8. In contemporary analysis, the patient's history is completed, corrected,

and created, with reorganization of the personality. The past takes on elaborate new meanings that could not have existed in childhood, so that experience and meaning are variously retrieved and reconstructed, reordered and created anew.

9. In this case the evidence pointed to the significance of the intrapsychic and developmental impact of the traumata, the conflicts activated and validated, the fixation to traumata, and the compulsion to repeat traumata. These consequences of trauma can be differentiated and have different clinical and theoretical implications. The transference revival of a trauma was associated with derivatives of other traumata. The trauma of childhood parent loss and the mourning process were reactivated in analysis and repeated on different levels of development and throughout the life cycle. Developmental challenge may evoke regression and/or renewed mourning with attempted mastery of trauma and conflict.

10. Inferences during and after the analytic process are at varying degrees of abstraction and distance from the data of analytic observation. Observation, inference, and conclusion should not be confused with one another. The manifest meaning to the patient of the conscious fantasy of massacre was fear of reexperiencing death in the family. He was unaware of his own impulses, his confusion of past and present with a compulsion to repeat, and the many other components of the fantasy, such as a compromise formation. The massacre referred to the unconscious meaning of his father's death as patricide, to the formerly repressed and the largely reconstructed trauma of a family massacre threatened by his mother's destructive behavior, and to the more remote reconstruction of his mother's presumed reaction to the massacre of her relatives in the Holocaust.

11. The more distant inferences are from their testing in the analytic process, and the earlier they are in psychic development, the greater the need for articulation with other psychoanalytic knowledge, explanatory fit, and cautious extension. The representation of the patient's childhood objects and the understanding of their contribution to his problems and to his strengths is at a different level of inference than transference conflict and its genetic interpretation.

12. The oedipal organization was hierarchically dominant, but analysis revealed important determinants of the patient's neurosis from the early preoedipal period through adolescence. All evidence and developmental phases should be considered; for example, the nuances of the relationship with the preoedipal mother must be coordinated with the father's death in latency in drawing inferences about the origins of the patient's depression.

13. The translation of manifest to latent content is both creative and yet deduceable from data that helps the patient recover—data that can stand alone, separate from its context and from the personality of the therapist. Clinical psychoanalysis leads to recovery through discovery. The multiple meanings and functions of the patient's psychopathology—for example, of a repetitive daydream of massacre, present prior to analysis—can also be understood relatively independently of the influence of the analytic situation and of the analyst's own personality.

14. The meanings of such a massacre fantasy at all developmental levels may be inferred from analytic data, with levels of inference at increasing distance from the clinical material. Analytic interpretation and reconstruction cannot be entirely free of suggestion or subjectivity. Nevertheless, interpretation is not arbitrary, preformed, or mystical but, rather, conveys rational understanding of the irrational. Clinical inference is linked to analytic explanation, which aims at objective com-

prehension of psychopathology and pathogenesis and of personality development and organization. Analytic explanation encompasses motivation and meaning, cause and consequence, fantasy and reality, and interdependent dimensions and levels of theory.

Summary

This chapter has illustrated and reviewed the nature of analytic evidence derived from the analytic process. The initial acting out of flight from analysis combined with an egregious lie later proved, surprisingly, to be analyzable. The lie of loss was a leitmotif in the analysis that revealed a neurotic structure strongly influenced by actual and threatened parent loss in childhood. Analytic explanation of psychopathology and pathogenesis is based on insightful inference at increasing distances from the direct analytic data. The meanings inferred and understanding achieved are progressively refined to minimize suggestion and subjectivity. Clinical inference can be tested in the analytic process, but inferences about the distant past or at higher levels of abstraction or generalization require consistency and coherence and articulation with analytic knowledge and principles. This case reemphasizes the reconstruction of traumatic experience as a significant dimension of analytic work, with reciprocal illumination of transference and resistance. The evidence was drawn from the totality of the analytic process, in which shared inferences become a part of the process in which they are further evaluated and extended.

2

Psychoanalytic Psychotherapy

Irwin L. Kutash
Jeffrey C. Greenberg

In this chapter we describe psychoanalytic psychotherapy and differentiate it from psychoanalysis. We survey newer psychoanalytic approaches, including the theoretical framework for a form of psychoanalytic psychotherapy, the drive/relational model (Kutash, 1984a), which draws on instinctual drive, interpersonal relations, and object relations theories. We then apply this approach to a case of a di-egophrenic patient (Greenberg, 1984), mostly involving "relational" issues, since cases involving or purporting to involve "drive" issues are well represented in classical psychoanalytic literature.

Differentiation of Psychoanalytic Psychotherapy and Psychoanalysis

Psychoanalytic psychotherapy has been differentiated from psychoanalysis in two ways. First, some therapists see psychoanalytic psychotherapy as a modification of psychoanalysis designed to treat particular disorders that are less amenable to psychoanalysis—for example, reconstructive therapy for disorders not previously approached by psychoanalysts. Kernberg (1982), for example, believing that "the structural characteristics of borderline patients defy applying the model of psychoanalysis to psychoanalytic psychotherapy, unless the model is modified," devised psychoanalytic psychotherapy modified to take into account "the defenses and resistances, the transferences and drive derivatives of patients with severe character pathology and borderline personality organization" (p. 21). Second, psychoanalytic psychotherapy has been differentiated from psychoanalysis on the basis of their goals and aims. For example, in ego psychology theory, psychoanalytic psychotherapy is intended to only partly resolve unconscious conflicts and resistances and achieve a partial integration of repressed impulses into the ego, with reinforcement of some defenses attempted. To these two differences from psychoanalysis we would add a third: psychoanalytic psychotherapy has added to psychoanalysis psychoanalytic approaches designed to help construct, as opposed to reconstruct, the ego, to facilitate the progression of the ego, as opposed to its repair. Kris (1952) talked about "regression in the service of the ego," and we similarly caution not to overlook progression as a service to the ego.

Wallerstein (1969) described psychoanalysis as attempting fundamental character realignment or revision of the total personality and psychoanalytic psychotherapy as having more discrete goals, such as modifying character structure for adaptive stability. Psychoanalysis attempts a full exploration of the unconscious and of genetic development; psychoanalytic psychotherapy focuses on the derivatives of presenting symptoms and their unconscious causes. Both utilize interpretation, free association, dream analysis and transference, but the former uses them more globally and the latter directs them more toward particular areas of conflict and with the aim of resolving particular symptoms. In structure, psychoanalysis uses the couch, with the analyst not visible, for three to five sessions a week. In psychoanalytic psychotherapy the meetings may be face to face, upright, and one to three times a week. In both forms of therapies boundaries are maintained in the relationship by the neutrality in stance struck by the therapist, but in the more intense psychoanalysis schedule this neutrality can lead to severe, intense transferences.

Newer Psychoanalytic Approaches

Psychoanalytic psychotherapy has evolved from psychoanalysis by the development of new techniques applicable to more restricted goals or to certain types of patients. These techniques are derived from theoretical models that include ego psychology, object relations theory, self psychology, and the drive/relational model. Some of the techniques are designed to repair damaged egos, as psychoanalysis was designed to do in neurotics, extending this goal to narcissists or borderlines— for example, those deriving from psychology and object relations theory. Others are designed to enhance ego progression for submerged, arrested, or not fully developed egos, a group ignored by orthodox analysts—for example, those derived from self psychology, which focus on affirming weak egos by affirming the self, and those derived from the drive/relational model, which help the client affirm his or her own ego, facilitated by a neutral therapist.

J. R. Greenberg and Mitchell (1983) have described two schools of thought in psychoanalytic theory: the "drive/structure model," in which relationships are entered and shaped by the need for drive satisfaction (for example, Freud), and the "relational/structure model," in which relationships in and of themselves are a primary motivating force (for example, Sullivan). These authors believe the two models are intrinsically incompatible and, for that reason, consider mixed models such as those of Kohut (1971), Modell (1975), or Sandler and Sandler (1978) failures.

Modell (1975) posited a two-factor theory accepting both instinct theory and a psychology of object relations and self, with each viewpoint fitting different disorders. He attempted to do this by suggesting two types of instincts: libido and aggression from the id and object relational instincts from the ego. Kohut (1977) replaced his two-factor theory, which was meant to complement Freudian theory, with his "self psychology," which was intended to replace the id/ego model altogether. His main difference was his belief in a narcissistic developmental line separate from psychosexual or ego development.

Within psychoanalytic theory the traditional idea that all behavior and psychic functions originate from and are secondary to instinct was first challenged by those who put ego functions on at least an equal footing (Hartmann, 1958a, 1964), and this modification is at the core of ego psychology, which posits ego functions as primary in importance.

That "drive/structure models" and "relational/structure models" are not incompatible and in fact complement each other is the position we take after having worked within such a combined model for many years. We have drawn on Greenberg and Mitchell's distinction in naming our model the "drive/relational model" but not on their conclusions. Drives and relational needs exist within each person and developmentally play different roles at different times. Both drives and relational needs can be thwarted or subverted, and thwarting of these two kinds of needs leads to different emotional problems.

An individual goes through two stages of relationship development, a primary stage and a secondary stage. The primary relational stage occurs before the individual's secondary drives have developed, such as curiosity or exploration or other characteristics equated with independence. In the primary relational stage all relationships are based on drive gratification. In the secondary relational stage, some primary drives have been sublimated, and some relationships are entered not only for primary-drive satisfaction but for gratification of relational needs. In short, it is postulated that the ego emerges to mediate between the id and the external world to help achieve drive gratification but that the more developed ego perhaps as early as the second year of life seeks gratification in contacting other separate and unique egos. Such relationships can lead to the discovery of new drive gratification strategies from the other but also satisfy the child's desire to establish relations that are pleasurable in and of themselves, and relationships later in life may involve attempts to reestablish these early relationships for various reasons.

What can go wrong in these stages constitutes the work of psychoanalytic psychotherapy. Sigmund Freud believed that a basic goal of psychoanalysis is to help the person's ego to appropriate to itself part of what was formerly functioning as id or instinctual drives. He put this succinctly when he said, "Where id was, there shall ego be." We would add to that what we see as the second basic goal of psychoanalysis. Psychoanalysis must help the person to distinguish his or her own ego from introjected parental pseudo egos. We must ask, if "where id was, there shall ego be," whose ego? Hence in therapy a person may gain greater control and delay over instinctual drives implicated in intrapsychic conflict, but if this has been obtained by a loss of self or a lack of individuation from parents, there is a "well"-functioning pseudo ego rather than a person with increased ego control. In 1976 Schafer reinterpreted Freud's remark, rendering *id* as impersonal *it* and *ego* as personal *I*. In Schafer's interpretation, the ego is helped to appropriate to itself that which was impersonal or disowned so it can be owned and experienced as part of oneself. In fact, "Wo es war, soll ich werben" can be literally translated "Where it was, there shall I become," wherein the ego alien drive becomes a sublimated personal desire. This comes closer to the goal of psychoanalytic psychotherapy in the drive/relational model but still excludes the effects of the hands that first "helped" the child turn instinctual drives into controlled aims—the parenting figures. They can help the child to learn to satisfy the child's own wishes or their wishes for the child. If the former is the case, the child can grow to be an autonomous adult. If the latter, the individual will become a socialized automaton with great ambivalence about any aim, since his or her aims actually belong to someone else.

Analysis, then, can be used to help one replace id with ego if one was never helped to originally do so and/or to replace pseudo ego with ego. The former is the case in more primitive patients with a building form of therapy, the latter in patients with less primary process but socialized pseudo selves. Instinctual drive theory is adequate to describe the process in the former patients, but drive gratification and interpersonal theory must be combined to explain the latter. Even after children can satisfy their instinctual drives, their sense of self and well-being can be shaped by early parental relationships, determining whether they will be self-affirmed, selfless, or pseudo-selved.

In the drive/relational model we go on to relate unconscious internal object relations to current interpersonal relationships. As therapists who practice within a drive/relational model, we are often analyzing the relation between unconscious internal object relations in our patient and the patient's distortion of present-day interpersonal relationships based on these internal objects. We never ignore instinctual drives, however. So far we have related drive to interpersonal theory, and now we will go into object relations theory.

Object relations are intrapsychic structures consisting of the mental representatives of self and the object, or other. This intrapsychic constellation has an overriding bearing on a person's interpersonal relationships. This constellation is formed during the early years of life and is based on the person's relationship with parental figures who helped to fulfill his or her early needs. This definition is in line with Freud's statement that the ego is "the repository of abandoned objects" ([1923a] 1961, pp. 1–66).

The relation of drive theory, or instinct theory, to object relations theory has been a central difference among object relations theorists in the emphasis given to drives. Some see instinctual drive as no more important than any other aspect of experience, requiring the same integration within the self, and with ego controls an outcome of this integration (Horner, 1984). Others, such as Kernberg (1984), emphasize constitutional factors and propose "that the units of internalized object relations constitute subsystems on the basis of which both drives and the overall psychic structures of ego, superego, and id are organized as integrating systems" (p. 85). In Kernberg's view, instincts, represented by psychologically organized drive systems, along with the overall psychic structures make up the systems of the personality constituting the suprasystem. The units of internalized object relations constitute an integrating system for subsystems including inborn perceptual and behavioral patterns and affective dispositions. Kernberg stresses that libido and aggression are the two overall psychic drives that integrate instinctive components and the other units of internalized object relations. Theorists from both extremes in the object relations school would agree with drive theorists that failure to control instinctual drives represents inadequate development of organizing processes that structure the ego, or self, and that drive and affect must be integrated within a cohesive object-related self-representation.

We are now left with three distinct categories of disorder: disorders in those who cannot integrate instinctual needs and drives with reality, having undeveloped or poorly developed egos or unenduring mental configurations of self, such as autistic children; those who cannot meet relational needs because of poor early relationships with parents, such as schizoid personalities; and those who cannot form internalized self-representations because their self was not affirmed, such as narcissists. To this we would add a fourth group, those who appear to integrate instinctual needs and drives with reality, form interpersonal relationships, and seem to have intrapsychic structures that continue throughout life to be modified by experience. In reality their own ego, or self, is submerged because of a particular type of maternal failure or parenting-figure failure. The di-egophrenic (Wolf, 1957; Kutash, 1984b; Wolf and Kutash, 1984) is a person who has learned to comply or rebel around parental needs, whose relations are built around meeting or thwarting those needs, and whose own sense of self has been submerged by a parental introjected ego, pseudo ego, or other. For him or her there are a submerged internalized self, an introjected pseudo self, and the external object, or other.

Differentiation of Di-egophrenia from Borderline Diagnosis

A lack of clarity in defining and understanding the actual disorder at hand appears particularly prominent with the array of disorders grouped under the label "borderline personality." Our first task with the case to be presented was such a differential diagnosis. Much is written about patients who fit into this "borderline" range of emotional functioning (see Leboit and Capponi, 1979; Meissner, 1984). In fact, confusion exists over what constitutes borderline pathology. Giovacchini (1979a, 1979b) describes the borderline person as having a lack of ego organization, characterized by a tendency to decompensate fairly easily into a psychotic state, and a lack of adaptive techniques in dealing with reality. Kernberg (1975) views the borderline condition as a personality organization that is stable but pathological. Searles (1965) views the borderline individual as vacillating between symbiosis and object relatedness. Blanck and Blanck (1979) view borderline pathology as comprising deficits in the organizing ability of the ego that vary so widely in degree of severity that they do not consider it a diagnostic entity. Masterson (1976, 1981) views the borderline personality as one that has introjected both accepting, "good" parental objects and rejecting, "bad" parental objects, with the ego "split" between these introjects. Although much disagreement exists over what constitutes borderline pathology, theorists generally agree that (1) splitting, projective identification, and denial are major defenses of the borderline, (2) borderline pathology is well entrenched in the personality structure, and (3) borderline symptoms are varied and can involve depression, rage, fear, anxiety, somatic concerns, impulsivity, helplessness, and feeling void, with primary problems centered on unstable interpersonal relationships.

Although agreement prevails that borderline conditions have their origins in the preoedipal years and that symptoms first manifest themselves in adolescence (Leboit, 1979; Meissner, 1984; Rinsley, 1980), confusion arises beyond this point. One reason for all this confusion about borderline pathology appears to be the variety of developmental issues that contribute to this disorder. The borderline category probably includes a multitude of disorders with different etiologies.

In order to better differentiate the various types of pathology labeled "borderline," we feel it is imperative to look at concrete developmental interactions between the child and his or her environment. It appears that the nature of the problematic interaction as well as when the problematic interaction begins will affect the type of pathology produced. This pathology can range from weak egos (narcissism) to borderline (splintered egos or split egos) or submerged egos (di-egophrenia). These developmental factors appear to determine and differentiate the type of borderline pathology in an individual or whether it is indeed borderline at all. Some theorists have focused on relating developmental issues to borderline pathology but usually have concentrated on one particular developmental issue with little regard for differential diagnostic concerns raised by the different types of pathology in patients who are diagnosed as borderline.

Giovacchini (1979b) traces borderline pathology to the presymbiotic phase of life (through the third month) and into the symbiotic phase. Whereas the psychotic had traumatic assaults, the borderline's early life experiences were characterized by a lack of available libidinal energy. Winnicott (1965c) terms this "privation" in that the person does not know gratification. The person consequently has "only limited ability to form introjects" (Giovacchini, 1979b, pp. 148–149). The self-image is imperfectly formed, and the person has few adaptive defenses. Unlike the psychotic, who withdraws from contact because of trauma, the borderline, in his or her symbiotic state, clings to others except when rejection occurs. Kernberg (1972) sees borderline pathology as a fixation occurring during the fourth through twelfth months, in which the self and object representations within an "all good" and "all bad" self-object representation split. "This is the stage where ego boundaries become more firm and effective in providing the capacity to differentiate the self from the outer world" (Capponi, 1979, p. 130). Kernberg attributes disturbances in this phase to excessive frustration and aggression due to constitutional factors and/or problematic parenting interactions; splitting serves to separate the good and bad parental images. This splitting reduces integration and synthesis of self and of objects, resulting in a weakened ego with poor anxiety tolerance, impulse control, and sublimatory defenses.

Masterson (1976, 1981), in line with Mahler's (1979b) works, views borderline pathology as developing in the rapprochement subphase (eighteen to twenty-five months) when difficulties in individuation and separation occur. Masterson views parental figures as providing adequate parenting skills except when the child attempts individuation, which is met by rejection and libidinal energy withdrawal. Thus regressive behaviors become reinforced, and the child's ego becomes split, one part introjecting the parents' rewarding part and the other introjecting the parents' withdrawing part. The person swings between feeling good when fostering dependency relationships and feeling angry, frustrated, depressed, and helpless when involved with others.

Differences in the type of aversive interaction that the child encounters with the environment as well as the timing of onset of that interaction create different kinds of borderline pathologies with regard to ego development. It appears that what Giovacchini describes as borderline is what Knight (1953a, 1953b) had in mind when he coined that term for patients who had very early emotional damage and who hover close to the edge of psychosis. With regard to ego development, these patients in essence have a lack of it. While inappropriate interpersonal experience has produced relational difficulties, problems in drive and instinctual control are readily apparent owing to a lack of ego development. Kernberg describes patients whose pathogenic influences occurred at a time when ego organization and structure were more developed and when a modest amount of interaction with the environment had occurred. Since interpersonal problems occurred at a time when drive regulation and self/object differentiation were developing, ego damage has resulted. These individuals have difficulty in regulating instinctual drives and difficulty with boundaries. Relational difficulties are present because structural impairment of the ego produces distortion in the view of the world and the self.

Masterson describes his patients as having damaged and "split" egos. Because their history involves a consistent object, particularly a consistent and accepting object before two years of age, when ego formation is occurring, it is questionable whether their egos are truly damaged as he indicates. Giovacchini (1979b) describes Masterson's borderline patients as character neurotics in that they are more stable and have adequate boundaries, psychic cohesion, and well-entrenched defenses. In fact, Horner (1979) states outright that rapprochement crisis is not where borderline pathology develops.

Many of the patients Masterson (1976) describes appear to have a developmental history and resulting pathology better understood with a di-egophrenic diagnosis (Wolf and Kutash, 1984, 1985), and that is the diagnosis we arrived at for the patient whose case is presented next. This point of view holds that many "higher level" borderline individuals are not truly borderline in that their egos are split; rather, these patients have submerged their own egos to protect them and have introjected a parental ego, which they alternately comply with and rebel against. Their egos are weakened in that submergence causes an arrest in ego development, but their egos are not damaged. With two years of appropriate parenting when instinctual-drive regulation was developing, these patients' pathology appears centered less on drive and instinctual concerns and more on relational difficulties. The di-egophrenic's conflict is centered on loss of self versus loss of object. Developmentally, these individuals experienced consistent, "good enough" mothering until the rapprochement subphase occurred, when separation and autonomy were threatening and unacceptable to parental figures. Strides toward autonomy were therefore met with disapproval and rejection. As stated by Wolf and Kutash (1984, p. 12), "The toddler looking for maternal approval if not love and fearful if he or she does not submit to [the mother's] will, denies his own perceptions and abides by her judgments. To the extent that the [toddler] submits to mother's persistence, he suppresses his own ego and incorporates her views as a negative pseudo ego against which he repeatedly and compulsively rebels with an equally protesting pseudo ego. Thereafter, the child and later the adult with these two superimposed pseudo egos, separate from his own real self and oppositional to each other is ambivalent about any suggestion of another person, projecting on him or her the original mother and parenting figure."

The di-egophrenic protects the "primary" accepting prerapprochement mother from the "secondary" rejecting postrapprochement mother through defensive compliance, but is at a cost to the self. Rebelling behaviors not only indicate the underlying anger created by the loss of self through complying but create a greater loss as alternating between complying and rebelling leaves little energy for expression of self. This loss of self is apparent in the patient's affect and in a lack of creativity, flexibility, or ability to use internal resources. When one's ego is allowed to emerge and strengthen, and as complying and rebelling behaviors are diminished, more constructive, appropriate, and organized behaviors emerge that express one's own genuine ego, judgments, appreciation of reality, and contentment with self. These behaviors, as well as others including more appropriate daily functioning, better interpersonal skills, and an intact observing ego, help to differentiate the di-egophrenic from the borderline whose own ego is split and damaged.

Case Presentation

We will now present such a case to demonstrate drive/relational theory. Psychotherapy is a process dependent on a multitude of variables occurring intrapsychically as well as interpersonally. Although this process occurs in the therapeutic relationship, work with patients and investigations into human behavior confirm how influential past environmental experiences are over behavior and emotional processes within and outside a psychotherapeutic relationship. Accordingly, a cohesive and clear understanding of a theoretical framework, based on drives, relationships, and developmental processes, should guide the clinician in treating a patient. The word *guide* is used because a balance should occur: rather than blinding the therapist to the individuality of the patient, theory should be used as a backbone in understanding the patient's pathology. Seeing the patient within his or her individualized context is essential to making the choice whether therapy is a building task-fostering ego progression and/or rebuilding, reconstructive to the ego based on that person's specific needs. We will present this case study with these guidelines in mind, integrating the therapist's understanding of the patient's psychopathology as well as therapeutic issues pertinent to our theoretical model. The case itself was seen by Greenberg (1984) with consultation by Kutash.

Identifying Data. Maria has been in psychotherapy for twenty months. She is very attractive, twenty-nine years old, of Protestant faith and American parentage. Her family is of Italian origin. She is of medium height, slender, and well developed. Her black hair is long, usually worn away from her forehead. Her dress varies from casual to professional and is always stylish. She is neat and appropriately groomed. She has a high school diploma and has been married for nine years. Maria and her husband, Jerry, separated twenty months ago. Currently she is living with her two children, a son who is of primary school age and a daughter who will be entering school in the fall, in a two-bedroom apartment. Maria is currently employed as a bookkeeper with a construction company.

Reason for Seeking Treatment. Maria sought professional mental health treatment through referral by her family physician after complaining of feeling lonely and depressed, with vague suicidal ideation. Precipitating factors included separating from her husband and quitting her job because she could not concentrate on her work. She reported feeling tense and anxious. She elaborated on these feelings in terms of feeling shaky and cold, having numerous crying spells, and having "butterflies" in her stomach. Maria also reported that she felt like a failure and was having sleeping difficulties, chest pains, shortness of breath, frequent headaches, and gastrointestinal problems. Further, she complained that everyone always tells her what to do and that she wanted therapy in order to feel better and to decide what she wanted to do with her life.

Summary of Previous Treatments. Maria had had minimal prior involvement with the mental health system. Some years ago, after feeling depressed, she sought the help of a local psychologist in a community mental health center. Seeing him for only a few sessions, Maria thought he was helpful in suggesting things for her to do but that therapy was not for her. Shortly before her present therapy she began seeing her family physician for medical problems, which included feeling "jittery," gastrointestinal problems, and heart palpitations. Numerous medical tests were performed on her as an in- and outpatient; no organic causes were found. Her physician concluded that her problems were psychological and, five months before the start of her current psychotherapy, prescribed Valium, 2 mg. twice a day.

History of Presenting Problem. Although Maria's current psychotherapy was initiated by a separation from her husband and termination of her employment, her presenting problems developed over many years. Maria has described feeling depressed and "empty" numerous times in her life. One of her strongest recollections concerned her mother's return to school part-time when Maria was in her early school years. She recalled feeling lonely and upset for a few days. A few years later these feelings recurred when her mother went abroad for a few weeks. Throughout the years Maria recalls having strong butterflies, stomach pains, and dizziness whenever people were angry or disapproving of her. Maria's feelings of loneliness, depression, and nervousness, as well as gastrointestinal problems, backaches, headaches, and severe dry skin, were exacerbated shortly after her marriage and particularly after moving out of state. Maria reported feeling unhappy with her living situation during this period and crying about it frequently. Six months before beginning psychotherapy, after she moved back to her original locale and took up residence with her in-laws, her depression and physical symptoms subsided briefly and then returned. Though manageable, particularly with the Valium, these symptoms intensified about ten days before beginning therapy, after Maria left her husband.

Developmental and Personal History. Maria's personal history was obtained throughout the course of treatment, although a modest amount of information was gathered in the initial session. Many background highlights unfolded in treatment, as initially she had difficulty recalling or elaborating on prior events.

Maria was born and raised in a predominantly middle-class suburban town. She is one of three children. The children and both parents comprise the family constellation. Maria is the youngest child, with a brother and sister respectively three and four years older. Maria was a full-term baby and reached developmental milestones at appropriate ages. She was never severely ill and never had a serious injury.

Her parents, both high school graduates, were married in their early twenties, eight years before her birth. Her father married after discharge from the service. He is currently retired because of a shoulder injury from a fall. He was a detective. Although he spent long hours working, Maria reports that he was a family man. She described him as conservative, strict, and authoritarian. Though usually quiet and reserved, he was outspoken when the children stepped out of line. Maria reports that he was the "muscle" in making sure the children obeyed their mother. When angry, he had a strong temper and used a belt, shoe, or hand for discipline. Maria reports that she loves and admires him, although she never feels comfortable when she is with him.

Maria describes her mother as warm, caring, concerned, and "motherly" and also as hypersensitive, anxious, and overly involved with the children and family. She has worked part-time as a lab technician, starting in Maria's elementary school years. Nevertheless, she was quite involved with the children and household, with the house kept in "immaculate condition." Maria also reports that, though caring and warm, her mother was demanding with the children, "always putting her two cents into everything," and that "the only right way is her way." Although Maria's father is described as the disciplinarian, her mother is described as an "expert in administering guilt." When upset, she would become either hysterical and emotionally "wound up" or withdrawn and depressed. Whereas Maria regarded her father as the head of the household, she viewed her mother as the center of it.

Maria's relationship with her brother and sister has been mixed. Maria has positive feelings toward her brother, to whom she was close as a child. In Maria's early teenage years, they grew apart because of his inability to get along with his parents. He began spending more time away from home, married in his late teens, and moved out of state. Maria views her sister as being close to her mother and being her mother's "eyes and ears." Her sister would report Maria's misbehavior to the mother, even fabricating stories at times. Maria feels her relationship with her sister has always been poor. As teenagers, each had separate friends, and they rarely did much together. Currently, Maria's sister is divorced. She and her children live in Maria's parents' home.

In the social domain, Maria had a group of girlfriends during her childhood and teenage years. A few of these girls Maria considered close friends, spending much time with her. Maria reports that her friends appeared more happy and outgoing than she was and she always thought they were more attractive.

Maria reports that she was usually well behaved while growing up and abided by her parents' wishes. She reports that the household was "warm" and that she got along with her parents, particularly her mother. She notes that she usually followed her parents' wishes and that this allowed for a comfortable relationship. Nevertheless, she recalls a few occasions when she became "fed up" with their demands and directly acted against their wishes. She recalls one incident when her parents would not allow her to sleep at a girlfriend's house. In opposition, she slept at another girlfriend's house for the entire weekend, facing harsh consequences when she returned home. During adolescence, Maria reports, her parents became more strict and concerned about her. Although she reports her friends disapproved of drug and alcohol use, her father was always concerned about her male friends, as he assumed they "only had sex on their minds." He did not allow Maria to date until she was seventeen, and before her marriage she had an early curfew. In spite of her parents' views, Maria dated during her high school years without her parents' knowledge.

Maria reached puberty at about age 12. She first experienced sexual foreplay at age fifteen. Her first sexual intercourse occurred at age nineteen, soon after her father wrongly accused her of going to bed with many of her male friends.

Educationally, Maria reports that she was an A student. Her parents were strict about grades and she worked hard in school. She reports that her teachers liked her and she was never a behavioral problem.

On graduating from high school, Maria enjoyed working as a waitress for a year. She met her future husband in the restaurant where she worked. He was a few years her senior, had just graduated from college, and seemed sexually attractive and financially well off. After a very short courting period, against her parents' strong objection, they eloped across the country and were married. She recalls feeling very ambivalent about the elopement but remembers feeling attracted to him and wanting to leave her parents' household. On returning, they lived at her in-laws' house, as her parents wanted little to do with her. Maria reports feeling upset in this house because Jerry and his parents gambled heavily and engaged in drug abuse. After a few months, with Jerry still an unemployed accountant, they borrowed money from his parents and moved out of state with the prospect of a good employment opportunity. Maria was upset by this move and felt ''it was for him.'' At their new residence Jerry was rarely home. Refusing to spend much time with Maria, he spent many nights ''around town'' with friends and often came home in the morning hours in an impaired state from marijuana and cocaine use. Communication between them became nil except when he wanted sex, a demand which she resented but with which she complied. Maria felt very lonely and spent her time doing housework, working as a waitress, or favoring the company of a few girlfriends. After two years of marriage, she became pregnant. Although the pregnancy was unplanned, she felt that she had always wanted children and that having a child might change Jerry. After the birth, Maria stopped working and felt more alone. When a daughter was born two years later, Maria began an affair, which she halted after a short period. Although she was depressed, Maria reports having worked hard at caring for the children. She reports that she frequently became intolerant of them and occasionally angry at their demands. Maria still wanted Jerry's support, but his involvement with the family remained minimal. When under the influence of drugs, he often became verbally assaultive toward her. Her response was usually crying and occasionally screaming at him. At times, particularly when upset, Maria went on eating and spending sprees, buying clothes for the children and herself, which only upset Jerry more.

During their first six years living out of state, Jerry was frequently unemployed because of his drug use, gambling, and overall noncommittal attitude toward his work. Nevertheless, with borrowed money they moved out of an apartment and bought their own home. After a short time, with the house near foreclosure, Maria persuaded Jerry to move back to the East. After they moved back in with his parents, Jerry continued to abuse drugs. Maria found employment as a cashier. She reports that Jerry and her in-laws continued to criticize her and provided only mediocre care of the children in her absence. After some months of tolerating this situation, Maria took the children and left Jerry, moving back with her parents against her sister's wishes. With difficulty sleeping and concentrating, and feeling more depressed, she followed her physician's advice and sought mental health services.

Theoretical Understanding of the Patient

Psychotherapy begins with the therapist's having a broad understanding of theoretical issues and the etiology of psychopathology. As the therapeutic relationship develops, more precise theoretical understanding of the patient should ensue, resulting in tailored treatment.

Clinicians (for example, Boyer, 1980a; Giovacchini, 1979b) note that similar symptoms can be characteristic of many types of mental disorders. True understanding of the patient develops over the course of treatment as the therapist obtains a total picture of the patient's intrapsychic and interpersonal functioning. The therapist ''has to be able to tolerate and sustain ignorance'' (Giovacchini, 1979b, p. 12). Understanding of the patient develops through formulation and reformulation of hypotheses; the therapist uses theory to anchor his or her confirmed hypothesis into a larger, more complete picture of the patient. As Giovacchini (1979b, p. 11) states, "A sound and scientific clinical picture requires a consistent conceptual background. It must be supported by theory which permits the observer to make sense out of an array of data which otherwise would be chaotic and overwhelming."

As understood through the treatment process, Maria's major dynamics and personality structure are di-egophrenic. Simplified for brevity, her issues appear centered on an unavailable and submerged ego, overshadowed by a need to comply with others and yet a need to rebel against them. Maria has submerged her own ego and incorporated her parents' wishes and symbiotic demands through developing a pseudo ego which is compliant with their views but which she opposes through the development of a rebelling pseudo ego. This internalized conflict is repeated in other significant relationships. While incorporating the opposing pseudo egos affects her ability to integrate interpersonal relationships into a whole, dividing her feelings to protect the primary (prerapprochement) mother from contamination by the secondary (postrapprochement) mother exacerbates this condition. Thus, Maria perceives significant people as good or bad, usually ambivalating between the two. With dependency needs great, owing to a loss of self and a history of rewards for regressive behavior, relations focus on recapturing the nurturing and accepting object. Yet, because Maria has experienced the emergence of the secondary mother, all relationships become suspect. Although Maria desires intimacy and sexual contact, these feelings are threatening to her. Gratification is hindered by anticipation of a rejecting object and by the fact that oedipal issues are not resolved. Maria forms close heterosexual relationships with men who are demanding and unable to meet many of her needs, thereby completing the repetition compulsion and confirming the secondary mother's message that autonomous behaviors have negative consequences.

Acting out is common in the di-egophrenic. Maria has engaged in numerous rebelling behaviors, such as drinking, eloping, and having an affair, particularly when complying behaviors do not result in need gratification. At times Maria's frustration tolerance is low, but this is not surprising when complying has not had the expected payoff. Furthermore, low frustration tolerance develops when in childhood the self has experienced intense frustration.

Maria's perceptions of herself are negative, highlighted by feelings of insecurity and inadequacy. With parental figures unable to accept her emerging, autonomous self, her self-concept is affected. Furthermore, feelings of abandonment, isolation, depression, and depersonalization develop out of the loss of self and emerge into awareness when Maria is involved with significant others as she anticipates and psychically reexperiences secondary objects. In addition, with the expression of anger unacceptable in the formative years, and with the rejection of self creating tremendous rage, underneath this depressed shell is an enraged woman with discharge occurring through somatization. Somatization also symbolizes Maria's conflict. It expresses her inner pain and simultaneously confirms the introjected parental message of weakness and vulnerability. And because of her underdeveloped and submerged ego, the intensity of her anger is a threat to her. Diffuse anxiety is therefore better tolerated while acting as a signal that the self is in danger.

In spite of Maria's symptoms, conflicts, and rebellious behavior, a healthier but submerged ego is present and is evidenced when Maria is not involved in rebellious behaviors. The primary object, stability, and many positive factors in the home account for this situation. Indicative of this intact ego is an intact observing ego that allows Maria to judge her behaviors, her perceptions, and others with relative accuracy, although she is not always able to convert this information to the emotional sphere. In addition, Maria is very personable, has developed some stable peer relationships, has adequate daily living skills, possesses a variety of mothering skills, has adequate work-related skills, and, outside conflict areas, sees life in a more integrated format. Further indications of the presence of a more stable, less damaged ego are noted when Maria is under stress. Although an exacerbation of symptoms occurs, with some regression, reality testing and stable ego boundaries never give way to psychotic thinking or processes.

Psychotherapy with Maria

The main thrust of a psychoanalytical approach is focusing on the therapeutic relationship and its developing transferences (and countertransferences) and relating the past to the present, with emphasis on insight, interpretation, and understanding the patient on many levels. As Giovacchini (1979b, p. 7) states, "The psychoanalytic method is an in-depth approach and can be compared to a microscopic examination." Technically, analytical work with the di-egophrenic is constructive. The primary work is constructive in allowing the ego to emerge and replace the pseudo egos. Reconstructive work also occurs in focusing on prior experiences and their distortions, since once the ego has emerged, it is weakened and may require some structural change. Overall, with a borderline the therapist is attempting to reconstruct the ego, whereas with the di-egophrenic the attempt is to allow the ego to emerge and strengthen. Whereas the main thrust of treatment with the borderline is toward increasing integration and organizational processes of the ego that is split and composed of organizational malformations, with the di-egophrenic the emphasis is on ego-enhancing techniques to foster emergence of the patient's own ego as opposed to reconstructing it. Accordingly, many clinicians have introduced numerous parameters (Eissler, 1953) in working with borderline patients, including confrontation (Kernberg, 1975; Masterson, 1976) and purely supportive approaches (Zetzel, 1971), but these are contraindicated with the di-egophrenic. The difference between ego-enhancing techniques and supportive psychotherapy is that the former makes an appeal to and forms an alliance with the submerged ego while the latter is more nurturing, gratifying, and/or controlling. The former fosters autonomy, the latter dependency.

In order to allow the patient's own ego to emerge, treatment must be conducted in the most orthodox manner with regard to what Freud ([1915a] 1958) termed relative abstinence. Failure to remain abstinent may be viewed by the patient as an alignment with either pseudo ego, resulting in treatment failure or termination because the patient feels loss of self or primary object. Particularly, being directive, supportive, or nurturing can create problems in that unknowingly one might support either pseudo ego or else foster a transference in which the patient complies to obtain acceptance, with unforeseen results. As the term *abstinence* may imply passivity, *neutrality* is more accurate whether the therapist is passive or active. *Neutrality* does not mean "listless indifference" (Freud, 1963) but, rather, "a sufficient degree of objectivity combined with an authentic concern for the patient" (Kernberg, 1979, p. 296).

These are the therapeutic guidelines used in treating Maria. In addition, and most important, "the therapist must be a real person" (Masterson, 1976, p. 90). Thus one must be oneself and adapt a procedure to one's own style. The therapy employed is geared not only to the dynamics of the patient but also to the therapist's style. Therefore, the therapist's training, style, and experience also set the treatment parameter. With Maria, the treatment approach has been psychoanalytically oriented psychotherapy with the goal of allowing her own ego to emerge and strengthen. This should decrease her anxiety, depression, underlying anger, and somatic problems and increase productive behaviors and positive self-regard. The treatment frame consists in face-to-face treatment in a low-lighted room, two forty-five-minute sessions a week.

Psychoanalytic psychotherapy is usually separated into three components: initial, middle, and termination phases. As Maria's treatment is currently in the middle phase, our focus will be on the initial and middle phases. The opening phase of therapy had as its main goal understanding the presenting and underlying problems, evaluating Maria's potential for establishing a therapeutic alliance, detecting anxieties and resistances to treatment, stabilizing emotions, and obtaining personal information. The first impressions of Maria centered on her overall appearance: she was well dressed, appeared well controlled, and gave an air of pleasantness. Once she was in the office, this appearance diminished, giving way to a distraught, helpless, sobbing individual who felt alone and frightened by her current state of affairs. Although she was organized in thought, her affect was intense as she spilled her story about separation and job loss. At times in the initial sessions she appeared overwhelmed with emotion and the need to tell her story. This overwhelming feeling was instilled within the therapist and was understood through the mechanism of projective identification (Leboit, 1979; Boyer, 1982). Maria was allowing the therapist to experience what she internally felt. In addition, the strength of her affect and her need to "spill" her story gave the impression of trying to "steamroll" the therapist. She was in need of protecting herself, and this behavior appeared to keep the therapist at a distance. When treatment is just beginning, initial transferences develop as the therapist is perceived in an uncertain manner. Paradoxically, Maria also appeared to make some contact, as noted in her leaning forward. She appeared caught between wanting contact and being fearful of it.

Although Masterson (1976) and Kernberg (1982) use supportive techniques throughout treatment with "primitive" patients, the guidelines of Boyer (1961, 1980b), Eissler (1953), and Langs (1973, 1974) were followed. Supportive psychotherapy can be warranted early in treatment to foster a therapeutic alliance and emotional containment and to help the patient deal with a crisis, but it should be removed once these objectives are met. Although initial therapy was mildly supportive, the stance was still neutral, the therapist being nondirective and withholding judgment or advice. Therapy initially focused on making Maria feel understood, allowing and fostering appropriate emotional discharge, providing some optimism for the future, helping her focus on how she was feeling (as many emotions were blurred), and helping Maria engage in a healthy therapeutic relationship on which treatment could build. Control over her life and feeling understood appeared particularly important to Maria—she repeatedly noted that people did not understand her and that she always had to do what others wanted her to do. This was understood to be her "prescription" for her treatment within therapy. Much of her early treatment was directed toward providing a "holding environment" (Winnicott, 1960) where Maria could feel some reprieve from her daily interpersonal experience and also providing some structure for her feelings. Ego-enhancing techniques were used to give Maria more control over her feelings—for example, "I understand how upset you feel, but these feelings can act as a force to help *you* find a way to resolve the situation *in a manner that's best for you.*" The neutral stance was particularly helpful during these initial sessions in that, as noted, closeness appeared to be a concern of Maria's. Neutrality allowed Maria to feel understood in a nonthreatening way as well as giving the therapist time to understand her issues and dynamics clearly without interrupting her projective field.

Testing the therapist and strong transferential reactions usually appear in the initial phase of treatment. This was evident in treating Maria. Although therapy was structured with reference to the frame, Maria had control over the content and direction of her sessions. Yet, she would start many sessions by asking the therapist what he wanted to talk about. Although therapy was directed at helping Maria focus on whatever she wanted to, the scenario outside treatment became evident within the therapy as Maria would discuss a particular problem and then ask: "So what should I do?" This behavior, besides demonstrating her feelings of helplessness, was viewed as an attempt to prove that the therapist was like others in her life and that to please them one must submit to their control. The therapist explored these situations, helping Maria look at various alternatives and allowing her to decide what she wanted to do. At times she was given a neutral ego-supportive statement such as "As we continue working, you'll figure out what's best for you." She usually appeared content with this approach but on occasion became anxious or withdrawn. One hypothesis is that when she was complying, parental figures' acceptance of her was forthcoming. The neutral stance prevented complying and may have evoked a feeling of object loss, as had happened in prior situations when Maria did not comply with another's wishes. The therapist remained somewhat active but neutral in an attempt to reduce abandonment depression, but on one occasion countertransferential issues interfered with therapy. Giovacchini (1979a), Shapiro (1978), and Searles (1979b) note that with more regressed patients counter-transferential difficulties are greater owing to these patients' heightened emotionality, less well integrated impulses, and feelings of helplessness. In needing to be the "helper" or "giver" on one occasion when Maria asked what to do, the therapist gave a suggestion. The following week Maria missed her appointments under a pretense. The therapist's suggestion may have been experienced as controlling, aligning with the secondary mother, as well as making her feel more helpless. Reexperiencing the transferential mother may have evoked a loss of self, with anger expressed through withdrawal from and rebelling against treatment. Therapeutic recovery occurred in that neutrality was reinstated. The therapist accepted this interruption, making Maria feel she could make decisions without consequences. Testing continued to occur; Maria asked a few sessions later how the therapist felt when she could not make an appointment as scheduled. Exploration of these feelings occurred with therapeutic neutrality maintained. Therapy in this and other situations was ego-enhancing, allowing Maria to focus on how she felt or what she wanted to do in a given situation, whether her feelings were similar to or different from others', and whether she felt she was acting or reacting, as well as allowing Maria to decide what was best for her.

Maria's response to interpretations was similar to her response to suggestions, a fact that led to our initial diagnosis and treatment plan. Although Giovacchini (1979b), Kernberg (1979), and Leboit (1979) view interpretations as the crux of analytic treatment, soon after therapy began, it became evident that Maria could make only minimal use of interpretations presented by the therapist. This is congruent with Blanck and Blanck's (1979) and Leboit's (1979) position that with pre-oedipal conditions interpretations are contraindicated in early treatment. Maria had difficulty incorporating the most ego-enhancing and horizontal interpretations. She would comply in accepting them, but internalization or focusing on them appeared minimal. She appeared to view them as the therapist's and not hers. It appeared that "digesting" was difficult for her in the fear of greater loss of self. Thus, therapy was established with Maria exploring what the given manifest content meant to her and, as treatment progressed, having her develop her own insights and interpretations. This was accomplished by jointly exploring events, feelings, and occasionally dreams. The conclusion of this exploration was left to Maria, the therapist at best elaborating or fine-tuning her insights. On occasion, when an interpretation was given, it was presented in question form, allowing for dismissal.

Dealing with therapist transferential issues was especially important during these months. In the early months of treatment Maria was feeling more helpless, and her view of self was negative. While well contained, the therapist needed not only to change her view of self but to do it in a timely fashion. These therapist transferential issues and their potential effects were explored introspectively in consultation. Dealing with these transferential issues allowed the therapy to proceed unhindered, as going against Maria's feelings would also go against the parental message, which would be a threat to Maria because the parents' message has been that she needs them. To feel more autonomous would also create greater feelings of abandonment and depression, as the secondary mother emerges when these autonomous feelings are felt. Furthermore, "convincing" Maria that she should feel better about herself might make her feel that she could not be herself in therapy, creating greater feelings of anger and inadequacy as well as confirming the parental message. Finally, change might be perceived as the therapist's agenda and not hers, so that Maria might comply and then rebel against therapy. Maria was very repetitive in her feelings and concerns, and this was understood as indicating her need and concern in being heard as well as a test: can the therapist be accepting of her, or will the therapist become the secondary mother, presenting his own agenda? It became apparent that the impetus for change would be the development of the transferential therapeutic relationship, in which the therapist can be accepting as Maria's ego emerges and strengthens. This strengthening of her own ego is of critical importance, as a submerged, weakened ego, by definition, is somewhat analogous to a negative, helpless view of self.

Crises presented themselves in treatment, and these were evaluated and dealt with within the therapeutic frame. One concern was Maria's suicidal potential, as this takes priority above all other issues. A concern in initially treating Maria was her statement in an early session: "I can't go on." Although any indication of suicidal potential must be therapeutically addressed, careful evaluation of the situation is imperative, as overreacting can have a negative therapeutic effect. To overreact with Maria could have created a negative transference in which the therapist was perceived like her mother, who was hysterical, overly concerned, and overprotective. This would confirm parental messages that Maria needed to be controlled and guided. In addition to exploring Maria's statement, the therapist used Shneidman's (1980) risk factors of suicide, which include concreteness of plan, history of attempts, and impulse control. Maria did not appear to be in actual danger. Her statement appeared to be a cry for help and a message of the pain her inner self felt. This evaluation was confirmed by a consulting psychiatrist to whom Maria was referred in order to evaluate and monitor her Valium use, as well as to confirm her physician's findings that the physical ailments were psychosomatic. Another situation with therapeutically destructive potential that was dealt with in treatment was a call to the therapist by Maria's parents ''so maybe you can put some sense into her head.'' This situation was handled tactfully, ensuring that her parents would not disrupt treatment. It was made clear that treatment is confidential, and Maria was told of their call to prevent a perceived alliance between therapist and parents.

The middle, or working, phase of therapy began in the latter part of the first year of psychotherapy. It was highlighted by a reduction in somatic symptoms, depression, and anxiety. A positive transference developed in that Maria appeared to enjoy coming to her sessions and was able to relax more, to feel less threatened by the therapeutic relationship, and to feel some emotional connectedness between herself and the therapist. During this phase of treatment, the supportive parameter was reduced—the therapist became less active, remaining neutral and guiding Maria to her own insights. Although Maria frequently came to her session feeling anxious, as the session progressed she would feel more relaxed, sometimes having difficulty terminating the session. This initial anxiety appeared to result from not knowing which mother might emerge in the session, as away from therapy the image of the therapist became more ambiguous. Through the session, the fact that the secondary mother had not emerged made Maria feel more relaxed, and she attempted to hold onto the primary mother through delaying termination of the session. The sessions always ended promptly and in an ego-enhancing manner—for example, ''If you like, we could pick that up next session.''

During this middle phase of treatment, although Maria still had days when she felt very depressed, she also had some positive days, which appeared to be slowly increasing as treatment progressed. Maria's most difficult days appeared when in overt conflict with family members. Maria would feel more alone and depressed. On days when she felt better, she would still describe herself as feeling empty—for example, ''Something's missing within me''—as the self was still submerged. Nevertheless, these contrasting periods were used to help guide Maria to an understanding of issues, conflicts, and their effects on her daily functioning. During difficult periods, focusing on the prospect that better days would recur was also ego-enhancing in that it allowed Maria to soothe and comfort herself within her own thoughts, as opposed to getting these needs met externally.

A central issue for Maria that emerged as therapy progressed was her disproportionate concern with what others thought of her and her actions. This concern was a defensive operation geared to protecting herself from the potential for future rejection and related to a complying pseudo ego. In addition, it was indicative of both her historical experiences and the submergence of her own ego and its perceptions. Treatment focused on Maria's being the judge of her own behavior (as well as incorporating the therapist's acceptance of the emerging self). The following condensed dialogue shows this type of treatment approach:

Maria:	I feel like I would like to go out with this guy at work, but I do not know if I should do it.
Therapist:	Do you feel you do not know what to do, or is something else preventing you from making a decision?
Maria:	I would really like to date him to see what it's all about again, but what would others think in that I'm only separated from my husband?
Therapist:	What do you think others would think?
Maria:	That I'm doing something wrong.
Therapist:	What does it mean to feel that someone thinks you're doing something wrong?
Maria:	. . . That they won't like me, that they'll think something is wrong with me.
Therapist:	If whatever you decided to do, you knew that people would agree with you, any thoughts about what you might do?
Maria:	I would go out with him.
Therapist:	What would you think if a friend were in the same situation and asked you what to do?
Maria:	I would tell them they have to do what they think is best.
Therapist:	What if your friend were concerned that what they thought might not be in line with what others thought?
Maria:	I would tell them that they have to do what they feel is best, as they probably wouldn't be happy until they did what they wanted to do.
Therapist:	I know you mentioned that with regard to yourself a concern would be that others wouldn't like you. Would you feel this way toward your friend?
Maria:	No, even if I disagreed with them, it would have nothing to do with friendship. I always feel that people should have the right to disagree, even though I'm scared if they disagreed with me that they might not like me. . . . That's how it was at home. If you disagreed, you got your head chopped off. . . . If only I could be a better friend to myself.
Therapist:	Is there any way that you can be your own friend?

Ambivalence was quite evident during this phase of therapy: Maria alternately loved and hated her parents, perceiving them as good in one session and bad in the next session. Nevertheless, in contrast to the initial phase of therapy, at times Maria's observing ego would emerge, allowing her to perceive parents and others in her life in a more consistent, realistic fashion. She had difficulty translating these observations to the emotional sphere, however. In addition, in therapy Maria's own ego was allowed to emerge, thereby reducing the need to alternate between opposite perceptions. Focusing on prior events and feelings that had been elicited in earlier therapy sessions was another vehicle used to foster her own more consistent feelings toward significant people in her life.

Although Maria's view of the therapist as the all-good, accepting primary mother was quite apparent, she simultaneously displayed a negative view of self and a fear of the therapist's becoming the secondary mother. At times Maria would remark, ''You must think I'm nuts,'' or ''How can you put up with me?'' Therapy would focus on exploring these feelings and having Maria evaluate her thoughts, concerns, and behaviors. Occasionally treatment focused on examining where her negative feelings might have come from, but in a nonthreatening, neutral man-ner—for example, "Did you feel that anyone else had difficulty putting up with you?"

Of particular difficulty for Maria is the emergence of her own ego for fear that the secondary mother will emerge. This was apparent in her dreams and her daily concerns. In one dream that exemplified her fears about the emergence of her own ego as well as other di-egophrenic issues, Maria was swimming in a lake, wearing a heavy overcoat saturated with water. While trying to keep her head (ego) above the surface and gasping for air, she had to constantly duck as a motorboat (secondary mother) kept heading toward her.

With regard to daily events, no matter how well she was doing—for exam-ple, getting a new job, enjoying dating—Maria would focus disproportionately on negative events from the past, such as having a brief affair and going on shopping sprees, which had occurred several years before beginning therapy. In incorporating the complying pseudo ego, Maria appeared to punish herself for her parentally disap-proved successful strides and also viewed herself negatively. Interventions were again ego-enhancing, allowing Maria to develop her own insights—for example, "Recently you've been feeling more comfortable with yourself. Do you think focusing on these past events is a way to take some of your enjoyment away?" After her affirmative response: "Any idea why this would occur?"

Introjection of the secondary parents' message was also seen when Maria was at work. She was fearful that she was not as good as the other employees (sister transference), that the boss did not like her, and that she would lose her job. (Rebel-lious behavior was also noted in that although she performed well, her work would deteriorate when the boss was present.) Other feelings toward self were noted in her fear that she was schizophrenic and a fear, which occurred years prior, of los-ing her hair. Concerns with schizophrenia appeared to be centered on whether she was the "sick one" and recognition of her ambivalent feelings toward others. Hair loss was symbolic of the loss of self as a grown woman as well as proof that she was the "sick one." Again interventions were neutral but ego-enhancing. The focus was on exploring her feelings and allowing Maria to develop her own insights into these concerns.

Testing the therapist through acting out presented therapeutic problems that were explored in treatment. During a four-week period Maria became very am-bivalent about her fixed appointment time. She would ask for a new appointment slot, but when it became available, she would ask for a different one, and so on. It appeared that, in addition to resisting treatment for fear that her true self would emerge, Maria was rebelling against the therapist in having to comply with the therapist's schedule, but after finding she could have her way, she began testing the therapist to determine whether the secondary mother would emerge. Other behaviors with similar latent content also surfaced on occasion, such as coming to her appointments late and being tardy in her payments. Therapy would focus on exploring these behaviors in a neutral, nonthreatening manner, discussing associated feelings and other, related situations in her life so that Maria could develop some understanding of her present behaviors. Maria usually came up with her own in-sights. Any interpreting by the therapist was done in a question form, allowing Maria to reject the interpretation.

Another major issue taking place in treatment that produced countertrans-ference issues occurred during the seventeenth month of therapy when Maria left treatment to enter a residential drug program. Maria was doing well at her job, was becoming socially active, was feeling less depressed and anxious, and had reduced her Valium to 2 mg. once a day, on some days taking none. Nevertheless, the fear of the self emerging and fear of further rejection from her parents were too great. In needing to see herself as the weak one and as the ''problem,'' she entered a drug program that had many secondary parents (very harsh and confrontive). Paradoxically, though a way of complying with her parents' message, her entry into the program became a form of rebellion. Although Maria first had reservations about her entry, this quickly changed as her parents tried to convince her that she did not have a drug problem. With the secondary parents in charge of the program, Maria found many ways to rebel. She began calling the therapist, staying up past curfew, and socializing with males, all against the program's rules. During phone conversations with the therapist Maria was ambivalent about staying in the program. While it was made clear that she would be accepted back into therapy, neutrality and an ego-supportive position were maintained, so that Maria had to decide what was best for her. With regard to therapy, Maria's entry into the drug program may have been another test of the therapist's acceptance of her autonomy, a check to see whether the primary or the secondary parent would emerge. With the therapist still maintaining neutrality, after six weeks she rebelled against the program by leaving prematurely and resumed her individual psychotherapy. This situation was used in treatment as a vehicle for Maria to better understand herself by helping her use the feelings in this situation to understand her feelings in other situations. Again the approach was discussing the events and feelings, allowing Maria to develop her own insights and awareness. Kernberg (1979) and Masterson (1976) discuss confronting the patient, particularly when acting-out behaviors occur. However, this therapy has followed the position that confrontation leads to compliance but not to changing internal emotional structures. Furthermore, opposition by the therapist to either pseudo ego can lead to further complying and rebelling behaviors. Of course, the therapist can encourage the patient to confront himself or herself in a neutral ego-supportive way—for example, by saying, ''What do you think would be best for you in the long run?''

Currently, therapy continues to focus on allowing Maria's own ego to emerge and strengthen. This process will be facilitated as the transference with the therapist becomes stronger and Maria experiences the fact that she can truly be herself without rejection occurring. As complying behaviors are reduced in that Maria realizes she can be herself, so should rebelling behaviors be reduced, as the need to rebel will diminish. Many more treatment obstacles and ''tests'' are expected, but these should diminish as the therapist continues to remain neutral and allows Maria's ego to emerge and strengthen. As her ego emerges and as Maria learns to evaluate her own behaviors and decide which are acceptable, ambivalence should eventually be reduced, because this defense will no longer be needed as Maria becomes able to tolerate not having the accepting mother. At this time the relationships she develops should be more fulfilling, as they can develop by choice rather than need and as Maria can tolerate closeness better. Furthermore, as Maria's ego emerges and strengthens, interpretations by the therapist will be better tolerated and digested, facilitating the working-through process. As the ego continues to emerge, Maria should feel more comfortable when her desires coincide with those of significant others. Currently, when this happens, as Maria is used to complying, the other person's desire overshadows her own, and desire or satisfaction diminishes.

Concerning specific issues, at present Maria has not been able to express much anger, particularly at its source, for fear of further loss or rejection as well as concern about the ability of her own self to tolerate this emotion. As Maria's ego begins to strengthen and the therapeutic relationship and transference continue to develop, anger toward the therapist should emerge. As her view of the therapist as primary mother is reduced, seeing the therapist as secondary mother is expected to occur, especially when she wants to be gratified but is not. Integration of others should be facilitated as therapy allows Maria to see the therapist as he is, rather than either the primary or the secondary mother. Integration should also be facilitated as Maria discovers that the therapist can tolerate and accept her anger and other negative emotions, thereby allowing her to better integrate and appropriately express her emotions. This should further reduce misdirected and often self-destructive rebellious behaviors, as well as somatic complaints. Oedipal issues also remain to be dealt with as therapy progresses. Problems in this area further contribute to heterosexual difficulties. A difficult relationship with father, lack of separation from mother, and a submergence of Maria's own ego have interfered with the oedipal process and resolution.

Conclusion

With the development of psychoanalytic psychotherapy, psychopathologies once considered outside the realm of psychoanalytic techniques are now being treated with favorable outcomes. In the drive/relational model, drive theory, relational theory, and object relations theory are found to be compatible and all important for a comprehensive treatment approach. This is in sharp contrast to the traditional position. Psychoanalytic psychotherapy is found to be of particular significance in the much focused on and debated disorders of those with personality structures that are described as "borderline." The drive/relational model with its consideration of drive and impulses can be applied with true borderline patients, who had early inconsistent parenting and chaotic developmental experiences. Furthermore, with its emphasis on relational issues and object relations, it can be applied to patients previously considered borderline but who have developmental histories that allow for containment and integration of drives and relational affects and who the authors consider di-egophrenic. For these patients, as discovered by Wolf and Kutash (1984, 1985), appropriate parenting occurred until autonomy and individuation were attempted and a submerged rather than a split ego resulted. Manifestly these individuals functioned well, but a split introjected complying and rebelling pseudo-ego was in place. While the pseudo-ego controls the patient's manifest behavior, the submerged ego is left in an unactualized depressed state. Thus the therapist's effort is to help the submerged ego emerge and this was the case with Maria. This di-egophrenic's treatment was tailored for this specific type of disorder as an example of the specificity of the techniques derived from psychoanalysis. Specialization in approach to different types of pathology is now becoming more of a reality.

3

Self Psychology and Psychoanalytic Phenomenology

Daphne D. Socarides
Robert D. Stolorow

Psychoanalytic self psychology is a relatively new and still evolving theoretical system to whose richness and complexity we could not possibly do justice in this brief clinical introduction (see Kohut and Wolf, 1978, for a summary of its basic principles). We wish to focus instead on what we believe are the two most fundamental contributions of self psychology to psychoanalytic therapy—the delineation of the empathic-introspective stance and the concepts of selfobject, selfobject functions, and selfobject transferences.

In a pivotal early paper that marked the birth of self psychology, Kohut (1959) argued that the empirical and theoretical domains of psychoanalysis are defined and delimited by its observational mode—that is, by its reliance on introspection and empathy to gain access to complex subjective states. According to this argument, only that which is accessible to empathy and introspection falls within the domain of psychoanalytic investigation. The empathic-introspective stance is a mode of understanding from *within*, rather than outside, the subjective frame of reference of the experiencing person.

In placing the empathic-introspective stance at the methodological heart of psychoanalytic inquiry, Kohut took a giant step toward the reframing of psychoanalysis as a pure psychology of human experience. The implications of this step have been developed in detail by Atwood and Stolorow (1984) in their proposals for a "psychoanalytic phenomenology" devoted to the illumination of meaning in personal experience and conduct. From this theoretical perspective, the goal of psychoanalytic therapy is the unfolding, illumination, and transformation of personal subjective worlds. The specific clinical focus is on the "intersubjective field" created by the interplay between the differently organized subjective worlds of patient and analyst or of child and caregiver.

Through consistent application of the empathic-introspective mode in treating certain patients who were thought to suffer from "narcissistic personality disorders," Kohut (1971) was able to illuminate two broad types of transference configurations, which he later (1977) termed "selfobject transferences." In one type, the patient required a sense of oneness with the analyst as an idealized source of strength and calm (idealizing transference), while in the other the patient sought the analyst's confirmations in order to sustain a grandiose image of himself or herself (mirror transference). Kohut concluded that these patients, during childhood, had experienced traumatic developmental deprivations and interferences, with the result that the maturation of their idealizing and mirroring needs had been obstructed. Through the establishment, interpretation, and working through of the selfobject transferences in the analytic situation, this arrested psychological growth could be permitted to resume once again (see Kohut, 1971, and Stolorow and Lachmann, 1980, for detailed clinical accounts of this therapeutic work).

Initially applied only to the analysis of so-called narcissistic personality disorders, the concept of selfobject transferences was later extended to the treatment of other forms of psychopathology (Kohut, 1977, 1984). Atwood and Stolorow (1984) suggest that the term *selfobject transference* should not refer to a *type* of transference manifested by a certain type of patient. Rather, it should refer to a *dimension* of transference—indeed, of all transference—that fluctuates in the degree to which it occupies a position of figure or ground in the analytic dialogue. The analyst's understanding of the often subtly shifting figure/ground relations among the selfobject and other dimensions of the transference will directly determine the content and timing of interpretations (Stolorow and Lachmann, 1984/1985).

What is critical in the selfobject dimension of the transference is that the analyst is not experienced primarily as a separate person who is the target of conflictual wishes and feelings. Rather, the analyst is experienced as a *functional part of the patient's own self-organization,*[1] and the patient requires a specific bond with the analyst to sustain his or her sense of self-cohesion, self-continuity, or self-esteem. Thus, when the selfobject dimension of the transference predominates, the analyst's listening perspective shifts from what the patient might wish to *ward off* to what the patient needs to *restore or maintain* (Stolorow and Lachmann, 1980)—to the archaic tie to the analyst through which the patient's self-organization can become solidified and undergo developmental transformation.

We wish to stress that the term *selfobject* does not refer to a caregiving agent (therapist, parent). Rather, it refers to particular psychological *functions* pertaining to the restoration, maintenance, and developmental transformation of self-experience. Thus, we use the term to refer to an object *experienced subjectively* as serving selfobject functions (Socarides and Stolorow, 1984/1985). We believe that the concept of selfobject functions is the central, foundational construct on which the theoretical framework of self psychology rests (Stolorow, 1983). Once assimilated, this critical theoretical concept radically alters one's mode of listening in the therapeutic situation (Schwaber, 1981).

---

[1]We conceive of the self as an organization of experience, referring specifically to the structure of a person's experience of himself or herself (Atwood and Stolorow, 1984). The self is a psychological structure through which self-experience acquires cohesion and continuity and by virtue of which self-experience assumes its characteristic shape and enduring organization.

In an earlier contribution (Socarides and Stolorow, 1984/1985), we offered an expansion and refinement of the selfobject concept that provided a bridge between self psychology and psychoanalytic affect theory. It was our contention that selfobject functions pertain fundamentally to the integration of affect into the organization of self-experience and that the need for selfobjects pertains most centrally to the need for attuned responsiveness to affect states in all stages of the life cycle.

The two broad classes of selfobject needs formulated by Kohut (1971, 1977) can be seen as important special instances of our expanded concept of selfobject functions, pointing to the critical role of attuned mirroring responses in integration of affect states involving pride and expansiveness and of soothing responses from idealized sources of strength in integration of affect states involving anxiety and helpless vulnerability. In our earlier work, we extended our concept of affect-integrating selfobject functions to other aspects of affective development that are central to the consolidation of the self. These are: (1) affect differentiation and its relation to self-boundary formation, (2) synthesis of affectively discrepant experiences, (3) development of affect tolerance and the capacity to use affects as signals to oneself, and (4) desomatization and cognitive articulation of affect states (see Socarides and Stolorow, 1984/1985, for detailed descriptions of these developmental processes).

In general it can be said that affects serve as organizers of self-experience throughout development, if met with the requisite affirming, accepting, differentiating, synthesizing, and containing responses from caregivers. An absence of steady, attuned responsiveness to the child's affect states creates minute but significant derailments of optimal affect integration and leads to a propensity to dissociate or disavow affective reactions because they threaten the precarious self-structures that have been achieved. The child, in other words, becomes vulnerable to *self-fragmentation* because his or her affect states have not been met with the requisite responsiveness from the caregiving surround and thus cannot become integrated into the organization of the child's self-experience. Defenses against affect then become necessary to preserve the integrity of a brittle self-structure.

It is our view that the integration of *depressive* affect is of particular importance for self development. The capacity to experience and withstand painful feelings of sadness and disappointment without a corresponding loss of self, fear of self-dissolution, or tendency to somatize the affect has its origins in the early affect-relatedness between the child and the primary caregiver. When the caregiver is able to tolerate, absorb, and contain the child's depressive affect states, which presupposes that they do not threaten the organization of *her* sense of self, then she functions to "hold the situation" (Winnicott, 1965a) so that it can be integrated. Optimally, if such responsiveness is consistently present, the child gradually internalizes the caregiver's selfobject functions in the form of a capacity for self-modulation of depressive affect and an ability to assume a comforting, soothing attitude toward oneself. Consequently, such affect will not entail irretrievable losses in the self. The expectation that restitution will follow disruption becomes firmly established, providing the basis for a sense of self-continuity and confident hope for the future.

When a parent cannot tolerate the child's depressive feelings—because they do not conform to the parent's own affect states, self-organization requirements, or selfobject needs—then the parent will be unable to assist the child in the critical task of affect integration. A child who experiences such protracted derailments of affect attunement may, in order to safeguard the needed tie, blame his or her own depressive feelings for the selfobject failure, resulting in a pervasive, self-hating helplessness and hopelessness or—if he or she responds by defensively dissociating the "offending" affects—in lifelong states of emptiness. It is here that one can find the origins of chronic depressive disorder.

Implications for Psychoanalytic Therapy

Two major therapeutic implications follow from our expanded concept of selfobject functions as pertaining to the integration of affect and from our corresponding emphasis on the fundamental importance for self development of the responsiveness of the early caregiving surround to the child's emerging affect states. One implication concerns the analytic approach to defenses against affects when these emerge as resistances in the course of psychoanalytic treatment. As we have stressed, the need to disavow, dissociate, or otherwise defensively encapsulate affect arises originally in consequence of a failure of the early milieu to provide the requisite attuned responsiveness to the child's emotional states. When such defenses against affect arise in treatment, they must be understood as being rooted in the patient's expectation or fear in the transference that his or her emerging feeling states will meet with the same faulty responsiveness that they received from the original caregivers. Furthermore, these resistances against affect cannot be interpreted as resulting solely from intrapsychic processes within the patient. Such resistances are most often evoked by events occurring within the intersubjective dialogue of the analytic situation that, for the patient, signal a lack of receptivity by the analyst to the patient's emerging feeling states and therefore herald a traumatic recurrence of early selfobject failure.

A second therapeutic implication of our thesis concerning affects and selfobjects is that once the resistances against affect based on the "dread to repeat" the damaging childhood experiences (Ornstein, 1974) have been sufficiently analyzed in the transference (in the context of "good enough" affect attunement by the analyst), the patient's arrested developmental need for the originally absent or faulty responsiveness to his or her emerging states will be revived with the analyst. The particular emotional states involved and the particular functions that the patient requires the analyst to serve in relation to these states will determine the features of the unfolding selfobject dimension of the transference. The analyst's ability to comprehend and interpret these feeling states and corresponding selfobject functions as they enter the transference will be critical in facilitating the analytic process and the patient's growth toward an expanded and enriched affective life.

It follows from this formulation that when remnants of early selfobject failure have become prominent in structuring the analytic relationship, a central curative element may be found in the selfobject transference bond itself and its pivotal role in the articulation, integration, and developmental transformation of the patient's affectivity. We can understand from this standpoint, the great emphasis that Kohut (1971, 1977) placed on the careful analysis of ruptures in the selfobject transference tie. In our view, the therapeutic importance of analyzing such ruptures lies mainly in the mending of the broken tie, which, when intact, provides a nexus of archaic relatedness reinstating the patient's derailed emotional growth and self development, in the medium of the analyst's empathic attunement.

The Case of Steven

The following clinical account (a more extensive presentation of a case discussed in Socarides and Stolorow, 1984/1985) exemplifies our conceptualization of and therapeutic approach to developmental failure in the area of depressive affect integration. Our focus is on how this developmental arrest gradually became understood, clarified, and transformed as it emerged as the central organizing feature of the therapeutic dialogue.

Steven began treatment at the age of twenty-six with a vague and generalized sense of doom and a pervasive fear that there was something terribly wrong with him. His fears centered specifically on his dread of becoming depressed, which he associated with "loss of control" over his mind and body. He complained of insomnia, failing graduate school grades, an inability to concentrate, and constant exhaustion from "covering over depression." Two events had precipitated his first visit to a psychotherapist: the broken engagement to his girlfriend of three years and the unexpected hospitalization of his mother. These two powerfully upsetting events took place on the same day, three weeks before treatment began.

From the first session, Steven was extremely sensitive to the therapist's verbal and nonverbal reactions to him. He was usually very serious and occasionally quite anxious and agitated during the sessions. He had extreme difficulty in focusing on what he wanted to communicate, and his conversation often took on a distinctly dry and unconnected flavor, revealing no apparent depth of feeling. He spoke incessantly about the "traumas" he had suffered—not only recently but throughout his life—and yet he was unable to provide any details of the events or recall how they had made him feel. All he knew was that his life was "not quite right." When he tried to look more deeply into this problem, the attempt would create an acute sense of anxiety, panic, and confusion, occasionally accompanied by dizziness, which then made him believe that he must have a "defective core" (that is, be psychotic).

He was intensely frightened that he would someday become massively depressed, since he believed his "defenses were failing" him. He knew he was depressed, but he "couldn't feel it." He remembered that once before he had "given in" to his feelings and had become so depressed that he had believed he would never recover. Steven associated this belief with a "downward spiral" into a dark, deep hole, a process that, once begun, could never be reversed. In general, this is how Steven conceived of his depressive states. Consequently, he could neither express nor fully experience them until long into the treatment.

Steven had been employed as a computer programmer after dropping out of graduate school. He held many other odd jobs, filling his days and evenings with perpetual work. His obsessional style and lack of connection with his emotional life were the most salient features of the early months of therapy. He desperately wanted to communicate an exact account of what he had experienced, and he showed an acute sensitivity to whether or not he was being understood. He explained that fears of being found "incorrect" or "inaccurate" were at the root of his anxiety, but it soon became clear that he believed that his feeling states, to the extent that he experienced them at all, were unacceptable and would eventually drive the therapist away from him and destroy the therapeutic relationship. The growing tie to the therapist was therefore continually in jeopardy. He believed that the preservation of the tie depended on his never making a "mistake," which was later understood to mean that he must not express any feelings which were not in line with what he perceived the therapist required and, more important, which might disturb her or make her feel inadequate. Thus, he was very compliant with the therapist's interventions, but his responses were strikingly devoid of affect. He was terrified that any spontaneous feelings that might be disjunctive with the therapist's state of mind would both be rejected by her and have a disorganizing impact on him. When an intense emotional reaction was evoked, he would become confused and panicky, seeming to be unaware that he was experiencing an emotional reaction and thus completely unable to recognize its significance as a signal to himself. After Steven had become able to express some feelings in the therapeutic situation, he nevertheless remained continually baffled by what he "should do with them" now that he felt them. "I don't know what I feel, if I feel at all—if this is what a feeling is!"

Additionally, Steven was convinced that although on the surface the therapist might appear to accept his feelings, nonetheless she would secretly feel hatred, disgust, and loathing for him—especially, he said, because "they represent my feelings toward women." Steven had never experienced a deep inner sense of trust in another person and consequently was unable to believe that the therapist was not using him to fulfill her own needs, as his mother had done throughout his development. This lack of trust was pervasive early in the treatment and increased his vulnerability to almost intolerable proportions.

Steven's early life was punctuated by pervasive feelings of loneliness and emotional isolation. He had few friends as a young boy, "preferring" instead to spend countless hours with his mother in what appeared to be an intensely enmeshed relationship. Throughout his life he fantasized that his only purpose in life was to take care of his mother and try to extricate her from her recurrent, prolonged states of depression. She emerged in his memories as a cynical, pessimistic, suspicious, and severely hypochondriacal woman. Most of his memories of his early experiences were vague and fragmented, but as treatment progressed, he recalled a number of times when his mother had been hospitalized for a variety of physical and psychiatric conditions, leaving him in continuous despair. Her first prolonged hospitalization took place when Steven was two, and she was hospitalized almost yearly throughout his childhood. Steven had both disavowed his affective reactions to these hospitalizations and repressed his knowledge of the reasons for them. In light of what was learned in the treatment about the mother's psychological state, it seems probable that many of these hospitalizations were for psychotic depressions. Steven recalled that his mother had been depressed as far back as he could remember, and yet he had no conscious awareness of her psychological unavailability, nor did he recognize its impact on him.

Steven's disavowed childhood feelings of loss and abandonment were powerfully replicated when his girlfriend unexpectedly broke off their engagement. The depressive feelings evoked had a disorganizing impact on him and were, he felt, completely ignored by those around him. His mother was in the hospital attending to her own needs, and his father remained as unavailable and stony as Steven had always remembered him. In treatment he could not understand why he was unable to "get over" his girlfriend and attacked himself mercilessly for this "defect" in himself. A few months into the therapy Steven recalled that he had been getting "deeper and deeper into depression" following the breakup. "I felt as though it was spiraling downward. I began to get depressed and it continued on where I didn't want to do anything. I had no interest. I had an intense desire not to feel and not to think. It's a slightly suicidal tendency that scares me."

Steven clearly had no capacity to integrate his depressive feelings following this traumatic experience of loss, nor was he capable of accepting these affects in himself. He believed that they surely must mean that he was "crazy," for no one else understood them. Throughout his life, experiences of disappointment and sadness had gone unrecognized as far back as he could remember. He firmly believed that his mother could not tolerate his sadness, and he remembered that she had often ridiculed and berated him for feeling at all. When close childhood friends moved out of Steven's neighborhood—a trauma Steven repeatedly suffered—both his parents would laugh at his distress, commenting on what a "joke" it was that he was so upset. Not surprisingly, in light of such early experiences, Steven was extremely sensitive to any laughter or lightheartedness in the therapist, believing that she was ridiculing him for his feeling states, as his parents had.

Both his parents, but particularly his father, had major difficulties maintaining stable relationships with others. Steven pictured his father as a reckless, self-involved man, unpredictable in both his personal and professional life and "completely unconcerned about other people's feelings." His father had abused his mother and had often become absorbed in grandiose and immoral financial schemes. Steven consequently had strong, conflictual feelings about him. He both felt a strong desire not to believe that his father was the unethical and uncaring man he was portrayed to be and, at the same time, was filled with anger, disgust, and extreme disappointment in him. His father was incapable of recognizing how disorganizing these experiences were for his son and instead became annoyed and angry that the boy was doubting his moral character.

Steven had lacked the kind of relationship he had needed with a father whom he could genuinely admire. His father's use of him to mirror the father's own grandiosity was prominent in Steven's recollections of their increasingly limited interactions. "He would sit me down to have father-son talks and he would go on and on. But there was one crucial thing missing. He was talking for himself, to himself, not to me. I was more of an object than another person." Steven's experience of his father as "distant," "erratic," and "unreachable" led eventually to his conviction at age twelve that there was no longer any hope for their relationship.

Even though Steven had little conscious awareness of his reactions to his mother's severe and repeated depressions, his low self-esteem and propensity to become disorganized by affect states of all degrees of intensity can be assumed to be products of prolonged enmeshment with a mother who was chronically depressed and unresponsive, compounded by the lack of a stable bond with his father. Steven's own disavowed depressive affect states can be seen as a natural response to chronically having no one respond to him. He shamefully admitted that he had been "depressed his whole life" but was "never able to feel it." He experienced "no zest for life, no glory in life," only a deep sense of isolation.

Steven's fears of his own depressive affects maintained a prominent place in the treatment for a long time. Initially he was somewhat aware of his dread of depressive feelings, believing that once he "got in touch with them," they would eventually destroy him. He feared that he would fall into a "dark hole," never to return, leaving him forever empty, helpless, and hopeless about his future. He believed that once he allowed himself to feel the massive disappointment, sadness, and remorse that had always lain beneath the surface, he would "go crazy" and end up like his psychotically depressed mother. Thus, his dread of feeling and acknowledging his depressive affects was based in part on his strong identification with, and incomplete differentiation from, his mother. In addition, the mother's own extreme vulnerability to depressive reactions had rendered her unable to provide any sustained, attuned responsiveness to *his* depressive feelings. Any such reaction on Steven's part had been met with ridicule, negation, angry scolding, or superficial apologies that left him feeling not responded to, worthless, deflated, unacceptable, and empty. Both his parents had been unable to understand or to tolerate his unhappiness, considering any such affect a vicious attack on their self-esteem and efficacy as parents.

During his many visits to his mother's hospital bedside throughout his childhood, Steven often felt extremely upset and frightened about losing her and being left alone. On such occasions, she could focus only on herself and how *she* was feeling, communicating to him quite clearly that what he was feeling was unimportant and unacceptable and that his affect state must somehow correspond to her needs. Nor could he at such times turn to his father, who always seemed too preoccupied with his own grandiose schemes and fantasies to respond to his son's distress. The emotional unavailability of his father exacerbated Steven's depressive feelings and intensified his enmeshment with his mother. No collateral pathway for affect integration was available. Steven thus came to believe that his depressive feelings were loathsome imperfections in himself. Since his parents could not tolerate painful aspects of his subjective life, he developed a firmly embedded conviction that painful affect must be "eliminated" and that "hurt must not be allowed."

Whenever Steven dared to show his emotions, his mother would accuse him of being too self-absorbed like his father and uncaring about the feelings of others, meaning principally her own. Her responses to his depressive feelings were always based on how they related to her own vulnerabilities and needs at the moment. She subtly communicated to him her own fear that his depressive feelings would lead to a psychotic regression, as hers had. Steven felt continuously alienated from his parents and peers alike. He eventually portrayed his childhood as lacking in any true, genuine feelings except pervasive emptiness and hopeless despair, coupled with a constant struggle to "survive just one more day." He commented often that "each man makes his own purgatory that he must live in," implying that *he* was fully to blame for his despair.

Steven's early memories were sparse and unarticulated, a phenomenon consistent with his massive early dissociation of affect, a product of the relentless lack of attunement to his depressive feeling states. He referred often to what he called the "missing links" in his history and in himself, imagery that was later understood to concretize (Atwood and Stolorow, 1984) the emotional disconnectedness he had experienced throughout his development. He spoke of life events as if they had happened to someone else and found it difficult to imagine that he was the same person now that he had been in his childhood. Thus Steven lacked an experience of himself as being continuous in time, because he lacked the organizing and stabilizing influence of integrated affects that solidify the experience of being the same person though in the midst of change. In the therapy, Steven would occasionally feel a loss of a "time frame," especially during separations from the therapist or at the end of sessions. Forty-five minutes would seem like ten, four-day separations like months.

Before the crisis situation that brought Steven to treatment, he had been a most obedient son, especially to his mother. When the mother found herself in intolerable social or professional situations, she would rely on her "bright, creative, and compliant" child to rescue her and "fix" what she had done wrong. Steven had become a very religious Catholic after his parents' divorce when he was eight, channeling all his energies into his religiosity. In this way he found an added source of structure for his increasingly chaotic inner world. His terrifying emotional reactions to countless disturbing childhood experiences (especially the divorce and his mother's hospitalizations) were dissociated and repressed, solidifying his obsessional, cerebral character style. A state of pure, affectless intellectuality became his ideal of perfection, embodied in his intense idealization of the *Star Trek* character Mr. Spock, whose life seemed completely free of the "imperfections of emotions." His struggle to attain this affectless ideal became poignantly clear as the treatment began to bring forth hitherto disavowed aspects of his emotional life.

For Steven, depressive affects of all degrees of intensity had become embedded in specific, dangerous meaning-contexts and consequently had remained a source of powerful anxiety throughout his life. In reaction to his mother's last hospitalization and being dropped by his girlfriend, he was unable to maintain his defenses against affect. An understanding of the dangers involved in acknowledging and expressing his depressive feelings evolved gradually in the course of treatment, finally centering on two separate but related dreaded outcomes. One was the expectation that his feelings would lead to further disorganization in his mother, precluding any accepting, affect-integrating responsiveness on her part. The other was his belief that, in the context of his merged relationship with her, he too would become psychologically disorganized, a hopelessly disintegrated self. Thus the emergence of depressive affect immediately triggered acute anxiety.

To summarize, Steven's inability to integrate depressive affect into his self-organization was seen to result both from profound selfobject failure in relation to his states of sadness, grief, and disappointment and from his deeply embedded association of depressive affect with the specter of disintegration—of both the self and the maternal object.

Steven's transference relationship with the therapist quickly replicated with distinct clarity his tie with his mother. He was in constant fear that the therapist would see him as a fragile, disintegration-prone individual who was at the brink of psychosis when he expressed any depressive feelings. He was afraid to tell the therapist his dreams, convinced that she then would clearly see the "crazy," disorganized qualities of his thoughts and feelings. Additionally, he was frightened of any depressive moods in the therapist for fear that she, like his mother and himself, would "lose control" and become psychotic. When Steven perceived a change of mood in the therapist, he would begin to feel anxious, as if it were he who was experiencing it. As with his mother, he believed that the therapist's failures and mistakes were his own and felt her limitations as fatal flaws in himself. This incomplete selfobject differentiation, in turn, made it all the more necessary to disavow any feelings of disappointment in the transference.

When depressive affects were evoked in Steven, along with the corresponding states of acute anxiety, the therapist focused on the specific meaning-contexts and dreaded repetitions of early selfobject failure to which these feelings were linked. Whenever possible, she clarified his fears that she, like his mother, would find his feelings intolerable and unacceptable and would therefore respond to them with spreading panic or angry belittlement or would become emotionally disturbed herself. Through this repeated analysis in the transference of Steven's resistances to depressive affect and the anticipated, extreme dangers that made them necessary, the therapist gradually became established for him as a selfobject who would comprehend, accept, tolerate, and aid him in integrating these feelings, regardless of their intensity.

Four closely interrelated consequences followed from this consolidation of the selfobject dimension of the transference. The first was that Steven began to show a much greater capacity to recover painful memories of his past. The second was that he began to feel and express formerly dissociated feelings of deep, suicidal despair. Despite the painfulness of these feelings, the therapist and patient were able to understand that they reflected a developmental step in affect integration.

A third consequence, following from the second, was the crystallization of his conviction that his emerging depressive feelings constituted a deadly threat to others—a remnant of countless early experiences in which he perceived that his sadness and disappointment were experienced by his mother as psychologically damaging. This theme was dramatically symbolized in dreams that followed immediately on the disclosure of his suicidal feelings. In the imagery of these dreams he portrayed his emerging feeling states as uncontrollable destructive forces that, once unleashed, would engulf and annihilate everyone around him.

Not unexpectedly, Steven's belief that his depressive affects were dangerous and destructive to others began to dominate the transference, as he became frightened that his feelings would inflict psychological harm on the therapist. As this fear was repeatedly analyzed in the transference, its genetic roots in his mother's extreme vulnerabilities and consequent inability to tolerate and "hold" his depressive affects became clarified in increasingly bold relief. This ongoing transference analysis, together with Steven's progressively solidifying new experience of the therapist's affect attunement and containment, made it possible for him not only to experience and express previously dissociated depressive feelings but to begin to reunite with ever-widening spheres of his affectivity in general and, in turn, to move toward an experience of himself as an emotionally complex human being.

The fourth consequence of the consolidation of the selfobject transference tie and the corresponding expansion of Steven's affective life was that he showed increasing capacity to immerse himself in intensely pleasurable experiences, most notably those that emerged at this time in his first sexual relationship. Analysis of his fears of experiencing and disclosing these pleasurable feelings provided insights into the impact on Steven of his mother's inclusion of him in her own paranoid view of the world. He remembered that his mother had told him repeatedly that she had brought him up with the overriding aim of providing him with "tools for survival"—that the world was a "very dangerous place" and that he must devote his life to protecting himself. She conveyed her belief that feelings must not be expressed—or even felt—because they indicated to her a loss of self-control that interrupted one's concentration on self-protection, thereby rendering one vulnerable to annihilation. His positive affect states were subject to the same maternal restrictions as his negative ones. Steven recalled only a "few moments" when his mother had allowed him to feel joy and unburdened pleasure in what he happened to be immersed in as a young boy. During these times, when he began to feel the normal expansiveness of fearless pleasure in mastery, his mother would soon become alarmed and warn him that he must not give up "preparation for tomorrow's dangers for happiness today." This theme was clearly replicated in the transference in Steven's expectation of the therapist's "severe disapproval" as he began to express his new-found feelings of excitement, happiness, and carefree self-involvement. He would refer to these states as "reckless abandon" for which he expected punishment—for example, when he disclosed to the therapist the enormous satisfaction and pride he had experienced in his first sexual encounter. Working through these fears of retribution in the transference and clarifying their origins in his mother's ever-vigilant alertness to danger strengthened the selfobject tie to the therapist, further expanding Steven's capacity to experience strong feeling.

A vivid example of Steven's progress in affect tolerance arose in the context of his decision to relocate to a distant city in order to resume his education at the only graduate school to which he had been accepted. He was immediately able to experience and express acute feelings of sadness and distress over the impending loss of the therapist—feelings that earlier would have had to be disavowed because of their links with early traumatic selfobject failure in this area. The understanding and acceptance of these painful depressive affect states led to two final important therapeutic transformations, the first consisting in a newly formed dimension of the transference. Steven began to feel the loss of a "true friendship," a kind of bond he had never before felt was possible, given the ingenuine nature of past relationships in his life, beginning with those he had with his parents. Such increased feelings of closeness and trust came as a direct result of Steven's growing awareness that his affect states, whether positive or negative, could now be understood, tolerated, and rendered intelligible by the therapist. It is notable that this new feeling of friendship crystallized shortly after intense depressive feelings had been fully expressed to the therapist. The bond had been further solidified by the affect-integrating responsiveness of the therapist, increasing Steven's sense of being worthy of her friendship.

The second consequence that followed from the integration of Steven's feelings of loss was an unexpected illumination of his heretofore unarticulated perception of his *father's* emotional states. He remembered for the first time that not only was his mother chronically depressed throughout his early years, but his father too had suffered from prolonged depressions punctuated by extreme agitation. "I grew up believing that depression was a way of life, there was nothing else." Steven had long attempted to avoid identification with either parent for fear of becoming like his parents. Since neither parent was available to provide any consistent responsiveness to his affect states, he had remained arrested in his affective development and had become increasingly enmeshed in a futile attempt to alleviate his mother's pain and suffering. In treatment, the therapist had eventually become established as the affect-integrating selfobject that Steven had sorely missed throughout his formative years. During the course of therapy, he seemed gradually to internalize the therapist's integrative attunement to his emergent feeling states and increasingly to identify with her accepting, understanding attitude toward his previously disavowed affective life. Steven's stalled emotional growth was thereby permitted to resume.

Conclusion

The central thesis that has guided this chapter is that the integration of affect is fundamental to self-development and that it is achieved through the attuned responsiveness of the caregiving surround to the child's evolving affect states. We have focused in particular on the developmental importance of integrating depressive affect into the organization of self-experience and have presented a clinical example of severe developmental derailment in this area. In the case of Steven, the principal resistances that emerged in treatment were found to be rooted in fears that his depressive (and other) feelings would be met with the same traumatically faulty responsiveness they had received during his childhood. When these fears were consistently understood and clarified in the transference, Steven was able to establish the therapist as the affect-integrating selfobject he had lacked during his early years, reinstating an arrested developmental process and resulting in significant enrichment of his emotional life.

⤙ 4 ⤚

Ego Psychology

Malcolm J. Marks

Psychoanalytic developmental psychology, also called ego psychology, is a natural outgrowth of Freud's unremitting effort to understand the mind in terms of our conscious and unconscious mental life. By developing his structural theory, Freud ([1923] 1961) moved from an id psychology to a psychology of normal development. Blanck and Blanck (1974) consider Freud's ([1926] 1959) new formulation of the theory of anxiety as a signal function of the ego to be integrally related to his structural theory. With this formulation superseding the toxic theory of anxiety, the Blancks note a natural evolution of the concept of repression as one of many defense mechanisms of the ego. This construction of the defensive function of the ego, elaborated and developed by Anna Freud ([1936] 1946), shifted the focus of analytic technique from uncovering primary-process thinking in the patient to attending to the ego and assessing structure by noting the patient's ability to exercise defenses in the service of the ego (Blanck and Blanck, 1974, p. 23). Bergmann and Hartmann (1976) state, "Anna Freud's outstanding contributions can be summarized as follows: she was the first to realize that an important implication of psychoanalytic ego psychology was the relaxation of the demand that the analysand associate freely from the beginning of his analysis. She understood that the way the analysand resists free association may be as informative as the associations themselves" (p. 39). So we see here a shift toward concern with the patient's ego and a movement away from an id psychology concerned with getting at the patient's primitive unconscious. Bergmann and Hartmann note Anna Freud's warning against excessive focus on translation of symbols and undue concentration on the analysis of transference resistance. They state, "With the publication of Anna Freud's book [*The Ego and the Mechanisms of Defense,* 1936], psychoanalytic ego psychology came into its own" (p. 40), and they add, "As to who were the real Freudians, all laid claim to being Freud's heirs. They all used free association and analyzed transference and resistance. They differed in the kind, the dosage, and the timing of interpretations. What to one analyst was a phase in Freud's development became to another the cornerstone of his whole approach. To Reik, the evenly suspended attention was crucial; to Reich, the analysis of resistance; to Strachey, the analysis of transference; to Alexander and Klein, the analysis of the superego. To Anna

Freud, equidistance toward ego, id, and superego—and the neutrality of the analyst toward those three structures—was crucial" (Bergmann and Hartmann, 1976, p. 40).

Blanck and Blanck (1974), in their chapter "Psychoanalytic Developmental Psychology," affirm Freud's successor and the founder of modern ego psychology Heinz Hartmann, whose work *Ego Psychology and the Problem of Adaptation* ([1937] 1958a) went beyond the defensive functions of the ego to how the person develops and uses his or her organizing ego in adapting to life (inner and outer).

To the concept of adaptation, Hartmann ([1937] 1958a) adds the use of the synthesizing ego function in what he terms "fitting together." We maintain our psychic equilibrium not by our organizing ego alone but by what we have internalized and made psychically our own. He writes, "The development of thinking, of the superego, of the mastery of internal danger before it becomes external . . . are examples of this process of internalization. Thus, fitting together . . . gains in significance in the course of evolution. If we encounter, as we do in man, a function which simultaneously regulates both the environmental relationships and the interrelations of the mental institutions, we will have to place it above adaptation in the biological hierarchy" (p. 40). Hartmann is referring to the importance of the synthetic function of the ego, or, more broadly, what Blanck and Blanck came to make their thesis in their text *Ego Psychology II: Psychoanalytic Developmental Psychology* (1979), the dominance of the organizing ego in its integration of and anticipation of the person's life. It is in this critical functioning system that Hartmann places the capacity for establishing and maintaining psychic equilibrium. Thus the synthetic function of the ego is considered at one with the integrating, organizing function. When the organizing ego is regressed or nonfunctional, the mind may run amuck and put together word salads, mixing cabbages and kings; and the synthesizing ego function is under the dominance of the primary processes. Hartmann's thesis is that it is the integrative capacity of the organizing ego function that enables us to effect psychic equilibrium and to adapt to our inner selves and stabilize ourselves so that we are not swayed by our primary processes to act on the pleasure principle without regard for or anticipation of reality. It is noteworthy in regard to this effort to understand "ego psychology" through Hartmann's work: "Psychoanalysis . . . does not, in general, have a high opinion of the individual's inborn adaptive abilities as guarantees of successful reality relationships and of mastery of the environment. . . . Our long neglect of this factor is due partly to a lack of means to deal with it and partly to the fact that the instinctual drive aspect of mental processes engaged our interest much earlier than their ego aspect" (p. 45). We see in the above statement the stress on "id psychology" and the significance of Hartmann's groundbreaking treatise *Ego Psychology and the Problem of Adaptation* ([1937] 1958a). Hartmann's work has had a major and definitive impact on theory and technique in psychotherapy as well as in psychoanalysis and enables us to approach the more damaged ego in psychotherapy with the goal of building structure that furthers adaptive processes and the possibility of developing a capacity for psychic equilibrium. This is in contrast with early Freudian technique, which aimed at undoing repressions and thereby bringing id content to consciousness. Many of those we try to treat today have shown little capacity for repression and thus need procedures aimed at helping them to build psychic walls and to contain their primary processes to prevent flooding of the fragile ego.

We owe much to Spitz (1965) and his pioneering work in bringing to his direct observation of babies from birth through the first year of life his psychoanalytic knowledge and scientific method. These innovative observations, begun in 1935, have been followed by the work of Mahler, Brazelton, Anna Freud, and other child researchers, all of whom support Hartmann's concept that work with children can enhance psychoanalytic investigation and theory building. Spitz's groundbreaking work *The First Year of Life: A Psychoanalytic Study of Normal and Deviant Development of Object Relations* (1965), as its title implies, focuses on the development of structure within the framework of the mother/infant dyad. This work delineates ego development according to ego organization. In this "slow motion" process of ego development, the focus is on the reciprocal child/mother relationship. Spitz notes that Freud rarely touched on this aspect of development. His libido theory focused on the dyadic relationship. Spitz writes of the "dialogue" between mother and child through which the child builds the first representations of the merged selfobject out of which identity is painstakingly formed. His formulations on the "stimulus barrier" that affords psychic protection and on the slow-motion aspects of the child's entry into the object world are of profound use in our work with patients lacking in firm boundaries and psychic structure.

As clinicians, we can apply these formulations to our work with patients designated "borderline" or "psychotic" who have not been adequately protected from psychic trauma and flooding of the ego in early life. To engage the ego of such persons, our techniques must be directed toward helping them to slow down, to avoid overstimulation, and to work toward containment. With impulse-ridden persons lacking in the ego capacity for neutralization of drives and self-regulation, the therapist becomes an external stimulus barrier, thereby hoping to provide time and space for the patient's ego to emerge and take hold.

Spitz concludes his chapter "The Precursor of the Object" as follows: "The emergence of the smiling response initiates the beginning of social relations in men. It is the prototype and premise of all subsequent social relations" (p. 107). Certainly this response, which depends on memory and on the percept-conscious and the synthetic functions of the ego, is critical for a developing capacity for object relations. Further, it is indicative of a happy and secure child who has been enabled to develop confident expectation (leading toward basic trust) through the very early dyadic relationship. Many persons who as adults cannot tolerate the centrality of the object in therapy, as in life (since it means remembering the loss of the central object and a blow to the child's budding narcissism), regress to the smiling response, which is unselective and nonthreatening: any reasonable facsimile of the smile will do. Our task as therapists is to help such persons take the risk of allowing the therapist a basic centrality, which renders them, for a time, vulnerable to the painful memory of early narcissistic wounds. Development requires the capacity for object love and object loss, for tolerating frustration, depression, and pain. The task of the therapist is directed toward early life and mood states, which have precedence over the matter of the Oedipus complex. Much of developmental ego psychology addresses the foundation for early development leading toward separation/individuation (Mahler, Pine, and Bergmann, 1975) and a solid core of identity formation (Jacobson, 1964). Even the more intact ego of the neurotic must address these wounds of early life as a foundation for mastering, subsequently, the Oedipus complex.

We are often put off by or find ourselves at a loss with patients with whom we are unable to establish a working relationship. Such persons may best be understood as having identified with the unattuned, indifferent (to the child) mother and as reenacting this dyad in the role of the mother to the therapist as the object of indifference. This is a subtle form of relating that, if understood, can in time enable the patient to take the risk of a real relationship in which his or her repressed affects can now emerge. What emerges, more often than rage or anger, is an almost intolerable sadness, a powerful, humanizing affect that had been lost (Bornstein, 1945).

Spitz would agree with the thesis of Mahler, Pine, and Bergmann (1975) that the child does the lion's share of the work of developing structure and separateness. Spitz affirms that drive energy and the ego need for mastery by the infant, not the mother, promote development of structure. This has relevance for our therapeutic technique, since we are often confronted with the drive for action on the part of our less structured patients. To understand that this aggressive energy can be put to the service of ego development and ego strengthening challenges us to find creative ways to enable such patients to channel their aggression so that this psychic energy is not used solely in the service of the pleasure principle for drive discharge but, rather, in the service of development. This is often effected when we are able to relate the action to the transference relationship and to engage the patients in secondary-process functioning by having them talk about their impulses and fantasies about the therapist rather than discharging outside treatment.

For example, Mr. Jay was complaining about feelings of being exploited at work and of having to do all the work while his supervisors and superiors did very little. After listening to this discharge for a half hour, the therapist suggested that Mr. Jay must feel that he was doing the major share of the work of treatment and that the therapist was not doing his share. Mr. Jay then spoke feelingly about the time and money he was spending in treatment and said he did not see the therapist as doing anything about his problem. The energy expended on complaints about parents, family, bosses was now directed aggressively to the therapeutic situation, where the distortions could be explored and the ego strengthened thereby. The patient manifested paranoid tendencies and allowed no one to exist for long in his mental life. The therapist understood that the total negation of the therapist's efforts served in great part as a defense against Mr. Jay's homosexual tendencies and wishes. At a later phase of treatment, as Mr. Jay was enabled to gain closer entry to the object world, he was able to speak of his wish to be held by the therapist and to be gratified by him. At this phase it was possible to relate this wish to Mr. Jay's possessive attitude toward his twin brother as well as to early symbiotic longings for his mother. In the phase described above, the therapist had been quite active in dealing with Mr. Jay and his various cleverly compelling defenses against object-relatedness. His projection of his own hatred and contempt and disregard onto all objects with whom there was a possible connection—mother, brother, boss (who was very kind and appreciative of Mr. Jay and therefore all the more threatening), colleagues—allowed Mr. Jay to tolerate and justify his hatred and his distance toward others. Of course, the therapist, during as intensive a procedure (three times weekly) as Mr. Jay could tolerate, was the one object on whom most of the contempt and alienation was focused, albeit as a defense against his powerful drive to merge as in the twinship and his equally powerful homosexual drive (narcissistically based, as Freud explicated it, wishing to join someone like himself as well as someone who was as he once was when he and his twin, as young children, had had their own language and communication system, which effectively shut out the out-side world). We might assume that such phenomena as Freud's "negative trans-ference reaction" may well be rooted in early developmental failures in the first year of life that induce a powerful unconscious attitude of distrust in such persons. Evidence of gross unattunement in early parenting is often manifested in the autistic-narcissistic attitude of such patients, who keep the therapist at a distance as a needs object who must be tolerated but not internalized as a good object.

There seems to be an essential component in our therapeutic attunement that allows us to feel the primary-process affect of such patients. Yet we tend to sweep this under the countertransference carpet rather than accept it as a com-munication from the patient. We address what Spitz labels diacritic, secondary-process material, which may often be a cover for intense instinctual impulses and affects directed to us as unconscious transferential representatives or replications (Blanck and Blanck, 1979) of early mothers or later-phase fathers as the patient experienced them. When Mr. Lee spoke of his resentment at having to leave home and wife to come for his regular early-morning appointment, his associations led to a memory of an intense libidinal attachment to a sexually exploitive mother. Anger, anxiety, separation, and loss were experienced in his conflicting aggressive drive toward termination and separateness and his libidinal drive toward connec-tion and merging. The therapist's attunement to Mr. Lee's conflict and his attitude of acceptance facilitated the working through of early feelings of helplessness and sadness at the memory of a preverbal experience of loss. This was indicated in his stating that he could not find language to express what was going on inside him. Reconstructive considerations related his feelings of loss, of helplessness, and of betrayal at the arrival of a sibling when he was thirteen months old. His mother must have withdrawn from him months before the delivery of his sister. This recall was facilitated by a basic acceptance of his hostility and negative therapeutic reac-tion within the framework of a schedule termination that Mr. Lee consciously wanted. Mr. Lee experienced the therapist's acceptance of his wish to terminate as indif-ference. This was explored and interpreted to the patient.

Spitz (1965, p. 138) writes of the impact of the mother's moods on the baby: "Affective signals generated by maternal moods seem to become a form of com-munication with the infant . . . without the mother necessarily being aware of them." Mr. Lee had come to treatment with a problem of rage reactions, depressive moods, and withdrawal symptoms close to depersonalization. His mood states, his tantrums and depression (through three years of treatment), were clearly derived from an identification with his powerful, aggressor mother that was so total it often over-shadowed Mr. Lee's persona and identity. The internalization or introjection of the mother's moods was powerful, and Mr. Lee did not wish to give them up, even though this was his manifest reason for seeking treatment. It would have been like losing his powerful early mother to give up his indulgence in these crippling mood states and rages. This loss, in turn, would mean Mr. Lee would have to come to terms with his essential helplessness, his aloneness, and a loss of omnipotence (Born-stein, 1945).

Spitz concludes his considerations of the role of the mother in early develop-ment by affirming the importance of optimal frustration for the child's develop-ment: "Frustration is inbuilt in development. It is the most potent catalyst of evolu-tion of which nature disposes. It is 'unpleasure' which impels the infant toward change'' (p. 147). In relation to the problem of Mr. Lee's moods, it became clear over time that he found it difficult to tolerate frustration. His mother had used him to gain sensual gratification and thrust him aside when he displeased her or when she did not need him. She was only nineteen at his birth and evidently had low tolerance for frustration herself. The patient suffered deeply, including many narcissistic wounds from his young mother, who was mainly attuned to her own moods and her own needs for discharge. Although Mr. Lee developed sufficiently to enter a profession and to marry, he struggled throughout treatment with matters of gender identity and with lack of sufficient organizing ego capacity to propel him forward in his profession. Without the support of his wife, who was more like his tolerant father of childhood, he would eventually have required hospitalization. His ''object hunger'' did provide a motivating force in his ability to sustain the treatment relationship and to extract enough from it to enable him to function at a more adult level in work and in marriage.

Spitz's study of the first year of life was a major contribution to our understanding of anxiety. Spitz considered the origins of anxiety within the framework of the mother/infant dyad as well as within the framework of his second organizer of the psyche. Thus the establishment of the libidinal object proper requires tremendous development of structure for the infant at eight months to invest in the mother as nonreplaceable and to differentiate her face from all others. Spitz relates this anxiety to the child's experience of loss of the central object rather than to fear. ''The eight-month anxiety . . . which appears in the second half of the first year of life, is quite different from the behavior of fear. In the reaction to the stranger, the child is responding to something or somebody with whom he never had an unpleasant experience before. . . . What he reacts to when confronted with a stranger is that this is not his mother; his mother 'has left him' '' (p. 155). So the child's capacity to perceive that he or she has lost mother, according to Spitz, ''reactivates wishful tension and the ensuing disappointment. Accordingly, I have called this response the first manifestation of *anxiety proper*'' (p. 156).

It is profound that anxiety proper and the emergence of the ego as more than just rudimentary (as in the smiling response of three months) are interrelated according to Spitz's research formulations. We find in our work that patients often express anxiety when they begin to feel the therapist as having centrality in their mental and affective life. Thus transference phenomena derive from these early memories of the identification of mother as central and irreplaceable. The adult patient and, perhaps, all of us experience anxiety and some threat as we come to create a central libidinal object in our lives, for this brings with it the memory of narcissistic wounds when the love object was lost.

Spitz postulates that drive development through drive differentiation and the fusion of the drives, working in concert under the reality-testing, organizing-ego function, require the capacity to delay drive discharge and to value object love more than instinctual gratification. To see this evolve within the first year of life—the establishment of the object proper—is truly impressive. It helps us to realize how low and inadequate is the level of structuralization in persons who cannot tolerate delay or even minimal frustration—for example, the patient who is always late rather than having to remember the experience of waiting (to be tended to). The fragility of the ego and the vulnerable narcissism of such patients invite careful attunement and infinite patience in the effort at structure building that will enable such people to tolerate delay of discharge and optimal frustration. The latter occurs within the framework of the rhythm of sessions as well as the frequency. It is always vital to acknowledge for such patients the reality of the long wait from the end of the therapy week to the beginning of the next treatment session. The patient may work out affective memories as the child who was made to wait unduly long and made to feel that his or her needs were too great for mother or as the child whose mother could not tolerate delay or frustration and anticipated her baby's slightest need or discomfort, thereby allowing no space for optimal frustration and differentiation of baby's discomfort and person from mother's.

One cannot leave Spitz's contribution without considering his concept of the third organizer of the psyche (the critical period when the child has first acquired the capacity of judgment and negation), which he relates to human communication. As the child moves toward upright locomotion and into the second year of life, he or she moves from a passive position to an active position. Spitz notes that once the child can move away from mother, crooning is replaced by prohibition, command, and reproach. The most frequent word is "No! No!," with a negative shake of the mother's head for emphasis (p. 182). Spitz writes, "For the child, this head shaking becomes the symbol and the enduring vestige of the maternal frustrating action. He will adopt and retain this gesture even as a grownup" (p. 183). Unlike such words as *mama* and *dada*, Spitz notes, "The negative head shake and the word *no* by contrast represent a concept: the concept of negation, of refusal in the narrow sense of this term. It is not only a signal, but also a sign of the child's attitude, conscious and unconscious" (p. 183).

Therapists often fail to understand the compliant patient when he or she begins to reject their interpretations, explanations, and interventions. If one listens closely, one begins to find out what is going on. When the therapist catches on and says to the patient, "Oh, you're saying 'no' to me," the patient invariably responds with a "no." Often, too, we find persons who do not possess a "no." In the logic of the unconscious this may signify that they do not wish to be reminded of the "no," which means to them, as it does to all children and to the unconscious, "no love." Psychoanalysts offer a fuller explanation, according to Spitz: First of all, the mother's "no" represents a frustration of the drives. The mother's prohibition is emotionally charged, and so is the child's memory of this experience of defeat and frustration. Spitz writes, "It is this affective cathexis which ensures the permanency of the memory trace, both of the gesture and of the word *no*" (p. 185).

Spitz explicates the concept of the "no" and the beginnings of a semantic communication through an integration of drive theory, object relations theory (in the dyad), and structural theory. Thus he writes of further dynamic determinants in the mother's thrusting the child, with the "no," from activity back to passivity, which the child opposes. The child resists. The affect of unpleasure induced by the frustrating "no" provokes an aggressive thrust from the child's id. "A memory trace of the prohibition is laid down in the ego and will be invested with this aggressive cathexis" (p. 183). Finally, the child is also thrust into conflict between the libidinal bond with mother and the instinctual aggressive thrust toward movement and action. The resolution of this conflict is seen as occurring through the mechanism of "identification with the aggressor." Actually, Spitz refines this concept, noting that the fifteen-month-old identifies with the frustrator (mother) rather than with the aggressor (self).

Many persons designated as having passive-aggressive personalities have initially opposed the object and subsequently, through frequent and excessive punitive treatment, have made a secondary adaptation of compliance in which they overtly have given up their "no." Here, the blunting of the child's healthy aggression and ambition to take on the mother's "no" and to function for itself is severely limiting of the person's development of good organizing ego and superego structure. The case of Mr. Lee, referred to above, is an illustration. Mr. Lee had great difficulty over the years of treatment in using his organizing ego to address the demands of written reports in his work. His failure to develop adequate superego structure was evidenced in his inability to regulate his mood states and in his difficulty in maintaining a reasonable sense of self-esteem. Jacobson (1964) indicates that the reaction formation through the identification with the aggressor and the effort to make the mother's "no" the child's own were the (first) precursors of superego formation. Spitz (1965) concludes that, beginning with the "no," the child has formed an abstraction, which he or she uses in exchanges with the mother. This, in turn, becomes the origin of verbal communication, which Spitz considers "the tangible indicator of the formation of the third organizer" (p. 189). He writes, "It would appear then that in acquiring the 'no' gesture the child begins to shift from exclusive reliance on the primary process to the gradual use of the secondary process" (p. 187, footnote). Hence, the third organizer of the psyche ushers in the use of language for communication and thereby secondary-process functioning in object relations.

It was the study of depression that led Jacobson (1964) to her work on understanding the process of identity formation. The roots of anxiety and depression are uncovered in the child's dawning awareness of separateness of self and object. As Hartmann, Spitz, and Mahler have established, it is the developing ego, not the drives, that brings the child to the painful awareness that the fantasized oneness of symbiosis must be given up. It is the whole mother, not just the breast, that the child feels he or she has lost during weaning. Jacobson agrees with Spitz that the child's associations include the sight of the mother's face as well as oral intake. It is the mother's face that becomes fixed and associated with the breast and is the beginning of the object representation of the good mother. Jacobson agrees with Spitz that identity begins with a sense of the selfobject and considerable ego development occurs on the way to Mahler's stages of differentiation of self from object before having one's own identity. She writes, "There is no doubt that long before the infant becomes aware of the mother as a person and of his own self, engrams are laid down of experiences which reflect his responses to maternal care in the realm of his entire mental and bodily self" (pp. 34–35). She reflects both Hartmann and Spitz as well as Mahler's findings when she adds, "Disturbances of the psychophysiological equilibrium, resulting in anxiety, may be caused by separation of the infant not only from the breast but from the 'whole mother' before the child can discriminate her from others" (p. 35). So we see that Jacobson's thesis makes the child's development of a self and identity an integral part of the mother/infant relationship—a central thesis in the work of the theorists of developmental ego psychology. The subtle affective interchange between baby and mother has its enduring impact on the psyche and on the child's patterns of object relationships.

We can see the patterns in which patients anticipate being set aside, forgotten, or abandoned as deriving from their condensation of the way they experienced weaning and how they adapted to their affective experience of object loss. For example, Mr. Ell spent several weeks of his therapy sessions objecting to a schedule change made by his therapist. The change was clearly to accommodate to the therapist's having a weekend holiday. Although Mr. Ell would have his three consecutive sessions in the same time slot, they were shifted forward one day to a Tuesday, Wednesday, and Thursday. For two weeks following this change as well as the preceding weeks, the therapist felt criticized, teased, and nagged by Mr. Ell about the change. Finally, a reconstruction was made. First, it was noted that it was not the schedule change itself that bothered Mr. Ell, but that, in the terminal phase of treatment, he felt or remembered a narcissistic wound at this reminder that the therapist had interests that did not involve him. Mr. Ell experienced the schedule change as arbitrary, capricious, and disregarding his needs at that time in treatment (termination). The reconstruction was that at a time when Mr. Ell had developed enough to clearly differentiate his mother from his self, he saw that she was more interested in being with her mother (Mr. Ell's grandmother) than with him. He was deeply invested in the libidinal ties to his mother and felt a narcissistic blow at this discovery. He needed his mother and her love and so had to comply with her schedule, as he did with the therapist's. But he felt deeply wounded at this early time—probably in Mahler's rapprochement subphase of individuation. This was not a new pattern. When he entered treatment, Mr. Ell had felt similarly wounded in his marital relationship when his wife expressed disinterest in his professional achievements. Now, four years later, he was remembering this early wound in the treatment relationship. Clearly, the very fact that the therapist had agreed to a termination of the treatment relationship was at the root of Mr. Ell's anxiety, protest, and hurt—a painful reminder of his separateness and aloneness as experienced in early childhood. Although he could cognitively realize that there had been much care, patience, and staying with him through the vicissitudes of his life and moods during the years of treatment, affectively Mr. Ell had wiped out the image or representation of the good, whole therapist and was focused on the bad, indifferent therapist as he had experienced his unattuned rapprochement-subphase mother. Mr. Ell felt that the attempted reconstruction and genetic interpretation were attuned to his current experiencing of the therapist, and there was some working through of this early narcissistic wound.

Jacobson (1964), using a schema of values, explains the child's development as he or she gives up the value of pleasure in the first year of life for the value of power when entering the second year. The shift from the whole loving and gratifying mother of the oral phase to the training mother who makes demands on the child in the broadly construed anal phase is facilitated by the child's developing ego and what Jacobson designates as "ambitious strivings" to function increasingly on one's own. This can be seen in the elation of the practicing subphase; Mahler, Pine, and Bergmann (1975) observe how the child feels excited and strengthened by the capacity to stand upright and to walk. So in time, Jacobson notes, "Expressive of the child's rapid body growth and the growth of his ego, ambitious strivings develop which no longer revolve exclusively about wishes to control magically the love objects on which he depends. In their stead, ambitious efforts for realistic achievements can be observed" (p. 49). The effort that ushers in the beginnings of selective ego identifications requires a libidinal investment in the object world as well as the aggressive wish to have the object's functions for oneself.

In establishing a developmental hierarchy of values, Jacobson shows how the child moves from valuing pleasure to valuing power, based on the attainment of selective identifications and internalizations. The next stage includes a loss of omnipotence fantasies and a sense of disappointment and disillusionment in the object world. This is a stage through which every human must pass, and it is related to Mahler, Pine, and Bergmann's (1975) formulation of the child's movement from the elation of the practicing phase to the low-keyed depression of the rapprochement crisis. The child's spurt in ego development compels the child to see the parents' limitations and his or her own. To negotiate this stage successfully, Jacobson says, the child must have firm, strong parents who thus relieve the child of the burden of omnipotence and bring him or her closer to reality. The next stage is idealization, in which the child's love for the parents takes precedence over the parents' human limitations. Jacobson notes, "The experience of learning how to function independently turns aggressive forces inevitably and increasingly away from the love objects and toward the self, since the child in his beginning independent activities meets with constant hurts and failures. What he once experienced as disappointments and frustrations, hurts for which he blamed the parents alone, he now begins to regard partly as injuries that he has inflicted upon himself. This attitude is greatly supported by his efforts to master his aggression and to build up enduring libidinal relations to his love objects" (pp. 78–79). She adds that the successful internalization of parental values and demands aids the process of superego formation and hence autonomous functioning (p. 79). The importance of healthy self-esteem rests on good object relations and the ability to seek autonomous functioning as well as the capacity to accept one's human limitations.

Jacobson (1964) notes that some children never adequately attain the capacity to differentiate omnipotence fantasies from reality in the self and the object world. Thus, the adult patient who sees the therapist and the therapist-self as invulnerable to life's vicissitudes is not testing reality well, and this deficit needs to be dealt with in the therapeutic situation. For example, Mr. Julio already had a history of two therapeutic relationships when he came for treatment on the verge of mental collapse and suffering from an ego regression. Both previous therapists had clearly helped him to cope better in his work life. They had been used as needs objects who were easily set aside when his jobs were terminated and he moved to other geographical areas. The presenting symptom, which he called "a loss of confidence," came after a two-year battle with his superior in which he was now on the point of submission and capitulation. He clearly looked to the new therapist—number three—to act on his behalf, to exercise ego for him, and to rescue him. The technical intervention and position taken by the therapist were meant to salvage what was left of a badly damaged ego in a severe state of regression suffering from a loss of self-esteem. This was complicated by a perverse wish to be beaten by his superior (who had been doing just that in viciously negating Mr. Julio's proposals) and then to get revenge on him. He readily associated to a time when his father had beaten him for an act he had not committed and his gratification at his father's remorse when the truth was discovered. So a perverse form of repetition compulsion was involved, and there was evidence that Mr. Julio was so caught up in it that he was not disposed to differentiate wishful fantasy (revenge) from reality. It took careful work to serve as a reality-testing ego for this man, the stated goal being to help him regain his self-respect (esteem) and find a realistic course of action in his work situation. This allowed him to withdraw from the job and yet to have a cushion of health insurance and six months of paid salary while he was recovering from his breakdown and seeking to reestablish himself in the work world. The primitive quality of his structure was such that he soon began to vie with the therapist as he had with his boss and his wife. He responded then to any intervention as something that was being shoved down his throat, as his mother had when she force-fed him as a child. This was interpreted also but with the statement that the therapist did not mean to force his understanding on Mr. Julio as his mother had forced food on him. The approach of respect for Mr. Julio's person and autonomy, which was carefully adhered to, enabled him over several years of intensive treatment to achieve a better internalization than he had in early parenting or his previous, more superficial therapies. His therapy—not analysis—helped him toward an autonomous work situation in which he was successful and made constructive use of his aggression with better maintenance of self-esteem. Although one could hardly say he mastered his perversions and the oedipal conflict, he was able to effect a better, more respectful relationship with his wife and to have a child (through adoption) and a family. I would consider that there was some gain in his reality-testing ego function and some easing of his quest for revenge and perverse gratification.

In conclusion, the present status of psychoanalytic developmental psychology reflects the profound impact of Gertrude and Rubin Blanck (1974) in their classic text *Ego Psychology*, which, for the first time, integrated the work of the great theorists who followed Freud. Some of the highlights of the work of these giants have been touched on above, with application of their theory to the therapeutic process. In their second text, *Psychoanalytic Developmental Psychology,* Blanck and Blanck (1979) furthered the theory of psychoanalytic ego psychology and its related techniques by focusing on the concept of defining the psychic systems by their functioning. They place special emphasis, as Hartmann did, on the ego's organizing, synthesizing, integrative function and how, when good object relations are present, structure is formed and identity strengthened. Their innovative chapters on normal and pathological narcissism and on resistance are in the tradition of Anna Freud, who stressed the whole patient over simply bringing material to consciousness. To appreciate the subtleties of ego psychology and the Blancks' application of this theory to their practice of psychotherapy, one must steep oneself in their now-classic texts.

One final word—it is all too often the tendency to find in a new theory or technique the cure-all or the omniscience we fruitlessly seek. The theorists of developmental ego psychology did not throw out the instinctual drives, as Jung did, but worked at the complexities of integrating drive theory and ego and superego development into understanding the full person. However, understanding the mind of another person, let alone one's own, is an impossible task. So the approach in applying the techniques of developmental ego psychology is stressed as aimed at respecting, protecting, and strengthening the person's autonomous ego functioning. The greatest contribution of ego psychology is its willingness to accept the complexities of the human psyche and to approach each patient with an essential respect and humility. In short, with the development of our Freudian theory, we must accept our limitations—that we are not omniscient, that we do not have the definitive answer on treatment or the human condition. Even as the child must give up the symbiotic myth of omnipotence, so must we give up the myth of magic and come, as did Freud ([1937a] 1964), to accept the limitations of the theory and technique of psychoanalysis. Freud wrote: "Our aim will not be to rub off every peculiarity of human character for the sake of a schematic 'normality,' nor yet to demand that the person who has been 'thoroughly analyzed' shall feel no passions and develop no internal conflicts. The business of analysis is to secure the best possible psychological conditions for the functions of the ego; with that it has discharged its task" (pp. 249–250). No more adequate statement of the goals of ego psychology need be made.

Demonstration Interview

The following verbatim extract from a demonstration interview is offered as an example of the application of the theory, technique, and philosophy of ego psychology.

The interview was conducted in an open room with the clinic director and staff, consisting of about fifteen persons, sitting on each side of the two persons involved. The initial format of this interview was framed in terms of an analytic ego-psychological approach to "Jim," labeled a schizophrenic in remission. Jim had been interviewed and treated by others—his main therapist being Dr. Lew Field, who was currently using biofeedback techniques for stress reduction. Jim had a 100 percent disability for service during the Vietnam War as a mechanic repairing planes stateside. In the interview he refers to this matter as causing him feelings of guilt, since his friends had gone overseas as mechanics and had come back mutilated or dead. This was one of his "secrets" that he came to share during the interview.

The beginning was something like two boxers being put in the ring without either having any measure of the other. There was a kind of sparring going on—each one trying to feel out the other and the situation itself, with staff personnel sitting at "ringside." It soon became evident that this "exhibition bout" was a tough one for the interviewer, whose "opponent" was a pro, very ringwise to the techniques and approaches of psychotherapists of varying persuasions.

The interviewer and Jim were introduced, shook hands, and sat down.

Interviewer: Well, it's good to meet you again.
Jim: Same here.
Interviewer: I have the advantage of receiving some notes from Dr. Field, which gave me some impressions, but of course, as someone who has been immersed in this field for a long time, I always feel I have to find what happens between me and the other person—and I see you have seen other people as therapists, so you must also have your own reactions. So let me ask you where you would like to start, what you would like to get out of meeting today. This is going to be psychotherapy, but it's time-limited. We meet this one time. Maybe you have some idea of how you would like to use this time.
Jim: Of course—to the advantage of something positive—but I really don't know where to start. Is there anything definite that—should be heading towards?
Interviewer: Well, one way we might bring up is, where you are at this time in

your life—how you see yourself at this time in your life, whether you have any thoughts about where you would like to go with you. Does that make any sense to you?

Jim: All right—physically and mentally?

Interviewer: Yes.

Jim: At this point, I have had a [remission?] in my condition. . . . [*Speaks of his "condition" as being pretty much under control at this time mentally and physically.*] At this time, I am at a point where I can accept pretty much what's happening to me. It seems to "minimize."

Interviewer: You put it pretty much in terms of what's happened *to* you—it makes me wonder whether you find your *"attitude"* [*Jacobson*] in your living day to day, even year to year, is in terms of what happens *to* you in contrast with what you might *make* happen.

Jim: Whether I make it happen to myself or it happens from outside, WHAT MATTERS IS THAT IT'S HAPPENING TO *ME*! [*A strong counter with some merit.*]

Interviewer: Yes—

Jim: [Strongly] So first of all NUMBER ONE [IS] WITH ME.

Interviewer: Yes—

Jim: HOW I FEEL—WHAT PHYSICAL OR MENTAL THINGS I AM GOING THROUGH—then I move out from there. I go through a step-by-step procedure *OUTWARD* from myself—my surroundings. Of course, being aware of whatever it is—PAIN—or anxiety or depression, whatever it is, IT'S *ME* FIRST—the symptoms are connected with *ME*, DIRECTLY. Then I'm aware of—so it becomes ME as NUMBER ONE! Then number two is to go OUT—to see what CAUSES THE DIRECTIONS—something to do with the present.

The interview was structured with regard to what it might offer Jim, but it soon became evident that Jim only hoped to prove once again how he could guard himself against a psychic invasion or intrusion. He thus began with generalizations and probably use of some ways in which therapy had been framed for him previously.

The initial intervention must have been felt as a sharp attack on the patient's characteristic defense of denial and his passive-aggressive personality structure. Jim was affable and relaxed on the surface when the interview began. However, he responded significantly to the probing questions, framed as an appeal to his ego, but clearly experienced as a thrust or as a surprise left hook, with an affirmative aggressive stance and a counterthrust. To the question "Do you have an attitude to life that things happen to you rather than you making things happen?" Jim said, in supreme narcissism, "WHAT MATTERS IS THAT IT'S HAPPENING TO *ME*!"

Behind the intervention was a focus on Jacobson's (1964) theory that what signifies a successful reaction formation in early and later life can be seen in the person's attitude. Many children and, later, adults comply with rules and standards externally but internally live out a "No!" The fact that Jim framed his attitude this early in the interview in terms of matters "happening to him" strongly suggested that he had adapted to life by this pseudophilosophical stance as an effective defense against feelings of ineffectuality and of low self-esteem. What emerges as the interview goes on is a pathologically based narcissism and an attitude that Jim comes first in Jim's mind. He avoids conflict by his surface compliance, which masks a deep attitude of scorn and contempt toward the object world. Note the power of his responses:

> Whether I make it happen to myself or it happens from outside, IT'S STILL HAPPENING TO *ME*!

and

> Whatever it is—pain—or anxiety or depression, whatever it is, IT'S *ME* FIRST—the symptoms are connected with *ME*, DIRECTLY . . . so it becomes *ME* NUMBER ONE!

The interviewer now tries to correct this intervention and to help Jim feel less attacked and feel less need to defend his image.

Interviewer: Let's go see what happened to you just now. I talked to you about an "attitude"—whether your attitude in life was focused on what happens to you or what you do with what happens to you. And I felt some reaction, as though you felt I was criticizing you or—

Jim: No—it's not a point of criticism—I like to explain things, to a point, maybe even sometimes going too fine into detail—may be a slight bit of misunderstanding.

Interviewer: Well, your response was to say: First, whether I make it happen or whether it happens, *I'm the one who's affected,* which I could not disagree with. But I thought you were affected [*meaning affronted*] by my posing this question to you on your attitude to life.

Jim: [Thoughtfully] I was affected? Sort of—being attacked?

Interviewer: Yes.

Jim: No—not really—

Interviewer: Or challenged?

Jim: Challenges I enjoy. I like challenges and criticisms. They're a route to positive effects. [*Sounds like the "power of positive thinking" approach.*]

Interviewer: [Slowly thinking aloud] I think very much about how one looks at life's problems. Everyone has difficulties and problems in life, and conflicts; no one is free from that. Can you think of some problem or conflict that is either here in your current life or that has been with you for a long time—something you struggle with, in yourself?

Jim: [Thoughtfully] For quite a while, I guess, as I was a youngster, I was more or less a "loner," all by myself, and I was satisfied at times with that—and then other times I wasn't. I'd just want to move out and see other people, talk with them, get to understand them, play games, whatever—and that, in the beginning, I guess you could say was a slight problem, moving in to—was scary. It was fine as long as I stayed with myself, in my room, all by myself with my art work. It was a little frightening to move out, to meet people, to play games with the other children. As I moved gradually into that, I ADAPTED—I found myself *blending* in. Well, that's a fast answer to your question. [*Jim appears to be much less defensive at this point, or he feels safe for the moment.*]

Interviewer: What *time* of life do you have in mind? You were talking about your childhood and this difficulty: feeling safe being alone, but when you'd venture out, you'd feel some fear. How far back does that go? Is that in early memory—two or three?

Jim: As far back as I can remember, as—when I could just about walk. [*Condensation is certainly working as a defense here. Jim's voice then picks up and he becomes an assured narrator—in contrast with a depressed quality later.*] There was only two of us in the family—my brother and I. We were pretty close as far as our ages and also as playmates. We played together very well and just seemed to—in that type of world that we were in—it was only the two of us, no one else ever existed. The two of us and our family—mother and father. I don't recall when it came time to go to school, meeting other students. I didn't feel as far as—not belonging in the class. I participated in everything. In the outside schoolyard events, recess, and also in school, but—I don't know—I guess there was *something missing*—something else INSIDE of me that I had to get out, and—the only possible way to do that was to GET INSIDE. So, as I got older, I sort of moved away from classmates and friends [*Condenses a whole life thusly.*]—and sort of isolated myself.

Interviewer: What age would you say this would have been? [*Still trying to get something that would offer developmental clues, but this proved to be a track that Jim was determined to cover over, or perhaps his vagueness resulted from a mix of childhood amnesia and the amnesia related to years of treatment, electroconvulsive therapy, medication, and conscious or unconscious defense efforts.*]

Jim: I would say the first signs of it started around maybe ten. [*So he moves from just learning to walk to age ten, I suspect to appease the questioner.*]

Interviewer: [*Trying to get back on the track*] And you said you became aware of something *inside* you that was troubling you?

Jim: Yes, I guess it was something troubling. [*Sounds evasive.*]

Interviewer: Anything specific? Anything you were afraid of? Anything that was happening in your life?

Jim: I don't think it was a *fear*. I think I might have realized something about my future and where I was going. [*It seems the time barrier has gone and he is thinking in adult terms. His response shows little sense of time with regard to childhood or adulthood. More likely, he is trying to offer acceptable answers while he keeps his distance. The interviewer experienced a sense of vagueness over this time.*] What I should do and a vocation, or job opportunities and so on—and I guess I was kinda mixed up and confused. I didn't know which way to go, as far as that was concerned. As a youngster I was interested in everything, no matter what it was, and at this point I think I still am . . . [*Speaks of having "multiple interests"*], and I just can't seem to settle down—like they say, "jack of all trades, master of none." I don't know whether that is a good way to continue my life or [Pause] an improper way [Pause] of continuing [Pause] my life. [*He has moved from childhood past to present with no awareness of this shift—failure of sense of time perception. Next mentions speaking to his family doctor and asking him:*] If it would be better in your opinion to be something like a doctor, where you do *one* thing constantly all the time, with few variations, or to be a person who can do multiple things in their life. He, of course, answered me, ''To be a doctor.'' And I don't know if he was answering that *for me* or *for him.* But I feel it's best to know more of everything or a little bit of everything than it is to know a lot about one thing. [*Here, it seems, there is something working competitively—and transferentially.*]

Interviewer: So you must be wondering about me.

This and the following intervention illustrate the technique of engaging the patient in the relationship between him and the interviewer. Jim was talking about his family doctor's narcissistic attitude that his way of life was the right way. Transferentially, the interviewer considered this a statement about himself. So even though this was a one-time session, the technique could be applied. Jim's response was a way of sidestepping the interviewer's direct confrontation. The next intervention seemed to reach Jim: the interviewer disclosed that he was failing to make a connection with Jim. Jim was then able to say that he was consciously holding back personal material. The technical intervention that followed aimed at ego strengthening in its support of Jim's ability to keep his secrets.

Jim: I wonder about everybody [*evading the issue of rivalry*].

Interviewer: Well, what I hope we could both be wondering about is—is my understanding that I'm finding it difficult to *reach* you, to feel that there's someone there that I'm really talking to—and I'm guessing now that it's completely understandable that you might be feeling some need to keep the more private, personal, even conflicted parts of your self to yourself. Are you aware, if you look now or think of it, of any sense of holding yourself back? [*Appeal to self-observing ego.*]

Jim: Oh, yes.

Interviewer: Oh, you are? Would you like to talk about it? [*Appeal to ego.*]

Jim: I'm aware that I hold back many personal things—I don't even speak with anyone about myself. I'm not afraid of those things. I don't think what I do or what I think is wrong with myself, and if I do, then it gets out—with my wife or Dr. Field or a close friend. But until this *secret* that I have [Voice more firm] becomes a worrisome problem, it remains hidden—secret.

Interviewer: I would say that you realize that it's good—a sign of strength—that you can keep this secret to yourself.

Jim: Yes, certainly. I'm able to really evaluate these secrets—to figure them out—which one of the several might be causing a problem—then you have to be releasing one of them or two or possibly all [*suggests that his defenses are slipping and the wish to confess, to tell all, is gaining power*]. I feel that I can hold on to some—say, there's seven [*magic number*] secrets, for example. I'll look at them and figure them out. I'll put one at the top of the list: well, this is the one that I believe is bothering

me the most right now, and I must speak about it—and I'll leave the
other six alone (*said as though he'd really solved a problem*].

Interviewer: That would be the one that is most expendable—

Jim: Yes, it's usually the weakest—

Interviewer: The easiest to give up—

Jim: Yes—the most serious is at the bottom—

Interviewer: Does—do you feel some tension when you feel some of these secrets
are pushing at you, somehow trying to get out of you?

Jim: What you're saying kinda—do I feel that I should release some of—

Interviewer: No. No, I'm not saying that. Sometimes we all have our secrets—
everybody—and especially secrets that are secret from ourselves [*a plug
for the unconscious*]—we don't know that it's there.

Jim: Do I feel that there's anything there like that? [*Asks interviewer.*]

Interviewer: No. I'm saying you might feel something pressing out that you can't
hold back—it back anymore. Do you get that kind of feeling?

Jim: Something that I'm aware of? Yes.

Interviewer: Yes. Well, it would seem to me at that time that you're feeling some
pressure to let go of what you're holding onto. So I wonder how you
deal with that internal pressure? [*An ego appeal—to self-observing ego: How
do you see yourself defending yourself from internal id drives?*]

Jim: I don't really feel it's essential to letting go. I don't want to let go
of 'em. It might be a point of a description of it—of an understanding
of it. Each person will have an understanding of something that's going on in their life and give you a definition, but an outside observer
might come up with one [definition] out of your three and it'll be a
hundred times better than your three [definitions], all three put together
[*a loss of organizing ego here*]—so under those circumstances I would—
bring it out and talk about it.

Interviewer: [*Trying to make this real*] You're being very general, of course, and I
don't want to invade your privacy—I want to respect that. But I wonder
if you could tell me whether you feel still in some danger, that you
have to hold back—or be careful of what happens between you and me.

Jim: Be careful for today? Oh, of course. Yes, I probably have some guards
up. I'm being cautious, but I think you're also asking me for an example of something of truth—something that I've already experienced
in relation[ship] that I used to keep hidden.

Interviewer: Well, that might be helpful, if you're comfortable in talking about it.

At this point it is evident that Jim wants to tell his "secret." As it evolved in the
telling, it was a constructive statement within the boundaries of ego psychology.
It was not an outpouring of primary-process material or thought, for even though
Jim talks of his wish to kill and destroy, he goes on to modify this through the account of his friendship with Harry and how it helped him feel better about himself
on a real basis. Hence, this material would suppport his fragile base of self-esteem
in a valid way.

Jim: Oh, yes. Certainly. It just happened to be that I had this thing, this
secret was inside me—this problem, that I happened to be aware of

for several years. In fact, I think it was almost a decade. I really ignored it, but I figured that there was more to it—it bothered me. So one day—I help this friend out at an auto body shop. While we're sitting there having little conversations—and—he had mentioned—I don't know how it started, but we sort of exchanged problems and difficulties, so I guess it was my turn, came up, and I mentioned to him that I had a *FEAR* inside of me about something. While I was in military— stateside—air force—my buddies were going overseas—some came back with obvious psychological—a few of 'em didn't return. Others were constantly going around mentioning same thing—what happened to them or what they had seen day in day out, and this kind of thing bothered me. I wanted to go over there and help—that's putting it mildly, I wanted to get over there and KILL, so I could get into the battle and DESTROY. So, I volunteered three times for a helicopter gunner, who had a life expectancy of something like six days—only ones who could volunteer for that were aircraft mechanics. Luckily now, looking back, I was not accepted, either one of the three times, and I felt that I was gypped—that I was left out—that I had lost something, that I had missed something. So I thought maybe at one point of my life that this could increase to a point that I could harm someone in the near future. So Harry (my friend) and I were talking about it, and he said something to put my mind at ease. He said, "You *did* help. You helped by putting together the banged-up and shot-up C-130s that came back to go back over there to assist the war effort." He said you might not have been over there physically holding the gun in your hand, but the aircraft is considered a *weapon,* and without the mechanic working stateside, it would not have been able to con- tinue with the battle. That kind of set me at ease a bit—that I really did help. It wasn't necessary for me to hold a gun and to actually blow somebody away—so that was discarded.

Interviewer: —through trusting another human being, who was very wise in his understanding of you—

The intervention here was once again designed to be ego-building through support- ing the value of allowing a real person to be in Jim's life. His schizophrenic adap- tation, as he had indicated earlier in the interview, was to live in his fantasy life and to avoid any real relationship. The interviewer supported the risk Jim took in letting there be a real object—his friend Harry—in his mental life.

Jim: He was very good as far as wanting to get involved, as far as any of my problems or difficulties were concerned. He's a very helpful per- son, too—a kind person.
Interviewer: So you say that helped you to let go of this idea and the feelings around it?
Jim: It did. I let go of a good bit—but not completely.
Interviewer: Do you want to tell us about—
Jim: How it's not complete?
Interviewer: Yes.
Jim: Well, it's not completely to a point. Well, I'm a disabled vet—100

percent disability—and I'm not sure so far as what the outcome would be if—let's say a war broke out—whether or not they'd accept me back. But I would join it—if they'd accept me, and *that's the bit*. I would want to get back and assist and help to the best I can.

Interviewer: So, in a sense, there's something that's still unfinished? Something that you'd like to get back [*some lack of closure and some fantasy of power*].

Jim: War is never unfinished [*he meant to say "finished"*]. It seems to have no end.

Interviewer: Yes. [Pause] Did you ever think of war with yourself or between yourself? Or is this *thought* really an idea of going over there and killing people? I guess you understand that you felt badly about your friends' having been injured or damaged in some way and that you wanted to go back and do something for them. But still the idea *stayed with you* for ten years or so—

Jim: Mm. Hmm.

Interviewer: [*Continuing in an effort to relate Jim's present thoughts to his affective state and possibly to his compelling need to value his "self" and to be valued*] And have you been aware, over the years of your life, of some battle with yourself? Because of this idea of destroying someone else [Pause] or yourself? [*This last phrase came out of interviewer's unconscious.*]

Jim: [Pause] Have I been aware of it? [*Seemed taken aback.*]

Interviewer: Yes.

Jim: Oh, yes. I've been aware of it—or that situation. I've tried to keep it as much under control as possible, but I have felt—I am saying here—I feel as though one of these SECRETS seems to be approaching uncontrollably—and I would urge someone else—[Stops] I try to evaluate it myself.

Interviewer: Yes—

Jim: —and as I reach the end—the end of my line—and as I need more answers—more questions—more different outlooks—because of the situation [*internal defenses are not working or have broken down*], then I will go to friends, relatives—medical profession.

Interviewer: Is that what part of your struggle is? Your *inner* struggle: to figure everything out yourself, or to have to turn to someone else? Do you feel you struggle with that? [*Addressing his ego—it would be felt as a blow to Jim's narcissism to have to admit he has lost control and failed to master himself and that he must then put himself in someone else's hands. Jim's response supports this hypothesis.*]

Jim: I think that it should be a "self" situation—whatever your problems or difficulties or goals or anything that you have during your life— from the minute you start taking your FIRST STEP as a child—IT SHOULD BE—ALL ON YOUR OWN—YOURSELF!!! Occasionally there are times—after taking that first step and then second step and third step as a young child, you'll FALL and *had* to be picked up and shown how to be picked up, near a piece of furniture. You constantly pick a child up near a piece of furniture and the child will catch on and say, well, I can pick myself up—will slowly go over to it—get up on the couch, up on his feet.

Interviewer: Yes. That means a lot to you. It means a great deal to you to be able to stand on your own feet.

Jim: I control my own life—my own feelings—my own thoughts.

Interviewer: When you talk to people like me here, does that go against that part of you that wants to be on your own feet? [*Note next how Jim depersonalizes the relationship and departs on a totally different topic and how the interviewer goes with him.*]

Jim: [*Denies*] No. I like people asking me questions—and I like time to answer them the best way possible—being an artist, I create. When you ask my opinion, it consists of multiple ideas, different styles of brush, pen, pencil sketch, et cetera.

An exchange followed in which Jim spoke of his work and self as an artist. Despite several interventions designed to engage Jim in the here-and-now reality of the interaction between him and the interviewer, Jim went on to expostulate about his theory of art. The interviewer once again tried to bring Jim back to the therapeutic encounter.

Interviewer: If you were thinking of characterizing what has been happening between us, between two human beings who are strangers to each other— we have met today—could you see how you've made an adaptation [*meaning "how you have defended yourself"*]?

Jim: [Long pause] How? I honestly don't know what to say.

There was then some discussion of a drawing that Jim had made of a primitive mask (see Figure 1.). When pressed by the interviewer, Jim spoke of his migraine headaches and said one was occurring right then. We see here a conversion symptom (Fenichel, 1945; Rangell, 1959) in the making. Jim is saying that the interviewer is giving him a headache and that he has had enough. In speaking of his migraine, Jim then admits to having had a headache when he awoke the morning of the interview, which indicates that his pretense of being at ease in facing the interview did not really work well for him. As the migraine symptom was considered, Jim was able to speak with more force and to respond in a more direct way to the interviewer.

Jim: I don't really ever want to have these—ever again—and I'm trying hard—[*refers to a lost key and release of his feelings*].

Interviewer: Do you hear yourself talking more vigorously just now? With more force—[*supporting his effective aggression directed externally rather than against himself*].

Jim: Yes—certainly—

Interviewer: I think you've taken a very forceful position. You said that you don't ever want to experience that migraine again. You want to find the key. How did you feel as you were expressing yourself [so] much more strongly?

Jim: [With confidence] And even though it [the migraine] is here, I do expect eventually it won't be.

Interviewer: Have you any afterthoughts about the migraine, about me—about

Figure 1. Jim's Drawings of a Mask and Himself.

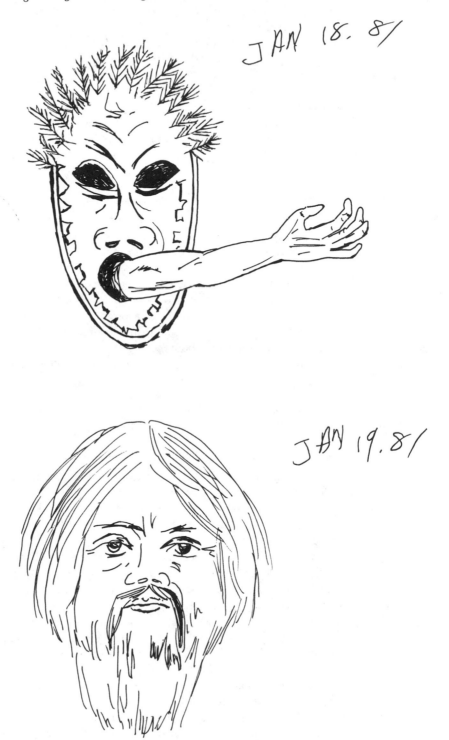

how you adapted here today? Just any way it may come to you. [*Jim became defensive again and appeared uncomfortable at the direct confrontation. He finally said:*]

Jim: I enjoy conversations [*making light of the interview*]. I like questions, and [*in a placating manner*] I believe a situation like this has helped in both directions.

The interviewer then made several lengthy statements in an effort to pull together what had taken place and to frame certain dynamics in terms of two issues: how Jim attempted to mask his aggression and how he had gained from a relationship of trust with his friend. (A number of interchanges are omitted owing to space limitations.)

Interviewer: Where I felt it very, very hard to reach you today, I felt maybe feelings that you feel, a kind of impotence—that I couldn't really use what I have to offer you, whether because of the "mask" or the way you're defending yourself. As you then shared this "secret" with me—about this idea you have—and allowed me to talk about the drawing you made, then I felt—some effective aggression—power—that I could offer you something. Now, I'd like to ask you whether you feel that offering is positive or [Pause] as a blow.

Jim: You, of course, mentioned things I might have sensed, but not really realized, especially about *masking* things—and releasing them, and trying not to release them, and trying not to release them because of the possibility of hurting others.

Interviewer: Yes—yes. [Pause] Do you feel that's something that you can use when you work with Dr. Field?

Jim: Oh, yes! That would be [Hesitates] a great deal.

The session was concluded shortly after that. A half-hour discussion followed with the staff during which the interviewer explained his technique and philosophy as follows: the direction of ego psychology is not to analyze but to synthesize—to put things together for the patient and to help him make his own connections through his synthesizing-ego function. To attempt to invade and to extract material is not psychotherapy.

Finally, it needs to be noted that the interviewer was not really prepared for Jim's basic attitude that he had no interest in being engaged as a patient. Although this could be said of all persons who come for treatment, what was different was that those who come for help are seeking relief from discomfort or seeking to regain their psychic equilibrium. Jim was seeking, rather, to maintain his equilibrium and not to engage in any feeling exchange. The interviewer, in his turn, tried to structure a situation in which Jim could find something ego-strengthening for himself. Blanck and Blanck (1979), in their chapter "Resistance Revisited," note the need to consider when the person is "resisting" the treatment process and when the person is appropriately defending his ego boundaries. The interview excerpts presented above offer a telling example of a person who is engaged in defending his ego boundaries and his sense of integrity by not pouring out all thoughts, fantasies, or feelings. It is of great technical and philosophical significance that Jim clearly experienced a compulsion to reveal more of himself and his secrets as the interview proceeded. His migraine headache suggests that as his attempts at repression began to fail, he fell back on a conversion symptom. The interviewer made an effort to support the right to privacy in his interventions. He also tried to present the concept that aggression can be used constructively. The interviewer offered that his own aggression in the effort to engage Jim in the treatment process might provide a model that Jim could consider for himself. In the postsession with the clinic staff, Jim was present, and it was here that Jim realized that the interviewer had been trying to effect a connection with him that would prove constructive and respectful of his boundaries.

This ended the interview with Jim.

Summary

The above verbatim transcription of a demonstration interview with a schizophrenic in remission has been offered as an example of the application of ego psychology in the initial structuring of the treatment relationship. The essential contribution of Freud's ego psychology lies in its attitude to the human condition and in its respect for the autonomous functioning of the individual. The theory and techniques of psychoanalytic developmental psychology are grounded in Freud's structural theory that encompasses instinctual life and its psychic development, the development of the reality-testing, the organizing ego function, and the internalization of values and standards that serve to regulate and to establish self-esteem and object constancy. In an extension of Freud's theory, the seminal work of Heinz Hartmann and the contributions of Anna Freud, Jacobson, Spitz, Mahler, and Gertrude and Rubin Blanck broaden not only the scope of psychoanalysis but of psychotherapy. Such work enables the psychotherapist to address the goal of ego strengthening and structure building through the use of the therapeutic dyadic relationship to further internalization processes. The focus has changed from extracting primary process material to strengthening the capacity for repression, particularly in those lower-level structures in which there is not simply "the return of the repressed" but an incapacity for repression. The intent in this chapter has been to highlight the profound contributions of the heirs of Freud and their significance for the technique of psychotherapy.

❦ 5 ❦

Short-Term Dynamic Psychotherapy

Manuel Trujillo

Short-term psychotherapy is enjoying once again the crest of popularity among clinicians and consumers, as manifested in the proliferation of new brief techniques (cognitive, interpersonal, and behavioral psychotherapies) as well as briefer modalities of such well-established forms as individual, family, and group psychotherapies.

The benefits of this expansion have reached—this time—the field of psychoanalytically based psychodynamic psychotherapies. Unlike earlier waves, going back to Freud himself (who was said to have treated the composer Gustav Mahler in a four-hour walk through the woods of Vienna), this expansion may yield a lasting transformation of the field for two fundamental reasons: it is fueled by a growing public appetite for psychotherapeutic services, and it comes at a time of increased demands by government and insurance carriers for accountability and cost containment. The chances of survival of this new wave of interest in short-term methods of psychotherapeutic help are also increased by recent research findings conclusively demonstrating the effectiveness of psychotherapy in comparisons with untreated controls (Smith, Glass, and Miller, 1980). The increasingly utilized ability to provide a lasting record of the psychotherapeutic transaction through videotape recording will undoubtedly help by allowing the field to systematize, define, and teach observable and replicable model interventions.

After Freud's original contribution of case material and his legacy of psychoanalytic metapsychology and techniques (Freud, [1905] 1953), mainstream investigative energies concentrated in the development of open-ended, long-term psychotherapies. Early in the history of psychoanalysis Ferenczi and Rank distinguished themselves by attempts to shorten the psychotherapy process (Ferenczi and Rank, 1925). These efforts continued in the late 1940s through the contributions of Alexander and French (Alexander, 1951; French and Alexander, 1946), which represent a significant advance in the quest for briefer, more efficient, and more specific forms of psychotherapy. Central to Alexander's concepts are the increased activity of the therapist with the aim of preventing regression and the importance of the role of emotion in fostering psychotherapeutic change. For Alexander, the corrective emotional experience, a reliving of the original trauma situation, is the basic vehicle for change.

In the 1950s the Tavistock group, under the fertile clinical leadership of Balint (1961; Balint and others, 1972), produced a series of clinical studies of short-term dynamic psychotherapy, which were elegantly documented by Malan (1963, 1975). Using two of the Tavistock studies involving more than fifty patients, Malan showed that standard analytic techniques and aims (to bring about clarification of the patient's conflict as it is played out with the therapist, to a specified psychotherapeutic focus) lead to deep work and successful outcome in no more than forty sessions. In his work, successful outcome is directly correlated with the number of interpretations linking the transference with the past ("T-P interpretations").

Sifneos (1972) has contributed a form of shortened dynamic psychotherapy (short-term anxiety-provoking psychotherapy, or STAPP) that he applies to patients who fulfill this selection criteria: (1) a circumscribed chief complaint, (2) a history of a meaningful relationship with another person, (3) ability to interact flexibly with the evaluator and have access to one's feelings during the initial interview, (4) above-average psychological sophistication and intelligence, and (5) motivation for change. Sifneos's techniques rely on development and extensive use of a positive transference and on active use of anxiety-provoking questions, confrontations, clarifications, and interpretations. Links between the present and the patient's past, as well as with the transference feelings, are also made.

It is to the everlasting credit of Davanloo that, over a twenty-year span and working independently, he has developed a form of brief psychotherapy, short-term dynamic psychotherapy (Davanloo, 1978, 1979, 1980), especially suited for the psychotherapeutic needs of patients suffering from severe neurotic symptomatology and character neurosis. Davanloo has developed a range of techniques that allow the clinician to confront and overcome the solid character resistances with which these patients typically approach psychotherapeutic work as well as other relationships of intimacy. Davanloo's systematic confrontation of character resistances in the initial evaluation, frequently aided by work with the transference, typically result in substantial increases in the patient's motivation and the development of the unconscious therapeutic alliance—two powerful indicators of the presence of active psychotherapeutic work.

Inherited Myths About
Short-Term Dynamic Psychotherapy

The short-term psychotherapy movement inherited along the way a number of myths that now may stand in the way of further scientific progress:

1. That short-term therapies are focal and limited, both in the material handled and in their therapeutic goals. The association of brief therapy with the concept of focal therapy seems to have two roots. One goes back to Balint's studies and the Tavistock group. They originally had proposed that some psychotherapeutic results could be attained by the therapist operating within one sector of the patient's mental life (a "focus"). Although the lengthy investigations of the Tavistock group later showed that brief therapies need not be restricted to material in any sector of the patient's life, the notion of focality was easily associated in the reader's mind with working on isolated sectors of the patient's mental experience. A second source of misunderstanding was a similarly incorrect interpretation of Sifneos's notion

of the circumscribed chief complaint. This concept, originally used by Sifneos to describe the patient's ability to organize the definition and communication of his or her psychological problems around clearly recognizable categories, has often been taken to mean a technical requirement to work on isolated sectors of the patient's psychic life. The current position of the field on the issue of focality, especially reinforced by the work of Davanloo, is that focality is merely a technical procedure and that far-reaching psychotherapeutic results are possible in dealing with patients whose psychopathology has multiple foci. The clinical studies of Malan and Davanloo provide the clinician with the techniques to become therapeutically ambitious. One's work need not be restricted to limited sectors of the patient's life. The substantial resolution of all foci of the patient's psychopathology is a legitimate expectation of the treatment.

2. That short-term dynamic psychotherapy should be applied only to a selected sample of patients and that patients should be accepted into this treatment on the basis of their suffering from uncomplicated oedipal psychopathology. The basis for this myth, prevalent in the anecdotal clinical literature, seems to be the natural caution of the responsible clinician navigating uncharted waters (*"Primum non nocere"*), an attitude that would "logically" reserve the most severe psychopathology for the theoretically deeper and more potent techniques of the full psychoanalysis. Some empirical findings documenting the potentially positive outcome of therapy provided by untrained therapists to patients suffering from relatively mild psychopathology have lent additional credibility to those clinicians in favor of using shorter modes of intervention for simple problems. The clinical studies of Malan and Davanloo as well as the formal research projects of Beck (1983) and Weissman (1979) have, fortunately, provided evidence supporting the application of short-term techniques to patients suffering from complicated psychopathology.

3. That the patient and the therapist in short-term dynamic psychotherapy should avoid deep psychotherapeutic involvement, including the use of the transference. This idea, though rapidly changing, may still be the prevailing opinion about the psychotherapeutic process and the transference in short-term, open-ended psychotherapy and even clinical psychoanalysis. Gill (1982) has advanced the view that the lack of consistent pursuit of the analysis of the transference may account for the poor technical quality of analysis as it is generally practiced. In this area, Malan has contributed one of the few empirically validated kernels of knowledge, if not the only one, about the psychoanalytically informed psychodynamic process. He has shown a positive correlation between the number of transference interpretations and the successful outcome of the therapy. Davanloo has established the centrality of the transference work to the successful treatment of severe obsessional and personality disorders. In his studies, transference feelings are identified and systematically pursued during the treatment. This constant attention to the transference prevents the development of a transference neurosis and adds depth to the psychotherapeutic process.

Davanloo's Form of
Short-Term Dynamic Psychotherapy

Though applicable to patients suffering from less severe forms of psychopathology, Davanloo's contribution is best studied in his refashioning of psychotherapeutic techniques to make them applicable to patients suffering from severe psychoneurotic disorders (obsessional, hysterical, or mixed) and character disorders. These patients are characterized by a deeply rooted need to avoid meaningful interpersonal contact. Consequently, the traditional psychotherapeutic process of these patients is often plagued either by detachment or by the stormy presence of negative therapeutic reactions. The classical psychoanalytic technique of free association meets with severe difficulties in overcoming the interpersonal walls of these patients in order to engage and increase their motivation and mobilize the unconscious therapeutic alliance. The key to Davanloo's technique is his understanding of the psychopathology of patients suffering from severe character disorder, its roots, and the resulting defensive structure. In classical terms these patients suffer from complicated oedipal psychopathology. Oedipal psychopathology is complicated by the presence of loss or environmental traumata and/or deprivation. In many cases, the therapist finds one or more foci of unresolved (pathological) mourning. These patients frequently present with a façade of interpersonal distance and a mixture of interpersonal defenses. In addition to repression, avoidance, and displacement, they make abundant use of intellectualization, undoing, denial, and projection. Their interpersonal distance is maintained by means of detachment, passivity, and helplessness. When relating, they frequently do so in a sadomasochistic form. The triad of projection, introjection, and denial is sometimes complemented by the use of regressive defenses.

Symptomatically these patients suffer from the whole spectrum of neurotic character problems and personality disorders. They earn Axis I diagnosis of anxiety disorders, including panic attacks. Depression is frequent, including characterological forms and major and recurrent forms. These patients are often mired in many forms of interpersonal failure. Their great difficulty in establishing intimacy brings about failure in marriage and other close relationships. The parent/child relationship is frequently impaired. Suffering, which is intense, is increased by unfulfilled cravings for intimacy and closeness. Work and other avenues of personal creativity and self-realization are also impaired by the neurotic process. These patients are involved in many forms of self-sabotage, affecting judgment, productivity, and key interpersonal relationships. Their stands toward authority display mixtures of submissiveness and lack of assertion, with dysfunctional forms of aggression such as defiance, stubbornness, and procrastination.

Patient Selection: The Initial Interview

Patient selection has been an area of fertile clinical insights in short-term dynamic psychotherapy. Sifneos was the first to abandon traditional clinical selection criteria, excessively focused on clinical diagnosis and difficult-to-observe psychodynamic constructs. He selected empirically a group of easily accessible clinical, historical, and process phenomena. In his experience the presence in the initial interview of these selection criteria correlates positively with successful outcome at termination. Sifneos's criteria are:

1. A circumscribed chief complaint.
2. A history of a "meaningful" relationship with another person during the patient's early life.
3. An ability to interact flexibly with the evaluator and have access to [the patient's] feelings during the evaluation interview.

4.   An above-average psychological sophistication and intelligence.
5.   Motivation for change. [Sifneos, 1978, p. 36].

Davanloo has compressed prior selection criteria into one, the "trial therapy technique"—the patient's ability to respond to the therapist's interpretations in an atmosphere of sufficient emotional arousal. These interpretations are of two types: transference interpretations, linking the transference with the present or actual life situation and the past experience of the patient, and core-conflict interpretations, linking the patient's conflicts in the present with their genetic antecedents in the patient's past.

In patients at the more severe end of the psychopathology spectrum, demonstration of these clinical indicators requires substantial amounts of psychotherapeutic work during the initial interview. These patients typically start the evaluation session as rigidly defended as they function in many other areas of their lives. Davanloo has taught that in order for the therapist to achieve meaningful contact with the patient's unconscious, the full panoply of defenses has to be clarified and systematically confronted. The typical successful sequence of work may include many rounds of systematic clarifications and confrontations of the patient's defenses against experiencing his or her impulses and feelings toward a particular meaningful figure in the patient's life. Holding such patients to their feelings about a meaningful figure in their lives, and systematically challenging any deviation from this focus, typically produces a mobilization and experiencing of the patient's impulse or feeling in relation to that person. Alternatively, mobilized impulses/feelings are experienced in relation to the therapist.

When either of these two sequences acquires a certain intensity, meaningful links can be made to similar situations and experiences in the patient's past. The completion of several successful runs going from patient defenses to impulses and feelings toward several meaningful figures in the patient's life, as well as toward the therapist, has the following verifiable effects: (1) an increase in the patient's affective experience and self-experience, allowing for sharper focusing of the patient's intrapsychic experience, (2) a rapid decrease in the use of particular sequences of resistances (in our clinical work we commonly observe shifts from lower-level to higher-level forms of defense), and (3) increases in motivation and in affectively tinged experience of the transference, followed by mobilization of the unconscious therapeutic alliance. These three factors combined allow both the patient and the therapist to enter into emotional exploration of the patient's unconscious conflicts.

In addition to the functions already described, the initial evaluation should allow the evaluator—

1.   To obtain a complete description of the patient's areas of disturbance, including a clinical diagnosis.
2.   To obtain a complete view of the patient's current dynamic functioning, including an evaluation and understanding of the internal forces that account for the patient's symptoms.
3.   To complete the clinician's understanding of the patient's neurotic functioning by providing a clear view of the core genetic structure that gives rise to both symptoms and dynamic functioning.
4.   To establish a psychotherapeutic focus.

A very important function of the initial interview is to obtain a complete descriptive/phenomenological history providing a clear description of all the patient's areas of disturbance. Symptoms such as anxiety, depression, and phobias have to be described, including their onset, development, intensity, and other phenomenological features. It is important to obtain a clear description of the patient's interpersonal function. Key relationships, including those with spouses, parents, and children, should be explored with a view to understanding their participation in the patient's unconscious conflicts. This exploration frequently meets with character resistances, which will require significant psychotherapeutic work, including clarification, confrontation, and interpretation, at times in the transference. The patient's ability to experience deep affect (anger and sadness) equally needs exploration and is typically impaired. The patient's capacity to give and accept in relationships of intimacy also needs mapping, including detailed knowledge of the patient's sexual behavior, fantasies, and history.

Through this process, knowledge is gained about the patient's current dynamic conflicts, as well as about the conscious and unconscious, internal and environmental forces playing major roles in the patient's problem. The relative contributions of conflictual problems and of developmental problems caused by deprivation need to be assessed.

The Unconscious and the Neurotic Process

In successful initial evaluation psychotherapeutic work at the level of present interpersonal conflict, one is led to an avalanche of significant unconscious material, including strong emotions, dreams, or memories, frequently loaded with meaningful information about the genetic structure of the patient's conflict.

Patient A. The following patient vignette demonstrates a typical sequence of this work. Patient A, who will be fully described later, became unproductive somewhere in the middle of the evaluation interview, during exploration of his relationship with his mother. His memories of her, close to age forty when he was born, involved her being chronically ill, fearful, and distant—a picture of his mother that had become the target of his unrelenting hostility. The following vignette will demonstrate the patient's resistances and the emergence of new material.

Patient:	We started out from home, the three of us together. Ray [patient's sister] was late for school, so there was running, and as the three of us got closer to school, Ray did run ahead, and I was younger and I was dragging behind, or I was pulling behind. I don't really know. My feeling at the time—I didn't want to be left with my mother.
Therapist:	Why not? What was she like in that picture at that time?
Patient:	[Pause] Controlling, an authority—
Therapist:	No, but how would you describe her?
Patient:	[Pause] Physically? I don't have much recollection of how my mother looked. [Pause]
Therapist:	You're talking about a picture in your mind. Can you describe the picture? [Pause] It's very striking that you remember Ray and the fence, but when it comes to your mother—

Patient: I don't have a picture of her.

Therapist: What was she like as a young woman, then! [Long pause] Have you
                noticed again you become slow?

Patient: I don't know what my mother was like then.

Therapist: "Don't know." Have you noticed your main defense? Helplessness and
                limpness.

Patient: I see I use it as an excuse. I can say, "I don't know," and if I don't
                know, don't bother asking me.

Therapist: [*Addressing the transference*] How do you feel when I ask you that question?

Patient: Feel like you put me on the spot. How do I feel? Inadequate.

Therapist: No. *Inadequate*—is vague. How do you feel? [Pause] Have you noticed
                how you constantly put a limp feeling in front of you in a way? You're
                hiding behind limpness. How do you feel? I got the feeling that you
                were irritated. Were you irritated?

Patient: When you asked the question?

Therapist: Yes. [Pause] You don't really like anybody to pry into your intimate life.

Patient: [Pause] I don't know if anyone ever has—

Therapist: It makes no difference, still you don't like it.

Patient: I don't like it. No.

Therapist: You don't like it. [Pause] But then again, have you noticed you don't
                like it, but then you become limp—

Patient: I noticed that.

Therapist: So in a way this is your major defense. A stubborn defiance behind,
                but then you put limpness— [Pause] What are you going to do about
                that?

Patient: Both of them have to go. Both of them have to go. No question in my
                mind.

The preceding extract signals the beginning of the exploration of the patient's feelings about his mother and his characteristic defenses, "No memory" and frequent
use of "I don't know," which the therapist challenges. The therapist next challenges
his stubborn defiance and adds a direct allusion to the transference: "You don't
really like anybody to pry into your intimate life." This work continues:

Therapist: [Pause] What was she like as a young woman?

Patient: [Long pause] She was scared of her own shadow—

Therapist: Again you're ruminating. What was she like physically? Could you
                describe her?

Patient: My earliest memories, she was sick. She had arthritis from an early
                age. She—

Therapist: What age?

Patient: She was in the hospital when I was in kindergarten.

Therapist: How long was she hospitalized?

Patient: I really don't know.

Therapist: [Pause] Again your memory goes limp.

Patient: That was a long time ago.

Therapist: I know. Now you—find excuses— [Patient smiles.] How do you feel?
                There's a smile there—

Patient: It's the first time I smiled at myself.
Therapist: How do you feel—
Patient: I smiled at myself—
Therapist: How do you feel? The words are there, but what was the feeling?
Patient: That I'm lying. That I'm lying. I mean I can say to you it was a long time ago. I would say, if you said it to me, the same thing. It's an excuse.

After renewed challenges of the patient's resistances (memory loss, passivity, "limpness"), there is a subtle emergence of the unconscious therapeutic alliance: the patient smiles as he catches himself at the stereotypic use of intellectualization and rationalization: "That was a long time ago." The therapeutic alliance intensified, the session proceeds.

Therapist: So, then, what was the picture of your mother at that early age?
Patient: Weak, sickly, overweight, white hair, didn't smile much, always telling me things not to do. [Pause]
Therapist: Was there any redeeming feature in that picture?
Patient: Any what?
Therapist: Redeeming feature. You are painting a bleak—
Patient: No.
Therapist: How fast you go to the "No." [Patient leans forward.] How fast you go to the "No." What was her body like? [Pause] Immediately everything goes limp again. [Pause] And your eyes again—avoid me. [Pause]
Patient: What was her body like? [Pause] Like it wasn't even there.
Therapist: I know. But it was there.
Patient: It was there. Yeah.
Therapist: Could you describe her?
Patient: Bent over at the shoulders. [Pause] Thin legs. Little stomach. Nondescript breasts. [Pause]
Therapist: What was she like earlier than that?
Patient: She was a very pretty woman.
Therapist: She was a very pretty woman? [*Patient:* Yes.] How do you know that?
Patient: Saw pictures of her.
Therapist: When did you see these pictures?
Patient: From when I was young.
Therapist: How did you get to see these pictures?
Patient: They were pictures my mother saved. They were in the family. At home.
Therapist: They were in the house on display? [*Patient:* No.] Where were they?
Patient: In a closet in my sister's room.
Therapist: How did you get to them?
Patient: Secretly. They weren't out.
Therapist: Can we look into how you got to them?
Patient: My sister and I would, every once in a while at play, we'd go into the closet with a flashlight and close the door and go through these old bins that had pictures.
Therapist: I see. Could you describe these pictures of your mother? What she looked like?

Patient: Uh—she had a very pretty soft face— [Appears very sad]
Therapist: Soft face—hm—
Patient: Nice smile, long curly hair— [Chokes with emotion]
Therapist: Nice smile, long curly hair—
Patient: Nicely formed jaw and neck. The only pictures we saw were down to
                here [Indicates breast]. Only her marriage picture, wedding picture—
                [Sobs openly]

By this time, the patient is opening the door to his deeply felt mixed feelings about
his mother. The positive memories emerge and with them the very painful mixed
feelings of the repressed craving for the mother of his early childhood, the forbidden instinctual impulses. The patient is now full of emotion, sad, and deeply engaged
in the psychotherapeutic process.

Therapist: What was it like in the marriage picture?
Patient: Attractive woman. She was wearing a dark suit; she stood straight. She
                had a little bit of an upturned chin. The picture was taken—she was
                posing for it. Her hands were up by her face, resting part of her face,
                not really touching [Illustrates with hands to face]. Her hair was long.
                [Pause]
Therapist: How do you feel at this moment?
Patient: [Weeping] Real sad.
Therapist: How do you explain that?
Patient: I never experienced softness with my mother.

It is essential that the therapist obtain a comprehensive and complete picture of the significant experiences of the patient's past that determine and explain
current psychopathological functioning. In a complete initial evaluation, the therapist
obtains repeated evidence of the patient's positive response to the trial therapy
technique—that is, of the patient's ability to respond meaningfully to transference
interpretations and core-conflict interpretations. The therapist also obtains a complete
phenomenological descriptive diagnostic picture of the patient's areas of disturbance,
including symptoms and interpersonal and sexual dysfunctions. Functioning at work
and in relationships of intimacy is explored. The psychodynamic diagnosis includes
a clear description of the patient's current dynamic conflict and central psychodynamic forces. A sharp picture of the core unconscious genetic forces completes
the evaluation and will act as a guide to the psychotherapeutic process.

For Patient A, a forty-two-year-old married professional man, the initial interview yields the following areas of disturbance:

1.   He has feelings of depression and despair precipitated by his sense that life
     is passing him by and that he is unable to feel meaningfully in control or con-
     nected with it.
2.   He cannot express his intimate feelings and instead lives at a superficial level.
3.   Chronic difficulties exist in his relationship with his wife. Married for ten years,
     the patient feels alienated from her and deeply disappointed by their inability
     to sustain closeness and intimacy. There have been episodes of infidelity on
     both sides. He is also troubled by the fact that his deeply felt need to have
     children is not reciprocated by his wife at this time.

4. At work, as a principal in a small professional firm, the patient is troubled by performance anxiety. When his activities require public exposure or speaking before large groups, he freezes, he suffers bouts of anxiety and self-doubt, and his considerable professional skills are paralyzed. His attempts at interpersonal assertion produce a similar response. He is equally anxiety-ridden and ineffective when facing interpersonal conflicts at work or in minor episodes in other areas of his life. A recent angry interchange with his landlord ended in intense anxiety and a response of "giving up."

In the initial interview, in response to the therapist's opening question, "What is the problem that brings you for treatment at this time?," the patient had started trying to describe his problems but was unable to do so clearly, because of the process of resistance. Defense mechanisms such as vagueness and intellectualization interfered with the patient's precise communication. The task of the therapist in such a case is to gently challenge these defenses by using a spectrum of technical maneuvers, including clarification and confrontation of the defenses, as in the following vignette.

Therapist: Perhaps the best way we can proceed is for you to tell me what are the problems that brought you here.

Patient: Basically, I have the feeling that I'm not dealing with stresses and anxiety in my life. I have had prior therapy, which I found helpful, but I discontinued it after a while. I find I was—I felt there are qualities of me, qualities of my personality, that have been long-standing and that I have never really addressed or dealt with that go back to—very early in my life that I have managed to deal and cope in my life and then develop and be successful ignoring them. And in relationships in my life, in my marriage, they have come up and they are getting in my way. They are getting in my way professionally. I have hesitations and I have these fears inside for reasons that I cannot identify. Like I know what I should do, but not—generally I have anxieties in my marriage. I'm married nine years.

Therapist: What is your wife's name?

Patient: Janice.

Therapist: So you are married nine years and there are anxieties in your marriage?

Patient: Yes, because—there are anxieties in my marriage because I don't think I have ever let myself go—I have always held back. I have always protected myself in some way. I've been secretive in our relationship. Uh— [Pause]

Therapist: [*Challenging the patient's vagueness*] Can we focus specifically upon what kind of a problem there is between you and your wife?

Patient: [Pause] Hm— [Pause; sighs] I don't know if I can be specific—uh—uh—

Therapist: Could you give me a specific example in which that problem that you are describing comes up? That you become secretive? You are married for nine years, and your wife's name is Janice. What is she like?

Patient: Uh— [Pause, sighs] She's kind of a held-back person—

Therapist: You mean quiet and reserved?

Patient: Yes.

Therapist: So then you are married nine years and you have known her for how long?

Patient: I've known her for fifteen.
Therapist: Fifteen. And are there any children?
Patient: No children.
Therapist: And one of the things is that from the very beginning you are aware that you are secretive and in a way that has created some problems in your marriage. Now, can you describe some specific event where that comes to a head in some way?
Patient: Yes. I had an affair that began a year and a half ago.
Therapist: And the name of this other person?
Patient: Louise. [Pause] And I saw her maybe a total of ten times, twelve times. Three, four weeks apart. I never told Janice about it, and it was driving me crazy. I would want to see her. I also found her very attractive in a physical sense, a sexual sense. Uh—I enjoyed being with her but I knew that it was just simply a release. That I was, in fact, being dishonest with Janice. Uh—and at the beginning of the summer, the middle of the summer, I called off the relationship. Uh, Louise was very upset about it. She had stated that she loved me and she didn't care if I saw her once a month or once every six months. And in the fall, maybe the end of October—I had written earlier in the summer, in June, kind of a diary in which I mentioned Louise. I wrote this particular thing, and as it turned out, it was home. I wasn't home and Janice found it among my papers.
Therapist: So she read about Louise. When was this?
Patient: October, beginning of November. And she found out and became very upset. Uh—and I acknowledged—
Therapist: How did you feel when she told you that she found the diary and she read it? [*The therapist now will stay in this area and try to help the patient experience his feeling toward his wife.*]
Patient: I felt caught.
Therapist: *Caught* is a word. What were your feelings?
Patient: Guilty, dishonest.
Therapist: But *guilty* is another word. How did you experience it? [*Therapist challenges defenses and holds the patient to his feelings.*]
Patient: How did I experience it?
Therapist: Did you have any feelings about the fact that she got your diary, which, after all, is a private book, and that she read it? Did you have any feelings about that?
Patient: Yes, I was angry that she had done that.
Therapist: You became angry—how did you experience your anger? [*The therapist is now using the holding technique; he is holding the focus on the patient's feeling of anger toward his wife and rapidly challenging the patient's defenses as they emerge.*]

A positive result of the therapist's challenge is that the patient becomes more concrete and specific and the interview focuses on a particular interaction with his wife. He describes a painful recent episode in which his wife, suspecting the patient of being involved with another woman, confronted him with evidence that she had obtained by reading his personal diary. He became infuriated. The interview has now focused on his feelings of anger in relation to a figure in the patient's current life (C).

As is the norm with patients suffering from severe obsessional psychopathology and character pathology, the patient is unable to experience his feeling of anger in relation to any object. The defense of dissociation of affect interferes.

Davanloo has discovered and refined a series of techniques to rapidly exhaust these elaborate defensive systems, allowing therapist and patient access to unconscious determinants of the patient's problems. This can be achieved by "holding" the patient to his impulse/feeling and confronting, challenging, and dismissing all the defenses that the patient will mobilize. Typically they include intellectualization, passivity, interpersonal distance, avoidance of interpersonal contact with the therapist (aversion of gaze), and subtle forms of character defenses involving the body (that is, extreme passivity, or woodenness). The following vignette illustrates the sequence of psychotherapeutic work with Patient A.

Therapist: You became angry. How did you experience your anger?

Patient: I didn't experience it, I—

Therapist: You said you became angry, you said you became angry—

Patient: Yes. But I was not immediately—that was not my first feeling.

Therapist: What was your first feeling when she told you about that?

Patient: Guilt.

Therapist: *Guilt* is a word. What actually did you experience?

Patient: A numbness. A numbness went over me.

Therapist: A numbness. That is intellectual. You said you felt guilty and caught, and all of that. What was your feeling?

Patient: I don't think I can describe it.

Therapist: You don't think—so in a way you became helpless. [*Therapist challenges the defense of helplessness.*]

Patient: I felt helpless, I felt caught, I felt weighted—

Therapist: Have you noticed that you are trying to describe—you said that you had an intense feeling, but when we are going to focus on the feeling, you become vague and general, and then you become totally helpless, but nothing comes? How did you feel inside when she called you on the Louise episode? [Patient sighs.] Have you noticed a very big sigh?

Patient: It's, you know— [Pause]

Therapist: And now you tighten your mouth and another big sigh.

Patient: I feel—I feel caught—I feel like I—

Therapist: Yeah, *caught* is a word.

Patient: I judged myself—

Therapist: Yeah, but all this is rumination. What was your feeling when she caught you like that? [Patient sighs.] Have you noticed that you take a totally passive and limp position in a way? [*Therapist now challenges passivity.*]

Patient: I noticed that. I noticed that about myself.

Therapist: So, then, what are you going to do about that passive and cut-off and limp position? Because one of the things is this: we still don't know your feelings.

Patient: That's the reason why I'm here.

Therapist: Yeah, but that's intellectual talk. [*Patient:* Yeah.] What are we going to do about that?

Patient: I think about it and I intellectualize it and I—I've always done that with feelings. I have never felt free to express feelings.

Therapist: Let's not ruminate any further. We are talking about an event which is very specific, which is that she called you about this. Janice called you about the episode with Louise that she read. Now what was your feeling at that moment? [Patient sighs.] Now again a big sigh and you become slow. [Pause] Hm? Another big sigh, and again you become slow [Pause] and passive.

Patient: That is the reason I am here, and I don't—I don't know what to say.

Therapist: When Janice called you, you must have had a lot of feeling about that? Hm?

Patient: There's also—I'm reacting—Now that we talk of anger, I feel I'm being pushed. I'm feeling anger here as well.

Therapist: You mean that you're getting irritated with me? [Pause] You say "here." [Patient says "here."] Have you noticed that you prefer to put it into impersonal in a way? [Pause. *Patient:* Yes.] But anyway, how did you experience your irritation with me?

Patient: I experience it by getting limp, by going away—

The therapist now is holding and focusing on the patient's impulse/feeling of anger toward him (transference). Davanloo's technique requires that this holding be maintained until the patient's defensive structures are exhausted and the impulse/feeling constellation vividly emerges into the open. This may require several runs of confrontation of sequences of defense, including intellectualization, passivity, helplessness, and interpersonal distance. Many of the interchanges reproduced here are repeated over and over until a meaningful breakthrough of the unconscious feeling occurs.

Therapist: We are talking about your feelings— [Pause] How do you experience your feeling of irritation with me?

Patient: I experience a certain tension—

Therapist: Where is the tension?

Patient: In my jaw—holding my body immobile, limp—

Therapist: So then you go limp, and obviously one other thing is this: you're tight like that. It is as if you are holding yourself like that. Hm? [Pause] What are we going to do about that holding? Because everything in you is totally held into a limp mask, now you have very precisely declared. There is a tremendous tension within you, your jaws—

Patient: There is.

Therapist: So what are we going to do about that mask?

Patient: Gone. The mask is gone.

Therapist: So, then, how do you experience this? [Pause] Have you noticed how you become slow again? [Pause] Hm?

Patient: I experience my irritation—

Therapist: And now your eyes—again avoid me.

Patient: I don't know—

Therapist: And now "I don't know." More helplessness. [Pause] And now you become totally limp. Because obviously your hand was tense like that. Have you noticed?

Patient: I experience it in another way, in that I seek to, either by smiling or by being limp, and I ingratiate myself—

Therapist:	But you are angry with me. That is very striking that you are very angry with me and then you want to bend over backwards, to ingratiate. [*By this time feelings are starting to stir up in the patient.*] What are we going to do about that façade? [Pause] Hm? [Pause] Now again a big sigh. [Pause]
Patient:	I'll get rid of it. I'll get rid of it.
Therapist:	Well. Again the big sigh. [Pause] How do you feel at this moment? [Patient is now very sad; lowers his head and sobs.]
Patient:	I just got a wave of sadness.
Therapist:	A wave? That came from very deep in you—hm? [*Patient:* It's—] Have you noticed that when the sadness hits you like that, your eyes move away from me? It's as if you don't want me to get close to your feelings. Hm? [Patient nods.] [Gently] Distance. So what are we going to do about all that distance? Because up to the point that we cannot get to that feeling, what's going to happen to our work together? To our relationship? Hm? I am sure that there are many failed relationships already in your life. Failed relationships. Hm?
Patient:	Yes, there are some friendships that have gone by the wayside. [Pause] Yes.
Therapist:	Now, one thing is this: that there was a lot of sadness in you. What thoughts came to mind?
Patient:	What did I feel inside? [*Therapist:* Yes.] [Pause] I felt— [Pause] Inside I felt warmth inside.
Therapist:	What came to your mind? I mean what triggered your sadness?
Patient:	Hearing myself and thinking afterwards and saying my façade has served me well. My mask.
Therapist:	That's very sad that you say that.
Patient:	I recognize that. [Sobbing; sighs]
Therapist:	It is a most painful thing. Obviously you are a man of feeling. [Pause; patient nods.] But then the whole thing gets—buried— [Patient sobs aloud.] It is most painful—all that façade and all that mask. Because you are a man of feelings, very deeply, as you pointed out. [Pause]
Patient:	It's locked up, [sighs] locked up. I don't cry easily. That's the way I see it's been. [Pause]
Therapist:	Now, one thing is this: we were talking about you and your wife earlier. [*Patient:* Mm-hm.] Can we focus on what are the problems in the relationship? Louise was—this was in October? [*After a significant breakthrough has been obtained in the transference, the therapist returns to the focus.*]
Patient:	In October my relationship with her ended.
Therapist:	So, then, what has your relationship been with your wife between then and now?
Patient:	Since October? [*Therapist:* Yes.] It's been better.

Following this breakthrough into the patient's unconscious feeling, the patient's speech becomes more specific, vivid, and fluid. He goes on to describe, in more detail and full of emotions, painful aspects of his relationship with his wife— their mutual alienation from each other. He feels unable to be giving, and in the past he was totally unable to listen to her wishes to have children. Sexually, he feels they have lost the ability to be playful. Further exploration of his sexual fantasies (which requires periodic, if much gentler, work with his resistances) reveals that during sexual intercourse with his wife he is frequently preoccupied with images of another woman—a woman with large breasts who is sensitive, responsive, and giving. A lot of repressed angry feelings also emerge in relation to his wife's earlier abortion of a pregnancy by another man.

The success of this phase depends on the therapist's active vigilance and his or her ability to identify and challenge the patient's defenses as they appear in rapid succession in the psychotherapeutic process. The end result is a momentary suspension of the patient's cognitive/affective disassociation, which often allows painful unconscious impulses and feelings to emerge and thus has a profoundly liberating effect on the patient. It is as if the neurosis has been lifted for a moment and the patient has an experience of freedom from neurosis. In addition to this impact on the patient's self-experience, this phenomenon has other measurable effects on the psychotherapeutic process. The patient's motivation, frequently dim at the beginning of the session, intensifies. There is a substantial increase of affectively charged meaningful material from the unconscious—memories, associations, dreams, and so on—that now allows the therapist a more complete exploration of the patient's areas of disturbance and the beginning of an understanding of the genetic roots of the disturbance.

There is also a visible impact on the unconscious and conscious therapeutic alliance; many times patients spontaneously report feeling deeply moved and touched by their work with the therapist, and a feeling of personal closeness emerges. Patient A reported that after this part of the initial interview he was very sad. While describing the session to his wife, and for several days afterward, he felt very emotional. For days he experienced waves of sadness and sobbing when remembering many of the issues touched on in the interview—his intense attachment to his mother in the earlier years, the failure of his relationship with his father, and the impasse in his actual relationship to his wife. He also remembered experiences of closeness and warmth toward the therapist.

Patient: Last week there was a time where I had a wave of feeling that came over me where I wanted to touch you, I wanted you to touch me.

After the therapist has gained access to the patient's unconscious process, a much more fluid ego is present, and then the evaluation session can shift to history taking in order to complete the picture of both the patient's areas of disturbance and the core neurotic structure. In Patient A the core, or central, neurotic structure includes an intense libidinal attachment to the fantasized mother of his early years, as proclaimed by the active, eroticized, large-breasted picture to which he had secret access in childhood. This intense libidinal attachment also extends to his sister Ray and other family members in both conscious and unconscious forms, including masturbatory fantasies. This libidinal structure is complicated by extreme ambivalence toward the father, now giving rise to pathological mourning since the father's death a few years before the start of treatment. A deep-seated craving for closeness and intimacy with the father finds expression in his tendency toward passivity. The patient's genetic psychopathology involves him in a pathological triangle in which the mother sides with her brother, who lives with the family, against the father. In this triangle the patient joins the mother in deriding and undermining the father. This triangle also accounts for the patient's identification with the defeated father (leading to masochistic behavior in the present) and intense hostile impulses against the mother (currently displayed toward his wife and other women).

By the end of the initial interview, the patient reacts with pensive sadness when some of these genetic structures are interpreted to him, thus successfully meeting Davanloo's criteria for a positive "trial interpretation." Following this initial uncovering of the core neurotic structure, therapy will consist in gaining progressively deeper knowledge of the core neurotic structure and its actual presence in the patient's life. For the therapy to be successful, the repeated working through of the multiple mixed feelings related to the core neurotic structure will have to occur in an atmosphere of meaningful involvement with the therapist.

Patient B. The initial evaluation of Patient B, a forty-six-year-old divorced mother of four, has required extensive work at the level of resistances before entering her world of intense suffering and despair. Now frequently depressed and lonely, she sought treatment in order to resolve her difficulties in relating to men. Divorced for four years after twenty years of an unsuccessful marriage, she is deeply disturbed by her seeming inability to express loving or angry feelings to a man or make a deep emotional commitment to a relationship. She also tends to gravitate to men who are ungiving, withholding, or otherwise unavailable, the realization of which often leaves her feeling enraged and deeply disappointed.

Her areas of disturbance include problems with feelings of anger. When disappointed and angry, she becomes distant, withdrawn, and passive. The outcome of these defensive operations is a façade of smooth, unruffled functioning and serious interpersonal distance. As a result, the self-experience of this patient is often plagued by loneliness and fear of abandonment. Raised in a foster care home between the ages of four and fifteen, she feels that these early experiences of abandonment prevent her from making unqualified commitments to people.

Though a dutiful mother, Patient B complains of some limitations in her ability to express and receive loving and tender feelings toward and from her son and three daughters. This pattern of dutiful performance and emotional distance also permeates her relationship with her two sisters and with her mother. This façade of distance barely covers very intense (but not experienced) feelings of anger.

Her past personal history includes very painful traumatic events, which (prior to intense confrontations of resistances) she recounts in a monotonous and unemotional tone. Born in Central Europe just before World War II, she was the second of three girls born to a marriage plagued by continual strife. The marriage ended when the patient was three, when the father, a professional man described as irresponsible, left the home, driven by his excessive drinking and compulsive gambling. The patient was placed in foster care, ostensively to allow the mother to go back to work. This state of affairs, first intended to be very brief, ended up lasting until the patient was fifteen, when she joined her remarried mother, who had immigrated to the United States five years earlier.

In the initial interview, the patient described few early meaningful memories. She stated that she was emotionally dead and that she didn't even bat an eye when notified by her foster parents of the death of her father. The initial evaluation of this patient required systematic confrontation of her interpersonal defenses both in relation to her actual life and in the transference. Following Davanloo's technique, this work required repeated sequences of clarification, confrontation, and interpretation of the whole panoply of defenses used by the patient. As much as half the initial interview was spent delineating and challenging her interpersonal distance, which in the transference had the function of keeping the therapist outside her deep feelings. Much as with Patient A, when the defensive structure was thoroughly interpreted and exhausted, it gave way to intense waves of sadness and longing for the father of her earlier years, before foster care placement. In addition to sadness and longing, feelings of anger also emerged, together with some indicators of a strong libidinal attachment to him: she had a memory of playfully rummaging through her father's pocket to get some money for her mother.

These vignettes from the initial interview point to the core neurotic structure of this patient's problem: the intense craving for and the libidinal attachment to the father of her earlier years and her repressed pathological mourning. There is also intense rage toward the father, who, having awakened the intense positive feelings, deserted her. From these elements of core psychopathology flow many of her current life problems: her inability to get close to any other man has the function of preserving the libidinal attachment and loyalty to her father as well as discharging sadistic impulses on these men. The picture is completed by her deep ambivalence toward her mother, who is unconsciously blamed for the father's abandonment. The deeply suppressed rage emerges in her stubborn determination never to call her mother "Mommy" again. Instead, she displays a dutiful, shallow compliance with the conventional mother/daughter relationship.

After the initial interview, the therapist has a complete descriptive/phenomenological history and an experientially vivid map of the patient's core neurotic problem. As a result of the interview, the patient has also developed an attachment to the therapist as a transference object, and her motivation has been substantially raised. The functions of the initial phase of treatment now include enlarging, solidifying, and completing the picture of the core neurotic structure developed in the initial interview, establishing links between current, core, and transference problems. Reawakening and the transference are used to gain increasing access to the patient's intimate feelings in preparation for massive working through and termination.

Early and repeated interpretations of resistance, ambivalence, and negative transference are important in maintaining the unconscious therapeutic alliance. The unconscious therapeutic alliance guides the behavior of the therapist during this phase. Its maintenance ensures that the psychotherapeutic process will continue to be an active one and will allow for a complete working through of the patient's core psychopathology. In the middle phase of therapy, the process requires, first, multiple interpretations of the triangle of the conflict in relation to current objects, to past objects, and in the transference. The cumulative effect of these interpretations is a freeing up of the ego, resulting in an experience of freedom and a capacity for joy and other affects and actions in reality. A second requirement is multiple links between experiences, impulses, and feelings at the level of the patient's current life, the transference, and the past. The net effect is the reduction of fragmentation of self, a typical clinical feature of severe obsessionals. Finally, increased ability to deepen the psychotherapeutic process is needed so that by the middle phases it will be relatively easy to shift from current to past in an atmosphere of emotional depth. This will allow the continuous and systematic working through of core genetic problems. All sources of resistances will continue to be monitored and addressed as needed, frequently in the transference. In patients with unresolved pathological mourning, the sources of resistances include the patient's unconscious feeling about attachment and detachment—in particular, their libidinal attachment to the actual and idealized object of childhood. In this patient instinctual loyalty to her father is buttressed by the severe ambivalence and rage that typically block normal mourning. These forces may now become an obstacle to the progress of psychotherapeutic process. In this patient the therapist needs to be vigilant about the transferentially based forms of sabotage.

The following vignettes from sessions 20 and 21 demonstrate a typical sequence of work. The focus of the work is on the patient's emerging sad feeling in relation to her father. She had always avoided such experiences in her past. The techniques used include gently holding the patient to her feelings with confrontation and clarification of resistances. Transference-current-past (TCP) links are made, and the deepening of the psychotherapeutic process occurs through a gradual shift to genetically structured material. A major defensive system (common to patients suffering from pathological mourning) is the tendency to derail the psychotherapeutic process as a form of self-sabotage. This defense system is gently confronted in this vignette.

Therapist: Maybe there is something within you that you would want to fail with me—and then what happens to your therapy?

Patient: It doesn't accomplish what I need to accomplish.

Therapist: It doesn't accomplish what you need to accomplish. Maybe there is a need in you to avoid success. It must bring tremendous pain, working together with me on this issue.

Patient: [In a deeply engaged and responsive mood] Yeah.

Therapist: If you look to your father's life—

Patient: I feel devastated.

Therapist: He could never have closeness with you. How could you now allow me to be successful when you and him—which started with a tremendous closeness ended up in a failure? Do you see what I mean?

Patient: I have been thinking about—the book. You know, Thomas Mann's book? I have started to read it. I am at the beginning. There is a young man who visits his cousin in a tuberculosis sanitarium.

Therapist: What were your feelings as you read this?

Patient: Oh, the character of the visitor. He goes through a tremendous amount of loss. His mother dies, his father dies, his grandfather dies. He is now a young man starting out on his career.

Therapist: How did you feel?

Patient: I want to avoid—there is so much pain [Averts her eyes].

Therapist: You also avoid me. You avoid my eyes.

Patient: When he went there, he didn't know—he didn't know how sick— [Slows down from sadness] does this sorrow ever end?

Therapist: What feelings came to you when you read about that man?

Patient: How could he survive?

Therapist: How do you feel now?

Patient: Sad—shaking inside—why, why, why didn't he do anything about his life? [Pause] I am involved with this man now, Harry, he is like my father in a lot of ways. Maybe that is why I am involved with him. He

Therapist: is so terrified of the relationship with me. My father did the same thing. He could have been in touch with us, but he wouldn't—it would have been so much more painful.

Therapist: It is also more painful for you to bring up your feelings rather than let everything remain buried.

Patient: My father was very devastated by where he was—he must have been devastated by where he was. The pain of not having us— [With sadness] I conjure up that expression between us. [Pause] It is unbearable to think that I lost him, but also it was his choice—I see myself in the convent, incredible that I am there and he is not with me.

Therapist: How do you feel?

Patient: [Deeply absorbed] It is so sad. I am so devastated.

This vignette is followed by the emergence of still another side to the patient's neurotic conflict: the positive libidinal attachment for the father of her early childhood and for the idealized father that has lived within her for a lifetime. The therapist here needs to promote instinctual decathexis. The psychotherapeutic process requires repeated exposure to her attachment and disappointment. Davanloo's techniques for this phase of treatment include the portrait of actual and/or fantasized experiences with the object ("How would you picture your relationship with him if he were alive today?"). The psychological work of the ego is to decathect the object in a process akin to the work of mourning. This patient's craving for tenderness appears through the transference in the following vignette.

Patient: I need a more caring response—from you, like more emotions reading in your face. I need to be held—someone to hold me—I have been craving for softness for so long. I don't know why, but you deprive me emotionally.

Therapist: You must have a lot of feelings about that. Your perception is that I am depriving you of something that is very important to you.

Patient: All my childhood I had to cry myself to sleep.

Therapist: When softness is not there, it mobilizes a lot of mixed feelings.

Patient: In some way it is the same with Harry. He doesn't look at me with tenderness either.

Therapist: How do you feel about that?

Patient: Mixed. I keep hoping that someday that it will be there, but then there is also rage, pure rage.

Therapist: If all this anger will come into the open, how will it get expressed?

Patient: I was thinking about that last night—so much rage—I would rip him up—with my own hands. [Sadness and tears appear] How could he do that to me—how could he do that to me.

Repeated experiences like this one encourage the patient to go deeper in her wish to overcome her core neurotic problems. Simultaneously the patient's problems with termination are brought to the foreground. The patient has been talking about her renewed wish to say her final goodbye to so many aspects of her life closely connected with the neurotic process. She is aware that closeness with the therapist brings sorrow and craving for more interpersonal closeness.

The following vignette illustrates these issues as they appear in the therapist/ patient relationship.

Therapist: Perhaps this sadness may have something to do with you and me. That is, if we keep working together, soon you will go your way and I will go my way.
Patient: Yeah.
Therapist: Maybe you have a certain feeling about that.
Patient: I have been thinking about that. When July comes and we finish, it will be our last goodbye.
Therapist: How do you feel about that?
Patient: Sad—very sad.

The last phase of treatment and the process of termination bring to a more intense pitch all the preparatory work that has gone on in the earlier phases. The task of the therapy is to complete the working through of the multiple dimensions of the core neurotic psychopathology as mapped in the initial evaluation. With this patient, as with patients suffering from severe character psychopathology, the issues include the final goodbye to the therapist, which brings very painful feelings to the focus. Any material left unresolved in her relationship to her father reappears at this time. If therapy is to be successful, the therapist has by now evidence of change in most or all areas of disturbance presented in the initial evaluation. The therapist can freely focus on issues relating to the current life of the patient, issues of the past, or issues in the transference. The techniques used at this stage of treatment include active frequent and deep genetic interpretations, as well as multiple inter-pretations of the ego defensive structure. By this time there should be abundant evidence of shifts from lower-level to higher-level defenses, as well as evidence of the resolution of many of the core genetic issues.

Two sessions prior to termination, at session 40, the patient brings to the session two pictures taken in the first three years of her life. In one of them she is sitting on a park bench together with her father and her two sisters. While the two sisters are sitting on their father's lap, the patient is seated two or three feet away, obviously sullen and sad. The second picture portrays the patient at age two happily in the arms of a smiling, warm, and obviously welcoming mother. The patient starts the session with great sadness and says:

Patient: When I look at myself, that is the way I am, angry.
Therapist: What goes on in the feelings of this man as he sits there? In a way he can hold only two of his girls, but his favorite is out.
Patient: I don't know—didn't notice it. It looks to me as if he's given up—he's lost—he is very sad—he looks sick and totally lost.
Therapist: If that picture were taken today, how would you portray the picture? Because in a way your deepest craving is to sit in that lap. Like in the earlier phases of your life with your father.
Patient: [Full of emotion] I would be sitting in his lap—no questions about that—and my arms—my arms—would be tightly around him.
Therapist: With your arms around him. Mm-hmm. And what would you say?

Patient: [Pause] Uh, I would just hold him. I'm so sad that I didn't recognize then that he was defeated, sick, and sad.
Therapist: But there has also been rage all your life.
Patient: Yes, he also let me sit over there, he didn't quite put his arms around me. Maybe he couldn't—after all, he had to leave me—it would have been so much more painful.
Therapist: How do you picture the life of your father if he would be alive? Because in a sense your last goodbye to him was from the position of distance and rage.
Patient: My own rage was so overwhelming at him. When he died, it was so deeply buried I was cold as ice.

After a while the patient shifts her attention from the picture displaying her father to the picture with her mother.

Patient: I went from here to there, from joy to sadness—I never forgave her for that.
Therapist: Again, how do you feel right now?
Patient: Sad, very sad, I was such a happy baby.
Therapist: There is sadness and there is rage. There is also another side which is very attached to that mother and has remained very attached to the mother of your early years. And in a sense you have never let go of that.
Patient: Yes.
Therapist: I wonder how your goodbye will be with me?
Patient: It will be sad, but I hope it will be complete—I like coming here, I like coming to see you, I look forward to coming to see you.
Therapist: Yes, but that must mobilize a lot of mixed feelings. How could you let me be successful with you when your relationship with your father died after reaching such a sad sorrowful state?
Patient: But there are so many feelings that I have now about myself. Sometimes I surprise myself in the morning or driving or when I listen to a particular piece of music and it is as if he is there with me. I feel his presence and then I feel so sad, but I also feel sort of serene and content.

Conclusion

The pioneering clinical work of Alexander and French, significantly revitalized by the insights of Sifneos and Malan, has acquired, in the laboratory of Davanloo, a new depth and maturity. The profound clinical and metapsychological rooting of Davanloo's techniques, as well as their obvious power to mobilize unconscious processes, may allow short-term dynamic psychotherapies modeled after them to find a lasting place in the spectrum of psychotherapeutic techniques.

Part Two 🙡

Neo-Freudian and Non-Freudian Analytic Therapies

In contrast to the therapies presented in Part One, which try to expand Freudian psychoanalysis, such as object relations psychology, or try to modify it using a shift in emphasis, such as ego psychology, Part Two contains alternative systems of analytic psychotherapy or analysis based on theoretical and ideological differences from Freudian psychoanalysis. These include non-Freudian systems such as the individual psychology of Alfred Adler and the analytical psychology of Carl Jung, as well as neo-Freudian systems based on cultural emphasis, including the holistic approach of Karen Horney and the interpersonal relationship school, with Harry Stack Sullivan as a forerunner.

In Chapter Six, "Adlerian Psychotherapy," Dorothy E. Peven and Bernard H. Shulman describe the case of a young woman, a victim of childhood incest, with a clinical dysthymic disorder, who suffered from intense feelings of inferiority, anxiety in social situations, and pervasive self-deprecation. The therapist used active techniques of exploration and confrontation to encourage the patient to make specific changes in her behavior and her goals. Certain Adlerian formulations and techniques are described: the Adlerian way of formulating the basic dynamics from the family constellation and early recollections, the understanding of dreams as metaphorical statements, the neurotic goal of superiority, the belief that the patient has the power to change (to select other behavior), and the belief that neurotic symptoms have a hidden purpose—either to protect self-esteem or to justify a demand on the social support system. An important therapeutic technique in this case was the use of humor—wit, irony, sarcasm, and nonsense—to maintain the relationship, deflect the patient's own gloomy approach, and dilute the patient's self-hatred.

In Chapter Seven, "Jungian Analysis," Mary Ann Mattoon develops the position that Jungian analysis facilitates development toward psychological wholeness through a "conversation" between the analysand's conscious and unconscious contents. The work makes use of the self-regulation of the psyche, which draws on the resources of the collective unconscious. Mattoon presents the theory of personality on which Jungian analysis is based along with the contributions of therapists who have followed Jung. She advances Jungian analysis as a framework for understanding highly varied personalities and for doing the therapeutic work necessary for each. The theory includes some concepts that are unique to Jungian psychology, such as extroversion/introversion, archetypes, and animus/anima, and others that are not unique but bear a Jungian imprint—for example, complex, persona, shadow, and Self. This chapter describes the setting in which one Jungian analyst works, examines the repertoire of procedures that may occur in analytic therapy (including dream analysis), and presents brief discussions of three cases from the author's practice.

In Chapter Eight, "Horney's Psychoanalytic Technique," Douglas H. Ingram explains that, for Karen Horney, psychoanalytic technique proceeds from an ever-deepening understanding of the patient. This understanding is grounded foremost in the quality of the analyst's attention, which, in turn, surpasses in priority even the analyst's theoretical outlook. The author advocates that analysts, developing their capacity to attend the patient, rely on their own and their patients' feelings, free associations, dreams, transference manifestations, blockages, and capacities for constructiveness. If understanding the patient leads the analyst to the considered judgment that suggestion, counseling, or inculcating values might attenuate the patient's alienation from his or her real self, then these techniques are endorsed. Ingram believes that extending the analyst's techniques beyond interpretation, clarification, silence, and exploratory questioning or other encouragement is no invitation to diminished rigor in the conduct of analysis and that there is no clinical justification for derogating other techniques as nonanalytic or as proceeding from countertransference difficulties.

In Chapter Nine, "Interpersonal Psychoanalysis," Stephen A. Mitchell describes interpersonal psychoanalysis, a broad, heterogeneous body of theoretical concepts and clinical approaches that were generated in the clash between European, classical Freudian psychoanalysis and the more operationally oriented American "interpersonal psychiatry" of H. S. Sullivan. A basic psychodynamic approach is preserved but recast within a framework that sees the establishment and maintenance of relations with others as the basic motivational thrust within human experience. The focus is on what people actually do with each other, in the patient's past and present and, particularly, in the analytic relationship. The analyst is seen not as a detached decoder of the patient's experiences but as a "participant observer"; the analysis is seen as providing not reconstructions and explanations but highly personal interactions and new experiences.

In Chapter Ten, "Existential Analysis," Herbert Holt describes existential analysis, a therapy designed for patients who have difficulty in finding meaning and purpose in life and in maintaining their identity. It is advanced as useful for people who need to find their individuality and separate themselves from mass society. It uses object theory, ego theory, and interpersonal theory to deal with the problem of "being-in-the-world"—in establishing one's identity in one's inner world of thoughts, fantasies, wishes, and dreams; in one's world in relation to others; and in one's experience in relation to the surrounding environment. Holt illustrates the technique in an existential analytic encounter with a patient.

6

Adlerian Psychotherapy

Dorothy E. Peven
Bernard H. Shulman

Late one summer, Sheri came to see me (Peven) for psychotherapy. She reported that she had had an incestuous relationship with her father from age six to age thirteen. Now, at thirty-three, unmarried, she found herself obsessing constantly about her father and their sexual experiences. She believed that the incest had colored her entire life and that, because of it, she could not make a long-term commitment to one man. A few weeks earlier she had broken up an intense year-long relationship; she blamed her own depressive behavior and "irrational" outbursts of rage and hostility.

Although she had been in treatment for a year with another therapist, she did not "feel helped." A male friend, a former patient, had recommended me. She was working as a schoolteacher; she said her work brought her no gratification, but she did not believe herself capable of doing anything else. She lived alone in her own apartment in the heart of Chicago's "yuppie" community and said she enjoyed her friends, some of whom were close, and did not lack for the attention of men. Her parents were divorced, both remarried; mother lived in Chicago, father out of state. There was one older brother who had a family of his own and was in business with father.

Sheri gave as her reasons for coming that she was depressed and "unable to get on with my life." She reported that she had "feelings of inferiority," poor sleep, and long bouts with diarrhea and had lost ten pounds in the past year. She denied suicidal thoughts or wishes. There were periods of time during which she isolated herself from social companionship because she "couldn't stand myself or anybody else."

Two years earlier, at the urging of a therapy group, she had decided to confront her father about the incest. When she did, her father responded by saying he thought she had forgotten. When she continued angrily, he retorted that she had enjoyed and encouraged the relationship, and finally he became angry himself. They had previously been on outwardly good terms with each other, but their relationship deteriorated to mutual recriminations and eventually to no contact at all. In contrast, Sheri had never before been close to her mother. After the fiasco with father, she told mother, who became supportive and encouraging to Sheri for the first time in her life. She now had a better relationship with her mother than ever before and feelings of hatred for father. She also told her brother about the incest, but they had never been friends, and the brother distanced himself even further from Sheri.

At one point in the session I asked her what she would do with herself and her life if she were free of symptoms. She answered that if her mind weren't "all confused and obsessed," she would change careers, study something interesting, spend more time with friends, marry, and "develop myself as a person, like taking up painting, reading, and sports."

Here she was, exactly what the media had been publicizing for the past few years—the sexually abused child who grows up psychologically "stunted." My first response was to question myself about how much of the story I was prepared to accept. Then I was curious to know how much this woman had been influenced by the media and what kind of treatment she had been exposed to.

As an Adlerian, I thought: How is this woman responding to the trauma of her childhood? Although I could not make light of what had happened to her, I felt responsible for teaching her that it need not make a tragedy of the rest of her life. I felt strongly that Sheri was in the process of making a "career" out of the "incest tragedy." So far, she had managed to upset a great many people; for example, after a "confrontation interview" with the previous therapist, father had refused to have anything to do with her, saying that all she wanted from him was his money. Her brother would not get in touch with her at all, treated her as if she were "crazy," and responded to a letter from her by saying she was "in the hands of the wrong therapist." The man she had been involved with was treated to violent, stormy scenes during which she accused all men of being pigs.

All this excitement creation, all the emotional arousal, all the ventilation in groups with other women with incestuous experiences and in the battles with her father, trying to make him accept the responsibility for his behavior, had added up to the creation of a clinical depression. What good had come of all the "Let's get it all out in the open," "Let it all hang out," "Don't leave any unfinished business around"? What had this done for her? My firm belief was that matters were far worse than they would have been had she not set out to "punish father."

So here was the dilemma: on the one hand father *had* exploited his female child, taken advantage of her desire to please, and, as Sheri said, father's incestuous attention to her had been "the only affection I got in the house." Father's stroking was designed to make her feel good, and it worked. What it did for him, I cannot speculate. On the other hand, Sheri wasn't getting what she wanted. She seemed to want revenge, but her idea of revenge apparently was to have father beg her forgiveness, admit he was a miscreant for doing what he did, accept full responsibility for his gross behavior, and feel shame and guilt and humble himself to Sheri so she could graciously forgive him. Then they would walk hand in hand into the sunset and be happy. I could see that she would never get this from the man she was describing as her father. But I saw no reason she should not get some revenge.

And so that very first day I did something perhaps rather startling. I suggested to Sheri that she try to get revenge, but in a "smart" way. Father was rich, so why not manipulate to get all the money she possibly could? Now, she knew he did not part with his money easily and had already accused her of bringing up the incest with an eye to making money out of it, and so I asked her to see a lawyer and find out whether there were any legal steps she could take. The psychological steps used so far had not brought her the revenge she wanted. Perhaps gaining revenge through legal means would help her feel better about herself.

Sometimes, in the initial interview, I seek to impress new patients, saying or suggesting something novel. I would like them to leave the first interview with something to think about. Occasionally I will make an interpretation that normally I would offer only after many long, hard months of working through. It does not matter whether the interpretation is accepted, only that the patient have something to think about. Usually I am a very interested, intensely alert, and caring listener. But I do listen to my own feelings, and in this case I thought I would like to give this woman a new way of looking at an old problem.

First I referred her to Women's Services, sponsored by the YWCA in Chicago. (They had been helpful in the past with other women's services, such as rape counseling.) Then I told Sheri that there were other ways to get what she wanted from father and that what I thought she should try to do was to get money as a form of reparation. She would not get the "confession"; she would not get the satisfaction of having him accept responsibility for his behavior. What was left? Money! Sheri seemed intrigued.

I asked Sheri what she would do if she were symptom-free because Adler (1958) taught that life offers three main social tasks that challenge each human: work (the need to sustain oneself and make a productive contribution to the common good), friendship (the need to develop mutually cooperative relationships in a supportive social network), and love and sex (the need to create a satisfying and harmonious relationship with a loved person of the other sex—an appropriate sexual bond). These tasks designate the field of action for the human being (Dreikurs and Mosak, 1966); they are the practical demands of social living (Way, 1962).

Adlerians ask a specific question designed to elicit the purpose of a symptom: "We ask patients what would be different if they were well? The answer to this question explains their complaints and emotional stress in a given situation. It indicates for what purpose patients are sick, against whom or what their symptoms are directed, and against which social threat or demand they defend themselves by being sick" (Dreikurs, 1956, p. 113). Sheri's answer told me she was hesitating to change careers, hesitating before the challenge of marriage, and not wholeheartedly meeting the tasks of friendship. Therefore, if I could help her be symptom-free, these would be issues for us to address and the "problems" we would have to solve together during her therapy.

The First Months of Therapy

During the first few months of therapy (sessions 4 to 16), Sheri gradually became more depressed. For weeks at a time she would go to work, return home, and "veg out" in front of the TV. At other times, when she did go out, she would complain that she felt self-conscious and got no enjoyment out of any social contact.

The men she dated were never "good enough—they don't change me, make me forget, or erase the black cloud I bring into the relationship."

In the sessions she often related dreams in which she and her father were engaging in some kind of sexual activity. The dreams were all set in the house she had lived in as a child and were full of hurt and anger at father (in one dream she saw him mangled) but also full of sexual acts that gave her pleasure. She would awaken upon orgasm.

The fact that she felt pleasure was another problem issue for Sheri. She knew she had *enjoyed* the sexuality with father, that she had had orgasms (as had he), and that what he had done to her had "felt very good." We discussed the fact that she was a sexually responsive woman and that this might very well be a result of the continual sexual arousal as a child. When very depressed, Sheri would complain that she felt no sexual longings and didn't "even masturbate"; but even during the worst of her depression she would dream about father, and almost always in her dreams the two of them were engaged in some sexual activity. She was furious with father, but her dreams revealed what she would never admit: she still loved him and longed for him sexually.

A few weeks after the initial interview, without further reference to the subject on my part, Sheri went to see a lawyer recommended by Women's Services. The lawyer, a woman, told her the statute of limitations had run out. Sheri could bring a civil suit against father, but the lawyer did not think it would hold up in court. Sheri looked at me strangely and told me, "The lawyer said the same thing you did: Why don't I make up with him and try to manipulate him so that I get a lot of money from him?" The congruence between the lawyer's advice and mine must have made an impression. Perhaps Sheri began to pay more attention to my advice from then on.

Four months after therapy began, Sheri's depression was so bad I urged her to see Dr. Shulman for medication. She had uncontrollable crying spells and a constant "lump in her chest," and she was talking about suicide. "It would be a relief to be dead," she said, but she promised to call me and go to the hospital if she ever really wanted to die. (She has never called me for any kind of emergency.) She spent many of our therapeutic hours telling me how "stupid, helpless, inept, unmotivated" she was and how she couldn't "help anything or change anything." Dr. Shulman prescribed a tricyclic antidepressant, and after a few weeks she began to feel a little better. She remained on the antidepressant thereafter.

This was the hardest time for me. Sheri was in the middle of a clinical depression, and experience has taught me that there really is not much I can do except be very supportive and encouraging, make frequent contact, be sympathetic, and perhaps offer a dollop of exploratory therapy. She listened when I talked about psychodynamics, but on the whole she was not ready to examine her own dynamics, even though I persisted.

During this period I used a formal structured interview technique to elicit Sheri's life-style.

The Style of Life. Rudolf Dreikurs (1897–1972) came to Chicago from Austria, a refugee from the Nazis. He had studied with Alfred Adler in Vienna and brought with him many of the techniques used by Adler himself, which he elaborated. For example, he designed a systematic questionnaire to elicit information about early childhood. Following this work, other techniques were evolved by Harold H. Mosak and Bernard H. Shulman. One such technique was the practice of using a structured interview to obtain specific information about the patient's formative years in the family of orientation. This information is used to formulate a family constellation. Of particular importance to Adlerians are certain family factors that influence personality development—birth order, behavior modeled by parents, family values, family atmosphere, sibling rivalries, and the way the child established its place in the family, its family "role."

From the fourth to the sixth week Sheri and I gathered and explored the information in the family constellation. Then we met with Dr. Shulman for the purpose of interpreting the childhood material to Sheri, to formulate a life-style.

The technique of using two therapists (a multiple therapy interview) at selected times in psychotherapy has been described by many authors. One indication we use for the multiple therapy interview is when information about childhood is to be assembled into a narrative summary. The two therapists review the information and construct a summary *in the presence of the patient.* The benefits to the patient from such a meeting have been described by Dreikurs, Mosak, and Shulman (1956).

Dr. Shulman, Sheri, and I collaborated to write the following summary of the family constellation:

> The younger of two and only girl in a family with a dictatorial czar for a father who was not able to relate to the family except as a dictator. Each family member responded to father's exercise of power in different ways: Mother played the role of an inferior female in order to be less threatening to father and used techniques that caricature femininity in order to establish her territory. Brother imitated father and thus came into conflict with him ("junior czar"), but he was supported by mother, who indulged him. Sheri imitated mother both in outward compliance and in inner resentment. Power over others was the highest value and was achieved by hook or by crook, and females were devalued.
>
> Sheri found herself in an inferior position because of her gender, because of her position as the second born, and because the family dynamics did not automatically grant family members a worthwhile place. One had to fight or finagle for one's place. Being the youngest and weakest, Sheri discovered that if she submitted to father, she could be his favorite and thereby achieve some vicarious power.
>
> This was a family in which no human being could trust another and all relationships were competitive.

In the same meeting we also reviewed the earliest childhood recollections I had elicited from Sheri. Adler pointed out that memory is selective and retrospectively reconstructed and thus early memories reveal current psychological issues: "His memories are the reminders he carries with him . . . . There are no chance memories; they represent his "Story of My Life"; a story he repeats to himself to warn him or comfort him, to keep him concentrated on his goal, and to prepare him . . . so that he will meet the future with an already tested style of action" (1958, p. 73).

Analysis of early recollections gives the individual psychologist the opportunity to understand patients' basic beliefs about themselves and their phenomenological worlds. Recollections also reflect patients' values: they tell us what patients find important and meaningful and where patients' central focus is when looking at the world. The individual psychologist is concerned with patients' "private logic" (as opposed to consensual validation), their final fictive goals (what confers significance), their guiding self-ideals (what they strive to be), and the methods they use for striving. Where these beliefs interfere with successful growth, we hope to change them. Eliciting early recollections at different points in therapy can show changes in perceptual outlook.

These are Sheri's early recollections taken in the first two months of therapy:

> Age 4. I'm standing up in my crib. Brother's bed is on another wall. I want a doll that I see across the room, and I can't get it. I cry. I feel frustrated. I'm alone in the room.
>
> Age 2. I was crawling around on the floor in the living room. People are there and the TV is going. I'm crawling around, stopping, looking around. Everybody else is watching television. I have a feeling of solitude.
>
> Age 5. In the house. My parents had gone out of town and were returning. They came in with a dog. I felt real happy. It was exciting and nice to have them come back.
>
> Age 6. First grade. I beat up a neighborhood kid, a boy. He pissed me off, so I grabbed him by the arm and was twirling him around; then I let him go and he bumped his head on a pole. Somebody came and helped him. I stood there feeling very bad, like a criminal. I said to myself, "How could you?"

If we interpret the recollections as conveying the meaning Sheri gives to her life, her subjective convictions, we can see her feeling of alienation from others and her frustration. She cannot attain her desired goals; she is not in the mainstream of her social network. Her actions lead to nothing useful. If she asserts herself, she does damage to others and feels like a bad person. The only happy memory is the one in which she passively depends on the behavior of others (her parents came back). In no memory is anyone glad to see her.

The following summary of Sheri's early recollections was suggested during the multiple therapy session:

> I am too small, too hemmed in, to achieve my goals, and there is no one to help me. Surrounded by others, I am still really alone. In my relationship with others, I, at least, want to be the person who acts justly and with consideration so that I can have some positive feelings about myself. I do not get much positive feeling from others.

The reason for this particular construction is therapeutic. Rather than say in the summary that she sees herself as causing hurt to others, we would prefer to use an ego-syntonic interpretation. We use the information that she feels guilty when others are hurt to attribute to her an ideal of acting with consideration for others (even though she often does not). In so doing we try to show her that we find something positive in her, and we hope that this will not only improve rapport but also oppose her own self-deprecation.

From the above material we infer faulty convictions that interfere with efficient adaptation to the developmental challenges of life. If we can identify these mistaken ideas and clearly reveal them to our patients, and the patients can recognize these mistakes and catch themselves making them, then change should start. As mentioned above, when we summarize the family constellation and the early recollections, we do it with two therapists and the patient in collaboration. Many patients report a profound emotional response to hearing their lives, beliefs, and feelings put into words.

However, when we construct the list of "Basic Mistakes," we do not ask for the patient's participation. The list grows logically out of the interpretations of the family constellation and early recollections. "Basic Mistakes" are errors, distorted perceptions, or mistaken meanings given to life, and it becomes a goal of treatment to change these cognitions and the behaviors that flow from them to more adaptive ones, or, at the least, to turn big mistakes into little ones.

Dr. Shulman and I thought Sheri's *Basic Mistakes* were these:

She has been trained to feel negative about herself.
She experiences her goals as impossible to attain and herself as impotent to do anything about it.
The only thing she feels able to do is to suffer and rage at heaven.

The Initial Phase of Therapy. Sheri had paid close attention during the summations of her life-style material and had agreed with or added to everything. She cried throughout the whole recitation, and she cried again during the summation. When I gave her a copy of the summary, she merely glanced at it and put it away. I took this to mean she was not prepared to deal with the issues raised and that I could expect long periods of depressive tactics. Unhappily, I was right.

Sheri spent the first six months of therapy deriding herself, complaining about herself and her life, and always, always, talking about men. "Men are never enough for me—they don't change me, make me forget, or erase the black cloud I bring into the relationship." I asked whether she wanted men to make up to her for her old hurts. "Yes," she said, "they're supposed to erase the old memories."

Sheri ventilated endlessly about how inferior she felt, how dumb she was, and how socially inferior she could be. After one blind date she assumed that since she had not been vivacious and charming, the man would never want to see her again. She had started taking courses in library science, and whenever she had an exam, I would hear comments such as "I can't concentrate," "I'm dumb," "I'll do what I have done with everything else and never see it through." (In fact she graduated with a solid B average.) In addition, she often repeated, "I'm too old for any man to want to marry me."

All this was accompanied by crying, sighs, reports of anxiety attacks, and constant obsession with the incest. She spoke of how much she hated father, what a "scum" of a man he was, how he had ruined her life, and how, because of him, she was unable to get along with anybody, especially men: "I think that everybody is looking at me and can see how sick I am. I obsess about how nervous and uncomfortable I am with every human being on this planet."

I was reluctant to carry on these discussions with Sheri, believing that such an endless recitation of symptoms and character flaws is not only useless but antitherapeutic. I tried various methods to get Sheri to stop the endless rumination. Once, listening closely, I began to understand something and said, "Sheri, do you feel flawed?" She responded with a deep sigh of relief, as if I finally understood everything she had been trying to tell me for so long. "Yes," she said, "that's exactly how I feel."

Sheri told me how horrible the shame of it had been for her and how for almost twenty years she had tried to put the entire seven years out of her mind. She needed (wanted) her father, and the truth was, she loved him. In her childhood, mother had been lavishing love and attention on older brother, who did his best to beat Sheri down. Mother was so intimidated by father's tyrannical demands that she often behaved like a simpleton. Sheri described sitting on father's lap in the living room on a chair, with a blanket over their lower parts. Mother was sitting in the same room, on the couch, and they were all ostensibly watching TV. But father had pulled off Sheri's pants and taken out his penis and was rocking Sheri back and forth, his penis rubbing against her genitals, until they both reached orgasm. Although she was worried that mother might notice and say something, mother did and said nothing. Nothing!

In that house Sheri gained love, attention, and affection from the "power" in the family by going along with father and his sexual games. Father rewarded her in many ways. He protected her and "flattered" her with his attentions.

Mother, probably quite disturbed by her inability to have any importance in the household, ran away with another man when Sheri was fifteen. During those early years there were constant battles in the house—one fight ending with brother hitting mother and mother having him arrested. Little wonder that Sheri believed her only salvation lay with her daddy.

There were several years when Sheri did not see or speak to her mother and she clung to her father. They had stopped the sexually explicit behavior when Sheri started to mature and pushed father away, but Sheri admired her father, thought he was wonderful, and believed in him and in his ability to keep everything in order. Small wonder, then, that many years later, when the media started to discuss incest openly, she was very reluctant to dredge up her memories. She had told no one about her sexual behavior with father and always felt that deep within herself she was flawed so deeply that no matter how she looked outside, her inside was rotten and anybody who got too close, especially a man, would notice.

I believed the truth was that Sheri still loved father and still thought of him as a sexually attractive man. She did miss him; she did think about him; and almost all her dreams were about him.

Dreams. Individual psychologists treat dreams as a projection of the patient's current concerns as well as of current mood. But dreams also have a prospective function for the Adlerian. The dream can be a "rehearsal for action" (Way, 1962) or a "trial solution" (Wexberg, 1929). The dream is a metaphor (Shulman, 1969) by which the dreamer "stores up a certain reserve of feeling and emotion . . . to sustain him in the pursuit of his own goal" (Adler, 1964, p. 17). Dreams, like any metaphor, can be interpreted and translated into rational language. They are used clinically to understand and define problem areas, to predict the near-future action of the patient, and to teach the patient to observe and understand his or her own internal dynamics.

About eight weeks into therapy, Sheri brought in the following dream: "I was in the bedroom [in her childhood home] getting clothes so I could leave. My father and I were in twin beds. He kept saying, "Good night, Sheri, good night, Sheri." I couldn't turn out the light. I kept thinking there's another light and yet another to turn off. My brother came in and looked around with an "I wonder what's going on" look on his face, "with these two in their pajamas." I didn't say anything. I just looked at father and shrugged, "Let him think what he wants to think."

A few nights later, she had a similar dream. "I was in the same bedroom at our old house. I was going to sleep. It was warm and I was going to take everything off under the covers. Father was there. I was waiting and wondering if he would come over and bother me. Sure enough, he did. Marvin walked in and father became very careful. I was aroused—that bugs me. I was going to stop him, but I was aroused."

These dreams demonstrate the recurring issues during the first six months of therapy. Sheri was concerned about her ambivalence in wanting father and wanting to get away from him. She dreamed that the lights were on, which, I think, was her way of saying she was going to turn the lights on the whole affair with father. When brother came in, she seemed to be saying, with her shrug, "Do I care who knows?" She still wants daddy, and she is "bugged" by it.

The one thing these dreams show clearly is how much Sheri still wanted father and how angry she was both at herself and at father because she felt that way. In each dream she reminded herself about the incest and refueled her unhappiness. In the dreams, she told herself, "I believe my father is still interested in me, and if I could get him in the right situation, I could prove it to him and make him acknowledge it."

One Year Later

A year went by. Sheri came to see me weekly. Her dreams showed little change, and she still spent considerable time reciting her list of her "inferiorities."

She was still pursuing her studies in library science, designed to help her change jobs; and although she suffered whenever there was an exam, she was really handling it quite well. She was dating intermittently but was always critical of the men and believed they were always critical of her, no matter what their behavior.

Slowly, gradually, she began to feel better, and some of the depression lifted. (However, she always claimed that the "good" days were just flukes.) We became friendly, and I found her charming and witty and possessed of a delightful sense of humor. I found I could tease her and enjoyed her company.

We had started taping our sessions because I wanted Sheri to listen to her self-derogation and perhaps listen to some of the interpretations I was busy making to no avail. The following excerpt is from session 60, almost one year after Sheri first came in. It is a good example of our interaction. I try first to show Sheri the fallacies in her logic and then, in a pixieish mood, enjoy making fun with her.

Patient:	Dorothy, everything is so bad, but what I really can't stand is the inconsistency. At least, at one time, my life was consistently—
Therapist:	Black.
Patient:	Black. Bad, and sad too. But now, periodically, I feel better, and I look at things in a very nice frame of mind.
Therapist:	Does that frighten you?

Patient: Maybe it does. Because I always blow it again. I always replace the good frame with the bad frame.

Therapist: You see, I'm encouraged by the fact that you have good times. You sound like you are *dis*couraged by the fact that you have good times.

Patient: It's not that I'm discouraged by it, but it is discouraging that somehow I decide to shift myself out of it all the time—

Therapist: You use exactly the right words. Do you mean that? "*I* shift myself?"

Patient: I *do* mean that. I *do* mean it.

Therapist: You understand, you are doing it to yourself?

Patient: I understand I am doing it to myself.

Therapist: What is the process by which you change yourself?

Patient: Do you mean, what do I actually do to do it?

Therapist: Sure. What do you think? What do you feel? What is your behavior?

Patient: Well, I'm not really sure. I just know it starts and then it is a ball that just rolls.

Therapist: Won't you please watch yourself and catch what you're doing?

Patient: I can't.

Therapist: OK. Now ask me "why?"

Patient: OK. Why?

Therapist: You are suffering because you lived a bad life in a past reincarnation.

Patient: You mean this is a new person right here?

Therapist: In your last life or the life before that, or whatever, you did something bad, and now you're suffering for it in this life.

Patient: In my last life?

Therapist: Or the one before that. [Laughter]

Patient: What happened to your degrees? You're starting to scare me. . . . You talk reincarnation, no more degrees. [Laughter]

Therapist: You mean you don't believe in it?

Patient: Not really. No.

Therapist: In the last class I taught, there were people . . . were telling me about reincarnation, and one of the girls sent me a book. . . . Have you ever heard of Edgar Cayce?

Patient: Yes.

Therapist: I have been reading it every night. And I'm all full of that stuff in my head. So now I have an answer for your "why"!

Patient: Dorothy, you're nuts!

Therapist: You noticed. [Both laugh.]

Patient: Back to reality. Last week I had a paper to work on. I sat at my desk at home, and I got myself so nervous, Dorothy, that my whole body was tense.

Therapist: Tell me how "I got myself so nervous"? Tell me about that.

Patient: It's like I said to you before, I shift myself in and out. You can ask me if I really believe I do that, and I could say to you I believe that I have a lot to do with it. . . . I sat there and drove myself nuts. All of a sudden it indicated to me that I was stupid. . . . Well, I got it after I went crazy for about a half hour. Then I stood up and gave myself a lecture.

Therapist: Which consisted of what?

Patient: . . . If you don't put this shit aside, you are just going to sit here like this the rest of your life. So, you know, it worked. For the next couple of days I felt good about what I had accomplished. More than getting the problem, I had dealt with myself. It was such a wonderful feeling! The next thing I knew, I was overeating to the point that I was feeling uncomfortable.

Therapist: Why do you think you do it?

Patient: I don't want to feel good.

Therapist: You don't want to feel good?

Patient: I don't want to look good.

Therapist: Yes, you do. You want to feel good, you want to look good.

Patient: I do? So why do I pack myself with food for days and days? My appearance is very important to me, and I am very unusual-looking. [*She is.*] When I do something to mar my looks, I am saying, "Look at me, I don't look good."

Therapist: Do you think, by chance, that you are caught up in the cultural thing that we are all supposed to be skinny—you are not supposed to indulge yourself, ever?

Patient: Indulging is one thing, but gorging is another—for five or six days, that's not just rebelling, that's anarchy!

Therapist: What happens after five or six days?

Patient: Then I get to a point when I say, "Enough is enough."

Therapist: Then you stop?

Patient: Then I stop.

Therapist: You don't allow yourself the slightest bit of leeway. "I'm not supposed to overeat, ever." "I'm not supposed to make mistakes when I do my homework." "I'm not supposed to—" whatever else you were telling me just now. I don't know, it seems to me you never stop picking on yourself. You are not very nice to yourself. Is a bubble bath all right? [*Patient shakes her head "no."*] A bubble bath is not all right? Why?

Patient: Bubbles are bad for your vagina. [Laughter]

Therapist: Well, what if the culture decides within the next couple of years that 150 is an appropriate weight for you?

Patient: I'll know exactly how to get there. [Both laugh.]

This segment shows an intense interaction between patient and therapist in a humorous and playful mood. The patient complains about various defects in herself—inconsistency, "driving herself nuts," compulsive overeating, and similar faults. The therapist tries to counteract the self-deprecating behavior by encouraging the patient to recognize that her self-criticism is exaggerated. When the patient seems to see that she creates a negative mood in herself, the therapist then introduces the question of why she does this. As can be seen in some of the later excerpts, this self-deprecation is a form of resistance. It is an expression of the patient's "spoiled" self-image and an example of Karen Horney's *self-contempt* (Horney, 1946). This type of behavior is also a form of overdramatization. In Adlerian theory, one might say that, feeling she has little to contribute in a positive way, she finds significance in being so "flawed." This allows her to have a sense of self that conforms to her self-image. She cannot yet accept certain improvements in herself—she does not yet feel like a whole person.

This session is notable for the playfulness in it, but there is a method in the therapist's madness. The playful mood permits a considerable amount of interpretation. It permits the use of exaggeration and of nonsense to drive home a point. Since the patient feels "flawed," the therapist offers the explanation that she is suffering from misdeeds in a past incarnation. As expected, the patient rejects this, but the therapist can then confront the patient with two important concepts: first, she is excessively self-critical and, second, she has been self-punitive and has the power to change that behavior.

(A later excerpt from session 60:)

Patient:	Last night I was sitting in this class, and I was on a bad roll last night. I was thinking, "Oh my God! This is it. This is the last class you are ever going to understand, ever." The frightening thing is, is that it is becoming so manageable that now I can get myself out of a state like that and even converse with people, where before I was so shaky and upset that I would think like that, that I would go home scared.
Therapist:	Well, I don't want to scare you, but could you be getting better, a little bit?
Patient:	I say I'm getting worse because I'm embracing this miserable attitude.
Therapist:	Let's go back to the beginning of the tape and listen when you told me how you're going up and down instead of always being flat and depressed. You have also told me on occasion, and again just now, that you have control of it.
Patient:	It seems to me that if you have control and you know you do and choose to have a shitty feeling, then you are worse off than if you are unaware.
Therapist:	You're right, you're not getting better, you are getting worse. Isn't that your logic? [*With irony.*]
Patient:	Yes.
Therapist:	OK, I agree with you. Would I fight such logic?
Patient:	Yes. [*The patient recognizes the irony.*]
Therapist:	It is very obvious you're right. That means you're getting worse. Because you have periods when you feel better and periods when you can talk yourself out of it, the logical conclusion is "I'm getting worse."
Patient:	It doesn't sound so logical as it did before. And I believe this shit. I really believe this shit.
Therapist:	It's hard for me to believe you really believe.
Patient:	With this you believe I am ready for a group? [*Therapist had been trying to persuade her to join her group.*] To sit for an hour and a half and be respectful and kind towards other people who have anything to say, when I know I'm a total basket case?
Therapist:	You'll be the only one in the group that will be respectful and kind to the others. Hurry up and come in.

This segment illustrates a common unconscious mechanism that can be considered a form of incomplete insight. The patient admits that she recognizes how her own style of thinking leads her to exaggerate the difficulties and thus to create anxiety. Now she recognizes that she has some conscious control over her thinking and thus over her production of the anxiety. Rather than see this as a hopeful sign, she now criticizes herself for continuing to engage in her habitual behavior even though she has learned that she does not have to. The self-criticism is simply a continuation of her previous behavior and further permits her to deprecate herself.

The therapist interprets this to her as a form of illogic. Trying to show the patient such mistakes in logic is an important Adlerian technique. "Since the person's difficulties emanate from faulty perceptions, learnings, values, and goals that have resulted in his discouragement, therapy consists of an educative or reeducative endeavor" (Mosak, 1979, p. 87).

Changes. About one year after Sheri had first come to see me, I became interested in evaluating what progress had taken place. Symptom complaints had subsided, and I wanted to know whether there had been a change in psychodynamics. Therefore (as discussed above), I collected another set of early recollections. They were as follows:

> Age 6. At a holiday dinner at aunt and uncle's house. The cousins were playing and having fun. We sat down. There were balloons on the backs of the chairs. The room was well lit. The whole family sat at the table and we were talking and eating. I felt happy.
>
> Age 9. My paternal grandmother from California was staying at my house. She and I sat on the patio and talked for a long time before we went to sleep. It was pleasant.
>
> Age 6. I grew big pumpkins. One morning I went out to tend my pumpkins and the biggest one was gone. I was very upset. I went outside and saw my pumpkin had been dropped in the alley. I felt better because if I couldn't have my pumpkin, then they shouldn't have it.
>
> Age 6. During a dance class, all dressed up in little costumes. I was paired off with somebody. I had a green wart on my hand and thought everybody would see how ugly it was. My partner said, "OOOH! What's that on your hand?," and we held hands with the other hand. We danced. I felt self-conscious and flawed.
>
> Age 7. Had a doll with a little fur piece from a furrier down the block. There was a little piece of fur lying by the back door as I walked out in the morning, and I went nuts. I thought it was a rat; we had had them. I screamed. Then I kicked it and saw it was my doll's fur stole. I picked it up. Felt silly and relieved.

The first recollections show considerable change in Sheri's social feeling. She is with people and enjoying herself; she belongs. Her "flaws" are ugly and openly apparent, but she is not rejected; in fact, accommodation is made ("held hands with the other hand"). Still, Sheri begins to realize she can make mountains out of molehills and is able to tell herself that she can misinterpret. And her desire for revenge is apparent: "if I couldn't have my pumpkin, then they shouldn't have it."

The individual psychologist believes that change in the recollected memories signifies that a change has taken place in the person's characteristic ways of perceiving the world and of acting in it.

Since the patient's psychopathology is considered the product of faulty learning, especially faulty learning about interpersonal relationships, we can be encouraged by the changes in the recollection. They show an increased feeling of belonging to human society (social interest). For Adlerians, social interest (*Gemeinschaftsgefühl*) is an important antidote to psychopathology. It is a sense of being embedded in a supportive social network, an attitude of openness to constructive social interaction, a readiness to experience positive feedback in human relationships and to give such feedback in turn.

Resistance. When the therapist begins to challenge the cherished beliefs of the patient, he or she "appears as the representative of the human community, as the herald of the needs of human fellowship" (Dreikurs, 1967, p. 32). Dreikurs says further that this image of the therapist will "call forth the spite that the patient feels against human society." This rebelliousness and the patient's desire to escape from the interpretations that point to this antagonistic attitude are two important roots of resistance.

Another frequent form of resistance occurs when patient and therapist have different goals and move in different directions. We will see this form depicted in the next description of Sheri's progress.

Several of Sheri's cherished notions reappeared constantly in the therapy. She believed she had been permanently impaired by her incest experience. Consequently, she had no confidence in herself; she spent most of the first eighteen months of therapy telling me about it. When I believed the therapeutic relationship was firmly established, I challenged her often about the constant restatements of her feeling of inferiority, which actually prevented us from moving to other issues. Once or twice, to dramatize my concern, I pretended to fall asleep and made loud snoring noises. She would laugh and continue her recital. I often tried to discuss with her the purpose of this behavior. She would listen politely and continue. I considered this resistance.

About one and a half years into the therapy, I spent one entire session discussing the *purpose* of Sheri's repetitious recital and her obsession with her feelings of inferiority. I offered one possible purpose and asked her to offer another. Between us we compiled a list of possible purposes for such behavior: it reinforced her old beliefs of not belonging with others, it served to impress her and others with her failings so others would not expect too much, it protected her against taking risks, it allowed her to claim special exception, and it fed her desire for revenge. Neither of us laughed during this interview.

The following week Sheri came in very angry at me. She told me that I had been irritable, that I jumped on her, that I contradicted her; she asked whether I was going through a "difficult time." I was taken aback but asked her whether she remembered what we had talked about the previous week or had listened to the tape. She had not and did not want to be interrupted. I asked myself what I had done. Had I been unpleasant or irritable? Whatever I had done, I didn't think I deserved quite as much flak as I was getting, and I understood her response as resistance to my interpretation of her behavior. I stayed away from any discussion of psychodynamics for several weeks, replying to her attack by suggesting she would have to learn to put up with me, since "I, too, am a flawed human being."

On consideration, I understood that Sheri had achieved her purpose: she did not want to discuss or pay attention to her psychodynamics, and I had accommodated her. Dreikurs (1967) taught us that therapists will encounter resistance whenever they fail to align their goals with the goals of the patient. My goal was to get Sheri off the subject of her inferiorities and onto the subject of her psycho-dynamics. Sheri's goal was to continue her neurotic strategy of deprecating herself, feeding her anger, and maintaining her posture as a "spoiled" person rather than making peace and beginning a more productive existence.

This particular manifestation of resistance to change continued throughout therapy with Sheri. She spent countless amounts of time in therapy telling me about everything she had done wrong and all the ways she could find fault with herself. The following exchange, from an interview in the twentieth month of therapy, il-lustrates her obsession with her inferiorities. She had just met a new man and was beginning to feel very attracted to him but had previous arrangements with a dif-ferent man for the weekend before our session. She is discussing the weekend:

Patient: But everything is going fine, Dorothy, and all of a sudden Sheri decides she feels uncomfortable, she feels weird around these people, she's not part of the group—she's flustered; she's unhappy; she's depressed; she's an egoist. Fuck.

Therapist: I've heard this before.

Patient: I know you have heard this. I just can't stand this anymore.

Therapist: You know you don't believe all this stuff.

Patient: I *do* when I can't talk myself out of it. I say, "What else is there left to do but to say it's true?" I don't know, Dorothy. I feel like such a nerd. Such a weak, helpless nerd.

Therapist: I don't understand what brought this on. First you're telling me how you began to feel slutty, trampy, et cetera, et cetera, and next you are putting yourself down. Are you telling me that you started to call yourself names because you have been with two men?

Patient: I don't know.

Therapist: I want to understand this. You started off by saying . . . my morals say I shouldn't be with two men at the same time. First you are having a good time, and then you tell yourself you are no good. Is there a connection?

Patient: No, I don't think so.

Therapist: But you start off by telling me, "I'm a slut, and on Sunday, I'm depressed, I'm no good, I don't belong with these people." There is a connec-tion. What is it? You don't start off your whole conversation with a story about what a puke you are and two sentences later come up with what you did Sunday without there being some connection.

Patient: We talked this through, Sonny [the new man] and I. And I said to him, "Look, I made these plans before I met you." And I told him I wasn't really comfortable about it but I was going to make the best of it. They were plans I just couldn't change at this point. I couldn't ruin the vaca-tion of three other people. I said I'm going to go and have a nice time. He wasn't pressing it, but at the same time I felt a little uncomfortable about it.

Therapist: I believe there is a connection.

Patient: OK.

Therapist: Why would you have done that on Sunday? Why did you wake up Sun-day morning and tell yourself, "I'm no good"? What was that about?

Patient: Yeah, let me think a minute. I think, Dorothy, when I was with John and Jane, I looked at them, and they have been seeing each other now for about two and a half years and they are very compatible and lovey-dovey. This is something I couldn't have with George; that is something I probably won't have with anybody, and that is what started working on me.

Therapist: What?

Patient: Just wondering how long does it take? I can't stand this.

Therapist: What's wrong with you? Repeat your list again. I missed some of it.

Patient: Dorothy, I just don't roll along with life. Everything is such a fucking, goddamn big deal for me. Everything.

Therapist: Why should you go along with life when you don't believe it is going to be nice to you? Now repeat your list for me. I'm sorry, I lost some of it. You're no good because—

Patient: I'm so fucking neurotic.

Therapist: You can be, but you and I may not agree about what is neurotic about you. Tell me what you think is neurotic.

Patient: I think I'm constantly obsessed about all the things that I'm not, and never will be, and what I can't do, and who has this and I don't, and I'll never be that, and I'll always be this. I'm such a fuckin' jealous cunt.

Therapist: Jealous? Where does jealous come from?

Patient: I'm sitting with three other people, we are all on vacation, and I get so insecure about the attention that other people are getting around me, you know, it's terrible.

Therapist: It is neurotic if you want to be the center of attention all the time.

Patient: Yes.

Therapist: Well, all right, but it isn't that you want to be the center of attention. It's that you want to be the center of attention *all the time*. What's the smile? [*Apparently Sheri had a "recognition reflex"; that is, she had an unconscious, uncontrollable grin on her face. Adlerians consider the recognition reflex a sign of sudden, not quite conscious awareness that an interpretation is correct (Dreikurs, 1967).*]

Patient: I don't know.

Therapist: Dr. Dreikurs used to put it this way: "It's a basic mistake if you add the words *only if*." So that it comes out "*Only if* I'm the center of attention do I feel good." If I tell you I like to be the center of attention, that's fine. So what? But I'm *only happy if* I'm the center, that's a neurotic shtick.

(A long discussion follows during which Sheri tells the therapist she has allowed herself to be intimidated by a store clerk.)

Patient: Dorothy, do you understand? The problem here is that I keep all this crap always inside of me and it never comes out and it brews and brews and brews, and I'm upset because I never spit things out.

Therapist: Sheri, if I thought that that was the reason why you weren't feeling good, I would discuss this with you, but I don't believe it. Because some days you spit those things out.

Patient: What is it, then? What am I doing this for? What am I going nuts about?

Therapist: I think things are going too well and you really like this Sonny and you want to make sure you are neurotic so nothing happens. You're so afraid to make a relationship that might turn into something that you have to make sure you have diarrhea all over it first. You could make a relationship, couldn't you? Something good could come out of it, couldn't it?

Patient: Yeah.

Therapist: So, what are you going to do to fuck it up?

Patient: I'm going to go through my mental trampolines.

Therapist: All your gyrations so that it ends up so that—what? . . . What are you afraid of? What's going to happen? Is he going to hurt you?

Patient: I think he is going to stop loving me.

Therapist: Why? Who stopped loving you? [*Referring to childhood*] Daddy never stopped loving you.

Patient: Yes, he did.

Therapist: When? Two years ago? . . . Talk to me about "when" in your early years. You might have been afraid you were going to lose daddy's love, but he certainly paid you a lot of attention. Now, I always have to be careful when I say things like this, because I don't want you to misinterpret that I think he was right in any way. But you did get a lot of attention. He did show you he cared about you.

Patient: Yeah.

Therapist: So you are not going to convince me that daddy took his love away. A couple of years ago when you had a scene, then he took his love away. But you know you provoked that. Or did he just reinforce what you always thought, "He really doesn't love me anyway?" How about "I'm not good enough to be loved"? I don't want to hear a list of your made-up stories, about your eyes and your hair. I have a song for you, "The Girl with the Picasso Eyes." [Laughter]

Patient: Dorothy, you're funny. Yeah, that is what it is, I'm not good enough. And eventually he is going to find out and he is not going to love me.

Therapist: You have no power to induce him to love you more. You have no power to keep him. If he finds out what you really are, he won't want you. What about telling him you are neurotic?

Patient: Well, I did mention to him something like "Don't let me fuck this up, it's really nice." He said to me, "You better not."

Therapist: Tell him when you start to fuck it up, when you begin to have inferiority feelings. He'll understand.

Patient: He's such a positive person. What the hell would he want with me?

Therapist: I'm not going to give you a list of your attributes; they're there. Can you give me one reason, one good reason that I'll accept, why he would not want you? A reason I'll accept.

Patient: Because I am making myself crazy.

The Letter. During this period there had been notable changes in Sheri's outward behavior. She reported that she felt much less depressed. She was more active socially and enjoying it more. She finished the library science course and was actively looking for new employment. Furthermore, she had started a new relationship with her father.

In the fourteenth month of therapy, Sheri made a comment about sending a letter to father to "milk him for money." I neither encouraged nor discouraged the idea, but I began to think about Sheri's "revenge." I always stressed that although father was never to be forgiven, she must not continue to devote her life to her obsession about the incest. I suggested she try to make father *want* her to forgive him. This would allow her to feel in a superior position in relation to her father. From this position, I hoped, she could begin to gain a sense of self-respect, self-esteem, and restitution.

I tentatively suggested to Sheri that she write to father in a completely conciliatory tone, accepting responsibility for the childhood sexual experiences, in order to reduce father's indignation. Sheri was very interested, and over the course of a few weeks we composed a letter. We chuckled when we wrote it and tried to outdo each other with what we considered outrageous sentiments. I never pressed Sheri to compose it and, after it was written, never urged her to send it. It read as follows:

Dear Dad,
   I've been in therapy a while now and I've had all this time to explore my childhood. I've sorted things out about our relationship when I was a child. One of the things that I realize is that I must assume some of the responsibility for what happened between us.
   I understand what I did as a child. I idolized you as the most wonderful daddy a little girl could have. To me you were the epitome of what a man should be—very masculine, strong, forceful, handsome, yet sensitive. To this day it's what I look for in a man, and today I understand that these are standards I'll never find in another man.
   I miss my daddy as part of my life. Not having you in my life has left me very empty.
   I don't know if it will ever be possible to be as close as we once were. But perhaps there is some way for you to be some part of my life again. I'm lonely without my daddy. I've been hurting for years because you haven't been with me and you don't seem to love me as you did when I was a child. It hurt me not getting letters for all these years. I want my daddy.
                                                  Your loving daughter,
                                                  Sheri

Then Sheri seemed to become uninterested in the letter. A few months later, when I asked about it, she didn't want to discuss it, and so I dropped the subject. Some eight months after we composed the letter, Sheri unexpectedly asked me for it. Father's Day was coming, and she wanted to copy the letter and send it. I gave her the letter and did not discuss it with her. Just after Father's Day, almost two years into therapy, Sheri announced she had sent the letter to father and had heard nothing from him.

Summer came around again, and Sheri was seeing Sonny regularly. She was so taken with him and he with her that they were discussing the possibility of marriage. "Could I feel this way after only two months?," she asked. "Definitely, yes," I told her. It was always my intention to encourage her to behave in "normal" ways, and what could be more "normal" than considering marriage? I was frankly concerned that she might interpose her ''neurotic shtick'' into the relationship and cautioned her. She agreed to watch herself closely.

Father called in July. He had been out of town and had come home the day before. He told her he was ''thrilled'' with the letter from her, and he blamed the previous therapist for the ''division'' between them. They talked for a long time. Sheri told me she had been very careful not to place blame on him. She felt she had handled herself well and was quite pleased with herself.

She quoted father as saying, ''I want you to have a gigantic wedding, and I'll pay for it, and I won't even have to be there.'' We both understood this to mean that father believed that once she married, he could believe that he had not inflicted any permanent injury on her, that she had been ''cured''—and he would be relieved of guilt. He wanted to see her, and they made arrangements for her to visit him (at his expense) for a weekend. She did not want to be with him too long, since she feared she would be unable to keep up the ''pretense.'' Sheri seemed happy with the results the letter had brought.

The Visit. We spent one session discussing how Sheri would behave while visiting, even though she did not seem apprehensive. I suggested that she stick close to father's wife, whom Sheri described as ''nice.'' I thought perhaps a small ''sisterhood'' could be established to help Sheri through the weekend. It did not work at all.

Father was late picking her up at the airport. When he finally did get there, they fell into each other's arms. They were able to get on very well indeed, but stepmother was cold and aloof, and all Sheri's attempts to be pleasant and friendly were met with almost open hostility. On the second day of the visit, Sheri learned why.

Father had told the immediate family about Sheri's ''charges.'' He claimed total innocence but confessed to Sheri that once, maybe twice, when she was about thirteen years old, he had ''fondled'' her, claiming that he had been having much trouble with his wife at the time. Several years earlier, when she had confronted him about the incest, he had said, ''I thought you had forgotten''; then he told Sheri that she had been ''sexy, sensuous'' and had ''teased him.'' He had said he ''couldn't help himself'' and denied responsibility.

Apparently, in the two years since he had last talked to Sheri, father had been able to use denial successfully. Surprisingly, Sheri did not take issue with him and did not discuss the incest. Father had called a few times since she returned home, and she was pleased with their telephone conversations. Sheri reported she had her feelings under control and felt able to cope with whatever would happen in the relationship with father.

I was content. Sheri seemed to be very pleased about the new relationship with father. She had managed to give herself the feeling that she was in charge, that she was the one in control of the relationship. This made her feel good about herself. For the first time in thirty-three years, Sheri was the one in the ''power seat.''

I thought that now Sheri could lay aside the use of the incest experience as an excuse for not getting on with her life. How naive I was!

The ''Repetition Compulsion'': Two Years

Two years after Sheri first came to me, we met with Dr. Shulman for a review session. Sheri described many changes in herself to Dr. Shulman: fewer symptoms, quicker insight, and more conscious control over her own thoughts. She talked about her current situation and feelings, showing a mixture of doubt and satisfaction as well as greater self-acceptance. However, she did not neglect to tell us about her continued feelings of inferiority. We spent considerable time discussing the possible purposes of the continuation of these feelings and concluded that her continued feelings of inferiority were a form of "insurance" against disappointment. Sheri, as usual (and especially when a male did the talking), accepted the interpretation but did not discuss it at any length.

The following week she walked in crying. It seemed she had been at dinner at Sonny's parents' home and believed she had not acquitted herself well. I felt frustrated—exasperated! After she presented a recitation of "what I did wrong at my boyfriend's house," the following exchange took place:

Therapist: Do you think those people are so critical?
Patient: I think everybody is very critical. Everybody is looking at me, and they can find some flaw when they look at me, [Pause] my eyes are two sizes, I'm bloated and fat, [Pause] it doesn't matter . . . there's something wrong with me . . . everybody can see that I'm flawed. [*I regretted I had ever used that word with her.*]
Therapist: I want to make an interpretation to you, but it is very unpleasant and I don't think you can take it.
Patient: Yes, I can. Go ahead.
Therapist: You seem to think everybody is looking at you and thinking about you and talking about you. It's as if other people have nothing to do but sit around and talk and think about you! . . . We've talked about how much you like attention, but how much do you want? Need?
Patient: [Laughs and looks sheepish] I like myself best when I'm at ease and comfortable and don't care what anybody thinks of me—but I can't be like that.

I took exception to Sheri's use of the word *can't*. I tried to help her see that the appropriate word was *won't*, and until she was ready to say "I won't" instead of "I can't," she was not accepting the responsibility for her own behavior. At this point I used my strongest maneuver: I declared bankruptcy. I told Sheri that I had tried everything I knew to help her, that although she had made some progress and was doing very well, apparently she didn't share my opinion. I told her I did not know how to help her get rid of her bad feelings, that since she was still claiming inferiority about whatever happened to her, she must still have good reason for continuing her behavior; but that I had exhausted all possibilities and could not think of anything else to do that might be of help to her.

I said I would continue to see her, but I was not so sure I could be of any help until she was willing to accept the responsibility for her own feelings and truly understood that she manufactured her oppressive thinking and could (and had many times in the past) stop herself as well as start herself.

Sheri seemed to be struck dumb (possibly for the first time since she had come in) and paid close attention. I went back to the original discussion of how she believed people responded to her in social situations.

Therapist: You know, Sheri, you're asking for special consideration. When you meet somebody new, why don't you hand them a card that says, "Treat me with special consideration"? Why do you think you do that, Sheri?

Patient: Because I had such a weird childhood?

Therapist: What should people do to make you feel better? How should people behave in order for you to feel that you're all right? Maybe Sonny's mother should say to you, "Welcome to my house, Sheri. You're the most gorgeous, charming woman any of my sons has ever brought to this house. I'm so happy to have you here."

Sheri laughed at the absurdity. She said she felt naked without the incest excuse. The session ended with the following exchange:

Therapist: So the way I see it, you make some very specific demands on people when you meet them. One is "I want special consideration because of what happened to me when I was eight years old." And the second statement you make to the world, and especially to me, is "I won't change unless my mother and father are different when I was eight years old."

Patient: I need an excuse for my behavior.

In the next session Sheri spontaneously brought in some new early memories that showed a further change.

> Age 7. In the classroom. Teacher was talking about some seeds the class has planted in paper cups. I felt nervous about it because I hadn't been there when they were planted. I started to poke the boy in front of me. He turned around and we started laughing. Teacher got upset and yelled at us. I felt foolish. Everybody knew I was doing something I wasn't supposed to.
>
> Age 7. The painter came to our house. I was in love with him. I hung around him and I talked to him and he was nice to me. I started to think he really liked me. Then he finished and left and said "Goodbye, it was nice knowing you." I cried when he left. It was as if he had done something to me personally.
>
> Age 7. Father, mother, and I were in the den. "The Stripper" (a record) was playing on the record player. I was parading around and dancing, pretending to strip. Father was laughing and mother was chuckling. I liked the attention. I knew he got a kick out of it.

The newly evoked memories certainly show that Sheri had heard my interpretation in the previous session. In each of these memories Sheri is making herself the center of attention and taking the responsibility for it. Each memory seems to offer a different facet of attention-getting behavior—by pleasing, by misbehaving, and, in the painter memory, by direct engagement. In that memory she also represents herself as the seductive one, who is disappointed when the other person is not as charmed with her as she had hoped. She does not claim to be abused or mistreated in any memory, but she does express guilt (the classroom memory). It would be tempting to explain her feeling of being "flawed" as a form of guilt for her sexual wishes. However, an equally powerful explanation would be to see it as a fantasy that she is constantly the center, that all eyes are on her, that everyone knows what she has been up to. Whether or not she feels "flawed" now can be seen as being influenced by the context. In a situation in which she gains the center by pleasing, she feels successful. *Where she is an outsider and unsure of her place*, she believes she will act inappropriately and draw attention to herself (the classroom memory). Thus, when she is invited to dinner with Sonny's family, unsure of their reaction to her, she expects that she will reveal some defect. In a social situation she expects others to either applaud or find fault.

Summary

The case we have described is that of a thirty-three-year-old single woman who suffered from symptoms of a dysthymic disorder. The main explanation she gave for her distress was an incestuous relationship with her father, which had left her "flawed." During the two and a half years of treatment she was able to put the constant obsession with the incest behind her, train herself for a new job, discover that she had more control over her thoughts and moods than she realized, reduce her self-sabotaging behavior, and come out of her depression.

She spent the first year in therapy complaining about both herself and others and bemoaning her fate. The early interpretations of the therapist seemed to have little effect. Eventually she began to seriously examine her own behavior. After two years of therapy, she sent a letter to her father and reestablished a relationship with him. About that time she discovered that she could *choose* to be less depressed. In the seventy-fifth session she remarked, "I decided I would feel better because my friend is coming to town to visit me." Shortly thereafter, she went through a period of resistance when the therapist was interpreting to her that she used the thought of being abused as a child to demand special consideration from others.

The latter half of therapy centered on her self-image as a "flawed" person. This period culminated in the eventual recognition that her intense desire for attention from others led her to use both pleasing and provocative behavior as ways of keeping others busy with her and that her actual complaint against her father was that he had withdrawn his love and attention.

At this time, she had met a new man and allowed herself to start falling in love with him. She still felt "flawed" and expected that her behavior would eventually destroy the relationship.

The therapist's behavior is noteworthy. After a number of sessions spent in listening to ventilation and complaint, the therapist became increasingly active. She gave the patient considerable attention and showed much caring. With the use of humor, irony, and conspiratorial assistance in writing the letter, the therapist succeeded in stopping the incessant complaints.

This particular therapeutic style is active, directive, confronting, and intrusive. The therapist offers clarification, interpretation, guidance, and support. The relationship with the patient must have been strongly positive, because the patient shows little hostility about the therapist's endeavors.

The therapist first allied herself firmly with Sheri. Then, acting as an ally, she began to interpret the unconscious plans and convictions that lay behind the behavior. She recognized resistance when it occurred, avoided stirring it up further, overcame it when she could, and consistently led Sheri to examine her own behavior and choose alternatives.

Transference phenomena did not become a problem in the therapy. The therapist's active supportive stance made it unnecessary for Sheri to make demands on her. On one occasion the resistance took the form of accusing the therapist of abusing her, but this was easily handled by the therapist's continued warm support.

Although the therapist's style was highly individual, the conduct and content of the therapy fit quite well into the Adlerian theory of therapy. The goals of therapy (Mosak and Shulman, 1974) include helping the patient develop "social interest"—a feeling of caring and belonging and active participation in constructive human endeavor. Another goal is to decrease inferiority feelings and overcome discouragement and pessimism. Implicit in both these goals is the goal of changing errors in perception and mistaken unconscious goals into more accurate perceptions and more appropriate goals. A more positive self-image, a more optimistic view of life and its possibilities, a more courageous attitude, and active prosocial behavior are considered desirable results.

The process of encouragement requires not a neutral but a friendly stance in the therapist. The therapist acts as if the patient could find better meanings to give to life. The symptomatic behavior is treated as a mistaken effort to adapt to the requirements of living. Such mistakes are treated as correctable.

Mistaken perceptions are sympathetically but thoroughly brought into the open for examination. Their sources are identified in the early childhood situation, and current troublesome behaviors are interpreted both as a relic of past learning and as having a current safeguarding value. These behaviors defend against loss of self-esteem and help avoid anticipated failures. Neurotic symptoms are considered misguided adaptive arrangements used by discouraged people.

Most important to the Adlerian therapist is to watch the patient's *movement*. The direction of movement reveals the goal—to avoid a feared task, to excuse oneself from an onerous task, to keep distance from what is not desired, and to approach what is desired. Thus Sheri used depressive and anxiety-provoking cognitions to nurse her wounds instead of going onward with her life. She created the self-image of a flawed/abused person who was bad and to whom bad things had been done, which allowed her to play the role of a tragic victim whose childhood experiences were blamed for her current inappropriate behavior.

In this mood she had no strong motive to get on with her life. She was not loving; she was demanding and vindictive. She would not give up her suffering; it was her justification for demanding.

Epilogue

At this writing, Sheri is still coming to therapy. She has read this paper and wants to see it published. (She still likes attention.) There is no depression. She has a friendly relationship with father and looks forward to his future generosity. Although she has not forgiven him, she no longer spends her time feeling abused. She half-believes that she is not "flawed." She and Sonny will be married next month, and her trepidation is no more than that of any other bride-to-be.

7

Jungian Analysis

Mary Ann Mattoon

Jungian analysis is a process in which analysand and analyst work together for the psychological development and, ultimately, the wholeness of the analysand (see Jung, 1966, 1969a, 1974; Singer, 1972; Fordham, 1978; Stein, 1982; Mattoon, 1984). Much of the work is similar to that of other schools of psychotherapy, with an attempt to gear all of it to the particular needs of each analysand. Because of its breadth of approach, Jungian therapy can be effective for persons with a wide variety of needs and pathologies.

All stages of the work are concerned with conscious mental contents (emotions, thoughts, behaviors, dreams, fantasies), as well as with some that are unconscious—that is, unknown by and beyond the control of the conscious personality. Analysis often means a process of separating, examining, and interpreting the component parts of the psyche, reducing the unconscious contents to their elements. To Jungians, however, the work is barely begun when this reductive process has been completed. The more important process is that of synthesis, the constructive phase of the psychological (analytic) work. In this phase formerly repressed contents must be recognized and acknowledged for their value—that is, integrated with conscious contents.

Jungians vary in their usage of the terms *analysis* and *psychotherapy*. Some consider analysis to be more intensive, longer-term, and more focused on dreams. I do not make a sharp distinction but often use the term *analytic psychotherapy* (or *analytic therapy*) to indicate that the work is a form of psychotherapy for which the analysand and I have available the entire analytic armamentarium.

The goal of Jungian analytic therapy is *individuation*. Individuation, for Jungians, is a process, not a state. It means coming to recognize one's uniqueness by integration of conscious and unconscious parts of the personality. (Jung specifically eschewed perfection as a goal because it implies the rejection of psychic contents that may be considered unacceptable.) Thus, as the word *individuation* implies, the goal is undividedness, or wholeness.

The hallmark of Jungian analysis is individuality (which is consonant but not synonymous with individuation). Each analyst has an individual style, which is adapted to the needs of each analysand. There are commonalities, of course, but no two analytic processes deal with the same set of problems or move at the same pace, in the same direction, or toward the same outcome. In addition, analysts differ among themselves in training and experience. Each has undergone a thorough personal analysis, which is central to the training process, and is changed further as the analyst accompanies each analysand in the search for wholeness.

The groundwork for analytic psychotherapy was laid by C. G. Jung (1875–1961). Many of his students and their students have contributed to the theories he outlined. The result is a fairly comprehensive, but by no means monolithic, theory of personality and psychotherapeutic practice.

It is often said that Jung was a "pupil" of Freud. Indeed, Jung occasionally described himself as such, evidently to indicate his willingness to learn from the older man and to acknowledge their shared confidence in the reality of the unconscious mind (often called "the unconscious"). Nevertheless, Jung originated and developed psychological theories independently of Freud before, after, and to a large extent during their association. Consequently, much of Jung's early as well as late work bears no Freudian imprint.

The discussions and illustrations of Jungian analysis presented here are necessarily limited. For example, I occasionally conduct therapy in groups or with couples, but the examples I present here come only from my work with individuals. My style of work draws heavily on the theory generated by Jung and those Jungians who have expanded and modified his work. I have found much less helpful the writings of Jungians who have borrowed heavily from such other schools of psychology as those identified with Melanie Klein, Robert Langs, and D. W. Winnicott.

Summary of Jungian Personality Theory

Many people who believe they know nothing of Jung's theories still recognize the terms *introversion, extroversion,* and *complex,* all of which designate concepts that Jung originated. Other familiar terms took on specific meanings in Jung's works: *persona, shadow, self, archetype,* and *collective unconscious.* All these concepts are part of the theoretical basis for Jungian analysis.

Jungian personality theory (see Jung, 1964b, 1970; Jacobi, 1973; Whitmont, 1978; Mattoon, 1981) focuses on the description of normal personality in its various forms. Problems are seen as both normal and necessary for movement toward individuation. Theoretical concepts and terms are rarely mentioned in analytic sessions, but they increase the analyst's awareness and understanding of the range of individual personalities, traits, and points of view that may come into the consulting room.

The individualized approach in Jungian analysis is possible and necessary because the psyche is *self-regulating*; that is, the conscious mind's contents are compensated by the resources of the unconscious. A one-sided conscious attitude elicits a balancing response in the unconscious. The result is a reduction of pathology and movement toward healing and wholeness.

A necessary condition for the working of self-regulation is *psychic energy.* Jung held that, just as living beings have renewable quanta of physical energy, so they have renewable quanta of psychic energy. Psychic energy manifests itself in motivation, attention, interest, and assignments of value.

A corollary of self-regulation is the view that neurosis is purposive. Whether neurosis is defined as unconscious conflict, as maladaptive behavior, or in other terms, it conceals the true source of the person's suffering by drawing attention to physical symptoms, undesirable behavior, or the nonspecific emotions of depression and anxiety. The resulting discomfort, however, can motivate self-reflection and open the person to psychological growth.

Fundamental to Jungian personality theory and psychotherapy is the fact that we humans are fully conscious of only a small portion of our mental contents. We can recall some contents erratically, but other contents seem to be permanently forgotten or to have never been available to consciousness. In the Jungian construction, the unconscious mind includes both personal and "collective" components. The *personal unconscious* consists of contents that are generated by one's personal experience. Some are subliminal and available to consciousness when attention is turned to them. Others are unacceptable and may be *repressed*—that is, pushed out of consciousness into the unconscious.

Jung hypothesized also a *collective unconscious,* which is composed of *archetypes.* These are ways (tendencies) of perceiving the world that are common to all humans. Archetypes are not memories, either of individuals or of cultures. Rather, they are predispositions to images and perceptions. They are constituents of the psyche's structure, just as the limbs and organs are constituents of the body's structure. Archetypes include needs that are generally accepted as basic, such as sex and bonding to parent figures. They also include needs, such as power and religion, that Jung—unlike many theorists—considered innate, or "instinctual."

The psyche is made up of several components, some conscious and some unconscious. Only the *ego* (what I mean when I say "I") is largely or entirely conscious; it is "the center of consciousness." The *shadow* is largely unconscious; it consists of psychic contents that a person prefers not to reveal or even acknowledge. To the ego, the shadow is unacceptable or even evil. Nevertheless, a content that is unacceptable to the ego and is therefore repressed can carry positive and even creative potentialities.

The *persona* (from the Latin word for mask) is the part of the personality that one shows to the world. It complements the shadow. Although it appears to be part of consciousness, it is not under ego control and is difficult to alter. It may take various forms corresponding to different roles.

Superordinate to all the components of the psyche is the *Self.* (The word is often capitalized by Jungians because of its central importance and to distinguish it from its different meanings in other psychologies.) Jung described the Self variously. When it is seen as the total personality, its relation to the ego is that of the whole to the part; when it is seen as the center of the personality, it is the "sun" around which the "earth" (ego) revolves. The Self's centrality and power may be best understood, however, when it is described as the integrating force of the psyche.

The best-known and most widely accepted Jungian theory is probably that of *attitude types:* extroversion and introversion. This theory contributes to an understanding of the different ways individuals perceive the world. These differences affect an analysand's relation with his or her analyst as well as other persons. Extroversion and introversion are equally healthy and important, but for each person one tends to be more accessible to conscious use than the other.

The extroverted attitude is characterized by a flow of psychic energy toward the outer world: an interest in people, things, and events. Thus, the energy flow (interest, attention, value) is toward the object. The introverted attitude is characterized by a flow of psychic energy inward: concentration on subjective factors and inner responses. Both attitudes are valuable. However, when two persons who are of "opposite" types seek to work together analytically or share their personal lives, the potential for misunderstandings and difficulties is high.

After Jung developed the theory of attitude types, he found that it still did not describe the varieties of individuals' relations to the inner and outer worlds. He expanded the types theory by hypothesizing that each attitude could be expressed through one or more of four *functions:* sensation, intuition, thinking, and feeling. *Sensation* (sensing) ascertains that something exists. *Thinking* categorizes and assigns meanings. *Intuition* suggests what the possibilities are. *Feeling* is not emotion but, rather, evaluation: determining whether an object or experience is desirable or undesirable and its degree of importance. Most people have one or two functions that are quite well developed and two that are relatively undeveloped.

Jung was an introvert, with intuition and thinking as his first two functions. His personality and psychological theory have tended to attract persons as analysts and analysands who are introverted and intuitive because his theory is congenial to them; moreover, some of their problems are due to their impression that Western culture has not valued them. Regardless of their own type, however, analysts find that the theory of function types helps them to appreciate the importance of the less-developed functions in themselves and their analysands.

The concept of *complexes* was so central to Jung's ideas that, initially, he labeled his body of theories "complex psychology." This label failed to be accepted, but the term *complex* came into common usage and was given varying definitions. For Jungians, a complex is an interrelated cluster of unconscious contents and, thus, is part of the shadow. It is emotionally toned and incompatible with one's conscious attitude. Jung considered the complex to be "the royal road to the unconscious" and dreams to be comments on complexes. Complexes are autonomous; they are like "splinter psyches" appearing in waking behavior as thoughts and actions that are foreign to the ego, such as disturbed memory, slips of the tongue, and accidents. They arise out of individual experience, but their force is augmented by their collective quality. For example, difficulties between an infant and his or her mother (a "negative mother complex") are intensified by expectations of mother that are based on an archetypal image.

Complexes and other unconscious contents are likely to become apparent when they are *projected* onto other persons or situations—that is, when one sees another person as thinking or acting as one does or might do, or when one expects that person to play a particular role (for example, mother) in one's life. Each instance of projection occurs involuntarily and convincingly, seeming to reveal truth about its object, the person onto whom the projection is made. Projections are omnipresent; they occur between analyst and analysand, as well as with other persons in the analysand's life. Although projections can lead to problems, they are also useful because of their contributions to initiating and shaping relationships.

One of the most controversial current issues in psychology is the degree to which the observed psychological differences between males and females are innate. Jung held, in accordance with the culture of his day, that women are innately more "feminine," men innately more "masculine." He hypothesized that each has an unconscious "contrasexual" psychic component, which he named the *animus* and *anima,* respectively.

Although there is no longer consensus on the definitions of masculinity and femininity, there is increased valuing of such traditionally "feminine" capacities as nurturance, relatedness, and receptivity, which are needed to complement the traditionally "masculine" capacities such as initiative, structure, and assertiveness.

A great deal is being written and said about the desirability of each person's having some of each—being "androgynous."

Many people find useful the concept of feminine and masculine principles. It may be that the feminine principle is more congenial to women, the masculine to men, with animus and anima largely unconscious. But there seems to be widespread agreement that each individual must find his or her own appropriate proportions of masculine and feminine qualities. Such a view is self-evident in a therapy that encourages the development of individuality.

Historically, Jungian theorists have tended to emphasize the negative expressions of the animus: a woman's opinionatedness, aggressiveness, and self-deprecation. This view has been helpful in understanding unconscious contents but sometimes makes for a distorted view of the animus and of women. Currently, there is increasing emphasis on the positive animus: assertiveness, initiative, and ability to provide structure. It has become apparent also that women's "masculine" qualities need not be entirely repressed.

A woman's "animus problem" has its counterpart in a man's "anima problem." The latter is often interpreted to mean that a man has not found his way to become free of his mother's influence. One of the more severe manifestations of this problem is the "puer aeternus" (eternal boy). Such a man holds back from taking on full adult responsibilities—family and work—apparently because he cannot bear to love a woman other than his mother and is "holding out" for someone to take care of him.

Most significant in the animus/anima theory, for me, is the Jungian view that both feminine and masculine qualities and values are essential to wholeness. These values are important beyond the individual psyche; they include concerns with ecology, peace, and other social and political issues.

Jung's theory of psychological development focuses on adulthood, especially on the "second half of life" (beginning at age thirty-five or forty). He pioneered in identifying the developmental tasks of that period when family and career have been established as well as they are likely to be. Often a person begins to dwell on the question of life's meaning and to accept mortality as a fact. Psychic energy turns toward concerns that have been neglected earlier in life. Although these concerns may vary with psychological type, many people experience an increase in introversion.

Since the rise in the 1960s of the counterculture and the women's movement, there has been a general recognition that spiritual matters are not the concern only of theists. This recognition was anticipated by Jung. He held that humans have a religious "instinct"; that is, he regarded religion as so essential to human life and mental health that neglect of this need is the primary cause of neurosis in the second half of life. Thus, in Jungian analysis, the search for life's meaning and for transcendent experience is of paramount importance.

Therapy

In my consulting room are an armchair for me and a recliner for the analysand. The use of two chairs (rather than a chair and a couch) reflects the Jungian attitude that analytic therapy is a cooperative process, a dialogue between two persons. The analyst is a companion on the way, not an "opaque screen" or a surgeon who dissects a passive patient. By providing a recliner, however, I recognize that an analysand may wish to close his eyes or look at the ceiling rather than at me, or simply put his feet up.

When I make the first appointment with a prospective analysand, I suggest that the initial meeting be an exploration of whether we can work together. My sessions are usually fifty-five minutes long, but I allow an extra ten to fifteen minutes in the first session, if necessary, in order to come to some closure on whether we should continue to meet and, if so, when and at what fee.

I start by asking the person what brings him to see me. His reply leads to a collaborative assessment of his psychological state. This assessment consists in identifying the problem areas and his aspirations for psychological development. I watch for indications of extreme pathology, but I prefer not to think of a person in diagnostic categories. To think so, I find, distances me from him and interferes with therapy, that is, healing. Often the assessment process includes discussion of a dream, preferably one that occurred after the appointment was made. Such an "initial" dream may indicate the response of the unconscious to the prospect of the analytic therapy. The decision to undertake therapy is made collaboratively and is based on the assessment that we have made and the subjective "chemistry" between us.

I usually see an analysand twice a week for the first few weeks, then once or twice a week as he and I perceive the need. Only when the analytic process is "tapering off" or when the analysand must travel a long distance for each session do I consider less-than-weekly sessions. Conversely, we do not meet more than twice a week except in cases of extreme distress, acute or chronic. Usually, the course of analytic therapy takes from one to three years.

In the first session (if I have not done so during the initial contact), I state my regular fee—the amount that I charge if the analysand has insurance coverage or can afford the fee out of pocket. If neither is the case, we negotiate down to a predetermined amount (about two thirds of the regular fee).

After we decide to proceed, I ask the analysand to write a "psychological autobiography" of two or three pages—concrete information about his life and the major persons and events that have shaped his psychological development. This information, to which I can refer frequently, enhances my acquaintance with him and expedites the amplification of dreams. I ask also for copies of all dreams that he wants to discuss with me.

What Happens in Analysis

Even though each person's analytic work is different, there are identifiable experiences some of which occur in each analysis. In the case material that follows, I describe and illustrate each experience in terms of my own practice, which resembles, to varying degrees, those of other Jungian analysts.

The framework in which all of therapy occurs is transference/countertransference. Some theorists have generalized these terms to mean all interactions between analyst and analysand, on the ground that even the most trivial or peripheral transactions are reflections of the relationship, positively and negatively. I consider the transference to be the projections of the analysand on the analyst (all projections, not just those that arise out of feelings toward the analysand's parents). The analysand gains increased consciousness about the transference through a cooperative process (with the analyst) of examination and reflection. The countertransference is comparable, except that the analyst's reflection on it is done alone or with the help of a colleague.

A strong positive transference is likely to produce a degree of emotional dependency of the analysand on the analyst. Jungian analysts, like other depth psychologists, are accused sometimes of "fostering" such dependency. It is more accurate to say that the analyst serves as a psychological "lifeline" while fundamental shifts are occurring in the analysand's psychic structure. Dependency is inappropriate only when it is prolonged by an analyst's need for psychological dependents.

Every adult who is not psychotic has a functioning ego. The ego may be weak, however. A weak ego is experienced in feelings of inadequacy (low self-esteem), which often underlie the specific problems that bring a person into therapy. Thus, an aspect of virtually every analysand's process is strengthening the ego—that is, attaining a clearer sense of her identity and values and more confidence in her ability to meet life's challenges. She needs a stronger ego to cope with the everyday environment and to confront the unconscious.

When her ego is sufficiently strong, the analysand can acknowledge that she is not perfect, yet avoid identifying with her inadequacies. At this stage, recognition and assimilation of the shadow can begin. Necessarily, changes occur in the content and balance of the unconscious. The task is lifelong; only a portion of it can be accomplished during the formal analytic process.

Much of the shadow is manifest in a person's complexes. Some complexes arise out of the less developed functions and the feelings of inadequacy and even evil that accompany them. Whatever the content of the complexes, much of analytic therapy focuses on bringing them into the analysand's awareness so that she can experience them consciously. Awareness of complexes often results from the analysand's discovery of her projections onto the analyst and other people, objects, situations, and events, current and anticipated. Conscious experience occurs when the analysand focuses on the choices she is making or could make, rather than on feelings of depression, anxiety, and inadequacy.

As the analysis proceeds, more and more previously unconscious contents are integrated into consciousness—that is, made available to the ego. Many such contents are unflattering to the ego, including those that are archetypal and, hence, reflect the fact that the ego is not the center of the universe. The result may be acknowledgment of the Self and, consequently, enhancement of the individuation process.

Termination of analytic sessions (but not of inner analytic work) occurs only when the analysand feels that the time is right. The most important objectives have been achieved or she has gone as far as seems possible and appropriate at the time; in no instance are all problems resolved. Occasionally, the limits of the relationship with the current analyst seem to have been reached, and the analysand seeks another analyst. (Sometimes, of course, change of residence necessitates termination.) The initiative for termination comes from the analysand; the decision is made after a careful cooperative appraisal of the factors that must be considered.

Procedures Used in Analytic Therapy

Much of each analytic session is spent in discussing the analysand's here-and-now problems. The analysand recounts experiences, some that occur in the sessions and some outside, and the emotions aroused thereby. Together with me, he attempts to understand the complexes that have been stirred by the experiences and the development toward which the situation is pushing him.

When the limits of conscious reflection have been reached, the analysand may recall spontaneously a dream that occurred within a day or two after the waking experience under discussion. Alternatively, I may ask about dreams. Discussion of a dream is not an attempt to reduce the experience to a shadow motive but, rather, an open search for the unconscious psyche's comment on an aspect of the dreamer's life. The comment often challenges the conscious attitude, but sometimes it confirms that attitude.

Dream analysis is of great importance in my work with most analysands. Work on a dream begins with a careful recounting of the images and establishing the dream context: the dreamer's associations to the images, parallels from mythology and other archetypal sources, consideration of the dreamer's conscious situation (which may be the same as the experiences already recounted), and recollection of other dreams that may be part of the same series. The analysand and I consider whether the dream should be regarded primarily objectively (a commentary on outer events and relationships) or subjectively (all images parts of the dreamer's psyche). We try to translate the dream language in order to receive the unconscious psyche's message on the dreamer's conscious attitude or waking behavior. If I introduce an interpretation, it is often in the form of a question, such as "Do you suppose the dream could be telling you such-and-such?"

A procedure that bears many similarities to work with dreams is that of Active Imagination. It can take many forms, including imagining the continuation of a dream or a conversation with a dream image. Other methods of active imagination are painting, sculpting, dance, writing stories or poems, and the increasingly widely used "sandplay" (using miniature objects and figures to make a picture in a sand table). Each such method enhances the therapeutic process during work with an analyst or continues it when formal analytic sessions have been discontinued.

The interactions and procedures discussed in this section are exemplified in the following case materials. The facts are disguised to prevent identification, and the cases are from work that is long past, but they illustrate the range of treatment offered in Jungian analytic therapy.

Jane

Jane was thirty-six when she sought me out. She had been having headaches. When a thorough medical examination revealed no organic basis, her physician advised her to undertake psychotherapy. Her minister, who was schooled in Jungian psychology, recommended me. She was aware that she had emotional problems, and she was interested in understanding her dreams. They were vivid and sometimes frightening: images such as a tornado about to strike, a hooded figure approaching her brandishing a knife. As our work proceeded, Jane reported some disturbing experiences of invasions from the unconscious when she was awake. For example, on more than one occasion when driving alone, she felt there were other people in the car with her. Pathological though some of her symptoms may have been, the foregoing description seems more helpful than a medical-model label for understanding the problems she brought to therapy.

Jane's current family included her husband, George, an attorney, and four children: girls of twelve, eight, and four, and a boy of ten. Her mother, with whom she had frequent and mostly unpleasant interactions, was sixty-eight and lived in the same city. Jane blamed herself for the difficulties between them. Her father, an alcoholic, had died at age fifty-seven of liver disease. She had an older brother who also lived in the area but with whom she had virtually no contact. Jane had left college after two years to marry.

The problems on which the therapy centered were Jane's anxiety, confusion about religion, stormy relationship with George, and belief that she was an inadequate, even bad, person. She reported many dreams, wrote me letters, and brought paintings of her dreams and other experiences. She telephoned sometimes until I made it clear that I did not welcome phone calls except in a genuine emergency. We met twice a week for about three years, with a third session during weeks when Jane was most distressed. After an additional six months of weekly meetings, the therapy was terminated. In this account I focus on the experiences in therapy that contributed to Jane's ego development and integration of her shadow and animus.

Jane was on an emotional roller-coaster during much of her work with me. When she was especially upset about an experience, she would report that she had been "clobbered." To me, this sounded as if she saw the distress as coming from the outside. When I asked her to tell me more, she would say, "I can't explain." Eventually it became apparent to both of us that the "clobbering," though often mediated by another person, was from a part of herself that could be identified as the critical animus.

The feeling of being assaulted by negative emotions was alleviated by my helping her to appreciate qualities in herself that she had deprecated. For example, she was competent in music, and she cared deeply about her children. Gradually, she learned to stand up to George's criticism and, later, to her own self-deprecation. Thus, as her ego became stronger, she could withstand the critical inner animus, which mirrored the hostility that she experienced from her husband. She also came to appreciate her strong intuitive and feeling functions and compared herself less adversely with thinking- and sensation-type acquaintances, including me.

Over time she came to understand that when I encouraged her to talk further about a matter, I was asking for a description of events and feelings, not a rational explanation that would stand up to her father's or husband's demands for logic. The respect and regard I evidenced for her helped her to develop similar attitudes toward herself. She began to realize that she shared the lot of all humanity in having emotions as well as thoughts, weaknesses as well as strengths, good qualities and bad. When Jane's ego became strong enough to tolerate these ambiguities, her undesirable characteristics became less shameful and overwhelming to her.

Between sessions with me, Jane was seeking out other people who were interested in Jungian psychology. One was a woman, Kay, with whom Jane said she could talk more easily than she could with me. Moreover, on three occasions Jane revealed an experience that she had "never told anyone," and yet the experience she revealed was the same each time. These facts made me reasonably certain that she discussed her inner life rather freely with other people, thus diluting the intensity of our work. I explained to her the Jungian metaphor of analytic work as an "alchemical vessel." Alchemists, who attempted to bring about a transformation in matter (for example, lead into gold), used a closed vessel to which they applied heat. For the transformation to occur, the pressure had to be maintained over a period of time.

Although the alchemical work evidently had little effect on the lead or other substance, it may have served as a projection of the alchemists' psychological transformations. Something comparable takes place in analysis if the analysand keeps confidential what happens in the therapy—that is, does not discuss with other people the problems and dreams that are brought into the sessions. (The analyst is bound ethically not to discuss analytic material with others, except for purposes of consultation to enhance the therapy.) Jane began to make a genuine effort to keep the material confidential and was rewarded with considerable psychological transformation.

Her very strong attachment to me was understandable as a projection of the positive mother, which compensated her feelings of rejection by her actual mother. This attachment also carried archetypal power. Indeed, much of the time Jane saw me as a kind of positive-Self figure, all-wise and all-loving. Inevitably, I did not live up to this image. For example, when I discouraged her from telephoning me, she saw me as not all-loving. Corresponding negative projections arose; she sometimes saw me as judgmental, rejecting, and even evil. She expressed her dissatisfaction with me by announcing on several occasions that she was terminating our work. Nevertheless, she would call, restore the appointment, and come at her usual time.

Jane struggled mightily with the conflicting emotions that these varying projections aroused in her. Each time she was able to transcend them enough to tell me about them, her self-awareness and, more important, her self-confidence grew. Thus, she became more of an ''I'' (ego) and less a bundle of chaotic emotions.

My role in this process was to encourage Jane to say whatever was on her mind and what she felt and to accept it nonjudgmentally as a fact rather than as a good or an evil. Thus, I was able to give her a stable point of reference from which to view the storm of emotions that buffeted her much of the time. When she saw that I was not overwhelmed by the storm, she became increasingly able to entertain the possibility that she did not have to be overwhelmed. She even began to give some value to the warmth and vitality that emotions contribute to a person's life. She came to understand that the invasions from her unconscious (for example, the "people" in her care) were reflections of complexes, which became less powerful when she acknowledged them.

As her ego strengthened, Jane was able to see that some of her traits were undesirable reflections of the shadow but they did not mean she was a totally bad person. These traits included the tendency to be too lenient with her children because she feared they would not love her or too strict when she felt she had to meet George's expectations of firm discipline. Finding that I could accept her with such a range of shadow qualities, she became better able to accept them in herself.

As Jane became more comfortable with herself and less frightened by unconscious material, she became more productive artistically. In addition to performing in public, she composed some songs and began to work toward getting them recorded commercially. Thus, her struggles with archetypal images and forces seemed to give her access to the creativity that has its source in the collective unconscious.

Jane brought dreams to nearly every session; we usually discussed one or two. Often our consideration of a dream went only as far as gathering associations,

but occasionally we worked out an interpretation together. (When we got no further than the associations, we moved to consideration of thoughts and feelings connected with the associations.) She began to understand that her frightening dreams
reflected the chaos and fearsomeness of the complexes with which she struggled.

Increasingly, her dreams came to depict images of positive inner figures,
often represented by personal acquaintances. For example, after about six months
of analysis, she dreamed: ''Max was wearing priestly robes and was very kind and
loving in a fatherly way. He told me that I wasn't crazy or responsible for everything
that had gone wrong in my marriage and that I must stand up to George.'' Max
was a minister, older than Jane, who had befriended her. She saw him as a kindly
father figure in waking life. The dream seemed to provide a positive animus figure
to help her stand up to the negative animus that she experienced in her relationship with her husband. As a minister, Max seemed to represent, also, a religious
resource to help Jane deal with her confusion about that area of her life, which
was all-important to her.

As the analytic work proceeded, Jane continued to be emotionally volatile
but became better able to deal with George. Despite his complaints about her
''kooky'' friends (people who shared her interests in psychology and religion), she
spent more time with them. She insisted on George's taking more responsibility
for the children and giving her more money for household expenses. She also took
a part-time job, mainly to pay for her analysis. As she became stronger, George
resented her independence and, consequently, became more hostile toward her.
When Jane suggested a trial separation, he insisted on their undertaking the marriage counseling that she had been requesting for many months.

In the marriage counseling sessions, as Jane recounted them to me, she became increasingly assertive, as she was doing at home. Eventually she and George
were divorced. The stormy relationship continued, especially the quarrels over
children and money, but Jane was able to pursue more of her own interests and
eventually to complete college and take a full-time job. Her assertiveness and initiative reflected an activation of the positive aspect of the animus.

Like all humans, Jane continued to have problems; some of them were severe.
By several indicators, however, the analysis had been effective: she had asserted
herself in the marriage, was less troubled by invasions from the unconscious, became
able to support herself, and had become artistically productive. Her relationship
with her mother changed little, but Jane now could see that they both contributed
to the difficulties. Her headaches diminished, evidently because she had more emotional strength to deal with the severe stress in her life.

Philip

Philip, a professional singer, was fifty-five when he entered analysis. He had
obtained my name from the psychology department at the university when he asked
for a Jungian therapist. He described his primary concern in analysis, as in life,
as a spiritual quest, with the ultimate goal of an experience of enlightenment. He
had read many of Jung's works and felt that the Jungian approach to psychology
was the most valid. Philip inferred that Jung had had the kind of experience that
he sought. Indeed, he saw individuation as the equivalent of enlightenment.

Philip suffered from depression and surmised that it arose from the conflict between his aggressiveness and his desire to be "nice." He felt that he got along well with most people with whom he had common interests, but he did not feel close to any of them. He wanted to have close friendships, but he did little or nothing to develop them. Indeed, he tended to avoid situations, such as parties, where he could meet new people. His attitude at work was one of ingratiating himself with people but avoiding both gossip and emotional intimacy. His ingratiating manner was an aspect of his persona; his shadow was reflected in his aggressiveness and resentment. Despite considerable confidence in his professional competence, underneath he was a frightened, yearning person.

We agreed to meet twice a week for six weeks and then reassess the decision. At the end of the six weeks his high degree of involvement in the process made him unwilling to think of meeting only once a week. We met twice a week for about thirteen months.

Philip's family belonged to a fundamentalist Christian sect in a western state. His father's sister was part of the household. She was even stricter and more rejecting than his parents. Philip had two sisters, one older and one younger, and a brother ten years younger. Philip had never married but had lived with a woman for several years; she was still a good friend. He regarded his "feminine side" as undeveloped. Indeed, his unfulfilled desire for approval from two mother figures (his mother and his aunt), together with his inability to form close, committed relationships, suggest that his mother complex was central and that he had much of the puer aeternus in him.

At age eighteen, Philip had left home to study music in New York. Three years later he had moved to Boston, where he had made his living in music for over thirty years. He had come to Minnesota under contract with a musical organization that seemed likely to give him broader opportunities than he had had on the East Coast.

His religious concerns had led him into the Episcopal church, which was satisfying to him for about twelve years but then ceased to be so. He still appreciated the symbolism in the liturgy but felt that it did not provide the means to enlightenment that he sought.

To our second session Philip brought a dream that had followed the first session and can be taken as an initial dream; it seemed to prognosticate positively for our work. He dreamed: "I am attending a play with my cousin Phyllis. I am happy because I feel that this time the play will be done right." Phyllis, he said, was the cousin who kept in touch with other members of the family, including him. She was happy with her husband and children, despite problems with finances and relationships with relatives. Philip and I concluded that Phyllis, whose name was similar to his, represented a part of him that had the potential to relate better to people and to be more contented with life. The play, which would be "done right," depicted his life, which he anticipated seeing more clearly and with a new perspective.

Throughout his analysis, Philip never used my first name. (He was correspondingly formal with other persons in positions of authority.) Although he may have been compensating for the difference in our ages (I was younger than he), such formality is unusual in my analytic experience. It may have stemmed from the fact that his transference was less to me than to the process and to the Jungian view of psychology. Nevertheless, this formal attitude seemed to reflect and perhaps contribute to Philip's less than full satisfaction with the therapy (a feeling that centered on his not achieving enlightenment during his therapy).

The positive side of this projection on the process was his openness to messages in his dreams. For example, in one dream the actress Kitty Carlisle questioned him about his sex life. Inasmuch as he associated her with the television program *To Tell the Truth,* he concluded that he was instructed to discuss his sex life with me. He spent most of that session telling me about his heterosexual and homosexual experiences and his problem with impotence. Thereafter, he seemed relatively at ease in discussing sexual matters as they arose.

The link between Philip's aggressiveness and depression became evident out of an episode in his professional life. He had had one of three lead roles in an opera. After the final performance, the other two leading performers (who played a married couple) received flowers and much applause. Philip received no recognition beyond that given to the whole cast. His recognition complex having been struck, he was furious. However, he said nothing to anyone at the time. (I was on vacation.) In our next session he told me about his depression, which had lasted two weeks. Later in the same session he mentioned sending off an angry letter to his landlord complaining about the noise from the apartment below his and then feeling guilty. I suggested that the letter might have been a way of venting his anger about the lack of recognition and that the guilt was a reflection of the self-deprecation that made him depressed. In the sessions that followed he became more aware of his fear and resentment of rejection.

During the remaining months of our work, he had further experiences that affected him similarly. As we explored each, the attention I gave to these manifestations of his rejection complex helped him to acknowledge the shadow qualities involved. Eventually he began to appreciate existing evidence (for example, the demand for his professional services) that his not seeing what life was offering him stemmed from his assumption that he deserved little.

During the time that Philip was working with me, his life seemed to move on three tracks: the public person, who was quite isolated and fairly unexpressive; the performer, who expressed emotions in each performance; and the inner person, who was full of passionate resentments, loves, hates, and hopes. He was probably a deeply introverted person whose artistic performances gave expression to parts of him that were otherwise hidden from the world. His search for enlightenment was genuine, but so were his struggles for a place in the sun and for feelings of closeness to other humans.

Much of Philip's inner conflict focused on his desire for recognition and love, which was incompatible with his wish to undertake a "journey of denial" to achieve illumination. My verbal responses included many that were meant to encourage Philip to stay close to his actual experiences, however painful, rather than escape into wishing for enlightenment. I was convinced that he might be able to have both but that enlightenment at the expense of facing the shadow would ultimately be destructive.

Philip's most forceful emotions centered on resentment of being ignored by the directors of the musical organization for which he worked. When these emotions were spent, however, he expressed feelings of being unloved and abandoned and wondered aloud whether such wounds could ever be healed.

His desire for a sudden transformation was evidently a response to this woundedness. A gradual healing seemed impossible to him; hence he wanted to leap across the abyss. By keeping his eye on a distant goal, he made it difficult for himself to see the path over which he had come and the stretch ahead of him.

The transcendent experience he desired seemed to be an expression of the collective unconscious. Evidently, however, he was unable to entertain the possibility that such an experience could come in a variety of forms—for example, artistic expression, a passionate love for a person or a cause, or a deep sense of the meaningfulness of life. Each of these can be an answer to the religious need, just as is the experience of enlightenment that Philip sought.

Despite the disappointment about his conscious goal, Philip showed signs of psychological development. His strengthened ego was reflected in increased certainty that his musical work was of high quality and appreciated by many people. His improved ability to relate to people could be seen in his friendlier, less suspicious feelings toward others and, in turn, increasing interactions with co-workers. Indeed, he was even able to acknowledge that many people, including me, liked him and had affection for him. He also seemed strengthened in his resolve to live his life according to his own values rather than collective norms. Thus, he became connected with the Self, a fact that may have made him more nearly ready for the more dramatic experience of enlightenment.

About a year after he terminated analysis, Philip wrote me that he had experienced the transformation he sought. It came about through his embracing an Eastern religion.

Beth

Beth's presenting problems were what Jung called those of the "second half of life." She and her husband, Larry, who owned a retail store, had six children. Although she had been trained as a teacher, ever since college she had worked for her family: in the house, with the children, in the store. Beth and Larry had a stable, loving relationship that held firm during her analysis. Nevertheless, she had been experiencing depression much of the time. She was bored with housework, felt guilty about not working efficiently, and yearned for some new stimulation and sense of meaning.

Reared with three brothers and a sister who was ten years younger, Beth had had a warm relationship with her father and grandfather but remembered little except criticism from her mother. Her resentment toward her mother had continued to the time Beth entered analysis and was the focus of much of her analytic work.

Beth's depression exemplified the "purposeful neurosis." It slowed the pace of her life by diminishing her physical and psychic energy so that she spent many hours lying on the sofa, staring at the ceiling, and hence she could not maintain the activity schedule that had been protecting her from examining her life. Now she had to face all the thoughts and feelings that "floated up" from the unconscious, including those that were unpleasant and those that threatened to disrupt the routine into which her life had fallen. She could not avoid considering questions of life's meaning and her goals for the next thirty to forty years.

Beth's fear of criticism, especially from a mother figure, was reflected in her concern, beginning after our first session, that I would think her too emotional, a sloppy housekeeper, and too depressed to relate to people. She also expressed her desire not to continue her lifelong pattern of trying to find out and act on what other persons—especially women—wanted. She seemed to be stating what she needed from me: acceptance, help in facing her shadow side, and learning more about being an adult woman.

Despite their problems, her teenaged children seemed to trust Beth enough to share their concerns with her. Consequently, she had repeated experiences of discovering her own naiveté. As a teenager, she had conformed well to adult expectations: being a good student, not drinking, and remaining a virgin. Her children and their acquaintances experimented with drugs, got speeding tickets, and accompanied their friends through pregnancy scares. Thus, Beth's exploration of what it means to be a mother was taking place on at least two levels, those of daughter and mother. The Jungian understanding of this situation is that the ''mother archetype'' was activated in Beth's psyche. Her ''mother complex'' was not something she could overcome ruthlessly; it was integral to many of the values that she needed in order to live the second half of life in a satisfying and meaningful way.

After hearing in a Jungian lecture that suffering accompanies analytic therapy, Beth became concerned that she was not suffering enough as a result of her analysis. She had been suffering when she came, but the sessions were largely a relief for her. She wondered whether she tended to escape problems. I suggested that she write down any that occurred to her that seemed to fall into that category. Before the next session, she wrote some ''reflections,'' which in effect described some of those problems and her feelings about them. They included being too concerned with what other people thought, giving in too easily to her children, being undisciplined and finding no joy in her work, and wanting more attention from Larry and feeling guilty about such wishes.

Beth, a lifelong church member, was reassessing her views on religion. She sometimes ran into difficulties when theological issues came up in conversations; she was torn between expressing her true opinions and not wanting to hurt the feelings of friends who were more conventionally religious. Even more of a problem was her tendency to see her husband as all-wise. Intellectually she knew that he was not and that her quest was for a god, but the wisdom projection on Larry remained.

Intermingled with the religious problems were her conflicting feelings about her shadow side. She had a strong tendency toward self-deprecation and an equally strong wish to believe that she had no undesirable qualities. Much of this ambivalence was projected onto Larry. She saw him much of the time as unimpeachable, the rest of the time as having problems that he was unwilling to admit.

Haltingly, she was able to tell me, one by one, the specifics of her undesirable qualities—often orally, occasionally by writing an account of an event, sometimes by bringing a dream that mentioned a relevant experience. Usually the telling depotentiated her guilt feelings, which were partly unwarranted, about her part in the unpleasantness. After a while she was able to accept these qualities as part of herself without concluding that she was a bad person.

Beth discovered some of her shadow qualities by her reactions to other people. One friend, for example, made a practice of finding something good in everything, however disagreeable; she expressed this attitude by saying ''Thanks be to God'' for every experience, whether rewarding or painful. Beth found this practice irritating. The irritation may have arisen from her own complex about facing negative facts, the complex that was the root of her naiveté. I did not state these thoughts to Beth. To do so probably would have resulted in further repression. Rather, I encouraged her to express her feelings about her optimistic friend and about the negative experiences that she told me only with difficulty.

At least one experience brought together her ambivalence about her shadow, some of her projections onto Larry, and her problem with religion. On this occasion she was angry at Larry; she felt that he deprecated her feelings and would not admit that he ever had problems. After telling me what had happened, she was able to face Larry and find common ground with him—the imperfections of both of them. As she saw his negative side, he became more human to her and less of a god. Consequently, her concept of God became more mature.

The primarily positive transference probably indicated that she experienced in me some of the positive mother who had been largely unavailable during her growing-up years. Such a transference seemed to be necessary in order for her to begin to accept her shadow.

Beth was vulnerable, also, because she considered herself to be a thinking type (I agreed) and was annoyed by people who deprecated thinking. Some of these people were in an encounter-type group in which she participated. As she was a thinking type, her inferior function presumably was feeling, and some of her experiences tended to validate this assumption. When buying clothing, for example, she did not trust her own choices but wanted to know what other people liked before she made a decision. When she was able to buy and wear with pleasure a dress that her children did not like, her feeling function was beginning to work.

Intuition seemed to be her second frustration. She was imaginative and intrigued by possibilities ''around the corner'' and felt correspondingly burdened by practical matters—the realm of the sensation function. Because she was intelligent, she could cope with the bookkeeping for her husband's business, and because of her sense of responsibility as a mother, she provided for the children's physical needs. Nevertheless, she often felt overwhelmed by the practical demands of her life and saw herself as constantly disorganized. This feeling arose, in part, from the size of her family and from her multiple responsibilities, which required a great deal of skill, efficiency, and organization. Beth's feeling of being overwhelmed arose around tasks that required a strong sensation function. As Beth came to understand this, she became more patient with her undeveloped sensation function, and it began to improve.

Beth brought dreams to nearly every session, and we usually worked on at least one of them. A dream sometimes opened a topic that Beth was having difficulty introducing. Quite often the interpretation would provide a helpful insight. Overall, the dream work gave Beth a sense of the power and resourcefulness of the unconscious. Some of her dreams and our work on them provide apt illustrations of the varying roles that dreams play in much of Jungian analytic therapy.

The first dream that we discussed came the night after our first session. The timing and its content suggest that it was an initial dream. ''I was in the basement of our house rearranging things. I told Larry I was going to redo it for an adult recreation room; another part of the house was the children's rec room. We were standing there in the basement when suddenly the whole wall seemed to buckle. We called the children and herded them out and then left ourselves. We watched the house from a safe distance, but it didn't fall down. At first I felt bad, but then I thought it would be nice to build a new house and have everything the way we wanted it.''

Beth associated the basement with the room there that she used as an office; she liked to have a place to get away from the family. She and Larry had talked about finishing the rest of the basement as a recreation room for children and adults. About the house as a whole, she said only that it was sound, as far as she knew. Additional amplification of the basement included its placement under the house: a darker, semihidden space that is essential to household activities but is not used every day. A recreation area is a place where recreation (creating again) takes place. The conscious situation at the time of the dream was, of course, the beginning of Beth's analysis—her journey into the inner world.

Having thus established the dream context, we translated the dream language. The dreamer is in the process of rearranging things in the lower part of her psychic house, the area where she has a place for herself, and plans to use the area for periodic renewal. She discovers, however, that a complete rebuilding is necessary. Thus, the dream seems to indicate that her decision to go into analysis is appropriate; it is necessary and possible for her to rebuild her psyche.

Two nights later, Beth dreamed that she adopted a child of four or five. Four or five years previously (the time of the child's birth) she had had the first rumblings of the discontent and desire for renewal that subsequently brought her into analysis. The adopted child can be seen as a child of the psyche, one that is not of Beth's flesh and blood. This dream indicates that the "psychic child" has been growing for those four or five years. (The dream could be taken concretely as expressing a wish for an actual child, but there was no other evidence of such a wish. Moreover, fulfilling such a wish would have been a distraction from Beth's task of the second half of life, which was an inner task.)

After about six months of analysis, during which Beth had expressed repeatedly her positive feelings for me, with no indication of any negative feelings, she dreamed: "My friend Rachel was being treated by a Jungian doctor. Another doctor (a male) thought the Jungian doctor was way off in her treatment of the case. Rachel was trying to be careful of what she said because she knew that I believed in Jungian medicine. I said, 'No, no, tell me all he said, don't be afraid of offending me.' I didn't like the man, but I didn't say anything; I just sat there feeling unimportant and insignificant." Rachel was a friend who had values and temperament similar to Beth's. Thus, her image seems to be that of an "alter ego." The dream evidently reflects the doubts, unconscious or at least unexpressed, that Beth was experiencing toward her "Jungian doctor" (me) and Jungian psychology. The dream ego defends the Jungian treatment, but another part of her psyche, perhaps her animus (represented by the male doctor), doubts and criticizes.

In order to bring the doubts more into consciousness, I suggested that Beth hold an imaginary conversation (a form of Active Imagination) with the non-Jungian doctor. In the next session she reported that she had had great difficulty in imagining such a conversation but she had written the following dialogue:

Ego: Why do you say that the Jungian doctor is off on Rachel's case?
Doctor: She just doesn't know what she is doing. Rachel needs a good, sensible treatment, not all this dream stuff and talk about emotions.
Ego: But dreams and emotions are important psychologically.
Doctor: Rachel's illness isn't psychological.
Ego: How do you know?
Doctor: She has physical symptoms, and the Jungian doctor is paying no attention to them.

Ego: Yes, she is, but she goes about it in a different way from you.
Doctor: Well, I don't think she knows what she is doing, so I'll keep on criticizing
           where I find it appropriate to do so.

After the Active Imagination experience, Beth still felt Jungian psychology was right
for her. Nevertheless, she more readily expressed her disagreements with me.

Often a dream series provides much of the context for an individual dream.
The series may comprise all the dreams in a given time period or several dreams,
perhaps experienced over many months, with a common motif (image). Beth had
periodic dreams of houses that seemed to augment the message of the initial dream.
About a year into analysis she dreamed: "I have a big, beautiful house, but I'm
not satisfied. I have a room for everything. The house is on a hillside. I go outside
and walk up the hill enjoying the scenery. I can't understand why I'm still feeling
restless when I have everything." The dream seems to indicate that much change
has occurred (the new house) and all the components are present for a satisfying
life, but she still must put the psychic components into proper relation to one another.

After another four months, Beth dreamed: "We had changed houses. It
seemed that we were on the same lot but had moved a different house in. I was
pleased with more room." In this dream she has gone beyond having everything
to having more room—an expansion of her vision and possibilities.

After about a year and a half of analysis, Beth had dealt with enough of her
problems that her depression lifted. She thought increasingly of getting a teaching
job. She began to have dreams in which she was interviewed for jobs and one in
which she was hired. We concluded that her dreams were supporting her inclina-
tion to reenter the teaching profession.

She took some courses to update her certificate and found that the inner push
toward resuming her profession increased. When she began interviewing for jobs,
she became anxious about the process and the adjustments in her family life that
a full-time job would necessitate. In our sessions she worked at dealing with the
inner conflicts and looking for the values that were intertwined with the disrup-
tions to her life, inner and outer, which would result from the new demands on
her time and energy. The psychic energy that had been tied up in her depression
now became channeled into her work life. Thus, the work was important for the
transition into a productive and satisfying second half of life.

That the individuation process is multifaceted but all of a piece was exemplified
in a dream of Beth's after about two years of analysis: "I was one of the older children
in a large family. My younger sister and I were trying to take care of the baby.
Our mother was behind a closed door; she had been away. She slapped us for the
poor way we had handled things in her absence. I was hurt not to get some love
from mother, but I felt that I at least deserved the reprimand because I was the
oldest at home and hadn't handled things well. However, my sister was blameless.
I took her and we left home. I decided that we would make our own way in the
world; we could get along without mother, who wasn't supportive to us anyway."

Taken as a picture of the dreamer's psyche, the dream seems to state that
the desire for someone to take care of her is still present. Nevertheless, she is taking
care of the new life (the dream image of the baby). She is acknowledging her shortcomings (those of the dream ego) but defending her positive qualities (those of the
sister image). She is becoming independent of the negative mother while manifesting

the positive mother to the younger sister as well as to the baby. (The dream conceivably could have been a foreshadowing of getting along without the analyst-mother, but there is no other indication of her seeing me as nonsupportive.)

Soon after this dream Beth began to feel that although she still had difficult problems, her inner life was moving at a steady pace, and she was confident that it would continue to do so. Sometimes she thought of terminating analysis. After she dreamed that she was going to die—a dream that was accompanied by strong feelings of fear and grief but also of freedom—I pointed out the connection with her conscious thoughts. The unconscious psyche seemed to be telling her that it was ready to terminate sessions, however fearful the ego was. At the same time, she was beginning a teaching job that would make it logistically and emotionally difficult to continue analysis. We discussed the possibility of termination and, within a few weeks, had our last session.

Philip and Beth are like many people who enter Jungian analysis. They are in emotional pain but have no severe pathology. They are eager to make the necessary changes to restore vitality and meaning in their lives. The success of the process for Beth is evidenced by a poem she wrote after about a year of analysis:

Analysis

Analysis is like
taking off a scab,
you find a sore
you'd forgotten.
It's like
scratching your inner ear
when nothing reached it
before.
It's putting down
what you've put up
And putting up
what you've put down.
It's putting the burden
square in your arms
where you can carry it
rather than weighting down
upon your head,
causing you to stumble.
It's like seeing unafraid
face to face
what scared you in the dark
from behind.
It's like seeing light
in the darkness,
and seeing darkness
in the light.
It's like getting
on a train

you can't get off
even when you're tired
of the trip,
and finding the weary miles
you've traveled today
bring you to the next station
tomorrow.
It's like knowing
which way the river runs
and going with the current
not against it.
It's like plugging into the
socket
and getting the power
or at least knowing
where the energy is.
It's like finding the time
to wait
when that's all
there is.
It's like planting
and resting in the faith
the plant will grow.

It's beautiful.

❦ 8 ❦

Horney's Psychoanalytic Technique

Douglas H. Ingram

Karen Horney's disaffection with Freud's instinct-based metapsychology sprang largely from the latter's insistence on penis envy as the primary determinant of feminine psychology. Repudiating the view that anatomy is destiny, Horney (1939) argued instead that the cultural impact on the developing psyche is of such magnitude that one might mistakenly ascribe its role to innate biological processes. With Sullivan, Fromm, and others, she argued that an adequate comprehension of personality and its disorders can be grounded interpersonally in the quest for safety, or, reciprocally, in the avoidance of anxiety. Horney (1937, 1950) regarded the various ideals found in a given culture as forming the underpinnings of particular personality trends. The ideal of love in our own culture, for example, gives rise to the wish to be loving and to be seen as lovable; masterfulness, likewise valued in the culture, manifests in the individual as a trend toward mastery, success, and ambition; the pursuit of liberty, the third major ideal of American culture, may be observed in the wish to be free from encumbrances of any kind, including personal relationships, material gain, and power. Parental and family influences, as well as a multitude of socializing forces, introduce cultural values and their associated impulses and behaviors.

In healthy growth, the child and later the adult adaptively integrates these values, appreciating his or her constructiveness, talents, and limitations. But in neurotic growth, an environment hostile to the emergence of health demands that integration give way to repression of broad areas of potential growth. This repression is not merely of memories but of entire ways of feeling, of attitudes toward the world, and results in deep feelings of alienation, elaboration of maladaptive defensive strategies or solutions, replacement of an authentic self-conception with a spurious idealized self, and a broad range of character pathology. Horney emphasized, as did Sullivan and Erikson, the critical role of experiences occurring after early childhood in shaping personality. Neurosis and the personality disorders are not so much a function of fixation as they are an ongoing process. Like Bowlby,

Horney believed that psychopathology represented a deviant path that, once started on, required the elaboration of structures necessary to maintain at least the illusion of an integrated self. Psychoanalysis, then, was directed more to the uncovering of actual personality structure, including defenses and repressed trends, than to recovering causal events for character pathology. In recent years, several writers have noted similarities between Horney's work and that of Bowlby (Paul, 1984; Ingram, 1984), Mahler (Lerner, 1983), Horner (Rosenthal, 1983), and Kohut (van den Daele, 1981).

Analyzing the present configuration of personality structure rather than the genesis of personality structure often means uncovering how the person's neurotic solution actually works against his interests. According to Horney, neurotic psychopathology entails the shaping of an environment that appears to gratify the person's immediate needs while worsening the longer-term overall impact. The suspicious person, for example, inevitably behaves in a fashion that generates concern in others about his intentions. In their concern, they behave in a fashion that not only justifies his suspicions but encourages them. The unwinding of "vicious cycles," of which this is a very simple instance, lies at the heart of Horney's psychoanalytic technique. Simultaneous with the exploration of these neurotic configurations is encouragement and support of the patient's constructive personality forces. At times, encouraging what is constructive in a patient's personality may call for suggestion, persuasion, ventilation, advising, and inculcating values. These techniques should be used only when the analyst has a very substantial appreciation of their likely impact on the patient's unconscious process. In psychoanalytic treatment, free association and interpretation of resistances, blockages, dreams, and transference are the principal techniques employed (Medical Board, Karen Horney Clinic, 1981). Horney emphasized the role of the psychoanalyst's attention, of free association, of resistance and blockages, of feelings in both patient and analyst, of dreams, and of the transference. Let us consider each of these in turn.

Horney (1952) approached the problem of psychoanalytic technique with caution, persuaded that technique can be taught only to a limited extent. Therapeutic effectiveness depended substantially on the quality of the analyst's attention, her inner freedom, her ingenuity, and her "fingertip feelings." To whatever extent psychoanalytic technique can be assisted through didactic instruction, underscoring the quality of the analyst's attention seemed to Horney most likely to be effective. Wholehearted attention by the analyst to the analytic session is not to be simply assumed. Distractions may readily arise because of personal concerns in the analyst or because neurotic factors inhibit concentration or interfere with her comprehensive receptivity. If, for example, the analyst has pride in theoretical understanding of a patient's productions, she may prematurely select material and overlook a far more valuable illustration of the patient's secret inner strivings.

Nevertheless, it is clearly necessary to selectively attend at times to certain aspects of what occurs in the analytic session. General qualities in the patient such as truthfulness, directness, diffuseness, self-contradicting tendencies, courage, self-indulgence, and the capacity to sustain anxiety all deserve attention. Nearly as important is the analyst's own flux of interest, his tiredness, irritation, hopefulness, and discouragement. Attention also needs to be given to the patient's attitude toward the analyst and to shifts in that attitude. Finally, attention needs to be paid to the patient's attitudes toward her problems and toward therapy as a whole. Does the patient want more and more help? Is she too proud to accept help? Does she deny problems, embellish problems, curse herself for having them, feel ashamed of them, or flaunt them? Does she tend to perpetuate her problems or reduce them?

If attention is wholehearted and comprehensive, it will also prove productive. The productivity of attention resides in its enabling a richer appreciation of the patient. In this process, the analyst's own resources are tapped. That is, the analyst's associations inevitably emerge in unexpected directions: "Perhaps it will be something from a play, or the Bible, or something from another patient, or from the same patient at another time, something from your own experience" (1952, p. 16). The productivity of attention includes the inductive crystallization into an insight from data about the patient that previously eluded clarity.

Demanding that the analyst's attention be wholehearted, comprehensive, and productive, Horney regarded notetaking as likely to be more a hindrance than a help. Certainly, notetaking would hinder free association and aliveness to feelings as they played out in the psyche of the analyst. Horney placed considerable value on free association as the cornerstone of psychoanalysis. For her, free association refers to the patient's revealing himself with utter frankness, without selection, without reservation, freely. The freedom of allowing one's inner self to emerge is an ideal dependent on many factors. As an ideal, it is prevented in the end by the patient's wish to repress, by his shame, or by the inevitable struggle between pride and truth. Overt encouragement of the patient to freely associate is necessary and must be done more frequently than many analysts think is proper. When free association is effective, the patient is able to concentrate on his inner self, and the quality of that concentration is likely to be more productive.

Helping the patient to free-associate may mean simply telling him, "Say everything that comes to mind," and repeating the basic rule time and again. But for some patients, such an injunction may be frightening. Some patients may need to feel that the analytic work is more a cooperative enterprise, and assisting patient communication may require more active participation by the analyst. Although use of the couch may assist many patients in free associating, the couch may not be helpful for others: "The couch may actually help certain patients to concentrate more on what is going on. But we don't see the couch as a condition of analysis *sine qua non*. We are flexible about it. Whatever is easier, whatever is conducive to greater concentration is all right" (1952, p. 35). Whether lying or sitting, a patient's attitudes toward his associations are as vital as the associations themselves. Does the patient use free association merely to ramble? Does the quality of the patient's interest in what is produced reflect the view that nothing has or should have meaning for him? Does the patient get lost in endless preoccupation with detail? Or does the patient interweave in his associations statements that attempt to prove that he feels all is known to him, that there is nothing for the analyst to add? Does the patient come with a program? Or does the quality of associations indicate dutiful compliance with the analyst's wishes, thereby expressing neurotic compliance as the patient's solution to life situations generally? Is continuity between his associations lacking? Or is the continuity so tight as to indicate his intense need to control? What indicates internal pressure, what haltings and silences intervene? Finally, what does the patient feel about what he presents? In this connnection, it may be crucial to ask time and again what his feelings are.

Attention to the content of sequential associations, particularly to sequences that repeat, can be exceedingly illuminating. Whereas at first a sequence of associations may seem to have no connecting elements, gradually—or quite suddenly—the common element may become clear and provide the essence for effective interpretation. Then, too, there are patterns of associational sequences that occur between hours. Finally, it is necessary to be aware of patterns of associations over still longer periods in order to discover, say, the unconscious arrogance of the self-effacing person or the secret wish for unbounded admiration in the narcissistic person.

Horney considered resistance or blockage a function of the neurosis and therefore subject to analysis. Nevertheless, some aspects of neurosis are more readily explored than others. What is perceived as a resistance amenable to analysis will depend on the patient's attitudes. The person who finds positive satisfaction in exploiting others must defend against awareness that such exploitations are taking place and will fight desperately to avoid recognizing what, in any case, would seem impossible to relinquish. In such instances, getting on the side of the defense, or at least not assaulting it, is the necessary technical position for the analyst.

The gradual unfolding of the patient's defenses and the elucidation of the patient's neurotic solution need to be accompanied in the patient by emotional experiences—a sense of aliveness, inner apprehensions, involvement in one's conflicts, a feeling of personal liberation, and so forth. Only when awareness is accompanied by such feelings can the analyst have some assurance that awareness has had an adequate impact. This does not mean, however, that every insight accompanied by strong feelings will have an important impact in modifying the patient's personality structure. Contrariwise, intellectual appreciation of inner processes without emotional involvement can serve as an important beginning for what will later become a significant structural change. Feelings that emerge in the course of analysis often hold little value for the patient, who, instead, may seek to justify the feeling, dismiss it, question its origins, or challenge the analyst concerning what can be done about it. Only rarely is the feeling appreciated and owned as properly belonging to the patient and as indicative of who the patient really is. It is this attitude toward feelings that we seek as signifying authenticity of insight. Feelings that the patient experiences but then rejects as somehow wrong or inadequate add little to therapeutic progress.

Horney viewed feelings not only as necessary data presented by the patient in the session proper but also as valuable when presented through dreams. Sometimes the analyst needs to ask how the patient feels at one or another moment in any dream offered in a session. Horney's appreciation of the function and value of dreams in illuminating the inner workings of the psyche was largely similar to Freud's. As Weiss (quoted in Horney, 1953, p. 18) noted, "In dreams we are closer to ourselves. Undistracted by the external world, we experience the inner world of ourselves—our anxieties, our rages, our conflicts—much as the stars become visible only in the dark, night sky." Four questions are raised by each dream a patient presents: What tendency or attempt at solution is expressed by a dream? What need is responsible for driving this tendency? What might have prompted this need? How might this sequence be typical of this person's way of reacting? Dreams function to find reassurance or compromise solutions for conflict currently experienced as unsolvable in real life. Rejecting the more usual sexual interpretations of symbols, Weiss, following Horney, might find a serpent symbolic of sin or knowledge rather than of the phallus; umbrellas might indicate protection; a pit in the ground might signify entrapment. Yet the caveat on interpreting dream symbols within context is a critical factor for Horney's approach to interpreting dreams: "A dream cannot be understood out of context. If we were to interpret it without background or associations, we would be forcing its meaning into the context of our own experience . . . the possibility of a valid interpretation could be said to increase in direct proportion to the clarity of the total contextual situation to the interpreter" (Kelman, 1944, p. 89).

As Horney valued dreams, she valued an appreciation of the transactions within the psychoanalytic relationship. Because the term *transference* was so enmeshed with drive theory, repetition compulsion, and the structural hypothesis, she allowed the use of the term only if it was understood in a much simpler sense: the reaction of the patient to the analyst and to the analytic situation. Implicitly, she rejected Sterba's (1934) view that the analyst/patient relationship was based mainly on a rational alliance between the analyst and that part of the patient's ego that sought improvement. Although such a rational basis for the relationship might be present, Horney believed irrational elements predominated. Horney believed that the patient and the analyst work largely at cross-purposes, the patient seeking to legitimize and fulfill neurotic strivings while the analyst seeks health and the possibility of self-realization in the patient. The sick patient idealizes the analyst despite disappointments, hanging on, as it were, in order to fulfill neurotic strivings. At the same time, the analyst's more constant values become internalized and replace the harsher and less well-integrated standards of the patient. Martin, following Horney, emphasized the value of empathy, conventional cordiality, and a wholehearted "being-with" the patient as necessary to the development of what Kohut later termed the narcissistic transferences. Externalization of the patient's idealized image to the analyst permits the establishment of a stable working relationship. The analyst, much like the Greek soldiers in the Trojan horse, can then fight from within the patient's neurotic strivings and thereby achieve restoration of health. Additionally, as the externalization of the idealized image is withdrawn from the analyst through successful therapeutic work, the patient sees more clearly the real person of the analyst and, consequently, more of his own real self.

In practice, analysts trained and certified by the psychoanalytic institute founded by Horney vary considerably in their actual conduct of therapy. This is not dissimilar from what casual observation suggests of other relatively cohesive analytic schools. Some Horney analysts, by dint of personality style and interpretation of theory, choose a more "classical" approach, whereas others opt for a more casual, freewheeling interchange. I am more the latter (although my patients think otherwise). As my own years of experience increase, I become more confounded by the question: What makes for effective analytic treatment? Borrowing from Spiegel's (1971) application of Dewey's epistemology, I find that the conduct of treatment may most usefully be regarded as arising in the transaction between patient and analyst, as determined by both and as inducing changes in both. It is from this point of view that I will illustrate my application of Horney theory and technique in a particular case. Two caveats: First, my intention is to illustrate something of how Horney's approach, in my hands at least, may be applied. Only those aspects of the case necessary to achieving this end are provided. Second, I regard what follows as a function of my patient and me, together. An analyst of another school, or even another Horney analyst, might well approach the case quite differently.

Ellie has been in psychoanalytic therapy for about three years, during which she has had 370 sessions. Sessions number 1 to 35 were conducted once weekly, sessions 36 to 360 three times weekly, and sessions 361 through 370 (the time of this writing) once weekly. Ellie began using the couch when she attended sessions three times weekly. Our sessions are of fifty minutes' duration. Shortly before the end of each session, a timer flips on a small light adjusted so as to catch my eye without disturbing the patient. Using the timer allows my attention to more fully engage the patient. The timer, too, enables me more effectively to use the feeling of duration as a tool for appreciating the moment-to-moment transaction in the session (Ingram, 1979). After each session, I have a ten-minute break during which I return phone calls collected on an answering machine and type a summary of the highlights of the session just completed. About every three to six months, I review these session summaries and prepare, for my own instruction, an analysis of trends and developments in each case.

In the last session of each month, I present my patients with a bill for services folded in a small envelope. Initially, Ellie presented a check at the beginning of each session. Her monthly statements always showed "Paid in Full." In our twenty-eighth session, she volunteered that paying in advance eliminated her feeling as if she owed something. Therapists, she emphasized, are like maids or prostitutes. If they are not paid, they will get it out of you in some other way. As the frequency of our work increased to three times weekly, she began paying at the end of each week's sessions. Only much later, as we shall see, did she trust the analytic relationship sufficiently to pay at the end of the month. How she paid for her sessions, like all else about her, is properly viewed as proceeding from her personality structure, itself a function of compromise solutions to seemingly irreconcilable inner conflicts.

Ellie phoned for a consultation because she chronically feared traveling to other cities, as her job required. She was then thirty-four years old, single, and worried that she needed to lose about thirty pounds in order to achieve her ideal weight. She showed no major body-image disturbance, but she did report an atypical bulimic pattern that I call pathological scavenging. On business trips, she felt driven to comb the halls for food remaining on room-service trays. It was the terror of hotels, where she would feel compelled to scavenge, that drove her to avoid business trips and to seek therapy. At home, binge eating unaccompanied by purging, diuretics, or laxatives was a frequent consequence of even the mildest stress produced by loneliness, social rejection, or occupational tension. Otherwise, the patient showed initially a history of depressive mood, conflictual family relations, rare one-night sexual adventures with rejecting men, and somewhat more durable friendships with women capable of offering support and solicitude.

The patient is descended of Rumanian aristocracy, humiliated first by the defeat of the Habsburgs in World War I and then utterly devastated by Hitler a generation later. When the patient was two years old, she and her entire family, including both pairs of grandparents, were interred in a concentration camp for political prisoners where, as she was told, her mother was the mistress of the camp's commandant. Ellie's mother was killed during an escape attempt. (She has been unable to recover memories of the camp experience.) When she was four, the camps were liberated and the patient, her father, and grandparents, fled to Austria, where her father had remarried and acquired a menial position with the occupying American troops. During the postwar famine, the patient was exhibited by her grandparents, who, like so many others, survived through beggary. Ellie's dancing and singing, pathetically dramatic, were apparently vital to the family's survival during these critical times. Despite her central role in the family's welfare, she was often mistreated and virtually ignored by her father. One evening her pet rabbit was deliberately served for dinner. The patient, now age five, developed rickets and was placed each night in a body cast. In order to achieve some mastery, however counterfeit, over her experience of impoverishment and abuse, she refused even the meager rations offered. Later when the family found passage to America and were guests of first one household and then another, conflict and poverty persisted. Ellie fell under the domination of her father's mother. Intense, persisting conflict between this woman and her son, the patient's father, effectively split the patient from her father, producing division marked by suspiciousness, silence, frustrated longing, masochistic submissiveness, and spiteful retaliation. Despite extreme hardship, Ellie succeeded brilliantly in the American public school system. Clever and generally submissive to what she accurately perceived to be others' wants, she was well liked by peers. But fearful of enraging her father and grandmother, she inevitably maintained a posture of social isolation. Not surprisingly, in view of her food-deprived past, she worked after school in a supermarket and contributed substantially to the family income. Her abilities, honesty, and diligence brought her to the attention of school authorities who intervened and effectively encouraged her continuing education. She won a scholarship and attended a prestigious college. Subsequently, she was pursued by a variety of management consultant firms and has been successful in her career despite the variety of her social inhibitions and idiosyncrasies. During early adulthood, she exhibited multiple substance abuse, including alcohol abuse, and exposed herself to humiliating relations with men. She entered therapy and joined Alcoholics Anonymous, successfully relinquishing drugs and alcohol. She withdrew from men but experienced her life as barren and dead. Assisting her during the early years of adulthood were a series of psychotherapists who provided weekly supportive therapy. During the three years of the current therapy to be partially described here, she showed sustained weight loss, improved relations with others, diminished binging, greater ownership of feelings, and increased inner aliveness. She appears somewhat happier and more femininely attractive than when therapy began. Nevertheless, she is often desperately unhappy and frustrated and is still searching for a man who will simultaneously create "razzle-dazzle" and yet provide security and genuine affection.

        When I first encountered Ellie, I was struck by two characteristics: first, her studied plainness. It was as if she worked deliberately at appearing inconspicuous. Her manner matched her style of dress. Her gestures were muted. At first, she smiled appropriately, too much so. Her voice was monotonal. She spoke spontaneously about her problems with eating but had little sense that she was also speaking of the inner barrenness of her life. After the initial session and for several sessions thereafter, she was always tearful. The second characteristic that struck me was her vivid intelligence. Listening to her speak, I would easily find myself transported into a deeply personal world of shifting images and personalities. It was because the associations she stimulated in me were rich and plentiful that I judged analytic treatment, rather than supportive treatment, would be beneficial. Ellie had a rich dream life and the capacity to weave dream elements into her therapy and to relate them to the events of her daily life. Nevertheless, she tended to dismiss as meaningless many of her dreams and feelings. Much as I wanted to help her, I recognized that any manifestation of that desire, itself induced by her, would succeed only in mobilizing suspicions in her about my motive. In order to secure a sense of the world as a safe place, she had needed to move into a schizoid, or detached, solution, one of the three basic solutions described by Horney and referred to above as proceeding from an internalization of the ideal of liberty. Only after several months of once-weekly therapy had elapsed did I feel that our alliance had developed sufficiently for us to consider working more intensely. The evolution of her detached solution resulted from her experience that those who love—or are supposed to love— are also likely to exploit. Affection is suspect. The experience of attachment, intimacy, dependency, and so forth could readily lead to her being exploited and abused. That, after all, had been her childhood experience. Better for her, it seemed, if all relations were contractual. Her paying me at the beginning of each session addressed this need, even though it caricatured it. Nevertheless, she experienced marked apprehension about becoming attached to me, launching into a description of herself as someone who never needed anyone. The analytic relationship, she feared, would put her in the position of Fay Wray, caught in the grip of a huge mechanical ape. A series of dreams depicted dusty weather, arid landscapes, and wounds that did not fully bleed, all in close association with lack of feeling. She wanted to be the "dry" sort. She wanted to repudiate feeling and yet found herself in the terrifying grip of an analyst with other intentions for her. Dreams and imagery suggested the critical value of avoiding closeness. Physical or emotional touching, dependency, responsibility were associated with the hand of her grandmother reaching for her from the grave. It was this hand that proved far more terrifying than that of King Kong. Often, Ellie felt as if she lacked a self. What she wanted was to be a well-oiled machine, the mechanical ape that she had projected onto the person of the analyst. That was her idea of health, and that was her goal for our work. She could not comprehend at this point just how much we were working at cross-purposes.

It was amply evident from our first sessions that feelings and intimacy threatened to do more than cause her subjugation. Feelings of intimacy threatened selfhood. Dissolution of self was concretely visualized in dreams of objects or people actually dissolving. Emotional and interpersonal detachment was the Horneyan solution to such a threat. Although one might drift into a discussion of borderline dynamics at this point in the case description, the concept of borderline defenses does not hold a place in Horney's theory. It is sufficient to affirm how vulnerable this patient's personality structure was and how alienated she had become. Emotional and interpersonal detachment was manifest particularly through her inconspicuousness. She worked at it. She wore black and drab dresses, avoided makeup, and hid from the world. She would go for weeks without opening mail, except to pay bills, and often allowed the telephone to ring without answering it. She could not bear attention directed to herself: attention meant that she was failing in her efforts to be inconspicuous. Yet she thirsted for attention and love in spite of her certainty that it meant abuse and exploitation. An unhelpful interpretation of her quest for inconspicuousness as a way of avoiding intimacy led to her purchasing a lavender dress, which, then, she never wore. A far more helpful interpretation, that intimacy was closely associated with exploitation, did succeed in releasing into subsequent sessions numerous memories of exploitation by family members. She also recalled a repetitive adolescent fantasy of boulders coming together and, when the last was in place, flying apart again.

It was only in the ninetieth session that I appreciated how fully detached, or unattached, my patient maintained herself. Her apartment had struck a friend, she said, as a place where nobody really lived. There was nothing in the apartment that distinguished it from a hotel room except perhaps for a few cacti on a sill. Anything personal—knickknacks, memorabilia, photographs—anything suggesting a home—was hidden from view. After all, a home is something one is attached to and hence is a source of potential hurt. Even her clothing was packed in a suitcase, as if she might need to leave on a moment's notice.

By and large, during this period of our work I avoided probing questions, restricting myself to mild questioning, casual interpreting, and frequent encouragement that she say what was uppermost on her mind. Ellie seemed to require that I not appear too interested. If I questioned closely, she felt too scrutinized; her need to be invisible was threatened. She idealized herself as perky, pretty Doris Day, the epitome of midwestern America. Her despised image, by far her dominant inner experience, was that of an Eastern European refugee, ugly and short. Nevertheless, her quest for freedom from emotions, relationships, and responsibilities was her paramount striving. At the same time that she idealized my comments and my assistance, she wished desperately to be free of me. But, she admitted she also wished to be free of Newton's Second Law! If I expressed appreciation of her constructiveness, she felt altogether too visible. She needed to flee appreciation because exploitation was never far behind, it seemed. Her idealization of me proved necessary because it established a safe distance. If she viewed me as a caring person, the inevitability that I would exploit her (or that she would feel dissolved in the substance of another self) would increase. Regardless, her sense that in this relationship, at least, she was not as likely to be abused seemed to be the chief means of enabling her to unwind the vicious cycle involving detachment, isolation, the need for love, the fear of exploitation and dissolution of self, and, once again, renewed detachment. Here she could begin to unfold what was on her mind and begin to acknowledge that her terrors were unfounded.

What did it signify, for example, when Ellie began to care for plants other than cacti? The cactus was the quintessential self-sufficient plant. Symbolizing the patient's own strivings for independence and freedom, self-sufficiency and detachment, cacti require little. (The prickliness of cacti did not appear in the patient's associations.) Already we had learned that dryness was associated with lack of feeling. The introduction of leafy plants that needed more care signified her acceptance of herself as likewise needing more care than she had hitherto admitted. Observing this shift, I felt encouraged in offering more overt help.

The ninety-seventh session began with Ellie's stating that she might have broken her thumb skiing and had wanted sympathy from others in the ski house. But she feared allowing others to know she wanted their support. She felt like a five-year-old, sorry for herself. She hoped I would feel sorry for her, too, as her grandpa had. That's what she liked about me—I reminded her of him. With her thumb broken, she felt like a wounded bird. I interjected that she often compared herself to a bird, but generally in connection with the freedom of flight characteristic of birds. However correct, this interjection introduced its own minor fracture into an otherwise intact session. Abruptly, she was reminded about how she had once tried to explain to her father that she felt like a wounded bird and he, as I had just done, interrupted her. He accused her of babbling. Nevertheless, Ellie was utterly unaware of the parallel she had drawn between her father and me. She noted that, in response to his cruelty, she began scrubbing the kitchen floor, and often, when she was in despair, scrubbing floors was still a source of relief. In the transference, she often shifted in her view of me first as grandpa and then as father, as the trusted and caring figure who would exploit her only a little and then as the darkly handsome, exciting figure to whom she was so often attracted, who filled her with aliveness, yet who inevitably abused and discarded her.

In the following session, she appeared with a short-arm cast to protect her fractured thumb. She noted how inconvenient it was. She felt scared, she said, but didn't know just what accounted for her feeling. Through the session, her associations concerned how someone she knew was trapped by social circumstances, her having been in a body cast as a young girl, her feeling like a grounded bird, and so forth. What frightened her, in my view, was the threat the cast presented to her major solution, the need to be free, self-sufficient, and detached. At the close of the hour, I offered her a plastic bag to place over the cast as protection from the drenching downpour she would face as she left my office, and I assisted her with her coat. I knew that these amenities would further threaten her strivings after self-sufficiency.

Indeed, she opened the following hour by noting how uncomfortable she felt, how certain she was that I held her in contempt. By my understanding, she had externalized onto me her own contempt for the neediness she had shown the session before. My assisting her in so overt a manner mobilized both gratitude and fear of exploitation. She idealizes self-sufficiency and holds neediness to be contemptible. In seeing me as having contempt for her, she proved to herself that one should never receive help. In this session and the next, her rage at me for regarding her as contemptible, itself a reaction to my assisting her with the cast, was manifest in her imagining me as excessively critical and judgmental. Why couldn't I simply be a computer, she asked?

Did I go too far in offering her a protection for her cast? Or in helping her with her coat? Should I have done otherwise, especially in view of her strivings for self-sufficiency? No, certainly not. It was precisely because I was aware of how my help would affect her that I felt confident in underscoring in this one instance, actually one of several, that accepting help need not result in dissolution of self or in exploitation. Her externalizations muted the impact of these "demonstrations." Nevertheless, there seemed to be some value in supporting an attempt of this kind. Whereas Ellie's earlier dreams were marked by aridity and bloodless wounds, in the 150th session she reported a dream in which she stabbed herself and saw blood everywhere. To a large extent, it seemed, she had relinquished her view of herself as a well-oiled machine: increasingly, she was flesh and blood.

On another occasion I offered a piece of advice on a minor matter. She took the advice and clearly benefited from it but, instead of expressing appreciation, related a memory in which she was unable to thank a helpful elderly lady. Her distrust of others' kindness was analyzed as her fear of being in any kind of debt. After all, debt meant loss of freedom and self-sufficiency. Ellie hated owing money quite as much as she hated having a debt of gratitude. Yet she needed the kindness.

Similarly, another's affection for her required that she respond somehow. Her affection for another meant that she was subject to exploitation. In the former instance, she would flee. In the latter, she would externalize contempt and develop a reactive indignation to the person she had burdened with that externalization.

Any form of commitment, implicit or explicit, struck Ellie as constricting. Her increasing awareness of this in the course of our work set the stage for a major insight when, in the 170th session, I mentioned that a person is always larger than the commitment he makes. Commitments can always be undone, but having made them frees us to move beyond. This kind of ordinary good sense does have a place in effective psychoanalytic technique, Freud's ([1912] 1958) dicta notwithstanding. Like simple advice and ordinary helpfulness, common sense can reconfigure a patient's experience of self and world, open new options for consideration, and promote the means for unwinding the vicious cycles that sustain neurosis. Ellie's insight that it was she who had the commitment, not the commitment that had her, effectively freed her to make new contracts, contracts of a kind she had never made before. But common sense, like advice and helpfulness, is likely to have little impact unless it meshes with the patient's personality structure, particularly the patient's major solutions and pride investments. Otherwise, it is inevitably repressed or deflected, or its effect is short-lived. The personality reacts to the analyst's comment much as the immune system reacts to challenge by an allergen: the comment is experienced as foreign.

In the session following Ellie's insight, she remarked that things had been going unusually well. Perhaps analytic work was not merely a business relationship, she said. Her associations during that hour oscillated between issues of trust and exploitation. In the session following, I wondered aloud whether Ellie would like to begin paying for her analytic work each month, instead of each week. Her reaction: "It strikes terror in my heart!" She would then feel committed to the work, that she was going to be here a long time. Paying each week meant she could leave whenever she wanted. In fact, she had been in treatment two years. It was like a marriage, she said, as in "till death do us part." She circumvented her terror by reminding herself that, for all practical purposes, it came to the same thing. She could leave whenever she wanted, even if paying monthly changed the quality, the feel, of her involvement. Predictably, she experienced virulent self-hate. In her agreement to pay monthly, she glimpsed her dependency. As before, when I had helped after the fracture of her thumb, she experienced self-hate in an externalized form: it was I, not she, who was contemptuous and critical. Not long afterward, she reported a dream in which she wore a wedding gown but was fleeing the wedding. A few days later, she reported another dream in which she was escaping from a former lover who was pursuing her. We explored these dreams as manifesting her wish to flee from the greater commitment she was now experiencing to her analysis. The therapeutic alliance had become sufficiently strong for her to appreciate how what occurred in our relations reflected what occurred in her other relations. She seemed more able to appreciate how her dreams reflected her wish to flee engagements generally.

Vulnerability to needing others yet fearing commitment had resulted earlier in barren sexual escapades followed by years of celibacy. Previously, sex had been an escape. The mere presence of a man was intensely stressful. On completing her catalogue of questions that she used to simultaneously engage and fend off the men she dated, she felt compelled to leap into sexual intercourse. As she put it, ''Fucking was easier than being with someone.'' After intercourse, no further avenue of escape remained except actual fleeing. In fact, while vacationing, she would regularly climb out of bedroom windows, literally escaping the presence of men with whom she had had intercourse. More sexual history and sexual fantasy entered the analytic sessions. We were vigorously interpreting and exploring transferential material, emphasizing her conflict between wanting to attach herself to me and fearing dissolution and loss of control. Over and over, we encountered the self-loathing and experience of being criticized that resulted from engagement with others and even from the passing thought of relinquishing detachment as a solution.

The behavioral effects of our work to this point were certainly positive but clearly not breathtaking. Ellie had lost excess weight, but binge eating and scavenging had not improved. Social relations and occupational functioning were enhanced somewhat and stabilized, and her inner world had grown more alive. Episodes of despair were fewer. Finally, she was attempting a durable relationship with a man other than her analyst. In this connection, it was quickly evident how much she was seeking to finally win paternal love by winning the affection of a seemingly rejecting lover. We had so substantially analyzed Ellie's predominant solution of detachment that we had gained admittance to an underlying conflict, a conflict between Ellie's need to triumph and her need to submit. We could now see how this conflict was manifest in all her relations. Detachment had been her primary means of avoiding the fragmenting anxiety associated with this conflict that now seemed so evident. Because her constructive personality forces had been underscored during our analytic work so far, she was in a position to move more forcefully into relations with others and to face another stratum of intrapsychic challenge. Material produced in our sessions consequent to her new love affair, the first of several similar affairs, illuminated aspects of her eating disorder and gender-related difficulties.

When she was reunited with her father at age four after the liberation of her family from the concentration camp, he greeted her coldly but offered her a candy bar. For everyone else in postwar Europe, a candy bar was a special treat. But for Ellie it was simply strange. She did not know what to do with it. For the next six years, Ellie secured a sense of mastery and selfhood by refusing to yield to hunger. ''I think, therefore I am'' was, for Ellie, ''I will not eat, therefore I am.'' Somehow, eating leftovers was permissible. In the session during which this history was explored and interpreted, Ellie developed intense lower back pain, reminiscent of the pain she had experienced when the doctor applied the body cast for rickets at age five. In America, the family became functionally divided. Ellie had become the handmaiden of her grandmother and was protected by her. Ellie's father and the woman he had married in Austria lived separately from Ellie and her grandmother in the same house. They had their own room, food, refrigerator shelves, and schedule. In stealing leftovers from her father's shelf in the refrigerator, Ellie unknowingly provoked overt antagonism between her father and grandmother. But at least she could witness a family united, however perversely, in quarrel. Otherwise, the two camps barely spoke. Stealing leftovers was for Ellie the means of securing some meager sense of unified family life, translating later as the means of securing a sense of unified inner life. Illuminating as this proved, it was associated with no insight or behavioral change. Exploration of relations with her father and with her seemingly abusive lover enhanced the patient's capacity to acknowledge feelings previously censored. For example, she was angry with me for taking my August vacation and was willing to own her anger even in the certainty that nothing she could do would alter my plans and that August vacations were, after all, standard fare.

Her tolerance for conflict within herself, sustained through time and circumstance, gave clear evidence that structural change was occurring. In session number 270 we find a richness of feeling, a newly discovered capacity for attachment, and the lingering intense wish for freedom: she presented a dream in which she and grandpa are escaping from Hungary to America. They join another group that is also escaping. In climbing a series of stairs, she sees that grandpa is falling behind. She calls out. He should leap from one landing to the next. He does so but falls and is injured; she finds herself wishing he were dead so she could keep up with the group and flee to America. He is taken to a hospital. Reluctantly, she goes with him and holds his hand. But that isn't enough. She wants to hold all of him and cradle him in her arms. He is going to die, and she is crying, and she missed the chance to flee to America.

Increasingly, Ellie's love affairs took a masochistic turn. Her attraction was to "razzle-dazzle," to the romantic and appealing womanizers who would phone her at any time of day or night, drop in on her, and abandon her. At no time did she suffer actual or threatened physical abuse or danger. What hurt her, and stimulated rage in me, was that she knowingly permitted and even encouraged her own humiliation. Our work so far had enabled her to progress from a highly schizoid solution to a masochistic one. The men she dated were, in the aggregate, a repository for externalized expansive strivings, and I was the repository for externalized judgmental attitudes. There were sessions in which I was sorely tempted to cry out: "How could you allow a thing like that to happen!" But because I appreciated her use of projective identification and how necessary it was for me to serve as a "container" (Langs, 1976) for her outrage, how much this "masochistic triangle" (Horner, 1979) needed to involve my having such intense reactions, and how "countertransference is the living response to the transference, and if the former is silenced, the latter cannot reach the fullness of life and knowledge" (Racker, 1968, p. 3), I was enabled to endure in my professional attitude without threatening her masochistic affairs or undercutting the analysis. The thrust of our work during this period in connection with these relations was twofold. First, we explored how much she was seeking to vindicate herself by extracting love from her unavailable, rejecting father. Second, we worked to recognize how much she needed these men, all of whom seemed tiresomely alike, in order to express her new neurotic solution to inner conflict: morbid dependency, as described by Horney. Idealized freedom had been replaced by idealized love as the predominant structuring feature of her thinking, feeling, and behavior. Her need for love from these men was coupled with her moral outrage projected into the countertransference. The analytic job at hand was to discover the value of her self-effacement and to gradually help her own the projected outrage. Because of my refusal to collude overtly with her projection, I was occasionally viewed as "one of them, like my father. You're all the same." Considerable care would be needed to successfully encounter this phase of our work.

Nevertheless, Ellie was beginning to sense that her self-effacing strivings were more to the point than any actual relationship: it was the yearning for a man, not the possession of one, that gave meaning to her life. The monumental submission to a male idol was what she sought. But it was the seeking, not the finding, that mattered. Finally, a man she admired took up residence with her and stayed beyond what they both had initially expected. In addition, his treatment of her was consistent with ordinary social standards. Her inner script called for his rejecting her despite all her efforts at loving submissiveness. She needed distance, either the horizontal distance gained through withdrawal or the vertical distance gained by his willingness to stand far above, on the pedestal she had constructed. To ensure that enough distance was maintained, Ellie provoked his leaving, insisting all the while that it was he who rejected her. When the facts were laid out in her analytic sessions, only the mildest suggestion was needed for her to recognize how she had sabotaged the relationship. This formed a major insight that sparked a negative therapeutic reaction and culminated in her decision to terminate analytic therapy.

Although the wish to leave analysis had been a frequent concern since Ellie had begun over 350 sessions before, it had always been possible for her to appreciate how the fantasized termination relieved anxiety arising from inner conflict. The analysis, in assisting the discovery of her motive for provoking her lover's departure, had seriously affronted her need to be seen as his victim. Simply put, the analysis of her expansive and controlling behavior was premature. She was still finding hidden gratification in her role as a victim of love. Eventually, if our work proved successful and complete, she would encounter in herself the wish for power and mastery and even sadistic intrigue. But to enable awareness that such trends were currently operating threatened her now predominant solution of morbid dependency and self-effacement. The analysis had successfully encountered her detached solution to unconscious conflict and, having explored its origins and continuing functions, succeeded in opening the door to this new solution, one that enabled far greater authenticity of being and of inner liberation. In leaping forward into an analysis of unconscious expansive tendencies where we would have been wiser to support and consolidate the solution of morbid dependency, we attempted too much. The patient provided her own legitimate corrective by terminating treatment for a brief period. The work in analysis had been successful and had opened entirely new areas of endeavor for the patient. She looked and felt better and reported how much her friends saw her as different. Analysis had become too expensive, she said, and after all, this was a thing that can go on forever. In my view, the analysis was incomplete, and I encouraged her to continue. Nevertheless, if it seemed best for her that we stop our work, we could also pick it up again in the future if it seemed helpful to do so. She had a man in her life and, for her, much of the immediacy of our work had waned. Our parting was abrupt, but she was insistent. Rather than challenge her wish to leave analysis by analyzing, for example, just what she felt was too expensive, I judged that far more would be gained by a friendly farewell with good wishes. Two weeks later, she returned. She had renewed fears that her lover would leave or that she would provoke his leaving. She also found herself obsessed with a parallel she drew in her mind between her stepmother and another woman in her lover's life. Would I be willing to see her once weekly? I encouraged her to resume at the same frequency as before. But no, she felt better and more in charge of her life. Once weekly was what she wanted.

At the time of this writing, Ellie and I have worked together for over three years, and it is very likely that our work will continue in one form or another for years to come. Much analytic work follows this pattern. The motive for initiating treatment is lost as the patient improves and, with the decrease in psychic pain, the patient chooses to attend less frequently, if at all. Only rarely does a comprehensive neurotic problem become entirely resolved. The patient is happier and more adaptive and has achieved important modifications in personality structure. Alienation is far less but still persists. This is an entirely acceptable outcome for analysis.

To require of our patients (or of ourselves) that a final resolution to neurotic conflict be achieved is to demand that they (or we) realize an ideal—the very thing it is our responsibility to attenuate.

9

Interpersonal Psychoanalysis

Stephen A. Mitchell

When the French historian Alexis de Tocqueville visited the United States in the 1830s, he was struck by the antiphilosophical quality of American culture. "In no country in the civilized world," he noted, "is less attention paid to philosophy than in the United States." Several decades later, when a distinctly American philosophical point of view did emerge in the writings of Charles S. Peirce and William James, it was something of an antiphilosophy philosophy, or at least a philosophy that cast a suspicious eye on the value of philosophizing in the abstract.

American pragmatism was a reaction to the broadly speculative expanses of nineteenth-century European metaphysics, the grand, elegant, formal systems and armchair visions of Kant, Hegel, and Schopenhauer. The pragmatists were wary of what they regarded as the presumptuousness and arbitrariness of philosophical systems and more concerned with the question of what one could *do* with any particular philosophical notion, what difference it made in everyday living. "A pragmatist turns his back resolutely and once and for all upon a lot of inveterate habits dear to professional philosophers. He turns away from abstraction and insufficiency, from verbal solutions, from bad a priori reasons, from fixed principles, closed systems, and pretended absolutes and origins. He turns towards concreteness and adequacy, towards facts, towards action, and towards power" (James, [1907] 1960, pp. 31–32).

Interpersonal psychoanalysis was heir to this pragmatic tradition. H. S. Sullivan studied medicine in Chicago, the hub of the tremendous fervor that pragmatism had begun to generate in American intellectual life and particularly in the social sciences, which were characterized by an orientation toward the practical, social reality, what can be seen and measured, rather than intangible abstractions. Sullivan's relationship to Freudian psychoanalysis, complex and ambivalent, was very much influenced by this sensibility.

Although Freud's earliest theory of psychopathology had stressed actual interpersonal events (infantile seductions), by 1897 he had come to believe that his patients' memories of seductions were, for the most part, a product of fantasy. The cause of neurosis was not actual transactions between people but wishes derived from instincts, generated from within the mind of the child; the pursuit of (and defense against) drive gratification became the dynamic underlying all human endeavors. Although a psychology of unseen, intangible forces was just the sort of theory likely to make any good pragmatist cringe, Freud's ideas were by no means unwelcome among Sullivan and his contemporaries.

Sullivan had been involved in the treatment of schizophrenia; between 1923 and 1930 he ran, with great personal care to detail and staffing, a small ward for male schizophrenics at the Sheppard and Enoch Pratt Hospital in Towson, Maryland. This experimental ward, the first example of what is now called a "therapeutic community," influenced the attention to the social and interpersonal setting that characterizes most progressive psychiatric hospitals today. Psychiatric thought during the first several decades of the twentieth century was dominated not by Freud but by Kraepelin, the "father of modern psychiatry," who viewed the various forms of what we today refer to as schizophrenia (his term was *dementia praecox*) as reflecting a common underlying, irreversible deterioration. Schizophrenic phenomenology and symptomatology were meaningless murmurings of a nervous system undergoing a relentless, inexorable disintegration.

For Sullivan, Freud's theories were a breath of fresh air. Freud had shown that seemingly bizarre neurotic symptoms like conversions and obsessions were not the result of random and meaningless neurological discharge but expressed the patient's wishes, intentions, and conflicts. Similarly, Sullivan had come to regard schizophrenic phenomenology and symptomatology not as a sign of meaningless degeneration but as expressing important aspects of the patient's emotional life. Freud's psychodynamic theory gave Sullivan a powerful tool for understanding his patients, and Sullivan's early papers were written largely in a Freudian mode. Yet, Freud often tried to account for that which was tangible and visible in terms of unseen forces. The schizophrenic break with reality, for example, was understood as a product of withdrawal of libidinal cathexis from the external world, rather than as reflecting, as Sullivan came to view it, the intense and distorted realities of the patient's interpersonal, familial context. Freud's explanation in terms of drives seemed to miss too much of importance and, particularly with respect to schizophrenia, led to a therapeutic pessimism. What Freud saw as derivatives of instinctual forces, Sullivan came to see as residues (sometimes distorted) of real, interpersonal events.

Sullivan's work attracted the attention of several theorists and clinicians, trained in Freudian psychoanalysis, who had begun to grant more weight to social, familial, and interpersonal factors. In the 1930s and 1940s considerable collaboration and mutual influence occurred among Sullivan, Erich Fromm, Karen Horney, Frieda Fromm-Reichmann, Clara Thompson, and others. Nothing like a comprehensive theory or distinctive, systematic therapy ever emerged from these efforts; the pioneers of interpersonal psychoanalysis were an individualistic lot, each with his or her own emphasis and way of putting things. There has also been enormous cross-fertilization between interpersonal psychoanalysis and other schools of psychoanalysis. Many of the major innovations in psychoanalysis in recent decades (particularly in ego psychology, the British school of object relations, and Kohut's self psychology) cover much the same ground opened by the early interpersonalists in the

1930s and 1940s, and conversely, contemporary interpersonal clinicians have absorbed many of the theoretical and technical contributions from these psychoanalytic schools into their ongoing clinical work. Consequently, sharply delineated lines of approach are impossible to draw.

Nevertheless, something of a consensus did emerge, or at least a shared sensibility, and it is this generally shared attitude toward theoretical concepts and the analytic process that I hope to convey in this chapter. I must caution the reader that what I am selecting reflects what in the interpersonal tradition has been most useful to me, rather than necessarily being representative of this richly diverse and heterogeneous tradition. Moreover, limitations of space make it necessary to present complex ideas in collapsed form, with the hope of conveying, not the full line of thought, but a taste, a sample, of a way of thinking.

Interpersonal Theory and Technique

The way an observer approaches and defines the object of study goes a long way in determining what sort of data he will come up with and how he will account for them. The portrait painter with her brush encounters a very different human body than the pathologist with his scalpel; the carpenter with his tools engages matters in a very different fashion than the particle physicist with her cyclotron. For Freud, the object of study in psychopathology was the individual mind. His "intrapsychic" model traced neurotic symptoms to processes and structures arising *within* the mind of the patient. Sullivan felt that Freud had incorrectly framed the phenomena in question. Psychopathology is best approached, Sullivan argued, not in terms of *a* person but in the context of actual interaction *among* persons, in terms of what he called the "interpersonal field." Personality and psychopathology do not exist in germinal form within the child, simply unfolding as a bud into a blossom; personality and psychopathology derive from, are composed of, interactions between the child and significant others. Interpersonal interactions and their residues (representations of self and others) are the very stuff of mental life. Let us consider a schematic outline of Sullivan's account of personality as an example of one kind of interpersonal approach to the human condition.

The infant's earliest organization of experience is based on the distinction between the caretaker's anxious states (bad mother), which arouse anxiety in him, and the caretaker's nonanxious states (good mother). As the child's cognitive capacities mature, he begins to anticipate these affective states and to link his behaviors with them. Some areas of experience and behavior meet the caretaker's needs and approval, evoking tenderness; therefore, through what Sullivan terms the "emphatic linkage," they make the child feel secure. These areas of the personality are experienced as "good-me." Some areas of experience and behavior make the caretaker anxious and therefore, through the empathic linkage, make the child anxious. These areas become "bad-me." Some areas of personality evoke intense anxiety in the caretaker and thus create intense anxiety in the infant. This experience is dreadful for the infant and produces an amnesia for the events leading up to the precipitation of the intense anxiety. Such experiences remain completely unknown and unintegrated. This area of the personality, Sullivan designates "not-me." All the infant's characteristic experiences become colored by the affective response they generate in the caretakers and, through the empathic linkage, in the infant. Eventually the intervening stage of the caretaker's response is no longer necessary. Experiences within good-me are accompanied by a sense of security and relaxation; experiences within bad-me are accompanied by relative anxiety; not-me experiences are enshrouded in intense anxiety.

The "self-system is a complex organization of experience derived from but not lifted out of the child's interactions with significant others" (Greenberg and Mitchell, 1983, p. 97). The self-system controls anxiety by attempting to limit awareness to experiential content within good-me, steering a course toward experiences and behaviors associated with parental approval and away from areas of experience and behavior associated with parental anxiety. As the child matures, the functioning of the self-system becomes more complex, no longer drawing simply on the control of awareness but now using a whole set of processes, which Sullivan terms "security operations." These processes function by distracting attention from anxiety experiences onto other mental content that feels safer and more secure, often imparting an illusory sense of power, stature, and specialness. Most security operations include "an extravagant, superior formulation of the self" to aid in overcoming anxiety (Sullivan, 1940, p. 121). Through these devices, the self-system tends to preserve the limiting shape it took during early childhood. New kinds of experiences and needs, drawn from bad-me and not-me, arouse anxiety and hence are avoided.

In Sullivan's system, anxiety about anxiety is at the core of all psychopathology and constitutes the earliest organizational principle of the self, which takes shape in complementarity to the character of significant others. In classical drive theory, intrapsychic conflict is predetermined and universal, a product of the inevitable clash between psychosexual and aggressive drives and social reality. For Sullivan, both the qualitative and quantitative factors in personality organization derive exclusively from the particulars of the interpersonal matrix within which early development takes place, from the character of the parental figures and their relationships with the child. The contours of the child's personality tend to perpetuate themselves throughout life; the patient extrapolates from her early experience, assuming that the avenues of contact and avoidance in her family are representative of the species in general. Repetitive patterns of living keep the patient within the realm of the familiar, attached to early representations of self and others, protecting her from the anxiety associated with personal growth and enrichment. What is most fundamental motivationally is preservation of the shape of the self, the characteristic patterns of integrating relationships and the recurrent stance toward life. What is most fundamental therapeutically is the inquiry into these repetitive patterns of experiencing and living, particularly as they manifest themselves in the analytic relationship.

The analytic process represents a movement from the more superficial, manifest level of the patient's experience to what is hidden, latent, unknown. How is this movement possible? In the classical theory of technique, free association provides the route in: the patient reports on her experience without concern for appropriateness or coherence, and the analyst reads in the chains of association the latent meanings. Questions play no major part in most accounts of classical technique; all the information is there in the associations. Questions merely interfere with the natural emergence of unconscious content. Sullivan, with his pragmatist sensibility, was doubtful about this process. Free associations, he felt, often serve less to express unconscious content than to perseveratively repeat habitual preoccupations and characteristic patterns of avoiding real interpersonal exchange. Further, it is very dangerous to assume that one knows what another actually means by the words he or she uses. Language is very idiosyncratic; the words a person uses to describe experiences, particularly those of greatest emotional import, are filled with personal meanings, unexamined assumptions, and inattention to salient data. Therefore, for Sullivan, questioning is crucial and provides an alternative route into the latent recesses of the patient's experience.

A good deal of interpersonal psychoanalysis entails what Sullivan termed "detailed inquiry." Much of what the patient needs to know about her difficulties in living is potentially available to her, but selectively inattended to. Hence, interpersonal psychoanalysis tends to be very phenomenological in tone, focusing more and more closely on various areas of the patient's experience, attempting to get beneath the language the patient uses to gloss over crucial subtleties of feeling and important circumstances and perceptions.

The past is examined in an effort to arrive at some understanding of the major facets of the patient's early development. Who were the caretakers and other important influences? What was it like to be in relation to them? The interpersonal tradition puts great importance on arriving at a reasonable determination of what actually took place. Much of the patient's difficulties are traceable to a discordance between what actually occurred in her interactions with others and what she was told and was required to believe (Sullivan, 1956; Levenson, 1983). The analytic process helps to disentangle this web of hypocrisy and mystification both in the past and in the present. The detailed inquiry explores gaps, inconsistencies, and improbabilities in an effort to make sense of the patient's past in relation to his current characterological patterns of living.

The present is examined to reveal rapidly shifting sequences of responses and behaviors of which the patient is only dimly aware. Who are the main people in the patient's life? What does he actually *do* with them? How are these relationships structured? The patient who comes into treatment reporting chronic quarrels with his wife, for example, may be experiencing anxiety concerning intimacy, which is being covered over by belligerence. A careful inquiry into their fights might reveal a sequence of tender feelings, anxiety, and a rapid shift to devaluation and contempt. When the patient arrives at the latter point, he feels comfortable and secure (if also sad). In Sullivan's terms, such a sequence comprises a point of anxiety followed by devaluation as a security operation. Perhaps the wife experiences similar anxiety in connection with intimacy and a similar ease with belligerence. Their collusion constitutes what Sullivan terms a "hostile integration." At the beginning of treatment, such a patient is likely to be aware only of the contempt and disappointment—the sequence happens quickly and outside awareness. The detailed inquiry enables the patient to become more aware of the nuances of and shifts in this experience. When did the latest fight begin? What was the patient feeling before that moment? What were the anticipations of the interaction that developed into a fight? The inquiry attempts to stretch time, to separate out the components of the sequence. Eventually the patient comes to experience the original affect and the anxiety connected with it, to understand how he uses security operations to escape from that anxiety and to appreciate the way the security operation (like all security operations), while minimizing anxiety in the short run, perpetuates difficulties in living in the long run. This appreciation becomes the basis for different choices and character change.

In the classical theory of technique, cure operates through "insight"; interpersonal theory stresses, in addition, the crucial ameliorative role of the personal relationship between patient and analyst. That the patient can more use experience with the therapist than any interpretation or explanation is a major theme of Fromm-Reichmann (1950). The patient's difficulties are understood as deriving from constricted and mystifying early relationships with others, leading to problematic patterns of experiencing and integrating relationships throughout life. These patterns inevitably manifest themselves in the analytic relationship as well, and the transformation of the relatedness between patient and analyst into something more open and collaborative helps the patient to enrich his life in general. Insight is crucial in this process, not only as information but also as a vehicle for opening up possibilities for greater mutual understanding and intimacy. Although interpersonal theory regards the relationship as curative, it is not a deliberately contrived relationship of the sort that Alexander proposed under the rubric of "corrective emotional experience." The struggle to arrive at an *authentic,* collaborative inquiry into the patient's experience provides a unique interpersonal encounter that helps to undo the constrictive effects of past interpersonal experience.

In interpersonal theory, it is not considered possible for the analyst to remain thoroughly and consistently objective, always outside the patient's difficulties. The patient's psychopathology consists of problematic patterns of integrating relationships, and if the analyst is to engage the patient at all, she will inevitably be drawn into these patterns. The analyst is a part of the interpersonal field, a "participant" as well as an "observer." The analytic stance is not experienced by the patient simply as an absence, which allows uncontaminated projections from the patient's past; even the analyst's silence is a very real and powerful form of participation, with implications and consequences. Hence, personal feelings the analyst finds herself experiencing with the analysand and the forms of interaction she finds herself participating in are regarded as crucial data enabling the analyst to understand firsthand the nature of the patient's integrations with others and difficulties in living.

How is the analyst to *use* countertransferential data? What is the appropriate analytic demeanor? There is a broad continuum within interpersonal psychoanalysis on this question. Though generally agreeing that observation of one's own feelings, impulses, wishes, and so on provides crucial data for understanding the patient, different authors take very different positions on the use of such observations. Sullivan, who might be regarded as a conservative on this issue, urged the maintenance of the stance of "expert" throughout; the therapist uses his experience to gain understanding but does not act on it except interpretively. Fromm tends to put more weight on the active, intensely personal encounter between analysand and analyst, defining the latter's role as an "observant participant" (in contrast to Sullivan's "participant observer"). Tauber and Green (1959), Wolstein (1967), Epstein (1979), and Searles (1979a), each in his own fashion, take a more radical view, stressing the therapeutic value of a judicious acting on or sharing of countertransference experiences. Levenson (1983) has developed the intriguing argument that the analyst inevitably and often subtly acts out the countertransference no matter what he tries to do or thinks he is doing. Consequently, an authentic mutual sharing and inquiry into transference/countertransference patterns is the only basis for conducting analysis in good faith. The endless intricacies of the analytic relationship and its most therapeutic utilization continue to be one of the most important areas for new developments in theory and technique in the interpersonal tradition.

Roger: A Pseudoheterosexual Conversion

Psychoanalysis with an analysand who has been in a previous analysis with someone else combines, at least temporarily, the freshness of a honeymoon with the protected sagacity of the Monday morning quarterback. Luckily, all the issues that beset one's predecessor eventually find their way into the current treatment. A careful examination of earlier treatments, therefore, often provides clues to current and future impasses, detours, and temptations. In the case of Roger, the previous treatment highlights, by contrast, some of the major foci of interpersonal psychoanalysis, since the earlier treatment stressed behavior at the expense of character issues, sexuality over the quality of relatedness, and the past at the expense of the present.

Roger, an intermittently employed photographer, had originally entered treatment (with another analyst) in his midtwenties because of chronic, deep depressions with suicidal ideation. These depressions were often connected with his participation in short-term, homosexual relationships in which he appeared to be looking for an older man to take care of him, only to be repeatedly and painfully disillusioned. Over the course of this earlier analysis, Roger had given up his homosexual activities. He no longer acknowledged homosexual fantasies, and he had sexual relations with and eventually married a woman who was a colleague of the analyst. The analyst moved, somewhat precipitously, to another city, forcing what analyst and analysand both felt was a premature termination of their work. After a year's hiatus, Roger returned to treatment, complaining of a general sense of purposelessness, lack of assertiveness, and work inhibitions. Sexual activity with his wife had all but ceased prior to the announced departure of the analyst, but this did not seem particularly troubling to Roger.

Roger was the youngest of three children born to an upper-middle-class couple, both professionals, living in a large eastern city. Roger's mother was an extremely depressed woman who, because of maternal deprivation she had suffered, saw herself as a particularly hurt and "sensitive" person. His father was a very detached, secretive, and resigned man, a severe martinet with his children who on rare occasions exploded in bursts of anger. The mother had suffered a severe postpartum depression after the birth of her second child; she was hospitalized for two years, apparently mute most of that time. The father pleaded for her return to life to no avail, until she finally emerged from her depression with the resolve to have another child, who she assumed would be a girl. Roger was born instead.

The most striking feature of his childhood was a very intense, mutually idealizing relationship with his mother. She was greatly preoccupied with his cleanliness and reported having given him suppositories at the age of seven months in an effort to control his bowel movements. As he grew older, they shared a world view in which they were very different from everyone else and exquisitely attuned to each other, particularly in their "sensitivity" to the mother's depression. The father, who had felt guilty and somehow responsible for his wife's hospitalization, apparently gave over his youngest son to his wife's ministrations. Roger was a very "good" boy.

He felt himself to be different from the other boys and men, more "sensitive," caring, and refined. Although the content of his earliest sexual fantasies was homosexual, he would masturbate into one of his mother's old bedspreads, which he concealed in his closet and later buried. He was quite talented as a photographer, although he had great difficulties in committing himself to his work. He began having homosexual affairs on leaving home for college, and it was the frustration he felt in connection with these relationships that led him increasingly to the despair in which he sought treatment for the first time.

In interpersonal theory, the salient features of personality are determined not by the preferred mode of instinctual gratification but by the predominant patterns of integrating relationships in general, which are understood as established in repetitive interactions with early caretakers. Sexuality and aggression are understood not as independent energy sources but as modes of experiencing and behaving that serve as vehicles for integrating relationships with others. The patient's sexuality is seen as a crucial source of data, not because it determines the rest of personality development but because it tends to be representative of the way the patient integrates his relationships with other people. Sexuality is a function of character, not vice versa.

Of the clinical data presented so far, the following would stand out for the interpersonal analyst. Here is a man whose early life was dominated by his deeply depressed mother. His existence was her reason for living, yet by virtue of his gender, he was necessarily and inevitably a disappointment to her. She seems to have been preoccupied with a particular image of him as clean, sensitive, and exquisitely attuned to her. In many respects, Roger became the child she had wished for on reentering life from the hospital. One would suspect that she would have approved greatly of any gestures on his part toward caring, perceptiveness, and artistic expressiveness, while any gestures suggestive of stereotyped male behavior or any movements toward independence would have met with disapproval and anxiety. Her premature and invasive efforts to regulate his bowel functions indicate the extent to which she sought total access to and control over his mind and body in a desperate effort to buoy her own fragile sense of self. What of Roger's sexuality? Certainly, any masculine identification would be difficult to maintain; preserving his connection to his mother, essential as the only context in which he had ever experienced himself, seemed to require eschewing any sense of community with other men. The homosexual fantasies and secret masturbation were the only areas in his life in which he operated outside mother's purview and control.

These hypotheses concerning the history would be regarded as an important feature of the analysis, having emerged from and, in turn, guiding the detailed inquiry; the analyst would attempt to arrive at a consensus with the analysand about what had taken place. However, the interpersonal clinician would be particularly interested in using the historical data as a take-off point for exploring the way the analysand operates now. What is his characteristic mode of integrating current relationships? Does his sense of purposelessness and passivity indicate a perpetuation of the original self-surrender to the mother? Why was the active sexual relationship with the wife so short-lived? Roger's previous analysis clearly had an enormous impact on his life. One would expect that an inquiry into the nature of that relationship as well as the current analytic relationship would provide crucial clues to the way deleterious features of Roger's early interpersonal relationships were currently perpetuated in his characteristic difficulties in living.

The initial presentation of the first analyst to me was of a highly idealized figure who had saved Roger's life by his kindness and wisdom. Roger felt that he had a special facility as a psychoanalytic patient and that he had become his former analyst's prize patient. He spoke of psychoanalysis as if it were a religion to which he and both analysts belonged, which gave meaning to life and offered a suitable explanation for everything. He spoke of his "neurosis" and particularly of his former homosexuality as if he were speaking of sin, now renounced and behind him. Despite this account, his first dream in his second analysis was: "I was at a carnival or boardwalk. Nixon was there in his shirtsleeves, passing out leaflets, asking people to vote for him. I'm there feeling very sorry for him. I want somehow to protect him." His associations to Nixon were to the first analyst, although he had trouble accounting for the meaning of the pathetic huckster image in the dream. It was only much later, after considerable work had been done, that he was able to talk about negative feelings about the first analyst, and, finally, similar feelings about me. He saw both of us, allowing for some differences in details, as rather incompetent, depressed, and lonely figures, filling in their lives with patients.

The initial transference to me was characterized overtly by a pervasive compliance, in which I was idealized, in a fashion similar to his idealization of his wife and his first analyst. The analyst was all-knowing and perfect, and Roger, by being a good patient, was safe and protected in his care. As long as he handed over to me what I desired, his "dirty secrets," he would eventually be "cured." He would provide, with great facility, interesting dreams, slips, associations, and interpretations of his own, always ceding to me a final interpretive statement, which he would receive as truth and work assiduously at elaborating. However, his status as a patient also entailed his endurance of what Roger felt were various humiliating indignities, such as my notetaking and relative reticence. The compliance and pseudo collaboration were punctuated by outbursts of rage and a deep contempt when he felt particularly misused or insulted. The affects and thoughts within these rages, it soon became apparent, were split off from his ordinary state of mind, and after the rages he would have great difficulty remembering them, dismissing them as some strange, "neurotic" aberration.

It gradually became clear that Roger used his sexuality in the service of his compliant/defiant transference. He saw the analyst (I will use the singular to stand for both analysts) as representing "normality" or society at large, pervaded by a deep sense of moral righteousness, taking a highly condemnatory stand toward his former homosexuality and any current homosexual fantasies. Homosexuality was sinful and unquestionably bad and wrong. The analyst demanded his renouncing this evil and converting to heterosexuality, and his involvement as a patient in psychoanalysis entailed an apparent surrender to this moral demand. When these beliefs were clarified, his deep conviction and insistence that the analyst did indeed have such a moral investment in his transformation emerged. As I questioned this conviction, Roger gradually became aware of the following underlying beliefs: heterosexuality is boring and vapid; the analyst's own life is empty and dismal; he needs to pretend it is "good" and "right" and particularly to have the patient join him in this self-deception. The surrender to what he felt were the analyst's desperate needs was experienced by Roger as motivated by the deepest love, entailing his transforming himself to accord to what he felt were the moral standards of psychoanalysis as a world view. Nevertheless, he also hated the analyst/mother for his weakness, vulnerability, unavailability, and self-deception, and he used his homosexuality as an ultimate defiance of the mother/analyst—a defiance that he kept hidden. Despite his overtures to heterosexual transformation and his self-mortification for his "sinful" homosexuality, he secretly felt homosexuality to be superior, more exciting, more vital, more alive. It became clear that it was in his homosexual fantasies, which he kept for himself, that he felt most spontaneous and real. This part of himself, which the mother/analyst could not reach, even with her cleansing and regulating suppositories/interpretations, was where he secretly lived. The heterosexual transformation that had taken place in his first analysis was a "pseudoheterosexual" vehicle for the expression of his submission and surrender to the analyst/mother and a defense against the deeper, more vital, and also hostile and defiant homosexual feelings, which he felt he needed to keep out of the appropriative grasp of the analyst.

Freud's discovery of the pervasive influence of the past on the present marked, perhaps, the beginnings of all dynamic psychotherapy. For the interpersonal clinician, uncovering the past (filling in the amnesias, as Freud depicted it) does not itself constitute the focus of therapeutic activity. The past is important because it illuminates the way the patient integrates current interpersonal situations. A brief example of one key interchange during Roger's treatment will illustrate this difference in emphasis.

Roger began this particular session, several years into the therapy, in good spirits, reporting excitedly on various of his experiences. At some point I became aware that Roger's affect had changed—he seemed uneasy somehow, a bit shaken. Having no idea what had happened, I asked. He denied any change. Being quite convinced that something important had shifted, I pursued the matter. With a greatly pained, anguished expression, Roger acknowledged that something *had* happened but said he couldn't possibly talk about it. I tried to get him to talk about why talking about what had happened was out of the question. His vow of silence, he finally conceded, was not out of self-protection but out of a concern for me. No matter how much I might think I wanted him to tell me what had happened, it would be disastrous to me for him to do so. He *had* to refuse—for me.

As we continued to talk around the event itself, exploring his sense of my vulnerability and his protectiveness toward me (and, in my pursuit and his reluctant surrender of "material," acting out once again the central transference/countertransference configuration), the following account emerged. I had used a word Roger was unacquainted with. This filled him with terror. He immediately concluded that the word was a schizophrenic neologism—my psychosis was showing! As the inquiry deepened, it became apparent that he experienced me not simply as needful and as using conventionality as a status enhancer but as quite mad, desperately using my social role and therapeutic function to conceal my madness from others and from myself. On occasion he saw through this ruse (he *was* quite discerning about various ideosyncrasies and madness in me and others) and quickly undid his perception, both concealing it from me and almost instantly forgetting what he felt he had seen. To see what he took to be my psychosis was like peering into the heart of darkness, undoing the very presumptions about himself and others on which his world rested. "This is transference, I experienced you as my mother," Roger argued; "it was my mother who was crazy, not you." It was clear that talking about his mother's craziness was immeasurably more comfortable for him than talking about mine, that the genetic interpretation was a defense against the anxiety aroused by uncovering the structure of his pattern of integrating relationships in the here and now. (See Racker, 1968, and Gill, 1982, for similar accounts of the use of the past as a resistance to the transference.)

From the interpersonal point of view, what was crucial in this interaction was not the uncovering of the past or filling in gaps in memory but the elucidation of the predominant pattern of integrating current relationships with others. Roger had developed his sense of self in the context of his relationship with his mother, whom he experienced as extremely brittle and troubled, desperately holding herself together by tending to him, being a "normal," somewhat sanctimonious agent of the social order. Roger's personality shaped itself in complementarity to his mother's character. He became a devoted son, fashioning himself into his mother's image of him, which, on some level, he sensed kept her afloat. His surrender of self to her was an act of love; it also provided him with an enormous sense of power and importance. Other kinds of relationships seemed banal in comparison and also anxiety-provoking, as options outside the borders of the familiar, not based on what he felt most valuable to others about himself—his capacity for protective devotion. Roger's relationship to his wife was based on the same pattern as his relationship to both analysts; he felt deeply connected to someone only when he could experience that person as well-meaning but deeply troubled, buoying himself or herself by assuming some position of authority and knowledge, to which he could devote himself as an eager disciple, always reserving some secret defiance, often eroticized, where he felt more fully real. It was very important to perpetuate the idea of the other as deeply flawed and floundering, as it gave him a sense of meaning and importance; yet, he could never allow the other to know, because he believed—and needed to believe—that his view of the other as desperately self-deceiving was true. From an interpersonal point of view, the problem with the first analysis was in its emphasis on sexuality itself instead of the underlying character issues and in its undue focus on the past; it did not reveal and challenge the perpetuation of Roger's recurrent pattern of integrating relationships through pseudoheterosexual conversion in the transference.

The initial transference of compliance/defiance reemerged at intervals throughout the analysis, particularly in the service of resistant retreats from newly emerging anxieties. Throughout, the idea of psychoanalysis as a set of ethical and religious norms, with the analyst as priest, was a persistent transferential obstacle to authentic self-inquiry and spontaneous development. There were many dreams of churches and priests, and after a highly significant fight with his wife in which for the first time Roger really challenged what he had maintained was her infallibility, he said, "Last night I lost my temple—I mean temper."

As the central transference configuration of compliance/defiance was worked through over the course of the second analysis, homosexuality was freed from its use as a previous bastion of vitality and defense against surrender to the intrusive mother. Homosexual fantasies and activities emerged, with new dynamics and transferential meanings. Subsequent themes connected with homosexuality included the following: (1) The emergence of feelings of playfulness and competitiveness in the context of male camaraderie (for example, a pissing contest) and a playful teasing in the transference. (2) A longing for recognition from the father, expressed through fantasies of exhibitionism and voyeurism, within and outside the transference. Homosexual activities and fantasies played an important function in maintaining the belief that Roger's father had abandoned him to the mother's needfulness and in keeping alive the hope that he would one day reclaim him as a man among men. (3) The use of homosexual fantasies in the transference and provocative, seductive behavior to re-create the original erotic/sadomasochistic tie to the mother. (4) The use of homosexuality as a defense against newly emerging heterosexual feelings toward the mother and other women, so as to preserve the mother as pure. His homosexuality also served to protect her from his rage at her for what he felt had been her seduction and betrayal of him. Sex was seen as dirty, powerful, and dangerous—a woman could never survive being the object of his sexual desire. Homosexuality also preserved, in his fantasy, his flimsy relationship to his father, since it represented his renouncing his own sexual claims on his mother, allowing the father to keep her. (5) The use of nonheterosexuality as a symbolic and apparent sexlessness, preserving his role as the daughter who rescued the mother from her psychosis and his identification with what he experienced as the dead, depressive core of his mother, to which he felt eternally bound.

As the recurrent patterns in his structuring of relationships were clarified and worked through and the role of his sexuality in perpetuating those patterns illuminated, there was an enrichment of Roger's relations both with men and with women. He developed, for the first time, deep friendships with men, who were no longer only an occasion for a sexualized defiance of the mother/analyst/wife. In his relationships with women, Roger no longer acted only in a submissive or defiant way; he began to allow himself more spontaneous reactions to them, including sexual and aggressive feelings. It became possible for him to experience women as having an authentic sexuality of their own and a substantiality to them, making it unnecessary for him to either flee or buoy them up.

Paula: A Bumbling Allegiance

Paula, a woman in her midtwenties, sought treatment because of conflicts in her pursuit of a career, emotional constriction in her relations with others, and sexual dysfunction. She was very bright and hard-working, with a well-disguised, subtly superior, and disdainful attitude toward most people. She came from a deeply religious southern family whose missionary zeal and ascetic ideal set them apart from most people in their community. Paula was the eldest of three children; her brother and sister had remained in close proximity to the parents. Paula had sought a wider world and a professional career in law. Two incidents, one early in our work, the other toward the end, illustrate the kinds of issues that interpersonal theory tends to highlight and the kinds of entanglements and interactions that promote growth.

During the first six months of treatment, Paula had approached analysis and me cautiously but dutifully, always with at least some preselected material for discussion. Some work had been done on, among other issues, her ambivalence and considerable anger and scorn concerning her parents' religiosity and rituals and her forced participation in them. I had noticed, but not commented on, a brief smile, almost a sneer, that would flicker across her face as she entered the office. In the particular session I want to recount, Paula had come unprepared for the first time, itself a significant event. She was very anxious about not having anything to say immediately, and this time the smile persisted for a while. I asked her about the smile, but she could not account for it. She said that the only thing she was thinking of was how *she* was always supposed to start the session and how I was *always* initially silent. The rest of the session consisted of a number of detailed forays into various aspects of what she experienced as our ritualized, stylized, and rigid interaction and her fantasies of why sessions went in such a fashion. I eventually brought together the various lines into an interpretation: She felt that our relationship was ritualized, coercive, and silly in some ways; her smile reflected those thoughts, which were frightening and disturbing to her because she had had similar thoughts about her parents and their religion. Any expression of such thoughts had been treated in her family as blasphemy. She was worried that I took *my* religion, psychoanalysis, as seriously and humorlessly as her parents had taken theirs, demanding her total compliance and deference. That made her both angry and scornful but also frightened and dutiful. Although she had provided the raw data, Paula at first greeted this interpretation with some disclaimers, but over the course of the session she was able to do some work on various aspects of it, and to allow its possible credibility. Over the next several weeks, as this work continued, she seemed more relaxed, somewhat more accepting of her own conflictual feelings both toward her parents and toward me, and even a bit more playful.

What happens in this sort of interaction, a commonplace example of the nitty-gritty work of psychoanalysis, that may be useful? Ideas were communicated—she became somewhat clearer about her feelings, past and present. This is insight. There was also a moment of intense contact between us. The interpretation was given at points with a raised eyebrow and what I imagine was something of a twinkle in my eye, reflecting my bemusement at how seriously she believed I took myself. There was an implicit communication and demonstration that I was not the patient's image of her father and that she did not have to act with all men in the constricted fashion in which she felt compelled to act with him. Something changed the quality of the relatedness between us at that point. The insight and the shift in the relatedness are two different features of that identical moment, that same process. The ideas are inseparable from the analytic engagement in the inquiry. From the interpersonal point of view, interpretation is a form of participation, and forms of interaction convey interpretive messages. The interaction between Paula and me might be looked at from either angle, but a full appreciation of the event and its ameliorative effects requires an appreciation of both the information conveyed and the participation experienced.

Several years later, Paula had been going through a period of time during which she had been feeling increasingly self-confident and satisfied in various areas of her life. She had been functioning quite well on a job that brought her into just the sort of interpersonal situations which had caused her the greatest anxieties, and she had responded in a way that greatly enhanced her sense of her own resources and capacities. Limitations inherent in this particular position became apparent, however, and Paula began to consider inquiring into other job possibilities. The best way to go about this seemed to be to call up several contacts supplied to her by various friends and to sound them out on whether they could be of any help. She opened a session by reporting on her decision to pursue this route. A friend had given her the name of a friend of his who might be able to help and who was awaiting her call, but she experienced considerable anxiety in anticipating making this call, the kind of anxiety that had characterized her earlier fears of making contacts with others. Oddly, the anxiety about the call seemed little affected by her recent successes and growing sense of confidence.

An inquiry into her anticipations of the phone call revealed the following dilemma. Making such calls is impossibly awkward, she argued. This was a friend of a friend who was only vaguely aware of her situation and intention to call. She had two choices. She could state her purpose and ask for help immediately, without allowing time for them to chat and get to know each other; this seemed too abrupt and presumptuous. Or she could start off by trying to engage the other in a friendly chat without announcing the purpose of her call; this seemed likely to be puzzling and irritating to him. No, there was no way such a call could be made that would feel at all comfortable. Paula felt stymied and chagrined that nothing seemed to have been gained by her positive experiences.

I felt a matching bewilderment, not at how such a call could be made, but at how something relatively simple had become so convoluted. Surely, making such calls is somewhat awkward and anxiety-provoking for many people. In Paula's case, such a situation had multiple dynamic meanings, all of which had been explored to some extent in our work: a phobic attitude to even small degrees of anxiety and discomfort; fantasies that others were able to function in a perfect, seamless fashion; fears of her own aggressiveness, connected with a sense of fragility in her parents as well as a dread of angry, punishing retaliation from them for any diminution of deference; fears of intruding on others, linked to a sense of the parents as over-burdened as well as a wish to intrude and make her needs known in an angry, peremptory fashion; conflicts involving gender definitions of womanhood; and a secret identification with an image of the father as sadistic. However, *this* situation had a peculiar, paralyzing intensity, which seemed puzzling. I said that I could appreciate the tension she described between friendliness and purposiveness; it seemed to me that most people announced their purpose at the beginning of the conversation in a general fashion, entered into some friendly conversation, and then returned after a while to restate their request more explicitly. What would be the problem with doing it in such a fashion, I wanted to know, an approach that I was sure must have occurred to her? She responded by describing a desire to be "stubborn" about this issue, to *not* figure it out. Surely, there were other people who could interact that way—cool, suave types who "have it all together" in social and business situations. She did not want to be that way; it was better to be sincere and bumbling. After a considerable silence we determined that she was (understandably) annoyed at me for suggesting, even if somewhat obliquely, an "obvious" solution. It reminded her of her parents, who were always telling her the "right way" to do things.

Paula spent quite a bit of time mulling over these events between sessions and began next time by acknowledging that she felt defensive about what she felt were gaps in her early social experiences. It was difficult for her to come to terms with how "out of it" she had felt in high school, for example, since her family's values were so different from those of her peer group. There was so much she did not know about how to dress, how to behave, and so on, and there was nobody who would be receptive to her asking. She had to go it alone. After exploring this facet of her "not knowing," I pointed to another dimension of what had happened in the previous session. She had got angry at me for telling her what seemed obvious, and in thinking about it, I felt she was right. At times, I realized, she spoke as if she could not imagine where to begin in dealing with social situations, which, particularly more recently, was not true. In my own bumbling fashion, I had unwittingly tried to offer her concrete advice, which, I realized on reflection, she did not really need but somehow seemed to elicit. In the previous session she had spoken of a sense of stubbornness and disdain for conventional socializing. It seemed that part of her "not knowing" was an active defiance, a wanting to not know.

She too had been struck by her defiance and had been thinking about various other aspects of her life in which she seemed to cultivate the image of herself as a bumbler, not "sophisticated" like those who were more socially and sexually successful. She was becoming more aware of how anxious she was about her growing interpersonal skills and particularly her enjoyment of them. To be comfortable with other people and to take pleasure in them ran counter to the basic values that had been stressed over and over in her family—the importance of self-discipline, humility, menial labor, of being an outcast, a gadfly to the social order, and so on. Her recent experiences and satisfactions ran counter to all that. By remaining a bumbler, Paula thought, it was as if she were telling others, and also telling herself, that she never really liked her social and professional activities that much, that she did not spend that much time at them or value them.

In the following session Paula presented a long, complicated dream that included the following highlights.

> She was teasing one of her younger siblings—her mother criticized her—she told her mother to go away—mother kept it up—she "blew up" and screamed at her mother to go—later her mother came up to her and said, "I finally know now what the problem is—I left you alone too much when I took you to church." Paula didn't know exactly what this meant and somehow never was able to clarify it with her mother in the dream—later there was a dog with a dislocated paw—Paula tried to help, but the dog was in too much pain and was drawing away—she couldn't fix it.

One set of the multiple meanings in this dream seemed to reflect Paula's efforts to work through some of the issues of the previous sessions. Paula felt imposed on by her parents' values, interfered with. She had absorbed them deferentially, with a secret defiance. Now she was in the process of throwing them off, reclaiming her own strengths through her current activities. She feared this would be damaging to her mother and her feelings about her mother. Could they both tolerate facing how alone Paula had really felt as a child despite the familial and religious trappings? Would Paula's mother be able to tolerate her differentiation and her anger, or would she recoil in pain so that there would be no way for Paula to reconcile herself with her, to reach her? Similarly, I too acted in a manner that felt critical and interfering. This response was partly invited by Paula's way of presenting herself as a perpetual bumbler who needed active guidance. It was also desired in some way, as Paula felt that I too left her too much alone, that beneath the trappings of psychoanalysis she sometimes felt lonely and abandoned. Better that I be interfering than withdrawn. Yet she also resented the interference and had told me to stop. Was I resilient enough to tolerate her dismissal and to stay related to her as she found her own way? Or would I retreat into an unreachable pain? Was I one of the "sophisticated" community, forever remote from her, or a bumbler whom she could secretly identify with yet despise? Or could we work out a way of interacting that contained both effectiveness and some awkwardness for both of us?

Among the various issues raised by this series of sessions, I want to call attention to the participatory nature of the analytic role. The analysand's paralysis called forth a response that operated as an interference. She became annoyed and told me so, and the interaction became the basis both for gathering important information and for deepening our relationship. The patient's self-presentation was aimed at eliciting a response that she both desired and was enraged at. My participation in re-creating this paradigmatic interaction allowed a fuller understanding of what had happened between Paula and her parents, as well as a medium through which Paula and I struggled to relate to each other in a way that was intimate yet respectful of boundaries. From the interpersonal point of view, the analytic position is not established someplace outside the entanglements of the patient's neurosis. The analyst pursues the inquiry and, in so doing, finds himself enmeshed. It is the patient's and analyst's collaborative efforts to disentangle themselves from the patient's characteristic patterns of integration that constitute the most important therapeutic action of clinical work.

Sam: Depression as Ideology

Sam, a physician in his early thirties, came to therapy because of compulsive overeating, recurrent depressions, and a long-standing romantic involvement with a woman considerably more overweight and depressed than he, whom he wanted to leave but could not. The most striking feature of his life was its marked unevenness. He was an extremely capable and creative person, highly successful and respected in his career, and yet his most intimate relationships had been adhesive, joyless attachments to others seen as disadvantaged in some important respect. He and his lover would spend a considerable portion of the time they were apart on the telephone with each other, not talking, but listening to each other breathe, keeping alive the contact.

Sam was the older of two children born to second-generation Eastern European parents who had both felt deeply crushed by life. His mother's family had been impoverished and dominated by her tyrannical, repressive father. Sam's mother, frightened and terribly shy, had led an isolated, sheltered life, finally marrying, quite late, a man who seemed to offer some hope of escape. Sam's father, in his younger years, was a vital, expansive, somewhat manic character who offered Sam a lively and crucially important alternative to his mother's anxious attempts to control and protect him. When Sam was four, a sister was born, who came to represent all the mother's hopes and dreams. Although it was openly denied for years, it slowly became apparent that a traumatic birth had left her severely brain-damaged. This blow, in addition to several crushing business failures and illnesses, led to a deep, depressive withdrawal by both parents. They would take hot baths for hours, lie around in bed, often with the damaged child, and take joy only in gluttonous eating. The family members, apart from Sam, became slovenly and inactive. Sam was viewed ambivalently. On the one hand, he was the family's emissary to the real world, he would take care of them and save them; on the other hand, his involvement with life was viewed suspiciously, as an abandonment and betrayal.

Of the many areas we explored over the years of our work together, I would like to focus on the function of Sam's depression as a mechanism for maintaining his attachment to his family and one crucial interaction between the two of us that illustrates how this attachment was established and eventually relinquished in the analytic relationship. Sam and his family, as we gradually discovered, had come to make depression a credo, a way of life. The world was seen as a uniformly painful place, filled with suffering. People who enjoyed life were shallow, intellectually and morally deficient by definition, frivolous and uninteresting. Sam was drawn to people who seemed to suffer greatly, was extremely empathic with and helpful to them, and then felt ensnared. The closest possible experience between people, he felt, is to cry together; joy and pleasure are private, draw one away, are almost shameful. Although we had explored various fantasies concerning *my* suffering, his solicitous ministrations, and our languishing forever together in misery, the mechanism of self-perpetuated depression was expressed most clearly in one particular session. He had come in one day feeling good, following some exciting career and social successes. As it happened, on that day I *was* feeling miserable; I had a bad head cold and was consoling myself as unobtrusively as possible with cough drops and tissues. Soon into the session, his mood dropped precipitously and pervasively as he began to speak of various areas of painful experience. I stopped him, and we were able to reconstruct what had happened, to trace his depressive response back to the point of anxiety. With hawklike acuity, he had perceived my congestive misery. He felt horrified to find himself feeling good and excited in the presence of my suffering. An immediate depressive plunge was called for. To feel good and alive when someone else was hurting seemed a barbaric crime, risking hateful retaliation and the destruction of the relationship altogether. His approach to all people he cared about, we came to understand, was to lower his own mood to ''the lowest common denominator.'' To simply enjoy himself and his life, without constantly toning himself down and checking in with the depressive pulse of others, would risk his being seen as a traitorous villain and, as a consequence, total isolation. I asked him in that session whether it had occurred to him that I might *not* resent his good mood but that, from the misery of my cold, I might actually feel enlivened or cheered by his enthusiasm and vitality. This *had* never occurred to him, seemed totally incredible, and provoked considerable reflection. Through this and similar exchanges our relationship gradually changed, articulating old patterns of integration and exploring new possibilities.

Thus, Sam's depression came to be understood as a means of perpetuating his characteristic mode of integrating relationships with others and as a means of controlling anxiety. In his family, people felt connected to each other through psychic pain, inadequacy, and defeat. The sense of depressive fusion between the parents and the despairing caretaking of the damaged sister became models of human intimacy. To relate in other ways and to take full ownership of his own resources and successes were pervaded by intense anxiety—the anxiety of the unfamiliar and the anxiety of options incompatible with the familial mode of contact.

In one session, after several years of treatment, Sam experienced for the first time a deep sense of euphoria, which precipitated an anxiety attack. He moved from feeling intensely joyful and buoyant to feeling lighter and lighter, less and less substantial, to a terror of floating off into space, losing touch with others altogether. To feel joy placed him outside the family, outside the realm of deep human connections. From an interpersonal point of view, what was most deeply repressed in Sam was precisely his capacity for joy, which had become "not-me" because it aroused the deepest anxiety in his parents, the greatest threat to their characterological patterns of living.

Sam presented the following dream toward the end of treatment, during a period when he had been experiencing himself and his relationships with others in a more positive way. Like all important experiences that stretch the boundaries of the self-system, these changes made him anxious. He feared that it was his depression and sensitivity to depression in others that made him a desirable person.

I am on a small island off the mainland with my parents and sister. I take a boat to the mainland to pick up some things or do some errand. There is a carnival going on. I walk around, watching the people, participating, having a great time. Then I remember that I must return to the island. I get in the boat and try to go back, but insects come and sting me. If I move back and stop rowing, they stop. I start to move toward the island and they sting again. I stop; they stop. I am very conflicted about what to do. After a long time of trying and stopping, I give up with a sense of relief and rejoin the activities on the mainland.

The dream seemed to capture Sam's experience at that point in treatment. He had begun to feel a sense of the rich possibilities that life and other people offer. Yet he also felt bound by his loyalties to his family and their ways. The connection to them was maintained through a stinging pain. As long as he suffered as they had, remaining isolated from others, he was bound up with them. To live more fully was to abandon them and the security that the tie to them provided. From the interpersonal point of view, characterological change comes not in renouncing infantile wishes but in the anticipation that tolerating anxiety long enough to make satisfaction possible (the mainland) will be less painful in the long run than the illusory security provided by the familial (the island) and the familiar.

❧ 10 ❧

Existential Analysis

Herbert Holt

Existential analysis serves a contemporary need of many people as one modern approach to psychoanalysis. It is addressed to patients who have difficulty in finding meaning and purpose in life and in maintaining their identity. This form of therapy is helpful to people who need to learn to separate themselves out as individuals from contemporary mass society.

Each historical period has therapies that can help individuals overcome the pull of their families, friends, and institutions and so maintain their own identity. Freudian psychoanalysis originally addressed itself to problems of repressed sexuality and hostility in Vienna and middle Europe from the 1880s to the 1920s. At that time, people needed a new therapy that was not religiously or philosophically grounded but found its strength in being underpinned by a method of treatment based on biological and scientific assumptions of their time.

Alfred Adler and participants in the beginning interpersonal schools were socialists who were idealistically interested in the welfare of the underclass (*Lumpenproletariat*) and of the blue-collar working class who could not afford expensive individual psychotherapy. Later the impact of World War II on society included political and economic upheaval as well as the destruction of moral values and expectations of the reliability of society. Existential philosophies provided the foundation for therapies that addressed themselves to the alienated, fragmented, broken individual who found no succor or reliance in family or the institutions of society during this time. These resentful, alienated people worried not only about their economic and political survival but about how they could survive from day to day and maintain their identity. They needed therapies that addressed their own daily needs and problems more than dealing with their sexuality and aggression. Psychoanalysis started to move its focus away from issues of unconscious, repressed libido drives and unconscious aggression toward an ego psychology that dealt more with the problem of living in an uncertain world where parents did not have standards to successfully raise children in a constantly changing environment. These new therapies, therefore, focused on preoedipal influences and on developing theories that would serve new needs through interpersonal analysis and eventually through existential analysis.

Some of the contemporary therapies tried to maintain theoretical continuity, adjusting Freudian theories to the new realities, and tried to deal as well with issues such as loneliness, isolation, fear of death, and fear of life. Among the psychoanalysts who tried to keep the Freudian heritage was Ludwig Binswanger, who based his existential analysis, which he called "Daseinanalysis," on the work of Freud. He and his associates, however, maintained that their generation had to focus on problems of isolation and dislocation of whole societies and groups that the original Freudian psychoanalysts had not had to deal with. Existential analysis is one of the few contemporary therapies that accept and use the findings of object theories, ego theories, and interpersonal theories as a basis for existential therapy.

Existential analysis deals with the problem of being-in-the-world (or *Dasein*) in a threefold manner, establishing an identity with and over and against the subjectively experienced world. The three ways of being-in-the-world that one experiences psychologically, either one at a time or simultaneously, are the *Eigenwelt* (one's inner world of thoughts, fantasies, wishes, and dreams), the *Mitwelt* (one's world in relation to other people), and the *Umwelt* (one's experience of the surrounding environment). We experience this psychological threefold expression of being-in-the-world from different points of view as we shift automatically and without awareness, as in a rheostat, from one to another of the three parts of the biological triune brain.

MacLean (1964) recognized that the large forebrain of the human is the result of millions of years of evolutionary development and that we have three living brains, which usually work together to adapt to the constantly changing environment. MacLean's theory of the triune brain led to the recognition of three modes of being-in-the-world corresponding to the three brains. The first brain, which MacLean labeled the alligator brain, gives rise to the magic mode of being-in-the-world and has the most restricted view of oneself in one's world. It is an impulse, action brain that leads to immediate action and reaction. It knows only one time, the here and now. The person experiences himself or herself as the center of the universe and other people as existing to meet his or her needs.

The second mode, the black and white mode, is based on the midbrain, classified by MacLean as the emotional brain or childbrain. There is an effort to control the archaic, primitive brain. The world is no longer magical; a sense of intentionality, more self-reliance, and self-confidence appear. The person still experiences himself or herself as the center of the universe, but since there is the beginning of an identity and a sense of separateness from other people and the self-created world, other people are experienced as potentially for or against the person, and negotiation is possible.

The third mode of being-in-the-world is the holistic mode. The world is seen from a different perspective. It is seen as larger, with many more possibilities, not just black or white, love or hate, good or bad. The person becomes conscious that he or she is not in the center of the universe. The person knows that he or she is a separate being, living and dying in his or her own skin, as other people are living and dying in theirs, and that we are thrown into a world of being together, where communication is possible. The person can become consciously aware of the network of historical, cultural, religious, and social thoughts, which go beyond immediate cause and effect. Through conscious awareness, a person can make appropriate rational and emotional decisions, not based only on the here and now but considering past development and projecting plans for the immediate and long-range future.

The findings of MacLean (1948), with his focus on the living triune brain, are a new underpinning of Freud's clinical and intuitive knowledge of unconscious, preconscious, and conscious phenomena. Existential analysis focuses on the total brain, taking a Gestalt position. Even the smallest unit (a dream, an illusion, a delusion, or an interpersonal experience) is a holistic experience and must be understood in the context of a network of thoughts and feelings that occur in time in our mind, with or without awareness. They can be made conscious in therapy as part of a larger view of the human being and his or her relationships, desires, and beliefs. Conscious, authentic awareness of self in one's experience with other people in one's world is an essential goal of existential therapy.

First Encounter with Nancy W.

After phoning me for an appointment on the recommendation of a former student of mine, Nancy W. presented herself on time the next day in my New York office. She was a very attractive thirty-nine-year-old woman with blue eyes and blond hair, wearing a light blue, expensive-looking suit with proper accessories and carrying a mink coat even though it was only October. Her personal appearance was surprisingly different from what I expected. On the phone she had sounded harassed, depressed, unhappy, claiming that she had come from a southern city to New York to escape life with her husband. To me, the inconsistency between the desperate way she sounded on the telephone and her appearance and strong, direct communication seemed paradoxical.

I inquired what brought her to New York. She told me that she had two children, a boy aged twelve and a girl aged six, and a husband, a prominent realtor, who she claimed had married her because he wanted a young wife (not older than twenty-eight) who was intelligent and charming and who could and would give him children. (It appeared to me that he had married her not for her own sake but for the function she would be capable of performing for him, as in a business partnership, and that her attitude had been much the same.) She told me that their first meeting had been at the bar of a large and prominent hotel where she worked as an assistant to the general manager. She had just recently come there, having finished studying hotel administration at a well-known university.

She said, "A few nights ago I ran away from my husband in the middle of the night. I couldn't stand living with him any longer." I asked her what had happened. She told me that she came from the north, from a prominent family of bankers. She was used to freedom from control and had a master's as well as a bachelor's degree in hotel administration from a prominent university. She was an adventurous young thing and went down to a prominent southern hotel, where she met a thirty-six-year-old "southern gentleman" who impressed her with his verbal and emotional ardor and his desire for her. She had never met a man who, on the second date, said that he wanted to marry her and have children with her, that he thought she was the most wonderful woman he had ever met. Even though she was a little scared and suspicious, she was flattered and her adventurousness overcame her. When she saw his estate and the style in which he lived, she agreed to marry him. I asked her in a kind but firm way why she had gone off the main point of her story. I felt that she had a story to tell that was very important to her, but instead of answering my question about what had happened, she had avoided coping with it by trying to impress me with her background, education, and status. I was interested in why she had had to "escape" from her husband and how she had managed to come here.

She told me smilingly, "Excuse me. A few days ago my husband began to beat me again in a drunken stupor and called me names like 'slut' and 'cheap New York whore.' He started to rape me and threatened to shoot me. It just became too much for me, so I decided to leave then and there while my husband, after raping me, slept in an alcoholic stupor. I gathered my children, took some of my clothes, and, driving all night, came to New York vowing, 'I will never go back!' I was scared, but my depression gradually began to leave me as I drove. I felt liberated at last, but infuriated and brutalized. I didn't drive immediately to my parents' home but went to a childhood friend whom I knew in college, and she promised me not to reveal to anybody that I was here in New York."

I expressed my genuine sympathy for her plight of being married to such an abusive man. She looked at me with great hostility, expressing an inner state of anger, and said, "I will never return. This is a lethal relationship. He's mad. He tries to drive me crazy." I asked her whether anyone in the town where she used to live knew about her disappearance. "No one does as far as I know," she said. She had called her parents and told them she had left her husband but had asked them not to reveal that she was in New York. She did not tell them where she was staying and with whom. Since she had cash of her own (she had taken with her all the cash she could find in the house, from a strongbox, and her jewelry), she felt temporarily safe until her parents told her that her husband had called them, saying that she must be with them, that they were "in cahoots" with her, that they had probably encouraged her to run away with his children, that nobody leaves him, that he would come up with a gun and take her back, and that if she did not come back, he would kill them. "He verbally abused my parents on the phone and said that it was all their fault for having raised such a daughter who was nothing but a 'slut.'"

I became quite uncomfortable and wondered why her husband was filled with such hatred and fear. Was he a latent homosexual who hated women? Why this paranoia and desire for revenge?

She said her father, who was seventy-eight years old and suffered from heart disease, had got very upset. He told his daughter, after listening to her story on the phone, that he was happy she did not tell him where she was, that he could not take it and did not want to know. It was too much for him, and he was afraid of having a coronary if he became too involved. Her mother, in her usual calm way, reassured her on the phone that she had done the right thing. She told Nancy firmly that she would give her all the support she could, both emotionally and financially. Nancy was their only child, and the mother told her she would leave $20,000 with Nancy's aunt who lived in Westchester County. Nancy was free to pick up the money any time she wished. Her mother wanted her to get the best possible lawyer, and since her husband was threatening their lives, they would hire a detective to guard Nancy and her children. They would also go to a lawyer friend to see what action they could take against her husband, because under the façade of being a gentleman, he was a potentially violent person, and they were afraid he really would come up north and try to kill them.

When asked how she felt about her mother's generosity in trying to help her, Nancy exclaimed, "I hate my mother. She is a killer. She is a dominating bitch. I'll fight her to the death. She wasn't and is not a good nurturing mother. She is like a wolf destroying her own young." I was aghast at this outbreak of preconscious and unconscious material so early in our relationship. The degree of hostility she felt and communicated was very strong. She seemed to have very brittle defenses against unconscious experiences. Her fear and hatred of her mother appeared very intense and sincere to me.

Nancy started to cry, and her voice became high-pitched. In front of my eyes, she regressed to the state of infancy. She lost her sense of orientation and said, "I'm really scared he might get me. You must help me! This is horrible!" She sank to the floor, sliding off her chair. "I can't understand this. Why does this have to happen to me? I've done nothing. He will come up! He will shoot my parents! He will shoot me and my children!" She jumped up from the floor, grabbed her mink coat, and said, "I better leave." I calmed her down, reassuring her that no one could enter this office with a shotgun, that we had doormen and locked doors, and that she was suffering from imagination that takes over. She surged toward me, crying aloud, "You must protect me!" and, trying to embrace me, cried bitterly on my shoulder. At this point, I felt even more uncomfortable and began to be scared myself. I said to myself, "This is too complicated a situation. This is not only an analytic situation but predominantly an interpersonal, realistic problem, and maybe I shouldn't or don't want to be involved in it. I don't need it."

I pulled myself together and said to her, "Look, it's understandable to get panicky; you're a brave woman." But she said, "No, I am not. You're just trying to make me feel better. I brought this all on myself. I'm a lousy mother. I took my children away from their father. They need him very badly. He is a good father to them." I asked her how she could say that. She avoided the issue by saying, "Proof of the pudding is that I cleared out the strongbox of $65,000 in cash, that I threw into my two suitcases the most expensive clothes for myself but barely took a change of clothes for my children. I am a mean, selfish, greedy woman." At the same time, she began to pull her hair with both hands.

I sat down and said, "Look, I'm a psychoanalyst and don't practice psychiatry any longer. You may need, in addition to me, someone who will give you medication to temporarily calm you down until you are ready and capable of functioning without these severe, angry anxiety attacks." She said, "No, I don't want medication. You're trying to get rid of me. You're like the rest of them. You only want easy cases. I'm not a case. I'm a human being who needs help. I had my pills. They don't work for me. They only make me listless. My previous doctor wanted to increase the dosage so I should be calm and collected and probably more servile and smacked around by my husband. He's a brute! All you men are brutes!" I said nothing and agreed to see her the same day again for another appointment in the afternoon. I felt exhausted but realized that this self-rejecting woman needed someone professionally who would take the responsibility of seeing her through a very trying life situation.

In existential analysis one tries to understand the other person (client/patient) and oneself from the subjective point of view of the other and, using the therapist's abilities of sympathy, empathy, intuition, and personal experience, to understand the encounter with the other person. Every encounter is a kind of invention, a scenario between two persons. It is an imaginative narrative, communicated from one human being to another in verbal and nonverbal form. We are trying to understand the communication of another person to us, to understand the emotional and circumstantial behavior of another person. This ability to link events into a structure and to create a communicative narrative is found not only in dreaming but also in conscious communication. We try to understand the verbal communications and give them a frame of reference and an order.

The effort to give meaning and purpose to our lives is uniquely human and is built genetically into our triune brain structure (MacLean). Without this capacity, we could not understand or create patterns in life, and we would conceive of life as a kind of meaningless chaos. We impose on the world our own concept of time and space in order to orient ourselves in the world.

The encounter with Nancy W. starts with the therapist's getting a phone call, and like most therapists, I experienced the phone call through the mode of being that I was experiencing at that moment. It appears that she had sudden mood shifts, which could follow each other in short sequences, showing different aspects of her personality, but she was aware of her shifts. She appeared very dramatic, a self-confronter who described her problem in the social context of her marriage. Her relationship to me was a direct, naked confrontation of the truth she saw at the moment and was communicating her panic and other life experiences. She forced the therapist to experience her in dramatic confrontation with his own personality.

Session with "Lost in the World" Dream

A few weeks later, Nancy brought me a dream without my asking for it and started the session by saying:

Nancy: Dr. Holt, I don't know if you're interested in dreams, but I had a horrible dream which I want to share with you. I've had similar dreams quite often during the last couple of years in one form or another, and I feel lost, confused, and scared in them. I usually try to forget them as fast as I can because I feel uncomfortable with them. They are not nightmares, but I wake up about 4 A.M., usually not knowing where I am for a moment, and I'm so relieved to find myself in bed. I get up, go to the bathroom and back to bed, and it takes me at least an hour to fall asleep again. I'm fearful I will start this intense dream sequence again.

Dr. Holt: Would you be so kind as to tell me the dream first as an experience without comments, and later on I'll teach you how to handle dreams yourself if you want to learn to. You can give me your spontaneous associations to the dream later if we need them.

Nancy: Well, before I tell you the dream, I will tell you that I don't know if I can trust you enough with my inner life to tell you the dream. I never tell dreams to anybody. I'm not basically a trusting person.

Dr. Holt: I understand. I think trust has to be earned mutually. Did you not tell any dreams to your previous psychotherapist?

Nancy: No, he wasn't my psychotherapist. There is nothing wrong with me. He was just a pill pusher. I felt very bad taking the pills and refused to take them regularly.

Dr. Holt: What kind of pills did your doctor give you?

Nancy: Oh, some kind of pills for anxiety, like Librium and Valium. When I was agitated, he gave me some tranquilizers, but I told him I didn't want them. I refused to take them. They'll poison me, and I refused to go to him.

Dr. Holt: Do you permit me to call him and find out what his impression was about your case?

Nancy: Definitely not! I resent your thinking of me as a case. I'm a human being who suffers greatly! I am no case! That makes me more suspicious of you. I wonder if you think of all the people who come to you for help as cases.

Dr. Holt: I apologize. I didn't mean it in the sense that you experience it.

Nancy: Well, anybody can say that. You are a professional person. You have been recommended to me. You know how sensitive patients are.

Dr. Holt: I apologized before and I apologize again. I didn't mean that you are a case in the sense that you mean it. I mean an oral or written report that he would give me. You don't have to give me permission to speak to him, but I thought it would just clarify for me how he experienced you. Do you mind going on telling me the dream now?

Nancy: I don't know. I'm really upset. Maybe I expect too much of you, and you know by now that I have difficulty in trusting. I feel like a cat going around a hot plate of meat.

Dr. Holt: Well, let's try. You can always stop your communication if you don't feel like talking.

Nancy: I don't know. What I actually wanted to tell you is that my mother left a message with my aunt that my husband has arrived in New York and is staying at the Waldorf Astoria. I had previously given my phone number to my aunt with explicit instructions not to reveal the number to my mother. My husband made a great scene on the phone, saying that he doesn't want me back, that I'm a slut, that he wants his kids back, and how could I do this to him. He seems to have been very angry with me. He ranted and raved about how he gave me everything he could and it was never enough, that they raised me like a princess, and that he wanted his children back. And then he broke down and cried bitterly. My father couldn't take it. He had an angina attack and went to the bedroom. My mother claims she calmed my husband down and felt very angry with him. She told him not to call anymore, that whatever problems he has, he can go the legal route, and that I'm not ready to see him or send my children back.

As she said this, Nancy sounded very angry and at the same time looked scared, spouting it all out in a staccato tone and frequency. She started to cry, but this time she did not lose conscious awareness of who she was, where she was, and who I am. After crying for a few minutes while nothing was said by either of us, she began again:

Nancy: OK, I'm ready to tell you my dream, but keep it strictly confidential. I'll try out if I can trust you a little.

Dr. Holt: My God, you really have courage and patience. But can you tell me

Nancy: [speaking as gently as I could] where are the children? Are they with you? Have you somebody taking care of them? Will you continue to live with your friend? Or do you intend to move?

Nancy: I don't know what's the matter with you! I wonder if you really want me to tell you the dream. Twice you have already interrupted my thoughts by bringing up issues that would interest you. Once about the pills which my doctor gave me, and now you ask me where my children are. You're like my husband!

I thought, "Oh, boy! I think it was too early to help her project images onto me." The first scenario, or "set-up," I used was to facilitate her projecting a previous doctor image onto me, which gave her a chance to vent a lot of hostility but mildly confused her, probably because it was too early. Now, by asking her where her children were, I set her up again, I believe prematurely, and interrupted her thoughts about her dream, which she had great difficulty in dealing with anyhow. At this point in the session I wondered whether I wanted to hear her dream then or later.

Dr. Holt: You're right. It is very painful to work through, not only for you but also for me. We are two living human beings who are imperfect and are trying to establish a different and new mode, an analytic mode, of relating to each other, and in time we can hopefully establish a greater degree of trust.

Nancy: You talk too much! I don't want to relate to you socially! I don't care what you feel! I pay you a horrendous sum of money. I would like you to see yourself as a service person of mine—like a servant. What is this! Look, get it clear in your mind. I'm a troubled person. I'm in pain!

Many patients cannot stand consciously to have the analyst relate to them in a friendly way. They experience friendliness as a negative set-up, not as part of a human relationship. Not everything between patient and analyst is transference/ countertransference. There are direct conscious communications with their own emotional tone. In common with Freudian psychoanalysis's position on the automatic, compulsive feelings of the archaic brain and midbrain, we do not believe that a person is fully determined by his or her impulses. However, we do not think or agree with existential philosophers who believe in absolute freedom. Unaware of MacLean and his associates and untrained in the biology or physiology of the human brain, they came to erroneous conclusions. Medically trained analysts see that their theories about freedom apply only to the functions of the neocortex.

After Nancy's last remark, I did not say anything. I felt it was not the right time. Instead of pursuing further remarks and questions, I wanted to give her a chance to tell the dream. I continued:

Dr. Holt: Please tell me the dream. We'll eventually have a professional, human relationship.

Nancy: [Pulling herself together and putting her hands on her knees] I am in a city, like New York, a big city which I feel I know. It is a world which is familiar to me, or should be, but I am alone. People are walking in every direction and pass me by. Cars come and go. It's daytime. The sky is gray, but it doesn't feel cold and wintery. I don't know anybody; nobody knows me. My children are not with me. I feel vaguely sure that I know where I am going. I want to visit my parents, who live on the East Side, but the streets have different names and I can't find their house. So I take a bus downtown, or I think it is downtown, but I don't know where I am. But I do know who I am. I'm at my present age and well dressed. So I approach a cop and say, "Isn't this New York?" He looks at me suspiciously and says, "Of course, madam. Can I help you?" I look in my pocket and open up my purse and give him the address of my parents. He says such a street doesn't exist in Manhattan. I ask, "Are you sure?" I get confused. I feel woozy and a little anxious, and a cold sweat goes down my face. I say, "Well, I have the phone number." I say thank you to him and go to the nearest phone booth, which, to my amazement, only takes quarters. I'm sure it is the number of my parents. I call and a strange voice answers, "This is the New York Public Library. You have the wrong number." I look through the phone book to see if I have written the wrong number down, but their name is not in the phone book. I call Information, and they say the number is confidential and cannot be given out. But at least I have established that I am in New York and that my parents have a phone number. And this is my dream. I awake mildly anxious, sweaty, and confused. I think I know the city, I think I know where I want to go, and then everything gets confusing. I feel very upset. I'm lost in the dream. Doctor, what do you make out of this?

Dr. Holt: In existential analysis, we believe that the dream is like a theater play in which the background and foreground in the dream and the people who appear in them express the mode of how we experience being-in-the-world while dreaming at that time. What does the dream mean to you?

Nancy: I'm lost. I'm lost in the world. I'm lost in New York. I'm lost in a world which should be familiar to me but which I find out isn't. It only appears so. It isn't really familiar to me. I can't find my parents. I can't go home again.

Dr. Holt: You know, we dream intentionally.

Nancy: You mean that I intend to have this lousy dream? That I intend to make myself miserable while dreaming? I had a hell of a life. Why would I intend that? Why don't I dream about a beautiful world, not a world where I get lost?

Dr. Holt: I don't know yet what purpose you intend and what meaning you give it, but one thing is sure, you are aware in the dream that you think and feel you should know the world of the city you create, the city in which your parent images live, which symbolizes the way you felt at home while you were young and where you want to return. But it seems that you arranged it so that you cannot find the way. Therefore, we must assume that you don't want to find, at present, where they live and that you prefer to feel lost until you have a dream where you are ready to confront your parent images and all the attitudes they represent. We will see in future dreams when you are ready to confront the attitudes you have been raised with.

Session with "Bobcat" Dream

A few weeks later, Nancy began:

Nancy: I have a suspicion that you lie to me. I don't like liars. I get angry if you don't do what you say you will do.

Dr. Holt: Tell me, what kind of relationship do you expect professionally?

Nancy: Well, I want you to be objective, impartial. I don't want a social relationship with you. I don't want to worry about you personally. I just want to talk about what's on my mind, and I want you to listen. The last dream upset me a great deal. It showed me how empty and lonely I feel, how confused I am deep inside. I want to talk a little more about this feeling. Before I married, I was so adventurous, full of life, and look at me, just barely fourteen or fifteen years later.

Dr. Holt: Are you confusing how you feel *now* about yourself with how you felt *then* and how you are experienced and appear to others? You might feel very empty, but you might act spunky. You claim one thing, that you want a professionally distant relationship, and on the other hand, in actuality, with me, you behave in a challenging, mildly aggressive way in the sessions. You seem to want a personal response from me, not only emotionally but also intellectually, and right now.

Nancy: Gee, you make me very angry! Are you trying to control me? Are you telling me how I should feel or behave?

Dr. Holt: Look, we've discussed the triune brain. Is it possible that you might feel empty with one brain and angry with the other?

Nancy: You know, it takes a lot of guts for me to talk to you this way, but I must talk to you. I have nobody else. I'm in terrible psychic pain. I need somebody to help me to orient myself in this world, get my bearings, so to say. I probably annoyed my husband for years without knowing it, so he should get rid of me, but instead he started drinking and beating me. I feel sorry for this poor man, and I hate him at the same time. We were ill matched from the beginning. I married him predominantly to get rid of my dependency on my parents, at least financially and emotionally. I wasn't ready to go out on my own, but I was adventurous. I'm mostly angry with myself and my parents. Here I was, a good-looking, intelligent, educated girl when I was young. I was scared of life, but I hid how I really felt by my behavior. Look, I don't like myself. I have made a mess of my life, contributed to the mess of my husband, and messed up my children. You know, I had another dream. Again, I hesitate to tell you, but you helped me a little bit in understanding my inner feelings of loneliness and confusion. This dream really scared me! Even after I woke up and had to do an errand, I was scared on the street. I'm afraid I'm getting worse. Doctor, you're not helping me very much! When I came here, I wasn't so scared. [*Many patients in analysis, when working through some of their problems, become aware of an inner anxiety and self-hostility. This is necessary in order to separate out from images.*]

Dr. Holt: Do you think that because you came to me for a few weeks so far, I've made you worse?

Nancy: Gosh, doctor. I wish you wouldn't be so defensive all the time. Let me blame you and attack you without your having to respond. I thought you were analyzed! Just let me blame you, for God's sake! Better you than I. After all, I pay you for that. I have to get it off my chest. I can't go around being so angry and blaming myself or my parents or my poor husband or children. But you're a paid hand. I don't want to fight with you and waste my time, so here's the dream. [*By projecting her anger onto me, she began to feel stronger and was able to work through her internal images. She could then verbalize in interpersonal space and avoid physically acting out without awareness.*]

I'm walking on Madison Avenue to buy some clothes for my children. It is again a gray day, no color. I feel drab and slow-moving, and to my amazement, very few people are around on the street at 10 A.M. The stores are all closed. Suddenly, I realize that it must be Sunday. I turn around to go home where I live now, when suddenly I am confronted, to my shock and amazement, by a big, female, wild-looking bobcat. My God, a bobcat on Madison Avenue, and she is looking at me! I get so scared that I start to run, yelling, "Help! Help! Help!" All the stores are closed. The doors are locked. Some people are walking in the distance, but apparently they don't hear me. The bobcat, who is four feet tall, chases me, and I, in desperation, throw away my purse and shoes and climb a tall street lamp. The cat tries to climb up after me. I hold on for dear life. Fortunately, I'm a strong person and can hold on. I yell for help, but people just pass by. They evidently don't hear or see me. Am I in a warp in a different space and time? I can't hold on anymore. I begin to slide down.

And, doctor, I fell out of my real bed and bumped myself hard, thank God. What's the matter with me? I must be nuts! I scared myself to death. Nobody came to help. Do I only see and hear things other people don't see? Am I the other people who don't see, as you have told me, since I'm everyone in my dream? Please don't teach me and talk down to me. Just help me to understand. At last, illuminate the situation with me. I can't go on always being so scared or so distant, or so angry, or all three at the same time.

The patient in this dream is in more familiar territory than she was in the other dream. This time, the street is named and corresponds to what she experiences in interpersonal life. It is Madison Avenue. Again, the day appears gray with no color. She experiences the world as gray while dreaming. When I asked her whether she likes the color gray, she said yes. It calms her down and makes her feel more "together." Her world is known to her. She is calmed down a great deal but feels drab and slow-moving. So the world she creates in her dream is in the morning, and on the stage of the dream she is amazed to find that there are very few people around. She is oriented not only to place (Madison Avenue) but also to imaginary clock time (10 A.M.). The *Mitwelt* is represented by the people on the street, but she feels distant and places them far away. She not only becomes aware of clock time but comes to the logical conclusion in the dream that it must be Sunday. The world she portrays in the dream (which represents a certain calm mood) is the background to her awareness that she is also a person with a purpose—to buy clothes for her children. She sees herself as a mother with a function, and the symbols of the children represent her intention to experience herself as a mother. When confronted with the realization that it is Sunday, she turns around to go home. She thus reverses her direction and loses for an instant her purpose of being a mother. This reversal causes her, through regression, to split into two images: one image becomes a big female bobcat; the other becomes herself, but a scared self-representation standing over and against herself. (The use of Freudian terminology such as *regression* and *splitting* represents Nancy's change of being. The experience is of her being on the interface between the alligator brain and the midbrain. The brain constantly shifts from one mode of existence to another, intentionally.) By splitting, she cannot function now as a mother, only as a scared, smaller image, and the bobcat image stops her in the dream from returning to her independent home.

When she becomes aware of the split of her being into two images—the bobcat and herself—she becomes anxious and sees herself as scared and helpless without help from people in the world (other self-created images), especially since this bobcat image turns against her and snarls menacingly. When I asked her what comes to mind when facing the bobcat, she associated: "I was always scared of my mother. She used to beat me and chase me when I didn't do what she wanted. I was really scared of her. I was little, and she is a five-foot, eleven-inch fat woman. I never wanted to be like her. I hated her. She tried to boss and control me. Gee! Her attitude reminds me of my husband. This 245-pound brute! This booze hound with a temper who used to beat me, too. I wonder if I married him because he is emotionally similar to my mother. I can't believe it. I can't accept it. It's too much!"

The association helped her understand that her mother was represented in her mind by a dangerous animal that wanted to kill her and eat her. (She experienced her mother as granting her independence as an adult only resentfully and begrudgingly. The mother did not want her to have an independent home, but wanted to control her and demanded that she live in her mansion with the children. Giving in to this demand would have further diminished her identity.) We are now seeing a further regression, to what the Freudians call an oral state, where the mother image is not seen as the good, benevolent mother but as a killing mother.

Nancy: Gosh, was I scared of my mother! And my father was like a dishrag. He never came to my help. Whatever my mother said, he didn't want to interfere. He didn't want to be involved. Even then, when he didn't have any angina. I had nobody to protect me against her. [Starts to cry with deep sobs] To rescue myself, I had to disappear. I was too scared. Gee, I hope I didn't lose my mind. Even as a kid, I had a tendency to faint. I lost awareness of who I was and where I was. Gee, I must be really sick. It goes back to early childhood. How can I trust anybody if I couldn't trust my mother?

It is no wonder that Nancy regressed further to living in the primordial brain, where she felt she lived in a time warp, where her concept of time, place, and object disappeared, and where she felt scared to death. I tried to explain to her that this projection of old emotional tendencies dating back to early childhood is very common and often changes our feelings about people in the interpersonal world in full consciousness. Such archaic feelings as terror and anger can color even our conscious mode, and we often wake up angry or terrorized, not knowing that we had a dream. We might feel angry all day.

Nancy: Gee, I feel better now. I'm beginning to trust you a little more. You're really not like my mother. I feel more hopeful that I can do something and I will probably be a better mother and wife than I was before. After all, I projected childhood feelings onto my husband, but then, God, I'm such a strong person that, in spite of my neurotic tendencies which I often acted out, I now know who I am. No! I will never return to my husband! I want to start a new life.

This experience felt to her like a religious conversion, like being newly born, living by new values and no longer seeing the world in an anxious, paranoid way as dangerous.

To summarize this session: Nancy W., who had a tendency to have nightmares since childhood and who felt that, while dreaming, she was being overtaken by a different state of being that was alien to her, made visible in a symbolic way in this bobcat dream strata of her mind that she had never been aware of before. She experienced the bobcat, which symbolized her mother image, as an ogre who threatened to overtake her, and she became aware in the dream of the distorted aggressive impulses that she projected onto the bobcat image. She could not cope with these feelings even on the natural dream level but had to descend to deeper layers where other people did not see or hear her. According to classical Freudian theory, these self-aggressive impulses as experienced by her were incestuous wishes so powerful that they had to be repressed even in a dream. Helpless rage and anxiety is a reversion back, according to Horney, to the preoedipal phase and might begin very early after the first year of life. Such fears represent how a small infant sees the world that is not the "good mother."

Summary of Nancy's Progress

During the five and a half months that Nancy was in therapy with me, we laid the groundwork for a further therapeutic relationship in which guilt, anger, and frustrations could be wholeheartedly expressed without her being afraid of being rejected or controlled. In addition, I helped her give up living predominantly on the boundary between the dream and the daydream world (alligator and child brain). She was able to live mostly in conscious awareness for long periods. There were many ups and downs and regressions. When her emotions were not involved, especially in the area of business, she functioned quite well. When upset with her parents or with her husband, she returned to function in her midbrain. She was "stuck," so to say, was not aware of what she was doing, could not free herself from her obsessive-compulsive thinking, and acted out her internal self-aggression. She then experienced the emotions and values of a small child and saw the world from the perspective of the midbrain, which experienced the adult world of people as hostile, rejecting, and controlling. With the help of therapy, she was able to free herself from the grip of her compulsions for long periods. She became conscious and experienced her new values as coming from the interchange of adult human relationships and, therefore, was quite often able to separate herself out from her dream and daydream impulses.

She was able to find the source of her nightmares which were symbolized by her mother image (bobcat). She remembered a daydream from age four in which she felt very anxious. This fantasy occurred quite frequently when her mother scolded her for not fulfilling tasks her mother had assigned her. The daydream was: She was walking through a forest, and every tree was a bobcat snarling at her. She was very scared but realized that these bobcat trees (mother images) could not bend down far enough to reach her. She crawled on her belly through the grass feeling like a snake, and was able to reach the fields, laughing hilariously that she had frustrated the bobcat trees. It gave her great satisfaction and joy to do this.

Since early infancy, Nancy had been in conflict with her mother. This conflict showed itself beautifully in her daydream, in which the mother image and the world (the forest) were fused so that she could not differentiate them. The world, therefore, was experienced as hostile, standing over and against her, and she dealt with this self-created world by reducing herself to a snakelike animal while still having human form. The purpose was to be able to deal with her self-conceived frightening world while being so young. This way she was able to overcome the dangerous forest-world of her daydream and feel triumphant. "Gee!" she said to me, "how smart and powerful I was as a kid. My mother couldn't do a thing. I surely fixed her. She could only snarl and yell and scream, but she couldn't reach me."

In existential analysis, we try to work through patients' preoedipal feelings by clarifying and discussing, in the here and now, the unconscious problems in the analytic situation. I have observed that, for many patients, their preoedipal, intrapsychic experiences have a far more intense emotional reality than feelings of the postoedipal situation. For example, Nancy had the following memory from age six and a half: She awoke in the middle of the night, convinced that a bad witch was under the bed. She woke up her father, who came into her room, turned on the light, and showed her that there was no witch. But Nancy insisted that as soon as he would leave the room, the witch would come back, and she pleaded with him to stay with her in bed, which he consented to do until she fell asleep.

At that time in her life, Nancy felt rejected by her mother and turned to her father for closeness. This acting out in the interpersonal world was based on a projection and confusion of intrapsychic space and time into interpersonal reality and had the purpose of making her feel secure. She was not able to separate the witch image from her attitude toward her real mother, whom she experienced, even then, as dangerous. By persuading her father to sleep in her bed, she triumphed over her mother in reality.

Nancy recalled another experience, from age eight and a half: One Sunday afternoon she said to her father, "Dad, do you really love me?" He answered, "Of course, Nancy." She said, "Am I really your hunky-punky?" He said, "Of course, Nancy. Aren't we playing together all the time?" Nancy asked, "Is mamma your hunky-punky?" "Of course not," her father answered, in a playful tone, according to Nancy. "Daddy," she said, "am I your flesh and blood?" He said, "Of course you are." "Is mamma your flesh and blood?" "No," he said. And then she said, "Then what is she, then?" And he said, "My wife." Whereupon, according to Nancy, she became very angry with her father, yelling, "I don't want to be your hunky-punky! I don't want to be your flesh and blood! I want to be your wife! You say you love me. You're lying to me. You sleep every night with mamma, not with me!"

This memory of a feeling that it is better to be a wife, or to be "loved," than to be a playmate, haunted her all through late childhood and adolescence. In reaction formation, she began to resent her father and to feel that he was not her friend, that he did not defend her against her mother, that he was a weakling, and that her mother triumphed again for the control and possession of the father. In therapy she recognized the anger she had had toward her father and saw that she transferred it, as an adult, onto her husband, whom she had begun to reject personally and sexually.

Intrapsychic experiences are often remembered by patients as real events and true memories. When Freud first analyzed the early childhood memories of his patients, he assumed that they represented real events. Later in his career, he came to the conclusion that some of these were memories of intrapsychic events that his patients thought were real events, and that most of the early childhood memories of his patients were "screen memories." Nancy thought the two experiences she had had at ages six and a half and eight and a half that she related to me were real events. It was not until she dreamed and then believed when awake that her husband (who, in actuality, was living in another city at the time) was beating her that she understood that she could misconceive of intrapsychic experiences as being real. She began to question whether many memories of her past had actually happened or whether she had imagined them.

Close to our forty-fifth session, she said, "You know, Dr. Holt, I feel much better. I am not declaring myself unilaterally healthy, but I've legally separated from my husband, I've organized my life with my children, and I've reestablished myself in New York City. My children are well taken care of and are happy. They have even visited my husband, who has cooperated and sent them back after two weeks. It is true that my daughter misses him a great deal, but she feels loved. So I think we should, for the time being, discontinue. How do you feel about it?"

I suggested that we see each other a few more times and perhaps resume after an interruption of three months to see how she would function without me. On further discussion, we agreed that much more work remained to be done but that she could now function better than ever in the past, even before her marriage.

She told me, "I wasn't going to tell you that I have found a fabulous man as a friend. I met him at the international office of the hotel chain where I'm working part-time. He is single, a widower, and has one daughter. We hit it off from the first time we saw each other. We felt attuned to each other and natural. He's my kind of a man. He's my intellectual and cultural equal, and I've been going out with him for the last few months. We not only enjoy each other but also sex, which to me is very important." I asked her why she had kept things to herself so long and had not let me know she was having an affair. She said she liked existential analysis because she did not have to tell everything that came to her mind but had the freedom to communicate to the analyst only what she wanted and when she was ready.

Since we were dealing with interpersonal events, not with inner material coming from the deeper layers of the brain, I agreed that this freedom of choice helped her to reinforce her individuality and identity and was an expression of herself as a unique person. It appeared that she was no longer driven to secrecy and that her value system was no longer that of a child who has to tell everything that comes to her mind. She could now select what was adequate, appropriate, and timely for her. Existential analysis does not reinforce dependency needs. Material coming from deeper layers of the brain is of such intensity and force that it often breaks through the conscious being, has to be expressed immediately in the here and now, and does not fall into the realm of conscious, voluntary communication.

We finished this segment of analysis five sessions later, feeling that she had worked through and faced, in the interpersonal space between therapist and herself, feelings that she had not dared to face by herself. She was freer as a human being to live her life more spontaneously.

In this beginning segment of an existential analysis, I have tried to give the flavor of what happens in the shifting relationship as analyst and patient take on different roles in different sessions within the therapy. The analysis continued for more than 500 sessions. The problems Nancy W. had with herself, her world, and other people, including her growing children, were more or less resolved over the years we worked together.

Some Comments on Techniques of Existential Analysis

Since in existential analysis we assume that the three stages of being-in-the-world are represented by three different perspectives and points of view and three different ways of emotionally experiencing the world, the "techniques" used here help a patient who is fixated and rigidly stuck in one mode of being-in-the-world. For example, the analyst's intervention and communication can free a person to move intentionally and consciously from the level of the "alligator brain" to another state of being if it seems appropriate to the patient. Then the person is no longer at the mercy of compulsions and obsessions. Existential analysis asserts that freedom of thought and action is an expression of the conscious living neocortex and can be analyzed through the concepts of existential analysis. It follows that the unconscious impulses that manifest themselves through illusions, delusions, and hallucinations as well as thinking and feeling patterns of the midbrain or through rigid should/ought systems have to be made conscious and dissolved by methods of Freudian and neo-Freudian techniques. Existential analysis is a method of modern psychoanalysis that focuses its therapy on the preoedipal and oedipal problems which interfere with the natural development of the human being. We follow Melanie Klein's theory in our therapy. Our major work is done intrapsychically, using dreams, daydreams, fantasies, and body sensations.

When we use the word *technique* to describe a communication of the therapist to the patient, we see the therapist shifting from a silent, observing pattern of relationships (which focuses on deep material coming from the alligator and midbrain) to the position of an observer participant (which focuses on the should/ought/must systems) and a participant observer (which focuses on the meaning and purpose of life-and-death experiences); this is our proper focus. The decision of how and when to use this technique is based on the proper analysis of the analyst, his state of mental and physical well-being, his experience as a therapist and as a human being, and his capacity to be flexible enough to relate to and attune himself to the shifting needs of another human being.

There are two special techniques that I often use very successfully. One is the scenario (or set-up) method, in which the analyst creates a scenario in the analytic session to bring out the way the patient really feels underneath the façade of social communication. Very often, the patient has to be angry at the therapist even though the technique has been explained in advance and the patient's cooperation has been solicited for the miniplays to take place. This approach is based on what in existential philosophy is called the "epoché," or "bracketing." The patient learns to separate out from her experience, acknowledging that it is her experience and becoming conscious of the meaning and purpose of the experience and the effect this experience might have on other people.

The second method of bringing out preconscious or unconscious patterns is the creation and illumination of guided fantasies and daydreams. The patient learns, for example, to furnish an imaginary apartment that she likes or dislikes or to create imaginary events and adventures in a place such as a forest, meadow, or seascape. The stories that the patient invents show a great deal about how in imagination she approaches other people, the world, and her relationships in it.

Many other techniques are available to the existentially trained psychoanalyst to facilitate and bring forth attitudes of the patient that he is not aware of. When he becomes aware of them, he can trace them back to the source and give himself a chance to imagine a potential future according to his own value system. Existential analysis as a method is successful only when it helps a human being to be conscious and free in the context of his relationship to himself and other people in the time, place, and culture in which he now lives.

Part Three ✌

Postanalytic
Psychotherapies:
Humanistic Psychology

Humanistic psychology is both a theoretical perspective and a social movement. It gives priority to human experience, values, intentions, and meanings while promoting personal growth and change. The founding fathers of this social movement are Carl Rogers, Abraham Maslow, and Rollo May. Rogers believed that a therapeutic relationship that included unconditional positive regard, empathetic understanding, and honesty could overcome blocks erected by socialization to a person's intrinsic self-actualization. Philosophically this group embraced Rousseau's concept of human nature as good but corruptible, rather than the traditional Freudian/Hobbesian view of human nature as more evil and as requiring intervention from society. The humanistic view contrasts sharply as well with the Lockean/behavioristic view of the human as a "blank slate" molded by environmental conditioning. Rollo May added to this movement the influence of existentialism and phenomenology, drawing on Tillich, Kierkegaard, and Heidegger. Outgrowths of humanistic psychology are the human potential movement and the encounter-group movement.

In Chapter Eleven, "Client-Centered Therapy," Carl R. Rogers puts forth the client-centered approach as a way of being that finds its expression in attitudes and behavior that create a growth-promoting climate. This approach is a basic philosophy, not simply a set of techniques—a philosophy that does not follow the medical model. Rogers believes that when the philosophy is lived in the relationship, the therapist is a companion to the client in a self-exploration leading to greater self-understanding and constructive change in behavior. This process is illuminated in an interview with Jan, who presents two major problems. In the interview she moves from describing her problems to experiencing them; from a variety of disconnected experiences to an integration of them; from desperation and hopelessness to a degree of empowerment of herself; from confusion to insight. The therapist remains sensitive to and accepting of her feelings, goes step by step with her in her search, and at one important point makes an intuitive response that brings a flood of insight.

Chapter Twelve, "Gestalt Therapy," presents "the case of Florence," chosen by James Simkin for this collection shortly before his death in the summer of 1984. It is taken from a transcribed videotaped session with a patient during one of his intensive residential Gestalt therapy training workshops at his home in Big Sur, California. The chapter was subsequently completed by his widow and two additional authors. His work demonstrates his use of a wide range of Gestalt therapy concepts and techniques. By following the process of what *is* for Florence, using past events as they become foreground in the here and now, she explores and begins to know and trust her own experience. Simkin demonstrates Gestalt therapy's main concern with the patient's awareness and the role of the therapist as a coexplorer in the therapy process. The therapist helps the patient change by directing her attention at every turn to what is in the now, in the belief that change then occurs in a self-correcting way.

In Chapter Thirteen, "Existential-Humanistic Psychotherapy," James F. T. Bugental uses a case to demonstrate the existentialist concern with presence, the quality of being genuinely accessible and truly self-expressive in a situation. Eric is a young man who unwittingly keeps his life hypothetical, avoiding the actualities that would confront him with the incompleteness and unsatisfactoriness of his way of being. In therapy he manifests this pattern in many ways, among which his use of vague language and ambiguous concepts stands out. The therapist shows Eric how he "protects" himself in this self-defeating way. As the patient recognizes this, he goes through periods of anxiety and then of anger. The latter emotion comes to a climax in a stormy therapy session, after which Eric begins to find greater access to his own inner experiencing and, as a consequence, the author feels, starts on his way to a more fulfilling life.

✥ 11 ✥

Client-Centered Therapy

Carl R. Rogers

What do I mean by a client-centered, or person-centered, approach? For me it expresses the primary theme of my whole professional life, as that theme has become clarified through experience, interaction with others, and research. This theme has been used and found effective in many areas, until the broad label "a person-centered approach" seems the most descriptive.

The central hypothesis of this approach can be briefly stated. It is that the individual has within himself or herself vast resources for self-understanding, for altering his or her self-concept, attitudes, and self-directed behavior—and that these resources can be tapped if only a definable climate of facilitative psychological attitudes can be provided.

There are three conditions that constitute this growth-promoting climate, whether we are speaking of the relationship between therapist and client, parent and child, leader and group, teacher and student, or administrator and staff. The conditions apply, in fact, in any situation in which the development of the person is a goal. I have described these conditions at length in previous writings (Rogers, 1959, 1961). I present here a brief summary from the point of view of psychotherapy, but the description applies to all the foregoing relationships.

The first element is genuineness, realness, or congruence. The more the therapist is himself or herself in the relationship, putting up no professional front or personal façade, the greater is the likelihood that the client will change and grow in a constructive manner. Genuineness means that the therapist is openly being the feelings and attitudes that are flowing within at the moment. There is a close matching, or congruence, between what is being experienced at the gut level, what is present in awareness, and what is expressed to the client.

The second attitude of importance in creating a climate for change is acceptance, or caring, or prizing—unconditional positive regard. When the therapist is experiencing a positive, nonjudgmental, accepting attitude toward whatever the client *is* at that moment, therapeutic movement or change is more likely. Acceptance involves the therapist's willingness for the client to be whatever immediate feeling is going on—confusion, resentment, fear, anger, courage, love, or pride. It is a nonpossessive caring. When the therapist prizes the client in a total rather than a conditional way, forward movement is likely.

The third facilitative aspect of the relationship is empathic understanding. This means that the therapist senses accurately the feelings and personal meanings that the client is experiencing and communicates this acceptant understanding to the client. When functioning best, the therapist is so much inside the private world of the other that he or she can clarify not only the meanings of which the client is aware but even those just below the level of awareness. Listening, of this very special, active kind, is one of the most potent forces for change that I know.

There is a body of steadily mounting research evidence that, by and large, supports the view that when these facilitative conditions are present, changes in personality and behavior do indeed occur. Such research has been carried on in this and other countries from 1949 to the present. Studies have been made of changes in attitude and behavior in psychotherapy, in degree of learning in school, and in the behavior of schizophrenics. In general, they are confirming. (See Rogers, 1980, for a summary of the research.)

Trust

Practice, theory, and research make it clear that the person-centered approach is built on a basic trust in the person. This is perhaps its sharpest point of difference from most of the institutions in our culture. Almost all of education, government, business, much of religion, much of family life, much of psychotherapy, is based on a distrust of the person. Goals must be set, because the person is seen as incapable of choosing suitable aims. The individual must be guided toward these goals, since otherwise he or she might stray from the selected path. Teachers, parents, supervisors must develop procedures to make sure the individual is progressing toward the goal—examinations, inspections, interrogations. The individual is seen as innately sinful, destructive, lazy, or all three—as someone who must be constantly watched over.

The person-centered approach, in contrast, depends on the actualizing tendency present in every living organism—the tendency to grow, to develop, to realize its full potential. This way of being trusts the constructive directional flow of the human being toward a more complex and complete development. It is this directional flow that we aim to release.

One More Characteristic

I described above the characteristics of a growth-promoting relationship that have been investigated and supported by research. But recently my view has broadened into a new area that cannot as yet be studied empirically.

When I am at my best, as a group facilitator or a therapist, I discover another characteristic. I find that when I am closest to my inner, intuitive self, when I am somehow in touch with the unknown in me, when perhaps I am in a slightly altered state of consciousness in the relationship, then whatever I do seems to be full of healing. Then simply my *presence* is releasing and helpful. There is nothing I can do to force this experience, but when I can relax and be close to the transcendental core of me, then I may behave in strange and impulsive ways in the relationship, ways which I cannot justify rationally, which have nothing to do with my thought processes. But these strange behaviors turn out to be *right,* in some odd way. At those moments it seems that my inner spirit has reached out and touched the inner spirit of the other. Our relationship transcends itself and becomes a part of something larger. Profound growth and healing and energy are present.

This kind of transcendent phenomenon is certainly experienced at times in groups in which I have worked, changing the lives of some of those involved. One participant in a workshop put it eloquently: "I found it to be a profound spiritual experience. I felt the oneness of spirit in the community. We breathed together, felt together, even spoke for one another. I felt the power of the 'life force' that infuses each of us—whatever that is. I felt its presence without the usual barricades of 'me-ness' or 'you-ness'—it was like a meditative experience when I feel myself as a center of consciousness. And yet with that extraordinary sense of oneness, the separateness of each person present has never been more clearly preserved."

I realize that this account partakes of the mystical. Our experiences, it is clear, involve the transcendent, the indescribable, the spiritual. I am compelled to believe that I, like many others, have underestimated the importance of this mystical, spiritual dimension.

In this I am not unlike some of the more advanced thinkers in physics and chemistry. (For example, see Capra, 1982.) As they push their theories further, picturing a "reality" which has no solidity, which is no more than oscillations of energy, they too begin to talk in terms of the transcendent, the indescribable, the unexpected—the sort of phenomena that we have observed and experienced in the person-centered approach.

The person-centered approach, then, is primarily a way of being that finds its expression in attitudes and behaviors that create a growth-promoting climate. It is a basic philosophy rather than simply a technique or a method. When this philosophy is lived, it helps the person expand the development of his or her own capacities. When it is lived, it also stimulates constructive change in others. It empowers the individual, and when this personal power is sensed, experience shows that it tends to be used for personal and social transformation.

When this person-centered way of being is lived in psychotherapy, it leads to a process of self-exploration and self-discovery in the client and eventually to constructive changes in personality and behavior. As the therapist lives these conditions in the relationship, he or she becomes a companion to the client in this journey toward the core of self. This process is, I believe, illuminated in the case material that follows.

Jan—and the Process of Change

Occasionally one interview will illustrate several aspects of the therapeutic process as it occurs in the changing relationship between therapist and client. Such an interview was the one I held with Jan. It was a half-hour demonstration therapy session, held onstage before a workshop of 600 participants in Johannesburg, South Africa.

Several individuals had volunteered, and the next morning, shortly before the interview, my colleague Ruth Sanford told Jan that she had selected her as the client.

Jan and I took chairs facing each other, so that the audience had a side view of our interaction. We adjusted and tried out our microphones. Then I said that I wished a few moments of quiet to collect myself and get centered. I added that she might also like that time to become quiet, and a nod of her head indicated that she would. I used the time to forget the technicalities and to focus my mind on being present to Jan and open to anything she might express.

From this point on, the material is taken from the recorded interview. The excerpts given contain the main themes and significant points. The material omitted consists of further explication of some theme or the pursuit of some issue that was dropped.

The reader will find it profitable, I believe, to first read the interview as a whole, looking only at what Jan and I said, and skipping over the comments on the process that are interspersed from time to time. A second reading can then be done by segments, stopping to consider the comments on each segment.

Carl: Now I feel more ready. I don't know what you want to talk with me about, because we haven't done more than say hello to each other. But whatever you would like to bring up, I'd be very ready to hear. [Pause]

Jan: I have two problems. The first one is the fear of marriage and children. And the other one is the age process, aging. It's very difficult to look into the future, and I find it very frightening.

Carl: Those are two main problems for you. I don't know which you'd rather pick up first.

Jan: I think the immediate problem is the age problem. I would rather start on it. If you can help on that, I would be very grateful.

Carl: Can you tell me a little bit more about the fear that you have of aging? As you get older, what?

Jan: I feel that I am in a panic situation. I am thirty-five years of age, and I've only got another five years till forty. It's very difficult to explain. I keep turning around and I want to run away from it.

Carl: It's enough of a fear that you really—it really sets off a panic in you.

Jan: Yes, and it's affecting my confidence as a person. [*Carl:* Mm-hmm.] It's only started happening in the last eighteen months, two years, that I've suddenly realized: Hell's teeth, everything's catching up on me. Why do I feel like that?

Carl: And you didn't have those feelings very much until perhaps a year and a half ago. [Pause] Was there anything special at that time that seemed to set it off?

My initial responses have two purposes. I want to make it completely safe for her to express herself, and so I recognize her feelings and ask nonspecific, nonthreatening questions. It is also part of my purpose to refrain from anything that would point in a particular direction or would imply any judgment. The direction the interview will take is completely up to her.

Jan has moved from *stating* her problems to beginning to *experience* the panic she is feeling. Her attitude is clearly that the help, if any, will come from me.

Jan: Not that I can recall, really. Well, my mother died at fifty-three, [*Carl:*

Mm-hmm.] and she was a very young and very bright woman in many ways. But I think maybe that has something to do with it. I don't know.

Carl: You sort of felt that if your mother died at that early age, that was a possibility for you, too. [Pause] And time began to seem a lot shorter.

Jan: Right!

Already Jan is using the safety of the relationship to explore her experience. Without being aware of its significance, her nonconscious intellect moves her into a consideration of her mother's death.

My response shows that I am beginning to feel at home in her inner world, and I go a bit beyond her description. My sense of her world is confirmed by her "Right!" If she had said, "No, that's not it," I would immediately have dropped my picture and tried to discover the meaning her statement did have for her. I have no investment in the correctness of my responses as I try to understand.

Jan: When I look at my mother's life—and she had many talents—she unfortunately, towards the end, became a bitter woman. The world owed her a living. Now I don't want ever to be in that situation. And at this point in time, I'm not. I've had a very full life—both very exciting and very sad at times. I've learned a lot and I've a lot to learn. But—I *do* feel that what happened to my mother is happening to me.

Carl: So that remains sort of a specter. Part of your fear is: "Look what happened to my mother, and am I following in the same path. [*Jan:* Right.] and will I feel that same fruitlessness, perhaps?"

Jan: [*Long* pause] Do you want to ask me some more questions, because I think that will help you to draw information out of me? I just can't—everything is a whirlwind, [*Carl:* Mm-hmm.] going around in circles.

Carl: Things are just going around so fast inside of you, you don't quite know where to [*Jan:* Where to begin.] take hold. I don't know whether you want to talk anymore about your relationship to your mother's life, your fear of that, or what?

A long pause on the part of the client is frequently fruitful. I wait with interest to see what follows.

First comes a clear indication that in her mind I am the authority, I am the doctor. She will fit into my wishes.

For my part, I don't refuse verbally to follow the medical model, to be the all-wise doctor. I simply do not *behave* as an authority figure. Instead, I show that I understand her confusion and leave her with a nonspecific lead.

It is interesting that she interjects to finish my sentence for me. It is an indication that in her *experience* she is recognizing that we are together in this search— on the same side of the table, as it were, rather than the doctor on one side, the "patient" on the other.

Jan: The older I get, though, the stronger I feel about the marriage situation. Now whether the two are related, I don't know. But the fear of getting married, and being committed, and children—I find very, very frightening. And it's getting stronger as I get older—

Carl: It's a fear of commitment, and a fear of having children? And all that seems
          to be a growing fear, all those fears seem to keep increasing.

Jan: Yes. I'm not afraid of commitment. For instance, when it comes to my work,
          to friendship, to doing certain things. But to me marriage is very—

Carl: So you're not a person who's irresponsible or anything like that— [*Jan:* No,
          not at all.] you're committed to your work, you're committed to friends.
          It's just that the notion of being tied into marriage—that's scary as hell.

The long pause leads Jan to open up and explore her fear of marriage.

The client "increasingly differentiates and discriminates the objects of his
feelings and perceptions, including . . . his self, his experiences, and the interrela-
tionships between them" (Rogers, 1959, p. 216). Jan certainly illustrates this statement in my theory as she recognizes her fear—not of commitment but only of a
special commitment.

We now are definitely companions in the search to know her self, her deeper,
inner self. We are free to take part in each other's statements.

Jan: [After *long* silence] Do you want me to speak?

Carl: I wish I could help you get a handle on some of those things that are going
          around in your head.

Jan: Um, [Pause] I really didn't think I'd be called up here today. Otherwise
          I'd have made a list! [Pause] Would my problem be— My love is for the
          arts, right? I'm very much involved with music and dancing. I'd like to
          be able to just throw everything up and devote my life to music and danc-
          ing. But unfortunately the society that we live in today forces one to work
          and live up to a certain social standard. It's not something I regret. It's
          something I miss, something I really want to do. But how do I do it? Has
          that got something to do with—as I say, I'm getting older, and I keep turn-
          ing around and running back.

Carl: So what you're telling me is, you *do* have a purpose in life, you *do* have
          something you really want to do— [*Jan:* Oh, yes.] to commit yourself to
          music, to the arts, but you feel society prevents you from doing that. But
          what you would like to do is to throw up everything else and just concen-
          trate on your love of music.

Jan: Right.

When Jan is struggling to know in which direction to move in her exploration,
she endeavors to give the responsibility to me. I simply express my very real feeling.

Her next statement is striking evidence that there is great advantage in letting the client take the lead in the interview. The first long silence led to her exploration of the marriage issue. This one leads to a surprisingly positive aspect of
her self-image. For someone who has seemed unsure, her love of the arts seems
sure and certain.

My response has the advantage of bringing fully into awareness her positive
aims and goals. There is value in holding up a mirror to the client.

From the point of view of therapeutic process, Jan "experiences fully, in
awareness, feelings which have in the past been denied to awareness, or distorted
in awareness" (Rogers, 1959, p. 216).

Jan: In the last eighteen months everything—it's quite strange, but—the situation is becoming *vital.* I was led to believe that when one grows older, one became more patient, more tolerant. I've really not had a care in the world. It's only now that I have a real *problem,* and I don't know how to cope with it.

Carl: It seems to me that in the last eighteen months, everything seems very, very important—every moment, every aspect of life [*Jan:* Yes.] seems more vital and more significant. And the question seems deeper: "What am I going to do?"

Jan: [Pause] Can you answer a question for me, Dr. Carl? Can you see the two related: the marriage issue, the aging process, or not?

Carl: Yes, it seems to me that they're related in your talking about them, and that you're saying the fears grow stronger, as time goes by, both of marriage and of children and of commitment, as well as a fear of aging—that it seems a package of fears. And alongside that, you've been saying that "I know what I want to commit myself to—I just can't."

Jan *experiences* the urgency of the issues in her life and her helplessness in dealing with them. Following a familiar pattern, she turns to the authority for an answer.

She has already related these two issues in her conversation, and I simply feed back to her the essence of her own feelings and their meanings. It is not obstinacy on my part that refuses to give any answer from me. It is a profound belief that the best answer can come only from within the client and that Jan is, in fact, answering her question by what she has been saying.

Jan: Mmm. And it's not—it's got absolutely nothing to do with giving. Just the fear of being trapped. As I am trapped in my age right now.

Carl: You get this feeling of being *trapped,* trapped by the year you're in, trapped by the age you are, and the fear of being trapped by marriage as well. [Pause] So life has become a frightening prospect.

It is interesting to follow her search for the right word—the right metaphor—to match her feelings. She has tried out *fear, panic, feelings being vital,* and now *trapped.* Finding a word, a phrase, a metaphor that exactly matches the inner felt meaning of the moment helps the client to experience the feeling more fully.

I am now quite comfortably moving about in her inner world, sensing the way she feels, even when she has not put it fully into words.

Jan: Yes. [Pause] I still carry on, [*Carl:* Mm-hmmm.] you know, and I try to keep this deep down inside of me. [Pause] I don't walk into the office and say, "Help, please, I'm thirty-five. What am I going to do?" It's not that at all. I can still, if I want to put my shorts on and wear my pigtails, but that's not it. It's—it's fear of being trapped.

Carl: And those fears that you have, they don't prevent you from functioning in the world. That goes on OK, but nevertheless they are fears deep inside, and the biggest fear of all is the fear of being trapped, in so many different ways.

I failed here to respond to her growing awareness of the incongruence between what she is experiencing and the façade with which she faces the world. I also missed the casual reference to shorts and pigtails, clearly another positive facet of her self-concept. Usually the therapist is given another chance if he misses significant meanings, and that opportunity is given to me in the next interchange.

Jan: And yet people say to me, "Jan, you're in your prime. You've got everything going for you!" And little do they know inside what I feel.

Carl: That's right. So that outside and to an observer, you are in your prime and you have everything going for you. But that's not Jan inside. Jan inside is quite different from that.

Jan: [Long pause—whispers:] Do you want me to say something else? [Laughter from Carl and audience] I'm just nervous as hell up here!

Carl: You can take all the time you want, because I feel I'm getting acquainted with that frightened little Jan that is inside.

Jan: So the more I talk, the more I'm helping you to get through to me, is that right?

Carl: The more you're getting through to *me*.

Jan: This may be related, and it may be able to help you: whether it's something to do with the amateur dramatics that I used to be involved with, I don't know, but I love playing the naughty little girl. And whenever I want to get away with something or I want something, I would play that naughty little girl.

Carl: That's a part that you know very well. [Jan laughs.] You've acted it in many plays. [*Jan:* And it works!] It *works*—the naughty little girl can get away with things. And one other thing that you said: that you're trying to help *me*. I guess I hope that what we're doing here will help *you*. [*Jan:* Thank you.] [Pause] Because—I feel that when you're telling me things, it's not for my benefit. I hope that you can get better acquainted with yourself by telling us some of those things.

Here is Jan's clearest statement of her view of the relationship: that she, if told to do so, will give me information so that I, the expert, can then be the external agent of help for her. The successfulness of my attempt to shift the locus of responsibility to her is uncertain. I do not believe she understands what I am saying, and her "Thank you" makes it clear that to her I am still the active helping agent.

What has play-acting a naughty little girl to do with her problems? I do not know, but I deeply trust that her nonconscious mind is taking a path that will lead us to the areas most relevant to her fears.

Jan: I have discussed this problem with one other person, who has been through this experience. She knows the traumatic effects that it has on a person. She herself went through similar feelings. And she said, "You know, it's very strange, but I have been able to overcome that, over a period of time—with the help of one or two people." I think the important thing is [Pause] to be able to relate to somebody that you can trust and have confidence in, who can spend the time with you. But it's very difficult to find.

Carl: But what you would like is someone you really could trust to help you go through and grow through this difficult period.

Jan: Mmm, of being trapped. [Laughs] So, I just don't know how to cope with it. I really don't.

Carl: Feel that it's a little too much for you.

Jan: Well, it's a part of my everyday life, you know, from the moment I wake up to the moment I go to bed. Obviously I don't discuss it with many people. For fear of the reaction, really, I think. It's important to try and find somebody who's been in the same boat—who knows what you're going through.

Carl: So you really are seeking—somebody, the somebody you need, the somebody you want, the somebody you could trust.

She describes very well the kind of nonjudgmental, understanding, caring, trustworthy relationship that everyone desires. It is a good description of a truly therapeutic relationship, another evidence of the fact that, fundamentally, "the client knows best."

Jan: Yes. I am trying to do it on my own, but I find it's not easy. [*Carl:* That's right.] To have somebody pushing me, saying, you know, "I *know* you can do it, you *can* do it, you *will* do it, you *are* going to do it," and that would—

Carl: That would really help.

Jan: Just one person who can believe in me.

Carl: One person who believes in you enough to say, "Sure you can do it—you're OK. You're going to get through it!" But you can't tell that to yourself.

Jan: No—and I try to be positive, and joke about it. But I, I'm just very scared. I'm going backwards. I'm not going forwards— [Long pause] I have tried to—push it to one side. I have tried to—wash it by the wayside, erase it. I've tried stopping myself when I think about it. But even that doesn't work anymore. [Pause] It's almost, metaphorically speaking only, as if I am walking into darkness. I'm coming out of the light and into the darkness. [*Carl:* Ahh.] Do you understand what I mean. [*Carl:* Yes, I surely do.] Because I fear again now—

Carl: And it's so risky, coming from the lighted spot into the darkness, into the unknown. [*Jan:* Right.] Such a chance, and so frightening.

Jan: [Pause] I can't think of anything else to say, other than—how do I overcome it? [Pause] I do feel at the moment it's a very lonely problem—I'm sure other people have been through it. Other people haven't. And they probably think, "Hell, what's the *problem?*" I even joke about it sometimes, to myself, and say, "I think I'll put an ad in the paper—you never [Laughing] know what response you'll get!" [Pause] It's the laughing and, you know, I tend to try and laugh it off.

Carl: But you wish so much that there was this other person, this person from outside, who would give you confidence, who could help you through this tough time.

Jan: Yes, because although I do pray—I have my own feelings about religion—I believe in spiritual development. And maybe for me this is a karmic conditioning, I don't know. That's another thing, of course, that's going on in my mind: it's a part of my development, as it were. But I feel that it's not enough; I must have physical contact. [Pause] Somebody I can relate to—

Throughout this segment she experiences the full depth of her hopelessness, her inability to deal with her fears, her desire for a helping relationship with another,

her conviction that help must come from the outside, the laughing face with which she hides her pain.

I walk with her, psychologically, along this path of discouragement. I do light up at her use of the light-into-darkness metaphor. The reason is evident in my next response.

Carl: Somebody you can relate to. And I guess that—this may seem like a silly idea, but—I wish that one of those friends could be that naughty little girl. I don't know whether that makes any sense to you or not, but if that kind of sprightly, naughty little girl that lives inside could accompany you from the light into the dark—as I say, that may not make any sense to you at all.

Jan: [In a puzzled voice] Can you elaborate on that a little more for me?

Carl: Simply that maybe one of your best friends is the you that you hide inside, the fearful little girl, the naughty little girl, the real you that doesn't come out very much in the open.

Jan: [Pause] And I must admit—what you have just said, and looking at it in retrospect—I've lost a lot of that naughty little girl. In fact, over the last eighteen months, that naughty little girl has disappeared.

This was the kind of intuitive response that I have learned to trust. The expression just formed itself within me and wanted to be said. I advanced it very tentatively, and from her initial blank and puzzled look, I thought that perhaps it was completely irrelevant and unhelpful, but her next response shows that it touched something deep in her.

I have come to value highly these intuitive responses. They occur infrequently (this is the first one I have captured in a recording), but they are almost always helpful in advancing therapy. In these moments I am perhaps in a slightly altered state of consciousness, indwelling in the client's world, completely in tune with that world. My nonconscious intellect takes over. I know much more than my conscious mind is aware of. I do not form my responses consciously, they simply arise in me, from my nonconscious sensing of the world of the other.

Carl: Has disappeared. Uh-huh, uh-huh. [Laughs] Then I wasn't so far wrong. Maybe you ought to look her up! (Laughter)

Jan: Would you like her number? [Laughter]

Carl: I would! [Laughter] I think she would be fun, and I don't think she would be so frightened. She sounds pretty sassy! [Laughter]

Jan: [Dubiously] So even though I'm getting older, I can still be a naughty little girl?

Carl: Well, I don't know—I'm only eighty, but I can still be a naughty little boy. [Much laughter and applause]

Jan: [Laughing] I won't make any comments! [Pause] Would that change my feelings about marriage?

Carl: I think that's a very significant question you're asking yourself. If you were a better friend of the little girl inside of you, would that make you less fearful of the risk of marriage? I feel badly that she's been missing for the last eighteen months, I really do.

Jan: [Pause] You're so right. You've really hit the nail on the head. And—

It is clear that our relationship has become a comfortable, companionable joint search. We can be humorous about serious things. It is an open, trusting relationship.

For Jan the realization sinks in that she has been denying a significant part of her experience, of herself, and that this is a deeply important fact.

I like my responses. They are spontaneous and funny but entirely serious in their intent.

Carl: I'm sorry, but we're going to have to stop in a few minutes.
Jan: OK—I'm fifteen minutes fast, because I'm always late. [Laughs]
Carl: Fifteen minutes older? [Much laughter]
Jan: [Laughing] Let's see, it's ten to—
Carl: Yes, then I think we'll stop. Is that all right?
Jan: Yes. You've been a great help, and I'd like to thank you very much indeed.

The ending seems abrupt, but time was up, and her willingness to joke about the situation seemed to indicate that she could close without feeling deprived. In addition, this was a point of real closure in the interview itself.

Significant Elements in the Interview

This interview contains many elements that are characteristic of a person-centered approach to psychotherapy or to any helping relationship. I will mention some of them.

1. A nonjudgmental acceptance of every feeling, every thought, every change of direction, every meaning that she finds in her experience. I believe this acceptance is complete, with one exception, which it is useful to note. I show real acceptance of her desire to be dependent, to rely on me as the authority who will give the answers. Notice that I accept her *wish* to be dependent. This does *not* mean that I will behave in such a way as to meet her expectations. I can more easily accept her dependent feelings, because I know where I stand, and I know that I will not *be* her authority figure, even though I am perceived as such.

But at one point my acceptance is not complete. She says, in effect, "I'll talk more to help you in your task," and instead of completely accepting her perception of the relationship, I make two futile attempts to change her perception. I respond, in effect, "What we are doing is to help you, not me." She disregards this, and no damage is done to the process.

2. A deep understanding of her feelings and of the personal meanings she finds in her experience, bringing to bear all the sensitivity of which I am capable. I am sufficiently successful in entering her private world that she feels increasingly safe in the relationship and able to express whatever comes to mind.

This sensitive empathy is so deep that my intuition takes over at one point and, in a way that seems mysterious, is in touch with a very important part of her with which she has lost contact. At this point we are perhaps in a mutual and reciprocal altered state of consciousness.

3. A companionship in her search for herself. As a therapist, I do not want to lead the client, since she knows, better than I, the pathway to the sources of her pain. (Of course, this is a nonconscious knowing, but it is there nevertheless.) I do not wish to fall behind in my understanding, because then the exploration

would become too frightening for her. What I wish is to be at her side, occasionally falling a step behind, occasionally a step ahead when I can see more clearly the path we are on, and taking a leap ahead only when guided by my intuition.

4. A trust in the "wisdom of the organism" to lead us to the core of her problems. In the interview I have a complete trust that she will move into the areas that are relevant to her distress. No matter how shrewd I might be as a clinician, I could never have guessed that her mother's death or her love of the arts or the role she played on the stage years ago would have any relevance to resolving her fears. But when trusted, her organism, her nonconscious mind—call it what you will—can follow the path that leads to the crucial issues.

So, as a therapist, I want to make it possible for my client to move in her own way, and at her own pace, to the heart of her conflicts.

5. Helping the client to experience her feelings *fully*. The best example is when she lets herself experience, quite completely, the *hopelessness* of being *trapped*. Once such a troubling feeling has been felt to its full depth and breadth, one can move on. It is an important part of movement in the process of change.

It is worth noting that when she says, with great conviction, "You've really hit the nail on the head," it is clear that she is *experiencing* something definitely helpful to her, and yet she does not verbalize what this is. No matter. It is the experiencing that is important, and the therapist doesn't need to know precisely what it is (although in this case she informed him the next day).

Perhaps pointing out these elements will have made it clear that a person-centered approach in therapy leads to a very subtle, often intricate process, a process that has an organic flow of its own. For the therapist to be fully present as an understanding, caring person is highly important in making this process possible, although the most crucial events take place in the feelings and experiencings of the client.

The Outcome for Jan

Immediately after the interview, in describing her experience to the participants, Jan said, "For me, strangely enough, though I'm very nervous, I found it very exciting. I needed help, and I think I've found an answer, thanks to Dr. Carl." This might be taken simply as politeness were it not for a subsequent conversation.

The next morning Jan told me that the interchange about the "naughty little girl" had initiated a self-searching. She realized that not only was the naughty little girl missing, but several other parts of her self had also disappeared during the past eighteen months. "I realize that to face life as a whole person, I need to find those missing parts of me." She said that for her the interview had proved to be a "soul-shaking experience." The process that started in the interview appears to be continuing in her.

12

Gestalt Therapy

James S. Simkin
Anne Nechama Simkin
Lois Brien
Cynthia Sheldon

James Simkin died of leukemia on August 2, 1984, before he was able to complete a commentary on his Gestalt session presented here. His widow, Anne, and Lois Brien and Cynthia Sheldon, who both have been frequent guest trainers at the Simkin Training Center in Gestalt Therapy, worked together to finish the analysis of this session with Florence.

The following session with Florence took place in 1979 at the Simkin Training Center. In viewing the videotape of this session, we were struck by the subdued and depressed quality about her. She is a heavy-set, older woman with white hair who gives the impression of someone waiting for life to happen to her. The pace of the session is slow, gentle, and exploratory. There are a few quick moments of aliveness, and at these times Florence looks younger. However, most of the time she seems depressed and contained—very much the opposite of the brazen hussy she discovers within herself near the end of the hour.

Florence is fifty-one or so, came from an alcoholic family, was married to an alcoholic, raised two adopted children, and was later divorced. During the first five years of her marriage, her sexuality flourished with men other than her husband. Later her sexual enthusiasm virtually disappeared, and she felt old and lonely—the issues she deals with in this session. Florence is a marriage counselor who works with alcoholic families. She has done previous Gestalt work with Jim.

The main concern in Gestalt therapy is the moment-to-moment awareness of one's self. The therapist is a *coexplorer* with the client, encouraging her to fully experience who she is at the moment. This is done by paying attention not only to her thoughts about who she is and what she says her problems are but also to her posture, her gestures, and her inner physical and mental experience. In the following session, Jim demonstrates time and again how they mutually explore what is true for her. He never leads her or pushes her. At no time does he ask or encourage her to be different (see Simkin, 1976b). He stays with her as she gets clearer about *how* she holds back her playful, sexy, warm, and tender self. He provides experiments for her to do in the hour so that she can check out within herself what fits. At the end of the session, when Florence declares or promises that she will stop holding back, Jim feels sad and tells her so. He then comments on how he differs from some therapeutic approaches in which the therapist sides with the client's wish to change and encourages it. Gestalt therapists believe that declarations of intention to change only set up a conflict within the person (superego versus id, critic versus rebel, parent versus child), which usually is unproductive. Only through constant full experiencing with awareness will the client want to do something different. If she tries to change because she thinks she "should" or "should want to," she will probably sabotage herself (see Simkin, 1975). These comments will become clearer with the following transcript and commentary.

Session with Florence

Numbers after sentences in the transcript of the session refer to the corresponding sections in the commentary that follows.

Florence: Thank you for seeing me today. [Pause]

Jim: When I look at you, sometimes I see an old woman, and sometimes I see a young woman, or a young middle-aged woman. I'm impressed with the differences that I see. (1)

Florence: I didn't know that. I watched the tapes and I felt shaky. Once in a while, I am a kid, a twinkly little kid, and a lot of the times, I am lonely. Watching the videotape [a tape from a previous session] is good for me.

Jim: If you were looking at yourself right now, who would you see at this moment? How do you feel from the inside?

Florence: Uh, a middle-aged woman. [Videotape is stopped and played back at this moment.]

Jim: Did what you saw agree with what you imagined? (2)

Florence: Someone a little older than a middle-aged woman but not really old, like on some parts of the tape I look really old.

Jim: Yeah, to me you were looking older than I have seen you at other times. And I think the difference has to do with something around your eyes. (3)

Florence: I am having trouble with my eyes—they are puffing up—in the morning they are puffed.

Jim: As if?

Florence: I have been crying a lot. I know at times my eyes are puffed up or look very angry.

Jim: Does either of those feel right for you at this moment?

Florence: Uh-huh.

Jim: That you are angry or crying a lot?

Florence: Uh-huh. I haven't been as in touch with my anger as my sadness this week.

Jim: Just hold that pose for a moment. See if you can get in touch with how you are. [Videotape is again played back.] What is that posture like for you?

Florence: Cold. I've got my feet up like I am starting to run a race here. I brace myself with my hands, and my head is to the side, like balancing myself.

Jim: So, if your posture could talk, what would it say? (4)

Florence: My feet would say I better stay on my toes. [Looks to her left]

Jim: And you looked over there. Did something attract you over there?

Florence: I'm worried—get away from you—worried—get away from you.

Jim: All right. I better stay on my toes away from you.

Florence: I'm hanging onto the chair like it might be a rocky landing.

Jim: And you're smiling. Are you pleased? I'd like to understand your smile.

Florence: Not pleased with the idea of the rocky landing as so much pleased at— oh, stepping aside and watching myself, maybe come up with the right— bright answers or something like that. (5)

Jim: Hmm. You'd be pleased with yourself when you are bright or come up with bright answers?

Florence: Uh-huh.

Jim: And the rest of you?

Florence: I just feel neutral here. I'm certainly crooked. My head's at an angle.

Jim: So you are braced, perhaps getting ready to run, holding on, looking away, pleased that you might come up with some bright answers, neutral, crooked. What would you like today? [Adjusts posture] (6)

Florence: I would like to be more comfortable.

Jim: What would you like me to do as you're getting yourself more comfortable?

Florence: I, let's see, what do I want from you? I would like to explore with you inner structure—which procedure or structure or program to use— [Sighs] I'm split. [Sounds teary] *I don't want to do what I am doing.*

Jim: Right now?

Florence: Right now, which is crying, [Sighs] and that other split part of me, I want to—I will get on and listen.

Jim: Uh-huh. If this feels right to you, I want you to say: "I don't want to cry and I *am* crying." (7)

Florence: I don't want to cry and I am crying.

Jim: "And I want to get on with living."

Florence: And I want to get on with living. I don't want to cry and I am crying, and I want to get on with living.

Jim: How can I be useful, or how do you want to use me in this process?

Florence: When I think of getting on with living, I think of Chet and I start to cry. When I am away from here. That is the only time I cry.

Jim: When you think of getting on with living and you think of Chet, you start to cry. Does Chet have anything to do with living, getting on with living?

Florence: No. Well, nothing that comes to my head, I guess.

Jim: Chet, I am interested in getting on with living, and when I think of you, I start to cry.

Florence: "And crying is part of my living," I would say to finish that sentence.

Jim: Have you any experience of getting on with your living without Chet?

Florence: Yeah.

Jim: What's that like?

Florence: Good, I'd be living good. A couple of things, one thing's missing.
Jim: What's missing?
Florence: My sexual drive. [Pause] I'm getting warm.
Jim: Is it true that without Chet your sexual drive is low? Or does that have nothing to do with it? (8)
Florence: He has nothing to do with my sexual drive. To me.
Jim: So one of the ways you keep yourself from being fully alive is dampening your sexual appetite or interest.
Florence: Uh-hmm. Everything else is just *really* fine.
Jim: Uh, how would I be for you as a sexual partner? (9)
Florence: I don't know. There are things, I, I, the only way I think of it is that I would be very scared, I don't know.
Jim: Tell me what you would be scared of.
Florence: [Long pause—looks more animated] I'd just be scared of coming close to you. [Pause] I feel it's the anger. I feel OK if I could get through the initial scare of getting physically close.
Jim: How would John [observer sitting in on the session] be as a sexual partner?
Florence: [Pause] I don't think I would be as afraid of getting close to you, John.
Jim: What's the difference?
Florence: [Looks younger; pause] I don't know. You may be more aggressive than he would. I think you would be harder to please than he would.
Jim: Sexually?
Florence: [Smiling; looks in her forties] Yes. Right off the top of my head.
Jim: You look pleased.
Florence: Well, I'm enjoying talking about it.
Jim: Some of the other men here? Mike? [Meaning other trainees in the program who are not present at this particular session.] How would Mike be as a sexual partner?
Florence: As far as being turned on, no. I'm not turned on.
Jim: Could you put Mike there and say that to him?
Florence: I'm not turned on. You've got a nice body. I liked looking at you without your shirt on last night, and I'm not turned on.
Jim: And I'm assuming that there is the potential for turn-on with the two of us, with John and me. With me the problem is that you're afraid that I'd be too demanding. Am I right that there is that potential there?
Florence: [Now notices her aliveness, whereas it was noticeable to the observer before] Yup. The potential is there. With Mike the potential is there, too. I'm feeling a little more alive as I'm talking about this. (10)
Jim: How old are you when you get to thinking of other people when you are feeling more alive?
Florence: About middle-age. I don't know, I don't know. [Video is played back so she can see how she looks.] [In tiny voice] You scared me now—
Jim: How are you scaring yourself?
Florence: [Long pause—tears] (11) I mean I know I'm old.
Jim: A good bit of the time.
Florence: I feel very old and I feel very young and I feel very young, too.
Jim: How old are you?
Florence: [Pause] I'm fifty-one.

Jim:	You have difficulty knowing your age?
Florence:	I forget it within three or four years. I'm fifty-one. I'm not so scared anymore. [Sighs] Sometimes I look like somebody's grandmother.
Jim:	Whose?
Florence:	I don't know. I've never seen my grandmother. Sometimes I look like my grandmother and see stuff around my eyes and my chin and my mouth—I forgot about my grandmother, but I lived with her for a long time; I look Irish and I'm Irish when I'm there. I look Irish. I look like an old Irish woman. (12)
Jim:	Does she have any sex drive?
Florence:	No, she left her husband, lived with us. The one thing I remember her saying is, I couldn't show my ankles and stockings. I used to go bare-legged. She wanted me to wear hose. She didn't have any men in her life.
Jim:	About how old was Grandma Gorman when she came to live with you, approximately?
Florence:	Oh, maybe forty? Forty, fifty, about my age. I was like a young kid— (13)
Jim:	Would that be OK with you to finish off like she did?
Florence:	No. Uh. She just stayed around the house, taking care of the house, fighting with my mother.
Jim:	There is some excitement in that.
Florence:	[Laughs] Not enough for me.
Jim:	What would be enough excitement for you? (14)
Florence:	I think excitement for me would be to have some type of relationship with a man I loved. To have a normal, healthy, sexual relationship— caring, sharing, and all the rest of those things that go with—I'm curling my toes. [Eyes bright]
Jim:	I am just wondering if you can imagine yourself saying that to a man: "I'd like to have a normal, healthy, sexual relationship with you."
Florence:	Oh, that would be very scary for me. I could imagine myself saying that here.
Jim:	Put an imaginary man here and say— (15)
Florence:	OK. I'd like to have a normal, healthy, sexual relationship with you.
Jim:	How do you sound? (16)
Florence:	Businesslike. How did it sound to you?
Jim:	A little pugnacious.
Florence:	Give me another word for pugnacious.
Jim:	Aggressive.
Florence:	Uh-huh.
Jim:	A little tiny bit of a chip on your shoulder.
Florence:	I was noticing a bit in the work that I was doing in that tape—that my jaw gets like that.
Jim:	Say that again: "I'd like to have . . ."
Florence:	I'd like to have a normal, healthy, sexual relationship with you. [Sounds softer and more tender]
Jim:	How did you sound?
Florence:	A little softer. [Elfish smile]
Jim:	Are there any men around you that you would like to say that to if you dared, or whom?

Florence: There is just one young man around that I, yeah, that I would like to say that to. ''Ken, I would like to have a normal, healthy, sexual relationship with you.''

Jim: Does he respond in any way?

Florence: If he did, I think that he would respond, uh, ''I'm scared, scared as you are,'' whatever that would be.

Jim: My reaction when you say what you just said: normal, healthy, et cetera—I, I—

Florence: Clinical? [Smiles]

Jim: [Embarrassed laugh] I couldn't measure up to those standards. (17)

Florence: Oh, yeah.

Jim: Normal, healthy. [Florence chuckles.] I'd like to have a normal, unhealthy, sexual relationship with you.

Florence: That sounds much better. That I could go for. [Highly animated; laughs more]

Jim: Are you blushing?

Florence: Yeah, I'm blushing. There would be more excitement in a normal—I mean abnormal, unhealthy, sexual relationship with you. (18, 19)

Jim: Yeah, that is more of a turn-on, I imagine. My guess is that one of the ways that you keep yourself turned off and have a low sexual drive or energy is this ideal or prescription or whatever—''normal,'' ''healthy''—''Let's first shower, put on deodorant, brush our teeth''—What's going on now?

Florence: I'm just thinking about what you are saying and wondering. One thought that went through my head—about—I'm not normal if I'm not sexual. I'm playing with words. *Normal, sexual,* and how all of my good sexual experiences have been the opposite of that. And the others have been kind of boring, but the ones I am remembering were *not* like that. [Long pause] (20)

Jim: Um, this potential friend, uh, see what happens if you tell him what you really want. (21)

Florence: [Mischievous—laughs] Right now?

Jim: Sunday?

Florence: That would be a risk for me, and I am going to take it.

Jim: What would be a risk for you?

Florence: Reach out and tell him what I really want from him.

Jim: This year?

Florence: No, Sunday!

Jim: I was teasing you.

Florence: Oh! I took you literally. [Laughs] I'm back to normal, healthy, da-*da,* da-*da*—

Jim: Make the experiment here. [Long silence]

Florence: I got what I would like to say in my head, and I'm not putting it out. OK. ''Ken, I'd like to *fuck* with you.'' [Smiles]

Jim: What's happening? (22)

Florence: Uh, I felt warm as I said that.

Jim: Are you feeling a little bit turned on?

Florence: All over my body but not in my genitals. [Jim snickers, Florence laughs.] I'm not very good in anatomy.

Jim: You have—

Florence: [Laughs] I saw flashes of my mother, my grandmother, uh! Like that, you know? That exclamation. Fireworks. (23)

Jim: I am imagining that you *have* had periods of times when you felt very turned on, and as you look back on those, is there anything that is a red thread or that runs through those experiences for you—that you experienced excitement and/or interest? (24)

Florence: Uh-huh. When I first was married, the first five years that I was married, I was really turned on and with sexual experiences. These were, when I was married, with men that were what I call I couldn't live with them, but it was nice to fuck with them—they were always turned on, men that were always turned on. Not too responsible, sort of sociopathic, psychopathic type of men. But they were men. I don't know if you are following me. (25)

Jim: They were charming.

Florence: And they loved all women, including me. And then I've been very turned on.

Jim: Uh. The first five years of marriage, when did your first child come?

Florence: My two children are adopted.

Jim: When did you adopt your first child?

Florence: When I was about thirty-five—twelve years after we were married.

Jim: So in your first five years there was a lot of excitement. No children, and there is a lot of excitement when you are with men who are not very responsible and who like your own excitement and who don't make any great demands, don't obligate you in any way. [Pause] How old are you now? (26)

Florence: [Responds immediately] Fifty-one.

Jim: How old are you? How old were you looking just then?

Florence: Probably about seventy-two, sixty-five.

Jim: Where were you?

Florence: Where was I? In my head.

Jim: Where were you when you were looking so old? What were you doing? (27)

Florence: I was trying to figure something out.

Jim: My *guess* is, when you are with some sociopathic man, you're not about to try to figure something out.

Florence: [Laughs] Just having a good time.

Jim: So for you figuring out is aging, ages you.

Florence: That fits. To get on with living, I stop trying to figure out how to make the past work, and I just get on with living instead of trying to figure things out. Trying to figure things out prevents me from getting on with living.

Jim: That's very true for all of us. I can own to that. I had a *fantasy* of you being somewhat psychopathic with your friend. Saying, "I would like to fuck with you," and not figuring out and that you were in a sense identifying with the way in which you had a good time or the men you had a good time with, not busy figuring things out, you were just—and what was true of them was that there—that there was not only you but any woman, a lot of women, so you could imagine that there was not only Ken, but ten, fifteen other guys? (28)

Florence:	That is one of the things I fear.
Jim:	That you would fear? Aha! It is not a wish, it is a fear.
Florence:	It is a fear. (29)
Jim:	That you become an abandoned woman.
Florence:	Brazen. (30)
Jim:	Tell *me,* "I have *no* wish to be a brazen hussy."
Florence:	[Laughs weakly] I have no wish to become a brazen huss—y, hussy—I can't even say it. I have no wish to become a brazen hussy. [Smiles] (31)
Jim:	True? False?
Florence:	*False.* I'd like to experiment with what it would be like to be a brazen hussy.
Jim:	And?
Florence:	I would have to change my life-style a *bit* [our emphasis] to do that. (32)
Jim:	And what I thought was—and you don't.
Florence:	And I don't want to change my life-style.
Jim:	You don't experiment.
Florence:	I don't experiment. No. (33)
Jim:	You stay turned off. [Long silence]
Florence:	[Muffled] OK.
Jim:	So where are you so far in terms of, uh, what you wanted, how you are using this hour, using me?
Florence:	I am using this hour and using you to talk about my problem of what I do instead of getting on with living.
Jim:	What I do instead of getting on with living is—?
Florence:	Trying to figure things out.
Jim:	I thought I heard you say—talk about your problems.
Florence:	Talk about my problems.
Jim:	I know some people who literally do that instead of living—spend their lives talking about their problems. They are workshop bums.
Florence:	I could see myself doing that around this problem, thinking about, talking about, rather than doing. Talking about the problem—getting on with it. I don't want to do that. (34)
Jim:	I won't do what?!
Florence:	Keep talking about the problem.
Jim:	Raise your right hand. [Florence laughs.] "I, Florence, do solemnly swear . . ."
Florence:	I, Florence, do solemnly swear to get on with living.
Jim:	Um. I'm feeling sad right now. And I often get a feeling like this kind of sadness when I hear people making *declarations of intention.* (35) This is one of the areas that I quarrel with certain therapy approaches. I sometimes get angry with them. I am feeling sad. And I was attempting to get you to experience the promising. (36)
Florence:	The redecision and the planning.
Jim:	Or whatever it is called.
Florence:	Thank you for sharing your sadness and—
Jim:	My belief is that this might be an appropriate stopping place. I want to leave some time for feedback, and I am wondering how that sounds to you. (37) Does anything feel unfinished, or that you got a start of something—
Florence:	I had a start of something and this would be a good place to stop.

Commentary

The following discussion covers the how and why of Jim's work in this session with Florence.

Jim begins the session by observing that Florence looks older and younger at different times (1). He uses his own keen awareness of her physical appearance and posture to direct her attention to herself. (Gestalt therapists are trained to notice even very small movements that untrained observers would probably miss; see Simkin, 1982.) His observation highlights a polarity within her: young versus old. Encouraging Florence to experience both sides of the polarity allows her the opportunity to expand her range of feelings and behaviors. No one is a fixed personality. Many clients come to therapy saying they want to find their identity, as if that were one thing! We are all different people, at different times, in varying circumstances. The sum of us is greater than our parts; we have many sides and polarities. Gestalt therapy gives attention to the observation and awareness of our different parts, to knowing ourselves more fully. Jim is pursuing this approach with Florence on the issue of age. Using instant video replay, Florence checks out her imagined view of herself with how she actually sees herself (2). Gestalt therapy focuses on the difference between imagining/thinking and actually seeing, hearing, and sensing. *Congruence* is important: are the client's words, tone of voice, and posture saying the same thing? If not—if there is incongruence—it is clear that some parts of the person are not within his or her awareness. Jim observes Florence's puffy eyes; she recalls her sadness and anger (3). Later, he asks her to give her posture a voice (4), and she discovers her desire to come up with bright answers (5), which is quite different from her earlier words about sadness and anger. She was remembering these states, and yet at the moment she was more concerned about her performance with Jim, a concern he had observed through her bodily posture. We lie a lot with words, but our body never lies; it mirrors and expresses present needs more clearly.

At this point in the session, Jim asks what she wants from herself and from him (6). His question gives her the responsibility to be in charge of what she wants. It also implies that he is there as a coexplorer, to help her with her issues, not as the authority to tell her what she *should* address. She then tells him in generalized concepts that she wants to explore her "inner structure" and what procedure to follow. She acknowledges being split, which leads to tears and then to her saying, "I don't want to do what I'm doing." She is not accepting where she is and wishes to be elsewhere (see Simkin and Yontef, 1984). In an effort to help her experience this present-versus-future split more fully, Jim gives her the sentence "I don't want to cry and I am crying" (7). By giving her a simple, clear sentence to repeat, he is helping her become aware of how she is deflecting from experiencing her crying. When a client says, "I want" (or "I do not want"), she is deflecting from the present into the future and, therefore, diminishing her experience of what is true at the moment. This does not imply that one should not consider future goals and wants. However, what we see here is Florence stopping her momentary experience by leaping into the future. It is important in Gestalt work that the client experience with her entire body. By saying a sentence out loud, one brings the whole body into play and can discover whether the sentence feels true or hollow. This is a way of testing congruence. To have a thought or sentence only in the mind does not produce a full experience.

Many people have the idea that Gestalt therapists do not deal with the past, which is not correct. In this situation, Jim encourages Florence's past thoughts to come forth into the present (see Simkin and Yontef, 1984). Jim goes further and asks her for more history about her life with Chet (8). Then he goes another step, using the information Florence gave about her sex drive being low, and asks her how she feels at the moment about him, John (the observer), and Mike from the workshop (9). As she deals with her feelings with the present men, she begins to feel livelier and younger (10). Here again, Jim has brought her back to the present reality to test her actual experience.

After Jim has her see herself again on the video replay, Florence says that he had scared her (11). Jim asks, "How are you scaring yourself?" Here he puts the responsibility back on her (see Simkin and Yontef, 1984). She cries and understands that she is scaring herself with her age. Statements like "You scared me" or "You hurt me" are common in our culture, and they imply that the other person is at fault. Gestaltists focus on taking responsibility for how one reacts—hurt, scared, rejected, and so on. Another person may influence you, but you are the one who has the emotional experience and is therefore responsible for it. As Florence acknowledges her age, she imagines herself to look like somebody's grandmother. Jim goes into the past again by asking, "Whose grandmother?" As Florence's own grandmother's life emerges, he wonders whether she is taking on her grandmother's fate and so questions her more specifically (12 and 13). Being specific is very important. Being general distances her from fully experiencing, whereas being specific focuses her feelings more clearly. Jim does not push her to deal with her grandmother's history but leads her back to her excitement and her wanting more than her grandmother had (14). Florence then states that she wants a normal, healthy, sexual relationship with caring and sharing—a cultural cliché. Jim brings her back from this idealized expectation to the moment and asks her to say this *to* someone (15). He pays close attention to her voice (16) and asks her to say the sentence again; repetition often clarifies experience. She sounds less pugnacious the second time, more open and tender. She realizes her tough approach cuts off her soft side. Jim does not stress this discovery. What is significant to him is her high expectations of herself and others. He uses himself again and tells her *he* could not measure up to her standards (17) (see Simkin, 1975a). She gets out of her thought and chuckles with more presence, including blushing (18). They explore the alternative of an unhealthy relationship (19), and she begins to feel more lively. Then she wanders back into her thoughts and makes an interpretation of not being normal if not sexual (20). Jim ignores this mental construct, brings her back to the session with him, and asks her to tell her friend what she wants (21). When she says, "Ken, I'd like to fuck with you," although it may seem uncharacteristic, she sounds and appears real. At this point, she smiles (22), and Jim realizes even more how much of herself she has kept hidden.

In the midst of her awareness of the warmth from saying, "Ken, I'd like to fuck with you," Florence flashes back to her mother's and grandmother's obvious disapproval (23). Jim does not pursue this; he stays with her energy and excitement (24) (see Simkin, 1975). With a low-energy and depressed client, staying with her aliveness is often indicated. Florence could too easily wallow in her family's disapproval. Jim wants her to feel the positive part of her polarity, the part she experiences least. So he asks for more history and discovers her involvements with a number of charming but irresponsible men (25). He mirrors back to her what she has said, and the message seems to be that she enjoys being sexual without obligation (26). Jim brings her back to the present by asking her age again. She was in her thoughts, trying to understand her sexuality, and she feels older doing so (27). Jim follows an idea of his own and wonders how she might feel with "ten, fifteen other guys" (28). He has a hunch she might feel like a woman behaving with abandon (29). She identifies with this thought when she immediately says, "brazen" (30). So he encourages her to experiment with this hidden part of her (30) (see Simkin and Yontef, 1984). After she says the sentence he gives her, he gets further clarification by asking whether it is true or false (31). When she acknowledges that there is a brazen hussy hiding inside her, she runs away from it. Jim does not take an obvious choice and encourage her to role-play this character at this point. Instead he tracks her next move, which is to jump into the future by claiming she would have to change her life-style "a bit" (32). Jim begins to summarize what emerged during the session: how she actually is in her life now, how she stays contained and depressed, unalive and not sexual. She spends a lot of time trying to figure things out, talking about her problems, and not taking many risks (33). As she listens to this summary, she leaps into the future again, claiming that she wants to change (34). At this point, Jim has her exaggerate her future intentions by asking her to begin a sentence with "I, Florence, do solemnly swear . . . " as a way for her to experience more fully how she jumps from the *now* of the brazen hussy to what she wants to do at some undefined future time (see Simkin, 1976b).

If Jim had pushed Florence to play out her hussy role, he would have been ignoring the process of how she runs away from this part of herself. Jim expresses his sadness about making future promises, which is a way to set up the critic/rebel process again (35). Some therapeutic approaches allow and encourage such promising; Gestalt therapy discourages it. Jim's intention at this moment is to get Florence to *experience* her promising (36).

Jim tells Florence that he is ready to conclude the session and asks whether she is ready to stop (37). He stresses the importance of completing anything that might be unfinished. Leaving an issue incomplete is seen as binding energy that could be more fruitfully used to meet the next emerging process. Sometimes it can be useful to encourage a client to stop a session without a sense of being finished— for example, when the client is very defensive or protected and is unwilling or unable to acknowledge what is happening. Florence is open to seeing herself in this session, and so Jim makes sure they have reached a full and complete conclusion.

Looking over this session, several questions come up. Why did Jim not help Florence adjust to her age and loneliness? Why did he not challenge her more strongly about her attraction to irresponsible men? Why was he so tolerant of her depressed nature? Why did he not offer more hope for change in the future? The following is a minilecture given by Jim to his trainees in 1982. It was recorded, and the transcript has been edited by Thomas R. Layne, one of Jim's graduates. Jim discusses some of the basic theories and goals of Gestalt therapy and provides at least partial answers to these questions.

> I want to say a little more about the existential philosophy that underlies Gestalt therapy. Until less than a hundred years ago, the accepted philosophy in the Western world was Aristotelian, to which

Isaac Newton made important additions. It was a cause-and-effect system of belief, and this concept spread to psychology. The belief was that all behavior is motivated and that there is a reason for everything we do. Sometimes, if we cannot find the reason, it is believed to be *hidden,* and so we look for what is *behind.* In human behavior, most people believed that if they could find the cause of why they behave in a certain way, they could then change that cause, and the effect would be that their behavior would change. Everyone was looking for causes, or a *root cause.*

Einstein's theory of relativity and other subsequent work in the area of nuclear physics moved away from causality toward a more observational and existential basis. Gestalt therapy came into being during this period and is based on the same principles. In Gestalt, we look at *what* and *how*; the question of *why* is irrelevant. The *what* means paying attention to what is occurring. You need to look at raw data; simply allow what *is,* and observe it. What you do as a good Gestalt therapist is teach yourself and your clients how to observe what is—how to pay attention to the obvious. That means paying attention to what is going on. If a person is aware of some feeling, then that is his process at the time.

This awareness is not ever-present. At times you or your client are not in touch with, or aware of, where you are. We call that being out of touch, out of contact, or withdrawn. But it comes down to the reality that when a person is unaware, he is usually not conscious of his unawareness. One of the ways the therapist can be helpful is by feeding back his impressions of the client—how he appears to you. So when I ask you what you are aware of, and you are not in touch with what you are aware of, you might guess—correctly—that you were out of touch with reality.

If you can collect this kind of data and teach your client to do so, without passing judgment, you are both on the way to becoming good observers, aware and nonjudgmental. Simply noticing what you are actually doing is the key. "Why?" is not a useful question. Once you understand *how* you do what you do, you have the means to correct it. That is, you can do the reverse. If I keep myself in a state of unawareness by thinking, then one of the ways I can reverse that is to interfere with my thinking. I can do anything else—look at something, taste something, smell something, focus on something other than thinking. When I become aware that I have lost touch again, that I am thinking again, I am at a very crucial point. If my reaction is a judgmental "Aha! I have been thinking again!," I can easily get myself back into a judgmental cycle. If I simply observe, "Ah, I have been thinking," then I am collecting data and am on the way to being in control.

I do not change by deciding to change or by being willing to change or by making New Year's resolutions. I change by being what I am and noticing it, by paying attention without judging. If I taste my behavior and it is distasteful, that is all I need. I will organismically and automatically change what I find distasteful. However, this self-correcting change will not occur unless I have tasted the full toxicity of my issue. Most people only begin to taste, then they run from the problem. They just take tiny tastes, and so their problem does not self-correct.

The Gestalt therapist's job is to observe the client, feed back the observations, and encourage the client to become more aware—to take a complete, full taste. That is all that is needed; it is very simple, and it is extremely complex. It involves changing from an Aristotelian mode of behavior to an existential mode; moving away from talking about, thinking about, and the *shoulds*; staying with what is real and tasting it fully. "What are you aware of?" is a profound question, and awareness is our only tool. The support for awareness is an existential mode of looking at the world and teaching ourselves and others to become phenomenologists, to pay attention to the *now*.

13

Existential-Humanistic Psychotherapy

James F. T. Bugental

What does it mean to be alive? To be *truly alive*? What are the limits of being alive? How much aliveness is possible for me, for you?

It is familiar to all of us that some days we feel livelier—more alive—than others. It is a commonplace of language to speak of some people as having more "vitality" or "spirit." Eastern traditions often use the image of awakening, and we in the West shout at other drivers to "Wake up!" All these words point to a profound and widely experienced dimension of human consciousness but one often neglected in our psychologies. I want to introduce a word that links aliveness to the work of psychotherapy. That term is *presence*. "Presence is the quality of being in a situation in which one intends to be as aware and as participative as one is able to be at that time and in those circumstances. Presence is carried into effect through mobilization of one's inner (toward subjective experiencing) and outer (toward the situation and any other person/s in it) sensitivities" (Bugental, 1978, p. 36).

The kind of psychotherapy that the case presented in this chapter will illusrate is intended to aid clients in becoming more alive, more spirited (Bugental and Bugental, 1984), more vital, more present. Paradoxically, for this psychotherapy to be effective, the client must be genuinely present! Or at least as much so as he or she can be at the time. The paradox is more apparent than real, however, since the therapeutic work revolves around disclosing the ways in which the client avoids genuine presence and the costs to vital living that those avoidances exact. This effort to seek aliveness takes client (and therapist) into many of the main life areas, and this journey is made not abstractly but very concretely—that is, vitally—in the interactions in the consulting room.

A few words of background may help to put all this in perspective: For the past 300 years there has been a steady trend toward mechanization, toward impersonality, and toward the objectification of persons. This trend has brought with it many benefits and not a few curses. It has made life more comfortable for much

222

of the western world and has introduced dissatisfaction on a worldwide scale, as it has promised but not delivered greater happiness from obtaining objects—and from making oneself an object.

Concurrently, there has been an opposite (but not an equal) reaction: Individualism, nonconformity, uniqueness, rebellion, and anarchic terrorism have become familiar news fare. In art, politics, justice systems, education, religion, and many other arenas, there erupt innovations and experiments that defy easy classification as creative or destructive. And individualistic crimes (terrorism, berserkers, crimes against persons) have increased. As Paul Tillich wrote, "Man resists objectification, and if man's resistance is broken, man himself is broken" (1951, p. 98).

Humanistic-existential psychotherapy sees it as its task to evoke the latent aliveness in our clients. We do not seek to teach them something so much as to call on them to listen better to what they already know but to which they do not attend, owing to lack of presence. This view contrasts with the perception of therapy as the repair of an ailing or broken being.

Parallel to this contrast are the beliefs, on the one hand, that the healing/growth potential resides in the client and, on the other hand, that it is in the power of the therapist or the therapist's techniques and the substances she or he brings.

It needs to be explicit that this is not necessarily an either/or situation. There are indeed conditions for which the introduction of external measures (medication, drugs, hypnosis, surgery, restraint, hospitalization) is in the best interests of the patient, the society, or both. However, it is my belief that there are many more client concerns in which the greatest and most lasting service to the client can best be sought through the kind of evocation illustrated here.

In this work we find that almost everyone is incompletely awake or present much of the time. Even when important life issues are at stake, there is a tendency to distance oneself from those matters, to deny the emotional costs, to avoid the naked confrontation. Working with clients so "resisting" presence will often disclose the earlier experiences that have led them to these patterns of avoidance, but solely understanding their roots no more stops the destructive evasions than does knowing the lake from which a river flows dam the floods that sweep along its path.

Another aspect of the task of working with clients' lack of presence is important to appreciate: the therapist must herself or himself seek to be as present as possible if the work is to go forward. A detached, uninvolved attitude tends to breed or reinforce its complement. A vital, attuned awareness, by its very quality, contributes to the evocative impact. Moreover, the therapist's own inner sensitivity is crucial to his or her so tuning in to the client's experiencing as to be able to mirror back elements of which the client is as yet unaware (see Walsh, 1984).

In summary: The human seeking for greater depth and richness of living is a primary force in all we humans feel, think, and do. This hunger for vitalness in being impels us to therapy or to other efforts that may bring us the inner experience that we call spiritedness. In seeking toward it, a primary issue is presence, the quality of being truly in a life situation (for example, in the psychotherapeutic encounter). To the degree that one is able to so enter into this engagement, to that degree the likelihood is good that there will be an outcome of enlarged being and potency. Thus presence is the central goal and the primary focus of much of humanistic-existential psychotherapy.

Eric: The Struggle to Be Actual

Eric comes to me on referral from a colleague who is a consultant at the junior college clinic in which Eric is a counselor. In all, we have 171 interviews in just short of two years. The presentation that follows does not trace all aspects of our work together, a manifest impossibility for such an intensive and extensive enterprise. Instead, it focuses on a characteristic issue of existential-humanistic psychotherapy (Bugental, 1976, 1978, 1981): the client's struggle to be genuinely and concernedly present to and in the therapeutic engagement.

What follows is a re-creation of the therapeutic work. All identifying details have been disguised; typical dialogue has been reconstructed from notes and memory.

Monday, 1 June. "I want to be a therapist myself, and so I thought I should get some therapy so I'd know what it's like, you know. I have some problems, of course, but not too many or anything, nothing that would make me go into therapy if it weren't—well, you know how I mean."

"I'm not sure that I do. Why don't you tell me?"

"Yeah, well, you know, I don't have any big anxiety panics or flaky compulsions or obsessions or any of that stuff. Just the plain old problems we all have, you know. But anyway, I wanted to know more about your way of working, so I thought it would be good to come in for a while and see what it was like, you know."

"You want to try out being in therapy with me."

"Well, yeah. I mean, I've read some of your stuff, and I figure that's what I'd like. I mean the kind of thing you describe, the humanistic approach, and all that." He smiles engagingly at me, and I find a responsive smile coming to my face.

So Eric tells me how he comes to be in my office this overcast day in early June. Although it's midmorning, the office light is on, and it shows me this good-looking young man, with long hands and feet, casual jeans and sport shirt, and a rather vague, distracted manner. He sits loosely in the big patient chair, looking at me earnestly at times as he talks and then apparently forgetting himself and examining the office with frank curiosity.

Allowing him to proceed pretty much as he chooses results in a rambling personal history. Eric has a master's degree in counseling from a midwestern university, is working as a counselor in the campus clinic of the local junior college, and lives with a young woman who is a secretary at the college. He came to California with his younger sister and his divorced mother four years ago and has worked in two generally similar settings before his present position. Although he is thirty-three, Eric has never married and is still attached to his family of origin. Toward the end of this first interview, he returns to his vaguely indicated "problems."

"Well, like I told you, I want to get my license and go into practice before too long." He pauses, looks earnestly at me in an appeal for an approving response—a response I am reluctant to give. He's trying to short-cut being explicit by getting me to implicitly say "I know" when actually he has provided very little information. Indeed, this is the first I've heard of his intention to become a licensed practitioner.

With Eric there is a persistent ground haze over our communication that makes everything shifting, indistinct. Often it seems his phrases come out mechanically without his examining them—let alone selecting them—to fit his actual inner experience. A nagging example is his continually interlayering his talk with "you know" when often there is no way I could know what he means.

Since I have still made no reply, Eric resumes, "Well, it's like I have some problems too. You know, the kind everybody has. I mean, no biggies, just sort of worries, you could say."

"You seem anxious to play down the importance of your concerns."

"Oh, no," too quickly. Then he pauses. I wait. He seems troubled; so I'll try to help him out: "What are you thinking right now?"

"Well, I kind of wonder how you mean?" It's not quite a statement, nor is it truly a question.

This is too soon to let him struggle; so I clarify my intention: "Whenever you mention these 'problems,' you make a point of how minor they are; yet you don't actually say what they are, either."

"Oh, sure, I see." He isn't interested, however. Instead he moves on quickly. "Well, I always worry that I'm not going to do things well enough, you know. It's no big deal, you know—oh, I just did it, didn't I?"

"Um-hmm." A good sign: he is using my observation promptly.

"Yeah, I see what you mean. But I really mean that I don't have too much anxiety or—it's no big neurotic or—I mean I don't get all obsessive about it or anything. It's just that I kind of worry about it. I think it's because my father was such a perfectionist. He always was criticizing everything I did. Never could really satisfy him. It makes me mad to think how he always was demanding more than whatever I did do. When I was eleven, he—"

It's time to find out more about his readiness to use my interventions. I interrupt: "You don't seem mad as you tell me about it."

"Yeah, well, I guess I'm used to it; so it doesn't come out very much."

"Eric, I can tell you've done a lot of thinking about yourself, but—"

"Oh, no—well, yes, in a way. But not really, you know. I mean I don't dwell too much on things. It doesn't do any good, you know."

"You sound a bit as though I'd accused you of doing something wrong." He's so vigilant, so afraid that he won't come across to me as doing things right.

"No, no. It's OK. I'm glad to have you point out things like that to me. It's just that I wouldn't want you to think I was one of those obsessive types, you know."

I sit back and let him go on. I have a slightly irritated feeling, as though I were being subtly teased or misled. I know that's not his intent, but I can't make contact with Eric. He has such a façade of words and understanding about himself that I feel eluded whenever I try to make genuine contact with him.

In the same way that he described his self-doubts, he now tells me of his troubles in relating to the woman with whom he lives. This leads to a similar account about his relations with his mother and sister. In all this, Eric mentions but never displays feelings, seems only vaguely connected to what he is describing, and is continually concerned that I not see him as troubled in any serious way.

Thursday, 2 July. After a dozen sessions, Eric and I have developed a working pattern. Today is typical: He comes a few minutes early and, at my suggestion, does not read in the waiting area but uses the time to try to get inwardly focused before our session begins. When he enters the therapy room, he plops down in the

big chair with an exaggerated exhalation of breath. Then he looks briefly but pene-
tratingly at me, after which he leans his head back, closes his eyes, and begins to
report on what he finds within himself.

"I was thinking about what we were talking about last time, and I wanted
to ask you just what you meant when you said that it was hard for me to be really
here. I mean, it seems to me that I do what—"

(Interrupting) "Do you think you will?"

"Will what?," startled, opening his eyes to look at me.

"Will ask me."

"Oh," vaguely. "I guess so. Uh—uh, what did you mean?"

"Eric, I'll answer that in a minute, but right now will you see whether you
can really get in touch with where you are inside yourself?"

"You mean, what do I feel? Well, I guess I feel kind of confused. I mean,
I'm not sure just what you—"

(Interrupting) "No, Eric, wait a minute. Did you notice that you said, 'I
guess I feel . . .'? It was as though you were talking about someone else and saying, 'I guess he feels . . .' It didn't have any sense of inner recognition in it."

"Oh, sure. I see what you mean. I should have said, 'I feel confused.' It's
just a kind of habit I have, you know. Anyway, I'm not really too confused."

When carefully examined, that last response of Eric's is a compendium of
nonpresence. With his "Oh, sure," he quickly agrees without really examining
whether he has a similar felt meaning (Gendlin, 1962) within him. "I see what
you mean" when he has mistaken my meaning completely. "I should have said"
translates my observation into a moral instruction, and he follows that injunction
by simply rewording his former statement with no apparent recognition of its meaning. "Just a" dismisses the importance of the matter, and "kind of" avoids any
definitiveness in his own statement, keeps it mushy. "Habit" makes it something
that functions automatically without his attention (here, at least, he's accurate but
scarcely in the way he intends.) "You know" is Eric's standard way of sliding past
being complete and explicit. Finally, his use of "too" ("not too confused") keeps
the whole issue of his possible inner distress in the ambiguous place where Eric
lives much of the time.

Given all this, to what shall I respond? Certainly it would be pointless to
go for any of these specific instances. Eric would only translate my comment into
a further injunction about word choice. Rather, I need to get back of these to the
underlying inability to be fully present with me and in his own life. That is a much
more difficult and time-consuming process on which I can only make a beginning now.

"It must seem to you that I'm making a lot out of a rather trivial matter."

"Well, no. I mean—well, I do wonder why it's important, but I guess you
have a reason. It's just that I sort of wonder what that reason is. I suppose I shouldn't
ask, really, because you'll tell me when—"

"Let me interrupt you again, Eric." He looks surprised and then, quickly,
attentive, the good student. "I want you to ask me when you don't understand
what I say or what I am suggesting to you. This is your psychotherapy, and you
need to be able to express whatever you're experiencing here—including being
puzzled by what I say."

Eric's face changes, eyes focusing on me more seeingly, expression attentive. He's beginning to be aware of the actuality of the two of us being engaged

at this moment. "Well, I don't think I know just what you mean. I thought—" He drifts off uncertainly. Already, the more familiar vagueness is returning.

"Right now, Eric, you're confused and not sure what I want."

"Yes." He's considering; then he brightens, and the tempo picks up—as my hopeful feeling slows down. "You want me to ask you questions when I don't understand you instead of beating around the bush. OK, that sounds good to me."

Not a complete miss. I do want him to "stop beating around the bush," but I don't think it's just a matter of giving up a bad speech habit, as he regards it. As he quickly goes on, he demonstrates his earnest intention to learn and his failure to grasp what I was trying to help him recognize.

"You know, I've been feeling bad lately because Janet is always complaining. I don't know how I keep getting with women that don't like me."

"Janet doesn't like you?"

"Well, I guess I don't really mean that. Oh-oh, I shouldn't have said 'I guess.' I mean, that's one of those things, isn't it? Anyway, I think she likes me kind of, but she's always saying I'm selfish, and I think she's pretty selfish herself. I mean she . . . ''

Although Eric seems unaffected by my interventions, I know that gradually they are reaching him, and so I turn my attention to his by now familiar account of his difficulty with his lady. He's already shown that repeatedly he goes through a pattern of discovering, wooing, and winning a Miss Special. Then, when she has been won, he finds that she is not who he thought her to be, and he becomes restless and unresponsive, while she is disappointed and complaining. Yet he professes to be baffled: "I don't know why every woman I'm with gets this way. Do I just pick them bad, or is there something I'm doing?"

After Eric leaves, I sit for a time thinking about him and his lostness. He is a well-intentioned person whose life is somehow blunted and lacking in fulfillment. Whatever he may say of his reasons for being here, underneath is, I believe, a yearning for more vividness, more spirited living (Bugental and Bugental, 1984).

Eric's effort to gain control of his life is complicated by two interwoven factors: first, his absence from the center of his life and therefore from the ability to direct it as he wishes and, second, his insulating himself from actuality, with the semantic sawdust that takes the place of meaningful thinking and speaking.

First, since he treats himself as an object, critically standing apart from his own experience, he is a back-seat driver finding fault with the route his life is taking but not taking the wheel to direct it otherwise. He is almost as helpless to guide himself as he would be to guide someone else. He has so little access to his living inner experience that he is constantly dissatisfied with his own actions, with his relations with others, and with what he is able to bring about in the outer world.

Second, he continually keeps his experience in limbo, in a hypothetical mode. Thus he insulates himself from the lived reality of his being. His use of "like" ("It's like I'm afraid"), of "sort of" ("I sort of tried to tell her what I was thinking"), of "just" ("It just made me kind of mad"), of "too" ("Oh, I wasn't too upset about it"), and of many other verbal insulators serves to decrease the actuality of his living. It is not the words themselves, of course, but the underlying need to put padding between himself and the shock of actuality.

To be sure, our culture is filled with such distorting influences: the TV news shows us war and tragedy but with the sound modified for living-room consumption, with the camera skimming past the agony and the blood, and with a bright commercial quickly diluting the human experience that has just been suggested but not depicted.

Tuesday, 28 July. Our work for some time has been divided among three areas: Eric's recounting his earlier years, his present difficulty in forming a satisfying love relation, and my repeated efforts to bring him to more genuine presence in our sessions and in his life.

Eric enjoys telling me about his earlier years in what was then a loving family. He is sad and somewhat bitter when describing how that family was eventually broken apart by his father's rages, which kept everyone uneasy and which eventuated in his parents' divorce. These accounts are familiar stories with familiar emotions; there is little sense of immediacy in their telling.

The inability to develop satisfying relations turns out to be the "problem" to which Eric devotes most of his conscious energy in therapy. He describes his current companion, Janet, with whom he lives, in phrases that portray affection and exasperation going both ways. The same ambivalence is apparent in his work situation, where he is functioning much below his potential and where he fluctuates between the desire to seek an advanced degree and the impulse simply to stay in his present nondemanding position.

Finally, we work to help Eric gain a greater sense of being truly in his life. I make it a point in each session to spend some time in demonstrating to him his lack of focused awareness and his inauthentic phrasing of much that he says. I am not interested in the wording itself, of course, but I am certain that what the language patterns cover is fundamental to Eric's sense of futility, dissatisfaction, and incompleteness. This last—and, to me, most important—phase of our work is again the focus of our attention today.

"Janet says that I should talk to you about why I seem to be so absent-minded."

"So?" I want to draw his attention to another indirect approach to a topic.

"What do you mean? I guess I'm saying it wrong again or something." He seems vaguely annoyed.

"You seem to be using Janet to tell you what to talk about here."

"Oh, no. Of course not." His voice is sharp; then he pauses and swallows, and his voice becomes more conversational. "No, I don't need her to tell me what to do. I don't know why you'd say that."

"Eric, you're swallowing down your annoyance with me right now."

"No. I mean, well, I was a little surprised that you—that you would think—"

"Wait, feel inside. You were upset, annoyed, not simply surprised. Is it hard to let yourself feel that?"

"Well, not really. I suppose that—"

"Go slow, Eric. You start to talk too soon. Feel in your throat, in your stomach. (Pause) Now you can still find the echoes of the feeling if you let yourself."

Well," he pauses, considers. "Well, yes, I guess so. But I don't want to—I mean, you know what you're doing, and so—"

Keeping my voice quiet but insistent: "Yes, but still it can be irritating to—" I let the sentence hang there incomplete.

"I guess you want me to be angry, and you're right, I was kind of annoyed and—"

"It seems hard to let yourself have your anger unless it's because I want it."

"No, that's not so." Again he pauses and swallows, and his face changes. "I don't need your permission to be angry!" He watches my face intently.

"I can feel you're pissed with me right now." My tone conveys recognition and acceptance.

He is slow to respond, and then he shifts into his usual mode. "Well, yes, I guess I was for a few minutes, but really it's all right, and—"

"Now you're sliding back into your more familiar and comfortable way of being."

"Well, you know, it was no big deal."

"Eric, go slow. You were really here with me, feeling your feeling, letting me know you and what you were feeling. That was a big step. Can you let yourself know the difference between being here with me that way and the smooth front?"

He starts to speak, stops, seems to be attentive inside. "Yes, I guess so." His voice is unsure, but he's really trying. He glances at my face almost shyly. "It feels kind of—kind of too personal—"

Quiet voice: "You're right. It is personal. Very personal. But it's the way you need to risk being here a lot more of the time."

Voice equally quiet as he is sensing deeply within himself: "I don't know whether I can do that." He is quiet again. I wait. "I mean, I—" Another pause. "I see what you mean, I think, but—" We're silent several minutes—not a long time by the clock but a very long time in the circumstances. Then: "I think it makes me feel frightened." His voice is gaining strength.

"You 'think' that. Don't 'think' it, Eric. Reach down inside yourself and find out directly."

But his voice is rapidly coming back to its usual timbre. "Yeah, sure. Well, I guess it does."

"Eric, you just pulled out of the place you were in."

"No, I don't think so." The familiar façade is back in place.

And that's as far as we'll get today. I moved in too fast with that pickup on his use of "think." He wasn't ready. I was too pleased to see him into himself and pushed too soon and too much.

Thursday, 30 July. When Eric comes the next time, he looks troubled and intent, in contrast to his usual breezy manner.

"I've been thinking about what we talked about last time. You know, about being personal here." He pauses and looks to me for encouragement.

That's easy to give, for this may be a sign he's really beginning to hear me. "Um-hmm," manner interested and supportive.

"It's—I'm not sure just how you mean, and I remembered you're telling me I should ask you when—I mean I thought maybe you were—uh, I'm wondering—like maybe you were telling me—" He stops, vastly uncomfortable.

"It seems very hard to say what you were thinking or to ask me what you want to know." (Sympathetic tone.)

"Well, not really. But—yes, I guess it is. I mean, I wonder whether you were telling me that—" He stops, looks down at his hands in his lap, swallows with difficulty, glances quickly up at me. "I mean—"

"You're feeling a lot of tension about what you want to ask me." His anxiety radiates from him like heat waves. Whatever is troubling him is a lot bigger than I thought at first.

"Yeah, well, uh—I mean, it seemed like you maybe were saying—well, I wonder if you were saying I shouldn't be here, that I'm—'' Again he stops, his misery manifest.

"You wonder if I'm saying—?"

"That I'm too sick to be in therapy like this?"

Of course! No wonder he's in agony. "You're worrying that there's something so wrong with you that I'm going to tell you that—"

(Interrupting) "No, no! I mean, I kind of thought that, but I don't really think—well, is there?"

This is no time to prolong his distress. "No, Eric, there is nothing so wrong with you that you shouldn't be in this kind of psychotherapy. In fact, there is something very right in you that you have chosen to be here to get more out of your life."

He exhales a very long, very slow breath as his face suddenly drains of tension. He looks as though he might cry. Then I see him gather himself. "Yeah, well, I guess I didn't really think—"

"Wait, Eric. Wait a minute. Breathe. You've been holding your breath. You were really frightened, and now you're busy putting back the mask—"

"Yeah, I guess I was. I really was scared. I have always been afraid that—" He pauses, feelings welling up in him. Now his eyes swim, and he slumps in his chair. He stares straight ahead with pain obvious in his good-looking face and an aura of defeat about him. "Yes, I've always felt like sooner or later someone would tell me that—that a psychologist would look at me and say, 'You're nuts,' or—"

"How much courage it must have taken for you to come here and see me with that fear inside you!" I let him see my appreciation. Our clients have such guts in confronting their deepest anxieties!

Eric is weeping now. Recognition of his long, lonely fight with his self-doubt has broken the floodgates. I keep quiet, looking at him warmly but leaving the action totally with him now. He's in himself, and that's the important thing.

After several minutes, he takes some of the tissues I've put beside him, dries his eyes, blows his nose several times with trumpetlike blasts, and then straightens in his chair. He still hasn't looked directly at me since his emotions overwhelmed him. I take that as a good sign that he's really in his inner experiencing.

"Would you tell me again what you were saying to me Tuesday?" His voice is so quiet that it takes me by surprise. He still isn't looking at me.

"Eric, I certainly will tell you, but it would be more helpful if, first of all, you tell me what you remember of it. I'm not testing you, and you don't have to get it right. Still, if we knew just how you received it, perhaps I could say it so you could hear it better."

"Yeah, well, OK. I think you were telling me that I am not really here a lot of the time. And that's—(he swallows) that's when I thought you were saying I kind of flipped out or something."

"Oh, I see." I pause and briefly feel sorry that I didn't sense how he was hearing my words. But, of course, he heard them as he needed to; the net result is a positive one. "Sure, I can see how what I said could have sounded that way, but it's not what I wanted to put over to you."

"What did you mean?"

"I meant that you—and I and a lot of us—learned to treat ourselves as though we were things. Often when you talk to me about yourself, it's as though you were talking about an object or, at least, another person. Frequently you are not in touch with your own inner experiencing. You think about yourself and speculate about what you are feeling, but it's hard for you to just be in your inside, living the way you've been today for the last ten minutes.''

"I guess I understand, but—''

"Look, Eric, you just said, 'I guess I understand,' and then I interrupted you. Can you get the feel of that 'I guess'? Can you sense what it was doing in what you said?''

"Well, sure, I—'' He's starting too soon.

"Go slow, Eric. Give yourself a chance to really reach down inside. You don't have to have an answer, and you don't have to have it right away.''

"Yeah, well—'' And now he stops and seems to go inside more. I wait.

"Well, I think it means that I'm not sure, and so I kind of guess about it.''

"Sure, I can see that. That happens a lot, doesn't it? Notice what you just said, 'I think it means that I'm not sure, and so I kind of guess about it.' The 'I think' is like that 'I guess,' isn't it? Then the 'kind of' is another.''

"Yes. I didn't know I did that so much. Why is it important?''

"Hold off on that question for a little bit. I want you to try to feel again what those 'I thinks' and 'I guesses' and 'sort ofs' do for you. When you do something that much, it must be important to you.''

Eric looks puzzled, seems about to answer. It's too soon, and he's not into himself. I want to help him while he's so accessible. "Wait, Eric. I can see you about to answer me, but I think without your noticing it, my question has slipped you into the thinking-about-it place. Is that right?''

He shakes his head, starts to speak, but stops! That's a big step. He's quiet, checking into himself. Then, "Uh, I started to say, 'no,' but then I, uh—I, uh—I kind of got what you—oh, there I did it again, didn't I? I said, 'kind of,' and—and I think—(*sotto voce*) Again! and some way it feels sort of dangerous or naked if I just think of saying things without—without—well, you know.''

"No, Eric; I want you to tell me.''

"Yeah, well, like without protection.'' He's inwardly focused. I keep quiet. After nearly a minute, he straightens and draws in a long breath, looks up at me for the first time in quite a while. "Some way I feel safer when I say things that way. I don't know why; it just feels that way.''

"And you know that from the inside, not by thinking it out *about* yourself.''

"Yes,'' hesitantly. "Yes, I guess you could say that. Oh, there it is again. I said, 'I guess,' because—because I wasn't sure. No, wait. I'm pretty sure it was from the inside, as you say, but—''

"Yet you still wanted some protection.''

"Uh-huh. Why was that?'' Again he considers. "If I just agreed, then you'd—you'd win!'' He's surprised at his own words.

"And some way you didn't want me to win.''

"That's silly, I know, but still—''

"Don't desert yourself, Eric. It isn't silly; it's what it feels like inside you that counts.''

He is silent again. Several times he starts to speak and each time drops back. When he finally does, his voice sounds less introspective. "I don't know, Jim, I really don't. I just feel kind of tired and confused inside.''

"You've been working hard and in an unfamiliar and frightening place in yourself. It's okay to take a breather for a bit. Besides, our time's about up.''

We talk in a more casual way briefly, and the hour ends with Eric gradually sliding back into his usual manner, although some residue of greater engagement remains.

Thursday, 8 October. Now for some time Eric varies in his authenticity during our sessions. Sometimes he seems to be more truly accessible, more in touch with his actual experience, and less operating out of an ungrounded image of himself. Other days he is more as he was in our earlier sessions: vague, excessively qualifying everything, scarcely aware of himself or of me except as characters in a play he is passively watching. Overall, however, I am encouraged; he is gaining in sensitivity to the importance of this dimension and in alertness to his fluctuations on it.

Today is a bright, hot day that seems as though it should be mid-July rather than post–Labor Day. Eric comes in cutoff jeans and a shirt that announces he or someone ran in the Bay-to-Breakers Marathon some year. He is wearing sandals, which he kicks off almost at once as he reclines in the big chair, feet up on the hassock. His face conveys a mixture of impressions.

"You're wearing a face I can't read today, Eric."

He considers briefly before answering, a clear indication of his changed perspective on himself. "Yeah, well, I don't know whether I know what's on my face or—or in my feelings today." He shifts his position, fidgets with his shirt, which sticks to the chair back. "I mean, it's like something is going on inside, but I don't know what, you know."

The same Eric but with a difference. I'll just take it slow: "Um-hmm?"

"I feel kinda restless, you know. Like maybe I want to go do something, or—or like I'm—well, like I'm angry or something." He pauses, again wiggles, seeking a more comfortable position. I keep quiet. "I mean, I can't figure what I'd be angry about, but—"

"Don't 'figure' it out, Eric. Take time and just feel into yourself. At some level you already know."

"Yeah, I guess so." He sounds dubious, but he is taking time to try to get into himself more. "Whatever it is, it sure makes me feel restless. I mean, I just don't know why, but—" And he continues to fidget in the chair, seeming unable to find a comfortable posture.

After another interval, Eric lets out an immense sigh and addresses the wall opposite him, clearly avoiding looking at me. "Yeah, well—I—what I mean is, my dad was over last night—"

"Uh-huh."

"Oh, he's all right, you know. I guess he wants to be helpful and all. I mean, I think that he thinks he's—" He stops and stares again at the opposite wall.

"You sure get to the 'I guesses' and 'I thinks' when you talk about him, don't you?"

"Yeah, yeah." He's not interested; his tone is distant and sullen.

"You sound a long way off."

"What do you want?" There's annoyance in his voice.

"I want to hear you talk out of you. I'm not interested in a report on you."

"Yeah, great. If I could do that, I wouldn't need to be here." He pauses, looks pouty. "Why don't you tell me how to do it?," challengingly.

"You can do it, but it's frightening to let go of what you called your 'protection.'"

"I suppose so." He seems dispirited and distracted.

"You 'suppose.' Don't you know what you're doing?"

"I guess I know. You keep telling me that I do, you know; so you must be right." There's more of the challenge now.

"You 'guess' you know. You don't take responsibility for knowing but try to put it on me."

He pauses, turns to look at me. Then his voice comes out fast and hard: "Jim, I wish the hell you'd quit bugging me about the way I talk!"

He seems as startled as I am by his sudden outburst. For a moment he is staring straight into my eyes; then abruptly his gaze wanders, his eyes drop, and he pulls back physically and emotionally.

"You really were here just now. You really told me I was bugging you." I say it with some force, looking intensely into his face. "Now you're disappearing."

"Yeah, well, great. So I was here. So what? What's different? How does that change the price of pot in Peoria?" He is half-withdrawing, half-continuing to complain.

"Where are you going? You're fading." I put a slight taunting quality into my voice.

And Eric hears it and reacts to that tone: "Look, how come you feel you can always tell me what I'm doing? Suppose I tell you what you're doing: You're just playing the same old song over and over, 'Eric, you're not really here. (Mocking tone) Eric, you're making yourself an object. Eric, you're afraid to be real with me.' Christ, Jim, why don't you get yourself a new tune? It's no help to me to come here and pay you a lot of money just to have you nag me like my father. He does it for free, at least."

"It really pisses you that I get after you in ways that seem just like your father's."

"Yes, it really pisses me that you get after me in ways like my father's." His tone is mocking and angry again.

"And you're pissed right now when I feed back—"

"Oh, come on, Jim, don't keep doing it. I know I'm pissed, and you know I'm pissed; so what's to be gained by saying it twenty thousand times? Shit! Don't you have anything fresh to say? Can't you be some real help to me?"

"You can't see any help in what I'm doing now, can you? You're mad, and you want something that makes more—"

"Oh, shit! You're still doing it." He's on his feet, looking around with a combination of anger and desperation. I stop speaking and wait quietly, just looking at him. Inside, I feel questions and alarms: Have I pushed him too hard? Will he be violent? Have I messed up our working relationship? Will he abort therapy? Then I quiet down, knowing that he's doing exactly what he needs to be doing and that he's quite adequately in control.

Eric takes a few steps indecisively up and down the office and then drops down to sit on the hassock, looking up at me. (I'm struck that after his outburst he puts himself in a physically lower position.) His face is averted, but still I can see his jaw muscles working, his eyes filling.

"Look, Jim, I know you're doing what you think is best." His tone is controlled, almost formal. "But I don't think it's helping me. In fact (voice rising, tempo increasing), in fact, I'm pretty damn sure it's not helping. It's making things worse. (He draws himself up to look at me more eye-to-eye.) Do you hear me? It's making things worse! You're making things worse. Goddamn it, listen to me! You're making things worse, and I want you to stop it.''

He's on his feet again. Again there is a desperate, restless quality to his movements. He glances at the door, and I know he's considering bolting.

"Sit down, Eric.'' My voice is firm—not loud but insistent.

"I don't want to sit down.'' He paces the length of the room and back. Then drops into the chair. "All right, so I'm sitting down. So now what?''

"You're mad as hell right now, and—''

"I know I'm mad. I don't need you or anyone—''

"Wait, let me finish. You're mad right now, and you feel as though something's gone wrong, and you're thinking you ought to get out of here and get yourself back to normal.''

"Yeah. You're damned right something's wrong, and it probably would be best for me to get out of here.''

"Nothing's gone wrong, Eric.'' I say it quietly, firmly, flatly.

"What do you mean, 'nothing's gone wrong'? Do you want to drive me crazy or make me do something stupid?''

"You're not going crazy, and you're not doing anything stupid. You're mad, and you are showing that you're mad, and you're doing so appropriately. What scares you is that you're letting me really see you, and you hardly ever let anyone really see you.''

Eric draws in his breath sharply, looks at me again; his face drains of all evident emotion. We are quiet for twenty or thirty seconds. "Yeah, yeah,'' reflectively.

Again we wait quietly. He's busy inside, and I want to stay out of his way. Finally he looks up. "So you think it's okay to be mad at you, huh?''

"It's okay if it's really you who's mad.''

"Yeah.'' He breathes the word, still intent in his experience. Another pause. Then he looks at the clock on the little table. "Yeah. Hey, we're over time. I've got to go.'' He's shoving his feet into his sandals, standing, moving to the door.

"Okay, Eric. But remember I've seen you really, and I'm not blown away, and neither are you.''

His reply is muffled as he shuts the door behind him. I sit stunned for a minute. I'm amazed that the time is really over. It seems just a bit ago that I noticed that we had twelve, thirteen minutes left. I must have been much more intensely involved than I realized.

Friday, October 9. While I'm at breakfast, the phone rings. Exchange says she has a client on the phone who says it's important to talk with me. Shall she put him through? Yes.

"Jim?'' His voice is tight, high. He's not getting enough air.

"I'm here, Eric.''

"Yeah, well, have you got any time today? I think I ought to come in and talk with you, you know. I mean—well, yesterday was kind of heavy-duty, and—''

"I know. OK. Three-fifteen, OK?''

"Yeah, sure. See you then. Thanks.''

"I've been thinking of what you said: you saw me, and it didn't blow me away. Seemed a dumb thing, but I guess I know what you meant. Hell, I don't 'guess' anything. I know damned well what you meant.''

"Yes."

"You know, I—like you said, I'm scared to have people really see me. Remember one time I told you that I was scared you'd tell me I was nuts? Well, I expect that nearly anyone who gets to really know me will find out I'm really wrong some way."

"What a miserable load to carry around all the time!"

"You better believe it!" He settles back in the chair for the first time. He seems to have the same outfit on he had yesterday, but somehow he fills it out better. He's physically more in the room because he's emotionally more in the room.

Eric has been inwardly attentive; now he looks up at me with a shy smile. "I'm glad you didn't get blown away either."

"You were plenty strong, and that felt good, and I wasn't knocked out."

"Yeah, you know, it did feel good!" He smiles, reflecting. "I wasn't sure whether you'd be mad or—"

"But it was more important for you to be you than to be what I wanted."

"Yeah," slowly, tasting it. "Yeah, it was. It still is, in a way." His face changes. "Yeah, but I don't want you to think your feelings don't matter to me."

"I know, Eric, but the important point is, do they matter so much that you'll give up your own feelings to try to make me have the feelings you want or need me to have?"

"That sounds like a dumb question, but I know that the answer has mostly been yes. It's been important to make everyone like me, to keep anyone from being mad at me or disappointed in me or anything like that."

"You say, 'It's been,' past tense. Is it past?"

"Yes. Or at least I hope it is. But, you know, I don't really know whether it is or not."

"That sounds realistic to me."

So the session goes, reflecting on yesterday's intensity and setting our sights for the work ahead.

Monday, November 30. It's a drizzly day, gray and unrelenting. Eric is wearing old cords, a sweatshirt, and canvas shoes that look as though they had been gleaned from the refuse pile. He has chosen to recline the chair today so that he is nearly flat on his back. He hasn't looked at me since he greeted me as he came in. Instead, as so often lately, he is busy with his inward searching.

"Dad always had to top whatever anyone else said. Fact is, he still does. Don't know why it bugs me so. Always made me feel like I was being put down or put in my place." He pauses. "Yeah; 'put in my place' feels like it leads to something else, but I can't—oh, wait. I feel like I am always going to get put in my place if I—if I don't—if I—wait a minute, I'm losing it." Another pause. "Oh, right! I'll get put in my place if I don't keep everybody feeling good or liking me or if I'm not kind of charming."

He falls silent, and I reflect that a lot of Eric's verbal phrasing still has the marks of his old "protection" but how unimportant that is now that he's so much more emotionally present. Perhaps at some point we'll need to turn our attention again to those signals, perhaps not; but for now what's important is his ability to focus his awareness in inward exploration and to gain genuine inner vision.

"In junior high every Friday afternoon I used to tell my teachers, 'I hope you have a nice weekend, Ms. Bellin; I hope you have a good weekend, Mr. Simmons.' I liked to be charming and make them think I was a nice kid. But—but you know, inside I thought I was fooling them. Of course, in a way I was. I used to get into trouble doing things, like dumping people's garbage cans or swiping porch furniture and putting it on other people's porches. One time the cops came and chased us, and we ran through yards and jumped over fences and got away and hid in a vacant lot. We were scared, but boy, were we excited! Still, you know, that didn't seem like really me either. It's funny, now I think about it, I didn't know what really me was. I just knew that I couldn't let people see it—see me. I mean, I somehow felt I had to keep from being seen. I don't know why, but—"

"For some reason the real you had to be kept hidden."

"Yeah." Silent, he's listening within himself. "Yeah, 'for some reason'—what reason? I can hear dad's voice in me, saying, 'You better shape up, young man, if you know what's good for you.' 'Shape up'—'Shape up or ship out!' That's what he used to say. I didn't want to have to ship out—no, that's not right. I mean, I don't think I worried about that. I just let the words kind of fool me then."

"Um-hmm."

"Janet says she likes it that I'm straighter with her nowadays, but she says she doesn't know whether she really wants to stay with me anyway. I don't know what I want. Oh, damn. It makes me mad not to know. I want her to want to be with me, but I'm not sure I want her. I don't want her to ship me out or to leave me, but I think I'd be scared if she said she really wanted to stay with me or to get married or anything."

"You *think* that would scare you."

"Yeah, I think so. Oh, I did it again, huh? Well, I'm not sure. I don't know what I feel."

"So—?"

"So I just don't know. (Pause) Well, wait, wait. Let me see if I can get into that—"

For now Eric has a way of trying to understand himself more fully, a way of getting more in touch and of guiding himself more effectively. He is only beginning to use this way, but he is recognizing its potential more and calling on it more promptly.

Summary

This description of the work with Eric has focused on the central process issue of his lack of presence in the therapy hour. The account has not tried to deal with many other issues that occupied our hours together. This focus may seem to be on a minor matter when contrasted with his inability to make a lasting and satisfying relationship with a woman—a more familiar example of a "real" life issue. It is not minor; I believe it to be pivotally important to Eric's life.

This matter of what is "real" is very central to psychotherapy, and particularly is it critically significant in an existential orientation (Bugental, 1976, 1978, 1981; Edwards, 1982; Yalom, 1980). Within this perspective, the fact of be-ing (Tillich, 1952), of existence itself, is the primordial fact beyond all others. It follows that how genuinely or authentically one is in one's be-ing, one's existence, is a question of the most basic significance. So viewed, Eric's lack of genuine presence is a lack of reality in being, a concern importantly affecting every other part of his living.

Part Four ❦
Postanalytic Psychotherapies: Behavioral and Directive Therapies

At the other end of the spectrum from the postanalytic humanistic approaches are the postanalytic behavioral and directive approaches. Behavior therapy is therapy that aims to alter a person's maladaptive behavior through experimentally derived procedures such as conditioning. This approach contrasts with the psychoanalytic model's concern with treating intrapsychic organizations or underlying factors that lead to maladaptive behavior as a symptom. A new trend in behavior therapy is cognitive behavior modification, which emphasizes cognitive processes as mediators of behavior change, including thoughts, images, self-statements, sets, and response strategies. Biofeedback extends treatment of behavior from the clinician's control to the individual, who learns to use monitoring instruments to become aware of and eventually to control some physiological responses in order to function more healthfully. Hypnotherapy is another avenue to direct behavior control through the use of suggestions administered to patients in trance states. A complex form of hypnotherapy is hypnoanalysis: hypnoanalytic procedures are used to reach unconscious conflicts that seem intransigent and still are evidenced by continuing symptoms. Finally, psychopharmacologic therapies, derived from the medical model, involve prescribing and monitoring medications given to control emotional problems.

Julie M. Kuehnel and Robert Paul Liberman present two quite diverse cases in Chapter Fourteen, "Behavior Modification." The first case illustrates the use of behavior therapy principles and procedures with Andrea, a young woman suffering from bulimia and depression who was treated as an outpatient. The second case is that of Al, a young man suffering from a schizophrenic disorder and treated as an inpatient. The two cases convey the intertwining of assessment with interventions in conducting behavioral treatment. While the case presentations illustrate the use of a wide variety of behavioral techniques, an empirical approach is forwarded as the key element that binds the technology together and is the distinguishing feature of behavior therapy.

Chapter Fifteen, "Cognitive-Behavioral Sex Therapy," presents a case study detailing the cognitive and behavioral interventions used in the treatment of erectile failure. W. Charles Lobitz and his associates include session-by-session descriptions with a focus on the particular cognitive and behavioral strategies used. They also describe problems that the therapists encountered during treatment and elucidate the therapists' thinking and choice of interventions. The authors' intent in this chapter is to give the reader an appreciation of the role of psychotherapy issues in the "simplistic" application of cognitive-behavioral techniques.

In Chapter Sixteen, "Rational-Emotive Therapy," Albert Ellis advances rational-emotive therapy (RET) as a comprehensive theory and practice of psychotherapy that uses many cognitive, emotive, and behavioral techniques to show people what they are thinking and doing to make themselves disturbed and what they can think and do to undisturb themselves. In the case presented, the author treated a woman of twenty-seven with severe social and work anxiety. He used several RET-oriented cognitive methods, including the revealing and disputing of irrational beliefs, the use of coping self-statements, referentiating, psychoeducational methods, problem solving, and humor. He also used emotive methods: rational-emotive imagery, shame-attacking exercises, role playing, group socializing, forceful self-statements and self-dialogues, and unconditional acceptance. And he used behavioral methods: activity homework, reinforcement, penalties, and skill training. After nine months of RET, mainly in the form of group therapy, the client had lost most of her anxiety and self-hatred, was ready for a career change she had previously dreaded, and was able to participate more freely in interpersonal relationships.

In Chapter Seventeen, "Biofeedback," George Fuller–von Bozzay demonstrates how electronic instrumentation aids the individual in becoming aware of and then controlling physiological variables such as muscle tension, skin temperature, brain-wave activity, galvanic skin response, blood pressure, and heart rate. The aim is to give the person the ability to participate actively in his or her own health maintenance. This is demonstrated in cases of back and neck pain, muscle-contraction headaches, migraine headaches, Raynaud's disease, and stuttering.

In Chapter Eighteen, "Hypnoanalysis," Lewis R. Wolberg presents hypnoanalysis as an adjunct to psychotherapy, whether it be supportive, reeducative, or psychoanalytic. Among the ways hypnosis is purported to advance the therapeutic process, (1) it can exert a positive influence on the patient's relationship with the therapist, (2) it can enhance suggestibility, (3) it can expedite catharsis, (4) it can be used to lift resistances to verbalization and free association, (5) it can enhance cooperation with therapy rules, (6) it can expedite insight techniques such as dream or memory recall, (7) it can expedite transference, (8) it can expedite the working-through process, and (9) it can be helpful in the termination of therapy, since the patient can continue to use self-hypnosis to carry on the therapy process alone. Wolberg demonstrates its use through case material.

In Chapter Nineteen, "Psychopharmacologic Therapy," David S. Janowsky summarizes the case histories of six patients, illustrating treatment by a combination of supportive psychotherapy and psychotropic drugs. The cases illustrate the use of antipsychotic medications for an acutely ill schizophrenic patient and for a chronic schizophrenic patient, a tricyclic antidepressant for a patient with major depressive disorder and for a depressed borderline patient, an antianxiety agent plus a tricyclic antidepressant in a patient with panic attacks, and the treatment of a manic patient with lithium carbonate. The author describes techniques for enhancing drug compliance as well as strategies for monitoring and managing drug side effects and toxicities.

❦ 14 ❧

Behavior Modification

Julie M. Kuehnel
Robert Paul Liberman

The principles and techniques of behavior therapy constitute an emerging scientific and humanistic foundation for effective psychotherapeutic practice. Controlled clinical research from myriad studies across the full spectrum of psychiatric and psychological disorders has confirmed the efficacy of behavioral approaches that were earlier heralded in anecdotal collections of case studies (see Rosenbaum, Franks, and Jaffe, 1983; Liberman, 1978). The growing literature on behavioral assessment and therapy—now surpassing fifteen distinct specialty journals plus dozens of books each year—underscores the vibrant momentum of this field.

This chapter will not further add to the experimental and evaluative evidence that has validated a wide range of behavioral methods for promoting personal and social adaptation as well as ameliorating symptoms among those suffering from mental and emotional disorders. The reader interested in the scientific evidence is advised to peruse such journals as *Behavior Therapy, Behavior Research and Therapy, Journal of Applied Behavior Analysis, Journal of Behavior Therapy and Experimental Psychiatry, Behavioral Assessment, Behavior Modification,* and *Journal of Behavioral Medicine,* as well as more generic journals devoted to clinical psychology and psychiatry. Instead, we will introduce two patients whom we have treated with behavioral psychotherapy and then provide a clinical journey through their therapy and progress. We intend, in this fashion, to evoke the reader's interest in the behavioral approach to analysis and treatment of two quite different disorders—bulimia and schizophrenia. The first author treated the bulimic, and the second author headed the treatment team responsible for the care of the schizophrenic. After the patients are introduced in capsule summaries, a detour will be taken around the landscape of behavioral principles, which are so much more important to grasp and appreciate than are specific behavioral techniques. In this way we will provide a context for the more detailed account of the assessment and treatment of our patients to follow.

Case Vignettes

Case 1: Andrea. Andrea was an attractive, single twenty-one-year-old college student who came into treatment because of her concern over daily binge-vomit episodes that had begun about a year and a half before. She also suffered from periods of depression that qualified as a dysthymic disorder. She was the middle of three daughters. Her parents had been divorced since Andrea's early childhood, and her younger sister was still living at home with the mother and also attending college. When we began therapy, Andrea was preparing to quit her job and move back home to her mother's in order to attend college full-time.

Case II: Al. Though lacking close friends and never dating, Al graduated from high school with honors, intending to pursue a career in science. Within two years, however, he had increasing difficulty concentrating on academic work and dropped out of college. Expending great effort, he held a succession of menial jobs but felt tense and fearful, had strange thoughts of being a leper, and heard voices commenting on him as a "loser." He was admitted for inpatient care when he stopped talking, urinated in his pants, and sat immobile, gazing into space.

Behavior Therapy Principles

Behavior therapy is based on experimentally derived principles of learning that are systematically applied to help people change maladaptive behaviors. Fundamental to behavior therapy is the view that psychiatric disorders result when learned behaviors interact with biological vulnerabilities and inadequate environments to yield maladaptive life patterns. Hence, the therapist's task is to use all that is known about human learning to facilitate the replacement of maladaptive behaviors with more adaptive ones.

The therapist uses an empirical approach to understanding and treating clinical problems. The distinguishing characteristic of behavioral practitioners is firm and systematic adherence to specification and measurement. Without specifying and recording problems and goals along the various behavioral, cognitive, affective, and interpersonal domains of interest to a clinician, there is no true behavior therapy. As a reading of the literature shows, techniques in behavior therapy are ephemeral and should not be used after they are superseded by more effective methods. By adopting the strategy of specifying and monitoring our patients' symptomatic and healthy behaviors and expressions, we can be more accurate in planning our clinical interventions. As long as our practice is linked to frequent and regular measurement of the various levels and modes of human behavior, we provide ourselves with a self-correcting feedback loop that can help guide our work with individuals, families, groups, and social systems. Figure 1 outlines the empirical procedures integral to behavior therapy.

Behavior therapists try to facilitate functional improvements by changing the interaction between the patient and his or her environment. For example, instead of avoiding feared situations, the phobic is helped to gradually expose himself to the situations and not to leave them until anxiety abates. The withdrawn, shy, process-type schizophrenic is provided models who demonstrate and actively coach how to initiate social contacts and conversations. The parents of a hyperactive child are taught to use tangible and social reinforcers to increase their child's attention span in study and play situations. The relatives of a depressed person are instructed to reduce their attentiveness to her complaints of helplessness and hopelessness and, instead, to prompt and reinforce the adaptive, small, graded steps she takes toward improved functioning and positive verbalizations. Behavior therapists encourage

Figure 1. Behavior Therapy Process.

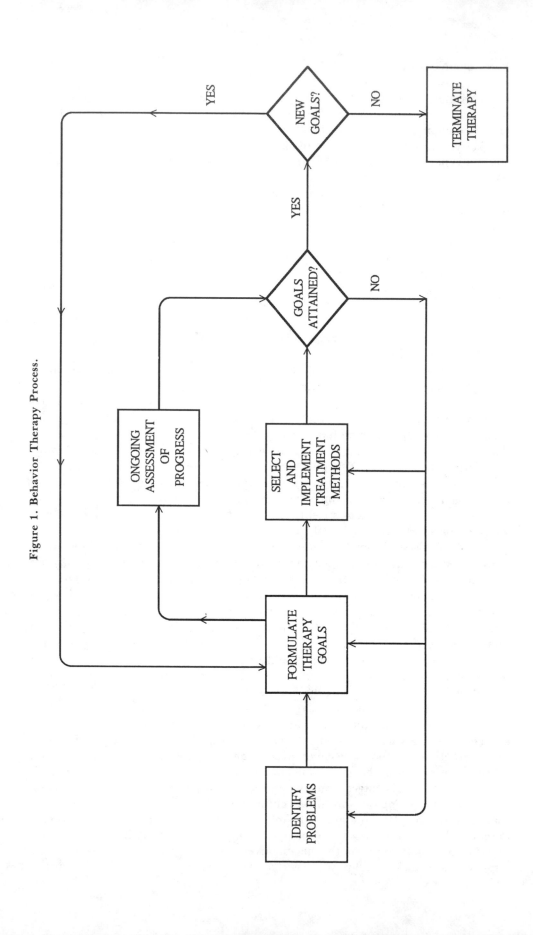

their patients to take an active role in modifying their environments and the contingencies of reinforcement that impinge on them. Behavior and the environment influence each other in a reciprocal fashion. The individual thus functions both as an agent and as the target of behavior change.

Although behavior therapists were historically antimentalistic, currently they recognize the importance of affects, cognitions, and imagery as well as the external environment in determining an individual's behavior. Behavior is defined in a broad, multimodal manner to include affects, sensations, imagery, verbal and nonverbal elements of social interaction, thoughts, and biological phenomena, as well as instrumental and observable actions. Internal events such as cognitions and feelings must, however, be capable of being operationalized and monitored in much the same way as overt behaviors. For example, the depressed, bulimic patient introduced above historically would have been treated by monitoring the number of binge-purge episodes, rearranging antecedent environmental conditions, and applying externally imposed consequences as rewards. Currently, in addition to these techniques, the behavior therapist might help the patient assess and monitor internal cognitions and assumptions ("self-talk" such as "Nobody will ever respect me because I am too fat"), which might also be antecedents of the binge-purge behavior.

Behavioral Assessment

Pinpointing and specifying a patient's behavioral problems—in all domains of instrumental, affective, cognitive, and social functioning—is the first step in behavioral assessment. Behaviors are often considered maladaptive, psychopathological, or problematic because they occur with excessive frequency, intensity, or duration. For example, it is not sufficient to determine that a patient is anxious in social situations. The behaviorally oriented clinician helps the patient to pinpoint the particular situations in which she becomes anxious, how often this occurs, how this anxiety is manifested, and how long the anxiety lasts. A patient may also present problems because of behavioral deficits. A depressed person, for example, may feel alone and suffer symptoms because he has no friends. The clinician must identify which specific behaviors could help him make and maintain some friends. For example, does the patient know how to initiate and maintain conversation? Does he smile when he interacts with people? Does he try to meet people? Alternatively, the patient may experience problems because he does not discriminate the appropriate time or place for certain behaviors. For instance, it is appropriate for a person to laugh at jokes in a social gathering but inappropriate for him to laugh indiscriminately or in somber settings.

The second step in behavioral assessment is to determine the patient's assets and strengths. What emotional, motoric, or interpersonal behaviors does the patient exhibit currently, and what behaviors has he exhibited in the past? What behaviors or activities make him feel good? The therapeutic task here is to use and build on those strengths that the patient already has to assist in the attainment of therapy goals.

As the third step in assessment, the information gathered thus far is put into the context of situations in which the problem behaviors occur. Specifying the probable antecedents and consequences of behavioral problems leads to the following questions: Under what conditions does the behavior occur? What are the environmental cues for or precipitants of the symptomatic behavior? Who reinforces the problem behaviors with sympathy, help, attention, or emotional reactions? What reinforcers would the patient gain if the problems were removed? In what situations can the patient control problem behaviors?

The fourth step in behavioral assessment is to set up a measurement strategy for each of the identified problem behaviors. Assessing the frequency of selected problem behaviors, through either direct observation or self-monitoring, produces a baseline evaluation, which can be used as a benchmark to determine the effectiveness of a therapeutic intervention and to decide which areas should receive the major (or the initial) emphasis in therapy. It is often advisable to conduct ongoing measurement of positive, desired behaviors that are the inverse of the patient's target complaints; regular assessment and feedback on adaptive and functional behaviors will strengthen movement toward therapeutic goals. If there are many problem behaviors, behaviors are initially targeted that seem likely to exhibit more rapid change so that the patient will receive positive feedback about his progress as early as possible.

As the fifth step in assessment, the patient's potential reinforcers are surveyed to identify those people, activities, and things that can provide motivation for treatment and for maintaining the new behaviors after therapy. The therapist may use tangible reinforcers and/or social reinforcers, such as praise and attention. Self-administered privileges and informational feedback may also be effective.

As the sixth and final step in behavioral assessment, treatment goals are formulated. The clinician and patient explore alternative behaviors that may offer solutions to the problem situation. Often the patient's realization that alternatives exist and are attainable is a major part of the solution to a problem. The alternatives selected become the initial goals for therapy. In formulating goals with a patient, it is helpful to remember the process of shaping. Breaking complex behaviors into more manageable units, or subgoals, can allow the therapist to frequently reinforce the patient's progress in working toward the long-term goal. If a patient is not fully capable of selecting an appropriate goal (for example, a young child or someone who is severely retarded), the clinician or informed and responsible relatives may help to select one for her. Goals specify the behaviors, attitudes, and feelings that the patient will have at the end of therapy (see Keefe, Kopel, and Gordon, 1978).

Once a behavioral assessment has been completed, the therapist selects interventions to help the patient reach the goals that were set. We now return to the two cases introduced above to illustrate the process of behavioral assessment as well as interventions based on principles of behavior therapy.

Behavior Therapy for a Case of Bulimia

My first appointment with Andrea lasted two hours. She was very soft-spoken and articulate but obviously tense at first. I asked her about her present living situation and activities. She told me that she was an A student majoring in biological science and interested in medical school. She was getting ready to move back to her mother's home.

Her mother had successfully supported Andrea and her older and younger sisters by working as a realtor and investing successfully in real estate. During her childhood, her mother's busy schedule meant that the three girls were home alone a fair amount of the time. Andrea's older sister had become dependent on drugs and alcohol during high school and ran with a "rough crowd." This sister had made positive strides with job training and sobriety, but she intermittently stirred things up at home with calls in the middle of the night threatening suicide and with periodic falls "off the wagon." Andrea's younger sister had few problems and was popular with boys.

I asked Andrea about the primary reason for our appointment. With some embarrassment, she reported that she had been binging and vomiting almost every day for over a year, usually in the late afternoons or evenings when she was alone. She felt caught in a trap between her perceived obesity and her food cravings. Although she was not model-thin, her weight was within the normal range. She also complained of loneliness and lack of close relationships outside her family and admitted that she felt depressed much of the time. Toward the end of this first session we had identified and agreed to focus on the following behavioral problems: (1) binge-purge eating pattern and (2) lack of friendships.

I felt that further sessions would confirm my suspicion that an inability to be assertive with males and family members would also show up as an important deficit area. Additionally, I believed that an excess of unstructured time would come out in the self-observational data I was going to have her collect over the intervening week. At the end of the session I asked her to keep a daily/hourly log of her activities (this included binge-purges) and to rate her mood during each hour on a scale of 1–100 (1 = "the lowest I've ever been" and 100 = "on top of the world"). I have found data of this type to be very useful, especially with depressed and eating-disordered patients, in identifying problem areas, environmental and social contexts, and areas of strength.

I also had her fill out the Beck Depression Inventory (Beck, 1972). Her score on the Beck was 30, placing her at the clinically depressed level. Some key items that contributed to her high score were these:

- I feel quite guilty most of the time.
- I expect to be punished.
- I blame myself for everything bad that happens.
- I cry all the time now.
- I believe that I look ugly.
- I am very worried about my physical problems and it's hard to think of much else.
- I am much less interested in sex now.

I consulted with a psychiatrist about the possibility of antidepressant medication, but I decided to wait for a few sessions before trying medication to see how she responded to therapy. This proved to be a wise decision, as the initial supportive contact and hopeful structuring of the self-monitoring produced a substantial improvement in her mood. At the start of her next session, we reviewed and discussed her daily log, which is partly reproduced in Figure 2.

It seemed that times at home in the afternoons and evenings were low mood points. Andrea said that she usually had studying to do but no other activities. This time was boring and lonely—prime binge time. Most of the time she would sit at the kitchen table and eat and read. Sometimes she would call her younger sister, but the sister's response was often impatient. Andrea considered her younger sister her best friend, and they had characteristically spent a lot of time together until

Figure 2. Daily Log I, Including Numerical Mood Self-Ratings.

	9:00	11:00	1:00	2:00	3:00	4:00	5:00	6:00	7:00	8:00	9:00	
Tuesday	Wake up (7:00) 75 Class 75	Class 50	Class 45 Would rather be home	Class (favorite) Good grade 75 Ate lunch	Class 75	Class 75	Home 50 Call sister	Home 40 Study, binge	Home 40 Study	Home TV 40	40	
Wednesday	Class 60	Class 60	Home Lots to do but bored 45	Home Energy level low 45 binge	45	Study 45	40		30	Gone to Mom's for *Dynasty* party	Mom's Acted happy but . . . 20	Home 40
Thursday	Class 75	Class 60 Break 40	Class 50	Home House-clean 75	Study 50	Lonely 40	Binge 20	20	Binge 20	Binge 20	Binge 20	Binge 20

the sister began dating her present boyfriend. Andrea felt hurt and somewhat abandoned, although she claimed that she "understood" her sister's need for a boyfriend
and not having the time to chat on the phone. The younger sister invited her along
when she and her boyfriend went dancing. Andrea always went but said she felt
uncomfortable. When she tried to decline invitations, her sister took it personally
or pouted, and so Andrea found it easier to go along if she didn't have a "legitimate"
excuse. During the threesome dates, Andrea felt embarrassed and put down by
the teasing manner of the other two. However, if she looked hurt or uncomfortable, she was accused of being a poor sport or "sensitive."

The lowest point of the week had been a Wednesday night family gathering
at her mother's house to watch the season opening of a TV serial, *Dynasty*. Andrea
said that she had "acted happy" and found this made her feel lonely. She said
that when she showed feelings of sadness or anger, her mother took it personally—
asking why Andrea was treating her that way or pointing out that Andrea's feelings were invalid. In discussing a variety of situations involving the ways Andrea
related to family members, it became apparent that certain self-talk behaviors were
maintaining her passivity and dependence; for example, she would say to herself,
"Fighting back isn't nice," or "I'm just overly sensitive."

It seemed clear from the assessment information to date that Andrea demonstrated a lack of assertiveness with family members and a lack of activity and stimulation in the afternoons and evening. To summarize the results of the assessment
with Andrea so far:

Behavioral excesses

1. Binge-purge episodes six out of seven days in the late afternoon or early evening when Andrea is alone and bored at home. This behavior anesthetizes her
to feelings of loneliness and social anxiety; the escape and avoidance of these
dysphoric affects are maintaining the bulimic behaviors.

Behavioral deficits

1. Lack of ability to initiate friendships with acquaintances from school. Fears
of rejection and disappointment maintain this deficit.
2. Lack of assertiveness with mother and younger sister. This is maintained by
their withdrawal or attacks when she does not comply with their wishes in her
behavior or emotional expressions.
3. Insufficient structuring of free time and lack of initiation of activities to fill it.

Assets:

1. Very intelligent and skilled academically.
2. Committed to getting an education and having a career.
3. Attractive.
4. Articulate and responsive in conversation.

Andrea and I agreed on the following short- and long-term goals for therapy:

Short-Term Goals (One Month)

1. Reduce purging behavior to two times a week.
2. Initiate one outside class activity with classmate every week (for example, a
cup of coffee).

3. Practice assertiveness with sister and mother in sessions and at home, based on situations that have come up during the week.
4. Learn to monitor her self-defeating cognitions.
5. Plan and implement a variety of regular, constructive activities for afternoons and evenings.

Long-Term Goals (Six Months)

1. Eliminate purging behavior. Reduce binge behavior to once a month.
2. Develop two companions to spend time with outside school (not family).
3. Be assertive in responding to sister and mother 60 percent of the time.
4. Be able to replace self-derogating attitudes with more self-affirming and realistic self-talk, especially in relating to her family.
5. Establish and maintain activities during afternoon and evening hours.

It is apparent in looking at these goals that the overall goal of therapy for Andrea is to move her from a position of passivity and dependence on the goodwill of others to a position of self-initiative and independence. It has been my experience with eating-disordered clients that when they engage in assertive behaviors, take control of the reinforcers in their lives, and generally act constructively on their environment, their self-esteem goes up and their depression goes down. Increased self-esteem and elevated mood, in turn, tend to reinforce the more adaptive behaviors.

As Andrea and I set the above goals for therapy, our discussion revolved around the following issues. The goal regarding the binge-purge behavior was set in terms of reducing and then eliminating the purging behavior. I explained to Andrea how the purging reinforced and maintained the binging behavior. Consequently, controlling and reducing the purging behavior would eliminate or reduce the binging behavior. This approach seems to work more quickly and efficiently than trying to control the binging first.

With regard to making friends, she could see that she had become too dependent on family members to fill this need. She also could think of several persons she had met at school who seemed "nice." She had had three serious relationships with men within the past two years, each of which had ended unhappily. She was still interested in having a boyfriend but was very discouraged about the possibility. We tagged this as an area to explore further in later sessions. As for the unstructured, alone time in the afternoons and evenings, she felt that moving back to her mother's house would help with this problem. She would be moving in a few days. I felt that she would still need some self-initiated activities and alternatives to binging for this time period.

On the basis of these goals, I devised the following treatment plan.

Goal	Treatment Plan
1. Reduce binging-purging.	Set frequency goals weekly; self-monitor hunger and reestablish hunger/eating relationship; discontinue "dieting" and weighing of self on the scale.
2. Develop relationships outside the family.	Set goals weekly and rehearse behaviors for initiating out-of-class contact with classmates.

3. Be more assertive with family members.

Read the popular book *The Assertive Woman* (Phelps and Austin, 1975); roleplay interpersonal situations calling for assertion that have come up in the previous week or are expected.

4. Learn new patterns of thinking to replace cognitive distortions that create anxiety/depression.

Read the book *Feeling Good: The New Mood Therapy* (Burns, 1980) and keep a structured journal as suggested in that book.

5. Structure time.

Set goals weekly and plan activities for after school and evenings that can serve as alternatives to binging.

Andrea was eager to begin implementing the treatment plan. She agreed to do the following homework assignments during the eight days before the next session. She would continue the daily log of her activities and mood level that she had kept the previous week (included on it are any binge-purge episodes). She agreed to reduce her binge-purge episodes to five in the next week (down one from the previous week). She wanted to set the goal at *no* binge-purge episodes, but I convinced her that it was better initially to set a goal she was certain she could meet. If she did better, then terrific for her! She also agreed, reluctantly, to leave her scale at her uncle's house when she moved home and not to weigh herself at all during the upcoming week. This was difficult for her, but I assured her that it would result in a great sense of freedom. She admitted that weighing herself resulted in anxiety and depression most of the time.

Her third assignment was to invite someone from class for a cup of coffee in the school cafeteria. She said that a girl named Anna in one of her classes had been friendly and she would suggest coffee on their way out of class on Wednesday. Her fourth assignment was to begin reading *The Assertive Woman,* which I lent her. Her fifth assignment was to find some activity to do late in the afternoon or early evening. I suggested some type of aerobic exercise. She thought that walking/jogging or putting on records and dancing might be workable for her. She had tried exercise classes in the past and liked them but felt she couldn't afford them right now. We agreed that on three out of the next eight days she would either take a brisk half-hour walk or dance for twenty minutes at 4:00 in the afternoon. She was to notice how she felt after these exercise sessions. She wrote down her assignments and left.

She arrived at our next session with her daily log. Before reviewing her log with her, I asked about each of her homework assignments. She had left her scale at her uncle's when she had moved home that week and had not weighed herself at all during the week. She said that there had been times when she was tempted to weigh herself but that she had indeed found it very freeing not to. She hadn't realized, she said, how anxious the morning and evening weighing ritual had made her until she gave it up. I told her that her accomplishment was even more important because of the effort involved.

She had enjoyed a cup of coffee with her classmate Anna, and they had made a tennis date for the weekend. She had read about two thirds of *The Assertive Woman* and found it very relevant. She saw that she frequently got caught in the "compassion trap" and generally let friends and family manipulate her. She had taken long walks before or after dinner with her mother since she had moved in. She had found these walks so enjoyable that she was going every evening. She said that she felt more energetic afterward and it was easier to study. As she described her homework completion, I leaned toward her, nodded frequently, and occasionally interspersed such comments as "Fantastic" and "Great progress!"

For the next week, she wanted to continue reading *The Assertive Woman,* continue her walks, and not weigh herself. We turned our attention to her daily log (see Figure 3). Her mood ratings had shown a significant improvement from the previous weeks. Almost all were 60 and above. She attributed much of this change to moving home and not being alone so much of the time. She had had only two binge-purge episodes this week, which was much better than the goal we had set. I smiled and said, "That shows you the relationship between your mood and your behavior, but don't expect constant, smooth progress. There will be some bumps in the road." Spending less time alone and being busy seemed to be key factors. We talked about the possibility of her working part-time. This would help structure her time and bring her into contact with more people, increasing her potential for making friends.

I asked her about the circumstances surrounding one of the binge-purge episodes, which had occurred late in the afternoon and was preceded and followed by mood scores in the 30s. She said that she had come home from school in the afternoon and found that her mother had rearranged all her dresser drawers in a way she was "sure" Andrea would like, since it was "so much more efficient." Andrea didn't like it but didn't say anything because she was sure her mother's intentions were good. This incident was one of many intrusive behaviors on the part of her mother that Andrea tolerated passively. Andrea felt uncomfortable with the lack of privacy but didn't feel she had the right to do anything about it. These ambivalent feelings had set the stage for the binge-purge episode. We reversed roles and I modeled how she might have handled the situation more assertively with her mother. She then rehearsed various strategies for dealing with her mother on this issue. We spent some time discussing her right to privacy and to set limits on others despite their good intentions (her mother, it turned out, locks her own bedroom door). Andrea agreed to try asserting herself with her mother over the privacy issue as we had practiced. She was to continue with her homework assignments from the week before, with one addition: she was to monitor the want ads for a part-time job and bring in any that interested her.

I continued to see Andrea weekly for two more months. I then saw her monthly for about three months. Following is a summary of the chief techniques and general progress during that time for each of the five goals we had set.

The first goal, to eliminate purging, was accomplished through weekly goal setting within the first month of therapy and has been maintained for the year since our last session. The urges to binge were not eliminated so easily, although actual binge behavior went down to about once a week by the end of the first month. Like most chronic dieters, Andrea tried to eat according to a set of very narrow, rigid rules and standards. She had totally lost touch with the hunger/eating connection. In order to begin reestablishing it, she agreed to monitor her hunger and rate it on a scale of 1 to 5. She was to record these ratings on her hourly/daily log. The next step was to try to eat only when she was genuinely hungry (hunger rating

Figure 3. Daily Log II.

Tuesday	Up and to school 75	Class (good grade on test) 80	Break 50 Class 75	Lab class Ate lunch 80	Lab class Baseball game at school 80	Home, dinner 70	Homework 60 Walk 85	65 Homework Bed at 11:00
Wednesday	Up and to class 75	Break Coffee with Anna 80	Class 75	Home, study, let cats and dog out 80	Nap	Study, dinner, D.O. called 80	Walk Homework 80	Watch *Dynasty* 80
Thursday	To class 75	Class and break 70	Class	Home 30 Binge	30 Binge	Dinner with family 40	Homework 45 Walk 70	Homework TV 60

3–5) and to slowly eat a moderate portion of whatever food she really wanted. After some weeks of practice she discovered, to her surprise, that she could satisfy her hunger with modest portions, that she was not hungry *all* the time, and that once she stopped eating according to a long list of "shoulds" and "should nots," the urges to binge diminished markedly.

Our second goal, to develop relationships outside the family, proceeded well. Each week we set a goal for her to initiate an activity or social contact with a friend or acquaintance. Some of them worked out and some didn't. By the end of two months she had developed a friendship with a woman named Lisa at school. They played tennis together regularly and often met for coffee or lunch between classes. They were not close confidants but had similar interests. As Andrea was initiating more contacts with people, a second problem in this area emerged. She could not terminate or set limits on relationships, partly because of her view of herself as a nice person and her irrational assumption that "nice people don't say no." This was the same trap she got herself into with her family. Each session we roleplayed situations that had come up during the week with her friends and family. Gradually she learned to say such things as "I would appreciate it if you would call and check before you drop by," "I appreciate your wanting to help me by rearranging my drawers, but I would prefer to take care of it myself," and "Thank you for asking me along, but I really don't want to go." She even began rehearsing more assertive responses to others at home with a tape recorder. Although learning and initiating more assertive behavior was difficult, she reported that afterward she usually felt stronger, more in control, and less resentful, even though the reaction of family members was not always positive.

In conjunction with rehearsing more assertive behavior, I began challenging some of the negative self-talk, putdowns, and cognitive distortions that were maintaining her lack of assertiveness (goal 4). It was important that she learn to recognize and restructure these for herself. To facilitate this, I gave her a copy of *Feeling Good: The New Mood Therapy*. Being very intelligent and motivated, Andrea was able to apply the techniques from the book to herself. Each week she brought in her "self-talk journal," and we went over it together as the first order of business in the therapy session. At first she frequently needed help coming up with rational self-affirmative alternatives to her negative self-talk, but she gradually became very good at generating such responses.

The fifth goal, to structure her time better, was accomplished with some help from serendipity. Andrea was asked to serve on a college committee to organize and put on an annual community event. This kept her busy for about six weeks, and she found it fun and rewarding. She liked being busy and found that her grades did not suffer and that she was not bored anymore. This experience persuaded her to take a part-time job after her committee work was finished.

Essentially, all our goals were met to a satisfactory degree; mutually, we agreed to terminate the therapy. I received a Christmas letter from Andrea about a year after termination. She had gone away to a four-year college in another city and was keeping "in touch" with a young man she was dating. She reported that the binging-vomiting was something "I don't even think about anymore" and said that her mother and sister "haven't changed, and the same issues keep coming up, but I'm handling them well."

Behavior Therapy for a Case of Schizophrenia

The treatment of Al, a young man with a schizophrenic disorder, illustrates the intertwining of assessment with interventions in conducting behavioral treatment for severely psychotic patients.

During the first days and week of his inpatient treatment, Al was given a neuroleptic drug and showed gradual improvement in his appearance and behavior. He resumed speaking, first in a whisper and only in response to questions, later in longer phrases and with occasional conversational initiations. His confusion and disorientation cleared. He took a shower and brushed his hair, albeit with some prompting. His eating improved and, after five days of hospitalization, he began smiling and looking at people. However, he avoided interacting with fellow patients or staff members and secluded himself in his room or in remote corners of the ward whenever possible. The medication appeared to improve his self-care skills and cognitive abilities, but he remained socially withdrawn and passive. He appeared to be returning to his premorbid personality—shy, quiet, and a loner.

Problem Identification. Like many schizophrenic patients, Al presented with severe and disabling problems in almost every sphere of functioning. Pinpointing these problems in operational and behavioral terms was the first step toward setting goals and instituting treatment. In fact, the decision to use neuroleptic medication at the time of his hospital admission was prompted by clinical observations of his catatonic immobility, mutism, and incontinence and by the history of characteristic delusions and hallucinations provided by his parents. The psychiatric evaluation of Al proceeded along multiple dimensions and is outlined in Table 1. A problem list was formulated with specific objectives, treatment plans, and a data base.

The information required for a comprehensive assessment of a schizophrenic patient comes from interviews of the patient and family, checklists and questionnaires filled out by the patient and family, and direct observations made by staff members of the patient's spontaneous behavior on the ward, in the home, or in community settings.

With an acutely and floridly psychotic patient such as Al, behavior therapy is aimed at cognitive and behavioral reconstitution so that more comprehensive assessment and treatment planning can be carried out with a reasonably attentive and socially responsive patient. The therapeutic environment, with proper programming, can lead to improvements in floridly symptomatic schizophrenics. Along with neuroleptic medication, the treatment team responsible for reducing Al's level of symptomatology also arranged for him to be removed, at least temporarily, from a possibly stressful family environment; to receive clear and concise messages from the staff about daily needs; to spend time in a quiet, unstimulating part of the ward; and to receive prompts for making small movements, with positive feedback for any sign of awareness, communication, or self-care.

Once Al's catatonic symptoms subsided, efforts were made to pinpoint his remaining problems, establish priorities for treatment goals, inventory his assets, locate reinforcers, conduct a functional analysis of his problems, monitor his progress, and determine when treatment techniques and settings could be changed. This is the empirical approach to treatment embodied by behavior therapy and shown in Figure 1.

Table 1. Outline of Behavioral Approach to History Taking,
Assessment, and Therapy.

I. PROBLEMS AND GOALS
    A. Define problems and goals and translate them into *behavioral terms,* using as dimen-
        sions their frequency, intensity, duration, form or quality, and appropriateness in
        their context.
    B. Develop a *multimodal* inventory of the problems and goals, in which all levels of human
        behavioral expression and experience are covered:
        1. Overt motoric and instrumental behavior
        2. Affects
        3. Sensations
        4. Interpersonal relations
        5. Cognitions
        6. Imagery and fantasy
        7. Biological, somatic, and physiological responses.
    C. Determine *behavioral deficits:* which behaviors need to be initiated, increased in fre-
        quency, or strengthened in form?
    D. Determine *behavioral excesses:* which behaviors need to be terminated, decreased in
        frequency, or altered in form?
    E. Determine *behavioral assets:* consider strengths in multimodal terms.
    F. Determine whether the patient's self-description of the problem is congruent with
        that of other observers.

II. ANALYSIS OF CONDITIONS MAINTAINING THE PROBLEMS
    A. *Antecedents* of the behavioral problems: what settings, situations, stimuli, or people
        serve as occasions or precipitants for the occurrence of the problems? Ask patient:
        Where does the problem occur? When? With whom? What life events have recently
        occurred that might be stressors?
    B. *Consequences* of the behavioral problems: sometimes called "secondary gains," these
        are actually the primary and important ways the environment responds to maintain
        the problem behaviors or make less likely movement toward the desirable, alternative
        goals. Ask questions such as: Who responds to the problems with sympathy, help,
        attention, or emotional reactions? Who persuaded or coerced the patient into treat-
        ment? What would happen if the problems were ignored? If the problems went away?
        How would the patient's life be different if the problems were diminished? What
        reinforcers or benefits would the patient gain if the problems were removed?
    C. *Self-motivation:* How is the patient affected by the problems—comfortable, ambivalent,
        or troubled? Does the patient acknowledge the problems and desire change?

III. ASSESSMENT INSTRUMENTS
    The purpose of assessment instruments is to ascertain the correspondence between *verbal
    self-report* by patient and *actions* observed by assessor and others.
    A. *Fear Survey:* This instrument determines degree of fear associated with a wide range
        of items, places, stimuli, situations, and interpersonal events that patient may avoid.
    B. *Reinforcement Survey* and *Pleasant Events Schedule:* These instruments determine activities,
        places, people, foods, and things that can be used to motivate progress.
    C. *Behavioral diaries or logs:* Counting frequencies or intervals promotes self-observation,
        self-monitoring, and more accurate depiction of scope and timing of problem
        behaviors.
    D. *Symptom ratings and interviews:* Examples are the Target Complaint Scale, anxiety in-
        ventories, Symptom Checklist, Marital Adjustment Test, Self-Rating Depression
        Scale, Beck Depression Inventory, Hamilton Depression Interview, and Present State
        Examination.
    E. *Physiological measures:* These include heart rate, blood pressure, fingertip skin tempera-
        ture, skin resistance, and other indexes as measured by biofeedback devices.

**Table 1. Outline of Behavioral Approach to History Taking,
Assessment, and Therapy, Cont'd.**

IV. BIOLOGICAL ASSESSMENT
  A. Relevant medical and surgical problems
  B. Physical limitations and handicaps
  C. Psychotropic drugs—they interact with behavioral interventions as well as affecting behavior directly

V. SOCIOCULTURAL ASSESSMENT
  A. Recent changes in milieu—migration, intergenerational family conflicts, changes in residence or work
  B. Recent changes in relationships—divorce, death
  C. Language and values

VI. GOAL SETTING
  Shift focus from problems to goals as soon as possible. Behaviors selected as goals should be, when possible:

  • Specific and clear
  • Chosen by patient
  • Short-term as links to longer-term goals
  • Frequently occurring
  • Salient and functional
  • Attainable

VII. MONITORING PROGRESS
  Using behavioral measurement means keeping track of changes in the behaviors targeted as problems and/or goals. Measurement should be practical, convenient, and relevant to the clinical problems. Data may come from the treatment session or the natural environment. Observing and recording can be done by the therapist, the patient, or significant others. Some types of recording progress are:

  • Frequency counts of the behavior
  • Intervals noted when the target behavior has occurred
  • Duration or latency of the behavior
  • Intensity estimations (for example, "How much did the anxiety bother you during the last week?")
  • Permanent products—tangible outcomes that show that the behavior occurred (for example, ticket stubs indicate patient went to a movie; clean face indicates face was washed)

VIII. BEHAVIOR THERAPY TACTICS
  A. Develop trusting, caring, warm, and mutually respectful therapeutic alliance, which serves as the foundation and lever for many of the behavioral techniques.
  B. Develop time-limited treatment program.
  C. Use behavioral rehearsal or roleplaying to simulate real-world problem situations.
  D. Prompt, cue, signal, and coach patient to make improvements.
  E. Give "homework assignments."
  F. Reinforce small, discrete steps in adaptive directions.
  G. Use therapeutic instructions and promote favorable expectations of outcome.
  H. Have patient repeatedly practice the desired behavior.
  I. Feed back information on behavioral changes to patient and periodically reevaluate progress and reset goals.
  J. Reinforce progress, underplay reversals.
  K. Generalize gains to natural environment by involving family members and other aspects of the real world.

In reviewing Al's problem list, the staff operationalized his problems so that an ongoing assessment could be made of their severity. Gauging the severity of the problems enabled the staff to establish priorities for goals and to monitor progress.

Cognitive Problems and Psychopathology. Once a week, Al was interviewed by the unit psychiatrist, who rated him on twelve dimensions of psychopathology, using the Brief Psychiatric Rating Scale (BPRS). The BPRS and a host of other convenient and valid rating scales can be found in an assessment manual published by the federal government (Guy, 1976). To supplement the ratings of delusions and hallucinations, the psychiatrist also used a measure of response latency during the weekly interviews, timing the elapsed time between his question and Al's response. Initially there were pauses of up to thirty seconds, but as Al reconstituted, the latency was reduced to five seconds or less.

During daily sessions of social-skills training, therapists kept a record of the number of correct and incorrect responses Al made to questions probing his ability to solve interpersonal problems. For example, after a family or peer interaction situation was roleplayed, Al was asked such questions as "Whom were you talking with?," "What did the other person want?," "How was the other person feeling?," "What was your short-term goal in the situation?," and "What alternatives could you have used to deal with the situation?" Al's ability to accurately perceive and process the information in the interpersonal roleplaying gradually improved: his error rate declined to zero, reflecting his growing attentional and cognitive abilities.

Affective Problems. Each day Al checked off (on a Target Complaint Scale) the magnitude of his tension, fear, dysphoria, and discomfort. This was graphed by the late night shift on the inpatient unit and revealed a decrease from "Couldn't be worse" to variable levels between "A little" and "Pretty much." It is of interest that a similar type of global rating of dysphoria, after "test doses" of neuroleptics, has been shown to accurately predict a schizophrenic patient's compliance with and hence eventual clinical response to the neuroleptic (Van Patten, May, and Marder, 1981). Thus, early and systematic assessment of the affective domain may not only reflect stress levels but also enable clinicians to predict effectiveness of neuroleptic treatment.

Social/Interpersonal Problems. Four times daily, the nursing staff unobtrusively observed Al on the ward, completed a Social Interaction Schedule, and recorded his level of activity, interaction, and inappropriate behavior. During his first week, Al was noted to be isolated and inactive for 90 percent of the nursing staff's observations. He showed several inappropriate behaviors, such as posturing, rocking, and grimacing. When initially approached for two- to three-minute conversations at these four daily Social Interaction Schedule sessions, Al actively moved away and closed his eyes. As time went on, observations revealed his more active engagement with the environment, although he was still isolated from others. By the third week of hospitalization Al was interacting with other patients and staff about 40 percent of the time and was responsive in conversations with staff.

During the social-skills training sessions, which began after a week of drug treatment, Al was rated on the adequacy of his performance in roleplayed scenes. He was rated as satisfactory on eye contact and voice volume but needed improvement in voice tone, fluency, and facial expression, which reflected his blunted affect. He also filled out an assertiveness inventory before starting the training and again at the end of the training (Rathus, 1973). The inventory showed an increase

of 15 points, moving Al up into the near-normal range, by the time his three months'
hospitalization was over.

Instrumental Behavior. Al's self-care and work skills were evaluated by the nursing staff numerous times a day within the context of a credit incentive system,
a type of token economy. The number of prompts that were required to get Al
to satisfactorily wash himself, shower, brush his teeth, comb his hair, and dress
himself in appropriate attire were recorded. Full credits were given for satisfactory
completion of these tasks without prompts; half credits were given for satisfactory
completion after one prompt. Varying numbers of credits were also given for room
maintenance and ward chores, depending on the quality of the performance and
the number of prompts required to instigate their completion. Thus, Al's credit
earnings reflected his instrumental role performance on the unit and served as an
ongoing assessment of Al's progress.

Sensory and Imagery Problems. Every week the psychiatrist rated the severity
of Al's hallucinatory experiences on the BPRS. Al self-monitored the frequency
of auditory hallucinations by activating a wrist counter for each occurrence during
the day. By the time of discharge, hallucinations were no longer occurring. Al's
fantasies and hypochondriacal delusions were followed during weekly recreational
therapy sessions by his drawing a picture of himself. The first few drawings revealed
distorted body shapes and numerous sores placed on the figure's hands and face.
Later drawings showed a figure isolated from others but with coherent outlines and
no sign of lesions.

Assets. Al's premorbid history indicated that he had good academic skills and
was conscientious and reliable in meeting commitments. He had a concerned, albeit
overinvolved and critical, family who were willing to be involved in the treatment
process. These assets were duly noted by Al's treatment team, who individually
tailored and set goals and monitored his progress through the inpatient unit's credit
incentive system, social-skills training sessions, and family therapy. The fact that
Al had completed a year of college and had held, though briefly, jobs in the competitive marketplace were also viewed as assets to be built on for aftercare goals.

Goal Setting. Initial goals, such as reducing Al's catatonic, delusional, and
hallucinatory symptoms, were set primarily by his psychiatrist and the treatment
team. Once neuroleptic medication and the consistent and optimally structured
hospital environment effected behavioral and cognitive recompensation, Al began
to participate in setting goals for himself. This was done with his psychiatrist and
at biweekly patient/staff planning meetings. Al worked out a series of problem situations that he wanted to work on in social-skills training—starting conversations with
strangers, maintaining a friendship, asking for a job, making small talk with co-
workers, and communicating his concerns about medication side effects to his doctor. He also indicated when he felt ready to start family therapy and suggested a
number of family scenes in which he needed improved communication skills. These
included telling his parents that he was annoyed and embarrassed by their discussing his illness with neighbors and requesting time and space to be alone when he
felt under stress.

Priorities for treatment goals were guided by the principle of ''shaping''—
reinforcing small steps, approximations to the desired level of functioning, in each
of Al's social and behavioral deficits. For example, before working on maintaining
friendships in the social-skills training, Al first had to learn more rudimentary con-

versational skills such as asking open-ended questions, giving "free" information about a topic, judging the appropriate level of self-disclosure to use, and sensing when it is time to end a conversation. Similarly, in the credit incentive system, initial goals of improving his grooming and room maintenance with immediate feedback from staff members preceded more complicated work tasks and autonomous self-evaluation of his personal hygiene.

Because the goal-setting enterprise is paced by the patient's progress, ongoing assessment of change is critical for decisions about goals. In Al's case, the monitoring of his progress in the multiple dimensions listed above enabled the patient, his family, and his therapists to rank-order treatment objectives in an orderly and efficacious sequence.

Functional Analysis of Problems. What environmental antecedents and consequences were influential in developing and sustaining Al's clinical problems? Axis IV in DSM-III prompts clinicians to assess antecedent stressors that may have a role in the development of psychopathology. Without speculatively reconstructing Al's life history (which was likely formative in determining his premorbid personality, assets, and limitations), it appeared that his increasing social isolation, lack of a peer network, and parental criticism all contributed to his symptomatic impairments. Many who have studied schizophrenia believe that either *under*stimulating or *over*-stimulating social environments can lead to symptoms and their worsening. Al was exposed to both types of stressors, alternating between total isolation and family criticism and overconcern.

It is also likely that his parents' cajolery served as a reinforcer of his growing negativism and isolation; that is, their emotional responses to his attempts to reduce intolerable levels of arousal may have inadvertently increased his withdrawal. Al's lack of peer relationships deprived him of age-appropriate models from whom he could have learned social skills to use in acquiring friends. In trying to reduce external pressure on Al, his parents may have gone too far by "excusing" him from reasonable work responsibilities. Instead of receiving recognition and acknowledgment for chores and continuing in a remunerative job, Al received his parents' concern and solicitude for being increasingly helpless and dependent.

A functional analysis such as the foregoing, despite its reliance on retrospective guesswork, can be helpful in the goal-setting process. In Al's case, it seemed important to alter the contingencies of reinforcement and communication patterns in the family, to find a reasonable work role for Al to develop, and to start Al on the pathway toward social relationships with peers.

Reinforcement Survey. Reinforcers that could be used in Al's treatment program were of two general types, social and symbolic rewards and more tangible rewards. Once neuroleptic medication had restored Al's responsiveness to reinforcers, nurses, psychiatrist, therapists, and family members were able to use social attention, recognition, and praise to reinforce Al's progress in attaining his treatment goals. For example, therapists liberally praised Al for giving correct answers and responding assertively in the social-skills training scenes. Praise was paired with credits to reinforce Al's improvements in self-care and work. Tangible reinforcers, such as Al's favorite beverages and candy, were effective in backing up the value of the credits he received for grooming, showering, dressing, and interacting. As time went on, Al experienced reinforcement from higher-level rewards, such as the feeling of mastery at having successfully engaged a stranger in a ten-minute conversation on the hospital grounds. A high-probability behavior of Al's, social isolation, was identified as a reinforcer and was used contingently to build up social involvement. Al was given access to his room for privacy *after* he first engaged in brief conversations with three different staff members or patients on the unit. This was part of a "contract" that Al negotiated with the unit treatment team as a prerequisite to being promoted to the highest level of autonomy and privileges in the credit system.

Monitoring Progress in Therapy. Al's progress was assessed continually through methods that were integral to his treatment program. The nursing staff evaluated his getting up, dressing, washing, grooming, and bedmaking, noting the number of prompts required for his completing these tasks. The number of prompts was the criterion for his receipt of credits. His credit earnings were another indication of his level of functioning: initially they were nil as he required constant one-to-one prompting and assistance; later they increased as he moved up the hierarchal credit system to higher levels of self-evaluation, individual responsibility, and privileges.

In the social-skills training sessions, the counts of errors made in answering questions assessing his perceptual and cognitive processing abilities reflected his progress. His ratings of verbal and nonverbal emotional expression also showed improvement. At one point, when he encountered interpersonal scenes involving assertion with his parents, his error rate went up and his nonverbal performance deteriorated. This was an indication to his therapists that these situations needed to be broken down into smaller steps and that he required more modeling and positive feedback for his efforts. Perhaps the most important method of monitoring his progress through the social-skills training was his completion of homework assignments. Al had little difficulty completing assignments related to talking with hospital staff and store clerks. However, when he was given assignments to converse with peers, he reported several times a failure to follow through on the assignment. Again, this was useful information for the therapists, who increased their level of intervention, accompanying Al into the field to provide closer prompts and feedback for his peer contacts.

In the weekly family therapy sessions, Al and his parents were observed for signs of spontaneously using the communication skills that were taught in the group. The leaders looked for examples of giving positive feedback for desired actions, making positive requests, and expressing negative feelings directly and nonaccusatorily. Figure 4 shows an example of a homework assignment, with recording form. When a failure of spontaneous unprompted expressions of negative feelings by Al and his parents was noted in the therapy sessions, the therapist modeled "owning up" and "feeling" statements in relation to a common problem that was irritating to all—the components of effective expression of unpleasant, negative feelings.

The Social Interaction Schedule, with ratings of Al's socializing four times a day, provided a good indication of generalization, or "transfer," of learning from skills training sessions to the more spontaneous give-and-take of the unit. When the data revealed an increase in social isolation, it was a signal to the staff to inquire of Al what might be stressing him. The BPRS enabled the psychiatrist to monitor Al's level of psychopathology and to modify his neuroleptic dose accordingly. Questions drawn from the Present State Examination elicited core symptoms of schizophrenia and other types of psychopathology (Wing, Cooper, and Sartorius, 1974). When the characteristic positive symptoms of schizophrenia had disappeared,

Figure 4. Sample Homework Assignment.

CATCH A PERSON PLEASING YOU

Day	Person who pleased you	What exactly did the person do or say that pleased you?	How did you acknowledge it?
Monday			
Tuesday			
Wednesday			
Thursday			
Friday			
Saturday			
Sunday			

Examples:
Helping at home
Showing interest
Taking medications

one month after admission, the psychiatrist used that information to make the decision to discharge Al from inpatient care. Five years later, Al remains on maintenance neuroleptic drug therapy, though on an intermittent basis. When his psychopathology shows signs of recrudescence, he is returned to a modest dose of an antipsychotic drug. Regularly monitoring his symptoms provides informational feedback to the prescribing psychiatrist, who may then increase or decrease drug dosage. Al was able to obtain part-time work in a public library, establish friendships in a social club for ex-patients, and move out of his family home into an apartment. His earlier academic promise has not been fulfilled, but he is living an independent life with satisfaction and has been able to work collaboratively with a psychiatrist, on a monthly basis, to keep his symptoms under good control.

Summary

Practitioners of behavioral analysis and therapy firmly adhere to specification and measurement in their clinical work. Ongoing observations and ratings enable the therapist and clinician to detect changes in behavior and judge the effectiveness of the treatment and the appropriateness of the goals.

The two cases presented in this chapter illustrate the application of a variety of behavior therapy techniques. The treatment techniques are varied bibliotherapy, assertive and social-skills training, self-monitoring, cognitive therapy, contracting, behavioral family management, and environmental restructuring—but there are some key elements that are essential to the behavior therapy process. The first is a thorough behavioral assessment, not only of the presenting problems but of the individual's strengths as well. For example, Andrea would not have responded so easily to the reading assignments if she had not been as intelligent and academically oriented as she was. The cohesive relationship Al had with his parents made behavioral family therapy feasible and effective.

Behavioral assessment comes both from observations and interviews as well as from data that the patient is asked to record. Assessment data are obtained during the initial evaluation period and from ongoing monitoring of progress through therapy. In this way, behavioral assessment is continually used to aid in relevant goal setting, refinement of goals, and determination of time for change or termination of therapy. Continual measurement of progress, in some form, is an essential element of behavior therapy. It allows the patient to see progress and provides information to the therapist for implementing and modifying the treatment plan. The third essential element in behavior therapy is the use of homework assignments to facilitate application and generalization of behaviors learned during therapy sessions. These three key elements provide the necessary conditions for behavior therapy to occur.

The field of behavioral psychotherapy, extending from office-based treatment of anxiety disorders to the organization of entire inpatient treatment units, has made substantial contributions to clinical disorders of concern to psychiatrists, psychologists, and other mental health professionals. Behavior therapy does not stem from a unitary learning theory but instead reflects a diverse set of conceptual and technical approaches, including systems theory and cognitive and developmental psychology. Behavioral psychotherapy is primarily an empirical and operational strategy for the understanding and treatment of the full range of clinical problems. Based on the measurement of behavior as a means of *initial assessment* and *continuing monitoring* of progress, behavior therapy has within its methods a self-correcting feedback loop, whereby effective techniques gradually emerge for both the individual patient and the field as a whole.

Behavioral psychotherapy is now clearly the treatment of choice for anxiety disorders, at times in combination with time-limited psychotropic drugs that block panic while the patient undergoes a corrective therapeutic learning experience. Further, in the areas of sexual dysfunctions, enuresis, tics, stuttering, and habit disorders, clinical research has documented that behavior therapy produces definitive relief and remission of symptoms. Long-term follow-up studies have shown that remissions in these disorders are durable. With autistic, psychotic, and retarded children and adults, behavioral methods provide effective management and training tools for increasing the adaptive repertoires of these severely disabled populations. More recently, cognitive behavior therapy, social-skills training, and behavioral family therapy have shown great promise in reducing disablement, producing remissions, and improving the quality of life of patients and families coping with depression and schizophrenia.

It is unlikely that any one set of principles will very satisfactorily explain the onset, duration, and amelioration or remission of psychiatric disorders. We must accept the overriding fact of individual differences and learn to tolerate the untidy likelihood that, for the wide range of individuals presenting with signs and symptoms of mental disorder, many different biological, environmental, and behavioral factors are responsible. Interventions, to be truly effective, will have to blend techniques that derive from the biological, environmental, and behavioral spheres. As long as our work is linked to frequent and regular measurement of behavior—just as our colleagues in medicine are guided by fever charts, EKGs, and laboratory assays of blood and urine—we can creatively steer our interventions and accumulate positive and negative experiences for improving the efficacy and durability of therapeutic outcomes.

15

Cognitive-Behavioral Sex Therapy

W. Charles Lobitz
Joseph LoPiccolo
Gretchen K. Lobitz
Jacqueline S. Brockway

When people first began to turn to psychotherapists for help with their sexual inadequacies, their dysfunction was usually considered to reflect a deep-seated personality disorder. As a result, the therapy, generally psychoanalytic in approach, did not focus on their current behavioral deficits but on the presumed dynamics and historical roots of the current symptoms. Over the last few years, an emphasis on learning-theory determinants of human behavior has led to new direct treatments for sexual dysfunctions (Wolpe and Lazarus, 1966; Masters and Johnson, 1970). In this behavioral approach, the dysfunction is seen as a behavioral deficit, caused by lack of skills, anxiety about performance, and guilt induced by societal conditioning. Treatment does not focus on uncovering childhood events, lifting repressions, and working through the transference but on providing information, changing attitudes, and teaching new and adaptive sexual behaviors and skills. Behavior therapy of sexual dysfunction has been found effective (Lobitz and LoPiccolo, 1972; Masters and Johnson, 1970; Obler, 1973) and can be completed in as little as two weeks (Masters and Johnson, 1970).

This chapter presents a case study in the treatment of sexual dysfunction, focusing not on generalized treatment strategies but on how these strategies were modified and adapted to fit the needs of a particular client couple. Although the overall treatment strategy is uncomplicated (perhaps even simplistic) and seemingly could be implemented by anyone who has read the available literature, the therapy process is complex and involves clinical and interpersonal skill. In order to cover a major area of sexual dysfunction, we present a case of erectile failure.

Treatment of Erectile Failure

The basic treatment strategy for erectile failure is well established in the literature and is basically an anxiety reduction procedure. Erectile failure is viewed as resulting from anxiety about performance, or fear of failure. Masters and Johnson (1970, p. 196) state: "The prevalent roadblock [to erection] is one of fear. Fear can prevent erection just as fear can lead to diarrhea or vomiting." If a man is frightened or anxious about achieving an erection, he is not likely to become sexually aroused. Obviously, if a man is not aroused, he will not have an erection. Thus a self-maintaining vicious cycle is established: anxiety about erection actually prevents an erection. Each successive failure of erection leads to greater anxiety on the next attempt at intercourse, which ensures maintenance of erectile failure.

This anxiety has a number of side effects. The man may closely monitor his state of penile erection, leading him to take a "spectator role" (Masters and Johnson, 1970, p. 196) in sexual activity. Being a "spectator" interferes with becoming an aroused participant. Similarly, he may become quite depressed about his lack of "manliness" and his inability to satisfy his wife. His wife may become hostile, derogatory, and demanding toward him. All these factors invariably act to further elevate the client's anxiety about erection and to exacerbate the pattern of erectile failure.

The treatment paradigm for this syndrome has been perhaps most elegantly described by Masters and Johnson (1970). However, the paradigm is not new, having been similarly described (ignoring difference in terminology) by many others, including Wolpe (1958, p. 131), Lazarus (1965), and even an eighteenth-century British physician, Sir John Hunt.

Basically, the treatment strategy involves eliminating performance demands by forbidding the client to perform. Initially, all sexual activity, except some kissing, embracing, and body massage (not including genitals), is proscribed. The male is explicitly forbidden to have an erection. Even if he should have an erection, the couple are jointly forbidden to have intercourse. Once the man has learned to relax and enjoy the low level of sexual activity, with all performance fears and demands eliminated, erection will occur even in the absence of direct physical stimulation. Treatment then consists in rebuilding the couple's sexual behavior step by step.

This treatment sounds simple, as if it could be applied to any couple merely by giving them some simple instructions in one session. Although occasionally it can, far more often the basic program must be extensively modified and elaborated to produce a successful outcome. In this particular case, such modifications and elaborations focused on four factors:

1. These clients were an older (late fifties) couple with age-related physiological changes in sexual functioning.
2. The wife was dominant in the relationship and was quite resistant to treatment.
3. Both husband and wife had a number of unrealistic expectations about sex.
4. They manifested a number of fairly serious, nonsexual marital problems with potential for disrupting therapy.

Case History: Mr. and Mrs. T

The clients were a married couple in their late fifties who were seeking treatment for the husband's erectile failure. They had been married about two years.

This was their second marriage, both having been divorced. Both clients were college graduates, and Mr. T held a master's degree in his professional specialty. They were referred to the clinic by a local psychiatrist whom the husband had seen briefly for his erectile problem. A complete urological evaluation had revealed no physical basis for his difficulty.

The clients reported that during the two years of their marriage they had been able to have intercourse successfully four or five times. Currently they were not attempting intercourse more often than once every month or two. Early in their relationship they had initiated intercourse more frequently, but because of the erectile problem they had almost discontinued sexual relations. The husband reported that he was sexually aroused by and attracted to his wife. However, to his great frustration, when they would try to have intercourse, he was almost invariably unable to achieve an erection. On those occasions when he did achieve an erection, he would lose it almost immediately, so that intromission was rarely possible. The wife reported being extremely frustrated by this pattern and, at the time they began treatment, was considering discontinuing sexual activities entirely. The husband did not like her suggestion and was extremely motivated to find another solution.

Sexual History: Mr. T. The husband had been married previously for some twenty-five years and had never experienced erectile problems in that marriage. His marriage had ended traumatically when his wife informed him that she was having an affair with another man and wanted a divorce.

After his divorce, the client remained celibate until he met his second wife and began dating her. As their relationship progressed, she initiated sexual activity, which pleased and surprised him. However, to his great dismay, in their first attempt to have intercourse, he did not have an erection. As he said, "I couldn't believe I didn't have an erection. I had never had this problem in my life before." To his bewilderment, the problem continued during their courtship. Both believed his failure was due to his feelings that premarital and extramarital sex were immoral. However, when his erectile problems continued after they were married, Mrs. T became upset and began to pressure Mr. T for sexual gratification.

Around this time, Mr. T tried masturbating, which he had not done in many years, to see whether he could obtain an erection. To his surprise, he experienced absolutely no erectile difficulties in masturbation. He continued to masturbate two or three times weekly over the next two years, until entering treatment.

Sexual History: Mrs. T. Mrs. T's first marriage, of some twenty-five years' duration, had also ended in divorce. She reported that her husband had been an alcoholic and had beaten her severely on several occasions in their last year of marriage. Her first husband had been an unskilled, violent, and inconsiderate sexual partner who had frequently forced her to have intercourse against her will. Consequently, although she had been raised in a family that was relatively relaxed and accepting about sexuality, Mrs. T had come to dislike sex. Most relevant to Mr. and Mrs. T's current sexual problem was the fact that Mrs. T's previous husband usually had an erection before beginning any overt sexual activity and never allowed Mrs. T to touch or manipulate his penis in any way.

During the three years between her divorce and her marriage to Mr. T, Mrs. T had sexual relations with two or three other men. She enjoyed these sexual encounters but, as had been the case all her life, did not reach orgasm in intercourse. She did attain orgasm in both oral and manual clitoral manipulation during these encounters, as she had during her first marriage.

Mr. and Mrs. T's current sexual behavior. At the time the clients entered treatment, Mrs. T was clinically depressed, with symptoms of weight loss, insomnia, low energy level, and pervasive sadness. She reported feeling suicidal at times and was receiving antidepressant medication from a local physician. This depression was partly related to her husband's erectile problems but was more centrally related to Mr. T's impending unemployment due to a reorganization of his company. Mrs. T feared that they might have to move to another city for a new job and that their economic status would suffer.

Because of Mrs. T's depression and Mr. T's erectile failure, sexual activity between them had become quite infrequent by the time they entered therapy. They estimated that they were having sex about once every six weeks, at Mr. T's initiation. Mr. T attempted to initiate sex two or three times a week, but Mrs. T usually refused. In their sexual sessions, Mr. T would use a variety of sexual techniques to bring Mrs. T to orgasm, including manual and oral manipulation. In contrast, Mrs. T was quite unwilling to manipulate Mr. T's genitals manually or orally, as she found those activities mildly repugnant. Mrs. T had not masturbated since adolescence. Mr. T masturbated two to three times weekly, with no erectile difficulties.

Course in Treatment. Mr. and Mrs. T were seen daily by a male/female cotherapy team (JL and JB) one hour a day, for a total of fifteen therapy hours. On each day of treatment they were given a "homework" assignment of sexual activities to be carried out in the privacy of their home. Mr. and Mrs. T each separately filled out a daily record form in which they described the activities performed, rated them for arousal and pleasure experienced, and made comments. These forms were returned to the therapists before the next appointment.

After a brief initial intake session, separate histories were taken from the husband and wife. Actual treatment interventions began with session 3.

Session 3. In this session the therapists explained the general dynamics of erectile failure to the clients and personalized this formulation in terms of Mr. and Mrs. T. It was pointed out that both of them had some rather unrealistic expectations about sexual functioning. On the basis of her experience in her first marriage, Mrs. T expected her husband to have erections before beginning sexual activity and in the absence of any direct penile stimulation. The therapists remarked that very few men functioned this way and that it was an undesirable behavior pattern in any case. The female cotherapist emphasized the pleasure she obtained from caressing her husband and arousing him to the point of erection. The male cotherapist revealed that he did not have erections before beginning sexual activity and that he very much enjoyed his wife's caressing his genitals. Both therapists emphasized the research finding (Rubin, 1968) that older men become erect more slowly and require more stimulation; thus Mr. T was unrealistic in expecting himself to perform sexually as he had in the distant past.

Although Mr. T seemed relieved by this discussion, his wife was negativistic and at times argued and disagreed with the therapists. Her negativism became more marked when the therapists discussed how Mrs. T contributed to her husband's erectile problem by making hostile and derogatory remarks about his sexual functioning. The female cotherapist tried to be supportive and nonthreatening in this discussion, saying that she understood how Mrs. T's sexual frustration precipitated these remarks without her realizing their impact on Mr. T. At this point Mrs. T became quite upset and began to cry. She denied making such remarks and insisted that she had always been supportive of her husband. When the male therapist asked Mr. T to repeat what he had reported in the history interview about his wife's remarks and pressure to perform, he instead made several conciliatory statements to his wife. The therapists thus found themselves in a seemingly untenable position: For treatment to succeed, Mrs. T had to realize and accept her role in Mr. T's problem. However, she refused to do so, and Mr. T was unwilling or unable to confront her.

The therapists first tried reminding Mrs. T of several derogatory remarks that she had made during the history interview. Mrs. T steadfastly insisted that such statements as "My first husband was much more masculine" and "Even when Mr. T gets an erection, it's not very big" were not threatening or hostile to Mr. T. She continued to cry, while Mr. T continued to comfort her and undercut the therapists by saying that such statements really did not bother him.

The therapists escaped from this impasse via a two-pronged approach. The female therapist supported Mrs. T by agreeing that, indeed, she had never meant to be hostile or derogatory to Mr. T but that many of her statements had inadvertent negative overtones or connotations in spite of their positive intent. Mrs. T was able to accept a partial role in Mr. T's difficulty through this face-saving maneuver, and a larger confrontation was avoided. At the same time, the male therapist capitalized on the female therapist's supportiveness and insisted that, whatever Mrs. T's intentions, her actual statements were quite harmful to Mr. T's sexual functioning. As Mr. T would not speak for himself (in the presence of Mrs. T), the male therapist spoke for him at some length. The male therapist reflected how he would feel if he were Mr. T and capped his remarks by saying, "I don't have any erectile problems at all, and I never have had, but I'm afraid I would if I were married to you." This statement essentially forced Mrs. T to rethink her role in their sexual problem.

At this point the overall treatment strategy was briefly outlined to the clients. Mr. T was eager to begin; Mrs. T expressed reservations, citing her depression and busy social schedule as reasons for her reluctance. The therapists had anticipated this reluctance and previously had discussed a number of possible tactics for dealing with it. The male therapist simply agreed with Mrs. T, saying that the demands of treatment were probably beyond her present capabilities. At this, Mrs. T visibly bristled and insisted that she could carry out treatment successfully. The female cotherapist agreed with Mrs. T, and the male therapist then "reluctantly" allowed himself to be argued into commencing treatment.

For their first assignment, Mr. and Mrs. T were told to go home, bathe together, and give each other a complete body massage while nude, excluding the breasts and genitals. All other sexual activity was forbidden, except masturbation if desired.

Session 4. The clients reported pleasure but little arousal during their assignment. The next assignment was increased to include some hugging and kissing and a complete "visual examination." Each of them was to examine the other's nude body while massaging it (again not including breasts and genitals) and to talk more or less continuously about what he or she saw and how he or she felt about the various parts of the body. This exercise was included to break down the embarrassment that each of them felt about their bodies.

Session 5. The clients reported considerable pleasure in their "homework" activity. To their great surprise, Mr. T had experienced a partial erection. The therapists repeated that erection would naturally occur, provided Mr. T was not pressured to perform. Forbidding Mr. and Mrs. T to do anything but their assigned activities was reemphasized as a way of removing the performance pressure.

Mr. T reported that Mrs. T had been quite aroused during their activities. Specifically, he had observed heavy breathing and nipple erection. Mrs. T did not report arousal and suggested that she had probably been cold. As it was approximately 32 degrees centigrade in their bedroom, this explanation seemed unlikely. The therapists suggested to Mrs. T that people frequently mislabel their emotional states and that she should allow herself to psychologically experience her obvious physiological arousal. The female therapist added that Mrs. T had learned to "turn herself off" in the past to avoid disappointment and that she now must allow herself to "let go" and become aroused. The male therapist then suggested that treatment might also focus on enhancing Mrs. T's sexuality, since she had never been able to experience orgasm in coitus. Mrs. T did not like this suggestion, saying she was happy with her present mode of reaching orgasm. After much discussion, the therapists reluctantly agreed that therapy would not focus on Mrs. T's ability to reach orgasm. To insist on this seemed too threatening to Mrs. T, and in any case the clients had not sought treatment for her.

The clients' new assignment repeated the previous day's but included genital caressing for both of them. It was emphasized that Mr. T should not try to have an erection, should not expect one, and should not "watch" for one to occur. He was simply to enjoy Mrs. T's caressing of his flaccid penis.

Session 6. The clients did not appear for session 6. Mr. T called and explained that Mrs. T had been hospitalized following what appeared to be a stroke or epileptiform seizure. For the next two days, Mrs. T had an extensive series of medical and neurological tests, which revealed no physical basis for the seizure. Mr. and Mrs. T then called and made an appointment with the therapists, three days after session 6 had been originally scheduled.

In this session Mr. and Mrs. T emphasized their belief that there was some organic cause for her seizure. They had rejected the neurologist's suggestion that Mrs. T was having psychogenic seizures to escape from life stress. The therapists did not become involved in this issue, and treatment was resumed. Their records indicated that the last assignment had been a success. Mr. T had orally manipulated Mrs. T to orgasm. In response to his wife's genital caressing, Mr. T had had two brief erections. He had been quite elated, but Mrs. T reported feeling resentful, since now that intercourse was forbidden, he was having erections, whereas he had not been able to for the last two years. The therapists pointed out that this was a rather hostile remark, typical of her earlier statements. Eventually Mrs. T admitted this and was able to verbalize pleasure that progress was being made.

Their next assignment was the "teasing technique" described by Masters and Johnson (1970), an exercise that demonstrates to the couple that if an erection is lost, it can be reestablished. The female caresses the male's penis but stops periodically, lets the erection subside, and then resumes. To reduce performance pressure, Mrs. T was told to "caress his flaccid penis, manually or orally, as you prefer. If he should get an erection, stop caressing at once and let the erection subside. Then resume caressing his flaccid penis. Repeat this as often as necessary for twenty minutes."

Session 7. The assignment was again successful. Mr. T had seven erections in the twenty minutes. Both clients were amazed at how quickly his penis became erect as Mrs. T caressed him. Mrs. T reported feeling no arousal, but also no repugnance, while touching Mr. T's penis; this was a positive change. Mr. T had also caressed Mrs. T's genitals, but she had not reached orgasm until she masturbated somewhat later in the day. Accordingly, their next assignment included having Mrs. T teach her husband how to manipulate her genitals as she did during masturbation. The therapists recommended that Mr. T teach his wife how to caress his genitals and discussed some genital caressing techniques. Mr. T's assignment was to have Mrs. T caress his genitals and to "try to maintain an erection for five to ten minutes, since you had erections constantly during yesterday's assignment." The perceptive reader will realize that this was a tactical blunder; the therapists had put a specific performance demand on Mr. T, ensuring that he would assume the role of anxious spectator instead of aroused participant.

Session 8. As a consequence, the activity session did not go well. Mrs. T had used both manual and oral manipulation, but Mr. T experienced only three brief partial erections, each lasting about thirty seconds. Mr. T reported feeling anxious, very conscious of having to live up to a ten-minute expectation and fearful that his erection would not last. The therapists reassured Mr. T by taking all the blame (which they deserved) for his difficulties. However, the episode did lead to a productive discussion of performance demands and their role in erectile failure. The therapists felt that, for the first time, Mrs. T really accepted this formulation. The rest of the assignment had been successful. Mrs. T had demonstrated her masturbation techniques for Mr. T, and he had quickly manipulated her to orgasm.

The next assignment was to caress each other's genitals while assuming the body positions recommended by Masters and Johnson (1970). In one position the male sits behind the female and reaches around her to manipulate her genitals. In the other position, the male lies on his back while the female sits between his legs and caresses his genitals. These particular positions help the client to learn to relax and simply receive pleasure "selfishly," with no obligation to give pleasure at the same time.

Session 9. The negative effects of the therapists' tactical mistake were still apparent in the previous day's assignment. Mr. T had had considerable difficulty in relaxing and focusing on his arousal. He reported being unable to avoid the spectator role, being very conscious of his wife's watching his penis, and having only partial erections, which he rapidly lost. At this point, he had suggested switching positions and his caressing her genitals. To his surprise, once he was sitting behind her, where she could not see him, he had a full erection during the entire ten to fifteen minutes he was caressing her genitals. During this time he was not receiving any direct genital stimulation. Mr. T then told Mrs. T of his erection, and she turned around and resumed stimulation of him. This time he was able to focus on his pleasure and maintained a full erection until ejaculation. Mrs. T was unable to reach orgasm during this session. However, given their progress, their next assignment was to assume the female-superior sitting position and to place his penis at the entrance to her vagina but not to insert it. Instead, it was stressed that because this was an exercise that could be done quite well with a flaccid penis, they need not worry about erection.

Session 10. The clients reported that the previous assignment had brought mixed results. Since they were both experiencing some genital soreness after several days of genital caressing, arousal had been painful. Mr. T had experienced some difficulty maintaining his erection. However, when he had caressed Mrs. T's genitals with his penis, he had obtained a strong erection. Unable to restrain themselves, they had inserted his penis and engaged in several minutes of vigorous intercourse. Both of them reported concern about breaking the ban on intercourse, which led them to stop before either of them climaxed.

The therapists responded to their violation of the ban on intercourse in two ways. On the one hand, they stressed that moving ahead too quickly usually brought disastrous results and that breaking the ban on intercourse rarely turned out to be a positive experience. On the other hand, the therapists reemphasized the positive aspect: as long as Mr. T did not have a performance demand to meet, he had no problems in achieving or maintaining an erection. Since both clients were reporting genital soreness, they were given a one-day "holiday" from sexual activity.

At this point in treatment, the therapists were becoming concerned about Mrs. T. Since Mr. T had been given notice that his job would cease to exist in about one month, Mrs. T's depression had deepened significantly. She reported that she was having difficulty in becoming sexually aroused, owing to her pervasive depression. She was also concerned because she had not experienced orgasm in their last few activity sessions.

Accordingly, after the "holiday" their assignment included Mr. T's caressing Mrs. T's genitals with the aid of an electric vibrator. In addition, Mr. T was to lie on his back with Mrs. T kneeling over him, and Mrs. T was to "stuff" Mr. T's penis into her vagina. They were to experience penile containment but not to engage in pelvic thrusting. The therapists again stressed that this activity could be carried out with either an erect or a flaccid penis; therefore, Mr. T was free of performance demands.

Session 11. The clients reported that all had gone well for Mr. T. He had maintained a strong erection during their entire session, and the insertion had been done with his penis erect. They had enjoyed the penile containment and had found it difficult to restrain themselves from pelvic thrusting. Mr. T had stimulated Mrs. T with the electric vibrator. She had been very aroused by his manual, oral, and vibrator stimulation of her genitals but again had not been able to reach orgasm. She insisted that she had never had such difficulty before and blamed her depression. The therapists tentatively accepted this explanation and told her not to try to reach orgasm, since this performance demand would interfere with her arousal. She was also placed on a program of Kegel's exercises (1952) to enhance her orgasmic potential by strengthening her pelvic musculature.

Their next assignment added slow pelvic thrusting to their activity. To avoid placing another type of performance demand on Mr. T, intravaginal ejaculation was forbidden.

Session 12. Results continued to be positive for Mr. T and mixed for his wife. They had had two sessions of intercourse with slow thrusting. Mr. T's only problem had been in keeping himself from ejaculating. Mrs. T reported arousal and pleasure but no orgasm, despite oral, manual, and vibrator stimulation by her husband.

Their next assignment was simply to resume a normal sex life with no restrictions whatsoever. Previous experience indicated that clients sometimes suffer a relapse at this point, since they perceive an implicit demand to function normally. The possibility of relapse was explained to the clients. The therapists predicted that, with all restrictions removed, Mr. T would experience some erectile difficulty at first but that experience indicated this difficulty was always short-lived. The logic of predicting failure to the client is as follows: by telling him he will likely fail to have an erection, the therapist virtually eliminates the demand on him for performance. If the prediction is correct and the client fails to have an erection, he is reassured by the therapist's statement that such failure is typical at this point in treatment and is always short-lived. If he does not fail, he is too elated by his success to be concerned about his therapist's mistaken prediction. Thus, the therapist cannot lose by predicting failure.

Session 13. The clients reported that Mr. T had been somewhat slow to obtain an erection because he was trying to get one preparatory to intercourse. However, once they discussed this, he had had no further difficulties. They had engaged in several minutes of vigorous intercourse, until Mrs. T insisted they stop (just as Mr. T was approaching ejaculation), since she was "hot and tired."

After a brief private consultation, the therapists directly confronted Mrs. T. As in the past, the female therapist was deliberately supportive, whereas the male therapist was more confrontive. The male therapist told Mrs. T that he was convinced she was deliberately sabotaging the treatment program and at some level did not want to resume a full sex life with her husband. The female cotherapist "disagreed" and suggested Mrs. T was just too depressed and physically frail to cope with a full sex life. Mrs. T vehemently argued that neither of these explanations was correct but that she had been hot and tired, since it was summer and their home was not air-conditioned. The male therapist indicated that he felt this was merely an excuse. He offered to prove it to Mrs. T by refunding a portion of their treatment fee so that they could spend the last two days of treatment (a weekend) relaxing at a luxurious air-conditioned motel. Mr. and Mrs. T accepted this offer and challenge.

Sessions 14 and 15. Whether the challenge worked because Mrs. T was right or because the therapists had finally succeeded in getting her interested in treatment will never be known. In any case, on both days they had successful intercourse, Mr. T ejaculating and Mrs. T greatly enjoying it. He also manipulated her to orgasm several times during the two days.

The final treatment step was developing a maintenance plan to ensure the clients' continued success after termination. To this end, Mr. and Mrs. T were each asked to develop two lists: one specifying what they had been doing that contributed to their difficulties and one specifying ways they had learned to correct these problems. These lists are shown in Tables 1 and 2.

Table 1. Mr. T's Lists.

Errors	*Corrections*
1. *Sex* was kind of a dirty word	1. Realization that sex and sexual activities are natural, essential, and a wonderful part of living
2. That a woman, particularly a "good" woman, either didn't want sexual intercourse or only wanted it in order to have children	2. Realization that a healthy woman has just as strong a need and (though latent) drive for intercourse as a healthy man

Table 1. Mr. T's Lists, Cont'd.

Errors	Corrections
3. That masturbation is a type of self-abuse and could or would result in physical or mental damage	3. Realization that masturbation in moderation is a healthy method to achieve a degree of sexual satisfaction, particularly when heterosexual intercourse is unavailable
4. That normal sexual intercourse is a manifestation of a male physically dominating a female solely for the male's satisfaction	4. Comprehension (and this was difficult to accept) that a woman intensely wants and needs penetration to feel fulfilled (completely apart from the needs for procreation)
5. That taking visual delight in the nude figure (or partially clothed figure) of my wife was sinful	5. Acceptance of the fact that a wife wishes her husband to enjoy the sight of her body
6. That an erection should "just come naturally" when circumstances indicate that intercourse may be consummated or that I can "will" an erection	6. Except for teenagers and those in their twenties, some type of overt stimulation is needed to produce an erection; that "willing" an erection is impossible
7. That personal gratification in and from intercourse was selfishly wrong	7. Acceptance that the only way for my wife to be completely satisfied sexually was for me to concentrate on my "selfish" desires

Table 2. Mrs. T's Lists.

Errors	Corrections
1. Hadn't been stimulating Mr. T by caressing his genitals manually or orally	1. Learned to do this and the places that it felt best
2. Unmeaningly [sic] undercutting Mr. T on occasion by unthinking remarks	2. Will be more careful of his ego
3. Trying too hard for climax	3. Will try to relax and just enjoy feeling
4. Start thinking of many things when Mr. T is caressing my genitals to produce climax	4. Will try to turn mind off and just participate

As a couple, they were also asked to develop a plan for their sexual activities over the next three months, after which a follow-up interview was scheduled. This plan is shown in Table 3. The therapists suggested only one addition to this plan. Since Mrs. T was now having orgasms during Mr. T's manipulation of her genitals, they recommended that the clients continue this manipulation during intercourse. In this way Mrs. T could experience coital orgasm.

Table 3. Maintenance Plan.

1. Frequency of lovemaking: At this time we don't know how often, on the average, we will make love. Initially, though, we intend to enjoy each other about two or three times per week, assuming near-optimum conditions. If this pace is not adequate or is agreed to be excessive, we will modify it.
2. Conditions: We will endeavor to make love under the most favorable conditions, such as:
   A. When there is no sense of time pressure and when we have no house guests (may have an exception to the latter if we are reasonably assured of privacy).
   B. Both will, as time and finances permit, read sexy books and see sexy movies together.
   C. "Set the stage" by taking phone off the hook, ignoring the doorbell, turning lights on dimly (or using candles).

Table 3. Maintenance Plan, Cont'd.

3. Signals:
   A. To indicate a desire, either may initiate by the oral invitation "Let's make love." (We have agreed that the request "Let's go to bed" will not mean a desire to make love.) The invitation to make love will be made only when the inviter really desires to carry through. The responding partner will be frank and candid in his or her oral response and will not deny the request to "get back at" the inviter for some unconnected "reason" or for flippant reasons. A full and clear statement of the actual reason for denial will be given.
   B. When or if either partner feels dissatisfied in any way with the other partner's sexual behavior, he or she will not "bottle it up" but will present a fair statement of the problem for candid and full discussion with his or her partner.
4. Positions: We have agreed we will experiment from time to time with a wide variety of positions and freely discuss our reactions and responses to each new position tried.
5. Loss of erection: We both realize this will happen occasionally. Upon occurrence, we will stop whatever particular activity was in process and go to a new activity, frequently shifting roles. (For example, if the penis is in the vagina, it will be removed and Mrs. T may begin general, nongenital stimulation.)
6. Slow orgasm for Mrs. T: Normally, Mr. T will continue to caress Mrs. T for up to twenty minutes, alternately using manual, oral, or vibrator method. At the end of the period, unless Mrs. T wishes him to continue, Mr. T will desist. If Mrs. T becomes tired or tender at any time, she will tell him so and Mr. T will desist. Mrs. T will not feign tiredness or soreness.
7. Spectator role: If either finds himself or herself in the spectator role, he (she) will try to relax and experience the sensations. If unsuccessful in this, he (she) will assume a new and positive role.
8. Mind wandering: Each will always try to concentrate his (her) attention on the sensations being experienced but may consciously use fantasies and mental images.
9. Performing role: Neither of us is to consider himself or herself a performer for the other or consider the partner a performer as such. Sexual play and activities are mutual efforts.

Assessment of Treatment Results

The clients filled out an assessment battery at the start of treatment, at the end of treatment, and three months after the end of treatment. This battery included a self-report questionnaire, the Oregon Sex Inventory (LoPiccolo and Steger, 1973), and the Locke-Wallace Marital Happiness Scale (Locke and Wallace, 1959). Scores from the self-report questionnaire and the Locke-Wallace (Table 4) all indicate that treatment was successful. Mr. T continued to be somewhat slower in attaining an erection than he would have liked, as reflected in his report that he had difficulty in achieving an erection on 25 percent of coital occasions. However,

Table 4. Responses on Written Self-Report Measures Before and After Therapy and at Follow-up.

Item	Time of Assessment		
	Pretherapy	*Posttherapy*	*Follow-up*
Frequency of intercourse	Once in 6 weeks	Daily	Twice weekly
Duration of foreplay (minutes)	1–3	7–10	16–30
Duration of intercourse (minutes)	1–3	7–10	4–6

Table 4. Responses on Written Self-Report Measures
Before and After Therapy and at Follow-up, Cont'd.

Item	Time of Assessment		
	Pretherapy	Posttherapy	Follow-up
Orgasm in coitus, percent-age of occasions			
Male	25	50	90 +
Female	0	25	75
Problem in getting an erection, percentage of coital occasions	100	50	25
Problem in maintaining an erection, percent-age of coital occasions	100	10	10
Rating of sexual satis-faction (scale of 1–6)			
Male	1	6	6
Female	1	5	5
Locke-Wallace marital happiness score			
Male	104	129	109
Female	78	112	104

he had little or no trouble in maintaining an erection and rated his sex life as extremely satisfactory. Mrs. T, though less satisfied at follow-up, was now reaching orgasm in coitus 75 percent of the time, provided clitoral stimulation was continued. Verbally, both of them reported being very happy now. Mrs. T reported that her depression had lifted once Mr. T obtained new employment.

Figure 1 shows the Oregon Sex Inventory profiles for Mr. and Mrs. T. Before treatment, Mrs. T was dissatisfied with their frequency of sexual activities (scale 2), Mr. T was dissatisfied with Mrs. T as a sexual partner (scale 9), and Mrs. T was also unhappy with her sexual responsiveness (scale 4). With the exception of scale 4, these scores were all in the normal, satisfied range after therapy. The fact that Mrs. T continued to be unhappy with her own sexual responsiveness after treatment suggests that the therapists should have tried harder to persuade the clients to include a treatment program for her in the course of therapy.

Long-Term Follow-up

One year after the end of treatment, the clients were contacted for follow-up. Mr. T reported that their sex life had been extremely gratifying to them both until Mrs. T's sudden death from a stroke some two months earlier. The therapists were shocked and saddened at the news. Mr. T thanked them for their help and accepted their condolences on his wife's death.

Discussion

The focus of the case history was a change in the sexual responses of the clients. The treatment strategy followed a general anxiety reduction, skills training model. However, the case presented problems in the direction application of this

Figure 1. Oregon Sex Inventory Profiles.

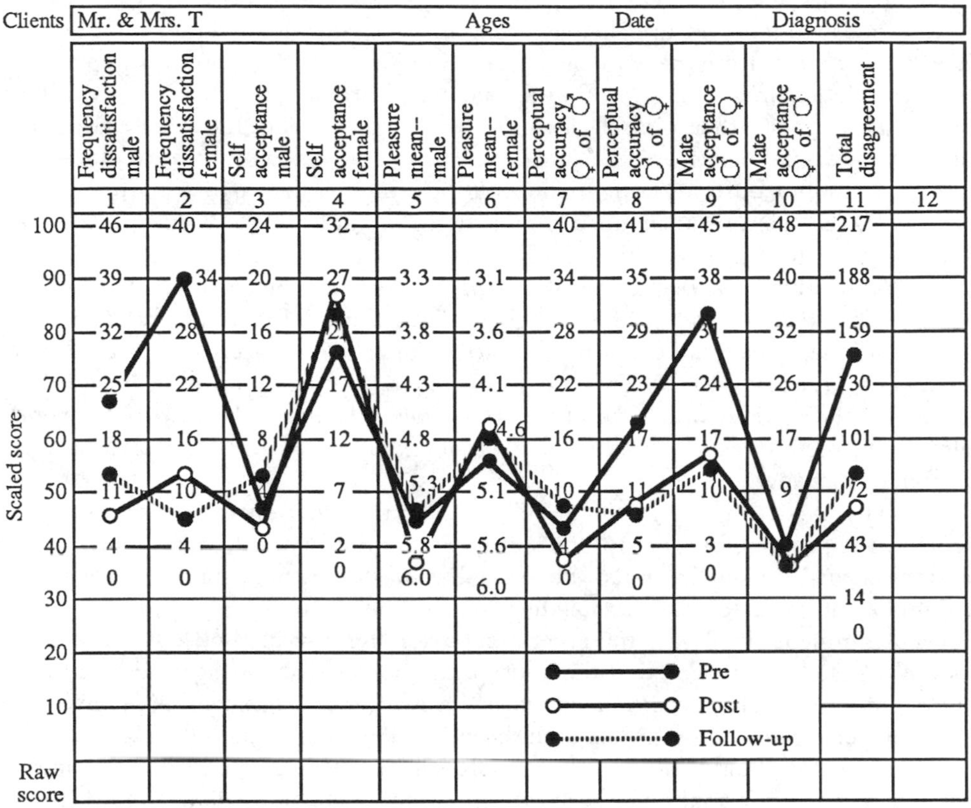

model. The husband's erectile failure was deeply embedded in the interpersonal dynamics of the marital relationship, and the general behavioral treatment strategy required moment-to-moment tactical modifications by the therapists. Some of these tactics were amplifications of the general anxiety reduction model and are common to behavior therapy, whereas others derive from cognitive, personality, and existential psychology. As presented in this case history, the therapists' tactics speak for themselves. However, a few of these tactics deserve special comment.

The general strategy for reducing performance anxiety followed a stepwise, gradual approximation to the sexual response, including initial prohibitions on intercourse (Masters and Johnson, 1970; Wolpe, 1969). In addition, the therapists further minimized the pressure to perform by predicting failure, thus limiting the clients' expectations. The latter tactic has been used by hypnotherapists and others (Haley, 1963) to present clients with a no-lose situation. The therapists further minimized performance anxiety by setting the clients' expectations for success no higher than their current performance at that point in treatment. Bandura (1971) has suggested that the self-reinforcement process is partly a function of the individual's expectations. In that sense, lowered expectations enhanced the probability that the clients would self-reinforce their progress.

In addition to tactics designed to motivate the clients' behaviors and to reduce their anxiety, the therapists directed much of their intervention toward client attitude change. One way of changing client attitudes is to appeal to relevant literature. The therapists did this to support the longer latency of erectile response in older men (Rubin, 1968). Another attitude-change tactic was the relabeling of certain physiological states. For example, when Mrs. T had defined her nipple erection as a response to temperature change, the therapists relabeled it as sexual arousal. This tactic derives from the work of Schachter and Singer (1962) on the importance of cognitive labeling in interpreting physiological arousal.

Throughout, therapist self-disclosure was used to change the clients' attitudes about their sexual behaviors. This tactic has been advocated by Jourard (1964) as a way of spontaneously reacting to the clients during the therapy hour. In the present case, the therapists extended this tactic to include self-disclosure about the therapists' own sexual behaviors in the privacy of their homes.

As Bandura (1969) and others have shown, behavior change in nonthreatening situations is a potent technique for changing client attitudes. In particular, behavioral rehearsal (roleplaying) has enabled clients to perform behaviors previously inhibited by anxiety (Lazarus, 1966). This use of roleplaying is analogous to Kelly's (1955) fixed-role therapy, in which the client is instructed to enact the role of someone else. In the present case, the role was a different sexual response rather than a specific personality change.

The use of different tactics at different points in therapy depends on several factors: the progress of therapy, the therapists' familiarity with various methods, and the clients' personality traits. While the first two factors are generally recognized as important variables in behavior therapy, the client's personality traits deserve special comment. In describing several behavior therapy methods, Eysenck and Beech (1971) have argued that the appropriate behavioral stratagem depends on the client's personality type. In a similar vein, Kanfer and Saslow (1969) have advocated a pretreatment assessment of the client's behavioral strengths and weaknesses to determine the appropriate treatment approach. In the present case, the therapists used personality information, as well as pretreatment behavioral data, to guide their therapy tactics. The therapists' challenge to Mrs. T that she was too depressed and frail to cope with a full sex life was based on their assessment of her personality pattern—that is, that her "passive-aggressive" style would lead her to resist whatever directives the therapists gave. This example illustrates that even when behavior therapists are not trying to change the client's personality traits, they need to be cognizant of them to best adapt the treatment to the client.

Though elucidating the therapy used in the behavioral treatment of sexual dysfunction, the present case does not establish the efficacy of the tactics employed. This case history is presented as a demonstration for the practitioner of the moment-to-moment tactics that complement the general behavioral stratagems. The relationship between the successful therapy outcome and the tactics used is correlational. A causal relationship between outcome variables and therapy tactics can be established only through experimental manipulation. The authors are engaged in research to determine what variables are necessary and sufficient in the behavior therapy of sexual dysfunction.

❦ 16 ❦

Rational-Emotive
Therapy

Albert Ellis

I created rational-emotive therapy (RET) in 1955, after being trained as an analyst and using classical psychoanalysis and analytically created therapy for several years and finding both these methods ineffective. I vainly tried to "reform" psychoanalysis and make it scientific (Ellis, 1949a, 1949b, 1950, 1956b) but was notably unsuccessful in my revisionism. Nor was I able to scientifically accept or effectively use the other most respected therapies of the early 1950s, such as those of Erich Fromm (1947), Karen Horney (1939), Carl Rogers (1951), Otto Rank (1945), and Harry Stack Sullivan (1953). Only Alfred Adler (1927, 1929) seemed to make really good sense; but his methodology was not active-directive or deeply philosophical enough for me, and he almost entirely ignored the findings and the techniques of the behavior therapists (Eysenck, 1953; Jones, 1924a, 1924b; Salter, 1949; Skinner, 1953; Watson and Rayner, 1920).

Believing that two main aspects of psychotherapy—the philosophical and the behavioral—were being sadly neglected, I began experimenting with these methods in 1953 and incorporated them into RET. Then, because I believed in a no-shilly-shally, evocative, confrontive approach (particularly after I had spent several years being allergic to the passivity of psychoanalysis!) from the start I made RET highly emotive; and I added to its emotive elements in the 1960s by adapting some of the main experimental and encounter techniques to its cognitive-behavioral approach (Ellis, 1969b). While many present-day schools of psychotherapy are distinctly eclectic in using a variety of techniques, RET is a pioneering form of psychological treatment which is truly comprehensive (or, to use Arnold Lazarus's term, multimodal) and which uses, with virtually all clients, several kinds of therapeutic methods.

Even RET theory is variegated and eclectic, since it has several main postulates that are not easily subsumed under a few major propositions. Thus, its hypotheses include the following (Ellis, 1962, 1971, 1973b, 1979a, 1979c, 1980, 1984a, 1984b; Ellis and Harper, 1975; Ellis and Whiteley, 1979):

1. Emotion, thought, and behavior rarely, if ever, are pure or unalloyed: each includes important elements of the others, and all three continually interact with and cause aspects of one another.

2. What we call emotional disturbances (especially neurotic feelings such as severe anxiety, depression, self-deprecation, and rage) are caused or contributed to by a complex of biological and environmental factors, and most seriously disturbed individuals have strong innate (biological) tendencies to over- or underreact to environmental influences and to exaggerate and/or minimize the significance of many events (especially the traumatic events) of their lives.

3. Humans are easily affected by the people and the things around them (the system in which they develop and live), but they intentionally also easily affect the people and things (the system) around them. To be affected, however, does not necessarily mean to be disturbed. Unfavorable conditions such as cruel parents, poverty, and bigoted teaching affect virtually everyone, but they hardly result in serious disturbance of all those affected. Affectability does not equal disturbability. Each individual's innate vulnerability to the system's influences also contributes to his or her disturbances—and often contributes more than environmental factors do. Because of their innate tendencies to react (and to overreact) to their surrounding system, people significantly *decide* or *choose* to disturb themselves—or to *not* disturb themselves—about the influences of the system in which they live.

4. Once people disturb themselves about the events or the other people in their lives, they almost always have the ability—if they choose to work at using it—of undisturbing themselves and of re-creating minimal (though not zero) disturbance in the present and future. Human irrationality and self-defeatism, however, are to some extent synonymous with the human condition. Consequently, virtually no humans are (or are likely to be) consistently and totally rational or undisturbed.

5. People disturb themselves emotionally, intellectually, and behaviorally. Thus, they often think, emote, and act in a manner that defeats their own best interests and those of the social group in which they choose to live. There is no one way in which they do this. But they can best understand and change their disturbed feelings and actions by clearly and specifically recognizing the most important cognitions by which they usually make themselves neurotic.

6. These disturbing cognitions consist largely of irrational Beliefs (iBs) or basic self-defeating philosophies which people, consciously or unconsciously, adopt or create and then strongly hold and which significantly motivate them to feel and act self-sabotagingly. The ABC theory of RET hypothesizes that people go to the stimuli, or Activating Events (A), in the system in which they reside with goals, purposes, or desires—especially the goals of continuing to survive and of living in a reasonably happy or unfrustrated manner. When they encounter (or think they encounter) undesirable things—especially failure and/or disapproval—they tend to tell themselves at point B (their Belief System) both rational Beliefs (rBs) and irrational Beliefs (iBs), and these lead to self-helping or self-defeating Consequences, or Concomitants (Cs).

7. When unfortunate or undesirable Activating Events (As) occur and when people have rational Beliefs (rBs) about these As, their rBs tend to take the form of preference or wish statements—for example, "I don't *like* this failure and I *wish* it had not occurred, but I *can stand it* and still lead a reasonably happy life." If they stay with these rBs, or preference statements, these people will have *appropriate*

feelings or consequences (for example, disappointment and frustration) that help them to take self-helping actions (for example, working to succeed next time).

8. When unfortunate or undesirable Activating Events (As) occur, people often also create irrational Beliefs (iBs) about these As, and these iBs tend to take the form of absolutistic "musts" and command statements—for example, "This failure *must* not occur, and because it did occur as it absolutely *should* not, I *can't stand it*; it's *awful*; and I am a rotten person for not preventing it!" If people add these iBs to their rBs, they will have inappropriate feelings, or Consequences (Cs)—for example, severe anxiety and depression that will encourage them to take self-defeating actions (such as withdrawal or desperate attempts to succeed next time).

9. When people feel disturbed and act self-defeatingly (at C), they have the ability to look at their As, rBs, and iBs and to Dispute (D) their iBs until they surrender them and change them back to rBs—thereby changing their inappropriate feelings and self-defeating behaviors (at point C). They can best understand (observe and figure out) their iBs cognitively, through empirical observation and rational analysis. Even when iBs are unconscious, they are rarely deeply hidden and can usually be observed, discovered, and logically figured out (if one uses RET theory) quickly and without too much trouble.

10. When people's iBs are logically and empirically discovered (and sometimes even when they are not clearly discovered), they can be counteracted and dissolved in a variety of cognitive, emotive, and behavioral ways. They can most effectively be eradicated or minimized by using several rather than only one of these thinking, affective, and action-oriented methods.

Briefly stated, this is the RET theory of emotional disturbance and its alleviation. Let me now show how I used RET theory and practice in treating a twenty-seven-year-old woman afflicted with severe social and work anxiety. When I first saw this woman, whom I shall call Jane, she was (as all the members of her therapy group agreed) unusually attractive. Hardly a day passed when some man (or some lesbian) did not try to pick her up at her office, on the subway, on the street, or in the stores where she shopped. In spite of all this attention, she was extremely shy with men, especially the ones she found most desirable, and reported that her mind went absolutely blank when she was about to talk to one. She was so self-conscious that she could hardly face storekeepers and often had her mother do her shopping. When men persisted in trying to date her—which they often did—she would first avoid them because of her shyness. Then she would desperately latch onto one who was most persistent and just wouldn't take no for an answer. When he proved (as he always did) to be an unsuitable mate, she would stay with him much longer than she wanted to, being deathly afraid to return to the mating "rat race."

Jane, who had quite a good sense of humor in spite of her conversational ineptness, referred to herself as a "basket case" in her vocational as well as her social life. She had been trained as a high school teacher but could not bear facing a classroom of kids and therefore had taken a Civil Service job as an administrative assistant—a job she easily got by scoring high on an examination. She would have liked to get any number of better jobs for which she was qualified, but she was terrified of job interviews and therefore never applied. She hated herself for sticking at her present low-level position, but this self-hatred only made her more convinced that she was incapable of adequate interpersonal relations.

Before my seeing her, Jane had had one year of Rogerian therapy with a college counselor when she was nineteen. She felt that it had helped her feel a little better but had not made inroads against her shyness. She had had two years of psychoanalytically oriented therapy by the time she was twenty-three but felt that it had only made her very dependent on her analyst and more than ever afraid to face the world on her own. She was disillusioned with therapy and was prepared to give up all hope of ever changing when her twin sister, who had very similar problems and who had had a year of RET, which resulted in considerable improvement, virtually insisted that she come to the Institute for Rational-Emotive Therapy in New York and even volunteered to pay for her first two months of treatment. Still reluctant to go into therapy again but not assertive enough to resist her sister's entreaties, Jane agreed to give RET a chance.

As is typical in my practice of RET, I used a number of cognitive, emotive, and behavioral methods with Jane, the most important of which I shall now describe.

Cognitive Methods of RET

The main cognitive techniques of RET that I used with Jane were the following.

Teaching the ABCs of RET. Because of her previous therapy, Jane held the common psychoanalytic belief that people become disturbed because of the traumatic events of their childhood. I used the first few sessions to disabuse her of this notion and to show her that we all strongly tend to bring *ourselves* —and especially our innate and unique proclivities to desire and to demand—to our parents and teachers in early life and they impart to us preferences and standards that we adopt and thereafter, as Pogo has aptly stated, we have met the enemy and it is us! Consequently, we take many of our preferences and standards from our early caretakers (and from TV!), but we add absolutistic musts to them and make those preferences into dire "needs" (Ellis, 1962; Ellis and Becker, 1982; Ellis and Harper, 1975). Moreover, I showed Jane that no matter how and where she originally acquired her irrational shoulds, oughts, and musts, she still had them today, and she had better acknowledge their power to upset her and work at understanding and surrendering them.

Although Jane at first resisted taking responsibility for her iBs because she found it more acceptable to blame her "dominating" mother for "making" her irrational and shy, she soon changed her tune when I showed her that her younger sister, who was even more dominated by her mother (because she was the "baby" of the family), had always refused to give in to this domination and turned out to be unusually outgoing and assertive—as, indeed, the mother herself was. Jane and her twin sister, in contrast, seemed to take after their shy and unassertive father, who was divorced from their mother when they were five years old and who thereafter had little to do with any of his three daughters. When, after our third session, Jane decided that she really had largely created her own iBs (for example, "I must never be disapproved by people I find significant") and that these Beliefs (and not her dominating mother) had made her pathologically shy, she "bought" much of the RET theory and started to look actively for her self-defeating philosophies.

Detecting Irrational Beliefs. In rational-emotive therapy, D stands for Disputing iBs (Phadke, 1980). But D can be subdivided into three main processes: Detecting iBs, Discriminating them from rBs, and Debating them. I first showed Jane how to detect her iBs—and particularly how to look for her absolutistic shoulds, oughts, and musts. She soon came up with some basic irrational Beliefs: (1) ''I must speak well to people I find attractive.'' (2) ''I must be interesting and clever.'' (3) ''I must speak easily and spontaneously without too much effort.'' (4) ''When I don't speak well and impress people as I should, I'm a stupid, inadequate person!''

These iBs, Jane was able to see, were the main and most direct contributors to, or ''causes'' of, her gut feelings of anxiety. But—as is commonly the case, and as RET always investigates—she also had some iBs *about* her anxiety. Whenever she experienced (or thought she might experience) anxiety, she almost immediately thought, first, ''I must not be anxious! It's terrible if I am!'' and then ''I especially must not *show* others how anxious I am. If I do, they will surely reject me—and that would be awful!'' These iBs *about* her nervousness led Jane to take her primary symptom (anxiety) and turn it into a deadly secondary symptom (anxiety about anxiety); and once she developed this secondary anxiety, she was so upset by it that her original nervousness escalated. She then went on to a tertiary feeling of panic and hopelessness, motivated by her tertiary iB: ''Now that I'm *so* panicked and can't get myself out of feeling this way, I'll *never* be able to overcome my anxiety. I can't stand this intense panic—and I can't change!''

Discriminating Irrational from Rational Beliefs. I showed Jane that she had not only iBs (musts) but a number of rBs (preferences) and that the latter were legitimate and self-helping. For example, on the secondary and tertiary level, some of her rBs were ''I don't like being anxious and showing it to others, but I can accept these feelings and work at getting rid of them'' and ''If people do reject me for showing them how anxious I am, that will be most unfortunate, but I can stand it.'' With the help of RET, Jane was able to see that these rational Beliefs (preferences) were quite different from her irrational Beliefs (unrealistic demands) and that she had the option of choosing to convince herself of the former rather than of the latter.

Debating Irrational Beliefs. I asked, and taught Jane how to ask herself, several logical and empirical questions to Debate and Dispute (at point D) her secondary and tertiary iBs. For example: (1) ''Even though my panic (and panic about my panic) is so intense and handicapping, where is the evidence that I *can't stand it* and that I *can't* overcome it?'' (2) ''Granted that my anxiety will turn some people off, will *everyone* boycott me for displaying it? And if some people do despise me for showing panic, will that really be *terrible*, and do I truly *need* their approval?''

As she Disputed these secondary and tertiary iBs that led to her anxiety about her anxiety, Jane also went back, under my guidance, to her primary iBs and actively and persistently began to Debate them in this vein: (1) ''Why *must* I speak well to people I find attractive?'' (2) ''Where is it written that I *have to* be interesting and clever?'' (3) ''Do I really *have to* speak easily and spontaneously, without too much effort?'' (4) ''When I don't speak well and impress people, how does that make me a stupid, inadequate person?'' She answered these Disputes as follows: (1) There is no reason I *must* speak well to people I find attractive, but it would be desirable if I do so; so I shall make an effort—but not kill myself—to do so. (2) It is written only in my head that I *have to* be interesting and clever, but it would be nice if I were! (3) I can speak *uneasily* and *unspontaneously* and still get by with most people with whom I converse. (4) When I speak poorly and fail to impress people, that only makes me a person who spoke unimpressively this time—not a totally stupid or inadequate person.

As she did the Disputing and questioned her own irrational Beliefs, Jane began to feel much better and to be more willing to speak up with people she favored.

Coping Self-Statements. I used another of RET's favorite methods with Jane—having her figure out, write down, and repeat to herself several times a day helpful coping statements (rational Beliefs) that she would eventually internalize (Ellis, 1962, 1973a; Ellis and Becker, 1982; Lazarus, 1966; Meichenbaum, 1977). Some of those she found most helpful were the following: "I *can* speak up to others, even when I feel uncomfortable doing so." "I would *like* to speak well, but I never *have* to." "No one dies of social anxiety!" "I'm an intelligent person." "When people I favor reject me, it often means more about them and their tastes than about me." "Even when I act stupidly and impress people badly, I can still learn a lot and enjoy myself with them."

Referentiating. An RET technique adopted from general semantics is referentiating (Danysh, 1974; Korzybski, 1933). Using this method with Jane, I helped her to write down and regularly review the advantages of making herself uncomfortable and overcoming her low frustration tolerance when she forced herself to act unsuitably. Normally, she referented to herself only the disadvantages (for example, her feelings of awkwardness) when she spoke up with desirable people. She now listed several benefits of doing so, especially these: (1) She would get practice in speaking and thereby become more fluent. (2) She would learn what it was best to say—and not to say—to others. (3) She would meet a larger sample of people from whom to choose friends or lovers. (4) She would see that many people were as shy and as conversationally backward as she was. (5) She could accept the challenge of doing badly and of then not putting herself down. (6) She would find her life more interesting. (7) Her anxiety would be more intense but less prolonged. As she continued to do this kind of referenting, Jane found that she was able to carry out her homework assignments of encountering others with much more ease than she had ever had in doing similar things before.

Teaching RET to Others. I used to warn my clients, when I practiced psychoanalysis, *not* to analyze their friends and relatives, because they almost always did so badly and thereby harmed themselves and their "clients." However, I now do the opposite and strongly encourage many of them to teach RET to their associates and to try to talk these others out of their irrational Beliefs, for as Bard (1980) has experimentally shown, teaching RET to others frequently helps the teachers learn its Disputing and other methods themselves. Jane particularly used RET with her mother, her younger sister, and her close women friends, and she reported that actively working with them to see and surrender some of their irrationalities significantly helped her to observe and effectively debate several of her own.

Psychoeducational Methods. RET has always promoted the use of books and audiotapes in teaching its principles to clients and members of the public. For example, RET encourages clients to record their own therapy sessions and to listen to them several times to remember better and to zero in more effectively on the points made by both the therapist and the client during a session. Jane found recordings of her own sessions extremely valuable teaching tools and regularly listened to each one a few times between sessions.

Problem Solving. RET sees people as having two kinds of problems: (1) practical problems, such as Jane's not having an interesting job or her winding up with unsuitable male partners, and (2) emotional problems, or problems *about* having practical problems. With Jane, as we do in RET generally, I started with the emotional problems and showed her how to minimize or eliminate them. Then I worked with Jane on her practical problems. For example, I went over her job-seeking problems with her, showed her how she could write a good résumé, and discussed the difficulties of how to get interviews, how to handle these interviews, and how to turn down some jobs and wait for the better ones she was actually seeking. We also discussed the practical issues of how she could look for a suitable male partner and how she could eliminate the poor prospects and do better with the good ones.

Use of Humor. According to RET theory, the irrational Beliefs (iBs) that people adopt and create with which to upset themselves emotionally usually arise from their giving due meaning or consideration to their desires and preferences (which is rational) and then going far beyond this to give exaggerated significance to these wishes. They take things much too seriously. As one of its main techniques to combat this kind of exaggerated, or "awfulizing," thinking, RET employs a good deal of humor. It reduces clients' ideas to absurdity, shows them how contradictory and ridiculous these views are, and gets them to sing (and preferably internalize) some rational, humorous songs that they can use to overcome their overserious cognitions.

Since Jane had a good sense of humor, I used many humorous sallies with her, and some of them proved quite effective. She particularly found benefit in singing to herself some of my rational, humorous songs when she had fits of anxiety or depression. Two that she found especially useful were these:

Perfect Rationality
(to the tune *Funiculi, Funicula* by Luigi Denza)

Some think the world must have a right direction
And so do I! And so do I!
Some think that with the slightest imperfection
They can't get by—and so do I!

For I, I have to prove I'm superhuman,
And better far than people are!
To show I have miraculous acumen—
And always rate among the Great!

Perfect, perfect rationality
Is, of course, the only thing for me!
How can I ever think of being
If I must live fallibly?
Rationality must be a perfect thing for me!

I'm Depressed, Depressed!
(to the tune *The Band Played On*, by Charles B. Ward)

When anything slightly goes wrong with the world,
I'm depressed, depressed!
When any mild hassle before me is hurled,
I feel most distressed!
When life isn't fated to be consecrated

I can't tolerate it at all!
When anything slightly goes wrong with the world,
I just bawl, bawl, bawl!

(Lyrics by Albert Ellis, Copyright 1977 by the Institute for Rational-Emotive Therapy.)

Emotive Methods of RET

As I have emphasized for many years (and as many writers on psychotherapy have nonetheless chosen to ignore), RET is almost always a multimodal school of psychological therapy and rarely treats a client without using several emotive and behavioral, as well as cognitive, methods (Bard, 1980; Ellis, 1962, 1969a, 1969b, 1973b; Ellis and Becker, 1982; Ellis and Harper, 1975; Grieger and Boyd, 1980; Walen, DiGiuseppe, and Wessler, 1980; Wessler and Wessler, 1980). Some of the main emotive-evocative methods that I used with Jane were the following.

Rational-Emotive Imagery. Using rational-emotive imagery (Maultsby, 1975; Maultsby and Ellis, 1974), I showed Jane how to imagine some of the worst things she could think of, such as meeting a man she found very attractive, having him speak to her, and then being struck dumb and unable to talk intelligibly. Imagining this, she would feel exceptionally depressed and self-hating. She then would work on making herself *only* feel appropriately disappointed and sorry rather than inappropriately depressed and self-downing. She would practice this kind of rational-emotive imagery several times each day for thirty or more days in a row until the image of this kind of social failure (or actual *in vivo* failure) quickly and automatically brought on the appropriate feelings of disappointment and regret—not anxiety and feelings of inadequacy.

Shame-Attacking Exercises. Jane derived a good deal of benefit from the shame-attacking exercises I created in the 1960s that have since been used by RET and several other forms of therapy (Ellis, 1969b; Ellis and Abrahms, 1978; Ellis and Becker, 1982; Ellis and Grieger, 1977). She first picked several silly things—such as yelling aloud the stops in the New York subway and singing at the top of her voice on the street—and forced herself to do them while working to make herself feel unashamed. When she could succeed at this, she then spoke to a number of strange (and attractive) men on buses, in elevators, in the supermarket, and in other public places, tried to get into conversations with them, and asked whether they would like to call her for lunch or a date. She was terrified to do this at first, but after she had done it about twenty times, she lost almost all her anxiety and shame and was able to meet several suitable men in this manner and to begin dating one steadily.

Roleplaying. I roleplayed several job-interview and social-encounter situations with Jane. I discussed with her what she was telling herself to make herself anxious and shy in these situations and what she could tell herself instead, and I brought out some negative feelings of which she was not fully aware and helped her change them. I also critiqued her skills in these situations and got her to reconsider and revamp them. Even better, when the members of one of my therapy groups, which she attended for six months, did roleplaying routines with her, they were able to get her to bring out more apprehensive feelings and to give her some excellent suggestions on how to deal with these feelings and how to improve her social skills. I often find it valuable for shy and inhibited people like Jane to join one of my RET therapy groups for a while, because they have more social learning opportunities in the group than they usually have in one-to-one therapy. In group she also learned to talk other members out of their irrational Beliefs—which helped her to dispute her own irrational Beliefs (Ellis, 1982).

Group Socializing. In one of my groups, Jane also learned to relate better to several of the other members, to call on them for help in between therapy sessions, and to try socializing activities with some of them that she might not have done by herself.

Forceful Self-Statements. RET theorizes that people disturb themselves not only by ideas, thoughts, attitudes, and philosophies but also by holding onto their "masturbating" beliefs strongly, forcefully, and vehemently. It therefore encourages clients like Jane to deindoctrinate themselves forcefully and vividly with dramatic impact (Dryden, 1984; Ellis, 1979a, 1979b, 1984a, 1984b, 1985a, 1985b). Jane was shown how to devise rational self-statements and to powerfully repeat them to herself (and to others) many times until she solidly began to feel them and to be convinced of their truth. Thus, she often vigorously told herself, "It's a pain in the ass to get rejected socially or in a job interview, but it's *not* awful!" "I want very much to find a suitable mate, but I don't *have to!*" "If people see how anxious I am, they will hardly run away screaming. And if they do, tough shit!" "I *can* talk to attractive men, no matter how uncomfortable I feel!"

Forceful Self-Dialogue. Another RET emotive technique Jane used was to have a forceful rational dialogue with herself and record it (Ellis and Becker, 1982). She would start with an irrational Belief—such as that she must speak easily and spontaneously, without effort—and then rationally, but with real vigor, argue against this belief, so that her rational voice finally won out over her irrational one and her feelings changed appropriately. She would listen to these tapes herself or let friends or therapy group members listen to them and check with them to see whether her rational arguments were good and to see how powerfully she put them across to her irrational self.

Sometimes, doing role reversal, I or a member of her group would play Jane's irrational self. She would play her rational self and try to argue us vigorously out of our dysfunctional thinking.

Unconditional Self-Acceptance. I always unconditionally accepted Jane, as this is an integral part of RET, no matter how badly she behaved inside and outside therapy. Even when she came late to sessions or got behind in paying her bill to the institute, I firmly showed her that her behavior was bad but that I never considered her a bad person. Going further, I taught her how to fully accept herself under all conditions and to rate only her acts and traits and never her totality, her being, or her self (Ellis, 1962, 1972, 1973b, 1976; Ellis and Becker, 1982; Ellis and Harper, 1975; Hauck, 1973; Miller, 1983). Of all the things she learned in RET, unconditional self-acceptance, she thought, was the most useful.

Behavioral Methods of RET

As with virtually all my clients, I used several behavioral methods of RET with Jane—particularly the following.

Activity Homework. From the start of her therapy, Jane was given activity homework assignments: to talk to men she found attractive, to go on job interviews, to make some public talks, and to tell her lovers she no longer wanted to see them once she was fairly sure they were not for her (Ellis, 1962, 1979c, 1984a, 1984b). She did many of these assignments even though she felt uncomfortable doing them— and thereby learned the RET maxim "There's little gain without pain." Whenever she did them, she soon got over her discomfort and even started enjoying some of them—such as talking to and flirting with suitable males. By doing these assignments, she also clearly observed how anxious and ashamed she was at first, and she was able to zero in on the irrational Beliefs behind her anxiety.

Reinforcements and Penalties. Jane was shown how to reinforce herself—usually with reading or going to a concert—after she did her homework and to refrain from this kind of reinforcement if she did not do it. She found reinforcements especially useful for helping her do rational-emotive therapy, because she would do it for several days in a row and then slack off and forget about it if she had no reinforcer.

RET uses penalties as well as reinforcers for clients who do not do their homework (Ellis and Abrahms, 1978; Ellis and Becker, 1982; Ellis and Grieger, 1977; Ellis and Whiteley, 1979). When Jane did not carry out her assignments, she chose to burn a twenty-dollar bill, and that quickly worked to help her do them.

Skill Training. Jane was given, in individual sessions, in group therapy, and in several workshops for the public that are regularly held at the New York Institute for Rational-Emotive Therapy, instruction in assertion training, in social encountering, in writing a résumé, and in communication skills. Skill training helped her in various areas—such as communicating better with her mother—that she never directly brought up as serious psychological problems. And partly because of it, she said, toward the close of her sessions, "I am very happy that I started RET for my social anxiety and other emotional difficulties. But the great bonus of these sessions has been my being able to actualize and better enjoy myself in several ways that I never even realized therapy could benefit me. But I am delighted to say that it really has!"

Summary and Conclusion

Rational-emotive therapy (RET) is a comprehensive system of psychotherapy that shows people that although they are born with strong biological tendencies to think, emote, and act in self-defeating ways, and although their environment usually influences them to adopt unrealistic and illogical views that may considerably add to their disturbances, they still have considerable freedom both to disturb themselves and to undisturb and actualize themselves. It helps them discover exactly how they consciously and unconsciously accept and invent rational Beliefs (rBs) to help themselves and irrational Beliefs (iBs) with which to emotionally upset themselves; and it teaches them a number of cognitive, emotive, and behavioral methods by which, with considerable work and practice, they can bring about profound philosophical changes that will enable them to lead significantly less disturbed and happier lives.

I saw Jane for nine months, first once a week for individual sessions of RET and then mainly in group therapy. By the time therapy ended, she was able to talk easily to the men she found attractive; she was preparing to take a teaching job, which she had always previously avoided; she had no trouble confronting salespeople when she shopped; she was able to change her unsuitable male partners after she had gone with them for only a few weeks or months; and she was in a public-speaking group, Toastmasters, and did so well there that she was made an assistant.

I no longer see Jane for therapy, but she frequently attends my Friday night workshops on problems of daily living and often participates actively in them, asking questions of and giving rational suggestions to the volunteers with whom I have public demonstration sessions of RET. She also stays for the coffee sessions we arrange for the workshop participants and easily socializes with people at these sessions. She is most grateful for her RET experience and refers a number of her friends and associates to me and our other therapists at the Institute for Rational-Emotive Therapy.

Jane's case is not entirely typical of clients suffering from social anxiety, because she worked harder at RET than many other clients do, and her improvement was therefore faster and more profound than it sometimes is in similar cases of overwhelming anxiety. But her progress does show that some of the most severely anxious people can help themselves considerably in a relatively short time if they accept and persistently use some of the main RET formulations and techniques.

✣ 17 ✣

Biofeedback

George Fuller–von Bozzay

Biofeedback is a learning procedure in which sophisticated electronic instrumentation aids the client in becoming aware of and in controlling certain physiological variables. With practice and integration into daily life this learning has lasting health benefits (Fuller, 1980). The purpose of this chapter is to introduce the clinician to clinical biofeedback, using actual case examples. For more extensive reviews of the experimental literature in this area, see Basmajian (1983), Hume (1980), Mathew (1981), Richter-Heinrich and Miller (1982), Rickles and others (1983), Mariella and Sovine (1981), Wentworth-Rohr (1984), and White and Tursky (1982). Recent publications in the emerging specialty of behavioral medicine have focused on biofeedback as the major treatment modality (Gaarder and Montgomery, 1981; Melamed, 1980; Olton, 1980; Pomerleau, 1979; Shapiro and others, 1981. The clinician interested in the historical development of the field is referred to the bibliography of "classics" in biofeedback, which capture much of its early enthusiasm and excitement.

Biofeedback involves the use of electronic instrumentation to monitor changes in physiological functioning. The attempt to modify these functions is the basis of feedback. The feedback loop is represented by the individual's interaction with the instrument. The loop may include other variables such as the therapist or facilitator, the environment and background, and the expectations of the individual. The essential components of the loop are the physiological parameter being measured; an electrode (sensor); shielded leads to a differential amplifier; filters; an analysis unit that can be set to give feedback of the desired limits; and a display unit that produces auditory, visual, tactile, or other feedback in relation to the measured parameter. The loop is completed by the individual's perception of the feedback process.

Although adjunctive instrumentation such as blood-pressure cuffs, heart-rate monitors, plethysmographs (to measure blow flow), and even simple mirrors are used in biofeedback training, the four techniques listed below are the major modalities in biofeedback, ranked in order of general applicability:

Special thanks to Sharon Kaitner for her editorial help in the writing of this chapter.

- *Electromyography (EMG)* involves the monitoring and training of electromyographic activity associated with body relaxation, chronic muscle tension, and states of muscle dysfunction. It currently has the most general applicability of the four major techniques, ranging from general relaxation to specific muscle reeducation.
- *Thermal training* (of skin surface temperature) has applicability in the monitoring and training of blood flow. This technique uses temperature as a measure of changes in peripheral circulation resulting from vasoconstriction and vasodilation and associated with relaxation and sympathetic arousal. Thermal feedback is helpful in Raynaud's disease, migraine, and other circulatory problems, as well as providing a correlate of ''resistance'' in psychotherapy.
- The *electrodermal response (EDR)*, more commonly known as the *galvanic skin response (GSR)*, and its most used variant, skin conductance level (SCL), involve electrical changes of the skin. Feedback of this response is of use in conditions associated with sympathetic arousal, as a demonstration device for desensitization, and in psychotherapeutic exploration of conflict-laden material.
- *Electroencephalography (EEG)* is used in the monitoring and training of electroencephalographic activity associated with states of mental relaxation, arousal, stress, cognition, and sleep. At present, EEG has somewhat circumscribed clinical usefulness because of the current limitations of its instrumentation.

Biofeedback gives a person immediate information about his or her own biological conditions, such as muscle tension, skin surface temperature, brain-wave activity, galvanic skin response, blood pressure, and heart rate, enabling the individual to become a more active participant in the process of health maintenance. The instrumentation of biofeedback collects information by means of electrodes or sensors on the appropriate areas of the body and differentially amplifies, analyzes, and displays this information through auditory, visual, or other forms of feedback. As a result of this process, the individual may learn to recognize the relation between psychological and physical changes and to relate them more objectively to their reactions of tension and relaxation induced by their environment.

Changes in physiology are often related to psychological factors such as stress, arousal, fear, sexual excitement, anxiety, and relaxation. The term *psychophysiological* conveys the mind/body interaction discussed by so many writers and yet rarely integrated into a unified approach by practitioners in the medical or psychological community. In addition to the many medical conditions that might be treated using biofeedback, the psychophysiological approach is directly applicable to psychotherapy, the psychotherapist becoming a part of the biofeedback loop. The availability of psychophysiological information to both members of the dyad can assist in diagnosis, exploration, guided fantasy, and other facets of self-understanding in the psychotherapeutic process.

The biofeedback learning process can be viewed from behavioral, personal growth (humanistic), and psychodynamic perspectives. Since the changes that occur in a person's physiology are normally beyond awareness, the accurate amplification provided by modern technological advances allows the person to hear, see, or otherwise identify signals not normally available to a person's consciousness, a first step toward controlling physiological processes. A simple analogue is the task of learning to throw darts to hit a target. A blindfolded person learns with great difficulty, if at all, since he or she receives no feedback. Through practice and various forms of reinforcement and shaping—as well as generalization of these processes to everyday life—a person is capable of learning and retaining volitional control over certain processes without further need for instrumentation. Such control is accomplished by working with the instrument using a strategy such as imagining feelings of relaxation, warmth, and so on and then slowly "weaning" the patient from the machine when changes in the desired direction are replicable at will. Once the person is able to produce those changes using an "internal loop," the instruments are no longer necessary. As in most learning, retention of the ability is partly based on motivation, degree of reinforcement, and extent of overlearning obtained.

Although the client might make some progress by simply interacting with the instrument alone, the guidance, knowledge of psychological and medical issues, interpretation, and cognitive structuring offered by a therapist allow the process to be useful and meaningful in the context of a person's problems and daily life. Thus, the ideal therapist is one who is experienced in biofeedback in addition to having other therapeutic expertise.

The following cases are clinical examples of the use of the major biofeedback modalities in the treatment of psychophysiological disorders. It should be pointed out that typically this treatment integrates psychodynamic and behavioral therapy, as well as relaxation and hypnosis.

Biofeedback Training with EMG

Back Pain. Low back pain is pain in the lower lumbar, lumbosacral, or sacroiliac region of the back and is often accompanied by pain radiating to the legs in the distribution of the sciatic nerve, which may be more severe than the back pain itself. One cause is a physiological condition elsewhere in the body, such as menstruation, infectious disease, and prostatic disease. Biofeedback treatment involves the strengthening through electromyography of opposing muscles for rebalancing both the posture and the weight/load-bearing capacity of the back and enhances generalized relaxation in order to interrupt the "pain cycle."

A thirty-six-year-old structural engineer had had back pain for twenty years with episodes of severe pain two or three times a year, each lasting about two weeks. For two years, treatment had consisted mainly of bed rest and the use of a back brace. He was later started on mild relaxants and lower-back exercises and then, until biofeedback treatment, hot packs, massage, traction, and anti-inflammatory and relaxant drugs.

When training began, medical treatment consisted of the use of a back brace and Robaxin and Tylenol with codeine.

Testing with the EMG showed a reading of 1.25–4 microvolts for the mid-trapezius, an indication for feedback training. Monitored hand temperature was reported in the 90s, and GSR readings showed a small but reliable reduction over the relaxation period.

By the fourth session, there was significant progress. Starting with an eighteen-minute relaxation sequence, hand temperature rose from 93.1 to 94.6, the GSR dropped from moderately high (30) to moderately low (20), and the midtrapezius EMG dropped from 2–3 to below 1. All three systems were reducing simultaneously with feedback only from the EMG.

The patient was then asked to think of a difficult situation. Immediately, there was a pronounced rise in arousal, the GSR rising to 24, the EMG to 1–1.5, and temperature dropping to 94. Two minutes later, he was instructed to "let go" again, and the reduction in arousal was seen in his scores of GSR 19, EMG .6–1.25, and temperature 94.4.

Homework cards were used with this patient to record (1) amount and time of day of relaxation practice, (2) amount, kind, and time of medications, and (3) subjective amount of pain twice daily on a scale of 0–10. After the fourth visit, homework was expanded to (1) reducing the number of hours wearing the brace to less than fifty hours a week, (2) giving instructions for the spouse, who habitually said, "Don't frown," to touch the patient's brow instead (the patient would then give a general relaxing response), and (3) practicing desensitization to anxious thoughts during relaxation practice periods (as had been done during training sessions). The patient continued weekly visits with hand temperature and EMG training using both frontal and trapezius sites. Training suggestions were aimed at increasing awareness of sensations and feelings to heighten a sense of internal control.

By the fourteenth session, the patient was lent a portable EMG for use at home, and during treatment sessions EMG and temperature training were given simultaneously. Continued training demonstrated how quickly EMG reduction could occur. By session 17, he dropped frontal EMG to 0 in two minutes with temperature feedback only. Homework consisted in involving the family in stress-reducing cues. (In session 18 the patient reported the referring doctor had discharged him.) He was discharged from treatment with instructions to request additional visits if symptoms recurred.

Muscle Contraction Headaches. In tension headaches, the individual has responded to stresses in his or her environment by maintaining chronic contractions, typically of the trapezius, frontalis, and other muscles, resulting in pain. Biofeedback treatment focuses mainly on the patient's awareness of and ability to discriminate tension and relaxation of these muscles and the learning of effective muscle tension reduction, both generally and specifically to the site. Once the patient is adept at lowering both the general tension and the muscular response in this area to outside stimuli, the persistent headache diminishes.

John, an unemployed college teacher, was a twenty-eight-year-old white male who had been suffering headaches daily for three and a half years. Medication had included a variety of painkillers, including 25 mg of Valium per day for the past three years. Concern over his medication and the continuing headache episodes had made him irritable, preoccupied, and tense, leading him to seek biofeedback training.

During the first session, a complete social and medical history was taken and his sources of chronic anxiety were discussed. At the end of this session, a baseline hand temperature and GSR were taken. The hand temperature was relatively nonsignificant (low 90s), but the GSR was high. More important, instrumentation showed an extremely high trapezius EMG of a minimum level of 25 microvolts. He was unable to lower this during his first session.

His second session showed an improvement. After training in progressive relaxation, his trapezius EMG fell from 25 to 16 microvolts. He was instructed to practice relaxation for two fifteen-minute periods daily. In the third session, he carried out the relaxation procedure without instruction from the therapist, with EMG showing a continued reduction in muscle tension.

In the succeeding fifteen sessions, John continued with EMG training, plateauing at a level of .75 microvolts. He was instructed to maintain the lower EMG level, not necessarily to reduce it further. Headaches dropped to mild occurrences once a week. Gradually, dependence on Valium also disappeared.

John was seen twice more, at four-month intervals following treatment. He reported occasional mild tension headaches after a hectic day of teaching. He had discontinued all medications and relied on his successful ability to reduce the tension by relaxation. This describes the typical case, in which the most significant drop in the EMG reading occurred at the beginning of training. Continuing training allows the patient to differentiate and maintain the tension reduction.

Thermal Biofeedback Training

Migraine Headaches. Migraine headaches are recurrent, severe headaches often accompanied by nausea, vomiting, and visual disturbance. Symptoms last from a few hours to a few days, with moderate to severe pain. Migraines may be preceded by a period of depression, irritability, anorexia, and scintillating scotomas. Clearest evidence of the cause of this disorder indicates that the symptoms relate to a functional disturbance of the cranial circulation. The prodromal symptoms (flashes of light and paresthesias) are probably due to intercerebral vasoconstriction. The vasculature itself is healthy, and evidence points to a disorder in the neural pathways regulating the vasomotor response.

Self-regulation of migraine headaches through training of hand temperature control is accomplished by taping a thermistor to the patient's finger and suggesting that the patient move the needle by warming the hands either by use of autogenic phrases or with visualizations, such as hands in warm sand on a sunny beach. The meter tells the patient about increases or decreases in blood flow. These fluctuations reflect changes in the neural firing levels in sections of the sympathetic nervous system. The sympathetically controlled vascular system in the hands is regulated by hypothalamic centers at a higher level in the neural hierarchy and controls vascular processes throughout the body. Migraine is thought to be ameliorated as a side effect of voluntary handwarming by a general resetting of vascular homeostasis.

Mrs. L, a thirty-eight-year-old executive, had experienced headaches for the past twenty years. She had been briefly hospitalized because of the severity of the pain and had been on the medications Ergotamine and Sansert intermittently for the past ten years. Relief was temporary at best.

Biofeedback training was started using temperature and simple autogenic exercises. Homework cards were used to extend practice to the home. Skin temperature baseline readings were recorded at the beginning and end of each session to illustrate the patient's progress more clearly to her. In the beginning, auditory and visual feedback were used during about 80 percent of the session. By session 4, feedback was reduced to 60 percent, and patient use of autogenic training was increased. As the patient gained greater control of skin temperature, reliance on the biofeedback equipment was decreased and use of self-induced relaxation was increased. By the fourteenth session, relaxation and autogenic training by Mrs. L composed almost the entire session. The pretreatment baseline average of 84 degrees had now been increased to 95 degrees. All medication had been eliminated.

Raynaud's Disease. Raynaud's is a functional cardiovascular disorder, usually of the fingers. It is characterized by loss of manual dexterity, coldness, and numbness or pain. It may appear after exposure to extremely cold weather. Other causes have been suggested: an overreactive sympathetic nervous system, a disorder of the local digital vessels, and, more recently, a heightened sympathetic discharge and a heightened sensitivity of the peripheral vessels to norepinephrine.

Customary medical treatment includes medications, such as reserpine, which may produce symptomatic relief, vasodilators, phenobarbital, and aspirin. Chemotherapy frequently has unwanted side effects. Often the physician simply has the patient avoid low-temperature environments, chemical irritants, and emotionally upsetting situations. Surgical treatment, such as a sympathectomy, is only 50 percent successful and should be used only for the most severe cases.

Self-regulation of hand temperature through biofeedback provides an important alternative approach to Raynaud's disease. During Raynaud's attacks there is a decrease in circulation in the digits and thus a decrease in skin temperature. Handwarming may be used for volitional peripheral vasodilation to prevent or terminate an attack.

Susan, a thirty-seven-year-old credit manager, suffers from Raynaud's. She first noticed the symptoms while in high school. At that time, her fingers were already changing color and it was difficult to touch or write. When she moved to the San Francisco area in 1977 from Chicago, the problem worsened, although her new environment is generally warmer. The stress of the move and a different environment from the one where she had lived most of her life were therefore taken into consideration. She had briefly been treated at the Yale Behavioral Medicine School, where she did receive some relief from the disease.

During the past year, she had started to notice little red spots developing on her skin, probably from the skin tissue not receiving enough oxygen. By the patient's report, dressing warmly from the start of her day helped, but once she did get cold, warming up was difficult.

Owing to the nature of this disorder, a preliminary workup in which to examine any environmental problems should be done. Susan stated that her apartment was drafty and heat was kept turned low. Instructions were given to warm up her apartment. Patients cannot warm up their hands when the room temperature is below 70 degrees or so, unless they are well trained. After twelve sessions, even skiers can ski with their hands warm by using the biofeedback techniques they have learned.

Next, her homework card, where she recorded hand temperatures in the morning and the evening taken before and after a relaxation exercise, showed that hand temperature would start low in the morning and remain low, while the opposite held true for evening readings. Additionally, then, the therapist must look to the situation the patient may be in at the time of the temperature taking. Susan took her morning temperature at work, during her most productive time. Evening temps were always taken at home, where she could relax. In this case, beginning hand temperature held as much relevance as the ending temp.

In this case, emphasis is placed on home practice, with recognition of the stresses in the patient's environment. This allows a generalization and a transfer from the office setting to the outside setting. The patient is allowed to "wean" away from instrument training and to carry her new skills into her daily routine.

Much progress has been made in this case since the first visit. Patient termination is expected within four more sessions.

Electrodermal Biofeedback

Stuttering. Stuttering is a speech disorder associated with anxiety and stress. It involves tension in the articulators, improper breathing, tongue thrusting, and/or vocal cord shutting. Stuttering has been viewed as an organic condition, a symptom of anxiety, a cerebral dominance problem, a perceptual difficulty, and a psychological expression of conflict. Therapy has included reinforcement for nonstuttering speech, punishment of stuttering behavior, delayed auditory feedback, metronome and rhythmic speech training, relaxation training, and psychotherapy. These methods typically take months of treatment, and outcome studies suggest that they are less than 50 percent effective. The galvanic skin response can be used with stutterers in a desensitization procedure. This is especially effective with telephone stutterers. In stuttering related to tension levels, a vicious cycle of blocking is developed. Using GSR rather than EMG avoids the difficulty of muscle movement, although a combination is sometimes used.

A thirty-two-year-old junior executive was a phone stutterer who stuttered as long as a minute before saying "Hello." Although he was bright and effective as a person, the stuttering interfered greatly with his life. His stuttering dated back to his childhood.

After relaxation training facilitated with EMG, and some exploration of the variables of the problem, GSR training and the phone desensitization procedure were started. He was to maintain a low arousal level, taking about fifteen minutes to have the GSR at a low level of conductance, and then he was to call someone. Alternatively, he would have his secretary place a call to him. If the GSR indicated an increase in arousal, he was instructed to stop until it was again below the predetermined criterion. This continued until he could perform an activity such as talking on the phone while keeping low GSR. In one example, he was able to call a girlfriend whose name he had never been able to say on the phone successfully without a stuttering episode. This was a rewarding experience for him and allowed an "on line" way of using the instruments.

Electroencephalography and Biofeedback Training for Insomnia

Insomnia is the inability to sleep for an "adequate" amount of time. This amount of time is individual and variable, and it is found that many who complain of insomnia sleep as much as the normal population. The most common presenting problem is delayed onset of sleep. Depression is implicated in sleep-duration insomnia, in which the person has early-morning awakenings. Commercial sleep preparations and prescription medications have both been criticized as adversely affecting the quality of sleep as well as producing side effects and dependency. Biofeedback procedures include EEG frequency shaping—a successive lowering of brain-wave frequency toward sleep. This technique is most effective with patients who cannot "clear their minds" of the day's problems or worries about tomorrow. The goal of this training is the relearning of the natural process of frequency reduction and "quieting" for rapid, effective, and nonmedicated sleep.

Dr. G, a thirty-five-year-old cardiologist, had suffered a ten-year history of insomnia, with both sleep-latency and sleep-duration disturbance. It would take him up to one and a half hours to fall asleep, after which he would sleep only three and a half to four hours uninterrupted. Dalmane, taken nightly, failed to diminish the sleep disturbance to any significant extent.

The first session's assessment procedures determined that depression was minimal and that Dr. G had a happy family life and adequate social contact. He was a fairly well-integrated, productive person. During the second session, a contract was set for treatment; the treatment plan was discussed. The patient was trained using a combined form of deep muscle relaxation and autogenic phrases. He was also instructed to maintain careful records of sleep onset and duration, to be corroborated by his wife (this precluded the need for a more thorough sleep laboratory investigation). It was found that Dr. G's obsessiveness, useful in his clinical work, was one of the main features of the sleep disturbance. The patient simply could not rid himself of thoughts from the previous day.

During the third session, deep relaxation was verbally reinforced and an EEG baseline of 16–18 Hz was recorded. Moderating an EEG reading is a simple procedure of gradually shaping brain-wave frequency downward and amplitude upward. Each successive week, Dr. G would need to produce lower and lower frequencies in order to obtain feedback. The fourth session showed an average EEG frequency of 10–11.5 Hz; by the sixth session, he was reporting the ability to "let go"—a sensation he had never experienced—at 7.5 Hz.

By the twelfth session, the patient was able to fall asleep in the office within twelve to fifteen minutes. His EEG pattern would drop below 4 Hz (sleep range). His sleep record showed six to seven hours of maintained sleep and sleep onset in about fifteen minutes. Dalmane use was discontinued. Treatment was discontinued by the sixteenth session. The patient's sleep record indicated maintenance of a sleep-time of seven and a half to eight hours.

A six month follow-up showed maintenance of good sleep with only occasional use of Dalmane (the drug serving as a crutch). The operant shaping procedure of EEG training had retrained the patient in the normal process of going to sleep.

Conclusions

The underlying philosophy of biofeedback involves returning responsibility to the individual. This self-control model differs from the traditional medical model, which gives responsibility to the doctor to cure the illness through drugs, surgery, or other intervention. Through increased awareness of stress responses and the ability to voluntarily control physiological changes, the individual can reduce or eliminate the need for these drastic or undesirable measures. Perhaps more important, one can develop an understanding of the relationship of one's physiology to the unconscious, emotional responses, interpersonal relations, and environmental influences. The therapist assists the client through the learning process and facilitates the client's recovery.

A biofeedback program should promote successful integration and generalization of the therapeutic process by the patient. Homework practice, the keeping of a homework card, progressive relaxation exercises, and psychophysiological diaries all help in the transference of techniques learned in the office to situations confronted in the patient's environment. Treatment programs and therapeutic techniques should stem from a multimodel approach that includes a patient's emotional, cognitive, and physiological responses.

The use of biofeedback in behavioral medicine promises to be the emerging specialty in the treatment of psychophysiological disorders and an area of study in the treatment of stress-related disorders. Behavioral medicine represents the integration and amalgamation of many techniques, traditions, and disciplines. To the extent that biofeedback merges psychology and medicine and removes the artificial division between mind and body, it may provide new power and direction to health care delivery. Biofeedback is the philosophy of self-responsibility for one's own health maintenance and facilitation of self-control through learning.

What of the relation of biofeedback to psychotherapy? It is important to restate the principle that the best outcomes seem consistently to occur where there has been an integration of "talk time" and biofeedback training for the symptom. The session is divided between discussion of conflicts, environment, and dynamic issues and direct training of the physiological process.

The biofeedback instrument can become a third entity in the psychotherapy interaction or can be seen as an integral part of the entire process. Any instrument that reflects responsiveness and arousal can be useful in exploring conflicts, but it is better to use relatively unobtrusive ones—that is, instruments that are small, are easy to apply, do not limit movement, and use threshold-level settings rather than constant auditory signals. In this regard, EMG is too subject to movement effects and is difficult to set for threshold feedback. Thermal feedback is rather slow in response to content, while GSR for this purpose is rapid and relatively artifact-free.

Psychotherapy is a set of procedures for changing behavior. Biofeedback is a method of physiological behavior change. Psychotherapy facilitates change in one's response to different kinds of situations. The purpose is not to add new responses and remove the old, unwanted ones; instead it is to rearrange the conditions under which different kinds of behavior occur. The goals of treatment are of two kinds: (1) modifying or extinguishing the undesirable response so that the patient will develop more effective alternative responses and (2) developing new, more effective behaviors.

Biofeedback and related techniques add to the therapist's currently available armamentarium. It is useful for the therapist to be aware of as many techniques and interventions for behavior change as possible.

18

Hypnoanalysis

Lewis R. Wolberg

Hypnosis is a specialized technique that, in the hands of professionals skilled in its use, can be employed with benefit in many forms of emotional illness. There are a number of reasons that hypnosis does not enjoy greater popularity. First, the aura of quackery and superstition with which it is traditionally invested has never completely disappeared. Many professionals either continue to expect miracles from its use or unjustly downgrade its effects. Second, few reputable training resources exist that can teach the essential techniques. Third, use of hypnosis requires not only an understanding of methods of induction (which is easy to acquire) but also, and more important, supervised experience in adapting the trance state to the special needs of individual patients. Fourth, the therapist must be able to recognize and deal with any resistances that precipitate out as a consequence of the hypnotic inter-personal relationship. Fifth, hypnosis not only stimulates transference in the patient but also powerfully influences countertransference in the therapist. Because of in-tensified countertransference, therapists who customarily function well in psycho-therapy may lose their objectivity in hypnosis.

If therapists seek to employ hypnosis, they need to attest to its effect on the individual when they pursue it with their patients. In some subjects hypnotic pro-cedures are particularly powerful in stimulating emotional responses that can con-taminate the therapeutic climate. Unreasonable expectations know no bounds, and fearsome feelings of being controlled or vanquished may erupt, particularly in borderline patients. Hypnosis may also bring out some startling changes in the analyst's feelings and behavior. The seeming helplessness of the patient and his or her apparent susceptibility to suggestions may liberate omnipotent, sadistic, and sexual strivings more easily held in check with conventional techniques. These im-pulses are bound to come through in some form, influencing the patient's responses. Should the therapist be unable to control such feelings, he or she had best pursue the path of caution and refrain from using hypnosis.

The subtle influencing of the patient's productions by verbal and nonverbal promptings occurs in all psychotherapies. It is especially prominent in hypnosis, where the suggestibility of the patient is enhanced. It is remarkable how sensitive hypnotized patients become to the therapist's designs and how quickly they discern from verbal and nonverbal cues exactly what is expected of them. Accordingly, they may oblige the therapist with phantasies or spectacular recitations that enthrall both participants.

Suggestibility during a trance is so great that subjects will demonstrate in their reactions both their prior knowledge of what constitutes hypnotic behavior (Orne, 1970) and what they believe the therapist demands of them. Some of the reactions displayed will require clarification or interpretation. The best hypnotherapists are thoroughly grounded in dynamic theory and practice and also have the wisdom to discriminate between fact and figment in the imagery that issues out of the trance state. The patient's illusions and sallies into phantasy need not be discarded, so long as they are put into proper perspective. Indeed, they may constitute a focus for understanding the operative dynamics.

There are many induction techniques through which a satisfactory trance can be brought about. These include, among many others, simple relaxing suggestions with a progressive releasing of tension in muscle groups, eye fixation on a variety of objects, and hand levitation. No method has proved of consistent superiority, and the therapist may experiment with a variety of techniques described in standard textbooks in order to select one with which he or she is most comfortable (Wolberg, 1948; Weitzenhoffer, 1957). Confidence in manner and tone and soothing, repetitive suggestions enunciated slowly and with gentle firmness will bring best results. The patient will respond adversely to any verbal fluster, apprehension, or uneasiness. Since most people equate hypnosis with general anesthesia or sleep, they will interpret their ability to hear sounds in the room, to think independent thoughts, and to find their minds wandering as evidence that they cannot enter into a trance. Reassurance by the therapist is therefore essential, emphasizing that a mild state of relaxation during which the patient can, if he wishes, retain complete control over his thinking is the preferred state for best therapeutic results. Posthypnotic amnesia, characteristic of somnambulism, is rare and generally unnecessary in most forms of therapeutic hypnosis. However, it is required for a concerted examination of unconscious ideation (hypnoanalysis).

As a tension-relieving procedure, hypnosis has few competitors. With the simplest relaxing techniques, a distraught patient can often rapidly be brought to a homeostatic equilibrium. Undoubtedly a variety of processes are implicated here, including the placebo effect, the idealization of the authority figure who chants soothing pronouncements, and the force of suggestion, which in itself can exert an astonishing impact on symptoms.

Pragmatically, it matters little whether generalized or particular anxiety is part of the patient's symptomatology. The majority of patients who undergo hypnosis report a diminution of tension, an enhancement of confidence in their therapists, and a more optimistic appraisal of their potential to be helped. These effects in themselves are bounties that may be of adjunctive value to conventional therapeutic maneuvers. Psychotherapists of different theoretical denominations report a large variety of procedures predicated on an endless fusion of technical maneuvers with hypnosis. In recent years much interest has been shown in Ericksonian methods (Rossi, 1980) and in cognitive approaches, especially in what is called ''neurolinguistic programming'' (Bandler and Grinder, 1975). Actually the creative therapist will adapt his hypnotic procedures to his style of working and after a period of experimentation may evolve unique combinations of techniques that have proved to work for him.

Major Uses of Hypnosis

In the main, hypnosis has been employed in three distinct ways. First, it is used as a tension-relieving, anxiety-ameliorating maneuver for patients who are distraught and upset or who are in a state of emotional decompensation. Sometimes only several relaxing hypnotic sessions will suffice to restore emotional equilibrium and resumption of habitual functioning, as the following letter from a patient seen for a few sessions indicates:

> First of all, I want to thank you for what you have done for me. With your help, I have been able to step through that invisible but altogether powerful curtain that seemed to keep the world just a little bit from my reach. It is not only back in my reach, but happily so, as it used to be.
>
> Because I feel I now understand the things that brought about my anxiety, it seems the next move is entirely up to myself. Most important of all, I *want* to get back out into the world of action rather than remain in the one of introspection. I sincerely believe that *action*, consistently and with a definite purpose, will prove the therapy I need most of the time. Therefore, I wish to discontinue coming.

Such expressions of being helped by relaxing hypnosis are not uncommon in those whose aim is simply to restore themselves to their previous adaptive level, hoping to avoid overwhelming stress or crises in the future that may bring on a relapse. Obviously, hypnotic tension control is best supplemented by methods aimed at resolving tension rooted in the environment or in inner conflict provided the patient is motivated for more extensive objectives.

Hypnosis may also provide a medium for implantation of suggestions aimed at alleviating disturbing symptoms that constitute the chief complaint factor. Particularly vulnerable to hypnotic removal are hysterical symptoms such as hysterical aphonias, visual disorders, anesthesias, motor disturbances, amnesias, and a host of sexual and physiological disturbances. Substitutive side effects or other casualties commonly warned against in the literature rarely are seen and, if they appear, are manifestations of bad technique (Spiegel, 1967). The way suggestions are phrased will often determine their effectiveness. Should the therapist order or demand that the patient yield his or her symptoms and by this communicate dictatorial authority, the patient with tendencies to defy authority may countermand these injunctions. Persuasive but firm suggestions that the patient will *increasingly have the desire* to relinquish his or her symptom and thereby benefit by better functioning and a healthier self-image are usually accepted more readily.

The alleviation of pain, even organic pain, as in burns, arthritis, or terminal cancer, may be a dispensation yielded by the adroit use of hypnosis (Hilgard, 1971; Hall and Crasilneck, 1978). In obstetrics the use of hypnosis produces a light anesthesia, facilitates relaxation, shortens labor, and helps restore normal bowel and bladder function. How hypnosis works in pain relief is not entirely known, but probably distraction of attention and reduction of tension are important factors.

Among the habit disorders that may respond to hypnosuggestion are smoking, insomnia, sexual malfunctioning (for example, impotence and frigidity), anorexia, and dietary disturbances, such as obesity and underweight. Here, although a standard technique may be used, the wording will have to be reconciled with the specific needs of individual patients as determined by their history and the dynamics underlying the disorder. A cassette tape made for the patient has reinforcement value (Wolberg, 1980).

Hypnosis for specific symptom relief merits the same modesty as in general tension control, particularly in relation to the impermanence of effects. Nevertheless, as the following letter of termination indicates, symptom alleviation may be all a patient desires or needs from treatment:

> A quick, positive report on my progress.
>
> The depression, the listlessness has virtually all gone. I'm functioning better, day to day, than I have for several, if not more, years. And I'm having a good time doing it.
>
> Not a headache, even one to require a couple of aspirins, since I began. With the one exception of the night I thought the tape was broken. It went away when I found I could put myself through the paces.
>
> The slowest thing was the sex, not because the drive did not return, but the tension that had built up between Edith and me made it extra difficult. But that has been overcome too, and surprisingly easily when it happened.
>
> Many thanks for the great help. I'll go on as is, and report back in a month or so, unless you think I should come in again.

A wide variety of orthopedic, neurological, and other medical conditions produced or accompanied by stress have been palliated by the use of hypnosis and self-hypnosis. The increase of suggestibility during hypnosis (and, in susceptible subjects, posthypnotically) is especially striking during crises or situations of great stress, the application of hypnosis resulting in elimination of symptoms and restoration of emotional equilibrium. This palliative effect is less pronounced or absent, as might be expected, when symptoms are related to long-standing inner conflicts.

Suggestion is used during hypnosis as a reinforcer in behavior therapy operating to enhance expectation (Lazarus, 1973). Systematic desensitization for phobias is especially expedited, thereby facilitating the extinction process. Other forms of behavior therapy, such as operant conditioning, stimulus satiation, and aversive conditioning, can be expedited by the judicious use of hypnosis.

Uses of Hypnosis in Analytic Therapy

Hypnosis is of some value in dynamic psychotherapy. Resistances to such analytic techniques as free association and dream exploration can often be rapidly resolved by hypnosis. Channels to subconscious conflictual reservoirs can be widened in patients whose repressive defenses in the waking state are impenetrable. It is often gratifying to witness the release of emotionally charged vocalizations, the recall of past traumatic incidents, and the stimulation of productive dreams in patients who are virtually at a standstill in therapy (Wolberg, 1964).

Understandably, the patient will respond to a therapist's use of hypnosis, for any of the purposes outlined above, with his or her own reactions and interpretations. These can be of the greatest significance. Not only do such reactions reflect customary defenses, but they reveal clues to how the patient will utilize the suggestions that are given. Dreams particularly will disclose transferential and resistance manifestations that may require immediate handling, since they are often sentinels of a potential disintegration of the therapeutic situation. Consequently, the therapist may use the hypnotic experience as a sampling of how the patient enters into a relationship with an authority figure, interpreting the patient's reactions as paired with his or her character structure in operation and possibly to the genetic determinants that have fashioned the reactions shown.

Nonanalytic procedures can be combined with dynamic concepts in various ways. For example, if a patient complains of an inability to execute an essential task that is unpleasant to her, she may be asked during a trance to visualize herself in situations where she can gain an understanding of why she shirks her responsibility. This may or may not evoke mental images which explain to her why she shirks the task or which have a true connection with past experiences or feelings. To facilitate these images, the patient may be asked to fantasize executing the aversive task and to allow herself to associate freely. In a number of my cases, the mental imagery that was stimulated concerned transference feelings related to my being a cold, unfeeling, punitive parental figure who was forcing the patient to do things he or she did not want to do. This provided a means of working on the transferential distortion in order to unblock satisfactory responses to the behavioral techniques.

Questions that understandably concern the dynamically oriented therapist who contemplates using hypnosis are these: Will not hypnosis subvert the noninterfering climate essential for undiluted transferential projections? Does not a technique that virtually puts the patient under the domination of the therapist tend to subjugate him and mobilize undue dependency? What about the fear expressed in the literature of precipitating a psychosis, particularly in a schizoid patient? Is there not an undue concern with the unconscious during hypnosis to the neglect of important conscious ego elements? Will not hypnosis merely succeed in liberating strangulated emotion in a cathartic outflow without, in any definitive way, altering the repressive forces that conceal the conflictual core? How can hypnoanalysis, which deals with the inner repudiated aspects of experience, succeed in effectuating essential alterations in character structure necessary for lasting change? How can hypnosis reduce the severity of the superego when the hypnotist functions in the role of the commanding authority? These and other solicitudes would seem to cast a shadow on experimentation with hypnosis in psychoanalytic therapy. The fears inherent in these questions, however, do not necessarily restrict the pragmatic use of hypnosis as a facilitating tool in psychoanalytically oriented psychotherapy when executed by a dynamically trained and experienced therapist who is skilled in the use of hypnosis. Indeed, the patient's reactions (including dreams) to induction, to the trance state itself, to elicited past memories, and to the therapist make excellent grist for the analytic mill. Resistance phenomena mobilized by hypnosis also lend themselves to productive exploration.

A legitimate question can also be raised about the permanent effect on the patient of recall of forgotten memories. Barricades to awareness of a traumatic incident or memory may be temporarily lifted with some emotional relief or symptom alleviation, but the influence is usually evanescent. Nevertheless, the experience of recall may motivate the patient to inquire further into his interpersonal patterns and difficulties. If he can be convinced that his problems stem from hurtful past experiences, that present-day reality is constantly being influenced by what has gone on before, that many of his existing concepts result from misinterpretations and fantasies of bygone days, and that his mind is a repository of anxieties rooted in past experiences, he may develop the motivation to challenge some of his present attitudes. The recovery of traumatic memories thus serves to create an incentive for change.

Resolving Resistance. Perhaps the most important use of hypnosis in psycho-analytic therapy is in the resolution of resistance to analytic techniques. Hypnosis often puts the patient into closer contact with the more repressed thoughts, emotions, and impulses. It is therefore ideal for encouraging and liberating unrestrained thoughts. A study of Freud's early explorations into the unconscious suggests that he was keenly aware of how hypnotic relaxation promotes freedom of verbalization. His early techniques drew liberally from his experiences with hypnosis. When a patient "dries up" and becomes unproductive in analysis, one or two sessions of hypnosis may put the patient back on the analytic track. For example, a spontaneous dream, occurring after the first hypnotic session in a blocked patient who could not recall her dreams, revealed an important oedipal conflict that permitted the analysis to proceed without further recourse to hypnosis:[1]

> I was asleep on a desk or a table in your office. I was lying on my side with my knees bent. You walked over to me. You were a shadowy figure that I could barely see through closed lids. I knew I should wake up, but I was curious to see what you would do and I lacked the will to awaken. You touched me. I had been covered, but you removed the cover, and I remember thinking, "I hope I have a pretty slip on." At first your touch was pleasant, sexuallike, and I felt rather guilty for not letting you know I was really awake. Gradually you began to change into another man who seemed to be a derelict, and I knew I *must* get up. I struggled to awaken myself, and I finally succeeded. I ran to the door and ran out of the room, but there were a lot of people. In a mirror there I saw an utter ruin. I looked eighty years old and terribly ugly and, I believe, scarred. All the people were old and ugly. It was a village of discarded, useless, and helpless people. A feeling of horror overcame me, and as I stared at that face, I tried to comfort myself that it was only a nightmare and I would soon wake up, and I found it very difficult until I wasn't sure anymore if it was a nightmare or real. I finally woke up from the dream so frightened that I wanted to wake my husband, but I decided to try to calm down. I fell asleep again and had a second dream. I dreamed I had stayed up all night writing a paper you asked me to do. I started to bring it into the room you told me to. It was locked. I decided to have some coffee and come back. I did. This time your wife was in the room. She told me who she was. I said I knew. Then she told me she was your daughter's mother as though this made her a figure of great importance and dignity. This made me feel guilty and gave me the feeling that I could not see you anymore. She didn't want me to, and in respect to her sacredness as a mother, I couldn't.

---

[1]Some of the material and case histories that follow is from Wolberg (1967).

A number of techniques have been described (free association, dream induction, drawing, play therapy, dramatics, automatic writing, regression and revivification, crystal and mirror gazing, time distortion, hypnoplasty, and induction of experimental conflict) that, implemented during hypnosis, have as their purpose the uncovering and working through of unconscious processes (Wolberg, 1964). These embrace a variety of tactics to which different patients will respond with greater or lesser enthusiasm. However, in actual practice only a few need be consistently used—namely, free association under hypnosis and dream stimulation geared toward the analysis of resistance to understanding inner conflict and to translating insight into action. Although occasional patients, possessing special propensities, will respond dramatically to regression and revivification, mirror gazing, hypnodrama, and other stratagems, these will not be employed for the great majority of patients. The reason is that they require a very deep or somnambulistic trance, a state relatively few individuals can reach. Fortunately, patients can be approached through other devices that require only a light or medium trance, to which all persons, except those who willfully oppose, are susceptible.

Facilitating Free Association. Free association, the chief tool of psychoanalysis, may, owing to resistance, come to a stop. The usual interpretive activities may not succeed in releasing the patient from inhibitions that restrain his or her spontaneous verbalizations. Asking patients to shut their eyes and to report any scenes or fantasies that flash before their minds may circumvent a temporary diversion. If this does not succeed, a light hypnotic state may suffice to eliminate the resistance. Where the pressure from inner drives and conflicts is great, the mere induction of hypnosis may bring forth a spontaneous outburst of violent emotion, perhaps accompanied by verbal content. Should such a sterile outburst occur, an attempt may be made to get the patient to report his or her associations through the use of certain releasing techniques, some of which have been described elsewhere (Wolberg, 1964). When free association is blocked by resistances impervious to the usual interpretive techniques, hypnosis may be advantageously attempted.

A patient started her session by talking about baby and childhood pictures that she had found in an old album.

Patient: When I look at baby pictures, I begin to panic. [Pause]
Therapist: Tell me about this.
Patient: [Breathes heavily] I can't think. [Long pause]
Therapist: There's something about those baby pictures that frightened you.
Patient: Yes. [Pause]
Therapist: Are they *your* baby pictures?
Patient: Yes, I'm in all of them, although my father is in some of them, also my brother and mother are in some of them. I feel very detached from them. I keep looking at and staring at them. When I go through them, they just don't seem like me. I feel like I'm looking at somebody else. I feel very detached from it. I can't use them to bring back anything. [Pause] The only thing I was able to do was to go back over diaries from high school on through to when I started analysis. I need to talk, but I am detached from it all. I need to talk about high school, the length of time I was with Dr. ———. I can't remember any of it. I feel frightened of this because I don't know what it is. [*Long silence, only unproductively interrupted by my questions. At this point I induce hypnosis to encourage*

her to associate freely in a trance state.] All kind of weird things that don't make any sense come into my mind. These are the sorts of things that come all the time and don't make any sense, so I always block them out. [Pause]

Therapist: What things?

Patient: That I am glad that my mother had cancer and had a breast removed. That I wish she was very fat. That at a certain point in my life it was very disgusting to me—and the picture of me with my father brings it back—that he had so much hair on his body. I never liked men with a lot of hair. This always nauseated me. Here my brother is so cute in the pictures. I'm getting dizzy. [Pause] Feeling any hostile feelings makes me dizzy. It really upset me because my mother called me at school today saying that I had to come home this evening to sign a tax form or something, and I told her that I had been feeling so tired that I had figured that I hadn't been eating enough, and I started eating more. Then she said, "You'd better not get too fat," and I felt like killing her. [Pause]

Therapist: You felt like killing her for saying that?

Patient: Yes, I've been extremely hostile toward my mother. I never feel that she accepts me the way I am. At school it is very frustrating because I want this director to kind of be my mother, and that just can't be. No wonder I feel so anxious every day when I leave. I have a separation anxiety. I didn't want to leave her when I went home. I want to be with her all the time. It's really a struggle to let out my feelings of hostility, but I'm letting them out and seeing that they are based on something and that people understand them. [Very heavy breathing] It's as if they both understand the teacher who I'm working with. She is over me. She understands that it is very difficult for me to work under her now, since originally I was the one running the group. I thought that she would be mad at me because I've been feeling so angry at her for coming in and taking over. Yet I took a chance and expressed this, and there was no retaliation of any sort. I told the director that I had been doing things my way and even though they may prefer another way, I was just furious that somebody was coming in and that there was a lot of things which she did that I didn't like, and yet they were her way of doing them, and I really couldn't do anything about them, since I wasn't running the group. I felt like screaming in there. Then she said, yes, that she understood this. [Pause]

Therapist: Don't you get disappointed when she doesn't act the part of your mother?

Patient: Yes, I do, but I inhibit this so much. I've really been pushing this under. I've been saying that I can't. I haven't been in touch with my feelings, which is why I've been coming in and saying that I don't have anything to talk about. I would like to think that I've worked out this situation with the other teacher. I am very upset, but I've accepted the fact that she is in her position and I'm in mine and that I will learn from her. But I guess I still feel very resentful. [Pause]

Therapist: You still resent her very much.

Patient: Yes, I guess I caught that at one point this afternoon, and I was very upset at seeing it. [Long silence]

Therapist: See if an image comes to your mind. Tell me what you see.

Patient: I keep seeing a leopard pacing up and down in his cage. He just walks back and forth and he can't get out. [Pause] I just had a vision of feeding my brother to the leopard. I saw him as a little boy, and I was going to throw him in the gate and he would be chewed up and then he wouldn't be around any longer. Then I would be loved.

Therapist: You would have mommy and daddy all for yourself.

Patient: Yes. [Pause] Thinking of it makes me very dizzy. That's what I feel, very guilty. I guess I hate him for getting married, because I didn't want him to be happy. And I hate mother. I keep closing my door every night so that she won't come in and talk to me. I feel so anxious when she is around. But I guess I do need her to like me because I have been dependent on her so that I feel very panicky when I think she is sensing the fact that I don't want her to talk to me. Then she starts to avoid me. I've just been feeling so angry at everybody. I can't stop talking about myself to people. I feel completely isolated. [Pause]

Therapist: What set off this reaction?

Patient: It was the history teacher I met, I kept writing in my diary how I loved him. It was the feeling, like a child, seeing older men and liking them and feeling that I loved them, and feeling very anxious when they were around, very nervous. Wanting them to talk to me and yet being petrified lest they talk to me. I pretty much feel the same way with fellows now. I still feel like a little girl. I still feel that I don't want to get too close when I see somebody that I like. I want him to talk to me, but I would be terrified if he said anything—that I would stutter and I wouldn't be able to say anything. Because, who am I? It's as if any man that I like talks to me only as a big favor, or they are talking to me because I am a little girl. In a way I am so terrified that I would like to be rejected, sick, and I would like the men to know this, and that I am very disturbed and they had better not have anything to do with me. I wasn't really aware that I still feel this way until I broke up with this guy and started reading some of this. When I went folk dancing, I saw a guy who I had been seeing over and over again, and I started shaking because I wanted to talk to him. And yet I was terrified of saying anything to him, and so I got very dizzy. I felt the same way then that I felt in high school with this history teacher. I like his looks, body, the way he moves, his smile, and his enthusiasm for dancing. He seemed to have a warmth about him. It kept going through my mind—he's a man and I'm a little girl. [Pause]

Therapist: Remind you of anything?

Patient: I have no exact idea, but I would guess that it is probably not until I was fifteen. I have a memory of being physically close to father for a very long time. As a matter of fact, when I was going with George, if he would kiss me on the neck, my head started spinning, because my father used to do that. I panicked when he did that. I would say "Stop it" over and over again. When he stopped, I felt all right. [Pause]

Therapist: Could you have had this same feeling toward your father? You've been denying the fact that you've had any deep, close feelings toward your father.

Patient: Which would, in turn, mean that if I had this closeness with him for so long, it would naturally make me furious at my mother for being around. As a matter of fact, I get a picture in my mind of his kissing her and of imagining that he hates it and that he would much rather kiss me. This still goes through my mind now. She is horrible. How can he kiss her? She's old, like his mother. I always think of her as his mother. I always think of him as if he were my age. I think I feel that it would be perfectly natural that I should sleep with him. This sends me into a panic that I should think that way. [Pause; visible agitation]

Therapist: What do you feel?

Patient: I feel absolute disgust and nausea. But my feelings are still, if only he would let me love him, take care of him, and that his whole life has been ruined by my mother. Also that I would make him feel strong and masculine, and that she has emasculated him and made him into nothing. No wonder I was feeling so in a panic about going home this evening.

Therapist: Do you think you may transfer any of these feelings toward other men?

Patient: It becomes absolutely out of control. It becomes overpowering. It's really—though I was never conscious of it when I wrote in my diary—this is what was getting me with all these men that I used to see and liked. I just couldn't stand it. Yet I wasn't the least bit consciously aware until halfway through college of any sexual feeling. Never. I must have had it, but I never admitted it.

Therapist: It may have been too dangerous for you to admit it.

Patient: I guess I solved the problem of competing with mother by deciding that it would be safer to be a boy. The sexual feelings were too overpowering. I guess that's why I decided that I would never get married. I was aware of having trapped myself somehow. I decided that after folk dancing that night that I could never marry somebody who wasn't special to me, and yet I could never relate to such a person. I would be too terrified. I have a feeling that this is all connected with taking a passive role sexually. I keep having a tremendous feeling of wanting to be raped, of not doing anything, just wanting to be taken over.

Therapist: Do you have fantasies about this?

Patient: A vision keeps going through my mind. Such as the man in the folk-dance place. Just lying there and enjoying it. I don't know why. I think in that way I don't think I can be rejected. Because I won't really be involved in it. As a matter of fact, I think that this is most what I complained about with George. I didn't know why it bothered me so much that he is so shy and unaggressive. In that relationship with him, I played a very active role sexually. Now consciously this made me feel very good, but I wonder if I didn't feel very angry because of his lack of responsiveness. There is always a mixed fear, desire, and terror about being raped. It's equivalent to dying for me. Just losing any sense of self. And yet it still seems like the most pleasurable thing that could happen to me. I wonder if at some point I didn't have fantasies about sleeping with my father. Something just passed through my mind. Try-

ing to go into my parents' room and finding it locked. I felt like tear-
ing the house down; it made me so furious. I didn't know why.

Therapist: Can you recapture what you might have been thinking?

Patient: Yes. That they were sleeping together.

Therapist: You knew that they were sleeping together?

Patient: I didn't know it consciously. I would never admit any of these things.

Therapist: Perhaps you wanted to be in your mother's position?

Patient: My God, I'm so dizzy.

Therapist: That's how you felt when you were dancing with this man—dizzy.

Patient: Yes. I now see the connection—when I was blocking out the fantasies
                 that I was having about my father. Nausea and getting upset. I get
                 that all the time now. I always get that around men that I like.

Mobilization of Transference. It is to be expected that hypnosis will tend to
mobilize transference, a contingency that can prove of help in repressed patients
who deny their projections. How hypnosis can help bring transference feelings to
the surface is illustrated by a patient with anxiety hysteria who gradually had circumscribed her activities to avoid attacks of panic and uncomfortable physical symptoms, which focused on choking sensations and pains in the upper extremities and
back. Free associations had come to a sudden pause, the patient professing a blank-
ness in thinking at the same time that she experienced a recrudescence of her symptoms. Just before coming to my office, for a few sessions, she had experienced vague
feelings of excitement and a frightening "lump in the throat." During the session
she had little to say, other than to talk about her symptoms and to ramble about
reality problems that were, she insisted, of important concern to her. Probings of
her resistance yielded nothing. She remembered no dreams, and she vehemently
denied any feelings about me other than that she trusted me and was sure of my
concern for her. At the end of one session, I decided to try to break the deadlock
by inducing hypnosis, giving her the suggestion that she would remember any important dreams and discuss them with me at the next hour. The suggestion was
successful, as the following excerpt from the session illustrates.

Patient: I was choking all Friday and I didn't know what it was, but I was work-
                 ing very hard and I didn't pay much attention to it. On Saturday it
                 got much worse. The result was I withdrew Sunday quite a bit, and
                 last night, in the middle of the night, I got up with such a nightmare,
                 fright and screaming. What is it? I almost trusted a man. I almost trusted
                 a man. It was a wild, wild nightmare. My shoulders and every part
                 of my body was shaking. [Pause] [*The patient apparently responded to my
                 suggestion that she recall an important dream.*]

Therapist: In other words, you had a nightmare in which you felt you trusted
                 someone?

Patient: Whether I wanted to trust him in sex or whether I was just trusting
                 him, I don't know. But I had the feeling that I was just about to trust
                 a man, and I was petrified. Can you imagine, after all this working,
                 Dr. Wolberg? [Pause] It was nice, fine, and good and wonderful, and
                 I was just about to trust him and I started to go all to pieces. [*I got
                 the impression at this moment that she was talking about her relationship with*

me, that she had begun to trust me, but that this threatened her defense against
men that had up to that time served to protect her against hurt.]

Therapist: Anything precede the dream—the day before?

Patient: Nothing except I had a date with this man. I have a problem with him even though I've had an affair with him two years before. As soon as I feel that his erection is good and strong, I must control from there on. In other words, as long as he is impotent, as long as he can't get an erection, I don't care and everything is all right. But the minute I feel that the erection is there, I panic. Now I think "This is it." [*Apparently her need to control is essential; impotence in a man removes his threat to her.*]

Therapist: Are you aware of the panic while it is happening?

Patient: No.

Therapist: This business of the old pattern of not permitting him penetration, how old is that?

Patient: The funniest part is that when I am in control, I allow it. Only when I feel that I'm in control. When I feel that he is not too erect. If he is really in there pitching, I turn to every other means to satisfy him and to do all sorts of things so as not to have him penetrate.

Therapist: What about this business of control? What comes to your mind as far back as you can go? Shut your eyes, relax, breathe deeply, and tell me what comes to your mind. [*A suggestion such as this can induce a light hypnosis.*]

Patient: [Pause] Oh, I can't [Gasping]. It was a bus stop. I remember what I was wearing. I was wearing a little coat, hat, and little red scarf. The man had a stomach, and he was heavy and fat and sitting down on the bench of the bus stop. He must have had candy in his hand. He said, "Come here, little girl." Then I did. Then he asked me to do that, to suck his penis. Then I did. I didn't understand what it was. Then all of a sudden something must have happened, because I ran away into an empty lot. I ran screaming. All I can remember is my scarf flying in the air, and my books flying, and I ran home. I don't think that I ever told my parents. I never thought of it since.

Therapist: It must have terrorized you.

Patient: Evidently it must have done something. All week I felt like choking. Just like now [Holds hands on throat]. Something about you [Gasping]. [*Transference feelings seem evident.*]

Therapist: What do you feel with me?

Patient: There was a time I felt in control.

Therapist: But not now?

Patient: No. Because when I got up in the nightmare, it could have been you. I don't know who it was. It was just men or a man. And yet I think that I associate this man with my father, because I remember saying once that my father was like this man. Therefore, I must have hated all men. [*The incident with the man at the bus stop may have been a cover memory for fantasies related to her father.*]

Therapist: Do you feel that you trusted your father at all?

Patient: Not really. Except when he was ill. When he was ill, he had to rely on me even to go to the bathroom. So that this was the greatest thrill of my life. We have the story pretty much, but I can't seem to do anything about it. It makes me weak thinking of all this. This is most amazing. Why did I put this on today? [Pointing to dress] I think I wanted to be choked. I had no business putting this on today. This is the highest-neck dress that I have. [*Masochism is a prominent aspect in this patient.*]

Therapist: Why do you think that you want to be choked?

Patient: Guilt feelings? I feel guilty, and yet it was guiltless.

Therapist: Then what could you feel guilty about? Right now, on the reality level?

Patient: Nothing.

Therapist: What could happen if you really let yourself go with a man? What is the worst thing that could happen in reality?

Patient: Nothing. It is so hard to answer. I can feel it all the way down in my guts. How am I going to overcome this?

Therapist: Perhaps if you talk about your feelings about me, it will help.

Patient: [Pause] It's all there. I mean you, and father, and this man. I say to myself that it would be the grandest thing in the world to have that kind of relationship, a good relationship with you, because it is normal, natural, and yet—I tremble, get panicky. It is understandable. There I am, and I have to work it out. At least one thing is good. We talk about it. There is nothing ever left unsaid now.

This session constituted a crucial breaking through of her resistance. The understanding that her associational block was produced by a fusion of images projected into transference enabled her to continue her analytic work. This was associated with a progressive bettering of her relationships with men, sexual and nonsexual, and with a consistent strengthening of other aspects of her personality.

Sometimes the hypnotic situation itself acts as the chief means for the working through of transference. A patient who easily entered into a deep hypnotic state became more and more recalcitrant to suggestions. He was submissive to his father (and to later male authorities), and his rage was internalized, with resulting depression and psychophysiological gastrointestinal symptoms. From his associations it was apparent that he had acceded to my suggestion that we use hypnosis to please me, as he had pleased his father by conforming to the father's whims. "For years I hated my father. He couldn't stand being contradicted. I remember needing to lose at cards deliberately so that father would not get upset by my winning. I never am able to be successful; it makes me too anxious." The resolution of his conflict with male authority was to a large extent worked through in transference. At first he fantasied resisting hypnosis; then he deliberately resisted it, finally being unable to enter the hypnotic state on any level. Accompanying this were dreams of triumph and feelings of love for his father. "It's a healthier dream to feel love than hate. For the first time I realize I loved my father. I cried in my sleep. I felt father really loves me, but we had this wall between us. I awoke feeling I really loved him." This change in feeling was associated with a complete abatement of symptoms and was soon followed by a capacity to relate more cooperatively with men.

Dream Induction. The stimulation of dream recall may be attempted through hypnotic suggestion. The quality of symbolism will depend on the depth of trance. In light hypnosis, the symbolic representations are like waking daydreams; in somnambulistic hypnosis, like night dreams. When a patient shows resistance to remembering dreams, suggestions by the therapist during hypnosis or by the patient himself during self-hypnosis may facilitate recall. Dream content may be suggested with a selective focus on special problems and conflicts.

For example, a man with a problem of impotence developed an ambivalent transference toward me. Because of his difficulty in remembering dreams, I induced hypnosis and suggested that he would dream about his feelings toward his wife. That evening he dreamed:

> Isabelle has injured her arm; actually it is her right hand. In fact, we are in a hospital room. She is in bed. I am sitting in an easy chair, waiting for her to become conscious. Actually her right hand had to be amputated. It was the result of an accident using a power tool while working on a piece of sculpture. She becomes conscious. She is unaware that her right hand has been amputated; the right forearm is heavily bandaged and she doesn't realize her hand is missing. [*The patient's wife has functioned with him as a mother figure. The patient during therapy has slowly been overcoming his submissive attitude toward her and has improved his sexual functioning. This may be equated with his having castrated her in assuming a more dominant position.*]
>
> At this point I awaken and then fall asleep again. We are back in the same dream. My father and another elderly man enter to visit. I am surprised, for one, that he knows of the injury and that he has bothered to make this visit. We embrace in greeting each other. The other man reminds me of a friend, John Davis. I say that as long as they are visiting, I will go out and repark my car, which I do by driving it up from a Riverside Drive–like location right into a building somewhere.
>
> I am back in the hospital room and ask my father, "Have you told her that her hand is missing?" He says, "Oh, no, not me, I haven't the courage. You'll have to tell her yourself." She is herself still unaware.
>
> I think I awake again, but I am not sure. I may have dreamed this. The scene is uncertain, but a man who could be a French-Canadian guide with Indian blood and I are looking at a fragment of a canoe that is made out of metal. He points out that the quality of work tells him it came from the Old Town Canoe factory in Old Town, Maine. I am surprised. I know they only work in wood there but somehow realize it's been thirty-five years since I was there, so times could have changed.
>
> We are now in your office waiting room, not here, but in a country village. I am talking with an unidentified person, perhaps a woman and the doctor with whom you share this office. This doctor is either a surgeon or some other highly technical practitioner of mechanistic medical skill. We are arguing about helping bums. I take the position that one who gives to a bum is really hostile to them, because the bum's pattern is to take and fail, and by offering giving-type help we keep him in that pattern. The doctor is derisive, contemptuous, and says this argument is really reaching too far and is either not intelligent or is overintelligent. But then, if I am there to see you, it is probably for some Freudian sort of reason [*said with great contempt!*], and that explains my unrealistic position. [*I am apparently fused here with his father.*]

In the midst of this argument my wife enters. She is wearing a blue and green plaid jumper, which she fills out appealingly. Her hipline is full, the bust is full and generous. She reminds me that we have to go somewhere and asks me to button the straps of her dress in the back. I button the straps and tell her to run along. I prefer to remain and continue the discussion. She is whole, there is no suggestion of the injury. In fact, she looks wonderful and healthy. [*This is perhaps indicative of a better relationship with his wife.*]

We, the doctor and I, are in a driveway by a big white station wagon. We are waiting for the woman to come out of the house, another house nearby, so that we can drive somewhere and continue the discussion. He points out that I must have been in the office to see you, and would I not now be missing that appointment? I say it is only 8 A.M. and my appointment is not until late afternoon, and I awake.

The patient's associations brought out his ambivalent feelings toward me, which he recognized contained many of the attitudes he had toward his father.

Summary

Used by a reasonably trained professional within the context of a structured therapeutic program, with proper awareness of the limits of its application, hypnosis can make a contribution as an adjunct to any of the manifold branches of psychotherapy—supportive, reeducative, or psychoanalytic. Hypnosis can facilitate the therepeutic process in several ways. First, hypnosis often exerts a positive influence on the relationship with the therapist by mobilizing the hope, faith, and trust essential in every helping process and by cutting through resistances that delay establishment of rapport. This is especially important in detached and fearful individuals who put up resistances to any kind of closeness and hence obstruct the evolution of a working relationship. Second, hypnosis, by enhancing suggestibility, will promote the patient's absorption of positive pronouncements, verbal and nonverbal, thus alleviating some symptoms that interfere with adaptive functioning. Third, hypnosis often expedites catharsis by opening up founts of bottled-up emotion, thereby promoting at least temporary relief and signaling some sources of residual conflict. Fourth, resistances to verbalization and free association are often readily lifted by even light hypnosis. Fifth, where motivation is lacking toward inquiry into sources of problems, hypnosis, through its tension-abating and symptom-relieving properties, may help convince patients that they can derive benefits from treatment if they cooperate with its rules. Sixth, through its effect on resistances, hypnosis may help expedite such insight techniques as dream recall and the release of forgotten memories. Seventh, hypnosis may light up transference, rapidly bringing fundamental conflictual problems to the surface. Eighth, by dealing directly with resistances to change, hypnosis may expedite the working-through process, particularly the conversion of insight into action. Toward this end, teaching the patient self-hypnosis may be of value. Finally, hypnosis may sometimes be helpful in the termination of therapy, enabling patients who have been taught self-relaxation and self-hypnosis to carry on analytic and synthetic processes by themselves.

19

Psychopharmacologic Therapy

David S. Janowsky

In contrast to the psychobiological hypotheses of psychopathology, the major tenet of the biological school is that biological factors are primarily involved in the cause of at least the serious affective disorders, such as major depressive disorder, bipolar disorder, and schizophrenia, and that the majority of serious affective disorders and schizophrenias are treatable by somatic means.

The therapeutic position of the biological school is that somatic treatment of emotional disorders is at least as advantageous as psychological therapies. At the heart of this perspective is the observation that such somatic manipulations as electroconvulsive therapy, antidepressant drugs (monoamine oxidase inhibitors, tricyclic antidepressants), lithium carbonate, antianxiety drugs, sleep deprivation, circadian rhythm manipulation, psychostimulants, and antipsychotic drugs exert therapeutic effects that appear to be relatively independent of interpersonal factors. Elaborate biological hypotheses have been developed to explain the effects of psychotropic drugs. For example, good supportive pharmacological evidence suggests that too much functional norepinephrine, a down-regulation of noradrenergic receptors, dopamine depletion, too little serotonin, too much acetylcholine, and imbalances in intracellular/extracellular sodium may be causes of depression.

Although representatives of the psychological and biological perspectives on understanding and treating depression have generally spoken only to themselves, not to each other, attempts have been made to synthesize the two frameworks into one, and considerable evidence from many studies indicates a natural overlap. There is no theoretical reason to believe that certain psychological and somatic therapies would not affect the same systems. Freud ([1895] 1961) envisioned a psychology that could be understood through its basic biological mechanisms but abandoned this effort because of lack of technological resources to explore this possibility. More recently, Akiskal and McKinney (1975) have proposed a "final common pathway" concept for psychological and biological theories and therapies of depression and their relationships to genetic and environmental influences. It is thus possible that somatic therapies and psychological therapies alter the same central biochemistry and that psychological therapies are capable of causing the same behavioral changes as drugs are (DiMascio and others, 1979).

The following cases illustrate a number of principles underlying the use of several psychopharmacologic therapies. Generally, an integrated approach, with attention to diagnostic, social, psychological, and psychobiological processes, was used in these cases. However, because of the designated focus of this chapter, the major descriptive emphasis is on their psychopharmacologic components.

Case 1: Recurrent Depression

Mrs. O, a thirty-five-year-old, Caucasian mother of two, had a ten-year history of chronic feelings of dissatisfaction, irritability toward her children and husband, and periods of withdrawal and lethargy, associated with sadness and crying spells. Although these symptoms generally were worse during the three to five days before her menstrual period, they occurred intermittently and generally lasted from several days to several weeks. The patient's family history was significant in that her father and sister had a history of unipolar, recurrent depression.

During the year prior to seeing me, Mrs. O began a trial of weekly psychotherapy with a licensed family therapist who treated her with a reality-oriented psychotherapeutic approach. Her need to evolve in her life, her ambivalences about her marriage, and her need to be her own person were explored. The therapist spent much time helping her to feel comfortable and not to feel guilty for her need to enjoy personal activities, such as aerobics, in spite of her husband's jealousies and protests.

In spite of a year of psychotherapy, in which the patient gained valuable insights about the origins of her tendency to be dominated and indeed became much more assertive and free, Mrs. O still suffered from periods of feeling inadequate, in which she questioned herself and wondered whether she deserved to be doing the activities she enjoyed. During these phases of self-doubt, she continued, as before, to be irritable and angry, especially toward her children.

The patient mentioned to her marriage and family counselor that one year earlier her father, a physician, had given her some of his imipramine and that she had felt less irritable and anergic after taking this drug for eight days. However, she had discontinued the imipramine after three weeks because she did not want to take medication, nor did she want her father to be in control of her life.

The patient said that she felt she was ready for another trial of imipramine "on her own terms." The marriage and family counselor therefore referred the patient to me for evaluation of the appropriateness of giving her medications, as well as for prescription of medications, stating that she felt the patient was benefiting from her psychotherapy and that she wanted to continue the psychotherapy as before.

Mrs. O arrived for her first appointment attractively and casually dressed and well groomed. She was a pleasant-appearing, obviously well-bred woman who was mildly seductive. She showed no evidence of suffering from depression and indeed said that she felt fine. She stated that she was somewhat chagrined to be visiting me while feeling well.

A review of her history was as described above. I made a tentative diagnosis of minor depressive disorder and encouraged Mrs. O to return in two weeks or sooner if the "depression" recurred. Two weeks later she returned, appearing moderately downcast. She said she was in her premenstrual phase and had been depressed, irritable, and withdrawn for one week. She was tearful at times and seemed mildly depressed. There was no evidence of suicidal ideation, although the patient appeared less certain of herself and less seductive than before.

Even though the patient still did not seem obviously depressed or suffering from a major depressive disorder, she and I elected to begin a trial of imipramine in spite of my reservations that it might not be effective.

The patient was sent to an internist for a laboratory and physical evaluation; results were normal. I decided to focus my therapy primarily on her drug treatment and to leave the major psychotherapy to her psychotherapist. However, since she and her therapist had explored in some detail the issues in her life, I also elected to speak with her about contemporary areas in her life, generally supporting the directions of her therapist in a reality-based manner.

One week later Mrs. O began a trial of oral imipramine 50 mg daily, with the dose increased to 50 mg twice daily after three days. One week after starting imipramine, she returned for evaluation. She reported having a mildly dry mouth and constipation. Her dose of imipramine was increased over the next week to 50 mg three times/day orally. On return, the patient said she had felt less irritable and more relaxed for about three days. She still complained of constipation and having a dry mouth. Imipramine was increased to 200 mg orally at bedtime.

One week later the patient returned, saying she felt much better, attributing her improvement to the imipramine. She stated that she was no longer lethargic and irritable and was less prone to feel picked on by her husband.

Since the patient continued to complain of a dry mouth and constipation, a trial of urecholine 10 mg four times daily was begun which alleviated the target symptoms. At this point it was agreed that the patient would see me every four weeks and would be monitored between times by her psychotherapist.

Two months later, having felt much less irritable and not depressed, the patient expressed a wish to try a less anticholinergic drug. She was tapered from her imipramine over one week, and a trial of desipramine was simultaneously begun, with doses increased over one week to 200 mg at bedtime. However, after one week of this treatment, the patient felt insomniac, jittery, and depressed again. For this reason the imipramine was restarted and increased to 200 mg/day, and the desipramine was stopped. The patient improved again over the next week and elected not to restart her urecholine. Consequently, she continued to have a mildly dry mouth, which was, however, much less bothersome than before.

Over the ensuing five months Mrs. O has continued to visit me at monthly intervals. At present she is doing well and generally is not depressed or irritable, although she has some irritability before her menses and when under stress. She and her husband have greatly improved their relationship, in part because she has become more cheerful. He is adjusting to her need for greater autonomy. She sees her psychotherapist twice monthly and feels the counseling has been more effective since she has been receiving imipramine. In four months she plans to move to another city, and much of her psychotherapy is now devoted to her feelings about this move. It is planned that she will continue on imipramine for at least another year, with referral to a psychiatrist in the San Francisco Bay area, to which she is moving.

This case illustrates the collaboration and interaction between a psychiatrist and a nonphysician psychotherapist. In this case, the psychiatrist provided pharmacotherapy in close conjunction with the patient's psychotherapist, who provided psychotherapy. However, the psychiatrist also provided a psychotherapeutic relationship, which was adjunctive to the use of pharmacotherapy. This strategy differs from the use of the physician as a "scripwriter" and allows for a more comprehensive and unified approach to the patient.

The case illustrates a number of psychopharmacologic principles. Imipramine (Tofranil) was used because this drug had been used successfully by a family member, and specific drug effectiveness often appears genetically linked. In addition, the patient had used imipramine in the past with positive results, a good predictor of future effectiveness.

Because the patient developed annoying anticholinergic effects, a trial of bethanechol (urecholine), a peripherally acting cholinomimetic drug, was used to antagonize peripheral anticholinergic effects, such as dry mouth and constipation. Since tolerance to anticholinergic effects can develop over a period of four to eight weeks, urecholine administration should be time-limited. Finally, the case suggests that it is important to provide continuity of care to patients who must move to other locations, especially when drugs are used (Jackson and Bressler, 1981; Berger, 1977; Bielski and Friedel, 1976; DiMascio and others, 1979).

Case 2: Panic Attacks

Mr. R, a forty-two-year-old, married, Caucasian city administrator, requested a consultation for treatment of his panic attacks. The patient described a long history of having periods of extreme uneasiness, consisting of sweating, a severe fearful feeling, a fast heart rate, occasional hyperventilation, and a feeling of dread, occurring when he was confined in closed-in places, such as elevators, or when having business lunches in restaurants. Between episodes, which occurred about once a week, the patient reported feeling mildly to moderately anxious but able to function well. He had previously been treated for his panic attacks and anxiety with diazepam (Valium) 5–10 mg every four to six hours. He had been carefully evaluated to rule out anxiety-producing medical causes, such as hypoglycemia or hyperthyroidism. Routine laboratory tests and physical examination were normal.

The patient felt diazepam had not worked for him and had discontinued his diazepam three months before his consultation. He had read that desipramine (Norpramin) was useful in the treatment of claustrophobia associated with panic attacks and wanted to know a specialist's opinion.

On the basis of the patient's history, I decided that a trial of desipramine was indicated as treatment for the panic attacks. A dose of 25 mg each day orally was increased to a dose of 75 mg per day over a period of one week and to 100 mg/day three days later. Since Mr. R lived in a distant city, without local psychiatrists available, it was decided that once medications were stabilized, a local family practitioner would monitor the patient's medications.

After two weeks on desipramine, the patient said he felt slightly more relaxed. He complained of a dry mouth and mild constipation. He was seen at two-week intervals over the next one and a half months and, by the end of the second month of treatment, was much improved, having almost no serious panic attacks. However, he continued to avoid elevators and restaurants because he feared that he might have an attack. To combat the patient's anticipatory anxiety over the possibility of having another panic attack, I decided to begin a trial of a low dosage of diazepam (Valium). Diazepam was therefore prescribed at a dose of 5 mg every four to six hours as needed to antagonize anticipatory anxiety.

Administration of the diazepam to combat the fear of having another panic attack, plus desipramine to alleviate the panic attacks, plus psychological support and behavioral deconditioning, allowed Mr. R to function with minimal uneasiness over the next year, during which time the diazepam was tapered slowly to nothing as he became less and less fearful of having another panic attack.

This case illustrates the somewhat unconventional use of a tricyclic antidepressant to alleviate panic-attack symptoms and anxiety in a patient without evidence of severe depression. Major drugs effective against panic attacks include desipramine (Norpramin), imipramine (Tofranil), phenylzene (Nardil), and aprazolam (Xanax). The doses of antidepressant drug effective in alleviating panic attacks can be relatively low, compared with doses needed to alleviate depression. The time course needed for symptom alleviation is often considerably longer than that required when depression is being treated.

This case also illustrates the fact that although a tricyclic antidepressant can effectively alleviate panic-attack symptoms, such a drug is not as effective in alleviating the anxiety and fear that a panic attack might occur in the future. Such fear may lead to a constriction of activity and function. A classic antianxiety agent, such as diazepam or chloridiazepoxide (Librium), may be effective in treating this "anticipatory anxiety," in association with behavioral deconditioning and desensitization techniques (Rickels, 1982; Maxissakalian, 1982; Zitrin and others, 1983).

Case 3: Intermittent Psychosis

Miss R, a twenty-seven-year-old, unmarried, Caucasian woman, presented with a history since age eighteen of intermittent psychotic episodes. Though premorbidly a rather shy person, she was able to finish high school, attaining B- to A-level grades, and to enter a private college. However, during her first college year, she felt she could not cope, felt homesick, and was extremely anxious. In addition, she began to experience vague paranoid symptoms such as ideas of reference. As a result, she dropped out of school and returned home. During the next ten years, which she spent in attempts to reenter college and to work at clerical jobs, she had intermittent psychotic episodes, mostly punctuated by paranoid ideation about people casting aspersions about her. For nine months of the year prior to treatment with me, Miss R was treated as an inpatient at a large private psychiatric treatment center, using low doses of haloperidol and psychotherapy.

In May 1982 the patient and her parents moved to the San Diego area, where she continued to live with her parents. She was frequently disturbed by hearing voices calling her name in a derogatory way or by hearing the letter *A*, which scared and annoyed her. She associated hearing *A* with being stupid, ugly, and incompetent, as well as with previous sexual activities she had engaged in that she considered immoral. She also associated the letter *A* with the novel *The Scarlet Letter*. In addition, the patient felt people in cars were spying on her and watching her. When she hallucinated the letter *A*, she would become extremely anxious.

An initial mental status exam revealed a well-nourished, attractive, alert, well-dressed woman appearing younger than her age. She appeared very anxious and said she was very scared by hearing herself being called "A." She showed constriction of affect, was shy, spoke without elaboration, and said she was somewhat depressed. She stated that she was mildly suicidal and displayed autistic thinking. She also displayed moderate mouth, tongue, and hand movements indicative of tardive dyskinesia. A diagnosis of paranoid schizophrenia was made.

In spite of the patient's tardive dyskinesia, she, her parents, and I elected to resume antipsychotic drugs, since her psychotic and anxious symptoms were disabling and extremely painful to her and were severe enough to make the need for hospitalization likely if they continued. The patient was fully informed of the danger that the antipsychotic drugs eventually would increase her tardive dyskinesia symptoms.

Trifluoperazine (Stelazine) was begun at 5 mg three times/day. This was gradually increased over a three-week period to 15 mg three times/day because at lower doses the patient's symptoms were inadequately alleviated. The basic strategy was to give as low a dose of antipsychotic drug as possible. Early in the course of treatment, Miss R developed Parkinsonian symptoms, chiefly akinesia and rigidity. Benztropine (Cogentin) 1.0 mg three times/day was begun, with moderate activation of tardive dyskinesia symptoms and alleviation of Parkinsonian symptoms. The patient and her family were informed that although the tardive dyskinesia symptoms would appear to increase if benztropine was given, it was likely that they were not being fundamentally affected by the benztropine.

At an antipsychotic drug dose of 15 mg three times/day, the patient's anxiety decreased considerably. However, she continued to hear herself being called "A" and had vague ideas that she was being followed by people in cars from the FBI.

Over the next three months, the patient's trifluoperazine was gradually reduced to 10 mg/day. During this phase, her tardive dyskinesia symptoms increased, probably owing to withdrawal "rebounding." I advised her that this increase in tardive dyskinesia symptoms was probably not due to a worsening of the underlying disorder. After two months of receiving 10 mg/day trifluoperazine, the patient expressed a marked and disturbing increase in psychotic symptoms and anxiety, leading to a realistic fear that she would need to be hospitalized. Her dose of trifluoperazine was rapidly reescalated over four days to 45 mg/day, and symptoms gradually decreased over a one-week period.

Over the next several months, Miss R continued to improve. In order to lower or discontinue her trifluoperazine and to attempt to maximize antipsychotic efficacy, I added reserpine to her regimen. The rationale behind this strategy was that reserpine is a mildly effective antipsychotic agent that apparently does not cause tardive dyskinesia. Reserpine was begun at a dose of 0.25 mg per day and increased to 0.25 mg four times/day over a two-week period.

Over the next several weeks, the patient's symptoms continued to improve, with an approximately 75 percent reduction in the frequency of her hearing "A" and a progressive indifference to the symptom. At this point the patient was encouraged to consider applying to a junior college and to expand her social contacts.

Over the next year Miss R continued in junior college, doing marginally in her courses. Because she felt that her thinking was impeded by the sedating effects of her drugs, she again requested a dose decrease. The patient's dose was gradually decreased over a six-month period to 1.0 mg reserpine daily and 2.0 mg trifluoperazine daily, associated with a decrease in sedation and mental dulling. Tardive dyskinesia symptoms gradually decreased to virtually none. After two months on trifluoperazine, 2.0 mg per day, the patient began to experience a mild increase in her symptoms. That was treated by increasing her trifluoperazine to 5.0 mg/day.

Because the patient had received a high dose of trifluoperazine without maximum benefit and because her hallucinations were of a derogatory sort and she was prone to feel depressed, I planned the addition of lithium carbonate. A one-month trial of lithium, at a dose of 300 mg three times/day and a serum level of 1.0 meq/liter, was completed, with no significant side effects and no beneficial effects. Lithium was therefore discontinued.

The patient was also treated with weekly half-hour sessions of psychotherapy. The major focus of the psychotherapy was on trying to get the patient to accept her symptoms and to develop strategies for not becoming frantic if she heard the letter *A*. Attempts were made to help her develop reality testing of her symptoms and to help her understand the symbolic meaning of *A*. Since the patient was generally rather noncommunicative about her situation and seemed anxious in my presence, I elected to engage a psychologist who specialized in art and body-movement therapies as an adjunctive treatment. This relationship worked extremely well: the therapist established a more easy and comfortable rapport, using art therapy and relaxation therapy.

Over the next year, as I saw Miss R monthly and the psychologist saw her twice monthly, she gradually improved. She stayed in school, making several friends, and eventually obtained a part-time job supervising children in a day-care center. At present she continues on trifluoperazine 5.0 mg/day, reserpine 1.0 mg/day, and benztropine 1.0 mg three times/day. She is getting Bs and Cs in school, is working ten to fifteen hours a week, and has several friends. She continues to live at home and to see me monthly and the psychologist twice monthly. She still occasionally hears the letter *A* and is mildly bothered by this. She tries to ignore such intrusions and is functioning adequately. She feels that her medications plus the art and movement therapy is the most helpful combination for her.

This patient's case illustrates a number of issues and controversies. Because of her long history of treatment with conventional antipsychotic drugs, Miss R had developed tardive dyskinesia, probably caused by the dopamine-receptor-blocking properties of the drugs. Thus, a needed treatment had caused serious side effects. The therapeutic dilemma for this patient was that although she appeared to need antipsychotic drugs to stay out of the hospital and to relieve ego-dystonic, disabling psychotic symptoms, such drugs would eventually increase her tardive dyskinesia symptoms. The patient and her family were included in the decision making, and the implications of the dilemma were outlined in detail.

Benztropine mesylate (Cogentin) was used to treat Parkinsonian symptoms due to the dopamine-blocking properties of trifluoperazine. Although in most cases such an anticholinergic agent can be stopped after six to eight weeks because tolerance to the Parkinsonian effects develops, a small percentage of cases require continuing anti-Parkinsonian drugs to alleviate ongoing Parkinsonian symptoms. Furthermore, although an anticholinergic drug such as benztropine can cause an apparent increase in tardive dyskinesia symptoms by shifting the dopamine/acetylcholine balance in a dopaminergic direction, no fundamental induction of the tardive dyskinesia process appears to occur.

This case also illustrates the principle that acute psychotic symptoms often require higher doses of antipsychotic drugs than those required when psychotic symptoms are either alleviated or controlled. For acute psychotic symptoms, a dose of 400–800 mg/day of chlorpromazine (Thorazine) or its equivalent dose of a more potent antipsychotic drug is required. Maintenance doses of antipsychotic drugs may be much lower, and yet some dose is required for prophylaxis, since cessation will often lead to relapse in chronic cases.

After controlling psychotic symptoms, I decreased the antipsychotic drug dose very slowly, so as to avoid "withdrawal psychosis." This withdrawal psychosis is a psychological parallel to tardive dyskinesia, in which an antipsychotic drug presumably causes upregulated dopamine receptors in psychosis-relevant brain areas, and these receptors are unmasked on abrupt drug withdrawal, leading to dopamine-induced psychosis activation.

In some patients with psychoses and affective symptoms, a trial of lithium carbonate may be useful.

Simultaneous with the patient's pharmacotherapy, a number of social maneuvers were used, including the offering of a warm, supportive therapeutic approach, social rehabilitation in the form of encouraging the patient to attend school and find work, and later, nonverbal psychotherapy. All these strategies were employed to appeal to and strengthen those qualities in the patient that were socially appropriate and healthy (Jeste and Wyatt, 1981; Gardos and Cole, 1983; Klawans, Goetz, and Perlik, 1980; Hogarty and Goldberg, 1973).

Case 4: Chronic Depression

Mrs. H was a thirty-eight year-old, married, Caucasian registered nurse and mother of two school-age children. Her formal psychiatric history had begun at age twenty-eight, when she began a series of hospitalizations for depression and suicidal ideation, receiving diagnoses of recurrent depression, borderline personality, and schizoaffective schizophrenia. From age twenty-eight to thirty-three, Mrs. H was treated with a variety of antidepressant and antipsychotic medications, with questionable results. Hospitalizations were generally relatively short.

At age thirty-three the patient began a course of psychoanalytically oriented psychotherapy, three times weekly, during which she received no psychotropic medications. She developed an erotic transference toward her therapist but continued in therapy. After three years, the patient abruptly ended therapy because she felt she was costing her family too much money. However, her course of dynamically oriented psychotherapy had been quite beneficial, leading to a cessation of her need for psychiatric hospitalizations. During the two years after stopping her psychotherapy, the patient functioned adequately as a nurse, although she was chronically depressed and anhedonic. On recurrence of anxiety and severe depressive symptoms two years after her psychotherapy had ended, her former psychoanalyst referred her to me for a trial of interpersonally oriented psychotherapy plus pharmacotherapy.

During our initial weekly sessions, Mrs. H gave a history of having been depressed virtually all her life. She spoke of extreme parental disapproval and criticism, of withdrawing into a fantasy world as a child, and of having felt and feeling worthless, hopeless, and useless, as well as chronically sad, since at least early adolescence. Furthermore, Mrs. H felt that she was being judged by others by others and that she had to be perfect in all her activities to prevent being criticized. She spoke of being obsessive about plans and details in her life, at times being incapacitated by her ruminations over small details. She felt adrift, having quit her job as an R.N. months earlier to pursue her artistic and literary talents.

On mental status examination, the patient appeared as a washed-out, drab, and sloppily dressed woman, wearing no makeup, who appeared sad and cried easily. She expressed feelings of hopelessness, worthlessness, and uselessness and was preoccupied with "doing a good job." She expressed some suicidal ideation but said that she would not commit suicide, owing to her strong Catholic religious commitment, although she wished she could do so. She spoke of dying as a release from the bonds of her life and illness and saw it as a cleansing, "like crashing through a glass window into a new life" and being destroyed in the process. She expressed no delusions or hallucinations.

During the initial two months of therapy, she saw me weekly. Our focus was to learn more about her, to work through the feelings of loss toward her previous therapist, and to attempt a trial of psychotherapy. We spent much time discussing her childhood relationships, her feelings of hopelessness and sadness, and her need to do things correctly to the point of incapacitation. Another direction of the therapy was to encourage her toward expressions of spontaneity, using humor and irony. I encouraged the patient to express her anger toward her life situation, rather than to feel depressed. Much time was focused on her relationship with her caring, yet emotionally distant, husband. Time was also spent reviewing her literary writings and offering generally positive support.

Over the initial two months, the patient showed moderate improvement. She ceased to be desirous of dying and showed some humor. Yet she still felt quite depressed. For several sessions we discussed whether to try antidepressant medication; the patient feared the use of drugs and felt she should be able to get herself together without such "crutches." Finally, we agreed on a strategy in which Mrs. H would maintain control by committing herself to receiving only one day's dose of a drug, and if she had side effects or was dissatisfied, she could stop the medications.

A one-day trial of desipramine (Norpramin) was started. After one 50-mg dose the patient called to say that she felt worse and had not slept all night. She said that her thoughts were racing and that she felt very agitated. Desipramine was therefore stopped with my permission.

One week later, a trial of amoxapine (Ascendin) was begun. The patient received one 50-mg dose without ill effects. By one week after starting amoxapine, she was receiving a dose of 50 mg four times a day without side effects other than a dry mouth. By the sixth day of treatment, the patient said she was feeling somewhat better—less sad, less obsessive, more optimistic, and more outgoing. By the second week of therapy, she said that she felt the best she had ever felt in her life and that her whole outlook had changed. She stated that things that had bothered her before no longer did and that she was feeling hopeful. She dressed in more colorful clothes for the session, seemed bright-eyed, and was only mildly depressed. She was no longer suicidal and displayed a good sense of humor. She attributed her change to the medication.

At the next weekly session, the patient parenthetically asked whether I thought the medication could cause a rash. She then displayed a maculopapular rash that covered most of her body. She reported that her face had been swollen and that the rash had progressed over a three-day period. She had not reported the rash for fear that I would stop the medication. She also reported nausea, diarrhea, and vague joint pains. A visit to a dermatologist at my behest led to the diagnosis of a drug reaction with possible serum sickness. The amoxapine was therefore discontinued. Considering the seriousness of the symptoms, I decided that a further trial of amoxapine was clearly not warranted.

Over the next four weeks, while the patient was off medications, her depressive symptoms gradually returned to their level before starting drug therapy. She was unhappy about the recurrence of symptoms, but her optimism continued as I mentioned that if one drug had worked, another probably would also be helpful. Eventually I decided on a trial of a monoamine oxidase inhibitor (MAOI), since MAOIs are chemically unrelated to amoxapine. I discussed the side effects of MAOIs, including the potential for hypertensive crises, and stressing the possibility of developing hypotension and sedation. After several weeks of discussion and after the patient had decided that the potential benefits were worth the risks, a trial of phenylzene (Nardil) was begun. The patient received a list of restricted foods and medications.

The patient was started on phenylzene 15 mg per day. Since no serious side effects occurred, the phenylzene dose was increased to 15 mg three times a day over a two-week period. Mrs. H noted that the medication made her feel lethargic and a bit dizzy. She said she did not like the phenylzene as well as she had liked the amoxapine. Her depressive symptoms began to remit after ten days of therapy and decreased further over the subsequent three weeks. Because of side effects, the patient expressed a desire to lower her medication dose. After a week on a dose of 15 mg twice daily, she felt that the side effects were slightly less.

The patient is now continuing on a twice-monthly regimen of psychotherapy with me, as well as receiving phenylzene 15 mg twice daily. Psychotherapy is directed toward her starting to plan her future and adjusting to the challenges and limitations of feeling better. Little time is spent on her past. Much support and encouragement is given. The current psychopharmacologic plan is to continue the phenylzene for at least three more months. I hope that, by that time, several of the newer nontricyclic antidepressants, such as nomifensine and bupropion, will be on the market, and these will be tried after a ten-day cessation of phenylzene. If these are ineffective over a three- to four-week therapeutic trial, phenylzene will be restarted.

After one year of effective psychopharmacologic treatment, a trial off medications will be considered if the patient finds her marital, vocational, and child-rearing activities acceptable. If relapses occur, an antidepressant will be restarted. The current plan is to start a trial of gradually decreasing psychotherapeutic contacts, with increased contact resumed as needed.

This case illustrates the strategy of getting to know a patient well and establishing a psychotherapeutic relationship before beginning a trial of pharmacotherapy. This was especially needed because the patient was strongly identified with her previous therapist. This strategy allows the development of a more comprehensive and, ideally, more trusting and collaborative therapeutic relationship and, at the same time, allows for the healing effects of interpersonal interactions without resorting to potentially problematic somatic therapies.

In this case, many characterologic qualities in this patient could have led a therapist to believe that interpersonal therapy, rather than somatic therapy, was solely indicated. However, the patient did not respond maximally to interpersonal therapy and did have symptoms of a major depressive disorder. An open-minded and empirical approach to this patient allowed for the use of antidepressant drugs along with a psychotherapeutic approach.

A number of technical points in this patient's pharmacotherapy deserve consideration. First, therapy with antidepressant drugs was markedly effective in alleviating a number of her depressive and characterologic features, such as perfectionism. In addition, since the patient was prone to develop drug side effects and had a fear of drugs and a strong need to feel in control, short-term drug trials lasting one to two days were initially tried to screen for appropriate drugs. A trial of desipramine (Norpramin) led to agitation and insomnia, not infrequent side effects for this noradrenergically predominant agent. A trial of amoxapine (Ascendin) was effective; symptom alleviation followed the expected time course, beginning between one and two weeks after starting therapy. The development of a serious allergic reaction precluded further use of this drug. A switch to phenylzene, which is not chemically related to amoxapine, was chosen to avoid further allergic reactions.

Fortunately, phenylzene therapy was useful in alleviating the patient's depressive symptoms, although side effects such as sedation were annoying. A lowering of dose was partly effective in controlling side effects, as is often true in the use of antidepressant therapies. The planned use of either nomifensine or bupropion, both nontricyclic antidepressants with low side-effect profiles, may allow a more comfortable treatment without the risk of causing a dangerous allergic reaction (Paykel and others, 1982; Bounsaville, Klerman, and Weisman, 1981).

Case 5: Chronic Schizophrenia

Mr. N, a thirty-three-year-old, unmarried Caucasian male, arrived at the emergency room at the university hospital complaining that spirits from God were controlling his mind. He was also noted to be hearing voices chanting and hearing God telling him to sacrifice his left hand and eye. The patient's affect was markedly flattened, he spoke with an obvious loosening of associations, and he showed mild to moderate agitation. History, as related by his sister, who accompanied him to the hospital, revealed that since age twenty-five he had had multiple psychiatric admissions, lasting from one to three months. He was unemployed but had worked intermittently as a waiter between episodes.

He was described as shy and withdrawn since childhood, with no current friends. His previous psychotic episodes generally had been similar to the current one and normally were preceded by his discontinuing his prescribed antipsychotic drugs, which generally had been administered by a local mental health clinic. Two weeks before the current episode, the patient had moved out of a board-and-care facility into a low-cost hotel and had stopped his haloperidol.

Mr. N was immediately admitted to the psychiatric inpatient unit. His mental status on admission was as described above. A physical examination was normal, and laboratory tests, including a chemistry panel, complete blood count, and urinalysis were also normal. A diagnosis of chronic schizophrenia was made.

Because the patient had heard voices telling him to mutilate himself, I decided that a rapid neuroleptization protocol was indicated. A regimen was begun in which the patient was to receive 5.0 mg intramuscular haloperidol every two hours until sedated and no longer a danger to himself. Furthermore, he was placed on one-to-one nursing surveillance.

Over the next six hours, the patient received three 5-mg haloperidol injections. By the time of his last injection, he said that he was tired and wanted to go to sleep. He also said that the voices appeared to be fading but were still present. The patient slept through his first night in the hospital. By morning, he appeared calmer, and although he still felt his thoughts were being controlled, he stated that he no longer was hearing God tell him to hurt himself. I decided that he would receive haloperidol orally in the same dose that had been given the previous day. Thus, the patient was begun on 5 mg oral haloperidol two times/day and 5 mg at bedtime. The one-to-one nursing surveillance was discontinued.

Over the next week, the patient improved considerably on a regimen of haloperidol 15 mg daily, decreasing nursing surveillance, and integration into the milieu of the unit. By the end of one week of hospitalization, the patient was more spontaneous and was saying God was no longer talking to him. He decided that the force that had been controlling his thoughts had found someone else to bother. He still believed that his hallucinations and delusions had been real.

A review of the patient's past revealed that he had a history of existing marginally when he was taking his medications but generally could be employed. Consistently, when he stopped his medications, a relapse occurred within one month. Furthermore, his cessation of medications generally occurred in spite of his therapist's and family's admonitions against doing so and were generally motivated by the patient's need to deny his illness.

On the basis of the above information, I decided to switch the patient to a long-acting and injectable antipsychotic agent, fluphenazine decanoate (Prolixin Decanoate). An injection of 25 mg intramuscularly was given, with plans for repeated injections every two weeks, and the oral haloperidol was given in decreasing doses over the next five days and then stopped.

Over the next two weeks, the patient continued to improve. His delusions and hallucinations almost stopped, and he began to talk of leaving the hospital to return to his board-and-care facility. He began to look for a job and eventually was rehired by a previous employer. He went to work from the hospital for one week and subsequently was discharged from the inpatient unit back to his board-and-care facility. I urged his outpatient physician to continue to give the patient intramuscular fluphenazine decanoate 25 mg every two weeks, which he agreed to do. The board-and-care facility and the patient's family were encouraged to report to the treating physician any resurgence of symptoms or avoidance of having his fluphenazine injection as soon as such behavior occurred. Over the subsequent six months, the patient has done well, continuing to receive treatment, to work, and to reside in his board-and-care facility.

This case illustrates the technique of rapid neuroleptization. Often, adequate doses of an antipsychotic drug can lead to a rapid alleviation of symptoms. A dose of 10 mg/day of haloperidol, for example, will often suffice. Haloperidol (Haldol) was chosen because it has relatively few anticholinergic and antiadrenergic side effects and thus is less dangerous with respect to causing serious hypotension, sedation, cardiac depression, or cardiac arrhythmic effects when given aggressively. The technique was chosen because this patient appeared in moderate jeopardy of mutilating himself. Some centers routinely use this technique without specific indications other than the presence of acute psychotic symptoms.

The amount of haloperidol given in the first twenty-four hours of treatment determined the subsequent daily doses of haloperidol given orally. This is a conventional technique used in rapid neuroleptization (Donlon and Tupin, 1979).

Since the patient had a long history of discontinuing his medications, I chose a trial of a long-acting antipsychotic drug as a way of undercutting his tendency to stop his medications. This technique is often effective for patients who are on the "drug merry-go-round" and relapse frequently, because it takes control for drug compliance out of the patient's hands.

Case 6: Bipolar Disorder

Miss E was a thirty-two-year-old, unmarried, Caucasian unemployed secretary. At initial evaluation she had a ten-year history of intermittent manic and depressive episodes, in between which she had been essentially euthymic. Episodes had increased in frequency over the years, occurring as often as twice a year. More often than not, these were manic episodes, but depressive episodes occurred approximately one out of three times. Episodes lasted about two months.

The patient was brought to the university hospital emergency room displaying hypertalkativeness, irritability, euphoria, grandiosity, and a recent history of planning to set up a transcontinental telegraph business, for which she had approached members of the New York Stock Exchange. She had been making numerous long-distance phone calls, overspending money, and sleeping about two hours a night. Her symptoms had begun approximately two weeks previously, at which time she had been faced with having to take a job that she considered demeaning.

On initial examination, the patient was dressed brightly in a red and magenta muumuu. She spoke rapidly about her numerous contacts and business dealings and showed euphoria, except when confronted on details, at which time she became irritable. She also showed flight of ideas. She noted that since moving to this city, two months ago, she had stopped taking her lithium. She said she had been lonely and depressed since moving until two weeks earlier, when everything had started working out for her.

I made a tentative diagnosis of bipolar disorder, manic phase. Initially, I felt that the patient might be able to be managed as an outpatient, but during the closing part of the interview, she began to insist that she did not need medications, since she was doing so well. I suggested hospitalization, and after initially resisting, the patient agreed, saying she wanted "to help those poor souls on the psychiatric unit."

During her initial two days of hospitalization, the patient continued to be hyperverbal, grandiose, and mildly euphoric. She was also extremely manipulative, dividing the staff into those who thought she was sane and charming and those who thought she was sneaky and a fraud. She showed a remarkable tendency to perceive accurately the deficiencies of the inpatient unit. On the third hospital day, amidst a regimen of three-times-weekly group and individual psychotherapy, a trial of lithium carbonate was begun. Lithium was started at a dose of 300 mg twice daily for four days. On the fourth day of lithium administration, a serum level taken twelve hours after the preceding night's dose showed a level of 0.4 meq/liter. Since an eventual level of 1.2 meq/liter was targeted, the lithium dose was increased to 300 mg four times/day for three days, after which time the serum level was 0.9 meq/liter. An additional increase to 600 mg three times/day led to a serum level of 1.1 meq/liter three days later.

During the first ten days of lithium treatment, the patient showed little sign of improvement. Because of her manipulative style, the nursing staff of the inpatient unit treating her requested that antipsychotic drugs be given. However, since the patient was sleeping well and only being annoying, it was decided, after several staff meetings, to try to avoid adding an antipsychotic drug if possible. It was agreed that if the patient became worse or if the staff felt matters were getting out of control, the decision would be reconsidered.

By the twelfth hospital day, the patient was slightly improved with respect to her grandiosity. She was no longer talking incessantly about her telegraph business and was less irritable. She was still hyperverbal and was showing mild flight of ideas.

On the sixteenth hospital day, a serum lithium level of 1.2 meq/liter was obtained, with the patient continuing to receive 600 mg lithium three times daily. At that time she was beginning to complain of frequent urination and was observed to be using the water fountain frequently. Furthermore, she had developed a fine tremor of her hands, which she disliked having.

A trial of propranolol, up to 50 mg/day, for treatment of the tremor was considered, as was a decrease in the dose of lithium. However, since the patient was showing diminishing manic symptoms and was not severely incapacitated, the lithium was continued as before. Because the patient appeared to be responding to the lithium, I decided to get twice-weekly serum lithium levels, since a switch to euthymia or depression would be expected to increase serum lithium level and increase toxicity.

By the twentieth hospital day, the patient was only very mildly hypomanic. She was no longer manipulative, had been elected community meeting president, and was now well liked by the nursing staff. Because she had improved and because her serum lithium level had now increased to 1.4 meq/liter, I decreased her lithium dose to one 300-mg tablet four times/day. Four days later her serum lithium level was 1.0 meq/liter. At this dose, the patient's tremor became minimal, and her diabetes insipidus syndrome disappeared.

At this point the patient began to speak of wanting to return home. Dispositional planning occurred, the patient meeting twice with her designated outpatient therapist before discharge, which occurred on the twenty-eighth hospital day. The unit social worker interacted with the patient to help her appropriately seek employment, as well as to smooth the transition back to her apartment. At discharge the patient's lithium level was 0.9 meq/liter. She was quite gregarious and cheerful but showed none of her previous grandiosity or hypertalkativeness.

The patient was subsequently followed in an outpatient clinic by a third-year psychiatric resident, who treated her with a combination of insight-oriented psychotherapy and supportive psychotherapy. She was seen weekly for four months. Lithium level was monitored twice monthly for two months and monthly thereafter. A dose of lithium of 300 mg four times daily yielded serum levels between 0.8 and 1.0 meq/liter.

At the end of four months of outpatient care, the patient began to talk about discontinuing her psychotherapy, since she had secured a job as an executive secretary and had been doing well. She also began to request that her lithium be stopped, as she did not like using a "drug crutch." Her therapist strongly urged her to continue taking her lithium for at least several years. This suggestion was based on the prophylactic need for lithium in view of the patient's history of frequent relapses and recurrences over the years. She reluctantly agreed to this. However, she convinced her therapist that she should be seen only twice monthly.

At the end of six months of outpatient care, Miss E began to develop mild symptoms of anergy. She began to experience early morning awakening and said she felt sad. She showed no cognitive manifestations of depression. Because the patient had not had laboratory testing since her hospitalization, a laboratory battery included T_3, T_4, serum electrolytes, and serum creatinine was obtained to rule out any renal damage and lithium-induced hypothyroidism. All results were normal.

Therefore, having ruled out a depressive episode due to lithium-induced hypothyroidism, the patient was diagnosed as having developed a bipolar depressive episode. At this point the patient and her therapist decided that she would come in for therapy twice weekly. Over a period of two weeks her depression stabilized in the mild range, less intense than during previous episodes. At that time she requested antidepressant medications. After a discussion of side effects and the risk of inducing a switch into mania or an increase in the frequency of cycling, the patient and therapist decided to begin a course of trimipramine (Surmontil). Trimipramine was begun in a dose of 50 mg daily and increased over a period of two weeks to 200 mg/day, a clinically adequate dosage.

The patient experienced mild sedation, a dry mouth, and mild constipation from the trimipramine but generally tolerated it well. After three weeks of receiving trimipramine, the patient reported sleeping better, and by the sixth week she felt euthymic. Trimipramine was continued for one more month in full doses and then tapered to none over a period of two weeks to prevent withdrawal symptoms due to "cholinergic overdrive." The patient did not experience a renewal of symptoms after stopping the trimipramine.

The patient resumed a twice-monthly schedule of seeing her therapist. She continued on her lithium carbonate 300 mg four times daily, with resumption of monthly serum lithium level evaluations and a lithium level of 0.8–0.9 meq/liter.

After two months a job opportunity in another city occurred, and the patient decided to move. It was agreed that she would continue her lithium as prescribed. A referral to a psychiatrist in the new city was made; the referring therapist telephoned the new therapist and described his management of the case and his thoughts about further care. The patient was told to call the referring therapist if the transition to the new therapist was not satisfactory.

This case illustrates a number of issues in the treatment of bipolar patients. At this time lithium is the treatment of choice for mania and hypomania, as well as for prophylaxis of future manic and depressive episodes. Since lithium may take from one to three weeks to be effective, short-term use of an antipsychotic drug may be helpful in decreasing manic symptoms until the lithium takes effect.

Lithium side effects may be bothersome and are a major cause of noncompliance. Among the frequent side effects are tremor and the development of a diabetes insipidus–like syndrome. Both these symptoms are at least partly responsive to decreasing the lithium dose, and the lithium tremor is treatable with a beta adrenergic blocking agent such as propranolol.

For unknown reasons, larger amounts of lithium are required when a patient is manic than when depressed to maintain a given serum level. Therefore, as a patient's mania remits, lowering the dose may be necessary to avoid an increase in serum levels into the toxic range. In addition, serum lithium levels of 1.1–1.5 meq/liter are usually necessary to treat acute mania, while levels of 0.8–1.0 meq/liter are necessary to maintain prophylaxis.

Although lithium is often an effective prophylactic treatment of manic-depressive illness, producing a decrease in the frequency and intensity of episodes, bipolar patients are often noncompliant. The patient often states that he or she misses the high of mania, or the natural denial accompanying a hypomanic state may cause the patient to be overconfident. For this reason it is extremely important that the patient have an ongoing therapeutic relationship and that the tendency to stop medications be dealt with psychotherapeutically.

Another issue of importance in using lithium is the question of when to stop lithium therapy. Generally, lithium can be stopped several months after the remission of symptoms following an initial manic episode, since a subsequent episode will not necessarily occur. However, if a pattern of relapse occurs, giving lithium prophylactically and chronically is generally indicated, as bipolar illness is a disease of considerable morbidity and mortality.

In this patient's case, as is typical, the management of swings into depression presented several problems. Use of a tricyclic antidepressant or monoamine oxidase inhibitor carries the risk of inducing a manic episode or a greater frequency of manic and depressive episodes. Lithium may be effective enough to prevent serious future depressions, but sometimes it is not. Frequently a tricyclic antidepressant or MAO inhibitor will alleviate depression without causing mania or rapid cycling. However, once the patient is euthymic or becomes hypomanic, the antidepressant should be stopped, and lithium should be continued throughout the therapy. An antipsychotic drug may be useful in treating antidepressant-induced manic or hypomanic episodes in conjunction with lithium (Cooper and others, 1979; Gaby and others, 1983).

Part Five ✑

Group Therapies

Group therapies are techniques designed to foster improved mental health through the use of a group setting. In some techniques, such as psychoanalysis in groups, the focus is on the individual patient, and the group setting is used to foster progress; in others the focus is on the group as a whole, and group themes are addressed. Psychoanalysis in groups and group-centered approaches are psychoanalytically derived techniques. This section goes on to cover encounter groups, which grew out of the humanistic and human potential movement; marathon groups, which can be of encounter, Gestalt, or psychoanalytic orientation; psychodrama, a forerunner to encounter groups; transactional analysis groups, which derive methods from Gestalt therapy, hypnosis, psychodrama, and behavioral psychotherapy; and finally conjoint therapy, an attempt to combine the individual and group modality with the use of separate therapists.

In Chapter Twenty, "Psychoanalysis in Groups," Alexander Wolf and Irwin L. Kutash describe psychoanalysis in groups—a technique for treating the individual's intrapsychic problems and exploring and resolving interpersonal psychopathology with other members within a group, rather than for treating ailing groups. Individuals can benefit from the multitude of transferences elicited within a heterogeneous group and then analyzed and from the use of such analytic methods as dream interpretations; with patient interpretations and associations analyzed as well, analysis of transference and resistance. A multitude of cases are highlighted that illustrate the use of psychoanalysis in groups with diverse individuals having diverse problems and defenses.

Leonard Horwitz begins Chapter Twenty-One, "An Integrated, Group-Centered Approach," by reviewing the controversial question of how analysts working with groups can integrate group issues and individual issues. Group psychotherapists hold a range of views on the nature and pervasiveness of a shared group tension or group theme. Some therapists believe that such a theme emerges only intermittently and that in its absence individual issues are of paramount importance. Horwitz, by contrast, believes that an omnipresent, common group tension exists that is fueled mainly by a processing of projective identification moving back and forth among the members. He believes that care for the individual needs of each member can best be assured by an inductive method in which a patient's contribution is interpreted individually until a shared group theme clearly emerges, at which time a group-centered intervention is offered. He illustrates this technique by presenting part of a group session.

In Chapter Twenty-Two, "Encounter Groups," Will Schutz advances the idea that encounter is "a way of life," not just a technique. It aims at helping people to be truthful, aware, and self-determining. It emphasizes feelings as well as thoughts and stresses body methods, nonverbal techniques, and guided daydream fantasies. Schutz offers a case example to illustrate a variety of methods and changing techniques as well as to follow the energy as it moves within the group and within the individual.

In Chapter Twenty-Three, "Marathon Groups," Elizabeth E. Mintz describes what goes on in a therapy group extended in time—one that may last for twenty-four hours without a break for sleep or for several days, usually with time for sleep. The therapeutic technique may be encounter, Gestalt, psychoanalytic, or, as in the author's own groups, a flexible approach. Special values of the marathon groups are a sense of warmth and safety that develops with prolonged intimacy and leads participants toward willing self-revelation, an opportunity for participants to regress and then return to maturity with new insight and often at a higher level of maturity, an opportunity for each individual in the group to undertake self-exploration and to experience emotional catharsis without the time limitations of conventional ongoing group therapy or the individual session, and the development of a sense of common emotional experience and shared humanity that frequently makes the marathon group a "peak experience" for its participants.

In Chapter Twenty-Four, "Psychodrama," Ira A. Greenberg describes psychodrama as an action therapy that enables people to reach the core of problems quickly through reenacting and reexperiencing traumatic events and through thrusting themselves into stressful situations while protected by the group and by the psychodramatic process. The enactment, Greenberg explains, calls for physical and emotional interaction with other group members who portray people connected to the problem. Basic conceptual components illustrated are spontaneity, situation (staging in the here and now), tele, catharsis, and insight. Psychodrama has two phases: the warm-up, in which the director helps would-be protagonists emerge from the audience, and the enactment, in which the director or the protagonist selects auxiliary egos to portray people involved in the problem, and concludes with audience sharing. Some important psychodrama techniques presented are role reversal, the double, soliloquy, high chair, empty chair, and future projection. Psychodrama derivatives described are sociodrama, hypnodrama, role training, spontaneity training, living newspaper, magic shop, and televised session feedback.

In Chapter Twenty-Five, "Transactional Analysis," John M. Dusay describes another action therapy, in which the therapist actively structures the milieu for redecision and change for successful life scripts. In transactional analysis, eliminating feelings is more important than providing interpretations. The therapist encourages the patient to reexperience painful life events and provides a nurturing atmosphere where the patient can work on them. Techniques from a variety of other therapies are used, including Gestalt, hypnosis, psychodrama, and behavioral psychotherapy. The technique is illustrated with two cases: a couple with marital difficulties and a woman with an unsatisfying social life.

In Chapter Twenty-Six, "Conjoint Therapy," Joan Ormont and Louis R.

Ormont describe the concurrent treatment of a single patient by two therapists, working in different settings; one sees the patient in group and the other individually. The authors believe that the efficacy of this approach derives from the many-sided possibilities that it affords. They can give the patient the benefit of having multiple observers, of having many people who can help him work through his resistances and with whom to exercise his developing maturity. The approach is also found to present special problems. With two therapists, the authors find there is nearly always a splitting of the transference, and the therapists must handle this to advantage. Moreover, they conclude that the therapists must not let their own individual transference and countertransference reactions undo them. They illustrate these points with conjoint case material.

❧ 20 ❧

Psychoanalysis in Groups

Alexander Wolf
Irwin L. Kutash

In psychoanalysis in groups, the creative growth of the individual ego is primary. *Group psychotherapy* is a misnomer for a technique that, though conducted in a group, is designed to aid an individual; it is a treatment of ailing individuals in a group setting, not a treatment of ailing groups, since only individuals have intrapsychic dynamics (Kutash and Wolf, 1983; Kutash and Wolf, 1984).

All group therapies share three fundamental ingredients: (1) a group therapist and at least two patients, (2) multiple interactions among the group members, and (3) limits on what takes place. Psychoanalysis in groups, originated by Alexander Wolf in 1938, shares these three parameters. An additional ingredient, however, is basic to psychoanalysis in groups: the exploration and working through of intrapsychic unconscious processes (Wolf, 1980). An excerpt from a paper written for a group therapy course by a supervisee of one of us (Nattland, 1983) illustrates this difference: "On the night of the interaction to be analyzed, three members are absent and two members arrive late. This sequence of interactions was selected because it involves only three members and one leader." (From the point of view of psychoanalysis in groups, even simple interactions involving few members tend to become complex rapidly.)

A begins to discuss the tactical aspects of leaving his wife. B asks for details. A says he feels guilty and worried that he may become seriously depressed after moving out of the house. He reveals for the first time in group that he has been impotent on several occasions. B tells A she is glad he is moving out on his wife because he "has been in turmoil for so long." She continues by giving him a great deal of support. Then she expresses her feeling that A has not yet dealt with the anger and jealousy he feels for a woman with whom

332

he had been having an affair. A ignores this comment. The leader points out that A has ignored B's last statement. A snaps at the leader and B admits that she, too, "skirts around issues." The leader persists in trying to get A to examine why he doesn't listen to others. A becomes increasingly angry and tries to close the topic by sarcastically retorting, "I'm glad I know I don't listen." A short silence occurs. C, the third present member, has been silent throughout this interaction.

A therapist with a "mass group process" orientation, such as Bion, might describe this interaction as characteristic of a basic-assumption "flight/fight" group. The therapist with an "interpersonal process" orientation, such as Yalom, might view this same interaction as an example of A's maneuvering to solidify his unique position in the group sociogram. A therapist with a psychoanalytic orientation, such as the present authors, would focus on each individual and allow other members to do the same in order to uncover unconscious elements of each individual's behavior as it becomes manifest in interpersonal interaction, and most importantly, what is behind the action on the intrapsychic level.

Throughout the rest of the chapter we will use individual cases to illustrate psychoanalysis in groups in practice. Because psychoanalysis in groups is designed to aid individuals rather than groups, we believe that the approach can best be illustrated by presenting cases of individuals being affected in their own individual ways by their psychodynamic interaction with other group members as facilitators, rather than following one group.

Constructive and Destructive Groups

Groups may be either constructive or destructive. According to the equilibrium-disequilibrium theory of stress-induced anxiety as developed by Kutash (1980) and Kutash and Wolf (1983), an individual experiences anxiety, or a state of disequilibrium, when he or she is not experiencing the optimal level of stress for his or her individual needs. Tranquility, or a state of equilibrium or malequilibrium, results when one is experiencing the optimal stress level for one's constitution, either in a healthy (equilibrium) or in an unhealthy (malequilibrium) balance. Stress can emanate from any of the four environments a person experiences—the interpersonal environment, the physical environment, the mental environment, and the physiological environment. The mental environment includes mental phenomena—conscious, preconscious, or unconscious processes or content: thoughts and feelings. This is, of course, the area focused on in psychoanalysis.

In psychoanalysis in groups the interpersonal environment, which includes familial, social, and cultural phenomena that surround or affect the individual, must be particularly considered. The interpersonal environment of the group can fall into a generally destructive balance or pattern of interaction, a generally constructive balance or pattern of interaction, or, perhaps most insidious, a generally comfortable but stultifying balance or pattern of interaction. The authors have termed these three group situations "group disequilibrium," "group equilibrium," and "group malequilibrium" to reflect whether the level of interpersonal and mental stress is destructive, constructive, or stultifying. Group disequilibrium takes the form of a transferential, pathogenic, uncomfortable re-created family; group equilibrium takes the form of a comfortable transferential family with a new look, as we shall see later; and group malequilibrium takes the form of a pathogenic but comfortable family with a new look.

Group Disequilibrium

Disequilibrium for the individual in the interpersonal environment occurs when a person experiences too little intimacy (for example, isolation) or too much intimacy (for example, engulfment). The person is left with an interpersonally derived stress level that is either too low or too high and experiences anxiety as a result of the imbalance. These feelings initially develop in the family and then, by way of repetition compulsion or projection, either are re-created by the individual or are projected to exist by the individual in his or her later life experiences. In the individual, this process can lead to the immediate investment of the group with frightening, familial transference in the first or second group meeting. When this happens, a patient may experience so much stress that he or she runs out of a session in terror. Trying to induce such a person to return to the group to face and analyze his or her projections may be a formidable task. Such a member has probably been prematurely ushered into the company of other patients. The analyst must try to discern in advance the patient's distortions of reality. This may be accomplished by waiting for the development of a working alliance and/or more positive transference in prior individual treatment, followed by more intensive preliminary study of the patient's particular projective devices. Apparently such an individual straightaway re-creates his own threatening family with its intimacy imbalance in any small cluster of strangers, where original conflict is forced speedily and dreadfully near the surface, so that he takes flight hurriedly. A patient who behaves this way is commonly shy, withdrawn, or schizoid. He is fearful of a collection of people who may renounce etiquette and the superficial social forms that offer him some safety. He runs from the brutality he is repeatedly reincarnating. He is more comfortable in an outside world that assures him a precarious security as long as it remains conventional or distant. He rarely shows up in a group, and if he does, his resistances finally give way to analysis, so that he constitutes no serious indictment of group analytic technique.

An example will show how this pattern may manifest itself and how it can be worked with. A woman seen by one of us entered group when instructed to do so by her analyst, to whom she had a hostile-dependent mother transference. She was living with her mother, and she felt engulfed by her mother but too guilty to leave; her husband, whom she unconsciously thwarted by gaining weight and being difficult and for whom she had given up higher education and career, but who remained symbiotically attached to her; and her divorced daughter and grandson, whom she cared for but resented, since she felt they drained her time and resources. She had no friends because she felt people were rotten and only used one. It was soon clear that she would become either engulfed or used by any relationship she had developed, as she had in brief forays outside the family relationships. She began group therapy by saying and doing anything that might put people off and predicting that everyone would soon hate her.

After observing her first two sessions, the analyst took the following stance: Care was taken never to be directive, as her mother was. The way she might act to alienate the group members was outlined and predicted to her and the group, by first asking her to describe her previous experiences with people and then asking her and the group to try to have something different happen. She was also asked to tell the group whether she was experiencing her old familial feelings. For many months she was her old self, but the members did not allow themselves to engulf her, tell her what do do, or reject her behavior. She was excused from alternate sessions, which she could not initially tolerate, but was assured she would be welcome at any time later. These therapeutic tactics allowed her to get past her initial family transference.

Furthermore, just as an individual may re-create his pathogenic family, there is the ever-present danger that the group, functioning as a re-created family, may become pathogenic as a family. Without adroit management, some groups end up this way. The therapist must watch for the elaboration of inbred and incestuous trends that bind members together as neurotically as in the original family. A recovering patient, for example, may be attacked as unready for discharge by a compulsively overprotective member who is parentally castrating. If a man and woman gravitate toward each other with erotic interest, they may be invested with father and mother roles, and other patients may react to them with detached respect, voyeuristic aggressive interest, or moralistic disapproval that corresponds to earlier ambivalent curiosity about intimacy between the parents. These investments can be dispelled only by persistent analysis. Occasionally a member or two will exhibit some reluctance to permit a patient who has recovered to leave the group. Such members show the same kind of envy or jealousy earlier directed toward a sibling and feel the family group or parental therapist is favoring the cured member with special regard that her performance does not deserve. The majority, however, generally welcome the improvement of anyone and take pleasure in her progress. Transference that denies discharge to a patient who has recovered is also analyzable.

An unfavorable situation that may arise in a group is the development of intense, generalized neurotic resistance, accompanied by hostile bilateral transferences and the formation of allies in groups of two or three, leaving some individuals isolated except for a relatively warm relationship to the analyst. Sometimes even this association becomes strained, because the patient blames the therapist for having been exposed to such a trying and antagonistic environment. Such forms of resistance must be analyzed; otherwise, the group may fall apart. Attendance may become low and demoralize those present. The therapist, while taking an analytic view of absenteeism, confronts those who stay away with the possibility of being dropped. He explores transferences that force aggressors into belligerent roles and points out their illusory character. He is equally vigilant about projective devices that impel the compulsively withdrawn to retreat further or to submit to the domination of other members. The analyst seeks to uncover the causes for resistance to participation on deeper levels, pointing out explicitly the destructive character of particular defenses and encouraging free emotional ventilation. All else failing, the analyst may be obliged to remove a patient here and there, one at a time, at varying intervals, introducing each retired member into a more constructive group. Such a crisis can usually be avoided by not organizing a group with a majority of strongly sadomasochistic patients. Too many such members in the same milieu provide an unfavorable climate for evocation of the positive resources that need to be expressed if the group members are to proceed effectively.

Group Equilibrium

Group equilibrium is achieved when the patients constructively re-create the family—but with a new look. Cultivating a permissive atmosphere in which mutual tolerance and regard can flourish will enable the earlier prohibitive character of the original family to be projected with less intensity and to be more easily worked through. Furthermore, the general acceptance and sense of belonging that follow will enable a similarly easy transition to correspondingly untroubled social relations beyond the confines of the group. The other patients, because of their numbers, provide more familial surrogates for transference evocation. Each patient comes to a realization of the extent to which he re-creates his own childhood family in every social setting and inappropriately invests others with familial substitute qualities. The number of participants also clarifies the variety and multiplicity of central and penumbral transferences. In individual analysis the therapist tries to see clearly what perceptual distortions the patient makes of outer reality and what internal factors contribute to this social disfigurement, but the analyst is often misled, because he or she does not see the patient in action. In group, the therapist also is interested in what is happening at the moment so that the patient's unconscious warping of fact can be observed in motion. The patient can then be confronted with his projective trends and the inciting role he plays in precipitating the environmental disturbances he resents so much.

An illustration of how a group helped an individual see his misperceptions of the present as if it were the past will be offered to show the usefulness of psychoanalysis in groups for this purpose and to show how group equilibrium can be achieved. A group member seen by one of us was transferentially viewed by one younger male member of the group as an immovable controlling figure (his father). A second younger male group member also viewed him as very controlling and irritating but experienced as well a positive feeling that he would like to help him to feel free to be less controlling (feelings he felt for his father). A younger female group member saw the person as manipulative and subtly controlling (like both her parents). A fourth group member saw him as talking down to her and treating her as if she were unintelligent (again like her parents), and yet a fifth group member saw him as a warm, good father (the father she never had). When the first four members described all began to express their feelings to this member, the recipient of so many transferences, and told him how he should behave, as a group they became transferentially his mother, who always had controlled him and told him how to act, and he resisted their efforts vehemently. Only after one by one each father transference was explored and the group came to see the defensive nature of this man's controlling behavior (warding off his own mother) and after his transference to the group was clarified did gradual progress for many group members occur. Many individuals came to see how they related to present-day figures as people from their past. These theoretical and practical problems of working through are one of the most neglected, yet most important, aspects of psychoanalysis both in the individual and in the group setting.

Group Malequilibrium

Group malequilibrium occurs when group members are all comfortable with one another but do not in any way challenge one another's defenses. The group itself is in an unhealthy stultifying balance. Conflict-laden topics are avoided and everyone, in an unconscious bargain, avoids stressful but potentially growth-inducing material.

An example of a patient in such a group is the following: One patient's love for the emotional climate of the group bordered on the ecstatic. He reveled in the luxury of what he considered an absolutely honest relationship. He was, *mirabile dictu*, in a family whose projections, having become at last analyzable and understandable, no longer alarmed or hurt him.

The danger in his case was that he ran from real life to the fabricated safety of an unreal laboratory. He found the group warmer and saner than most associations on the outside. He needed to be instructed in how to carry the affective closeness he had achieved in the group to larger segments of society, beyond the confines of his fellow members. This, by the way, is a common objection to working in concert with other patients. How, it is asked, can one transfer the good fellowship of the group to areas outside it? Analysis in a group lays no Pollyannaish or grandiose claim to making the world a big happy family. But group analytic technique offers the patient a means of making conscious the trends that stand in the way of his vigorous affective contact with others, whether loving or hating. We say "hating" as well as "loving" because there are some psychopathic influences in the world that can appropriately be hated.

Another example further illustrates malequilibrium in groups: A woman patient seen by one of us was placed in a group and arrived at her first meeting with a long cigarette holder and a very theatrical air and dress. After attending the session, she told the therapist, "These are not my kind of people. Haven't you a group of patients who have more in common with me?" The therapist, who was seeing a number of artists and theater people, was about to start a new group. He invited this woman and several other patients who seemed compatible into the group. Everyone immediately hit it off, laughed, joked, and had a marvelous time. Members never talked about themselves, their feelings, their associations, or their dreams.

This group was eventually disbanded and its members placed in more heterogeneous groups where the cultivation of the group came through the promotion of differentiated, complementary and uncomplementary, and conflictful and unconflictful personalities. People, through their growing individuality, learned through differences in realistic perception and unrealistic misperception to appreciate one another's mutually proffered gifts of vision, to appreciate their oppositeness and opposition, their mutuality and compatibility, the treasures of one another's perceptions, and the nonnarcissistic growth of one another's egos.

Treatment

We will now illustrate how to deal with resistance in group, acting out, transference problems, countertransference problems, dreams, and working through (see Wolf, 1949, 1950; Wolf and Schwartz, 1962; Schwartz and Wolf, 1963; Kutash and Wolf, 1983).

Resistance. Resistance manifests itself in the myriad forms encountered in individual analysis, but the group setting provides a special environment that lends itself to the elaboration of resistive forms peculiar to group analysis.

For Carol, a patient "in love with" the analyst, being in the group was enlightening. She was soon as emotionally attached to another group member as she was to the analyst. Her "unfaithfulness," the rapidity and completeness with which she moved from one man to another, confronted her with the irrational and compulsive character of her behavior. In time the nature of her activity became obvious to her as transference. Carol was rigidly blocked in neurotic interest in the analyst and insisted that she was truly in love with him and that she would be neurosis-free if only the therapist would return her genuine feeling; the group experience dispelled the illusion. In the group, if such a patient does not transfer her affective claim to another patient, she is led to examine her feelings more deeply in the face of similar resistance and transference to other members. Their falsification of reality makes its impression on her. In most cases, she is brought face to face with the "infidelity" that impels her to exchange the analyst for a patient and is obliged to plumb earlier emotional attachments. She then discovers the neurotic resistance implicit in every such episode.

Another manifestation of resistance is the compulsive missionary spirit. One group member, George, persisted in looking after other members in a supportive, parental way, using this device subtly to dominate and attack the other members and to repress more basic personal psychodynamics. The group resented this false charity and demanded and evoked more spontaneous participation by rewarding the messianic for unguarded slips of feeling and by rejecting dogmatic helpfulness.

This does not imply, of course, that warm and spontaneous offers of assistance are rejected. On the contrary, as long as supportiveness is not compulsive but is thoughtfully sympathetic, it is welcomed as a sign of good health.

An interesting example of this kind of resistance is provided in the following case. In one group a professional teacher, Harry, habitually preached to his fellow analysands until their hostility bordered on the explosive. Later he reported that during coitus sometimes an hour passed before his sexual partner had an orgasm. To him, the sexual act, like his compulsive stewardship in the group, was a gesture of generosity. The other patients encouraged him to be less providing and to strive to enjoy his wife's allure with more spontaneity and pleasure for himself. At the next session he reported an ejaculation within three minutes and a corresponding simultaneous orgasm from his partner. The group conjectured that his earlier largesse concealed unconscious hostility, to which his wife had been responding with equal frigidity. They also suggested that his benevolent preachments and ostensible advice contained the same kind of irritating and unprovoked aggression. He was urged in this situation as well to abandon his compulsive role for one that was more spontaneous and acceptable. After some time he became aware that his specious charity was a form of resistance preventing the development of real feeling. Variants of this theme appear in the self-appointed do-gooder, in the overprotective, typical "mom" in the group. It is also eminently displayed in the "mother is always right" dogma.

Voyeurism is resistance that is more general in group analysis. Robert tried to escape personal examination and engagement by taking a "grandstand seat," which gave him a gratifying view of what might have been the equivalent of the primal scene or its lesser familial counterparts. He seemed willing and even eager to allow others full interaction, while he assigned to himself a tremulous watchfulness. Instead of engaging in interpersonal exchange, he peered at it from a distance. But looking can be a prelude to participation. The group had little tolerance for a non-participant. It engaged Robert by its welcoming self-exposure. It moved him by inviting and provoking him to become involved in the warm emotional life of the new family. His resistance began to melt when the sideshow to which he was drawn by dubious surreptitious motives became a wholesome drama in which he was impelled to take a legitimate part. Projected aggression gave way to a recognition of reality, and he became prepared to act more appropriately in this unforbidding environment. In this fashion, voyeuristic resistance developed from an end in itself to a first step toward a normal relationship.

Hiding oneself behind the watchful analysis of others is a common form of resistance in psychoanalysis in groups. The group may provide a convenient setting for the exercise of this kind of resistance. Abe concentrated on the neurotic behavior of other patients while evading analysis directed toward himself. He cleverly shifted attention from himself to the associator in order to defend against disturbing examination. He was adept, when threatened by an observation that might become alarmingly penetrating, at neatly parrying the proffered insight. He managed to redirect the group's attention to any individual who dared to analyze him. He handled what was said of him, for example, by remarking that his critic had an interesting overtone in speech that he ought to examine. By endless devices he deflected what might add up to deeper insight into himself and tackled his examiner. Sometimes he produced brilliant, if compulsive, analyses in his own defense. Usually his techniques were so able as not to be easily broken down under critical examination. However, the group gradually dissolved his resistance by expressing its gratitude for his incisiveness and simultaneously demonstrating to him that behind his emphatic lecturing he made himself inaccessible, in terror of humiliation, to the helping hands of the group. It was pointed out that fear of castration or its equivalent by the parental substitutes in the group was forcing him into this compulsive role. To the extent that the members understood the frantic insecurity that underlay his bravado, they extended a reassuring friendliness that enabled him to relinquish his insistent critical study of others for self-examination. The maintenance of a compulsive complacency that regarded the other patients as neurotic inferiors could not withstand such an approach from the associated members. Their understanding enabled them to become friendly enough to help him, in time, give up his program of evasion.

The use of history as resistance deserves special comment. There is probably nothing in individual treatment more uselessly time-consuming and basically harmful to both patient and analyst than the practice of rehearsing the patient's past. Long, irrelevant biographies, usually distorted by the narrator, were Ted's form of continual evasion. He even used a recital of yesterday's events for this purpose. In a most unsatisfactory form the relationship between patient and group members was reduced to a day-by-day report of frustration that demanded nonanalytic advice on ways of circumventing it. This insistence on guidance instead of therapeutically valuable transactions was also used as resistance. Refusal to face the present with one's own reactive emotional and mental processes withstands only in extreme cases the impact of other patients' stimulation. Talk of what happened in childhood and even accounts of last night's dream became vicarious and pallid when compared with the dynamic interpersonal reactions produced by a suddenly articulate contact. Such dramatic provocation cannot be resisted by escape into the day before yesterday.

Of course, we do not mean that we regard history as unimportant. On the contrary, it is of the utmost importance. History has the greatest significance when evoked and recalled by the discovery and analysis of resistance and transference in the moment of their occurrence—that is, when history has a bearing on the present that is meaningful to both the patient and the analyst. The present neurotic behavior is envisioned as a multidimensional photograph of the significant past. Careful scrutiny of the immediate moment will recall pertinent traumatic events. Personal flashbacks may be vividly illuminating, and the exploration and understanding of the past in terms of its influence on the present are essential to creation of a wholesome present and future. But allowing a patient to indulge these proclivities is encouraging him in resistive subterfuge, his attempt to escape the resolution of similar conflict in the present.

Some patients, perhaps a majority of them during the early stages of treatment, discuss sexual material with patent reluctance. This is a kind of diffidence we try to dispel. Slighting or repressing sexual data reproduces the prohibitive role of the original family. Unless the patient frees his own sexuality, he cannot make an adequate recovery. Access to sexual material is obtained partly by intuitive free association. Once the initial resistances are broken down in this process, there is usually little difficulty in getting patients to discuss this fundamental matter.

An intimate relation exists between abnormal social behavior and abnormal sexual behavior. Access to sexual material is obtained by illustrating how a variety of interpersonal conduct that appears in the group has its sexual counterpart, perhaps as yet unseen. Since the average patient is wary, at first, of revealing her sexual predicament, and since she is hardly aware of either its extent or its complexity, group members are urged, early in analysis, to examine the interplay of their personalities on the social level. Then the analyst may begin to suggest that for each of the character traits revealed by cross-examination there is a sexual analogue. The analyst's ease in taking the parallel for granted, without criticism, tends to infect the group members with a like tolerance for otherwise socially prohibited intimacy. The analyst might indicate that a manifestation of social impotence implies the existence of a corresponding sexual impotence, that they are both signs of a similar psychodynamic problem in the analysand. Similarly, for example, excessive attitudes of male supremacy suggest a corresponding compulsive sexual excess, organized to conceal deep-rooted castration anxiety. A statuesque pose on the social level is probably accompanied by some form of sexual frigidity. When the therapist has thus schooled patients in the effort to uncover the usually concealed existence of these sexual correspondents of social forms, the members make numerous accurate guesses about hidden sexual data. By intuition, one after another uncovers sexual material. In the light of this relationship, nuances in curious social conduct are clarified in turn. One exposure excites release in others until, in a surprisingly short time, the cautious lose their caution and proceed to unburden themselves of the most intimate details.

A group afforded an illustration of an instance in which psychologically-induced impotence was accompanied by social ineffectiveness. One of its preeminently male members, Dave, physically powerful and imposing, exhibited evidence of extreme shyness. His emotional reactions were, to say the least, deficient. References to plays, art, and literature both annoyed and embarrassed him, and when pressed for an explanation, he characterized them as effeminate manifestations of weakness. He secretly regarded any display of feeling as soft and feared he might be seduced into affective response by any emotional stimulant. At an early age he had lost his domineering father and had been forced to go out on the streets to sell newspapers in order to support his mother, his sisters, and himself. Attacked repeatedly by anti-Semitic hoodlums, he spent years toughening himself until tenderness, sympathy, and, by extension, any emotional symbol that did not connote hard struggle were ruled out of his life. In group activity it was noted that he evaded those social responses that might betray any underlying emotional attitude. He was formally considerate, proper, and unreactive, except for a compulsive need to display his masculine excess. This latter consisted in exhibiting his masterful virility whenever possible, in missing no opportunity to engage in intellectual debate, at which he excelled, and in a general supportiveness simulating strength which invited the dependence of other members on him but which was unconsciously intended to dominate and exploit them.

During various sessions, the group speculated about the sexual counterpart of his deficiency in feeling and gradually led him to a not-too-painful admission of his impotence. He was moved so deeply by the friendly reception accorded his confession of weakness that he burst into tears, the first crack in his resistive armor. With this disruption of neurotic defense against emotional expression, he began dreaming, free-associating, and "going around" at deeper affective levels. This enabled the group, in time, to analyze his masculine conceit and striving for power as defenses against castration and passive homosexual submission. He was able to acquire insight into his compelling preoccupation with erotically tinged struggle between himself and other men that removed him from sexual engagements with women. He was able to trace his aggression toward men to his domineering father and his later and repeated compulsive strivings with them as the ambivalent expression of submissive and aggressive conflict. He learned, too, how the loss of his father removed a masculine image with whom he needed to identify, leaving him with three feminine figures who played their part in further emasculating him, partly out of their playing a phallic role and partly by providing him only with feminine examples. This was added to by their own ambivalent eroticism toward him. To all this conflict he reacted with repression, attempting ever to surmount unconscious affective claims that would not be denied until he was both impotent and apparently unfeeling. But the group members' action, with inserted a wedge into his formerly impenetrable façade, allowed him to relax restraints successively and steadily build up lively and cordial contact. The return of feeling allowed him to relate to others with intensity, to fall in love, and to consummate an erotic and wholesome heterosexual relationship with full potency.

One such confession has a catalytic effect in producing similar uninhibited discussion by others. With varying degrees of stubborn opposition, the members finally yield to the potentiating influence of self-revelation induced by the permissive aura pervading the group. Emboldened by avowals from all sides, each sees around him his counterpart in sexual embarrassment and exposes his particular variant of the sexual theme.

Not all varieties of resistance that appear in the group can be dealt with here, for they are as manifold and distinct as human beings, but we shall mention some other common ones. Some patients resist by trying to hide in the group, whether by attempting to escape into group analysis from individual treatment or by coming late and missing meetings. Some leave the room on various pretexts. Others cannot recall their dreams or fantasies. A few exploit their tears and other devious emotional or psychosomatic releases to evade more direct responses. Some maintain a compulsive complacency among patients whom they regard as neurotically inferior and hence not to be entrusted with important private matters. Their resistance takes the form of supercilious silence or contempt. Some try to overwhelm the group with endless outpourings of irrelevant talk that is neither self-revealing nor permissive of emergence of others, and some act out.

Acting Out

We must ask whether the group setting provokes more acting out and what values we are applying to patients in a group. Some analysts believe that any sexual behavior during analysis is acting out. There are probably some who feel that having sex seven, seventeen, or twenty-seven times a week is acting out. Others may think that not having sex is acting out. At what point is the particular sexual activity acting out—that is, contrary to the best interests of the patient's growing development, to the resolution of neurotic conflicts, and to the discovery of new, more fulfilling, and healthier ways of behaving and living?

When is masturbation a forward movement, and when is it acting out? Let us consider two cases.

A young man, Gary, had never masturbated and had never had a conscious experience of sexual feeling or fantasy or a sexual relationship with another person. The exploration of his sexuality led to the beginnings of masturbatory activity. The expression of himself in masturbation may, at that moment, be considered forward-moving. It would become resistance if, for example, he refused to continue to struggle to develop a heterosexual relationship or, after establishing one, returned to masturbation.

Another young man, Jeff, had a large number of girlfriends. His sexual activity was pathological. He was a Don Juan who would have a one-time contact with each woman and end up in bed with her. After entering treatment, he separated himself from women and concentrated on masturbation as his only source of sexual gratification. This was, in part, a healthy development. There came a time when to continue to do this was resistive to forward movement, to constructive change. It was an attempt to maintain the status quo. He had used masturbation to overcome the repetitive seduction of one woman after another and to avoid early confrontation of his fear of the father. It became clear that he was now using masturbation to resist having a sexual relationship with a woman and resolving his problems. His isolation from women was a form of resistance. He feared facing the anticipated violence for being sexual, in a transference with the analyst as the forbidding father. Rather than come to grips with his own felt and projected violence regarding the castrating father and resolving the conflict, he sought to avoid it. The persistent masturbation had to be approached by the careful analysis of these two factors, the resistive element and the transference element, and the relation between the two.

Transference

Perhaps the citation of a few examples of the transference process as it occurs in the group will be illuminating.

In prior individual treatment Helen evidenced erotic interest in her analyst that was associated with some fear and anxiety, mixed unconscious feelings originally directed toward her father in childhood. (There were never conscious feelings directed toward her father in childhood.) These were never conscious or expressed. During an early group meeting, the analyst complimented James on his brilliant intuitive appraisal of her. She felt, at once, that he was being favored, and she reacted with jealousy, feeling that he was more highly regarded for his intellectual talent. Immediately anxious, she challenged his statement and reacted with marked hostility toward both him and the analyst throughout the duration of the meeting. Despite her competition with him for the analyst's esteem, she felt that James would inevitably do better than she and that the therapist would just as certainly always promote him because he was a man. The compulsive nature of her conduct, together with its interesting sequel, came out at the next session. Helen said that on leaving the previous meeting she had gone automatically to a florist to order an elaborate bouquet for her mother. Suddenly confounded in the flower shop, she stopped and tried to realize what she was doing. There was really no occasion for sending her mother a bouquet, for the mother was not ill, nor was it a holiday or an anniversary. Understanding followed directly. She knew then that in the group the analyst had changed from a father to a mother image; James, the man the therapist had complimented, had become a substitute for her brother, with whom she had been in perpetual rivalry for her mother's attention. Praise of him elicited the projection of the mother figure onto the analyst. It also aroused a keen hostility toward James and especially toward the analyst. The gift of flowers was to propitiate a mother who was annoyed by her conduct, to conceal her welling resentment, and to appease her conscience for coming so close to fully expressing her anger against her mother. Of striking interest was her abandonment of the father image in the therapist as soon as the group provided a situation in which the analyst could reward a man, who was at once invested with a brother quality. Apparently Helen was able to re-create the father image as long as the analyst was alone with her. As soon as the original family was reanimated by the group setting and more particularly by the authority figure's approval of a man, a particular familial constellation was revived that necessitated a revision in her earlier investment in the analyst. A high estimate of a man unconsciously recalled greater admiration of her brother and disapprobation for herself. Her mother had been the prime agent in the construction of this historical configuration.

Later meetings brought out her mother's actual preference for Helen's brother because he was a boy. Helen's compulsive penis envy, her disregard for her feelings, and her excessive regard for excelling intellectuality, in the company of which she always felt doomed to come off second best, reproduced her relationship to mother and brother. By attention to the aspects of her shifting transferences to the analyst and to James, we were at last able to help Helen relinquish familial claims on her and to react in her own and others' right.

Another example likewise shows how transferences can change when the patient enters a group. In thirty preliminary sessions, Joe and the analyst got on famously. Joe was brilliant, serene, and exceptionally friendly. There was good rapport on both sides; they liked each other. He made rapid progress. There seemed to be no resistance. He interpreted a dream, and the analyst would add an additional point. Joe accepted it, usually with a modification that seemed appropriate. There were no stumbling blocks—it all seemed too unneurotic. The analyst proposed that he join a group, where certain areas of his personality might reveal themselves more adequately. It took the first group meeting to provoke the only indication of negative transference that could be discovered. He was a changed man. The harmonious relationship, his appreciation of what the analyst had done for him, and his willingness to act on insights vanished. He challenged substantially everything the analyst said, and his keen intuition, though extremely helpful in analyzing other patients, was unconsciously intended to forestall and belittle the analyst's contribution.

Whereas in prior private sessions there had been easy exchange, in the group Joe would hardly allow the analyst to speak. He interrupted, he anticipated and predicted (often accurately enough) what the analyst was about to say. The analyst held his tongue for the time being. But very soon the group noticed Joe's compulsive behavior and began discussing it. When the analyst called to his attention the contrast between his former complacent demeanor during individual analysis and his subsequent truculent attitude toward him in the group, Joe expressed surprise and embarrassment at having been guilty of such behavior. But even as he spoke, he was struck with a flash of historical insight: He recalled with what pontifical dignity and Victorian strictness his father had held court at the dining table when Joe was a child; how one had to tiptoe about the house when his father was napping on Sunday afternoons; how he was not allowed to speak in his father's presence unless spoken to. And he remembered other indignities, extending to his not being allowed to enter the bathroom as a very little child when his mother was bathing—a privilege, however, that his father permitted himself. At subsequent meetings he explained how all his life he could talk freely and easily with one person, just as he used to do with his mother. But in the presence of a group he felt driven to excel, to be the genius in the drawing room. In every social gathering, he habitually re-created the family milieu and automatically strove to become its guiding intellect. The group suggested, and Joe acknowledged, that he might now be playing an assumed paternal role in the new family. Then he remembered how as a child he had been almost irresistibly impelled to challenge his father in everything the latter did or said, but he had never quite dared to carry it off.

The reproduction of his relationship to his mother when alone with the analyst and to his father and family when in the group led to deeper insight into his oedipal conflict, his attachment to his mother, his repressed rivalry with his father, and his compulsive replacement of the father in every re-generated family. Certainly, Joe's transfer to a group revived old family ghosts that could not have been so easily discovered or dispelled without reproducing the household unit.

Helen's and Joe's stories raise at least three salient points. The first is the sudden appearance of occasionally unforeseen bursts of transference toward the therapist or another member after a patient has been introduced to a group. The second is the inevitable appearance of previously latent facets of personality, new and multiple transferences in the re-creation of the old family, so that movement into a group changes behavior. The third is the recall of significant incidents in early life by the flashback method in relation to the analysis of immediate transference.

Analyst's Transference and Countertransferences

Countertransference is thought by many to be the analyst's transference. The distortion is perceiving the patient or patients in a group as if he, she, or they were members of the analyst's original family. We consider the analyst's transference distinct from countertransferences but nonetheless of great importance. Kutash (Kutash and Wolf, 1983) coined the following terminology to cover some important types of analyst's transferences: *direct transference, projected identification transference,* and *introjected transference.* In direct transference, the analyst or group therapist reacts to patients or group members as if they were members of his or her original family. In projected identification transference, the analyst or group therapist identifies with the patient or patients and projects his own early feelings from his own family onto the patient. In introjected transference, the therapist takes on the role of his own parents in the way he ministers to the patient or group, who become original family members; influenced by introjection, the therapist acts as his or her own parent might as leader of a re-created family. The analyst who finds herself thinking, "How could he, she, or they have done this to me after all I did for them?," might find she is the victim of an introjected transference reaction.

The following is an example of transference in a patient in a group, met by transference as well as countertransference in the therapist. Bob, on the death of his sister, spent the next group session projecting the group as a family that, unlike his own, would comfort and be with him, to the point that he invited all the members to his house while he sat shiva. He called on the group leader to take the role of his long-dead father, who had shown him some affection, phoning him to ask him to call group members to let them know he was sitting shiva at his home. The group leader, under supervision with one of us, described how he identified with this neglected patient, now without the father from whom he had got some sustenance. He found himself encouraging group members to attend, and only when one gentleman said, "I'm confused—are we supposed to be a group or a family?" did the therapist catch his transference and countertransference and say, "A group. But you may, of course, have your alternate session at Bob's."

The following situation exemplifies the transference/countertransference cycle in a group setting. It is possible to illustrate this effect because we know the patients' transferences and their implicit expectations, as well as the analyst's psychodynamics. Mary lent Fred, a copatient, some recordings, which Mary claimed Fred scratched and Fred claimed were already damaged and hurt his hi-fi needle. These patients were both music lovers. Their transferences were similar in that both patients projected "bad mother" images on the other and turned to the analyst as the "good mother" who would side with each against the bad mother projected onto the other patient. The transference of the analyst was having to settle arguments between the symbolic mother and father, which always gave him some anxiety, but his countertransference was immediately to fulfill the passionful, irrational demand of Fred and Mary by trying to settle their argument. The chances are that the analyst could avoid countertransference if he were not also in transference. Most parents want the child to side with either father or mother. There is much opportunity and pressure in the group for the analyst to become an omnipotent judge as a way of handling his anxiety and helplessness.

Our transferences and countertransferences may account for many failures because they elicit copatient transference and countergratification and encourage patients to try to meet our transference and countertransference needs. Counter-transference may be concealed in what the therapist chooses to emphasize or analyze in the contestants when she is, in fact, favoring one or rejecting the other. Often, by some technical or theoretical device, she rationalizes the taking of sides or an irrational, inappropriate action in a contretemps between patients. Sometimes the analyst has a pressing need to solve a conflict immediately and thereby to cut off any interaction between patients. This is true of patients' expressions not only of anger but also of positive feelings, which may give rise to anxiety in the analyst and a need to interpret quickly.

Dreams

Dreams may lead to insight, provoke elaborate free association, and cut through resistance. But in the clarification of transference, dreams are also valuable therapeutic adjuncts (see Wolf and Schwartz, 1962).

Since a patient in a group tends to take up a large part of group time when he tells a dream and his associations to it, it is useful to ask the other members to free-associate to the dream so they do not feel bored or excluded and can also benefit. Then the members can explore not only the dreamer's but the nondreamers' associations for insightful psychodynamics and psychopathological material. Using this method rather than encouraging the exploration of the meaning of the dream to the dreamer alone welcomes this intrapsychic participation of all the participants. More is gained for each member than if the nondreamers simply offer their inter-pretations of the dream—often a resistance on their part to self-exposure and self-exploration.

A member, Bill, projected an associated woman patient in a dream, in a dual role: both as a menacing figure and as a lovable one. He did this before free association or biographical acknowledgment had given us any indication of his mother's ambivalent attitude toward him. Interpretation of the dream enabled him and the group to discover the castrating mother image with which he compulsively invested the woman. As he recognized the transference features of his vision of her and saw her as in fact a friendly associate, he was able to divest her of her threaten-ing aspect, and she became more lovable. As he progressively analyzed the com-pulsive character of his attachment to her, he dispelled even this maternal hold, and she became simply an engaging friend, stripped of maternal qualities but with an attractiveness of her own. In these instances, reality proved much richer and more rewarding to the patient than his illusion.

In psychoanalysis in a group, if a copatient is aggressive toward the dreamer, his dream, or his associations, it is good practice to explore the provocation for the attack in the dreamer and in the aggressor. In this way we attempt to arrive at some understanding of the encounter, so that the dreamer may be encouraged rather than discouraged to report further dream material. Generally, some members of the group see the positive in the dream. If, as on occasion happens, there are only negative reactions, the analyst ought to explore with each member this homo-geneous manifest response and search for latent material. At the same time the analyst may wish to emphasize what is constructive in the dream.

Patients may use a dream to break through or support resistance. Dreams may also be used as resistance by a patient. One patient, Irene, came to each session with a dream. Although these dreams were revealing of her psychodynamics and the group worked with them, resistance took the form of not expressing personal reactions to the analyst. This dynamic was acted out in her life in two ways. First, Irene maintained great distance from her father, really wanting him all the time but isolating herself in a remote part of the house and hoping he would come to her. Second, she never really related to a man. While in treatment, she finally began to build a relationship with a man. She has not yet reached orgasm in intercourse. That some part of her problem still exists is expressed by her putting the dream in the way of her relationship to the analyst. The fact that she tells her dreams, however, is in itself positive.

Working Through

In the advanced stages of treatment a central problem is that of working through vestiges of pathology. Here too a discriminating estimate of the uniqueness of each patient's disturbed psychodynamics and therefore the particular devices to be used to move him or her toward a more reasonable adjustment have to be studied, planned for, and employed.

Let us, for illustrative purposes, consider one member, John, who is extremely impulsive in expressing his feelings but who considers thinking things through as unspontaneous and controlling and regards planned activity as too frustrating compared with immediate yielding to affect. Working through this problem for John entailed a discriminative review of the kind of emotion he indulged. When this emotion was irrational, our struggle with him was to bring him, in time, to the expression of more appropriate feelings. But having progressed so far, he has not yet reached the optimal therapeutic experience. It is necessary, further, that we help him see the value not only of relevant affect but of thinking things through and of planned activity.

Let us now consider a second member, Susan, who withheld feelingful responses but exulted in her intellectual and interpretive productions. Here an adequate resolution of the problem called for an analysis of the patient's resistance to her own emotion in order to liberate it and a corresponding demonstration to her of how her compulsive intellectuality was equally defensive.

Reference has often been made in the literature of group psychotherapy to the emergence of group leaders and auxiliary therapists among patients, particularly later in therapy. A note of warning is in order to caution the analyst against the patient's exploiting such a role in resistance to participating affectively. By engaging as a leader and interpreter of other members' difficulties, the patient may well conceal her own affective detachment, her underlying compulsive seniority, or her competition with the therapist. The latter, in his ready appreciation of help from all resources in the group, may be too readily inclined to condone whatever analytic aid he can get in the group and accordingly be misled into tolerating what may at times be a resistive maneuver. This is not to say that analytic observations coming from patients may not sometimes be evidence as well of their budding resourcefulness, in which case their interpretations can be welcomed as therapeutic for both the donor and the recipient; but it would seem reasonable to say that only the analyst is the leader in terms of expertness, that although patients can certainly play reparative roles, they have neither the knowledge nor the training to be considered auxiliary therapists. If they are so regarded by the group or so regard themselves, their activity may well be examined for its disordered significance. And if the analyst looks on a patient as an auxiliary therapist, he may well explore his perception for countertransferential content.

A third member deified impromptu activity to the neglect of thought and feeling. He was accordingly very active physically in the group—he couldn't stop moving. Where another patient was verbally tender, this patient embraced; where one member spoke his anger, he was ready to throw something or strike; and where one man wept, he, rather, tore his hair. Here, working through involved the exercise of control over such indeliberate activity, the quest for more planned operations, and the pursuit of the uses of reason and affect.

A fourth member was compulsively devoted only to those activities that were, in essence, defenses against repressed material, rationalized as strategically reasonable. Here the resolution of the problem lay in the analysis of his behavior as defensive and compulsively repetitive, lacking in the sensible planning that might lead to fulfillment of his real potentials.

In all these instances, we are interested in each of the three dimensions of thought, feeling, and behavior, in the kind of intellectuality, affect, and activity, and in which form of these is pursued to the neglect of the others.

The same discriminatory emphasis is required in the study of what temporal accent the patient gives to her productions. If she is enmired in an exclusive preoccupation with her past, we are interested in her present and her future. If she is engrossed primarily in here-and-now experiences of the moment, we would lead her to an exploration of her history and a consideration of eventualities. If she is wrapped up with her future, we want to know more of her background and current necessities. If the patient is absorbed in sexual matters, we would direct her attention to her interpersonal relations apart from her sexual obsession. If she excludes sexual content from her revelations and seems exclusively consumed with social relationships, we would attempt to analyze the resistances that exclude consideration of her sexual needs.

One member, prepsychotic or psychopathic, may need stronger superego controls. A second, overconscientious and bound by rigid inner monitors, may need some relaxation of an incorporated sense of duty. A third, a borderline, whose ego has been weakened by schizophrenic parents, may require ego strengthening as the primary therapeutic intervention.

Another member, too readily given to value only his unconscious productions, may have to be led to lay store by conscious activity. Still another, inattentive to unconscious material, should be guided to a more serious contemplation of underlying motivation. One patient, preoccupied with dreams, may have to be induced to explore other dimensions of his life in waking experience. Another, who never reports dreams, should be induced to pay attention to this voice of her unconscious.

One member, too involved with the other patients, should be directed to develop and explore her extragroup contacts. Another, detached from the group but seemingly involved with people outside the group, must be induced to extend his interaction in the group.

One patient, haunted by his parents, may not be able to let others intrude on his continuous involvement with his forbears and may require a weaning toward admission of nonparental associates into his limited circle of experience. Another, divorced from her family and in reeling flight toward nonfamilial figures, may need a careful review of the real and projected defenses that keep her from a wholesome acceptance of her parents.

These examples are sufficient to illustrate the importance of the analyst's maintaining a discriminative view of the particular pathological dynamics of each patient, so that she can keep in mind the specially indicated means of working through. In so doing, she also makes group members aware of their uniqueness in terms of their needs as well as their potentials, so that they are not so commonly impelled to demand from the therapist that she treat them the same way. Even in the most homogeneously organized group, there are always enough differences in character structure, psychopathology, and resources to call for such differentiated study and treatment. Moreover, when the analyst is thoroughly aware of these distinctions and the need to treat them differently, she no longer feels threatened by the patient's complaint that ''you don't treat me the way you treat him.'' But if the therapist persists in making discriminating estimates of each member, she finds before too long that group members soon follow her lead, cease demanding undifferentiated responses from her, and, in their own interest, recognize the value of differences and complementation.

According to some group therapists, the leader is somewhat more active during the end phase than during the middle phase of group psychotherapy. Here again, we believe a discriminative view of the therapist's activity, passivity, or neutrality must be taken, and if he is any of these, consideration should be given to the timing of his interventions as well as to the kind of engagement he chooses to serve the patient's positive evolution at this moment or in the future. With a member who is initially silent, the analyst may choose to be active or passive, depending on which maneuver he believes will best call forth a response. With an initially verbally monopolistic member, the therapist may have at first to intervene very actively in analyzing his narcissism and, in a terminal phase, just as actively in esteeming his allocentrism. With a shy, withdrawn patient, the analyst may in the beginning be quite active in encouraging him to participate, in a middle phase be just as energetic in appreciating his more vigorous communication, and, nearing termination, be more passive as the patient appears to be doing well enough on his own. These differences in patient requirements point up once more why a nondiscriminative, stereotyped prescription for the therapist's role at so-called group phases can no more be appropriate to the needs of all than to the needs of one patient in different periods of his progress.

The analyst's or a patient's analytic comment to member A may apply as well to patients B and C. But even D and E may get something out of it by virtue of comparison, learning to appreciate their differences from A, B, and C and gaining insight by contrast. Understanding here occurs then not only out of identification but out of difference. The analyst is careful when she generalizes from one patient to the next. A collective interpretation tends to obscure specific differences that may vary with each patient. A generalization may enable a member to resist deeper and more refined insight into his unique dynamics. Still, the therapist seizes the opportunity, when a recollection or dream brings insight to one patient, to encourage exploratory reactions of other members to the same recollection or dream.

Experimental Techniques

We will conclude with a discussion of experimental techniques and their implications.

One of us has been experimenting with something we call the "minigroup" (see Kutash and Wolf, 1983). Since some individuals feel lost even in a group as small as eight because they were neglected in a family that may have numbered as few as three, an experience in a group setting where the leader can assure them a prominent role can provide a new constructive experience. Several persons who had previously found themselves overwhelmed in large groups were placed in a group with three or four individuals. The smaller size of the group was never mentioned as the reason for the invitation to these groups. These patients found themselves participating more and feeling a unique freedom. They were at last in a setting without overpowering mother, father, or sibling figures, while not feeling lost in the crowd. Later additional members were added, including less passive potential transferential mothers or fathers. At this point their egos were more secure because of their previous experience with the leader as a "good parent." They felt his respect for their participation and the regard of siblings who were not perceived as overpowering or parental favorites. The larger group then became the arena for their further growth.

An adaptation of this technique was tried in a group solely for treating di-egophrenics (Kutash, 1984b; Wolf and Kutash, 1984; for a description of di-egophrenia, see Chapter Two). Again overpowering mother, father, or sibling figures were not included, and only later were less ambivalent potential transferential mothers or fathers added. The members consisted of a man who works for his father as an accountant, who had years earlier studied fine arts but flunked out of school and who paints on and off as a hobby; a woman who is currently a teacher, like both her parents, who had been in the drug culture as a college student with much sexual acting out, who could write while on speed publishable songs and poetry of an angry, antisociety nature but who had not written since getting off drugs; a photographer who would work two days a week doing photography and three days a week on a job the family approved of (particularly his wife, who had taken over for his father), who put together double-exposure images of good and bad, God and the devil, and who, though quite talented, never made good commercial deals for his work; a professional artist who is a commercial success with his light art, who is less recognized for his truly creative work, which he does for himself but is bitter over its lack of acceptance and sometimes loves it himself and sometimes hates it. The other members are also di-egophrenic but are not in the creative arts. Nonetheless, they are also conflicted and have difficulty with the emerging of their creative production from their submerged egos.

All being di-egophrenic, the group members initially could count on resistance to whatever they interpreted to others, but it soon became apparent to them that all they needed to do was switch sides to bring out the opposite point of view in their antagonist. This left all feeling safe, not being locked into complying with or rebelling against any fixed parental positions. Furthermore, on any issue they found a person who was in favor for every person who was against, or vice versa, and again felt safe in the even division that di-egophrenia created. The analyst in the group, and before long the patients as well, observed what was going on in the group and knew that something quite different was happening behind this manifest performance. This allowed many patients to get past their initial fear of being overpowered by a parent or the therapist and encouraged members to let their own submerged egos emerge. The group therapy was combined with individual therapy—for some the one was an adjunct to the other.

The results to date include the following: The accountant is painting more and has become more assertive in the business with his father. The teacher/poet is again working but without drugs. Her anger toward society remains intact, but she has decided to marry the man she lives with, concluding, "This is not to comply with my parents but because I want to." The group had encouraged her to follow her own feelings and did not themselves try to persuade her one way or the other, demonstrating their evolving understanding of others' needs. The photographer is no longer producing his images of good and evil. His work is less creative objectively, but he is doing better commercially. His ego-syntonic creativity is more conventional than his conflict-ridden productions, but he is more content. The painter is doing more creative, noncommercial work and finding more success with it, as he believes in it more. The other members are progressing as well. In fact, one computer programmer has added some creative hobbies, including art. The group has had only one casualty—a man who could not be helped, as yet, not to see the group-as-a-whole as the parents he complies with and rebels against. His solution was to split off his anger to the group and his compliance to his home, and he quit the group. He has, however, not abandoned therapy altogether, and it is hoped that eventually his group experience will be integrated differently.

In another experiment, one of the authors had the opportunity to alternate sessions with a female analyst (see Wolf and Schwartz, 1962). The purpose in organizing a group with two therapists was partly to teach and learn and partly to see the effect of introducing what might turn out to be maternal and paternal images in the persons of the two analysts. There was no uniform response to them. For some patients, both evoked parental projection. Occasionally a patient would direct negative transference toward the male therapist if there was historically greater hostility toward the father, and toward the female therapist if there was early resentment of the mother. But just as often, it appeared that members reversed parental roles. And perhaps just as frequently, patients did not use the analysts as father and mother surrogates at all but used one another instead. This experience seemed to show that there is no special advantage in introducing two analysts of different sexes. When a single therapist conducts group meetings for the duration of treatment, patients may choose some group member of the other sex than the analyst's as a representative of the missing parent. Sometimes, if the analyst is seen as a mother image, the patient will choose another male or female member as a father image. Occasionally a patient discovers two or three father and mother surrogates in the group and variously any number of sibling substitutes. Sometimes the analyst is not regarded as a parental equivalent but as a sibling or child, and parental proxies are chosen entirely from the patient membership. However, there are some few members who never seem to unsex others in projection. For them the presence of both sexes among the membership provides a target for the investment of heterosexual transference reactions, which are elicited with more difficulty when patients are obliged to project them onto a parent or sibling deputy of the same sex. Thus a mixed group enables each patient to elicit, evolve, study, and analyze projected relationships to meaningful figures of both sexes in his or her past. From this we conclude that the choice of a particular patient or of the analyst as a target for some aspect of transference depends on the extent to which certain trends in the provocative personality most nearly resemble special characteristics of an earlier familial associate.

Conclusion

Psychoanalysis in groups tries to embody, integrate, and bring into concordance the intrapsychic and the interpersonal. In the group, the interpersonal interactions are presented for scrutiny at the time of their occurrence. In a group, the attendance of a number of analysands affords the concurrent presence of hierarchical and peer vectors. The bilateral, trilateral, and quadrilateral nature of transference responses become more apparent in a group milieu. The therapist is more remote to the patient, and the patient feels closer to his copatients. Each member can experience affirmation by the stimulation and animation of others in the group. In the group, interpersonal responses are maintained by the members, and the analyst can be the disengaged but active observer. In the group, the patient may withdraw unless the analyst promotes interaction and requires attendance at alternate meetings. However, it is more difficult for the patient to resist participation entirely, because other group members demand more action, reaction, and interaction. As a consequence, all the relationships of the members are magnified and amplified. The exchange among patients is followed by analysis of intrapsychic material. A genuine cohesion follows after the liberation of the suppressed ego in each patient and the working through of his individual resistances and transferences.

Psychoanalysis in groups is an approach that emphasizes harmony growing out of disharmony, reciprocity growing out of antagonism, ego growth through persistent emphasis on supporting the suppressed ego, self-respect and respect for others in the course of the struggle, appreciation of differences, and a sense of mutual regard as treatment goes on.

21

An Integrated, Group-Centered Approach

Leonard Horwitz

The debate among analytic group therapists has shifted from the issue of which orientation to emphasize—individualistic, interactional, or group-as-a-whole—to the question of how best to integrate all three into an effective rationale for understanding group behavior and intervening most effectively. In the not too distant past, polarities tended to be set up, particularly between those with a group-as-a-whole orientation and those who focused on individuals. As in the polarities that emerge in therapy groups, each of the two camps tended to see all the virtues in its position without recognizing its shortcomings. The Tavistock method of group psychotherapy, associated mainly with Bion (1959) and Ezriel (1973), made a genuine contribution to the theory of the system properties of groups but failed to appreciate the absolute necessity of working with individuals in a way that made them feel that their needs were distinctive and not subservient to the needs of the group entity. Similarly, Wolf and Schwartz (1971) took a vigorous position against recognizing or using the dynamics of groups in group psychotherapy and, in my view, failed to exploit the powerful therapeutic effect of a group's system properties.

During the past decade there appears to have been a distinct shift toward a greater recognition among most group therapists that one must understand and utilize group dynamic forces in order to do optimal therapeutic work. For example, Redl's (1942) concept of role suction, whereby an individual's behavior is viewed not simply in terms of his or her personal dynamics but also in terms of pressures within a group for certain roles to be filled and expressed, has become an important working tool for the group therapist. A corollary concept is that of the spokesperson who is speaking not just for himself or herself but on behalf of a segment of the group that is striving to find expression. Further, there is greater acceptance of the importance of the scapegoating phenomenon, in which ambivalent attitudes toward unconscious drives get played out by first eliciting the expression of such drives and then attacking the personification of the need (Scheidlinger, 1985).

The dynamic forces in groups described above have received additional impetus from the field of general systems theory (Durkin, 1981). The concept of boundaries, for example, has helped the group therapist to formulate better an understanding of how the entry and departure of members affects the equilibrium of the whole group. Similarly, the systems idea that any change in one subsystem will affect the system as a whole has turned out to be a rigorous way of stating what many group therapists have intuitively recognized: every event in the group, every contribution by the patients and the therapist (or failure to contribute or respond), has some effect on the functioning of the entire group. Group therapists are beginning to recognize that their job is not only to listen and respond to individual members but also to track the group's functioning as an entity in order to fully understand and interpret the functioning of individual members.

The early contributors to group-centered group psychotherapy, such as Ezriel (1952), have been taken to task, directly or implicitly, by a number of writers (Malan and others, 1976; Horwitz, 1977; Day, 1981). Using research data gathered at the Tavistock Clinic, Malan and others (1976) found widespread dissatisfaction among ex–group therapy patients with the prevalent method of the group therapy staff. Patients experienced their group treatment as focused mainly on how the group was functioning and only incidentally on the psychological needs that they brought to the group. Working with a group-centered orientation in Boston, Day (1981) reported that he gradually became disillusioned with the efficacy of a method that focused almost exclusively on the dynamics of the group, because his patients tended to feel that their individual needs were slighted. A similar experience was reported by the present writer (Horwitz, 1977), who found that groupwide interventions have to be liberally interspersed with individualized comments so that patients will feel that their individual needs are not being ignored and that the therapist is empathic and reponsive to them as individuals.

Diverse Views on Integration of the Individual and the Group

The existence of a drift toward integration of individual psychodynamics and group-centered forces does not mean that all group therapists view the integrative process in the same way. Each therapist, in fact, has his or her own special emphasis on how the two facets should be joined.

One of the first efforts at integration was proposed by Yalom (1975), and his approach can best be characterized as *alternation* between attending to group and individual issues. His view was that "mass interpretations" should be given only to remove obstacles obstructing the progress of the entire group, such as anxiety-laden issues or antitherapeutic group norms. He believed that "an issue critical to the existence or functioning of the entire group always takes precedence over a narrower interpersonal issue" (p. 131). But, significantly, he stated that there is no need for mass group interpretations when the group is functioning well.

Day (1981) expressed a somewhat similar alternation view, taking the view that there are significant points in the life of the group that affect its total membership, such as the beginning phases, entry of new members, therapist's absence, and reactions to a group interpretation. At these times group behavior is best understood in terms of the dynamics of the entire group, and the interpretations should be so geared. However, when the group is working cohesively and particularly after the group "envelope," or alliance, has been formed, individual transferences become more prominent, and it behooves the therapist to address himself or herself to individuals as well as to the group. Day has expanded the indications for groupwide interventions considerably beyond the ones proposed by Yalom and rightly notes that interventions by the leader as well as contributions by members have an effect on the group as a whole. He even observes the presence of "parallel transferences" in which the so-called individualized transference elicits similar reactions in one or more fellow patients. Nevertheless, his view is basically one of alternating between groupwide interventions when indicated and individual interpretations when group issues are not paramount.

In their recent book on psychodynamic group psychotherapy, Rutan and Stone (1984) move closer to adopting an even greater degree of integration than described above. They subscribe, for example, to the idea that it is possible to make individual interpretations within a group theme and later make a group-as-a-whole interpretation in order to bring together the diverse individual interpretations. However, they have not completely let go of an alternation approach when they observe that sometimes group-as-a-whole factors are most significant, as when boundaries are being changed, and at other times group-as-a-whole processes may fade into the background, although they never disappear. At another point they state, "Not all interactions are a product of group transactions. Some represent the specific pathological configuration that emerges in the group" (p. 66). In other words, they stop just short of adopting the point of view that unitary group functioning is present *at all times* within the group.

A point of view that espouses the idea of constant underlying "common group tension" is that expressed by Stein and Kibel (1984). They believe that the basic dynamic in a group is the group's relationship to the leader. However, they contend that this leader transference tends first to be expressed by displacement onto one's peers in the form of intermember interactions. Hence they recommend that peer transferences be interpreted before the leader transference. Their system of integration is very similar to the one I propose, although I would differ with their attempt to deal with individual transferences only by way of the intermember interactions. I believe that an individual's intrapsychic conflicts have a wide variety of manifestations and that the therapist may attend to these conflicts through whatever manifestations make their appearance.

My own effort at integration, described in a previous paper (Horwitz, 1977), is an outgrowth of Ezriel's (1973) idea of a "common group tension." This group-centered hypothesis makes the assumption that a common group theme is operative at all times in the functioning of the group. This point of view represents a special case, perhaps an end point, in a continuum that conceptualizes the relation between individual behavior and the system properties of the group. Whereas "alternation" theories view the group as sometimes being mainly a system and at other times being a vehicle for expressing individual conflicts, adherents of the group-centered approach believes that a common group tension is *always* operative and that individual needs are constantly interacting with this underlying tension. It is a shared common conflict, a set of unconscious wishes and fears, which each individual in a group attempts to cope with in his or her own idiosyncratic manner.

When Ezriel (1973) described the mechanism by which a patient contributes to the development of a common group tension, he spoke of each individual's attempt to "manipulate" the other into taking a role consonant with his or her own personal needs. "The fact that every member of the group tries to do this leads to an unconsciously determined process of selection, rejection, and distortion of one another's remarks until the group arrives at what I would call the 'common denominator' of the dominant unconscious fantasies of all its members" (p. 114). What Ezriel (1959) is describing is the mechanism of projective identification as it applies to group behavior. In a recent paper (Horwitz, 1983), I have tried to explain further the development of the common group theme through this important psychic mechanism. A complete explanation of this phenomenon has yet to be attained, but our increased understanding of primitive mechanisms like projective identification has brought us closer to this goal.

This group-centered hypothesis as first formulated by Ezriel (1952) and Sutherland (1952) described the technique as follows: once the therapist was able to uncover the common group tension as well as the individual modes of dealing with it, the therapist was in the position to give a groupwide interpretation that included individualized comments to each patient. Malan's study (Malan and others, 1976) raised serious questions about the efficacy of this method in attending to the needs of individuals within the group. One might characterize the Ezriel/Tavistock system as a deductive method of interpretation in the sense that a generalized principle, the common group tension, is the bedrock, or foundation, on which the individual comments rest. I have proposed that the interpretive sequence be reversed and that an inductive method be used (Horwitz, 1977). That is, the ideal framework within which interpretive comments are made would be to begin with interventions addressed to individuals, and only after working with a few individuals would the therapist introduce a common theme that bound them together.

Superficially, the method may not appear too different from a purely individualized approach that does not attend to groupwide properties. Certainly when an individualized interpretation is offered to a patient, one might be hard put to distinguish between a group-centered and an individualized approach. The group-centered therapist will not stop, however, with individualized interpretations but, rather, will silently begin integrating the common threads among the individual productions right from the start, a process that eventually culminates in interpreting the common group tension. In this sense, the group-centered therapist is constantly attending to the common underlying themes expressed by the patients as a whole while addressing his or her interventions to various individuals. In other words, the group-centered therapist's manner of conceptualizing the process, thinking about it and mentally organizing it, is quite different from one method to the other.

An important facet of the inductive method is that once the therapist has identified a common theme and interpreted it to the group, any number of patterns of moving back and forth between individual and group comments may follow. More often than not a particular common group tension will prevail in a group for more than one session, even though one might expect that each of these sessions is likely to show some facets of the groupwide conflict emphasized more than others. But once a given theme has been uncovered, the therapist will usually be offering some combination or integration of individual and group interventions.

Previously I discussed a number of advantages that the group-centered approach offers to the group therapist (Horwitz, 1971, 1977). In my view it contributes to a cohesive and cooperative group insofar as members begin to perceive that they are more alike than different. It provides a method of effectively dealing with patients who tend to get exploited by the group process, mainly through the mechanism of scapegoating, and the group therapist's appreciation of such dynamics makes it possible to forestall adverse consequences. The concept of common group tension also contributes to a deepening of therapeutic work by viewing each member's contribution as a further step toward the elaboration of an unconscious group theme. In fact, my experience in working with this approach has led to the frequent experience of having a fuller understanding of one patient's problems after hearing other patients who follow him or her elaborate on their own experiences. The latter are able to fill out and deepen the therapist's understanding of the previous patient's problems insofar as they are dealing with additional facets of a similar conflict.

An Illustrative Group Session

The session to be described is from a group of six patients, three male and three female, in an age range of approximately twenty-five to forty and length of membership ranging from less than one year to more than five years. Diagnoses are mainly character disorders within the neurotic range, with the exception of one patient who suffers from a borderline personality disorder. The group meets twice a week.

The important events preceding the session to be reported are, first, a month-long vacation break that had ended two weeks before and, second, that a couple of months prior to vacation one of the patients who had had the longest tenure in the group had begun making plans for discharge, the termination date being set for one month after the vacation break was over. When we resumed after vacation, his attendance became somewhat sporadic, and he was absent without explanation from the current session.

During the three sessions preceding the present one, the group was mainly dealing with its hurt feelings about having been abandoned for a month by the therapist. The theme that was developing was the wish to put one's worst foot forward in order to test the devotion of loved ones. Each patient wanted proof from a significant person in his or her life or from the therapist that he would stick by the patient despite the patient's anger, his or her childishness, and any other repugnant behavior he or she might show. This theme had been played out and interpreted by the therapist in two preceding sessions and continues into the session being reported.

The session is opened by Carol, a stout thirty-two-year-old divorcee with a ten-year-old son. She says she doesn't understand the theme that occurred in the group last week. In particular, she did not understand how she would get any gratification out of becoming even heavier than she is now, because any increase in weight would only depress her. So what would be the advantage of gaining acceptance from others if she can't accept herself? Jim responds obliquely to that question by saying that my interpretation to him had made a great deal of sense. He felt at the time that it captured his situation beautifully even though at the moment he is having some difficulty in holding onto it. Karen comments that she thought a great deal about things after the last session. Jim gropes to remember what the therapist had said, which he felt was quite meaningful to him, and rather than respond to the question directly, the therapist encourages him and the rest of the group to search their memories. Jim seems to be seeking some soothing and comforting words from the therapist, since he and the rest of the group are feeling deprived.

At this point Karen begins a rather long recitation of some recent feelings and events. She first refers to the therapist's comment in the previous session that the group were feeling guilty about their neediness. The other day she bought a $30 blouse and felt terribly upset about all the money she had spent. When she talked to her live-in boyfriend about this, he gave her a hard time about her irrational reactions. Continuing in this vein, she found herself talking to another man. She doesn't think she was flirting, but once again she felt overwhelmed by guilt afterward and was on the verge of tears when she thought about it. In these two comments the patient confirms the therapist's previous observation about guilt feelings over the need for love and attention. She goes on as follows:

> I was reading this book last week, and I was so obsessed with the damn book I couldn't even think of work or concentrate on anything but the book. It's called *Touch The Wind*, and one part in the book, the reason I didn't bring it up last time—it's so upsetting, it feels like it's really stupid. But in the book this girl fell in love with this guy, and he loved her so much that she was two and a half months pregnant—and I thought maybe this was farfetched—he knew it and she didn't know it. He knew her so well that he could tell when there was any slight movement or change in her body. For some reason I got overwhelmed with that, feeling that he loved her so much that he could tell that.

Then, with some hesitation and unclarity about how her feelings about the story are related, she tells of a terrible fight she had with her fiancé. It is necessary for the group to pull the details out of her, and the story is essentially incomplete. She was drinking too much wine and began to berate him. "I'm sure I must have called him every name in the book—a million times." When pressed about what led up to it, she says she is not sure why she got as drunk as she did. She goes on to say that the next night he informed her that if she was ever that bad again, he was going to leave her.

Once again, the theme from the previous two sessions is repeated. Karen is preoccupied, using the metaphor of the story, with finding a man who would be totally devoted to her, merge symbiotically with her, to the extent of knowing her body better than she knows it herself. And this intense wish has two related effects: she uses a form of brinkmanship to test her boyfriend's devotion to her, and she behaves in a thoroughly obnoxious way, which makes her feel extremely guilty.

Jim observes that Karen's anger at her boyfriend must be based on the fact that he is intimidating her or smothering her or doing things that she resents. (Note the readiness with which he makes these observations even though Karen has made no reference at all to provocation by her boyfriend.) Carol disagrees, saying that Karen is "just throwing fits for attention—she wants to be noticed and loved, and she feels so unloved right now." Carol and Jim continue the argument about their respective interpretations, and Jim has the last word: "She needs love—she needs a lot of it. Just like we all do. And he's not giving it to her, and she's very angry about it."

The group decides to check this out with Karen and wonders whether she is feeling sexually gratified in the relationship. She responds that she does not feel as if she is getting what she wants sexually and has felt reluctant since the beginning of their relationship to ask for more sex because of the criticism he had leveled against her earlier for being too sexually demanding. The group begins questioning her about whether her sexual frustration is based on a need for closeness or is something more purely physical. Karen is uncertain but proceeds with some reflection about her feelings toward the group.

> I think he [her fiancé] just gets what is built up in the group. I think the reason I was so angry at the group last time was that I was angry at Cal's leaving. He is the last of the original group, and now there is a part of me that feels like I don't belong here anymore. I guess it's because of the high-level jobs you all have and I feel like I am in a rut with mine [factory work] and I have no desire to go back to school. Part of me feels like you guys all have more in common than I do. I feel a lot of distance from the group. Probably because I feel like I don't belong here anymore. And partly I feel that you're all in a different league than I am.

Gary, an attorney, joins in her feeling of alienation: "Well, I feel the same way, so maybe there's a lot of distance in this group. We haven't gotten back together again since Dr. Horwitz left." At this point, about a half hour into the session, the therapist enters his first interpretive comment, addressed mainly to Karen:

> It is striking to me that you feel you don't belong in this group and that other people in the group are superior to you. Maybe because of your job, but you also imply the feeling that the group is not interested in what you have to say. This feeling has surfaced particularly since we resumed after vacation. You seem to feel that you shouldn't be talking in the group and that you are getting that message from others in the group. It seems like a general feeling that people in the group think they shouldn't be so assertive in here. I think it's related to the wish to get more from the group, to get more attention, more love, more concern, and again feeling guilty about all that greed to get it all for yourself. We were talking about that particularly with respect to Carol last time, and I think it is coming out again in your relationship with your fiancé where you feel that he's not attentive enough or loving enough or sexual enough and you put him to the test. You get drunk, you berate him, and then if he sticks around, you practically push him over the edge and defy him to leave. The fact that he doesn't proves to you that you're not as bad as you feel you are.

The most significant aspect of this intervention is the primary focus on an individual with a deemphasis on groupwide observations. The comment is addressed primarily to the main speaker, Karen, and is an effort to explain her feelings of being shunned by the group because of her inordinate wishes for love and nurturance, which induce guilt and feelings of worthlessness. In talking about the fracas with her fiancé, she herself had come close to understanding her frustration with the group and how she had acted out the transference with him. There is an implication in my comments that the patient's feeling of frustration and anger with me around the long vacation separation was a shared feeling in the group, but this is not made explicit and perhaps could have been. Her preoccupation with the story about the lover who knew the woman's body better than she did implies an eroticized transference to the therapist, which also could have been addressed. Probably I was responding to Karen's attributing her frustration to peer relationships, her feelings about Cal's termination, and her sense of inferiority to the other members, so that I focused on her feelings toward the group. In addition, since the group theme had already been explicated in the previous session, the relatively weak emphasis on groupwide feelings may be justified by the fact that each individual is now likely to translate the therapist's comments into personally relevant observations.

Carol responds to the intervention with the observation that she experienced a considerable resentment toward her ten-year-old son last night because he was demanding love and attention from her and since it was something she was wanting for herself, she had difficulty in responding to him. She was able to understand his special needs and even his right to make these demands. In fact, he has been able to make his transition back home after his annual summer visit with his father more smoothly than in the past. The therapist then encourages her to think about how my comments to Karen might apply to her, and she observes, without much conviction, that she attempts to test others' love by overeating. Gary tries to help her think about this: "How about this? You're making people prove they really like you because they like you even when you're fat." And Carol basically agrees by responding, "She gets drunk and I eat."

At this point the therapist reminds her of the breakup of a romantic relationship that occurred a few months earlier and suggests there is still more work to be done on that. Carol acknowledges the need to do so but rather quickly shifts to Brenda, who has been relatively silent during much of this discussion. Despite being coaxed by the group, all Brenda is ready to say at this point is "I'm very confused." Jim takes advantage of the lull to announce that he will be absent next session. Carol asks him for details and Jim explains that he is attending a family reunion. "I don't have much family left. They really care for me." Karen suggests that perhaps he has the desire to go home because of how he is feeling about the group. Jim denies this, stating that he feels as though he has made progress in the group and he hopes his family will notice the difference. The group is not ready to let him off the hook that easily and points out that the fact that his individual therapist (he is the only patient in combined treatment) is gone at the present time also makes him want to go "back to the womb." Jim is aware of such feelings himself and elaborates that he is not getting from his girlfriend what he needs. "I really don't want to talk anymore. I want so much in here that what I do is become overly aggressive as a way of reaching out and saying, 'Love me, too,' but I get too angry and then feel guilty." Carol reassures him that everyone in here does that. "I eat, Karen drinks."

At this point Gary joins in to observe that this weekend he drank too much and "maybe it was guilt about wanting so much attention." It was unusual because he has pretty much given up liquor and marijuana. The therapist notes that this is the first time Gary has mentioned this important change. Gary agrees that he had finally come to the conclusion that being in a half-drugged state was only perpetuating his difficulty in getting himself mobilized in his career. "It's hard to work and be stoned all the time." He speaks of his awareness that his new professional responsibilities require that he be as alert as possible when doing his work. He goes on for a bit about the strains he is experiencing in his efforts to establish himself as a professional.

At this point Karen turns to Brenda and wants to know what is so confusing for her. Brenda responds in a rather distraught and chaotic way that she is feeling terrified, her heart is pounding, that she is frightened of Dr. Horwitz and doesn't know why. She is feeling discouraged and "really pissed off." Why does she have to be so dependent, she asks? She has the feeling of having to start all over in the group. With some encouragement she begins to relate that as soon as she feels that she is doing well in something, such as her work, she experiences the need to start drinking or messing up in some way. She feels unable to stop. With regard to men, she has had some "male acknowledgment lately," but she has just pushed them away and doesn't know why or what she is looking for. Then she reveals that she has been getting a lot of attention from a man she has been seeing lately—the first time she has revealed it in the group. Karen becomes quite provoked with her for not having mentioned this before, and Brenda defends herself by saying that the relationship does not really mean anything to her. She is not interested in him, but he persists, and so she occasionally relents and goes out with him. Under some pressure from the group she acknowledges that she has slept with him on a couple of occasions, and the group, particularly the women, confront her with the fact that she is engaging in some very self-destructive behavior in having a sexual relationship with a man she does not care for. The therapist reinforces this idea by stating, "I think what might be going on is that you're feeling sad about yourself and badly about having sexual relations with someone you don't like." The patient acknowledges that she is feeling embarrassed about it, and the group then begins to focus on whether this relationship started just before the therapist's vacation. Carol puts it bluntly: "Dr. Horwitz, the love of your life, is gone, so screw him, I'll screw you." Brenda acknowledges her anger at the therapist for leaving and her difficulty in trusting him because "I just didn't want him to leave."

In a somewhat competitive way Jim wants to know whether Brenda has any difficulty in trusting him, considering that he will not be present at the next meeting. Brenda is not sure how she feels about that. Carol interprets this question to Jim with the comment that perhaps he is asking whether Brenda will still be here when he returns and then generalizes it to the group: Will the group bar the door when he returns? At this point the therapist makes the following intervention, mainly to Jim:

> The fact that you haven't talked about it is also an indication that you think it's not an interesting subject for anybody to care about your absence. After all, it's just for one time and isn't going to make any difference to anybody. Maybe they won't even notice it. It seems as though you almost forgot to tell us about it, and the lack of importance you are attaching to it expresses the fact that you seem to think that you have very little importance in this group. Now what I wanted

to say to Brenda was that I think your starting this sexual relationship with this man around the time of vacation is expressing the wish
to get more love from somebody since you are lacking love from me.
But at the same time I think it involves a kind of self-punishment in
the same way we were observing from the others, punishing yourself
for having such wishes.

Brenda responds by claiming that she has been relatively passive in the relationship with this man, although she is aware that she is doing nothing to stop it. The
therapist continues:

Also with this man you're in some ways giving him a signal
that you're receptive while at the same time saying to yourself, "He
doesn't mean a damn thing to me." That may be what you're also
experiencing in here, and you're turning the tables on him and treating
him in the way that you feel you're being treated here.

Brenda asks for some elaboration of that. The therapist explains, "Being encouraged
to express feelings in here and at the same time experiencing yourself as being
rebuffed." Carol attempts to reinforce that point by saying that Brenda is both
encouraging this man and at the same time pushing him away. Brenda acknowledges
that what she is doing with this man is not something she is proud of, and at this
point the time is up.

The last half of the session, which mainly involved Brenda and Jim, was
a further elaboration of the theme of hurt feelings experienced by the group in relation
to the therapist's vacation. Jim's belated announcement of his plans to be away
to attend a family reunion reflected mainly the wish to find a replacement for the
nurturance and comfort that he was not getting in the group. My interpretation
to him also stressed the low self-esteem that he was experiencing in the group, shown
in his minimizing the importance of his absence from the group. This dimension
had already emerged earlier in the session with Karen's feelings of inferiority vis-
à-vis the other members, seconded by Gary, who also felt that no one really cared
to listen to him. Another facet of Jim's absence that could have been further explored was Jim's competitive and retaliative wishes toward the therapist. He seemed
to be saying, in effect, that the therapist was not the only one who could take the
initiative in leaving the group, and the theme of guilt and self-punishment was apparent in his fantasy of being locked out when he returned.

Brenda's special contribution to the group theme was not unlike the self-
destructive acting out described earlier by Karen. Karen's guilt about her greed
for love and nurturance led her to behavior that threatened the stability of an ongoing
and valued relationship with her fiancé. She gained reassurance from his willingness
to tolerate her behavior, and she gained self-punishment from his disapproval of
her obnoxious display. Similarly, Brenda found a suitor to express his love, but
her contempt for the man vented her anger displaced from the therapist. She was
both identifying with the therapist as aggressor in leading this man on and at the
same time treating herself rather contemptuously in maintaining an intimate relationship with a man who meant nothing to her. Thus, the common threads that
ran through the session were the intertwined themes of seeking love and reassurance

to compensate for the therapist's abandonment, the guilt for having such intense needs, and the lowered self-esteem in relation to the abandonment and greed.

Conclusions

Earlier in this chapter I emphasized that the ideal model of interpretation is an inductive one in which the group therapist gradually builds up a series of individual interventions into an overarching groupwide intervention. The session just described illustrates this model but only in its general spirit and, I hope, not in a rigidified way. First, all models and rationales for clinical intervention are guides and ways of thinking rather than strict rules that must be adhered to at all costs. In effect, the group therapist should ideally establish his or her own preferred system of working in a group and integrating the dynamics of the group with interpersonal and intrapsychic material. Once having developed a method, the group therapist should respond flexibly and creatively to the changing context and varying needs as they are expressed at any given moment.

Second, therapy is an ongoing process that should not be segmented into individual sessions. Any particular session must be understood in light of significant events that preceded it. An inductive method is most relevant when a group theme is in the process of unfolding. Thus, the theme in this group had already emerged and had been interpreted; hence, my comments involved some degree of moving back and forth between an already explicated common group tension and individual conflicts that were being elaborated by the patients and explicated within a group framework. The therapist's interventions in this session emphasized individual content, but in each case the common group theme was either alluded to or implied.

There has been an increasing recognition in the group psychotherapy literature of the importance of group-centered thinking and group-centered interventions in trying to integrate the important dynamics of the entire group with the significant intrapsychic dynamics of individual patients. A rather wide range of models have been proposed to effect such an integration. These range from "alternation" views, specific and limited indications for when a group-centered intervention should be made, to the view expressed in this chapter that a common group tension is present at all times within the group. Many authors espouse the belief that a commonly shared group theme emerges only intermittently; on other occasions individual issues are of paramount importance. In this chapter I have attempted to develop the thesis that the preferred conception of integrating group and individual issues is a theory of an omnipresent common group tension, fueled mainly by a process of projective identification moving back and forth among the various members. Care for the individual needs of each member can best be assured by an inductive method in which a patient's content is interpreted individually until a shared group theme clearly emerges, at which time a group-centered intervention is offered.

❧ 22 ❧

Encounter Groups

Will Schutz

Although encounter groups have antecedents in many areas (see Schutz, 1973, for review), their most immediate predecessor was the T-group (for *training group*), developed in the late 1940s by a group of students of Kurt Lewin who formed the National Training Laboratories (NTL). The form evolved in several directions, primarily as sensitivity training and then as encounter groups.

The passions aroused by such groups often led to radical outbursts. In the heyday of encounter groups, the late 1960s and early 1970s, they were extolled and vilified with great fervor. The groups were praised/travestied in such motion pictures as *Bob and Carol and Ted and Alice*, bastardized as "nude encounters," transported to India by Bhagwan Rajneesh's ashram to aid in enlightenment, and eventually forsworn by the very institutions which had developed them and which had profited from their impact.

During the 1970s NTL attempted to distance itself from the T-group, preferring to identify its activities as organizational development. The UCLA business school, where sensitivity training evolved, has gradually diminished its emphasis in favor of sociotechnical and other less personally oriented approaches. Similarly, the Esalen Institute, in Big Sur, California, where open encounter groups became nationally known, made strong attempts to minimize encounter, even to eliminate it from its offerings.

Many reasons were given for disavowing the encounter form: too violent, too sexual, too confronting, too insensitive to social factors, too brief, performed by untrained leaders, too self-indulgent, too uncompassionate, too narrow a focus, too unintellectual, too hedonistic, leaders too exploitive and manipulative of group members, too unproved, too out of control, and, generally, too dangerous. In my opinion, there was some basis for all these charges, especially in the early days when the limits of the encounter form were being tested. Problems in groups were widely publicized, often startlingly exaggerated or distorted.

Because incidents could be culled from most psychotherapies to paint a lurid picture, the vehemence behind the criticisms of encounter suggested overdetermination. It appeared that, in addition to the legitimate shortcomings of encounter, there were some personal issues being elicited by the technique.

This vehemence was underscored by a remarkable phenomenon that occurs periodically in the history of science when the likelihood that some method is wrong or bad (or the desire that it be) is so high that research confirming its negative nature is warmly welcomed and uncritically accepted. Such was the case with a pivotal book called *Encounter Groups: First Facts* (Lieberman, Yalom, and Miles, 1973). Because this research report found that the ''casualties'' in encounter groups approached 10 percent, critics seized on this finding to give their opinions a scientific basis. However, more careful and scholarly considerations of the contents of the book (Rowan, 1975, Russell, 1978) revealed that by almost all scientific and experiential criteria the book was fatally flawed. And although the quality of the research was such that virtually no conclusions could be drawn, what could be salvaged from the work indicated that, contrary to the authors' assertions, encounter group methods are somewhat more effective than therapy group methods (Russell, 1978).

Although there were obviously many other factors as well, including a readiness to dismiss encounter, in retrospect this book played a significant role in diminishing the enthusiasm for encounter.

Despite this adverse trend, in the late 1970s and early 1980s encounter groups existed under a variety of names—process groups, human relations groups, consciousness-raising groups, communications groups, truth groups, and so on. They were not identical with encounter but were strongly influenced by it. Marriage encounter flourished, as did the human relations groups at NTL.

At Esalen, at least, there are new indications of a second look at encounter after several years. Some are seeing the values of encounter—truth, self-determination and self-awareness, in particular—as essential ingredients of any therapeutic or educational process, and an interest in reexamining encounter is detectable.

Now, in 1985, there seems to be a resurgence of interest in encounter, especially by professionals too young to have lived through its evolution. In at least one approach (Schutz, 1984) it is the basis for a very successful program for increasing organizational productivity and morale. It is particularly timely to see what encounter is really about.

Definition of Encounter

Encounter is a method of human relating based on truth, self-determination, self-awareness, awareness of the body, attention to feelings, and an emphasis on the here and now.[1] It usually occurs in a group setting. Encounter is therapy insofar as it focuses on removing blocks to better functioning. Encounter is education in that it attempts to create conditions leading to the fullest use of personal capacities.

Encounter usually takes place in a group of eight to fifteen persons in a room with a rug, almost devoid of furniture; all participants sit on the floor or on pillows, but some chairs are available. An encounter workshop usually consists of several meetings, each typically two hours long, spread over a weekend or over five days. Ages vary from fifteen to seventy-five; most participants are between twenty and fifty. The workshop is held in a residential setting where all participants live. There is no formal agenda. Group members focus on discovering and expressing their feelings

---

[1]Much of this material is adapted from *Elements of Encounter* (Schutz, 1973).

in the here and now. The group leader helps them to clarify these feelings. All these conditions for a group are quite variable. The workshop just described is typical of those I will discuss.

There are wide variations in groups called encounter groups and in groups that are called by almost synonymous names, such as T-groups and sensitivity training groups. Even the term *encounter* is used in different ways by authors and practitioners. The approach described in this chapter, I have called "open encounter," to distinguish it from the various other encounter groups. Rogers (1970), for example, has used the term *basic encounter* to name his approach. For simplicity, the term *encounter* will be used throughout, but it should always be understood to mean open encounter.

Principles of Encounter

Unity of the Organism. You are a unified organism. You are at the same time physical, intellectual, emotional, esthetic, and spiritual. These levels are all manifestations of the same essence. You function best when these aspects are integrated and when you are self-aware.

Truth. Truth is at the heart of encounter. Truth means both not lying to or withholding from others (honesty) and avoiding self-deception (awareness).

Honesty and openness are the keys to your evolutionary growth. Being honest allows your bodymind to become a clear channel for taking in all the energy of the universe, both inside and outside your body, and for using it profitably. You must expend great amounts of energy to hide your feelings, thoughts, or wishes from other people and even more energy to keep them from yourself. To withhold secrets requires a tightened body; it requires curtailment of spontaneity lest the secrets be revealed; it requires vigilance, shallow breathing, physical exertion, and a preoccupation with your own safety. As a result, you miss all sorts of stimuli because your bodymind is not relaxed enough to allow them in. The beautiful sights and sounds in nature must not be lingered on too long; the beauty or just the reality of other people cannot be seen clearly because their nuances are too subtle to be caught with rushed glance; the feelings and signals coming from within your own body are strangled by tense muscles, drowned in excess words, or starved from lack of air when you are spending great amounts of energy shaping your appearance in the world.

Self-Determination. Encounter stresses self-determination. We explore the possibility that you choose everything in your life. You choose it (1) because there is a payoff (2) both consciously and unconsciously (without awareness—you also choose what you do and do not want to be aware of). Saying that you choose is not a judgment. It is a problem-solving concept, a framework for discovering what is happening. If you feel guilty or ashamed of a choice you made, that is regarded as another choice, the choice to feel guilty, which also has a payoff.

Since you determine whatever you are, you can change. You are not the victim of forces beyond yourself.

The choice assumption is offered to you not as a right-or-wrong concept. You are invited to explore the notion and see to what extent it is useful to you. You are, of course, free to use or discard any part or all of the idea.

It is important that joining a group be entirely voluntary. If you, as a potential group member, do not feel ready to go to a group or if you have a dread of being brainwashed, denuded, robbed of all privacy, made dependent, or any of the other horrors vividly described by Koch (1971), Argyris (1966), and others, your path is clear: Don't go. As the group leader, I routinely announce that you are responsible for making the choice of entering the encounter group and that you are responsible for everything that happens to you during the life of the group. All choices about yourself are yours. You may choose to have your brain washed or to use your judgment, to go crazy or to be sane, to learn something or to be inert, to be bored or to be interested, to enjoy or to be miserable, to resist or welcome efforts at opening you up, to reveal your sexual intimacies or to keep them secret, to be physically injured or to remain intact. I regard you as capable of being responsible for yourself.

By assuming that you are responsible, I feel I elicit your stronger parts. If I assume that you are not capable of being responsible, I tend to infantilize you and elicit your weaker parts. The medical model, "I am your doctor, and I have the knowledge and ability to cure you, and you are the patient who is sick and requires my help," I see as often debilitating.

Awareness. A main purpose of encounter is to help you become more aware of yourself: to break through self-deception, to know and like yourself, to feel your own importance, to respect what you are and can do, and to learn to be self-determining. You achieve these best through self-awareness.

Awareness is a lifelong process. To live most fully, you must be able to feel all parts of your body, to be able to know what you are feeling at all times, to be aware of your needs and motives, no matter how petty or unacceptable, to recognize the personal consequences of your actions, and to integrate all parts of yourself. I believe that an organism in full awareness will choose those actions that are most beneficial for itself and that a group of organisms functioning together, all in full awareness, will form the most satisfactory society.

Self-deception leads to manipulative behavior, to exploitation, to dehumanization, and, ultimately, to unhappiness and lack of productivity. Awareness allows you to make decisions with a maximum of accurate data.

Naturalness. I trust natural processes. My reliance on natural unfolding extends to virtually every facet of human functioning. Encounter involves removing psychological blocks so that you can flow freely and naturally. Body methods used in encounter aim at removing physical blocks so that your energy can flow freely. Confidence in the natural flow of human energy extends to many areas of experience. The ideal diet is one that your aware body selects as its way of maintaining health; the preferred forms of medicine are those that remove obstacles to your body's processes for healing itself; the preferred group situation is one that lets you unfold; the preferred social organization is one that removes blocks to self-determination.

Way of Life. Encounter is a way of life, not just a therapeutic technique. It concerns itself with relations among people and offers an alternative to the present structure of society, a structure based on deception ("diplomacy"), masking feelings ("tact"), disowning the body ("rationality," "civilization," "taste"), avoiding responsibility ("luck," "fate"), and similar duplicities. It aims at helping people to be truthful, aware, and self-determining.

Encounter appreciates and emphasizes feelings as well as thoughts. It recognizes the central place of feelings in the internal and interpersonal aspects of people and devises means for recognizing and dealing effectively with them. It recognizes the centrality of the body in human affairs, the truth that resides there, and the body's role as the repository of a person's history and as the source of a person's pleasure. Encounter accepts the unity of the organism and the importance of working at all levels simultaneously. It recognizes the importance of naturalness and reality, of going back to the natural organism, and of knowing and accepting the truth of what a person is without overburdening a person with "shoulds."

Encounter differs from most other group methods in that it stresses body methods, nonverbal techniques, and guided daydream fantasies. It also emphasizes self-determination and expands the meaning of that term to include choosing for the state of your body.

The major reason for incorporating a large variety of methods into encounter is that nothing works for everyone. It is more valuable to determine the conditions under which each method works most effectively than to determine which among various methods is the "best." The idea that people are different from one another, though one of the least controversial ideas in psychology, is rarely thoroughly implemented. There are persons whose lives are dramatically changed through a weekend encounter and others who are relatively unaffected by several groups. The same can be said of persons who undergo psychoanalysis, psychodrama, behavior therapy, Gestalt, fantasy, rolfing, or virtually any other method. The challenge is to find out (1) for which people, (2) at what points in their personal development, and (3) with which leader each method or pattern of methods works best. My aim as an encounter group leader is to become proficient in as many techniques as I find useful and, through experience, to learn when to use each.

Technique: Follow the Energy

One of the most important phenomena to which a group leader must become sensitive is energy, both group and individual. As a leader, I am most effective when I follow the energy.

A look around an encounter group will reveal people in very different states. Some are relaxed; they have no pressing issue. If the group focuses on these people, the result is usually a dull and lifeless interchange without feeling or energy. Vital group interactions happen when the group goes to where the energy is. If you, as a member, are holding yourself tight, I, as the leader, may move on to someone else and count on the group interaction to loosen you up so that you can work better later, or I may choose to try now to help you break through that defense. My first step might be to ask you to relax by unlocking your arms and legs, if you have them crossed, by standing up and shaking yourself loose, or by jiggling and breathing deeply for several minutes. If a particular part of your body seems tight, either I or a group member might massage it. From this point on, I pay attention to how your body responds as you talk and act. I assume that your feeling is focused where you are tightening or jiggling, and that is where it will be the most valuable to work.

Sometimes you may be wound up too tight to be able to function. In this case, I encourage you to do something physical, such as beat on some pillows or scream. This action helps to drain off enough energy so that you can begin to work with the real problem. If the issue seems to be competition, an arm wrestle may help mobilize and focus the energy. The strength of your anger, jealousy, or competition may become apparent when your whole body is involved in combat, whereas sitting and talking allows you to hide this feeling from yourself.

You may be ready to work in a group but need support. When you clear your throat, it often means that you want to say something but you inhibit yourself. Throat clearing often functions as a request for attention. Or you may ask for support by looking depressed, by crying, by withdrawing, by making sarcastic comments, or by any behavior that calls attention to yourself. My interest and initiative may be sufficient to help you start to deal with your held-in energy.

Once you start to work, that is, to talk or act on an issue, I keep an eye on your energy. You may start to work but then begin to intellectualize, at which point the tone of your voice will change from one filled with emotion to one that is casual and controlled. Some of your visible body tension will dissipate or go deeper into your body.

Green Apples. Bullshit (the technical term for talk unconnected to feeling) is frequently a good fertilizer and makes other material grow more fully. It may permit a more complete working-through and may also give me clues to where to go next with the emerging material. The focus on the energy must be maintained, however, or defenses may take over and the value of the work will be dissipated. An inexperienced leader often falls prey to the "green apples" phenomenon. When I was a new leader, in my eagerness to test out my abilities I often seized the first feeling presented in the group and started to work on it with great flourish and virtuosity. The difficulty was that I frequently chose a shallow feeling not attached to much energy. After the first exchange, the feeling was gone and the action degenerated into shallow wordiness. My choice to pursue a given opening is better made after getting a sense that the apple is ripe, that the feelings being expressed are deep and are backed by significant energy. Dull groups result from the pursuit of energyless issues.

Less Is More. As I become more skilled, more happens in my groups with less effort on my part. When I am sensitive to where in the group the energy and feeling lie, I can help the group to focus its energy on them. Then every group event is meaningful and valuable. As others work through deep feelings, the group becomes a safer place to work. If you, a timid member, see others working ineffectually and with less feeling that you know you have inside yourself, the group will seem an unsafe place for you. Your feelings are deep, and you have no assurance that feelings of such depth can be dealt with in this group.

Completion. Energy also indicates when a person has finished working on a problem. When you really have resolved an issue, your energy is discharged, your body relaxed. Completion can be checked by observing your body; does it look relaxed, or are there still some parts that are tight? Are you still jiggling or picking at the carpet? Is your voice tight or relaxed? Does your face look relaxed, or is it still tight? Is your breathing full or shallow? These and other clues tell when the issue is resolved, and the indicators are usually quite clear. It is important to follow through until you are fully relaxed. If you still seem tense, even though you appear finished, I will explore the issue in greater depth. Completion is usually signaled by an involuntary deep breath.

Dissipators. The concept of energy clarifies how substances such as tobacco, aspirin, and alcohol impede group progress. They dissipate energy and therefore prevent its use in a profitable way. When you desire these aids, it is likely that your anxiety is aroused. Smoking and drinking flatten feeling. In a recent group, a girl started to light up a cigarette at the end of a meeting. I asked her what she might be anxious about.

"Nothing," she replied. "I always light up when I feel relaxed. I've been smoking for years. It's just a habit."

"Anything happen in the meeting that might have upset you?"

"No, it was a very nice session."

"Were you attracted to anyone in the group?" (I thought I had detected a flirtation.)

"Well, yes—one young man."

"Was he attracted to you?"

"I don't know." Her voice dropped.

"Who is it?"

She pointed to a young man who was just lighting up a cigarette. As this vignette unfolded, the anxiety around the possible unrequited attraction became obvious, and the significance of the cigarette as an indicator became apparent. Had she simply finished her cigarette, her anxiety might have been alleviated sufficiently that she need not have dealt with her attraction, and perhaps she would have been able to keep her anxiety out of her awareness. When I walk into an encounter group that is enshrouded in cigarette smoke, I expect that nothing of much significance is happening; much of the usable energy of the group has gone up in smoke.

As an energy cycle is completed, I look around the group for clues to where to go next. The cycle has probably affected many members. I focus on the persons with the most energy. This helps maintain a high level of energy in the group as a whole.

Decision Making. The concept of energy clarifies the group decision-making process. In making a decision, the group goes through an energy cycle. Completion of this cycle is indicated by the body relaxation of each group member. If such relaxation has not occurred, the group is not fully ready to implement its decision, and retrogression may occur. Completion of an energy cycle will usually make a permanent change in the person and in a group.

To ascertain whether the group members are ready to go along with a decision, I ask the members individually and note their reactions. Any response other than a clear "yes" almost always means "No, I'm not yet ready to go along with the decision."

Unreadiness to go along may be indicated by any occurrence that prevents an easy flow of the decision-making process. Expressions such as "Would you repeat the decision again?," "I don't understand the question," or "It's time for lunch," as well as nonverbal cues of discomfort or boredom, may indicate unreadiness. If this unreadiness is ignored, a decision can be reached more quickly. This speed, however, is illusory, since compliance with the decision is far slower.

When I detect your unreadiness, I encourage you to discuss your objections more fully. When you feel that your position has been understood and your feelings have been acknowledged and you see that the group still opposes you, usually you are willing to acquiesce, even though you still personally disagree. At this point, the group energy cycle is complete and each member is ready to comply. This situation is known as group consensus. Often, however, discussion of the dissenting view may influence other members to change their minds. You may be voicing a feeling that lay dormant in them.

First Feelings. When you fail to recognize the first feeling that occurs to you in response to some action, and you act instead off a second feeling, usually a defense, communication becomes distorted. In a recent group one person said to another, "I think what you just did was phony," to which the second replied, "Well, if you didn't like it, why didn't you stop me?"

"I didn't stop you because it's not up to me to teach you how to behave."

Since the first feeling was omitted from each statement, their verbalizing grew more and more irrelevant. If each man had been in touch with his first feeling, the interchange might have gone like this:

"I think what you did was phony."

"I feel hurt when you say that; then I feel angry."

"I'm sad that it hurts you. I don't want you to dislike me." The next interchange might have gone like this:

"Well, if you didn't like it, why didn't you stop me?"

"I feel guilty when you say that. I feel as you do. I feel sad and despondent. I feel that I never speak up when I should."

The overlooked feelings of hurt in the first case, and of guilt and sadness in the second, were the first feelings. The anger and debating were defensive reactions to hide the first feelings. Because the interchange continued at this defensive level, it remained relatively unproductive. Had the focus been directed to the first feelings, each of the men might have become aware of them, and the words and feelings would have been congruent. This would have been an example of productive verbalizing. The exchange that actually took place is an example of bullshit.

Nonverbal Methods. Use of nonverbal methods may rob you of your verbal defenses. When talk seems to be making things less clear, I may ask the principals to continue communicating but without words. When the anger is high, you may growl. At other times you may hug, shake hands, or turn your back. When nonverbal techniques are used, real feeling tends to emerge spontaneously.

When the first feeling is ignored, the interaction that follows may have a phony, wheel-spinning quality. A technique for redirecting the focus to the first feeling is to follow nonverbal cues, such as facial expressions, postures, and breathing. Ignoring first feelings is a frequent source of marital difficulties. One husband always came home and made an offhand remark to his wife, who then started nagging. When this situation was examined, it turned out that she felt he often belittled her intelligence. Not having gone to college, she was very sensitive about her intelligence. Her response was deep hurt, of which she was unaware. Her defense was to put him down at every opportunity, as if to say, "You see, you're not so smart either." When he became aware that he was hurting her, his whole attitude toward her changed, as did her attitude toward him. They were able to turn a fighting situation into one of mutual exploration; this transformation is a crucial turning point for any couple.

When the energy is directed to the first feeling, there is frequently an exchange of human warmth previously prevented by defensive behavior. One man had a fixed smile that irritated almost everyone. He was phony, unreachable, and saccharine, and many members simply withdrew from him. When he dropped his smile, the sadness behind it became obvious to the others. Their feeling of irritation changed to a desire for emotional and physical closeness. He relaxed and started to confide some of his fears about the present situation. Others were empathizing. These were feelings that they could recognize personally, and they began to feel closer to him.

Group Development. To assess quickly where a group is in its development, I use methods that combine energy fields, nonverbal behavior, and the concepts of inclusion, control, and openness (Schutz, 1984). To assess group *inclusion,* I ask group members to walk around the room silently, without trying to "figure out" what they want to do, until they find the place that feels most comfortable to them. This exercise quickly reveals who feels in the group and who feels out. Some members drift toward the corner, some seek the center; some turn their backs, some face one person and shun others; subgroups form. The important element of this exercise is the elimination of thinking and the use of body feeling to lead to the place of comfort and to avoid the places of discomfort. In terms of energy, this process focuses on the interaction of the energy fields of the group members. Compatible members draw each other close, and incompatible members repel each other.

The dominance line is an excellent procedure for assessing the *control* energies in the group. My instructions are "Without thinking about it and without words, arrange yourselves in a straight line. If you feel that you are a dominant person, go to the head of the line, and if you feel you are a submissive person, go to the back of the line. Find what feels like your proper place. If others are already there, feel free to remove them." Scuffles often break out in the front or even in the middle of the line. Some members back away, and some wait until the scuffling stops, then sneak in at the front. Control relations become clear through the use of aggressive energy.

To assess the *openness* area, I suggest, "Silently look into each other's eyes, then simultaneously explore each other's faces with your hands." This intimacy immediately informs you about how the others feel about you. You may hug; you may feel your energy merge with that of others; you may experience fear and hastily go on to the next face; you may become detached and begin an exploration of facial anatomy. However you react, your feelings about openness become clearer to yourself.

Thus, in twenty to thirty minutes, by using body energies and by blocking out verbalizing and cerebrating, it is possible to obtain a clear notion of where a group stands with regard to each of the three interpersonal areas.

Unity in Depth. As the group explores deeper feelings, it develops a feeling of the unity of humanity. When a group is allowed to stay at the level of defenses, the amount of human exchange is minimal and superficial, as at a cocktail party. As defenses are penetrated, a recognition dawns of the universality of the human condition, of the sameness of human needs, fears, and hopes. Criticism of others seems pointless, and the search for a mutual accommodation begins. Deep hatred toward anyone is very difficult to maintain when you are encountering that person. This does not mean that you will like everyone whom you encounter at this deep level. It means, rather, that your understanding is greatly increased and your fear reduced.

Although it may seem paradoxical, deeper groups are safer groups. When a group has shared deep feelings, the closeness that results gives you someone to go to, a friend, a roommate, a group member, should you find yourself in emotional difficulty. The sharing of humanity, the energy that comes from the center of each member, often gives this phase of a group a mystical or spiritual quality. As the feeling of the unity of humankind becomes a reality, the members who looked so strange, alien, and undesirable at the beginning of the group unfold into people who share with you the same psychological underworld.

Case Study

In order to make these theoretical ideas more concrete, I shall present an example of some work done in a group in which I was the leader. It illustrates a variety of methods and provides an example of changing from one technique to another to follow the energy as it moves, both within the group and within the individual.

Peony joined a five-day group of twelve members, some with group experience and some without. Peony was an attractive, twenty-seven-year-old woman. She came to the group with her male friend because she wanted to learn about groups, to improve her relationship with her friend, and to feel more comfortable around other people. She had grown up in a small town in England and was more experienced and comfortable with nature and animals than with people.

By the fourth day, she had said barely a word and seemed quite content with her passive role. No one in the group had made any attempt to bring her out.

Observing. Helen began working on a problem with her mother, using a Gestalt-psychodramatic technique. Helen let a pillow represent her mother and expressed her resentment at being pushed away from her mother too early. She became angry, pounded the pillow, cried. Then she changed roles and became her mother. As "mother," she explained to "Helen" (the pillow) the problem she had had in raising a family without a father. After working this through to a point of relaxation, Helen retired to a corner. At this point, several group members observed that Peony was crying.

Blocking. They were solicitous of Peony, but she would say little. Her voice was very tiny. I sensed that Peony blocked her feelings at her throat. A look at her body indicated a narrow chest, shallow breathing, and a tightness around the throat. Apparently, feelings were present in Peony, but she held them down through lack of breathing and tension in the vocal cords. I suggested that she scream. This is sometimes an effective way to break through and relax the blocking throat muscles. After a few futile efforts, Peony stopped with a look of despair. Some group members offered to scream with her if it would help. She agreed. We all screamed together. Then Peony screamed by herself, a loud, long scream that sounded as if it had been held back a long time. She took a deep breath, smiled, and looked pleased with herself.

Mobilizing. Peony was asked about the tears she had shed, and she looked very frightened and became immobile. She could say only that she could feel the same kind of anger toward her mother that Helen had felt. Peony's voice was now stronger, but she faltered quickly and withheld her breathing. I asked her whether there was anyone in the group similar to her mother. She said Josie. Then I asked her whether she would be willing to arm-wrestle with Josie. This was my attempt to mobilize both the anger and the breathing that Peony was suppressing. Arm wrestling requires a great deal of energy, deep breathing, and a strong contact with the other person through exchanging energy with that person. I felt that these requirements would help Peony become aware of her feelings and be able to express them more easily. In addition, her opponent had an important symbolic meaning, that of a mother figure.

Peony and Josie agreed to go ahead. I suggested that they lie on the floor, raise forearms, look each other in the eye, and make noises as loud and as primitive as they could while trying to put down each other's arms. Peony threw herself into the fray with great gusto, and amazing strength came from her frail body. After several minutes of struggle, they stopped, exhausted. Peony looked full of life. Her face had color, her eyes sparkled, she seemed very content. She and Josie spontaneously hugged, and Peony returned to her place in the circle. I interpreted her relaxed appearance in several ways. It meant that the problem with her mother was resolved for the moment. She had made a certain amount of progress, indicated by going from tears to relaxation. If she had still shown some body tension, I would have encouraged her to continue working. Either the mother problem was not very deep, or, more likely, the next level of working on this issue would wait to present itself at a later time. Peony's whole appearance was vital. It was as if, through the physical exertion and the group support, she had relaxed enough to feel comfortable joining the group.

Contact. Peony sat for an hour or so while other events went on in the group. At one point I sensed that there were several pairs of persons who had not fully resolved their relationships; I suggested that these pairs have lunch together and have two-person encounters (dyads). At this suggestion, Peony reported feeling terror. Her discomfort in meeting people directly had been tapped. Probably because of her earlier experience of screaming, she was now able to express her terror to the group. Her small-town background and orientation toward nature and "things" had not prepared her well for encountering people. I asked her whether she would be willing to go to each person in the group and make some kind of contact. This was an attempt to bring her generalized fear of people into the here and now so that she would experience it directly, rather than simply verbalize it. She could feel the fear with her whole body and could differentiate the kinds of fear she felt with different people.

Peony agreed, and the group members and I stood in a circle while she went in front of each person and made contact both physically and verbally. Everything was going very well; she was feeling more and more easy with people. She spontaneously hugged Josie when she reached her. Then she approached Philip, a small, kindly, middle-aged man. As soon as she reached him, she recoiled, covering her stomach, and looked terrified. She grabbed one of the women and started to shiver. I encouraged her to express her feeling, and she shouted, "I'm frightened. I'm afraid. I'm really frightened. I feel so frightened."

Fantasy. This was the deepest feeling that Peony had yet demonstrated. The earlier ones had been important, and they seemed to be related to allowing and expressing feelings, centering in the chest and throat. But now her terror was centered in her stomach at a different level of her being. The situation called for a technique that would allow her to go deeply into this terror. I decided to use the guided daydream (Desoille, 1965; Leuner, 1965), in which she would fantasize going into her own body and going to the area where her feeling, in this case terror, was felt. This fantasy method would allow her to explore below her conscious, verbal behavior and to build on the fact that the terror was localized in a certain area of her body.

Here is an account of Peony's fantasy in her own words:

> Will asked me to lie down on my back, shut my eyes, and imagine myself very small inside my body. I felt very small inside a big cave with black tunnels leading off. I felt like Alice in Wonderland—

there was a feeling of awe and excitement at being allowed in. I was trying to breathe deeply with help (Will was pressing gently on my rib cage to encourage deeper breathing so that I could contact the feeling more easily.) My jaw was moving a lot and I was still crying.

(Will) *Where do you want to go?*

I'm going down my leg.

How does it feel?

It's a bit difficult.

Do you need any help?

No. I want to do it alone. I want to be able to help myself.

Where are you now?

I'm in my feet coming out of my toes.

Is there anything under your toes?

There seems to be sand under my feet, it feels good.

Are you on the sand?

No, I'm going toward the sea.

Are you going to go in?

I don't know yet.

Have you decided yet?

Yes. I'm going in. I'm swimming slowly, I don't get very far, but I'm OK. It's calm and warm and feels good.

Are you going to stay there?

No, I'm coming out now. I'm going back to my feet. I'm inside my legs and traveling upwards.

Have you brought anything with you?

Yes. I've got my sack on my back.

What's inside?

I don't know yet.

Where are you going to?

I'm about here (I put my hand on my stomach) in between the front and the back. I'd like to fill up the space and stop feeling backless.

Can you do it alone?

I'm not sure.

Can you use what's in the sack?

It's full of sea, it's filling up the space.

Can you feel your back?

I can from the outside—someone is pressing it on the left side [Will was], but I can't from the inside.

Can you try to feel it from inside now?

I'm beginning to, it feels warm, and the front and back are together.

Do you want to come out of your body yet?

No, not yet. I can feel tingling down my legs, my knees feel strange.

Can you open your eyes and look around? (I hesitated.)

Would you like to go back into your body again?

Yes.

There's a mountain—can you see it?
Yes, it's here (I put my hand on my stomach).
Can you climb it?
Yes, it gets more difficult near the top. I have to breathe more.
That's OK, the air is thinner there. Do you want to stay there?
No, I'm coming halfway down, it's too far to fall.
Is there something there?
Yes, there's a soft shelf where I can stay.
Can you see some way to hold in the air?
Yes, it's here. (My hand was just above the "mountain" of
my stomach.)
Would you like to come out of your body now?
Yes.
Do you think you can stand up?
I think I needed help the first time—my knees felt uncertain.
I was helped up and was supported until I felt my knees were able to
support me. I had a lot of sensation in my legs, especially in my knees,
around the vagina, and in my hands—my body was extremely hot.
Will you look at each person?
I then met each member of the group in a way that felt very
different for me—I mean that I did not feel my whole being was
threatened by them. That is, except for Philip, who was similar in
stature to my father and held the combined identity of my mother
and father; I still felt very afraid of him. After further contact with
Josie I gained strength.
Would you lie down and now see if you can get up by yourself?
I got up by myself. Then I returned to Philip and felt unafraid.
I hugged him briefly. I was aware of the increased body sensation
and change in breathing. I felt I had come to life.

Integration. After she had completed this experience, the group showed their
pleasure with what I had done by putting me on the floor and expressing affection
toward me. When they were finished, Peony came over while I was still lying on
my back and offered to help me up. I accepted. Then Peony pulled me up and
hugged me.

The cycle was complete. Peony went from having to be helped up physically
to getting up by herself and then to helping someone else up. She and Philip went
to lunch together and reported having an excellent time. Later, she wrote:

I am writing this a week later, and my body is still feeling the
change. I've laid my foundations, which feel like firm ones at last.
The change in breathing still amazes me in the way that it really helps
me to know myself. I feel very much to be at the beginning of living
with myself, which means I am facing my adult self with a child's
experience.

After almost two years, she reports a lasting change in her personal security.
She has moved, traveled alone, and supported herself, and she reports general
stability and a continually increasing ease with other people.

Rationale. The case of Peony is a good illustration of encounter because of the variety of methods required to allow her to follow her energy. First, she simply observed her own feelings as she observed others work. It is important to let people move at their own pace.

When something moved her, Helen's psychodrama and Gestalt session, she indicated readiness to work. The use of a physical method, screaming supported by the group, helped to release a block.

Once the block was eased, arm wrestling was used to mobilize the energy, and the use of a mother figure helped focus the energy.

After the flood of new feeling, Peony chose to return to a passive position and assimilate what had happened. Her next strong feeling came with the prospect of having contact with people. Her report of feeling terrified was another request to continue her work. Inviting her to simply make contact with each person brought her feeling into the present in a form that made it possible to work directly on the issue. In addition, making a feeling physical usually brings out the specific issue very quickly, as it did here when Philip, her father figure, emerged as the point of difficulty. This method also capitalizes on the multiple transference figures afforded by a group.

Having reached a point of deep fear, Peony was ready for an individual technique. The group allows for both personal and interpersonal issues to be dealt with. To this point, the group interaction had been vital to stimulate, unblock, and identify the source of difficulty. Now she was ready to work individually. By this point the group was strongly identified with and supportive of Peony. This supportive group energy field made it safe for Peony to relax and allow herself access to her unconscious. The fantasy method is a very powerful technique for deep individual work, especially when the groundwork has been laid and the person is ready.

Peony clearly was ready and very quickly dealt symbolically with the issues of concern. The combination of group confrontation and support, physical and contact methods, emphasis on truth, and use of a variety of techniques—psychodrama, Gestalt, screaming, arm wrestling, contact, fantasy—allowed for a very rapid identification of the problem and a deep working through of the issues. Peony's reports years later indicate that a permanent change took place. The encounter format is at once very strong and, equally, very supportive and allows work to be done at both interpersonal and individual levels at great depth.

23

Marathon Groups

Elizabeth E. Mintz

A marathon is a time-extended therapy group.

It may last twenty-four hours or more, with no break for sleep. It may last three to five days or even longer, with time allowed for sleep and exercise. In its early days (late 1960s and early 1970s), the marathon was usually identified with encounter. But it can be used with psychodrama, transactional analysis, Gestalt therapy, bioenergetics, or any other approach that lends itself to group treatment. It has been used in residential drug treatment centers, with prison populations, with psychiatric inpatients, and in business firms.

This chapter describes marathon groups as used frequently in contemporary psychotherapy: ten to twenty men and women, attending voluntarily, functioning in society, and often in concurrent private treatment.

Marathon groups, compared with conventional once-a-week ongoing groups, have unique advantages, which will appear in my later discussion of what actually happens in a marathon. But first, since the choice of a time format is directly related to the marathon therapist's philosophy of treatment, we should consider how the marathon began. It was developed almost simultaneously in treatment centers for young drug addicts (Yablonsky, 1965) and in private practice by George Bach (1966, 1967). In both instances it was viewed primarily as a method for breaking down defenses through fatigue. Participants therefore remained in continuous interaction for twenty-four hours or longer.

Bach makes this philosophy explicit. His "Ten Marathon Commandments" include the edict "Tact is *out* and brutal frankness is *in*," and participants who seek to comfort one another are sardonically described as "Red Cross nurses" (1966, p. 1001). My first experience as a marathon participant, in 1963, was with Bach, to whom I still feel indebted for introducing me to this approach.

Since then, however, having conducted well over 600 marathon groups in the United States and Europe, I am sure of my own therapeutic philosophy, which in some respects is diametrically opposite to the battering-ram theory of breaking down defenses. My conviction is that the enormous power of the marathon is the development of trust and warmth, which enable participants to give up their defenses voluntarily, rather than as a result of fatigue and continuous group battering.

To foster this atmosphere, it is my endeavor to make the group physically comfortable. Fruit, cheese, coffee, and herbal teas are always available. Floor cushions, gymnasium mats, and chairs are provided. If the marathon lasts more than two days, free time is allotted for exercise or rest, and there is time for sleep.

A corollary of this approach is that ground rules are minimal. In the beginning of a marathon, a participant unfamiliar with the experience may inquire, "What are the rules?" And I reply that there are two "rules" only: no physical violence and no subgrouping, which means that while the group is in session, all communication takes place within the group and private dialogues are discouraged.

Another of my profound personal convictions, in which again I differ from some respected marathon leaders, is that the marathon experience is more meaningful if the leader does not impose a predetermined structure, such as conducting the group through a series of preselected encounter games or giving the direction "Now for the next half hour we'll all think about our mothers," followed by guided sharing of memories and feelings. Such approaches certainly have value, especially with patient populations who have difficulty in expressing themselves (for example, some psychiatric inpatient groups), but the guidance limits freedom and spontaneity.

Contemporary "growth movements," such as est, which have proliferated recently, seem to have developed in part as an offshoot of the therapeutic marathon. Typically they include large numbers (sometimes several hundred people) and require participants to go through a sequence of firmly guided exercises. Preferring a small group, I am able to allow my therapeutic interventions to be determined by the immediate situation, as with individual therapy or ongoing group therapy.

The format that seems to me most efficacious is a combination of free group interaction and therapeutic episodes, often very intense, in which I provide individual therapy within the context of the group and often with the group's help, as in a psychodrama episode. Every marathon, therefore, is different, and the marathon experience has remained an adventure to me after twenty years of experience.

Now, how are marathon participants selected?

Many group therapists like to offer an occasional marathon to their preestablished ongoing groups, finding that the therapeutic process is thereby deepened and accelerated. Other marathons, sometimes offered by nonprofessionals, are filled by people who respond to newspaper advertisements and large-scale mailings. Participants in these marathons, alternatively called "workshops," are admitted without preliminary screening, and the combination of a nonprofessional leader and an unscreened group has given rise to stories (some of them validated) of breakdowns, emergency hospitalizations, and spectacular sexual behavior.

In arranging a marathon, my own policy is to consider, as other therapists do when forming a new group, "Will these people fit together? Will they be able to communicate?" Diagnostic categories seem irrelevant, although I would screen out a participant who seemed fragile from a psychiatric viewpoint and whose personality would lead to overt rejection by the group, a combination that would probably be dangerous to the participant and disruptive to the group.

Two anecdotes will clarify this point:

A young man, referred by a colleague, telephoned to request a marathon. Because his voice seemed somehow unrelated, I invited him to my office for a fifteen-minute screening interview (no charge). In came a young, well-dressed man bearing the name of a well-known, wealthy family. His first words were "Will there be any blacks or Jews in this gathering?'' Our conversation for the next ten minutes was a comedy routine. He was trying to ascertain whether the other participants would be ''all right,'' as he put it, and I was trying to convince him that he would not be ready for a marathon until after several more years of individual treatment. The extreme inappropriateness of his question (not his prejudices in themselves, which, of course, are shared by many technically sane people) marked him as so seriously disturbed that he would certainly have disrupted the group. Some members would have attacked him; others would have sensed his fragility and tried to protect him. Later, his therapist (whom I telephoned with a professional complaint) told me that he had been unable to help his sick young patient make any kind of human contact and had referred him to me for a marathon in hopes of a miracle.

A miracle did occur in the case of another young man (call him Paul), whom I had accepted sight unseen because he lived too far away for an exploratory interview and because I knew and trusted the therapist whose name he gave me.

When Paul entered the marathon room, where the group was gathering, I was frankly alarmed. Tousle-headed, shambling, untidy, he was the very stereotype of the ''wild-eyed lunatic,'' and it was not surprising to learn that he had emerged from a mental hospital only a few weeks ago. He looked carefully behind some screens to find a secret recording device and then explained, ''There's one, of course, it's hidden here, but I don't think Elizabeth knows about it. I don't really think Elizabeth is one of *them*.''

''One of *them*, Paul?''

''No, Elizabeth, I think you're clean. I don't think that you're one of *them*.''

''Paul, who are *they*?''

Paul looked around cautiously and then answered in an eerie whisper, *''I don't know!''* It was comical and pathetic, but he was by no means joking, and we never did find out who *they* were. Yet, and here was the miracle, Paul actually turned out to be an asset. He showed surprising flashes of empathy, and he possessed a childlike, appealing quality that evoked affection from other participants, who were even able to tease him gently about his unseen enemies without upsetting him. At the end of the group, Paul said happily, ''It's been a great two days. The devil lets these good things happen sometimes! Bless you all.''

In mingled relief and irritation, I telephoned the therapist whose name Paul had given me. The therapist apologized profusely. Paul was indeed working with him, had seen a write-up of my marathons in a popular magazine, and had called me without telling his therapist, who was quite aware that Paul would not be considered an appropriate marathon participant. Indeed, my colleague had tried to alert me but by a series of coincidences had been unable to reach me. And both of us were pleased, because Paul had found the marathon a positive experience which proved that ''good things can happen'' and which gave him a helpful start in learning to live outside a hospital.

Here is an excerpt from a letter written by a man who had shared Paul's marathon:

> That poor guy! There was something so sweet about him.
> Elizabeth, this sounds sentimental, but I've always felt sort of con-
> temptuous toward people who were mixed up or in trouble. I felt pro-
> tective toward Paul, almost fatherly. It did me good to find out about
> a part of myself that I didn't know about and get together with it.

This letter, one of many hundreds sent to me spontaneously by marathon participants, expresses a feeling that is surprisingly common—a deep satisfaction in experiencing compassion for others, a feeling that somehow is often blocked in our society.

In a typical marathon, some participants have met before in an ongoing group or a previous marathon, but most of them are strangers. Although most marathon participants choose to attend more than one marathon, each of these groups is essentially a one-shot deal. A conscientious marathon therapist, in my opinion, should make sure that therapeutic help is available for follow-up work if needed by the participants. In my own experience this has *never* happened on an emergency basis, although many participants have decided to embark on individual therapy, with myself or some other therapist, after the marathon has led to awareness of personal problems. A unique value of the marathon, in comparison with a conventional ongoing group, is that it gives participants a chance to test out their reaction to meeting new people in an intimate situation, and they sometimes discover that they tend to pin unreal stereotypes on real people.

Here is an excerpt from another postmarathon letter:[1]

> At the beginning of the marathon I didn't like Sue because I thought she was a dizzy broad, and I didn't like Carl because he was a stuffed shirt. Funny, when the marathon ended and we all sat in a circle holding hands, I was between Carl and Sue. And by that time I knew she'd been through hell and she was a real peach, and Carl was a fellow who was really shy and scared to death but he'd do anything to help somebody else—give you the stuffed shirt off his back, ha ha.

Now that we are assembled, how does the marathon begin?

Some leaders begin with an encounter game designed to move the group toward intimacy and frankness, such as going around the circle and asking each participant to pick out a group member whom he thinks he would especially like and another group member whom he thinks he would dislike. Some leaders remain silent and passive, placing responsibility on the group to develop its own interaction. Over the years, having tried a dozen approaches, I have settled on a deceptively simple technique. I say, "Let's go around the circle. Introduce yourself by your first name. Then tell the group something you'd *like* us to know about you, something important, not your home town or that kind of thing, but not necessarily your worst problem either. Something you *want* us to know. We won't discuss anything until we've all spoken, so don't respond, just wait till the person on your right finishes up and then speak." Now I glance at the person on my left, having already tried to choose my cushion next to a participant who seems fairly well at ease, and we begin.

"My name is Elly. What I want you to know—well, I broke up with my boyfriend, I wanted to break up and I don't think I want him back, but I keep busting

---

[1]Nearly all the hundreds of letters in my files are positive. However, this does not necessarily mean that all participants are enthusiastic. Disappointed or disgruntled participants may not have bothered to write, since feedback was usually not requested, except in one brief study (Mintz, 1969).

into tears at funny times. . . . '' Elly, an attractive young businesswoman, was referred by another therapist whom she sees individually.

"Gary. I'm a workaholic, everybody says. It's crazy, but I just can't seem
to stop, my heart is not too good. Right now I feel I'm wasting time, I should be
working.'' He grins sheepishly, and there is a murmur of rather sympathetic laughter.
He is a burly, middle-aged man who was persuaded to attend the marathon by
his wife, a former patient of mine. He smokes incessantly.[2]

"My name is Lois. My shrink told me to come here. She says I don't get
out enough, don't make friends, guess I'm just shy. . . . ''

We go around the circle; the person on my right is the last of the participants
to speak. By a deliberate stratagem, I am at the end of the line.

"My name is Elizabeth.'' This too is deliberate; I would feel uncomfortable
here being addressed as doctor. Then, usually, I go on with perfect truthfulness
to say how I feel about this particular group—for instance, ''I'm always excited
when a marathon begins, and this time I'm a little nervous because so many of
you came from out of town, I hope you won't be disappointed. . . . ''

If I am troubled by something that seems inappropriate to share, I may mention it—for instance, ''If I seem jumpy, it's because I saw a dreadful traffic accident on my way here, don't worry, I'll calm down . . . .'' Never do I share anything,
such as a personal crisis, that would imply that I seek help from the group. In the
early years of encounter, some leaders took the position ''Let it all hang out.'' They
sought personal help, expressed hostility freely, and saw themselves as providing
role models for authenticity and freedom. My personal feeling is that I should keep
my own problems out of the group during working hours; at the same time, I do
not attempt to keep a formal professional distance.

In this half hour of the initial go-around, much has happened besides my
self-definition. We have moved immediately beyond the superficial get-acquainted
level. It has been established that participants are asked to share only what they
wish to share with the group, in accordance with my conviction that defenses should
be voluntarily relinquished rather than attacked. I have picked up clues to some
major problems and have an impression of who is ready to work and who needs
to wait a while. Most important, the participants have a foundation for getting to
know one another.

Usually a period of free interaction follows, as participants react to one
another's statements, often identifying (''My God, that sounds just like my marriage!'' or ''I thought I was the only one who had that problem!'') or asking for
more information. Unless someone appears to be in pain, I remain rather passive
during this phase, which is often marked by outbreaks of hostility, sometimes quite
sharp. Indeed, marathons often pass through a phase of initial hostility; next through
sharing grief, dependent needs, and frustrations; and finally through a concluding
phase in which members offer one another strong support and understanding (Mintz,
1969). These are generalizations. The course of a single marathon is not predictable, except that I have never yet seen a marathon that did not go to deeper and
deeper levels of self-exploration and warmer mutual acceptance as the time passed.

[2]In recent years, since the hazards of smoking have been publicized, I do not allow smoking
in the group; I require smokers to withdraw to an adjoining room. The account of Gary comes
from a marathon given before this policy was adopted.

One unique feature of a marathon, in comparison with ongoing groups, is that an individual can express problems, regress markedly, and then move on to a more mature level of development, a process which, ideally, takes place in most serious psychotherapy but which can be seen in its entirety in a marathon.

Elly, who in the beginning go-around had told us how she "busted into tears" uncontrollably, told us more about herself as the marathon moved toward intimacy, which typically requires about three hours of interaction. She always had trouble controlling her feelings, Elly said. She was capable at her work but had been told that she had missed a promotion because of her "nervousness." She had difficulty in not crying if her superior told her about a mistake, and she might lose her temper if someone pushed ahead of her in line when she was shopping. Even as a child, said Elly, she had had temper tantrums.

"How did they handle that at home? I mean, what did your parents do?" This question came not from me but from another participant. Most marathon participants develop rather quickly into good auxiliary therapists, although an occasional member attempts to show off pseudopsychoanalytic knowledge and is put down, not too gently, by the group.

In this episode, the question was appropriate. Elly said, "Well, they just took me to a room and shut the door and let me cry it out. I guess that's what they thought was right. But I felt awful. It was lonesome. I just cried and cried. Once I got sick, I cried so long, they had to take me to a doctor."

"What would you have liked them to do?"

Elly considered. "Just hold me, I guess. Not just for love, but to control me, make me keep from thrashing around like I did." She flushed; the memory was still painful.

It seemed to me that Elly's feelings were very close to the surface and also that her ego was strong enough to accept and assimilate a corrective emotional experience. "Elly," I asked, "could you accept me as your mother—for, oh, half an hour or so?"

"Yes," Elly said at once. In marathons I frequently play the "good mother" and sometimes the "bad mother," but I would regard this roleplaying as intrusive unless the patient has given me permission, especially if physical contact is involved.

"Then have a temper tantrum. Now." Using the gymnasium mat on the floor, I explained the movements of the classical bioenergetic temper tantrum—arms and legs thrashing alternately, head turning from side to side, deep breathing, and sounds that often turn spontaneously into sobbing.

This was not difficult for Elly. She kicked, screamed, and sobbed. When I felt she was ready for the intervention, I moved close and took her in my arms as if she were a child. She clung to me, sobbing on my shoulder, and I tried to hold her tightly enough to control her, but not uncomfortably tightly. I could feel her gaining control over her body. Gradually she became still, lifted her head, and smiled.

With the sensitivity that never ceases to amaze and delight me in marathon groups, another participant had moved close to us and held out a paper cup of milk. I took it and held the cup to Elly's lips. She sipped and gave it back to me. In a moment, I held it to her lips again. She sipped and tried to give it back to me. But this time I refused it and said gently, "No, you must put it down yourself."

She put it down, took a deep breath, and moved slowly out of my arms. Then she reached for the cup, drained the milk—and then actually put the empty cup into the wastebasket. She had regressed into a temper tantrum, had been controlled and comforted, had been fed passively, and finally had reached the level of mature group cooperation by disposing of the cup.

She smiled at me. "Thank you, mother."

"I'm not mother anymore. I'm Elizabeth now."

"Thank you, Elizabeth."

In general, I believe that cognitive integration should follow emotional experience in a therapeutic situation, but here the symbolism was so clear that discussion seemed unnecessary. Of course, marathon episodes are not always so symbolically beautiful as this, nor do they often bring about immediate therapeutic change. But for Elly the episode of the tantrum and the milk was a turning point. She was relaxed and helpful during the rest of the marathon, and her therapist reported later that Elly was working effectively on the development of self-control.

Obviously, this episode constituted individual therapy within the group, and yet I do not think it could have occurred in a one-to-one situation, nor would there have been time for it in a conventional ongoing group. The transferential aspect of the episode is worth noting also. Because I become intensely involved in roleplaying "good mother" or "bad mother," colleagues have suggested that patients may become stuck in a positive or negative transference and may not be able to move away from this fixation. My answer is that this simply does not happen. In my over 600 marathons, nobody has ever wished to leave his or her individual therapist to work with me as the good mother; and to my knowledge, nobody has ever borne a grudge against me after I roleplayed the bad mother.

The group itself, I believe, makes possible an intense therapeutic episode such as Elly's. Unconsciously, we are all afraid of our murderous impulses, our incestuous impulses, our wishes to be totally dependent or totally powerful. Unconsciously, I believe, the group is experienced as a protection against acting out these impulses in reality, and therefore they can be acted out on a symbolic level. This is in contrast to an ongoing group, which remains closer to the realities of job, family, and environment.

The story of Clem, who attended sixteen marathons over a period of four years while continuing to see his individual therapist, exemplifies the way a marathon can facilitate the working out of unconscious material and also the way such groups can function as a socializing influence.

"He's a dead man," said Clem's psychiatrist hopelessly, in referring Clem for his first marathon. And Clem, entering his first marathon at twenty-three, was indeed pathetic—eyes downcast, listless, pale, and certainly the most silent participant I had ever seen in any group. He sat near the door, because (his psychiatrist told me later) he wished to attract as little attention as possible if he had to use the bathroom. Overtures from me or group members were met with such a combination of anxiety and withdrawal that we eventually gave up.

Clem's history, as I learned it from his private therapist, was sad. Coming from a well-off family who had turned him over to the care of servants, he had made two serious suicide attempts in his late teens and spent two years in a hospital, where he met the psychiatrist who was now seeing him individually. He lived alone, worked as an accountant, and had an absolute lack of human contact, eating dinner alone every night and spending the evening with television.

He told us none of this. He remained in his corner. But shortly before the marathon ended, a vivacious young woman who had tried vainly to make contact with Clem had an inspiration. She took a roll of paper toweling from the kitchen, sat a few feet away from Clem, rolled it toward him, and said, "Play with me!" I was afraid Clem might feel ridiculed, but he smiled faintly and did roll the cylinder back and forth a few times. The young woman had given us a beautiful example of the natural therapeutic instinct that sometimes blossoms in marathons.

I was surprised when a note came from Clem asking to attend further marathons, which at that time I was offering about once a month. Nothing dramatic happened for a long time, but slowly Clem began to interact with the groups, which saw his shyness and did not push him. Gleefully, Clem's psychiatrist, a dedicated man who had despaired of ever helping his withdrawn patient, told me that Clem had actually joined a gym and begun regular workouts and was expressing fantasies that someday he might have a date, an adventure that he had never dared to try.

In his seventh marathon, Clem began to talk more freely. He spoke of his father, with whom he had never dared have any contact and who seemed totally indifferent.

"What kind of contact would you like, Clem?"

"I'd like to fight with him."

This was unexpected, from Clem. Fortunately, it was a request that can readily and harmlessly be gratified through the encounter technique of arm wrestling, in which the opponents lie face down on the floor, head to head, clasp hands, and try to force down the hand of the other. Carried out on the floor (rather than with elbows on a tabletop, a position that can lead to wrenched shoulders), this enables full use of physical strength with almost no risk of getting hurt.

"Who do you want to represent your father, Clem?"

Surprisingly, Clem picked out the burliest man in the group, who readily agreed but clearly felt that he would have to be gentle with Clem. But Clem's gym work had paid off. He lost but had put up an exhilarating fight, and he returned to his floor cushion with the happiest smile I had ever seen on his face. Thereafter, his psychiatrist reported, Clem went to the gym almost daily and was beginning to go out for lunch and coffee with his office mates.

After another year, during which he attended several more marathons, Clem was beginning to have occasional dates, had dinner with friends once or twice a week, and actually seemed to be enjoying life. In marathons, he showed an ironic sense of humor and became capable of interest in other people. To his psychiatrist, he confided that he would like to have sexual experience but was afraid of approaching a woman and did not wish to seek a prostitute.

Clem's breakthrough came when another marathon participant talked about how much he had resented his mother's seductiveness, although he thought it was unconscious. As every group therapist knows, patients can often deal with embarrassing or painful feelings after someone else has set an example, and now for the first time Clem told us that in boyhood he had had uncomfortable fantasies of sex with his mother, which he had never spoken of before, even in individual therapy.

It was essential to drain off some of Clem's anxiety. Because it sometimes makes things easier to pretend that a difficult conversation is taking place over the telephone, I asked Clem whether I could represent his mother and have a phone conversation. To my delight, Clem, who was familiar with this type of roleplaying through earlier marathons, not only accepted the idea but set the stage.

"That's fine, Elizabeth. I'll call you mom now for a while, OK?" Clem had to be sure of the distinction between reality and fantasy. "Okay, mom, you're home and I'm calling you. I'm at the airport, and dad isn't home. I've just got in. Hello, mom, it's me.''

"Hello, darling! How are you?" I tried to strike a note between seductiveness and motherly warmth.

"Fine, mom, I'd like to come home and sleep with you."

Astonished by his directness but reassured that he was greatly strengthened by his years of intensive combined therapy, I responded with equal fantasy-frankness.

"You mean, have sexual intercourse?"

"That's right."

"Why, darling, I'd love to! I always hoped you'd ask me."

"Well, I'm asking you now. Will you be in bed when I get there?"

"Why, yes, of course I will."

There was a long pause. Clem did not seem particularly anxious, but *I* was. Was Clem really strong enough to handle this frank expression of incestuous wishes?

The pause continued. Then Clem said firmly, "DIRTY OLD WOMAN!," and hung up the imaginary phone with an imaginary bang. The group exploded into laughter, which Clem accepted with the aplomb of a stand-up comedian.

A few months later, Clem began a sexual relationship with a gentle, sophisticated woman a few years older, who accepted his initial difficulties and whom he continued to see regularly. He decided that he needed no more individual therapy, and he attended a few more marathons, which he obviously enjoyed; it was difficult to remember the pale, terrified young man who had sat near the door at his first marathon. For a few years thereafter, his psychiatrist and I received appreciative, cheerful Christmas cards, and then he dropped the contacts and disappeared, probably to lead as normal and happy a life as most humans.

In the episodes just described, it was I as leader who took direction. But in most marathons, as the group interaction develops, therapeutic stratagems that are often brilliant may emerge from the group. So it was with Gary, who had described himself as a workaholic in the initial go-around.

Gary was older and more successful than most of the group, and some participants viewed him as a father figure. Although he was without previous group experience, he showed a warmth and sensitivity that drew affection. The group was disturbed when, still chain-smoking, Gary told us that his doctor had forbidden him to smoke because of a heart condition.

"How much?"

"Two packs a day." Gary grinned. The group began expostulating, reasoning, pleading, but nothing got to Gary. There was a hopeless silence.

"Look, this guy is as good as dead. Let's have a funeral." It was not I who said this but a participant. Quickly the group took up the suggestion, arranged cushions into a mock bier, and somehow persuaded Gary to lie down on it. Without directions from me, they lined up to pay their respects, as if at a funeral, and Gary's big grin gradually faded.

"Good-bye, Gary. You were a nice guy."

"Good-bye, Gary." Someone placed a pack of cigarettes on his chest and folded his hands around them.

"Gary, when you're looking down from heaven, maybe you'll see me dating Fran." This was Gary's attractive wife, my former patient, whom this participant had known from a previous marathon. "She's really something. Maybe I'll even get to bed with her—I'll sure try."

"Good-bye, Gary." I watched from the sidelines, with no need to intervene. The group was managing perfectly, and Gary could endure no longer.

"Enough already! It's stupid to be dead." He sat up, flung away his pack of cigarettes, took a fresh pack from his pocket, and ceremoniously put it into the wastebasket. Everybody clapped. For the remainder of the marathon, he did not have another cigarette.

But Gary's story does not have a happy ending. Despite his wife's efforts, he would agree neither to enter ongoing therapy nor to take part in a self-help nonsmoking group. He resumed smoking a few weeks later and eventually died of the predicted heart attack. Marathon therapy, even at its best, is essentially auxiliary treatment and should be supplemented by ongoing therapy if major problems exist. My feeling about Gary was that his smoking was not merely a bad habit but the expression of an unconscious death wish that could be worked through only in intensive psychotherapy, preferably psychoanalysis.

With Lois, also, the group invented a therapeutic stratagem which I have assimilated as part of my repertoire and which is called the Trial. It is a powerfully symbolic game, not only because every society develops some type of trial procedure to determine guilt or innocence but because within ourselves we are constantly praised, punished, and evaluated by the aspect of ourselves that is variously called the Adult, the superego, or the rational ego.

Lois, who had introduced herself as suffering from shyness, told us more on the second day. In her midtwenties, she lived with her widowed mother, had no dates, and saw almost nobody except her co-workers in the office. She was overweight, but her mother cooked delicious meals, and somehow it always seemed difficult to swim regularly at a nearby indoor pool, although she always planned to do so.

"It is," said Lois drearily, "a *nothing* life."

She talked freely now, and the picture grew clearer. Lois telephoned her mother each day from the office to inquire about her health (which was excellent). When Lois spoke of the indoor pool, her mother recalled an article about eye infections. On the rare occasions when Lois brought friends home, her mother was polite, but later she was critical. And this had been their life together since Lois was eighteen, when her father died.

"How were things before then, Lois?"

"Normal, I guess. I did have friends in high school. But mom's so lonely—and she's getting old—"

"How old is she, Lois?"

"She's forty-six."

The group burst into laughter. Two of the women, who happened to be successful and good-looking, confided their ages: well over forty. I also shared my age. Lois looked bewildered and tried another tactic.

"She's so good to me—cooks everything I like—helps me pick out my clothes—"

The group confronted Lois sharply with their perception of her mother—selfish, possessive, destructive. Lois became more defensive. Someone proposed, "Let's have a trial, hey, put mom on trial!"

As it happened, there was a lawyer in the group, and he immediately took charge. A judge, a prosecuting attorney, and a defense attorney emerged, either self-selected or nominated by the group. Because I wished to intervene if necessary, I asked permission to attend as *amicus curiae*. A maternal-looking participant named

Janet agreed to play mom, and Lois was to be star witness for the prosecution.

As defendant, mom stood before the judge, a part that the young lawyer had predictably selected for himself. The prosecuting attorney spoke.

"Mom, is it or is it not true that when Lois called up from the office to say she was going to the movies with another girl, you told her that you had an awful headache but just go ahead anyhow, so she came home?"

"Mom, is it or is it not true that if Lois wants to take a walk at night, you remember an article about girls being attacked?"

"Mom, is it true that you cook fattening, delicious meals when Lois is trying to lose weight?"

And so on. As mom, Janet admitted her guilt. The trial was fun, there was a lively spirit in the room, but it was not shared by Lois. She remained distant, almost sullen. A sentence was about to be pronounced when another group member, silent until now, asked permission to speak as another *amicus curiae* and said precisely what I had been planning.

"We've got the wrong person on trial. Mom shouldn't be defendant. The person who should be on trial is Lois."

Laughter, excited babbling. The judge pounded with a soda-bottle gavel. "Mistrial! Mistrial! Case adjourned." As mom, Janet stepped down from the low stool that had been serving as a witness stand, and Lois took her place.

"Lois, is it or is it not true that you just haven't got the will power to turn down those tasty dishes mother makes for you?"

"That you're just lazy about going swimming?"

"That it's easier to watch TV with mom in the evening than plan on something that takes energy?"

"And don't you just love having mom cook dinner and pick out your clothes? For God's sake, Lois, are you twenty-three or thirteen?"

Lois began to cry. Had the group gone too far? Unquestionably they were right, but could she face this well-intentioned, powerful confrontation?

After thirty years of practice, I am constantly relearning that if there is good will in a confrontation, it is rarely dangerous. Lois cried for a short while, and the group let her alone. Then she raised her head and said clearly, "Guilty, your honor. I guess I sort of always knew that I liked having mom take care of me. Besides— well, maybe I've got quite a lot to do with how we're stuck together. Maybe I helped it happen."

The group applauded. The judge pounded the gavel and gave his verdict.

"Guilty with extenuating circumstances. Defendant is released on probation, conditions being that she go swimming at least once a week, have dinner away from home at least once a week, and lose at least five pounds a month." He glared at Lois, who began to laugh.

"You know," she said, "I *could* go to a restaurant, even alone. It sounds exciting!"

After the Trial, the group spent a half day in a deeply meaningful discussion of how, even as adults, many of them still preferred an emotional dependency on their parents to the joys and perils of maturity. An interchange of this type, in which participants consider a common human problem, often follows an intense emotional episode such as Lois's Trial, and the marathon time format is uniquely suited to this process.

In the episodes described here, therapeutic procedures were often invented on the spot, to suit the moment's needs. There are also many encounter games that can be used to further group intimacy and individual self-exploration and can also be used to meet specific individual needs. Since these games have been described elsewhere (Mintz, 1973), only one representative game, with an illustration of its therapeutic use, will be reported here.

"Holding Down" requires the protagonist to lie face upward on a comfortable surface and be immobilized by the group, which usually requires five to seven persons, one holding the head and others holding legs and arms. The person being held down can put forth a surprising amount of strength in this position, and the participants are meticulously instructed to hold down the protagonist so as to immobilize him or her but cause no discomfort. The protagonist is told that she may yell, scream, and plead as passionately as she wishes, thus releasing her feelings, but will not be released until she says the "magic word," which has been agreed on beforehand; it is carefully chosen so that it cannot be confused with naturally expressed screams of fear and rage, coming from the deep sense of inner helplessness that all of us carry somewhere, even if it is unconscious. My favorite "magic word" is "Enough!," and group members are emphatically instructed to release the protagonist immediately at this word.[3]

Susan, a social worker in her early forties, limped rather badly but in general seemed to function well both professionally and personally (she was married, with several children) and was an interested and constructive member of the group. She waited until she felt fully at home and then told us that although she did indeed feel satisfied with herself and her life, she still had nightmares of being in a childhood crib where she had been immobilized by polio which had left her handicapped.

"I couldn't move," said Susan. "You see, I just *couldn't move.*"

We talked about it for a while, and then I proposed the holding-down, emphasizing strongly that this time she would be in full control of the situation and could be released immediately on request.

Frightened at first, Susan did understand the purpose of the game, and she agreed, after we had carefully ascertained that her bad leg could not be damaged physically by the stress. Nevertheless, as she lay down and submitted to the hands that were holding her down (with obvious tenderness and care), her eyes looked huge with fear. She sustained the pressure for a surprisingly long time and then began to sob with helplessness, instead of screaming with rage as some participants do. We waited for the magic word, longing to hear it, but Susan continued to sob for a long time.

"Enough!" she said at last, after her sobbing had subsided. Her tone was mature and controlled. The group released her instantly. Susan sat up.

"I get it," she said matter-of-factly. "It's obvious, and I discussed it in therapy for years, but now I *really* get it. I'm not that poor little crippled kid. I'm all grown up, and I'm in charge!" She and the group began to laugh together, and there was an exchange of joyous hugs, which often occurs at the end of a successful therapeutic game.

---

[3]Some encounter leaders believe that the childhood sense of helplessness can be elicited and released only if the protagonist is held down a long time *against his will.* I regard this as criminally irresponsible and as dangerous both physically and psychologically. The point of the game is to help dispel the archaic helpless feeling, not to reinforce it.

Because of the intimacy that develops in a marathon group and because physical contact not only is permitted but is an integral part of some group games, colleagues sometimes express curiosity or concern about whether sexual acting out takes place and what attitude the leader should take. Indeed, this concern is well justified by the fact that some group leaders, most of them untrained but a few of them professionally qualified, have encouraged sexual experience as a therapeutic procedure, a position that cannot be debated within the scope of this paper.

My personal attitude, when I began to offer marathons, was to request the group to refrain from sexual contacts during the sleep break, and indeed I went so far as to suggest, "If you'd like to see somebody again after the marathon, exchange phone numbers but wait a week before you call, because this is such a special situation that you might find yourself involved with someone you wouldn't really want to be with ordinarily." Before long, I decided that this policy infantilized participants. Now I let the group make its own decisions and have found that there is very little inappropriate sexual behavior. It seems to me that a marathon moves into a level of such intensity and sincerity that it does not foster superficial sexual contact, although several serious, long-term relationships have developed between persons who met in a marathon.

The marathon's closing phase is important. I set a definite closing time and warn the group that we will break promptly, because I believe that the acceptance of limits is part of maturation. Moreover, criticism of marathons has sometimes included the observation that participants tend to be depressed and to have difficulty reentering the outside world after the intense warmth and intimacy of a marathon, a letdown that can be avoided if the ending is planned carefully.

Several hours before termination, I tell the group that we are now in our final phase. If there are feelings they need to express about one another or about me or about their outside lives, now is the last chance. Having dealt with whatever response the challenge elicits, we discuss our individual plans for tonight, tomorrow, and next week. I warn the group that tonight they may be tired and perhaps irritable and probably should not act impulsively on feelings that emerged in the marathon. Indeed, I may be quite directive: "Lois, don't go home and tell your mother that there's going to be a new deal, let it get firm and solid inside you first. Sam, don't expect your wife to respond to your high feelings, remember she's been alone with the kids all day and she's probably worn out." And so on. Perhaps I ask each participant what are his or her plans for the evening, to help members make a smooth transition from the intense yet protected world of the marathon to the harshness and trivialities of the world outside.

As the marathon ends, group members usually form a circle and clasp hands spontaneously. Sometimes they invent an ending ceremony. One group began to chant, "Alive, *alive, alive!*" In another group, a minister asked permission to bless everyone, a request that was warmly granted by participants, who included agnostics and followers of other religions. If nobody has a current drinking problem, I may offer wine, and we all raise our glasses to toast one another.

These moments are often transcendent, and many of my postmarathon letters describe them in terms resembling Maslow's "peak experiences":

"I felt reborn."

"Life is beautiful, I am beautiful, people are beautiful!"

"I date my life A.M., *after marathon.*"

Some of these letters were written immediately after the marathon and may represent merely a postmarathon ''high,'' but others were written a year or more later. Research in psychotherapy is notoriously difficult, but there seems little doubt that a marathon group, conducted by a responsible leader trained in individual and group dynamics, can be a powerful therapeutic agent.

Marathons, however, are no substitute for individual therapy. They are most effective when a participant is concurrently in individual treatment, as Clem and Elly were, or has had such treatment in the past, as Susan did.

Nor does a marathon offer the same values as an ongoing group, which is typically more in touch with external realities and can help its participants through the vicissitudes of daily living. The unique values of a marathon, I hope, have been depicted here: it creates a very special atmosphere of warmth and trust, which allows participants to express their feelings freely; it offers an opportunity for deep regression followed by a higher level of maturation; and it provides an ideal situation for the exploration of terrifying archaic impulses and fears left over from the past.

❧ 24 ❧

Psychodrama

Ira A. Greenberg

Psychodrama is an action therapy in which the patient, also called the protagonist, acts out a problem by using other members of the group to portray people involved in the problem. Yet, psychodrama is more than an action therapy. It is an enterprise produced by a psychotherapist, who is the director of the drama, and presented—not acted—before an audience. Although some acting techniques may be used in a psychodrama, the enactment does not call for acting or theatricality by the participants. It is, rather, an extension of the reality of each that comingles and coalesces, foremost in the service of the protagonist and secondarily in behalf of the therapeutic achievement of all others present.

An eruption out of the creative fires of Viennese-born psychiatrist Jacob Levi Moreno (1892–1974), psychodrama first greeted the world before the eyes of well-functioning bohemians and upper-middle-class citizens of Vienna in the early 1920s. They were drawn to Moreno's Theatre of Spontaneity there and, after 1925, to their American equivalents who attended Moreno's institutes and the Theater of the Living Newspaper in New York City.

From these secular, rather than psychiatric, beginnings, psychodrama developed into both a therapeutic art form and a sociometric discipline through Moreno's work with psychotics at his sanitarium in Beacon, New York, which he founded in 1936, and through his research projects in intra- and intergroup relations in prisons, schools, and other communities (Moreno, 1934). Over the years to the time of Moreno's death, and afterward, psychotherapists came to study his methods in order to facilitate treatment of their own patients. Others drawn to Morenean training included social psychologists, sociologists, anthropologists, and theologians, all seeking to understand the wondrous results of sudden insight followed by positive behavior change that often accompanied a short, emotionally explosive psychodrama session. They sought to understand this phenomenon in terms of their own orientations and to incorporate it into their systems, which they usually succeeded in doing. And in so doing, they stimulated Moreno's further development of his therapeutic procedures, his understanding of the human being as found in a group, and his speculative philosophy that explains the human being in terms of spontaneity and the moment and in terms of our place in the cosmos (Moreno, 1934, 1940, 1956, 1964). Nevertheless, one result in the development of psychodrama, which perhaps should not be too surprising, is that although it is a highly useful treatment modality for mental illness and personality disorders, its greatest effectiveness and its most exciting deployment, according to my observations of more than twenty years, is to be found at psychodrama centers throughout the country to which well-functioning, verbally gifted professional and executive-level people are drawn. Why is this so?

To begin with, since psychodrama calls for some strong emotional involvement by all present, psychodrama centers serving both the general public and mental health practitioners tend to draw to themselves a daring segment of the population, a segment in some touch with feelings and ready to confront the pain behind the problems all of us experience. When a would-be protagonist comes forth from the group, he or she is ready to risk much, and so is the audience. Maxwell Anderson (1962), speaking through one of his characters in *Joan of Lorraine,* describes the theater as the temple of democracy, where a society's ills and aspirations are depicted and a sense of communion spreads among the assemblage. In a similar vein, the psychodrama stage may be seen as an altar of sacrifice in which the protagonist casts asunder his garments of success, his worldly achievements, his rituals of protection, and stands bare before the congregation—or audience—to face his greatest challenge, an encounter with himself and with his fears. In this there is magic in the moment, a sense of Aristotelian pity and fear and the Dionysian frenzy of triumphant spontaneity; there is also anguish and the outpouring of feelings; and there is revelation in the truths that emerge through pattern restructuring and configurational insight.

So, what, then, is psychodrama? Here is an example: During a session of televised psychodrama at Camarillo State Hospital, the protagonist, a slim, strong, twenty-five-year-old print-shop employee, who stood five feet eleven inches tall and who on occasion would sneakily attempt to strike female psychiatric technicians, was having a verbal exchange with a female nursing student in the role of his wife. His wife had run off with a football player, and while expressing his anger at this, he edged his chair closer to where the student was sitting. The director, trying not to be too obvious, eased a part of his body slightly between the two as the protagonist began clenching his fist. The protagonist immediately became aware of the director. "What's this?" he demanded. "Why are you standing there?" "This is where I want to stand," the director replied. "Does that mean you're my father?" "What if I am?" the director challenged. The protagonist quickly stood up and raised his fist threateningly. "Don't you dare raise your hand against me!" the director shouted, at which time the protagonist crumpled in his chair and, between sobs, complained, "Why are you always picking on me?" There followed a few role reversals between the protagonist and his "father" and between the protagonist and his "wife," and then the session concluded with the protagonist's seeing his fear and resentment of strong male figures in a new light, along with his attempt to retaliate against women for his inadequacies, rather than trying to deal with problems as they arose.

Psychodrama thus may be seen as a powerful modality that draws its strength from repressed drives and suppressed feelings broiling beneath the bonds of self or societally induced inhibitions. But, again, what exactly is psychodrama?

Parts and Aspects: Theory and Techniques

The opening statement of *Who Shall Survive?*, which many consider Moreno's greatest work, declares: "A truly therapeutic procedure cannot have less an objective than the whole of mankind" (Moreno, 1934). Grandiose as this may seem, it not only describes the potential of psychodrama, as Moreno saw it more than fifty years ago, but can be seen as a challenge for today. Presently, technical facilities exist in worldwide television and videotape recorders, not to speak of electronic marvels due before the century is over, that could effect a direct and immediate therapy for all of mankind, and womankind.

In psychodrama, everything occurs in the here and now, whether an event being dealt with occurred the day before or a dozen years earlier, whether the person with the problem, the protagonist, is anxious about an event occurring in the forthcoming week or five years in the future. In psychodrama, the dead can be brought back to life for whatever unfinished business the protagonist may have with them, and places, buildings, and smaller things, such as an overcoat, beautiful hair shorn from the head of a beloved, a robe, or a silver chalice, can be given a life of their own to meet the psychodramatic needs of the moment.

Conceptual Components

A detailed examination of Moreno's major works shows the key concepts on which are based both psychodrama and Moreno's theory of personality: (1) *spontaneity,* specifically, creative spontaneity, (2) *situation,* (3) *tele,* (4) *catharsis,* and (5) *insight.* When the personality is tossed into the pressure cooker of a psychodrama and therefore brought to a focus in a therapeutic setting, changes occur that enable repressed or suppressed material to emerge, at times with volcanic outbursts and at other times with whimpering realizations, and the insights that follow the sundering of inhibitions often bring about new ways of seeing oneself and improved ways of relating to others. It should be noted that the psychologist Ledford J. Bischof and Moreno himself organize the key concepts of Morenean personality theory differently (Greenberg, 1974, pp. 119–126), but the depiction herein presented seems the simplest.

Spontaneity. Spontaneity, according to Moreno, is an adequate response to a new situation and a new and adequate response to an old situation. The definition is so elegant in its simplicity that it bears repeating, since readers or audiences often take in the words and go on to the next matter at hand without giving the words the thought they deserve. Just as the ability to learn, accompanied by use of the opposable thumb, enabled our species to grow out of its prehuman past, so the spontaneability of some enabled them to deal with disasters better than others, and so it too has survival value. Our degree of spontaneity determines how well or poorly we might cope with such stressful situations as losing a job, being robbed at a bank or on a street corner, being caught in a flood, or being captured and held hostage by terrorists. A new and adequate response to an old situation might entail nothing more than changing one's way of greeting a spouse on returning home from work. This new and *adequate* response to the old situation could bring about improved and even exciting changes in a relationship. A very simple example is that of a dour person smiling at various peoples he encounters throughout the day and, after doing this for a week or so, noting the changes in her relationships.

Situation. The psychodramatic situation is what occurs on the stage, and, as noted, the natural barriers of time, space, and states of being are obliterated so that all occurs *in situ,* in the here and now of the present, in the psychodramatic *moment* of physical and verbal action and emotional interaction. The psychodramatic moment can be taken out of linear temporality as we experience it most of our lives and examined and dealt with from the viewpoint of another dimension. For example, an individual might complain to the psychodrama director of having been snubbed by a colleague as they passed in the corridor, an event that may have involved five seconds of actual time. The director may have the protagonist experience herself in this event—not linearly, where A and B pass each other and go on their way, but sidereally, where A and B approach each other and time stops as the protagonist explores her feelings about the situation, about this "important other" person, and about other people who were like this important other in various ways and at various times. Next, time again becomes linear as the protagonist returns to the incident of the "snub" as she perceived it when it occurred. This expansion and exploration of the moment is, according to Moreno (1965), investing it with *surplus reality,* the added reality of the psychodramatic situation.

Tele. Moreno defines *tele* as feelings of individuals toward each other across distance and uses the Greek word for "far" or "influence into distance" to depict the psychodramatic concept. Moreno calls it a "feeling of individuals into one another, the cement which holds groups together" (1964, p. xi), and, referring to a definition he gave for *tele* in 1914, also calls it "therapeutic love" (1964, p. xi).

The Sophoclean description of an awesome encounter is one way of describing tele. The closest English equivalent is empathy, an identifying with and experiencing of another, a "getting inside the skin" of another person. This could be equated with Moreno's more dramatic metaphor of seeing another through his or her eyes. In any case, tele is a powerful force that manifests itself in well-produced psychodramas.

Catharsis. In every good psychodrama, catharsis will occur as a natural part of the process. Moreno uses the term *catharsis* in the Aristotelian sense of an emotional purgation brought on by heightened fear or anxiety during the psychodramatic enactment. Moreno (1964, p. 18) notes that there is an element common to all sources bringing about catharsis and that he "discovered the common principle producing catharsis in spontaneity, spontaneous dramatic action."

Insight. Unlike catharsis, even in excellently directed psychodramas insight need not occur during or even immediately after the session; however, it will often occur within a day or two. Psychodramatic insight is seen in terms of the Gestalt psychology of the Berlin school of Wertheimer, Köhler, and Koffka, not to be confused with the modern Gestalt therapy, as propounded by the late Fritz Perls, an innovative psychiatrist who had learned psychodramatic methods from Moreno himself. Insight in psychodrama may occur during the enactment, especially toward its end; or after the enactment when participants share their feelings and reactions to what had occurred on the stage; or even hours, days, or weeks later.

This insight may be sudden understanding, such as "Aha, now I see why I've always been acting this way," or as the result of what Gestalt psychology calls perceptual or configurational learning that results in an immediate solution to a problem, whereas seconds before the solution did not exist. An oft-used example of this type of insightful problem solving, as opposed to an associational approach, is taken from Köhler's delightful and profound scientific work *The Mentality of Apes* (1959). After vainly seeking a basket of fruit near his cage but beyond reach, the ape picks up the stick he had handled previously and suddenly expands his perceptual field so that where earlier he saw the basket of fruit and the stick separately and unrelated to each other, now he makes a connection of the stick to his problem and, using it as an extension of his arm, brings the basket of fruit within grasp. Each time this occurred, Köhler reported seeing a ''Eureka, I've got it!'' expression on the animal's face, similar to the bulb lighting up above a cartoon character's head.

Staging and Cast

There are three basic parts to a psychodrama and in some instances a fourth. The basic categories are (1) the warm-up, (2) the enactment, and (3) the audience-sharing. The fourth is not essential in psychodrama, but a number of institute directors have found it useful, and it may be called ''postsession rapping.'' The ''cast'' involved in a psychodrama consists of four categories, namely, (1) the director, the person who produces a psychodrama from the many components that make up the finished product, (2) the protagonist, who is the person presenting the problem to be explored, (3) the auxiliary egos, the people portraying the important ''others'' in the protagonist's life, or even the protagonist himself, and in this case the auxiliary ego is referred to most often as the double but on occasion as the mirror, and finally (4) the audience, before which the problem is actionally delineated and from which various players are drawn.

The accredited psychodrama director is foremost a trained and experienced psychotherapist who has mastered the skills and incorporated the philosophy that constitute this Morenean discipline. The director's task and responsibilities are awesome when viewed by the beginning psychodramatist: to produce a psychodrama at a public or professional gathering, where most individuals, other than hospitalized patients, experience their first psychodrama, the director must stand before an assemblage of interested, skeptical, fearful, and at times hostile people and, through personal charisma, convert those people into a psychodramatic audience from which one or more protagonists are drawn and from which auxiliaries emerge. The room or lecture hall then becomes a theater of psychodrama, and a designated space thereupon becomes the stage.

All this takes place during the warm-up, which sets the stage for the action, which, in turn, prepares the way for the denouement, the discovery that often leads to insight, understanding, and potential behavior change. And although all psychodramas are different because the people involved change, as do the times and the situations, the general format of psychodramas remains the same.

Warm-up. The thought that often occurs to the would-be psychodrama director is ''Suppose I give a psychodrama and nobody comes?'' This translates to ''What if I try to do a psychodrama and I can't get anyone to come forth and be a protagonist?'' The consequences of such a nightmare can be disastrous to the beginning director.

How a director conducts a warm-up depends on many factors, including the type of person she is, how she is feeling at that time, both physically and emotionally, how she was affected by the traffic en route to the psychodrama center, her reaction to an accident or to the driver who almost forced her off the road or to the breakdown of disarmament talks as reported on the car radio, or any number of other things. The size and type of gathering also influence the manner of the warm-up. With a small, ongoing psychodrama group, the warm-up might be as simple as the director's saying, "John, you seemed to be getting into something as the last session ended, do you still feel pretty caught up in it?" If John says yes, the director might proceed with the enactment at this point, if no one else in the group has anything more urgent at that time. Or the director might say, "As I was driving to this session, my engine started sputtering right in the middle of traffic and I got a sudden panicky feeling, but then the engine caught and I continued without any difficulty. But part of that feeling of unexpected helplessness is still with me, and I'm wondering where everyone else is right now." And from the director's simple statement and question might come the matter of "making rounds," a term from the encounter movement, in which each group member is asked to make a statement about what he or she is experiencing at the moment. From these declarations a protagonist could be expected to emerge.

The "rounds" might go something like this: Tom: "I'm feeling a little nervous; I have to meet with my son's assistant principal after I leave here." Nancy: "My boss just said I'm being considered for promotion; I feel just great—and a little anxious." John: "Same old thing, I still can't plan anything until the strike's over." Alice: "I'm depressed; I still can't get my husband to see the counselor with me, much less come here." And so it would go, each group member presenting himself or herself to the group concerning "where I am at this moment" and to the director as a potential protagonist.

If it were a less experienced gathering, the director, after recounting her reaction to the sputtering engine, might get the people she was addressing to present themselves from a thematic perspective. She might say something like "You know, when I thought the engine was going to die out right in the middle of traffic, I got this helpless feeling and was just about ready to give up. I wonder whether anyone else has ever experienced something like this?" She can then wait to give individuals an opportunity to volunteer statements, or she can "make rounds," asking, "Jim, what about you, did anything like this feeling ever hit you?" and, after Jim replies, turning to the next person and the next until each has been heard from.

Enactment. The enactment begins when the protagonist steps onto the psychodrama stage or walks into the stage area. This may be a small specified area or the entire room, theater, or auditorium, depending on how the director utilizes it. Some directors confine themselves very effectively to a small area where intense scenes are often enacted, while others, including me, feel free to walk about the entire room or auditorium, directing from the rear or far side and at the same time encompassing the audience in the action on the stage. There are no rules for this; it depends entirely on what the director is experiencing at the time while subtly interacting with the audience during his direction of the enactment.

Now that the protagonist is onstage, the director must move the protagonist into the psychodramatic situation as quickly as possible, to better separate him from his passive audience-member role and get him into the action of the moment, the moment of the problem depiction. Consequently, the first thing I, as the director, do is to set the scene for the action. The director, who is responsible for everything that occurs on the stage (including the moving and arranging of furniture, which usually consists of little more than three or four light, easily handled chairs), will have the protagonist tell a little something about the person he is having the problem with—often simply the person's name, age, occupation, and relationship to the protagonist are sufficient—and then tell where and how he might be talking with or confronting this important "other."

For example, a man having a problem with his mother might set the scene, after describing her briefly, by telling the director, "Well, she'd be visiting me in my apartment," to which the director might further ask, "Where are you sitting? Oh, in the living room, OK; now where is your mother? You say she's facing you with her back to the kitchen. . . . " What the director is doing is not only getting the protagonist more deeply into the scene but also orienting the audience and the auxiliary egos to the setting. If the protagonist said something like "Well, she's always putting me down, never satisfied," while being very briefly interviewed as a potential protagonist during the warm-up, the group already has a feeling for what this important other is like. And after an auxiliary is called forth to be the mother, the experienced auxiliary might fussily complain as she takes her seat about "everything being so messy." If the auxiliary is correct, the protagonist will instantly be involved in relating to his mother, and the enactment will move quickly into areas of deep concern. The auxiliary might have guessed wrong or simply missed some cues, and the result of this opening thrust could be something like "Oh, mother would never have said anything like that; she would simply have sniffed disdainfully and gingerly held her skirt while seating herself." The clues in this instant would have been the way the protagonist comported himself, his manner of dress, speech, and bearing. After all, children, no matter how resentful or rebellious, are in many ways the reflections of their parents, and skilled auxiliary egos would be aware of this.

Nevertheless, there is room in psychodrama for mistakes, which is one of the many great strengths of this therapeutic modality. If a director brings in an auxiliary portraying a character who turns out not to be important to the protagonist's problems, the director simply removes the character from the stage and either introduces another or merely asks the protagonist whom else he might wish to talk to at this point. Sometimes the auxiliary ego is wrong in the role. If an auxiliary playing the boss shouts, "You've botched it again—can't you do anything right, you dummy!," and the protagonist responds with "No, that's not my boss; he would never say anything like that," the director solves the problem quickly and easily by saying the magic words "Reverse roles."

Role reversal is one of the most powerful tools of psychodrama, and it serves three purposes: (1) To enable the protagonist to educate all others present about how he perceives this important other person in his life. His perceptions may or may not be in accord with reality, but in psychodrama it is important that the auxiliary serve the perceptions of the protagonist during the enactment, letting reality rear its head elsewhere, perhaps toward the close of the enactment, when insight may be achieved, or at some time after the session. (2) To give the protagonist an opportunity to experience the world from the point of view of this important "other," especially in how this person views the protagonist. (3) To respond to or answer important questions that during the heat of the psychodrama, when spontaneity is at a peak, the protagonist, completely caught up in the action of the moment, throws at the auxiliary. Or the protagonist may demand a statement from the auxiliary ego in the role of the person important to the protagonist.

It is understood, of course, that most good auxiliary egos are intellectually, and at times intuitively, capable of coming forth with an adequate (that is, very appropriate) response to the protagonist's question or challenge. Yet, this response, no matter how good, cannot have the validity that a response by the protagonist in the role of the important "other" would have, mainly because the protagonist would be drawing from within herself, from all the fibers that went into the making of the relationship between the two, and by contrast the auxiliary's response can be considered merely shallow intellectuality. Another important consideration is that when the particular enactment ends, so does the responsibility of the auxiliary, but the protagonist must go on with her life after the conclusion of the psychodrama, and so any advice or challenge given the protagonist at this time is best if it comes from the protagonist herself, whether from the depths of her being or from her own intellectual and emotional reaction to what she herself has thrust on the important "other."

During an enactment, for example, in which an inhibited young woman is interacting with her forceful mother, the director may bring forth a double to help the protagonist deal with this overwhelming "other," as well as to help the protagonist get in better touch with her feelings. Later, the director may bring forth another auxiliary to help portray the mother, to make the mother even more formidable to the protagonist or to present another aspect of her, and still later the director may introduce others important to the protagonist's problems, such as a younger and more outgoing sister, an uninvolved father, a kindly uncle, and the young man she secretly has a crush on. Some directors are quite happy with a full stage at all times, but I find that the full stage is often a cluttered stage. I personally am quite happy with a lot of activity occurring onstage or even in the audience, but when a character is no longer germane to the problem, my procedure usually is to have him or her return either to the audience or, if the psychodrama theater is so laid out, to the section reserved for professional auxiliaries.

Having seen a number of Shakespearean plays performed in this country, as well as at Stratford-upon-Avon, I have been impressed and influenced by the Elizabethan manner of scene building. Because the Elizabethan stage is always open, not having the advantage of more modern theater curtain drops to end each scene, a center-stage action will drift off center as that scene is winding down, while off in a wing another group of actors can be seen interacting with one another and gradually moving toward center stage, their voices increasing in volume, as those in the earlier scene seem to drift off, their voices decreasing the farther they get from stage center. In a much smaller way, some of the techniques of this type of scene building can be incorporated into psychodrama, simply by bringing a character onstage, slightly off stage center, to wait until the protagonist has finished a statement to another—or even to interrupt the protagonist, if the director feels it is appropriate—and make a challenging or demanding or questioning statement to the protagonist. If this is well done, the protagonist may immediately respond, thus indicating he knows whom this auxiliary represents. If the protagonist does not immediately recognize this "other"—as often happens, even when the auxiliary is doing well—the director can simply add, "This is your ex-mother-in-law," or "This is the teacher who caught you cheating," and then let the protagonist take it from there.

The director during the enactment does not have to depend entirely on her spontaneity to produce a successful psychodrama that will meet protagonist and audience needs; she has many proven psychodramatic techniques to draw on. However, it is her spontaneity that enables her to keep the enactment moving forward at a pace appropriate to what the protagonist is able to handle, and it is her spontaneity that enables her to know when and how to use what procedure and how to deal with the new material a procedure may help the protagonist bring forth. Besides role reversal, some of the techniques that might be used in a psychodrama—but usually not all of them, or even most of them, in one enactment—will be detailed in a later section.

However, as the enactment progresses, as the protagonist penetrates some of his protective layers and exposes some of his secrets, his fears, his failures, his frailties, as he experiences his anguish, not only does he reveal his problems and his pain to the audience and others, who might, in Aristotle's words, themselves in their telic identification with him experience "pity and fear . . . and a proper purgation [catharsis] of such," but he also reveals himself to himself (insight). It is somewhere at this point or after the protagonist has gone as far as he is able at that time that the director will end the enactment. The director may herself close the session by stopping the stage action, after noting that it has gone as far as is appropriate at that time, or she might intervene after the protagonist has finished talking and instruct the protagonist to make a final statement to the important other and then end the scene with that other. When this is done, the director clears the stage of all auxiliaries and then, either with her arm around the shoulder or waist of the protagonist, if appropriate, or with her hand on the protagonist's arm, or holding the protagonist's hand, begins the third part of a psychodrama, the sharing and the structured feedback.

Audience Sharing. Although "anything goes" in a psychodrama, so long as it is in the service of the protagonist, is something the protagonist's ego is strong enough to deal with, and is under the control of the director, this is not so in the audience-sharing segment of the psychodrama. For one thing, the director must protect the protagonist at all times, and there is no time when the protagonist is more vulnerable to abuse, well intentioned or not, than after exposing his weaknesses to others, having "spilled his guts upon the stage," and thereby being emotionally drained and physically wilted. It is therefore easy for some, perhaps because of their own inadequacies, fears, and frustrations, to try to turn the protagonist into a "case" and, putting themselves in the role of a "counselor," distance themselves emotionally from whatever angst they experienced from the stage action.

The director's introduction to the audience sharing might go something like this: "John has shared something very personal with us, and now it's our turn to express our deep-felt appreciation for this. We do this by sharing with John some of our own feelings that may have been kicked off or stimulated by John's session. This is not a time to ask questions of John or to give advice or to make clever interpretations. This is a time to share with John some of our own failures or successes concerning problems we may have had that in some way may be similar to John's. This is a time to share the feelings—fears, frustrations, angers—in our own lives that we got in touch with during the psychodrama. Now, does anyone have anything he or she would like to share with John?"

While making her instructional statement, the director may be physically touching the protagonist as a means of letting him know she is *with* him, identifying with him, caring for him; or, as was stated, there may be no physical contact at all, depending on signals from the protagonist or what the director herself is feeling.

Very often the protagonist, by simple body language, will indicate whether or not he would be comfortable with being touched at that moment. In almost all instances when the protagonist has given fully of himself during the enactment, there will be a genuine caring for the protagonist by the director and others present. However, on the rare occasions when the protagonist has merely been acting, pretending, because of an underlying or manipulative agenda that has nothing to do with personal exploration or the attempt to deal with a current problem, the typical reaction by audience, auxiliaries, and the director is often negative, most often strongly negative.

Most good psychodramatists will attempt to use this ploy of the pretending protagonist to help him get from the surface need, the goal of the manipulation, into the problem beneath the overt problem, to help the protagonist explore the cause of the manipulation attempt. If the director succeeds and the pretender becomes a protagonist genuinely involved in trying to deal with his problems, then we have the making of a psychodrama, and at the conclusion of the enactment there will be an audience of caring individuals, many of whom may have resonated emotionally to the feelings expressed on the stage. During the rare occasions when the pretending protagonist is not caught up in the spirit of psychodrama, the director still must protect this individual during the audience-sharing period, but often the director will keep the sharing as brief as possible, just as she will have cut short the enactment on concluding that not much was happening or about to happen in getting the pretender to honestly attempt to deal with his problems.

But back to the session where much has happened during the enactment and where most if not all present sincerely care about the protagonist. Responses to the director's invitation "Now, does anyone have anything he or she would like to share with John?" might go something like this:

Bill: [After raising his hand and getting the nod from the director] You know, John, I had something similar with *my* mother; she was always putting down my friends to me after they'd left—no class, according to her, because of the way they dressed. One day I brought home a guy, sloppily dressed like the rest of us, whose father "worked with cars." Later, she made some remarks about the "mechanic's son," and I zapped her with "Mother, his father may be a mechanic, but he's also a vice-president of General Motors." That caught her up short. [Audience laughs.]

Director: Thank you, Bill. Jim, did you want to say something?

Jim: Yeah, my aunt was like that. Always putting me down, belittling my friends, complaining about my grades not being good enough. I tried every way I could to please her, to win her love, or at least her respect. But nothing I did was good enough. Finally, I just said, "The hell with it," and moved out. Went back to college with a month of vacation still to go. I just gave up with her. I got a job on the campus and just hung around until school began.

Doris: John, my dad was like your mom, never satisfied. I love him, but I can't be comfortable around him. He's cold, never satisfied.

Sally: John, I grew up in a warm and loving family. I felt cared for and safe. I wish you could have known my folks. They really would've liked you.

And so it would go, the director moving quickly from one audience member or auxiliary to another, encouraging each to share briefly, and then moving on to someone else, not letting this part of the psychodrama bog down in lengthy, detailed statements, and finally wrapping it up quickly after each person with something to share had made his or her statement, shared his or her feelings with the protagonist. During this structured sharing period, the only person not restricted in what he might say is the protagonist. He may ask questions of the director, of a person who has just shared a personal problem or experience with him, or of a silent audience member. The director's job is to protect the protagonist from audience members unable to share, but not the other way around in most instances.

Postsession Rapping. Though not a part of orthodox Morenean psychodrama, postsession rapping takes place at various psychodrama institutes and centers throughout the country. At my institute, the Psychodrama Center for Los Angeles, Inc., a nonprofit professional training and community service center, there is a standard procedure for postsession rapping. At the conclusion of the audience-sharing segment of the final psychodrama session and just after the director has thanked the protagonist for his participation, and while the protagonist is returning to his seat in the audience section, the director invites all present to remain at the center a little while longer. "We have coffee, tea, cookies for you," the director might say. "Have some of that, and while you're having the refreshments, this is a time to say something to someone you may have wanted to talk to but didn't get the chance, this is a time to get to know people, other than through psychodrama, through simple rapping or talking. So let's do it," he might conclude, as he himself leaves the stage and the lights are turned up if they had been dimmed earlier. This is something I learned from Lewis Yablonsky and the late Martin R. Haskell, both prominent sociologists at whose psychodrama institutes such social sharing was a part of the psychodrama sessions.

Actional Techniques and Derivatives

Techniques of Psychodrama

The eighteen psychodrama techniques to be described include all the major techniques and most of the minor ones used by psychodramatists throughout the world. These techniques well serve all psychodrama situations, but occasionally, usually during the "heat of the moment," often at the peak of spontaneity, the director may pull from within himself or from the stage action a new technique that fits the moment of the event and furthers the dramatic or psychological movement. It is a new discovery that worked well in that instance, and if it holds up through usage, it will become a part of the repertoire of psychodrama; if not or if it is not reported in the professional or academic journals, it may fall by the wayside, either to be "discovered" anew by another psychodramatist or never to be used again. Most of the eighteen techniques have stood the test of time.

Role Reversal. As already noted, the three functions of role reversal, perhaps the most important technique of psychodrama, are to educate those present about the protagonist's perceptions, to enable the protagonist to see the world through the important other's eyes, and to enable the protagonist to respond to questions and challenges the protagonist herself had posed. The role reversal is also important in its own right, apart from psychodrama, and has been used effectively in one-to-one counseling and in group therapy. An example of role reversal in individual counseling took place during the winter of 1965 at the Claremont Colleges' Psychological Clinic and Counseling Center, staffed by professionals and advanced psychology students at Claremont Graduate School. I was serving an internship at the clinic and was seeing an eighteen-year-old male who had appeared in a state of panic two weeks earlier because he could not decide on a major. During this third session, the youth, who had undergone many school changes in earlier years because of his father's Air Force career, lamented the difficulty of making friends and asked how one went about it.

We set up a situation in which I, in the role of another freshman in his dormitory, wandered into his room to get acquainted. "I notice you looking at the wall," he said. "Those guns are a part of my collection." "They sure look neat," I said; "you know, I used to shoot in high school." "Well," he went on, "let me tell you about them. Now, this rifle is part of a series . . . ," and on he went. I interrupted his lengthy monologue and had us reverse roles, although, in contrast to psychodrama, we did not leave our seats to assume each other's positions. I then proceeded to describe the guns in great detail until he began to fidget. "I must be pretty boring," he said. "We're all boring when we lecture when we should converse" was the reply, and he then began talking of some of his fears of peer rejection. Many other examples of the use of role reversal in individual counseling or psychotherapy come to mind as I write this, and most mental health professionals can come up with their own examples of how this and other techniques might be used outside the psychodrama setting, but role reversal is found foremost in psychodrama, and without it psychodrama would be a much weaker modality.

The Double. The double's purpose is to support the protagonist as he is seeking to explore a personal problem and also to serve as a link between the director and the protagonist. The physical position of the double is at the side of the protagonist away from the audience and slightly to the protagonist's rear, so that the double can observe the protagonist's actions and positions and assume the protagonist's body posture. Assuming the protagonist's posture is important, as this enables the double to better empathize with and know the protagonist. For example, if the protagonist is leaning forward in his chair as he intensively interacts with an important other in his life and the double is sitting back in his chair, comfortably relaxed, there is no way the double can know what the protagonist is experiencing. However, if the double is also leaning forward, his left hand braced against his knee and his right fist clenched like that of the protagonist, the double's muscles are telling him something he might not otherwise know. He is aware of the tightness in his stomach, the clenching of his jaw, and the strain in his arms, and although the protagonist might not be then aware of it, the double has to know that his, the double's, body is manifesting some of the results of anger.

Thus, assuming the posture and attitude of the protagonist is very important for effective doubling, but there is a danger in doing so. Although the double must assume the major changes in body position of the protagonist, the double must ignore many of the minor ones, and when he does change from one position to another in keeping up with the protagonist, he must do it inconspicuously, so that at no time is the audience aware of what he is doing. The danger in imitating all or most of the protagonist's movements is that from the audience's viewpoint it looks silly, as if the double were burlesquing what the protagonist is enduring, and no matter how agonizingly real the protagonist, the overeager and untrained double can turn it into low comedy, as the audience views it. Of course, a good psychodrama director should ensure that this does not happen through simple guidance of the double during the session; yet, sometimes the need to do so is ignored. I have seen a world-renowned director ignore it, and what should have been a meaningful psychodrama was destroyed by audience giggles.

Posture and position, however, are no more than tools of the double to help him better fulfill his purpose, and this purpose is to help the protagonist get in touch with inner conflicts, repressed feelings, forbidden thoughts. The telic bond connecting the double to the protagonist enables the double to be in tune with, to resonate with, many of the protagonist's feelings—the unadmitted frustrations, fears, and angers—and it is the double's responsibility to help the protagonist get in closer touch with his feelings, perhaps to acknowledge them, possibly to express them, even to vent them strongly. This the double accomplishes by speaking the unspeakable, perhaps softly at first—"I smile politely, mother, but you're wrong"—and then later, a little louder: "You speak forcefully, mother, but you don't know what you're talking about." After the protagonist has made some tentative statements in this direction, the double could add, "Mother, you go on and on and on, but you never listen!," and finally shout, "Shut up, mother, I've got something to say, and I want you to listen!" If the emotional escalation has been properly handled, the inhibited protagonist, prodded by the director, is ready to take over and vent the rage of many years' accumulation.

Thus the primary purpose of the double is fulfilled; this calls for a heavy emotional commitment by the double, and the director must ensure that the double does not get into his own problems in the process of trying to help the protagonist. The director, it must be understood, is always very closely involved in an emotional escalation procedure, and often she brings the protagonist's angry outburst to a physical climax by having the protagonist strike a cushion, either held by an auxiliary or placed on a chair or table, as hard as he is able and, while doing this, having the protagonist shout out why he is striking what the cushion symbolizes.

The double has another role, less spectacular than that in emotional escalation but also important, and that is to be *with* the protagonist, to give him added strength in dealing even with simple issues, to let the protagonist know and feel that he is not alone, whether on the psychodramatic stage or in life itself, that others connect with him and care about him. The double is important, where needed, but not all protagonists need a double, and those who do may not need one much of the time. Therefore, it is important that the double restrain himself, speaking only when it appears the protagonist needs an assist, and he must be very careful not to take over for the protagonist, not to intrude when the protagonist is doing well on his own. Some of the most effective doubles may spend much of their stage time in silence if the protagonist is holding his own pretty well.

The Mirror. Like the double, the mirror is an auxiliary ego who portrays the protagonist, but for entirely different reasons and in an entirely different way. The mirror is called for to show the protagonist both how she looks to others and what her actions can tell her of herself. The director will use the mirror when he notes specific and revealing behavior that he would have the protagonist become aware of. He will then instruct an auxiliary to observe the protagonist closely in order to mirror her, and after sufficient time has passed, the director will stop the action and inform the protagonist that he would like her to take a front-row seat in the audience and observe her mirror. The director then calls the mirror to the stage and has the mirror reenact the previous scene but with some exaggeration of the protagonist's physical movements and expressions. Then the director recalls the protagonist to the stage, either to reenact the scene that had been mirrored or to have her go into another scene. Usually, little needs to be said after a protagonist experiences herself being mirrored.

Soliloquy. The soliloquy is useful in helping the protagonist both clarify his thoughts and get in touch with feelings. On noticing the protagonist's confusion or indecision, the director may stop the action and ask the protagonist to walk about the stage in a small circle, either alone or with a double, and while doing this think his thoughts aloud. The soliloquy usually lasts only a short while but is often helpful, and after it has run its course, the director will bring the soliloquy to a close and resume the action.

High Chair. The high chair is most often used to give the protagonist feeling frail, weak, small, and inadequate an opportunity to experience a strength she may never have known. This is accomplished either during a scene or at its conclusion by having the protagonist stand on a chair and tower over the heads of those she had felt puny beside as she interacts with them from this new position of power. Often, after resuming her role from the floor, the protagonist will have with her some of the power she experienced while on the high chair. A chair is often used to enable an auxiliary to portray the Deity or other awesome figure, but this is not considered a part of the high-chair technique.

Empty Chair (or Phantom Other). The empty-chair technique is useful if (1) the protagonist is unable to interact with an auxiliary ego or (2) there is not an appropriately skilled auxiliary ego in the group, the latter often occurring in mental hospitals with a group of regressed patients and with no staff member to assist the director. The patient is asked to interact with an empty chair as if the important other were sitting in it; the director, from her standing position behind or near the empty chair, serves as the voice of the important other. The empty-chair technique, aside from its psychodrama employment, has proved effective in Gestalt therapy and in other modalities.

Audience Questioning. The director uses audience questioning when seeking additional understanding of the protagonist's perceptions of an important other. The procedure is simple. The director, when it appears appropriate, stops the action at a point when the protagonist has role-reversed and is now in the role of the other person, motions the auxiliary, in the role of the protagonist, either to leave the stage or to be quiet, directs the protagonist to face the audience, and says something like ''Bill, we have a group of people here who would like to learn something more about you and your relationship to your son, and so they'll be asking you a few questions.'' The director thereupon calls for brief questions to the protagonist, in the role of Bill, his father, and if there is a hesitation, the director will start things off with a question or two. ''Bill, what do you think of your wife?'' he might ask, and follow the response with another question or an invitation for *brief* questions from the audience. After a few quick questions, the director may either bring this to a close or, for a final question, have the protagonist, in the role of Bill, face the auxiliary and say something like ''Bill, take a good look at your son and tell us what you see, what you feel about him." When the protagonist has finished responding, the director may return to the interrupted scene, saying something like "OK, Bill, you were talking to your son; what else do you want to say to him?," thereby resuming the action where it was interrupted but perhaps with some new understanding or insights added, for the protagonist and for everyone else present.

Split Protagonist. The split protagonist is called for when the protagonist is indecisive about a pending action or is torn by many demands on his time and energy and therefore needs to assess priorities. In such an instance, the director will bring a number of auxiliaries to the stage, each to portray a particular aspect of the protagonist's personality or his problems, choices, needs, or responsibilities. A simple example concerns my difficulty in finding blocks of time to write this chapter, and when only one patient appeared for the televised psychodrama at Camarillo State Hospital in December 1984, I used this opportunity to work on my problem. This self-directed psychodrama had the director as a protagonist, a very conscientious clinical psychology intern portraying this chapter, and the patient portraying my lazy and self-indulgent side.

The protagonist argued with the Chapter, telling her, angrily in one instance, what a burden she has been and also how important he felt she was, while agreeing with Indulgence that his competing in a sport and other recreational activities was important, but he stressed that Indulgence was demanding too much and that Chapter at this time was much more deserving. The short session involved several role reversals, and at its conclusion the protagonist felt he had got something off his chest. Though still pressed for time—part-time hospital work, private practice of hypnotherapy, acting as host for a cable television show, to name a few time-consumers—he felt newly motivated toward completing the chapter. That night he squeezed out three pages; the following night, four; and so it went. No great insights came out of the session, but something obviously did happen.

A more involved split-protagonist example concerns a college professor and department chairman who had some important decisions to make. He liked where he was but wanted to live in another part of the state, where a very prestigious chairmanship was open at one university and a professorship at another, but he hated to leave his friends and the many interests where he was. These interests included his own institute, his important position at another institute, the many books he had written and others he planned to write, his family and the needs of each member, plus his academic and other responsibilities. The stage was full of auxiliaries, portraying each of the activities, the decision choices, and some personality traits of the protagonist. The session was fast-paced but lengthy, and at its conclusion the protagonist arranged the auxiliaries about the stage in order of importance to him, placing his family closest to him, and then he made some important decisions as the culmination of the earlier action.

The protagonist may be split among aspects, as defined as important either by the protagonist or by the director, such as fearful, industrious, idealistic, shy, and love-seeking, each of which can be portrayed by an auxiliary. He may be split among goals, among emotional conflicts, among needs, and in any combination of these, and from these splits may come a confluence of self-understanding and direction.

Multiple Protagonist. Strong confrontations with important others, usually at what might be thought of as the climax of the psychodrama, often set the stage for the multiple protagonists' emergence. Thus, when the protagonist has escalated his feelings to the point where he will let loose the rage, pent up and long harbored, such as the dutiful child at last shouting his frustration and anger at an unfeeling parent or the long-suffering spouse telling the partner where to go, an almost equal amount of anger may be found among various audience members. This strong identification often reflects frustration and despair from circumstances similar to those of the protagonist, and the director may respond to this in three positive ways. First, the director may have those sharing the protagonist's feelings double for him en masse, venting their feelings in the protagonist's behalf; second, she may have each of the angry doubles individually, one right after the other, speak his or her piece to his or her father or spouse, having the original protagonist stand aside for this, and, third, she may simply have the protagonist finish his scene and then call the others to the stage, each to interact with his or her important other in brief emotional psychodramas.

Obviously, the auxiliary ego confronted by the multiple protagonists must be strong and talented to be effective in this capacity. Walt Anderson, a world-class psychodramatist and a rugged writer and outdoorsman, has served in this capacity on many occasions, as well as having himself directed others in multiple protagonist situations (Greenberg, 1977). Anderson takes his cues for appropriate responses from the individual protagonist's statements, tone, and posture, as well as from his own reactions and previous experiences. And although the many who lashed out at him and whom he toughly talked back to might not believe it, Anderson, like any good psychodramatist, can also be gentle when called on; this gentleness is real, for he is a truly humane, humanistic social psychologist and political scientist.

Naked Before the Mirror. The protagonist was a teenager with boyfriend problems one night in 1970 or 1971, and the director, Joe Anderson (no relation to Walt), was setting a new scene for a psychodrama that had been in progress about fifteen minutes. The protagonist said, "Well, I'm up in my room now; I'm about to go to bed." "What exactly are you doing?" Joe asked. "Well, I'm brushing my hair. I'm standing naked before the mirror." "Stop!" Joe interrupted. "Stop brushing your hair. Stand there and take a good look at yourself. What do you see?" She then described what she saw, pointing out certain features she was dissatisfied with, mentioning that her schoolwork was not as good as it should be, noting some of her positive aspects, and generally taking a close, almost intensive look at herself, perhaps for the first time. Joe was so pleased with the results that he stopped the action and then called each one of us to stand on the stage alone, look closely at ourselves as we stood naked before the mirror, and describe what we saw. It was truly a revealing experiece, and so, out of the spontaneity of the moment, came this new technique.

Behind the Back. This technique is usually used at the close of a psychodrama, just before the audience sharing. The protagonist sits silent and alone on the stage, back to the audience, theater darkened, and listens as various audience members express their usually positive but occasionally critical feelings toward her. I have observed the technique only once, and my reactions were mixed. However, a very moving behind-the-back experience has been reported by Sam Osherson (in Greenberg, 1974), then a Harvard University graduate student in clinical psychology, who learned self-acceptance under the guidance of a Moreno Institute–trained psychodramatist and through the warm response of the audience overcame a severe stuttering problem and fear of rejection.

Director-Participant (or Director as Double). When a director wants an auxiliary ego or double to bring out a particular point or to turn the dialogue in a new direction, he will most often whisper into the ear of the one he is instructing, and the change is accomplished without any interruption of the scene or of the protagonist's train of thought. However, there are times when the action is so swift or intense that this whispering of instructions is not feasible, and the best solution to this situation is the director's making the intended statement, either in the role of the important other or as the double. This has proved effective, both in achieving the change desired and in keeping the action flowing.

Position Reversal. A father and his fourteen-year-old son were arguing about weekday curfew during a week-long encounter trip in the High Sierra led by Walt Anderson when Anderson suggested they reverse positions, which, unlike role reversal, enabled them to be themselves and use their own resources as they argued the other's position. This worked well then, and the issue was resolved. As useful a tool as this is, it does not quite have the power of role reversal; yet, it does have its place.

Multiple Double and Multiple Auxiliary. The multiple double is called for when the director seeks to add strength and volume to the double position or when he wishes different aspects of the protagonist to be emphasized at the same or near the same time. The multiple auxiliary serves the same purpose. For example, a protagonist having a confrontation with her father may need to experience a strong, strict aspect in conjunction with a warm and loving aspect, and there are times when two can do this better than one. Sometimes the multiple double, consisting of four to six persons, is used to overpower or hold in the protagonist to give her a sufficiently strong force to seek to overcome. The multiple double or auxiliary can also be used the way a coach uses a player he sends into the game to deliver a message. In this case, the director may send in an additional double or auxiliary with very specific instructions to meet what the director perceives as the protagonist's needs.

Future Projection. Since there are no boundaries of time or space in psychodrama, projecting the action into the future can help protagonists deal with decisions involving major commitments. In one session, a young lady, concerned about answering her boyfriend's marriage proposal, experienced herself five months into the future and married to him. She loved him but not intensively and in the future projection found herself being unfaithful to her husband with a former boyfriend. The auxiliary portraying the husband expressed his hurt, and the protagonist discovered his need for her. "He needs me," she said. "He really needs me! He needs me! He absolutely needs me!" she said over and over, seeming joyously overwhelmed at this revelation, and thus she made her decision to marry. During the audience sharing, one individual reported the reason his relationships were so poor was that he had never let himself really need anyone; he had never exposed himself to the risk of hurt.

Minienactment. The minienactment is something I discovered during the early years of the Psychodrama Center for Los Angeles, Inc., while conducting the warmup at the weekly Friday night sessions. The attendance ranged from a low of four to a high of thirty-six, but I followed a principle learned from Lew Yablonsky that, no matter how small a gathering, as long as people came for psychodrama, there would be psychodrama, and sessions were always held. And in the small gatherings, each person received the opportunity to talk about a particular problem he might be interested in working on or at least to tell "where he was," psychologically, at that moment. This could easily be done with a group of fifteen or fewer; and in the course of talking to each person, I, as the director, would occasionally assume the role of the important other the person was having a problem with. We would interact, occasionally reverse roles, and then do one of three things: (1) end it there, if warranted, (2) turn it immediately into a regular psychodrama production, or (3) halt it temporarily and continue "making rounds" and return to it later, using the mini-interaction as a preamble to one of the two or three regular psychodramas done that evening. Thus, the versatile minienactment may be an entity unto itself, existing only while "making rounds," or it may be part of a warm-up to an immediate or delayed psychodrama.

Ideal Other. I was introduced to the ideal other under the most ideal circumstances—namely, experiencing it under the direction of Zerka T. Moreno while studying with her and the late J. L. Moreno at their World Center for Psychodrama, Sociometry, and Group Psychotherapy at Beacon, New York. It was the first day of training in August 1964, and to get things moving, I had volunteered as a protagonist so another student could get directing experience before Mrs. Moreno arrived to instruct the class. This was my first time as a protagonist, and when Zerka arrived, she saw at once that I was resisting and that nothing much was happening on the stage. She immediately took over, and the next thing I knew, I was five years old and reliving the time of my mother's death. The session, more fully described in Zerka's preface to my first book (Greenberg, 1968), was quite complicated and an awesome experience for me. One of the things that had emerged was my frustration at not being able to have a close, caring, person-to-person conversation with my father, instead of the usual conversations in which we each talked out of our respective roles from entirely different points of view without respecting the specialness of the other. Zerka asked whether I would like to experience the ideal other, to which I assented, and first with some whispered instruction, she had a twenty-four-year-old trainee, who had portrayed one part of the five-year-old me earlier, assume the role of my father. The dialogue went like this:

Auxiliary Ego:	Hello, Ira, how are things going?
Ira:	Pretty well, dad.
Auxiliary Ego:	How's your love life?
Ira:	Not so good. I've broken off with _____ , or, rather, she and I agreed to call it off.
Auxiliary Ego:	That's too bad. I don't know her, do I?
Ira:	No, you've never met her, but I think you might have liked her; however, it's over with, and maybe it's for the best.
Auxiliary Ego:	Well, maybe so. How are things going otherwise, at the graduate school, for example?
Ira:	All right, I guess. I've just been officially accepted into the doctoral program, and that's taken a load off my mind. It's been a pretty rough year. They really work you hard at Claremont.
Auxiliary Ego:	I imagine they do. But that's why you went there, isn't it?
Ira:	Yes, it is, dad. I felt there was a lot I needed to learn.
Auxiliary Ego:	Well, you're doing what you want to do, and that's very important.
Ira:	Yes, it sure is, dad [Greenberg, 1968, p. xxx].

Zerka ended it there. It probably did not last more than a minute, but it was one of the most meaningful experiences of my life. It had fulfilled on the stage a long-felt yearning that at that time neither my father nor I was ready to achieve in real life. Because this was such an important experience for me, I have been very careful in how I employed the ideal other in my psychodrama sessions, and as a result I have not used it very often. The times I used it would be after an intense session in which I perceived the protagonist as both needing and being ready for this type of experience, and then I would always ask whether the protagonist wanted it. Some did not. When the protagonist accepted it, I would then carefully instruct the auxiliary to act warm, friendly, supportive, and genuinely interested in the protagonist and in what the protagonist was doing, thinking, aspiring toward. The auxiliary is always warned not to overdo this, not to be overly warm or "gushing," but to be closer toward the casual in approach and manner and yet really caring. The scene should not last long and is something that best fits after the audience sharing. At the conclusion of the scene, the protagonist should be left alone for a short while to be with the experience, even after leaving the stage. If it cannot be done properly, if the right auxiliary ego is not available at the time, it is better not to use the ideal other, to perhaps save it for another time, than to ill use it, which would result in a lost opportunity for that particular protagonist. Again, it should be used with care or not at all.

Derivatives of Psychodrama

The derivatives of psychodrama are known worldwide in the psychodrama community, and yet many are little used because psychodrama itself is such an effective modality that it suffices for most presenting problems and because most directors and professional auxiliaries have not developed proficiency in using these psychodrama progeny. There are seven major derivatives:

Sociodrama. Sociodrama is like psychodrama except that the protagonist or the group of protagonists deals with stereotypes or groups of people, portrayed by auxiliary egos, rather than with particular individuals. If the protagonist had a problem with a particular teacher of his, we would deal with it in a psychodrama, whereas if he hated teachers in general, the sociodrama would present the stereotype of teachers as he perceived them, and he would seek to work through his problem with this group. In sociodrama the protagonist may be either an individual or several individuals with one stereotyped viewpoint.

Hypnodrama. This modality, as first used by Dr. Moreno and psychologist James M. Enneis of St. Elizabeths Hospital, is very much like a psychodrama, but with the protagonist in hypnosis. This is useful in enabling protagonists to age-regress to early traumatic experiences and to help the inhibited protagonist better get in touch with experiences. As I developed this modality, hypnodrama involves a group hypnosis process in which the protagonist, auxiliaries, audience members, and even the director may together be in hypnosis during the session. Most often, however, for practical reasons, the director does not enter hypnosis during this type of hypnodrama.

Role Training. Role training is most useful in helping the protagonist solve surface interpersonal or intraprofessional problems, rather than having the protagonist probe within herself for underlying causes. The session begins like a normal psychodrama with the protagonist interacting with an important other, often a colleague, supervisor, or subordinate. After trying to deal with the problem, the protagonist, at the director's intervention, steps from the stage to a front seat in the audience and observes as various auxiliaries, volunteers from the audience, in her role, seek to solve the problem in their own ways. When the last auxiliary has finished, the director brings the protagonist back on stage to try again to deal with the problem, using any ideas that appealed to her from the earlier auxiliary ego attempts. Role training calls for a very strong auxiliary ego to portray the important other "against all comers" and never give in, unless it is to the protagonist, and then only if she has managed to psychodramatically overpower the auxiliary, a rare event.

Spontaneity Training. A seeming contradiction in terms, spontaneity training helps individuals deal with unexpected and highly stressful problems, set up by the director or trainer. These may involve an obnoxious waiter, an amorous plumber, a vicious holdup man, an intimidating panhandler, a sudden fire, an earthquake, or any other problem the trainer designs.

The Living Newspaper. This concerns the enactment of current societal problems as reported by newspapers, radio, or television.

The Magic Shop. The director, as the proprietor of the magic shop, opens for business by declaring that the would-be patron may purchase anything desired, including brains, beauty, courage, love, achievement (such as an advanced degree or a best-selling novel), sensitivity, athletic ability, or great wealth. Everything is available, but each has its price, namely, what the patron-protagonist is willing to give up that he already has or stands to get. The experience enables the patron/protagonist to come to grips with and better understand his own value system.

Televised Psychodrama. Use of television not only intensifies the psychodrama experience for some but makes the sessions available to large audiences not able to be present, as well as to participants themselves through later videotaped playback. The two mental hospitals I know as having outstanding closed-circuit television systems that lend themselves well to psychodrama are Camarillo State Hospital, located forty miles northwest of Los Angeles, and St. Elizabeths Hospital in Washington, D.C., the only federal mental hospital. In addition, St. Elizabeths offers annual psychodrama training fellowships to those with college and professional degrees, from B.A.'s through Ph.D.'s and M.D.'s.

At Camarillo State Hospital, where staff members, clinical psychology interns, and others interested get training through participation in weekly televised psychodrama sessions, the patients not only get to explore their problems through psychodrama but later can view themselves in action when the sessions are aired throughout the hospital. The closed-circuit television system reaches the television sets in the dayroom of every ward at the hospital. Very often the "glamour" of being on television will bring patients to psychodrama who would not otherwise come, but once involved in their enactments, they quickly lose awareness of the studio cameras, lights, and personnel. The patients, for the most part, like and gain from it, and the hospital staff finds it a useful modality.

Conclusion

Psychodrama is both an exciting and a rewarding discipline for those who participate, no matter what their role, but it calls for a certain kind of courage.

The director always runs the risk of being found wanting before the public eye, while the protagonist runs the risk of exposing oneself before others and, even more frightening at times, before oneself.

❦ 25 ❧

Transactional Analysis

John M. Dusay

Transactional analysis (TA) was created and developed by Eric Berne in the 1950s. Like many innovators of his time, Berne was trained as a Freudian psychoanalyst, and he originally envisioned TA as an adjunct to be used in group psychotherapy (Berne, 1966). He discovered that by using TA, his patients were getting better. As TA evolved as an entire theory of personality, Berne amiably parted ways with psychoanalysis to devote himself full-time to TA's theory and practice. Because Berne knew the advantages of hearing case presentations, critiques, and evaluations of new ideas, he originated a weekly seminar in 1958 called the San Francisco Social Psychiatry Seminar, which became the San Francisco Transactional Analysis Seminar in 1964. These seminars met weekly and they continue to do so. They attracted a large number of clinicians and other professionals who presented their work from various developing schools, among them Fritz Perls (Gestalt), Virginia Satir (family systems), S. I. Hayakawa (semantics), and many others from the rapidly expanding psychology centers in northern California of that era. The avant-garde therapists were tempered by input from classical Freudian, Jungian, and academic therapists. From these diverse origins modern TA emerged, and with theoretical and technical advances since Berne's death in 1970, TA is recognized as a complete theory of personality and an entire system of psychotherapy. Its parent body, the International Transactional Analysis Association, governs and certifies the therapists who have gone through its rigorous training program.

TA is practiced worldwide by both professionals and paraprofessionals and is successfully applied in nonclinical business and organizational development settings. Long-term prison inmates, regressed schizophrenics, and clients of drug treatment programs, as well as traditional outpatient clients from all socioeconomic groups, have been subjects of extensive TA treatment, and extensive literature including all of Berne's writing and the quarterly *Transactional Analysis Journal* is available for in-depth study.

Although it is therefore difficult to describe a typical TA practitioner, the theoretical backgrounds of practitioners remain intact and in agreement. TA is involved with the transaction (stimuli and related response) as the basic element of

413

communication. There are three dynamic ego states (Parent, Adult, and Child) that become involved in transactions. If a therapy is not concerned with ego states, it is not TA.

The following condensed case history segments from the author's own practice were chosen to illustrate the salient TA theory, maneuvers, and techniques.

Case Study: Donald and Mary

This is the fourth session in the evaluation and treatment of Donald (age thirty-five) and Mary (age twenty-nine), a married couple who came to see the doctor because, as Mary said on the phone, "our marriage is breaking up."

In the first session they came in together, seemed genuinely interested in preserving the marriage, and told of happier times in their seven years together. Their sex life was wavering, they argued more, and both seemed to be spending more time and energy in their careers (business) than with each other. They stated that they thought they still loved each other but that the fun had left their relationship. Donald recently had had an extramarital affair, which had precipitated the call to the doctor.

In the first session, the doctor watched carefully as they professed continuing love, for specific telltale signs that usually manifest in body language, such as negative shaking of the head while saying "yes," clenched fists, upward eye gazes, and tightened jaws. These are visual signs of inner conflict between the ego-state signs, and though respectful of verbal content, a therapist may find more importance in this nonverbal expression than in words.

Again in the first session, the doctor and the couple achieved a treatment contract (Berne, 1966)—an agreement between patient(s) and therapist about the goal of treatment, answering the question "How will you know and how will I know when you get what you have come for?" (Steiner and Cassidy, 1969; Dusay and Steiner, 1972).

Both Donald and Mary easily agreed that they wanted to stay together; yet, they had difficulty identifying their specific problems. Each acknowledged that sexuality had been very important for their first three years of marriage, and they agreed that they would have better and more frequent sex when they fulfilled their therapy contract. Donald and Mary agreed that "we will make love at least three times a week and I (Mary) will be orgasmic again."

Knowing that this contract would represent significant changes in their marriage for the better with many other side benefits, the doctor agreed to their treatment contract. TA therapists strive for a specific contract, which is stated positively, not negatively: "I'll have more friends" or "I'll lose weight." Contracts are crisp, not vague. Occasionally a treatment contract is not obtained in the early sessions; however, a basic attitude of TA therapists is that, regardless of what is said or done in treatment, the bottom line is a corrective behavior by the patient(s). In Eric Berne's early seminars, if a student offered a theoretically superb interpretation of a therapy session, Berne would quip, "So what?" He was less interested in interpretations than in cures.

The doctor then made individual appointments with both Donald and Mary for the second and third sessions. He did this intentionally so that each could speak freely and honestly without having to alter his or her concerns and problems to protect the spouse. The doctor also structured the conjoint sessions in such a manner that all three participants—husband, wife, and therapist—could be honest and candid. If a spouse has an ongoing affair or is seriously ambivalent about continuing the marriage, it is certainly more advantageous to schedule individual sessions to work out these problems in private. In the individual meetings the doctor ascertained that they indeed did love each other and very much wanted their marriage to succeed. Because of this knowledge, the doctor was able to proceed with conjoint treatment (patients in the same room at the same time with the same doctor). Had one or the other expressed doubts about his or her commitment, the doctor would have scheduled further individual sessions alone with the more doubtful of the two.

In the fourth session, the second time that Donald, Mary, and the doctor had been together, the process went as follows (the account here is condensed):

Doctor: Go ahead and discuss your situation, and don't hold back on what you think or feel is important.

Mary: Donald has been so critical of me.

Doctor: Talk to him, not about him.

Mary: Donald, you don't say anything about my looks now, except what you don't like.

Donald: I'm just being honest.

Mary: You mean you weren't being honest when we got married. You always said I looked great—now you never do. [*The doctor silently observes Mary speaking in absolutes—"always" and "never"—which are not Adult ego-state vocabulary but come from her Child, an insecure, hurting, threatened part of her personality.*]

Donald: I just told you today I liked your dress.

Mary: But I asked you, so it wasn't spontaneous.

Donald: [Plaintively turning to the doctor] See—she doesn't even listen to me. [*The doctor notices that their emotions are heating up rapidly; he sees that Donald sets his jaw in a grimace when under stress with Mary; Mary pulls her chin inward and looks up at Donald. This intensity of emotions is what the doctor facilitates so he can quickly get to script work.*]

Doctor: [With a caring attitude] I know that the session is painful now, but you both are willing to express your problems with each other. Donald, talk directly to Mary.

Donald: Well, damn it, Mary! You're goddammed busy—you don't even take time to listen—now you say you want to get pregnant—and work more and all that! [Grimaces again in a unique manner peculiar to himself]

Mary: I could do lots of things if you were more supportive.

Donald: What do you mean, "more supportive"? I told you that you have a great job—

Mary: [Tearfully] You don't pay any attention to my career!

Donald: [Looking tense] How can I help but pay attention? You bring a whole briefcase full of papers home every night. At least I don't bring my work home with me.

The doctor had two major options at this point. The first would have been to interrupt the *game* pattern. A game is an orderly series of transactions that has an ulterior level. Mary and Donald were playing a popular game among married couples, colloquially called "If It Weren't for You." In this sequence Mary complained that Donald held her back, didn't support her, and so on, and Donald criticized her. The transactional game model in Figure 1 illustrates their predicament. On the social level (solid lines) it seems that Donald is giving criticism to Mary from his Parent ego state to her Child, and Mary seems to be the innocent victim from her Child ego state. The psychological level (dashed lines) reaches the ulterior transaction. He is terrified of being unloved and abandoned, and she has a need to try to please him, always falling short. (This was the second predictable transaction sequence discussed by Berne, before the word *game* was chosen to describe this pattern of interaction in relationships, and was used to illustrate the characteristics of games in general in his historic book *Games People Play* [Berne, 1964]. The colloquial term *game* has met with varied acceptance by professionals, but its acceptance by the public was incredible. *Games People Play* still enjoys the all-time record for nonfiction on the *New York Times* best-sellers list.)

Everyone has his or her own repertoire of games, and these stereotyped patterns of behavior tend to reinforce one's basic belief about oneself vis-à-vis others. In this case, Donald believes that he was unloved and may be abandoned, and Mary believes that she was never able to get ahead and is continually being held back. The TA therapist knows that game playing arises from early childhood decisions that are colloquially called *script* decisions. Script implies that in certain crucial areas of life people are slaves to their past, and the goal of treatment is to allow the patient to become *autonomous* and free from these decisions (Berne, 1972; Goulding and Goulding, 1976; Steiner, 1974).

Figure 1. Diagram of Donald's and Mary's Games.

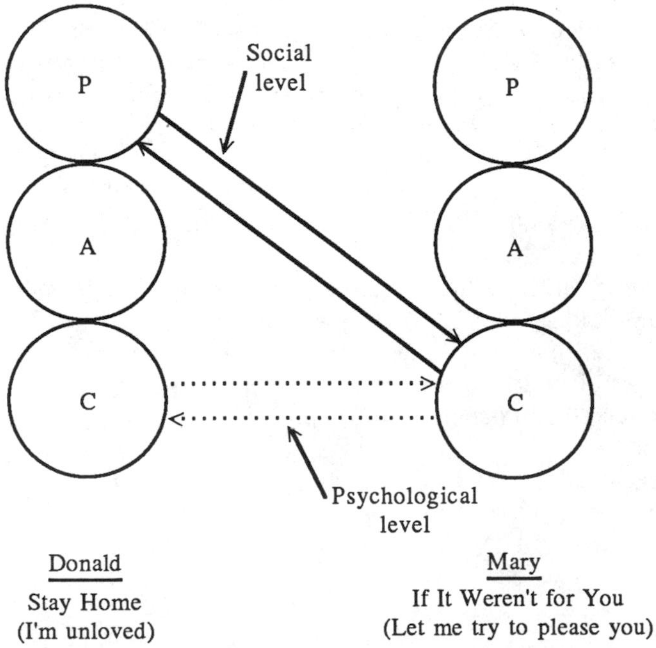

Donald
Stay Home
(I'm unloved)

Mary
If It Weren't for You
(Let me try to please you)

Because the doctor wanted to enhance the strong emotional tension between Donald and Mary, he did not interrupt their expressions or comment on the game aspect at this time but proceeded to structure a script redecision. Notice that the doctor asks very few questions in a treatment session, as question asking tends to focus attention on the asker and defuses the emotional tension in the patient.

Doctor: Donald, keep your jaw tight, real tight, like it is now. [Moving from his chair and grasping Donald's jaw] Keep your chin real tight. Mary, it's OK to cry now; keep your head down like it is now and keep your brow wrinkled. [Exacerbating the emotion connected with her wrinkled, tense brow by touching her and increasing the pressure] Say how you are feeling now.

Mary: I feel rotten, put down, awful.

Doctor: Donald, say how you feel now.

Donald: [Silent for several seconds before speaking] Bad.

Doctor: Keep your jaw tight—and put some words behind your feelings.

Donald: I'm alone, all alone—all alone.

Doctor: I notice some sadness behind your anger. [*Donald had a few tears in his eyes.*] Both of you close your eyes. [*The doctor wants to structure the situation so that both of them can temporarily regress, leave the room and the immediacy of the situation.*] Keep those negative feelings and let them go back through the years, back into your past. [*The doctor takes sufficient time for both Donald and Mary to let their "here and now" feelings go back with their pasts. Occasionally the doctor tightens Donald's jaw and Mary's brow with his hands and suggests, in a technique familiar to clinicians who use hypnosis, that they reexperience the negative feelings as they occurred in the past. The doctor watches carefully for signs of regression in their physical expressions such as deepening emotions, irregular breathing, sobbing, tight knuckles, and fetal positions. When they have regressed, he proceeds.*] Donald, you go first. Say what is happening. [*There is no set formula for which patient goes first; usually the one whose feelings seem more accessible is more ready for work.*]

Donald: She's working. She's not here.

Doctor: How old are you?

Donald: I'm about five.

Doctor: Talk as if you are there, and be five.

Donald: [Openly crying] I don't want you to go; I don't want to stay with Aunt Tillie—please—please—please.

Doctor: Say what you are deciding.

Donald: I'm always alone. I wish mom didn't have to go [to work].

Doctor: You are feeling alone.

Donald: I know she has to work, but I'm *always* going to be alone. [*The doctor has structured his consultation room so that he has ready access to several movable chairs. He takes one and places it about three feet in front of Donald, who is crying profusely, his jaw quivering.*]

Doctor: [Using words appropriate for the five-year-old Donald] This is a very painful time for you, Donald. Here, come over to this empty chair. [*Donald rises and sits in the empty chair. The doctor, who had previously touched Donald's jaw to increase the tension, now and only now lightly massages Donald's shoulders in a soothing, reassuring manner.*] Donald, in this chair sits the caring, nurturing, growth-promoting part of you. Say something to help the frightened five-year-old Donald.

Donald: I know you feel so alone, but mom will come home. She loves you.

Doctor: Go back to your original seat, Donald.

Donald: [Changing seats] I'm not so sure—sometimes she doesn't come back until after I'm asleep. [*The doctor senses that Donald isn't aware that his mother loves him and may even think he is unlovable.*]

Doctor: Are you sure that you are lovable? [*The doctor has been parsimonious in asking questions, and therefore his inquiries have greater impact than if he had habitually asked many questions.*]

Doctor: [Clenching his jaws again] She doesn't love me. I do so many things that make her mad.

Doctor: [Pointing to the empty chair] Go back and deal with that.

Doctor: [Moving to the chair representing his more nurturing self] Kids do lots of things that anger their mothers; you're not that different. Besides, your mother was under a lot of pressure.

Doctor: Mary, I know you've gone back in your past, too. [Mary nods affirmatively.] We'll go back to your childhood in a few minutes. Your feelings are very important, but if you are willing, come sit by Donald. [*The doctor provides a second empty chair alongside Donald. Mary almost leaps at the chance to nurture the "hurt little boy" ego state of her husband.*]

Mary: You're very lovable; you're cute and bright and just wonderful to play with. [Spontaneously reaches over and touches Donald affectionately]

Donald: [Wiping his eyes] Thanks, Mary— [Turning to the just-vacated chair representing five-year-old Donald] Maybe you aren't so bad.

Doctor: Maybe?

Donald: [To his five-year-old past self] You really are lovable. Mom was alone herself and had to go out sometimes. She really loved you, though.

Mary: Those were really tough times for you, Donald, but you are really great! I love you very much!

Doctor: Go back to the chair and say how you feel.

Donald: [In his original "little boy" chair] Better! [Jaw less tense, tears gone]

Doctor: Let's pause for a moment. [Donald and Mary hug and kiss each other.]

To review the entire process: The doctor began by encouraging Donald and Mary to escalate their bad feelings and immediately get into their arguments with each other. The doctor increased the tension and sought the characteristic signs of the Child ego state (technically the Adapted part of the Child, which is the script-deciding part, as opposed to the fun-loving Free Child part). The doctor had them regress to poignant moments of their early negative childhood decisions. This, in a non-cliché manner, is the *real* problem. Donald's problem was that of a five-year-old boy whose mother, herself abandoned by his father, had to work and leave Donald alone. Donald decided as a very young boy, much too young to take a lifelong decision, that he was unlovable. Mary, in witnessing this process, recognized that the problem was not thirty-five-year-old Donald but a five-year-old boy. Instead of being his adversary, Mary immediately became his ally and authentically nurtured little Donald. This process took only fifteen minutes—and they had been fighting for more than two years.

The childhood decision is colloquially called the "script decision" by TA therapists, and it is lodged in the Child ego state (Goulding and Goulding, 1979). The term *script* was chosen because once a profound existential decision (such as Donald's "I am unlovable") is made, then an entire life is lived to support that decision. Each episode of unrequited love as a young man then became a reinforcing trauma to Donald, and even Mary's development of an independent career was seen by the scripted five-year-old Donald as a threat to him. These childhood decisions have the quality of a hyperesthetic experience as discovered by Freud and Breuer as early as 1893, when they experimented with regression states under hypnosis (Breuer and Freud, [1893] 1962).

Occasionally, a TA therapist will offer cognitive feedback after a dramatic treatment episode, and for this purpose a chalkboard is used. For Donald the doctor could draw the script matrix in Figure 2. Mother, from her Parent ego state, gave Donald many important values that he incorporated, such as "Get married." He believed getting married was important. However, from her own anxious and insecure Child ego state, mother, by her actions, said, "You are not as important as my other concerns; that is, you are unlovable." Donald bought this message and decided by the age of five that he was unlovable. This decision became his script and has the quality of a self-fulfilling prophecy.

By playing a psychological game, Donald would reinforce his script decision. He would choose women who, like his mother, had other interests and therefore get himself rejected. On the social level, it appeared that he was in love

Figure 2. Script Matrix.

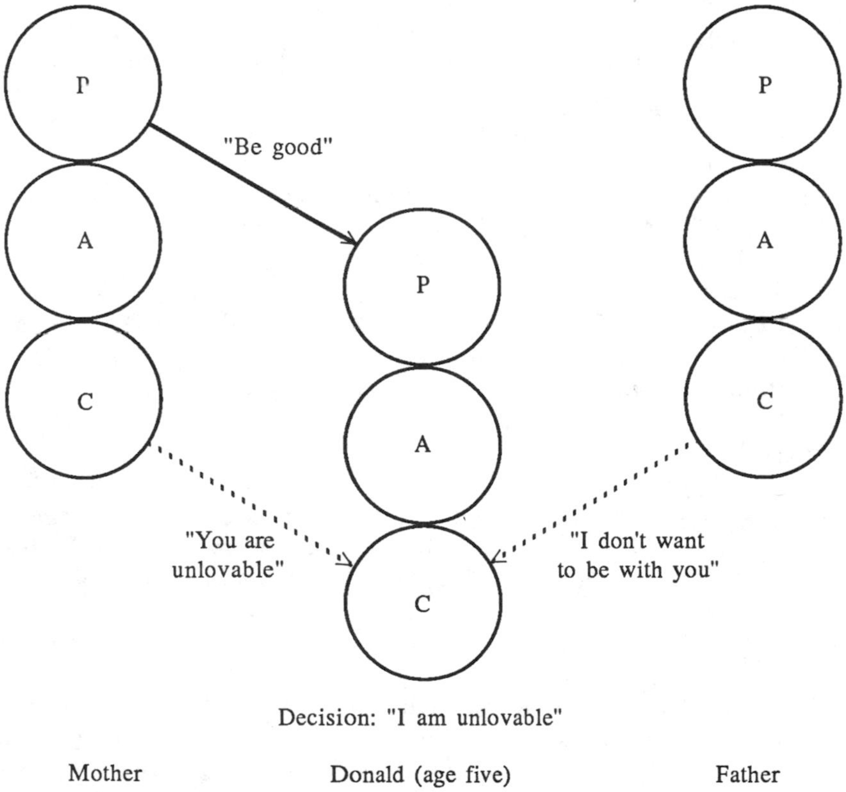

Decision: "I am unlovable"

Mother   Donald (age five)   Father

and was making progress toward a good marriage. On a hidden or psychological level, he created his own rejection *racket* (this is a maneuver designed to reinforce the script).

TA therapists do not take long, voluminous histories; rather, they encourage the patient to reexperience the early negative existential decisions so they can set up a redecision. Eric Berne once said that anything that has been learned can be unlearned. Through techniques such as observing ego states using hypnosis, Gestalt, regression, and psychodrama, one's negative script can be reversed. Goulding and Goulding (1978, 1979) have contributed much to TA literature on redecision models.

The doctor had allowed two hours for the session with Donald and Mary. He next turned to Mary:

Doctor: You have lots of work to do yourself. Sit back, make your brow tense. That's it. Go back to where you were a few moments ago.

Mary: [Again feeling some pain, with her brow wrinkled, her hands tense, and her chin pulled in] I'm seven, my father only talked about my bad marks in arithmetic.

Doctor: Speak in the present tense as if it's happening now and you really are seven. [Taking several minutes and enhancing her bad feelings by suggestion] Pull your chin in; your forehead is very tight.

Mary: I can never please him.

Doctor: Sit in this other chair and be your caring, nurturing part.

Mary: [Changing chairs] But you did so well in your other classes.

Doctor: Go back to your seven-year-old spot.

Mary: [Again changing chairs] He wants me to be perfect, but I'm not. I'm awful. If daddy could just say something nice to me and encourage me, I would do better.

Doctor: Come back to your nurturing chair. (He then nods to Donald to massage her shoulders a little.)

Donald: [Readily gets up and touches her affectionately] Mary, you are brilliant, you don't have to be perfect all the time; you're the most OK woman in the world.

Doctor: The two of you talk it over and tell the little seven-year-old something.

Donald: Instead of focusing on what you did not do right, it's about time to focus on what you *do* right. You have so many great qualities.

Mary: If only my father had been more supportive.

Donald: He was such a perfectionist.

Mary: Well, I'm not perfect.

Donald: You don't have to be.

Mary: I'm going to start believing that. I don't care what my father said. [Then talking to the empty "little Mary" chair] Mary, you're OK, because you're OK, not because father, Donald, or even the doctor says you are.

Donald and Mary kissed and hugged, and the doctor said, "That's enough for today."

Mary has a "Be Perfect" quality to her life script, and the process of redeciding is well underway and aided by her husband. When she was not perfect, she would feel the lack of support from her father earlier and now from her husband.

While Donald and Mary are rapidly experiencing this process to reverse their scripts, resistance to change frequently occurs, and this is common. Treatment continues to break down resistances.

Case Study: Edna

The case of Edna illustrates a severe resistance. Edna is a thirty-nine-year-old single woman who was in a TA therapy group because she had very few friends, male or female. A bright executive, she functioned well on the job, but her social life was bleak and she suffered from loneliness and recurrent depression.

She became very upset in a group treatment session because it seemed to her that another patient, Suzy, a perky, cute, younger woman, was getting more of the doctor's attention. Edna was showing anger and tears, and the doctor immediately had her, in her heightened emotional state, close her eyes and follow those angry feelings back through the years. Edna went back to age four, when her mother and newborn sister came home from the hospital. Her father, an insensitive man, actually spanked her because she was fussing about something. Little Edna retreated into the darkness of a clothes closet, where she decided "I hate them."

Doctor: [Encouraging Edna's expression of negative feelings] Say more.
Edna: I'll never love them again. [*She decided that she would never love (anyone) again and felt, in her little-girl way, that she was betrayed by her father and mother and a new baby sister.*]
Doctor: [Having her sit in an opposite empty chair] Do something for the little girl inside you.
Edna: Shut up and quit crying!

Obviously, Edna was not promoting positive change from her childhood resolution, and so the doctor placed another chair perpendicular to the original two chairs and directed her to this third chair.

Doctor: Describe what is happening. [*This is a process to allow her to gain immediate access to her Adult ego state.*]
Edna: I'm not being very nice to the little girl [pointing to the Critical empty chair].

The doctor agreed and suggested that Edna sit in another chair and nurture the little four-year-old girl. Edna attempted this but cried and clenched her fists in frustration.

This impasse, or resistance to redecision, is explained by a useful diagram called an egogram (Dusay, 1972, 1977), shown in Figure 3. Although Edna had experienced all her ego states (the five functional ego states are Critical Parent, Nurturing Parent, Adult, Free Child, and Adapted Child), she developed an imbalance in her ego-state energy. The egogram is a TA graph that represents the relative amount of energy emanating in one's personality. Each person has a unique egogram, which allows the TA therapist to gain clues to resistance. This energy model is a more physiological appraisal than the structural analysis of personality as seen in Figures 1 and 2 and is widely used in the clinical setting and by researchers as well.

Figure 3. Edna's Egogram.

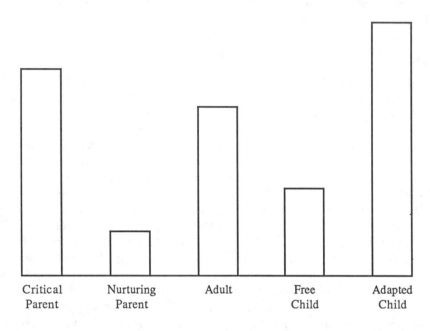

Critical	Nurturing	Adult	Free	Adapted
Parent	Parent		Child	Child

The part of Edna's Parent that is critical (CP, Critical Parent) was in full force and served her fairly well in business. However, her nurturing quality (NP, Nurturing Parent) was underdeveloped, hence a low energy on the egogram. Her Adult (A) was moderately high and also contributed to her business success. Her Free Child (FC), the part that is fun-loving, creative, sexual, and humorous, was likewise low, while her Adapted Child (AC), the part that still carried her hurt and resentful feelings, was the highest.

Her ability to nurture not only herself but others was low, and that is why she found it difficult to nurture the little girl in this redecision process. People who have great difficulty in forming relationships frequently have very low nurturing tendencies.

The doctor did not persist but retreated from the redecision process for the time being and encouraged Edna to practice and develop nurturing skills. In the group she practiced giving positive strokes to others; outside the group she joined a Big Sister organization wherein she took orphaned and disadvantaged girls to the zoo and ball games (Dusay and Dusay, 1984). Both the doctor and other group members exercised great patience in Edna's development of nurturing skills as, predictably, she did not take well to focusing positive energy on others. Strengthening weaker ego states is somewhat like exercising a muscle—it requires a great deal of practice both in and outside the consulting room. For those who succeed, the rewards of positive strokes from others are reinforcing, and the rewards are potentially high.

Conclusion

Although the preceding case material cannot do justice to the many vicissitudes of clinical TA, it does illuminate many of the important differences between TA and other therapies.

TA is an action therapy; the therapist is most active in structuring the milieu for redecision and change for successful life scripts. The therapist is more interested in eliciting feelings than in providing interpretations. The therapist encourages the patient to reexperience painful precedent events and then provides a nurturing atmosphere for the patient to do his or her work. Specific techniques familiar to practitioners of Gestalt, hypnosis, psychodrama, and behavioral psychology are used, and many students of these fields have been attracted to TA or a modified form of TA.

26

Conjoint Therapy

M. Joan Ormont
Louis R. Ormont

Psychoanalytic treatment has undergone radical changes during the last twenty years. Most of these innovations, as long as they adhere to the basic principles of analyzing resistances and transference, have had their successes. One that has won universal acceptance is group psychoanalysis (Wolf, 1949–1950). Another significant innovation has been conjoint analysis (Ormont and Strean, 1978). Conjoint treatment means different things to different therapists. In this chapter it refers to the concurrent treatment of a patient in two different settings by two different analysts. The analysts work separately to resolve the patient's resistances, one in a group setting and the other in an individual setting.

What unfolds in the individual sessions may be worked through emotionally in the group setting; what is touched on in the group setting can be explored in detailed depth in the individual setting. All the figures involved—the analysts and the group patients—tend to assume great importance to the patient.

Techniques of conjoint therapy have been successively refined. The method has proved singularly effective in resolving the resistances in preoedipal conditions, in borderline problems, in somatic conversions, and even in cases of severe character disorders (Spotnitz, 1976). We have discovered that structuring the therapeutic environment, based on the model of the psychological development of the child in the family setting, can facilitate the maturational growth of the patient's personality.

Because of the physical separation of the analysts and because each of them plays a part determined by the patient's history—for example, the individual analyst becoming the mother figure at times; the group analyst, the father figure—the two analysts can perform specific and totally different functions. One can analyze resistances while the other reinforces them (Weinberg, 1984). One can gratify libidinal yearnings while the other frustrates them. One can work to fulfill maturational needs while the other can study the effects of deprivation. Two analysts may become the

The authors wish to express their appreciation to George Weinberg, a fellow conjoint therapist, for his valuable suggestions.

maternal and paternal figures to patients in their different developmental emotional states. Or they may be seen as the same currently significant figure, split into contradictory functions. For example, one can be the good mother and the other the bad mother. Group members can serve the same function. They also can be viewed as siblings, as members of the extended family, or as other meaningful figures, such as teachers and nurses (Ormont, 1964).

Of the case illustrations that follow, the first typifies intense collaboration. As a married couple, the therapists were in constant contact. They went over many of the sessions in great detail. They used every opportunity to work through their countertransferential reactions to the patient. Together they fashioned interventions, mutually developed appropriate analytic attitudes, and monitored each other as they followed them through. In the second case, the conjoint analysts contacted each other only sporadically. Furthermore, each approached the patient with a different orientation and expectations. In the process of working with the common patient, they reached an effective working relationship. In both cases the results were judged satisfactory by all involved—especially by the patient.

In the first case, the patient saw his individual analyst once a week and the group once a week. In the second case, the patient saw her analyst four to five times a week and the group once a week.

The group sessions ran for an hour and a half with an occasional alternate session (meeting without the group analyst). In both cases, the individual sessions were suspended during the summer, during which time the group sessions (without the presence of the group therapist) continued.

An Individual Analyst Looks at Conjoint Therapy

The group analyst referred Harry, a thirty-seven-year-old man, to a woman analyst because Harry wanted to work more intensively on his inability to form a caring, rewarding relationship with a woman. At the time he entered treatment with the individual analyst, he did not know whether to marry his fiancée, Shirley. According to Harry, his fiancée was a "selfish, demanding woman, completely under the thumb of her mother." She did not work or engage in creative or volunteer activities but spent her days shopping, going to beauty parlors, and watching television. She coaxed Harry for a gold bracelet, a pearl necklace, and eventually a diamond ring. Harry felt there was something the matter with him because he didn't want to give her these presents. He imagined he was ungenerous. He gave them to her, but his heart was not in it. He questioned her values and he questioned the nature of his love. He felt put upon by having to fulfill her demands. When he discussed it with the analyst, he sounded compliant and childlike; in fact, he sounded as if he were as dominated by Shirley as he thought she was by her mother.

The novelty of seeing an individual analyst after eight years of group excited Harry, but almost at once he saw the analyst as a withholding, neglectful woman who reminded him of his mother. When he was a young boy, his mother had been away from the house in order to work and had communicated with him by leaving notes on the kitchen table. He experienced the same lack of maternal contact again. He complained about the analyst's silence and reported that he left the sessions with his mouth puckered up as if he wanted to suck milk. That early, though unavoidable, maternal neglect of him explained why he fell for outgoing, warm, manipulative women. They gave him a sense of nourishment and life. As the analyst explored his relationship with Shirley, his feelings about her demands, his hesitation about asking her to do things for him, he realized that Shirley's warmth flowed only when he was obedient. When he asserted himself, she withdrew and he felt rejected. When he understood this pattern, he broke his engagement. Shirley responded by lessening her demands and intensifying her warm and outgoing manner, and they resumed their engagement. This pattern had been repeated with other women several times in his life.

In spite of the analyst's lack of warmth and vitality in sessions, Harry began to see her as somebody who was always there to discuss things with him. When the first seven or eight months had passed and Harry's transference had intensified, he covertly conveyed his dissatisfaction with his analyst by constantly discussing group in his sessions. Moreover, he told her the group analyst was wonderful, brilliant, compassionate! In contrast with her, the group analyst was witty, generous—a perfect model for him. He complained that the individual analyst probably meant well but asked "dumb" questions. He told her about a woman in the group who understood him perfectly; he adored her; she had sexual feelings for him. He reported exchanges in the group word for word; he discussed the relevance of the group analyst's humorous interpretations. The individual analyst struggled with objective and subjective countertransference feelings. As the wife of the group analyst, she frequently and informally talked over with her husband Harry's development in individual treatment and her emotional response to his implied criticism of her (Ormont, 1961).

Subjective countertransference feelings of being dull, lifeless, stupid, humorless, inadequate swept over her. Harry had awakened in her latent feelings of uncertainty about her own effectiveness as a therapeutic agent. Feelings of inferiority and inadequacy provoked anger at and jealousy of the group analyst. Moreover, Harry's idealization of the group analyst awakened in her rivalrous feelings toward her brother who, in their childhood, had entertained the family and friends with card tricks, sleight of hand, and trumpet solos. That brother had always seemed to move into the spotlight.

Her objective countertransference reaction to being compared unfavorably with the wonderful male group analyst and those extraordinary group members was to feel punitive, irritated, and androgynous.

Her objective countertransference feelings were induced by Harry's narcissistic feelings. He felt nonsexual; so did she. He was furious at her for not being more giving; she was equally enraged at him. He wanted to punish her by telling her how terrific his group treatment was; she wanted to close her ears so she would not have to listen to one word he said. Harry put his thoughts and feelings into words. The analyst kept hers to herself and continued to listen patiently.

After fifteen months of treatment, Harry's transference changed. The individual analyst became the desirable object instead of the group analyst. She became the good mother figure, and the group analyst became the unreachable father figure.

At first Harry wouldn't verbalize sexual feelings toward her, but he talked about himself in a way that made her realize he had become competitive with the group analyst for first place in her affections. There were oedipal overtones in the way he courted her. In the following months he complained about his job as an account executive for a Madison Avenue advertising company. He said he had decided to change his career path because the company offered limited financial advancement opportunities. He went on to explore other professional options; he analyzed his strengths and weaknesses, concluding that he had excellent business judgment. Concurrently, he openly criticized the group analyst. He said that the group analyst did not pay enough attention to him, group members attacked him and the group analyst did not protect him. Harry saw flaws in all the group members. Now, in Harry's analytic world, only the individual analyst escaped his critical eye. She became the wonderful parent. She was no longer dull, humorless, stupid; she was intelligent, serene. Her faults had become strengths. Her silence now proved to him that she listened to him and accepted what he said. She was the one person who understood him.

Once Harry split his transference in this new way, it soothed the individual analyst's insecurities. This new attitude toward her poured balm on her suspicions of inferiority and, at the same time, heightened her intellectual curiosity.

She investigated his feelings toward the group analyst and his view of his experiences in group. She was able to analyze his resistance, which he was showing by arriving thirty to forty minutes late for his sessions in group. This turned out to be an acting out of his belief that he did not need as much attention; he was more independent of the group analyst, more autonomous, even superior. Afraid to verbalize his competitive feelings in the group, he was engaging in symbolic communication. Coming late and acting aloof were his way of demonstrating his superiority. The individual analyst helped him recognize and work through his resistance; he became able to tell the group how dissatisfied he was with them and with the analyst.

Emotionally, the individual analyst understood Harry's splitting better when she was the "good" parent. When she had been the "bad" parent, it was difficult for her to understand and accept the conjoint process. She had felt inferior and inadequate and had questioned her own technique. She wondered whether she would help him more if she were more interpretive and interactive the way the group analyst and the group members were. Although she had continued to follow her usual investigative method, she had almost totally believed that her approach was a poor second best to what the group analyst and the group members were doing. In other words, she tended to be defensive. The patient had picked it up. He said she was inadequate, and she was afraid she was. Compounding the problem was that she agreed with the things he said about the group analyst; he described that analyst's strengths accurately. When the switch in the split occurred and she became the "good" object, she felt more conflict-free. She knew she had not changed overnight any more than the group analyst had, but now she enjoyed Harry's admiration. As for his devaluation of the group, she took it with a grain of salt. She realized that her patient was painting his negative picture of the group with as distorted a brush as he had used for his original, idealized version.

She used the positive transference to encourage her patient to take responsibility for his relationship with the group analyst and for his experiences in group. This was done through a consistent examination of exactly what happened in group. As the patient talked about events in group, he would now correct himself and doubt his own view of what had taken place, often reaching a new understanding on his own. He felt, under the analyst's noncritical attitude, that he could explore his picture of group by talking to her about it. He would then go into group to check out his reactions with the other members. Harry modeled himself on the group analyst or at least on the way he perceived him because he had idealized him for so long. Fortunately, he was eventually able to integrate his rivalrous feelings with his feelings of admiration.

Next he tackled a new business—his own. He went about this in a creative but disciplined way—a combination he adopted from the group analyst. His competitive feelings forcefully propelled him forward. In a year he figured he was making three times as much money as the group analyst made. He was afraid to let the analyst know how successful he was, imagining that the analyst would not love him if Harry was not inferior to him. Behind this fear lay a death wish toward his father; he was symbolically showing off his sexual prowess to the individual analyst for her admiration.

In spite of his efforts, she felt detachment and indifference when he would try to induce admiration in her. She realized that this reaction was the very one that his mother had had to him. Apparently his mother had not enjoyed his growth into manhood, had found no joy in his accomplishments; her own worries and responsibilities plagued her, and Harry was one more burden. When the analyst questioned the validity of her patient's feelings, he began to question them also and finally to question his fears of the group analyst. Sensing his maturational need, the group analyst responded with enthusiastic admiration to his ability to make money, to change careers so flexibly, and to put his creativity into action. The group came to see him as capable and energetic and no longer as impoverished.

As he became sure of the cohesiveness of his own ego, seeing himself as a doer in the world and appreciating the constancy of the objects in his life, he was able to separate the individual analyst from himself. He found subtle indications that she had admirable qualities, although he would not praise her directly. He began to displace them onto fantasies of finding them in another woman. During this year Harry talked about the qualities he wanted in a wife.

Instead of making love to women on his first date, as had been his pattern, he postponed sexual gratification in order to know these women better. Now when he went on a date, he avoided being swept away by the blandishments of warm, outgoing women because he realized that this had interfered with his ability to discriminate between being castrated and being enhanced. In this fashion he found three women he liked. For several months he courted them and developed good friendships with all. As he continued to talk about these women in his sessions, he decided that two of them would not be good matches for him. Iris, the third one, grew on him. He admired her more as their relationship deepened. She was willing to listen to his needs and cooperate with him to try to satisfy them without sacrificing her own uniqueness. After he had known Iris for approximately a year, which coincided with his third year of treatment, they were married. The group and the group analyst supported this step.

Harry's self-understanding, acquired through his previous eight years of group treatment, his intelligence, industry, and perseverance allowed him to solve his problems and find a loving relationship in a relatively short time. Many patients need more time to resolve such difficulties with intimacy.

Harry's treatment in group and with an individual analyst aroused countertransference feelings in the individual analyst that are common to all individual analysts who work with patients conjointly. The importance of the group and of the group analyst to a patient may prick the vanity of the individual analyst. The tender blossoming of the transference in the first few months may seem to be weakened by the patient's transference to the group leader and the group members. Whatever latent competitive feelings the individual analyst has may be fanned by the patient's conjoint treatment. Patients are quick to read the analyst's unconscious and to release some subtle aggression by praising the group analyst to irritate the individual one. This is especially likely to occur the first time an individual analyst works conjointly.

Occasionally experienced analysts are caught in the competitive transference trap. One well-trained woman analyst has worked conjointly for twenty years. A pattern repeats itself with her. For five or six years the conjoint treatment works well; then slowly she begins to generate the patient's aggression toward the group analyst, who, by now, is the bad object. She polarizes the splitting. Since she is the good object, the patient responds to her desire to be the only analyst in his life and leaves the group. Such an unsatisfactory ending to conjoint treatment satisfies her competitive feelings; it is proof to her that she is a superior analyst to the group analyst.

When conducted properly, conjoint treatment has advantages that easily repay the burden of the analyst's having to endure unpleasant feelings. After all, the mother/child paradigm is predicated on the existence of a father in the background. The group analyst can provide the same balance in treatment. The group analyst and group members arouse memories, feelings, and conflicts that the patient brings into individual treatment; the relationship between patient and group adds another dimension to the analyst's understanding of the patient. The analyst encourages a patient who talks freely in individual sessions but clams up in group, in much the same way that a mother encourages a shy child to speak up in kindergarten. The patient who is outgoing and verbal in group but monotonous and without affect with the individual analyst is making a statement about early feelings toward the mother that are hindering interpersonal relationships in the present. Each patient shares his historical and present-day feelings in a unique way with the individual analyst, the group analyst, and the group members.

The Group Analyst Looks at Conjoint Therapy

In contrast with the first case, which was presented from the point of view of the individual analyst, now let us consider one somewhat different, told by the group analyst. This second point of view, added to the first, may furnish greater perspective on the conjoint process.

My first contact with Phyllis was with her individual analyst, a respected, classically trained professional. He wanted to know whether I had space in a group for a twenty-eight-year-old woman whom he described as a recluse. She had been in treatment with him for six years, four times a week. When they started, she had been withdrawn, almost catatonic. Although she had learned to talk to him, he had, to all intents and purposes, remained her only contact with the outside world.

From the tenor of what he said, I gathered that he thought the group could serve as a transitional socializing agent: she needed to know how to get along with people. He had reservations about the group as a therapeutic force and saw no need for us to be in any ongoing contact.

I agreed to interview her. Phyllis was an unusually attractive woman, dressed in a somber suit with no makeup. Her manner was well-bred and markedly self-reserved. She offered little information about herself or her background. She was by far the youngest of four and felt separated by age from the rest. Each of the others had been raised by nurses and packed off to school at the earliest possible time. She herself had stubbornly refused to leave home—mostly out of fear—and had attended a fine girls' school within walking distance.

Her mother was an active socialite, deeply involved in many cultural organizations. Her father, a partner in a highly respected law firm, seemed to do little actual legal work; he devoted his time to his extensive coin collection. Of the two parents, she spoke somewhat more warmly of her father.

Her teachers were the first to note her tendency to withdraw. She did not engage in any extracurricular activity, preferring to spend her free time in the library. However, her family had ignored the school's report and appeared quite content with her superb scholastic record. Despite this success in school, she made no attempt to go on to college.

At eighteen, on the death of both parents (within six months of each other), she withdrew from social life even further. For five years she lived alone in a brownstone, buffered against the outside world by a collection of maids and servants. Independently wealthy by inheritance, she had no need to enter the work force. Her sole outlets were reading and an avid interest in the visual arts: theater, movies, and exhibitions.

When she developed a number of physical complaints that were without serious physiological basis, her family physician—for whom she felt deep attachment—prevailed on her to enter analytic treatment. She proceeded to develop the same strong feelings toward her analyst.

Now, six years later, she felt pressured by that analyst to go into group treatment. She told me she considered a collection of more than four persons to be an "unruly crowd." I was not to assume that she would be in group any longer than absolutely necessary.

I formed a clinical impression of a rather likable, highly self-critical woman with a large reservoir of unexpressed anger. She set careful limits on everyone and everything.

Her phobic nature appeared at once in the group. In her first session, she sat by the door with her coat tightly wrapped around her. She spoke only when addressed and then in short, clipped phrases. In all respects she gave the impression that she had dropped in for a one-time visit. After each session she left immediately without a word to anyone.

In spite of her aloofness, one man, Roland, found her intriguing. He sought to put her at ease, sometimes inviting her into the flow of the group. But each time she made it very obvious that she preferred to be left alone.

After some ten sessions the members became restless, exasperated by her silence. One woman said she felt as if Phyllis were criticizing them, sizing them all up to judge whether they were acceptable. What did she think of the group so far?

She summed it up in a word: "Distasteful."

Instead of taking offense, several members wanted to know why she thought so. She turned red; her body stiffened. After a long moment of silence, a member reminded her that she was supposed to talk at least once in a while. Her face trembled in terror, and I intervened strongly on her behalf. She really didn't have to talk unless she wanted to; she was not to be pushed. At that, she looked surprised, even pleased, at my forcefulness.

Later that session, at a time when the group had momentarily broken into subgroups, Roland asked her how she saw the group now. Instead of giving him a personal reaction, she told him everyone looked frustrated, all the members were competing for attention. The others agreed in unison. She was visibly taken aback by this welcoming confirmation.

Over the following weeks members would occasionally turn to her for an opinion of what was going on. Though tinged with criticism, what she said was inevitably on the mark. Still, she wanted no credit. Whenever her admirer, Roland, praised her astuteness, she brushed him off. She told him, "These impressions aren't really new. I've gone over them with my individual analyst many times." And apparently the analyst had agreed with her that the group brought out people's self-indulgences. His support of her negative observations had given her a place to stand so that she could tell them off.

In the sessions that followed, she spoke even more derisively. She described the members, especially Roland, as shallow and called the whole group experience scattered. She constantly told members they thought too much about people's feelings. I surmised that her comments echoed the reservations of her individual analyst, who I already knew was skeptical about group analysis as a therapeutic tool. He told her she was in group for social skills, not to expect analytic work from group members. They were laypersons, after all.

Time and again, when someone in the group would admire an insight of hers, she would pass the credit to her analyst.

Accurate as her insights were, they grew increasingly scathing. Sometimes I would intervene, rephrasing one of her comments to a group member to mitigate the pain it caused. She seemed pandemically dissatisfied. If the group was supposed to make her a socially acceptable person, it had so far failed to do so. With the persevering exception of Roland, no one particularly liked her.

One woman questioned whether anyone could ever please Phyllis and whether her criticism of others didn't cover a profound self-critical attitude. Phyllis took the group member's question to her individual analyst, the only person in the world she still respected. When he confirmed that indeed she did attack herself unconsciously, she reviewed with him what everyone had told her. To his surprise, they were insights he had offered repeatedly with little effect. He proceeded to show her how she had done the same things with him and reminded her how they had gone over them before. Phyllis revised her view of the group. Perhaps it really could give her something.

She moderated her critical attitude somewhat and even found some things to admire about several members. She also gave more attention to what Roland said, even talking to him about a pressing problem he had with his parents.

In one exchange they discovered that they both liked foreign films. Although she had reservations about his favorites, they would gravitate to the subject time and again. Many found it disconcerting. Was this a coffee klatsch? They circumvented this complaint by arriving earlier than the others—sometimes as much as twenty minutes—to talk about films, writers, and directors. If anyone pointed out that this was a substitute for talking about feelings toward Roland, she would discount it, brushing aside any suggestion of intimacy between them. They just shared common interests, that's all.

One day her individual analyst called me. Were my group members in the habit of acting out? Did I condone socializing out of the group session? He sounded vindicated in his skepticism about group treatment, as if the true nature of the group experience were finally emerging. He cautioned me that he had not sent his patient to group to find a boyfriend. As an analyst, he was concerned only with her character resistance to forming relationships; he had no intention of arranging one for her. I was baffled. She hadn't shown the slightest affection toward anyone in the group. He said I had better give her behavior a second look. I told him I would bring it up.

I didn't have to. Phyllis opened the next group session by saying she had met Roland at a film festival three times in the last three days. She asked us what he was trying to arrange. Instantly, several group members pounced on Roland. He had been in group long enough to know this was a breach of contract. He protested that their meetings were really coincidental. He hadn't known she was going to be there. The film sponsors had served coffee, and they had taken theirs together. She was the only person there he knew. And they had just chatted about the film—nothing more. In fact, he would have felt awkward ignoring her. It was such a small crowd. If it would make her feel better, he would try to act as if she weren't there, although that would be quite a feat.

The members asked how she saw it. Apparently, from what she said, these meetings had aroused a number of fantasies in which she met the perfect man with tastes absolutely identical to hers—and he swept her off her feet. She found it so agitating that she couldn't sleep. She emphatically did not want the group to invade her real life. Nor did she think she could continue the film series unless Roland withdrew. The situation upset her too much.

Roland felt blackmailed and coerced. Then a group member suggested that it might be the other way around; perhaps Phyllis was the one leery of acting on her sexual fantasies! Phyllis outrightly denied it. But she did not appear at the next session, and Roland reported that she had not been at the film series. When I called her, I got only her answering machine, nor did she return my call.

After she missed the second session, I called her private analyst. What were her plans? He assured me that all was going well, that she was working on her fears, that I should be patient with this lapse. He even thanked me for calling. He was going to tell Phyllis about my concern for her and get her permission to talk more about her to me. His attitude had utterly changed.

She returned to the group the next session furious at her film companion. She was now convinced that *he* was the one acting on sexual fantasies. She got him to admit he did have sexual thoughts toward her, but he didn't see how he was acting on them. Phyllis wanted to know exactly what these fantasies were. She kept plying him with questions. Grudgingly, he revealed more details. One member finally broke in. This was a one-sided inquisition. What about *her* fantasies? Again she withdrew, this time feeling put upon and fuming with rage.

During her angry silence, a few members speculated about why she was so afraid to tell her thoughts. Roland wondered why her whole body had stiffened. He guessed that if she said something, it would probably be a forbidden thought. Phyllis sputtered that she felt more like kicking him than talking. Then, to everyone's surprise, she roundly cursed the whole group. Some members were shocked that this well-spoken woman knew such language. But most of them, delighted by the energy in her release, praised her for expressing such rage—putting her murderous thoughts into words. One man told her that he felt comfortable with her for the first time. She had joined the human race. Then, to ease her embarrassment, the members instinctively began to talk about something else. Quietly, she regained control of herself.

From then on she joined in more. She told them about her catatonic states and about her violent fantasies—about acts she felt on the verge of committing or feared she might if she allowed herself to. They were all struck by her new sense of freedom and the likability that they had never before seen in her.

About a month later she brought up some sexual fantasies. These were generally of a "me too" variety: they were parallel revelations. She would quietly inject them after someone else had spoken about sex. She intimated that she planned to talk more about sex in her individual analysis.

Soon afterward, she announced that her aunt had invited her to spend a month in Palm Beach and she was going. This would be her first time out of the city. She chatted with the women in the group about what to wear and what to take.

After that vacation, she sparkled with a new sense of liveliness and gossiped hilariously about the social life she had discovered. However, she confided that many of the men she had met seemed superficial, not half as interesting as those in her group. She took a lively, sometimes intrusive interest in the lives of the men in the group and would boldly tell them what she thought of their dress, their manners, their tastes in women, and their problems with intimacy. Her suggestions were often excellent. Even so, when any of the men got intimate with her, she would instantly back up, albeit good-naturedly.

One session she reported a dream in which all the men played roles. She told us how her private analyst saw it. Not surprisingly, each of the men had his own interpretation. Some chose to dwell on what it said about her "real" feelings toward them; others saw its sexual overtones; still others speculated about whom they represented in her past life—a brother, her father. She was delighted by the number of ways that single dream could be understood. She took these new interpretations back to her private session. Especially at this time, there was much bringing back and forth of material between the two settings.

Then a new man joined. She was the first to introduce herself to him. They liked each other at once; he came from her social set; although he had never met her, they knew people in common. However, Roland would intrude himself whenever things got close between her and the newcomer. Feeling hurt, he found fault with her over trivia. But that only consolidated her involvement with the newcomer.

As group analyst, I had felt strong reactions to the feelings she had induced in me. While treating this woman, I had found myself protective, annoyed, controlled, distant, even admiring, but I had never found her affectionate until now. That newly revealed side of her aroused sexual feelings in others as well. It gave her a fullness that she had not possessed.

Just at this time Phyllis suddenly announced that she was ending her private treatment. Since she had been lauding her analyst, it made no sense. When I questioned her, she reeled off a number of reasons, none of them persuasive.

I immediately called her analyst, who told me his impressions of what was going on. Things had been proceeding well. He had construed everything she reported about the group as if she had been talking about her family. He had repeatedly used group events as a springboard to enter her early life, and it had uncovered much new material from her childhood. Recently, however, she had stopped speaking about the group, except to say that she had met a new man there. Simultaneously, she began to take a great interest in the analyst himself, indicating that she harbored fantasies of spending time with him socially. She had looked up his professional biography, read his technical articles, and queried him about himself. Then, suddenly, after a number of static sessions, she had announced that she was cured. Her symptoms were gone. Her analyst didn't agree that the disappearance of her symptoms meant she was cured. We decided to discuss the case in detail. Together, we went over a number of impressions, dreams from many sources, putting together our best composite of what was going on.

We realized that she was in conflict over her sexual feelings. On the one hand, to experience them more intensely might propel her into unacceptable behavior—or at least being openly seductive toward her analyst. On the other hand, she *wanted* to act on them. She secretly hoped that by leaving treatment, she could meet the analyst and marry him—a quite acceptable behavior.

It seemed to me the group could help her over the impasse. We could provide an arena, free of conflict, in which she had confidence. In it, we could exert concerned influence, help her see the impasse from many angles. I briefed him on how we could do this.

At every opportunity I focused the group's interest on her decision to end her personal analysis. Roland was the first member to surmise the truth. She wasn't truly finished with her analysis but was fleeing her analyst. The newcomer refined the observation. She was fleeing her sexual feelings. The key was her fear of acting on these feelings. When these two men whom she liked saw eye to eye, she agreed. Other members joined in. They pointed out that there was little chance, given the nature of her analyst, that she could get into real trouble. Still others pointed out that the real unsolved problem was with her father.

Her private analyst was prepared to pick it up from there. He concentrated on exploring the differences between her father and himself. Now Phyllis was working on the same central relationship in both analyses. New memories surfaced, and these revealed a quite different picture of her early father—one of a man both seductive and aloof.

Her erotic feelings toward the individual analyst dissipated. She came to regard him as a somewhat distant but objective fellow who had a steadfast interest in her.

Phyllis herself attributed the change in her perception to her deepening attachment to the newcomer in the group. She added that she had met a wonderful man recently at a museum benefit and this too had helped give her distance from the analyst. With our help she had switched her feelings to someone in the real world.

Of course, there was still work to do. But her journey toward a new life, using conjoint treatment to help her, had taken her a long way. She now considered the two forms of treatment equally essential. The group served as her personal support system where she could get a diversity of opinions on whatever concerned her. And she had learned to give unstintingly to other people in the group. The world outside, which she had so feared and hidden from, had been turned into a world to be explored and enjoyed.

This case shows conjoint treatment succeeding even when the analysts have somewhat different persuasions. We started with different styles of operating and with slightly different theoretical orientations. We met in the common understanding of one patient. There was no question that the individual analyst was self-sufficient and competent. Yet, despite his initial reservations, he learned to appreciate what the group could contribute.

Together, we provided the patient with diverse benefits. Five stand out (Ormont, 1981). First, we offered her *multiple settings*. The group milieu served as an open forum. The individual setting gave her the space to explore the reactions that she felt in group but was hesitant to air there.

Second, we provided *multiple transferences*. The group enabled her to resolve a rooted oedipal resistance that had threatened her individual treatment. She saw in the group members aspects of her family. At times these members served as transference objects for her aggressive brother, indifferent sisters, meddlesome aunts, and distant but energetic mother. In the end, Roland, who never lost interest in her, evolved into the maturational father she had always yearned for.

Third, we offered *multiple observers*. Long before Phyllis came into the group, her individual analyst had discussed with her many of the same patterns that the members subsequently saw in her. Her hearing these descriptions a second time from the group members exerted a profound effect on her. She would spend the week between sessions mulling over the similarities between what the group and the individual analyst had seen.

Fourth, we provided her with *multiple interpreters*. The members offered her key interpretations which her analyst had offered but which she had warded off. In the group each member used his or her own unique imagery. The totality gave a powerful thrust to the process. She let down her defense enough to hear the group, and with her remarkable auditory recall, she recognized the similarity of the group message to the one she had been hearing (Strean, 1985).

The fifth advantage is that of having *multiple maturational agents*. The group experience had special value and contributed mightily because of her private treatment. Her individual analyst had said the right things but frequently without the right emotion for her particular needs. The individual in this case could not do enough. Perhaps no individual could have. Some patients can draw the emotional reactions they need from real life. But this patient's isolation made this almost impossible—and the individual analyst must have sensed this. Group members immediately met her emotional requirements. From one or another member Phyllis heard what was said in just the right dosage. We always knew when a member touched her emotionally because she would respond with a stream of feelingful reactions (Strean, 1985).

There are other combinations of therapeutic alliance between the analyst and an outside agent. That agent might be a personal physician, classroom teacher, or physical therapist, for example. It is doubtful, however, that any such combination could have offered Phyllis the rigor, the consistency, and the intimacy or could have instilled and sustained the motivation that this form of conjoint treatment provided.

Part Six ೫

Family System
and Marital Therapies

Family systems and marital therapies have dramatically changed the focus of earlier therapies geared to treat an individual. They have attempted to derive methods to treat a family or a couple. The principle of family techniques is that individual pathology has its roots in a disturbed family and that changing the patterns in a disturbed family will have a powerful effect on all its pathological members. Marital therapy as well shifts the focus from the individual to the interactional pattern of the two partners. These techniques are outgrowths of general systems theory, which in many fields has been applied to the interdependence of life forces and in the area of mental health has been brought into the treatment of the family and the marriage. Chapters in this section include cases that were treated from a family systems approach, conjoint marital therapy approach, couples group therapy, marriage contract techniques, and family strategic psychotherapy, including treating an individual alone within the principles of a systems theory.

In Chapter Twenty-Seven, ''Family Therapy,'' Joan K. Taylor presents the first task of the family therapist as assessing the family system in the belief that the person who seeks therapy or the situation that is problematic has to be understood and responded to in the context of that system. In the case presented, a woman seeks help for a problem that she insists is solely hers, not related to history, husband, or children. Yet, as the treatment progresses, the author illustrates how the therapist makes choices according to a systems perspective, and the entire network of psychological relationships is revealed.

James L. Framo uses a case history in Chapter Twenty-Eight, ''Couples Group Therapy with Family-of-Origin Sessions,'' to show how a difficult couple was treated by a sequence of conjoint marital therapy, couples group therapy, and a session with each partner together with his or her parents and siblings. The couple is used to illustrate how powerful, unconscious influences from family-of-origin experiences regulate marital choice and the course of a marriage. Particularly interesting in this case is how a woman's lifelong enmity toward her father (projected onto her husband's family) dissipated after her face-to-face encounter with her previously estranged father.

Clifford J. Sager begins Chapter Twenty-Nine, "Couples Therapy with Marriage Contracts," by briefly reviewing the concept of dual marriage contracts and then illustrates the use of the contracts as a basis for organizing pertinent data to guide the therapist's interventions and the couple's understanding of their relationship through a case history of the brief (ten-session) treatment of a couple. A panoply of therapeutic techniques based on psychodynamics and on systems, behavioral, and cognitive theories is demonstrated in the author's integration of therapeutic approaches. Employing the marriage contract concept in couples work is advanced as allowing the therapist to use those interventions that are consistent with his or her own therapeutic bias and comfort.

Chapter Thirty, "Strategic Psychotherapy," outlines some basic principles and concepts of strategic psychotherapy. These include circular causality, goals of therapy, the unit of focus, and the use of direct interventions and of therapeutic paradox. John J. O'Connor reviews three predominant schools of strategic therapy and then presents four cases with the essential ingredients of the therapeutic interventions outlined: a bulimic woman treated individually, an obsessional boy and his family, a problem of impotence in a couple, and a migrainous girl treated as part of the family system. The cases illustrate some of the basic strategic concepts as well as how a symptom can be related to and treated as part of a larger social system.

27

Family Therapy

Joan K. Taylor

Act One: The Person

I first met Eleanor Chapin a year before her family's therapy began, when she came to me by herself for twelve sessions. But because for me family, or "systems," describes a way of thinking, it was family therapy from the minute she walked in.

Eleanor is forty-three, married to Frank, a bank executive, and the mother of four children: Sue, fifteen; Ted, fourteen; Nell, ten; and Will, eight. Eleanor also had a management job, and she came in because of difficulty with her boss, Barbara, and anxiety attacks when she thought about the job.

Eleanor wanted to keep the sessions impersonal and was hesitant to describe her family, either past or present. That was frustrating to me, for while I believe a person's work system is important, I think the family system is much more so. What do I mean by *system*? It is the network of relationships in which a person is embedded. A system is a set of parts, related to one another in a meaningful, dynamic, and rule-governed way. It has a boundary that separates it from other systems, and yet it is in constant interaction with other systems. There is usually some sort of hierarchic relationship among its parts. Further, some parts within the larger system can align themselves together and form subsystems, with their own boundaries and rules and relations to other subsystems. No part of a system can adequately be described in isolation from the other parts, and a change in any one part of the system can produce change in any other part or can reverberate throughout the whole system. And lastly, an imbalance in the system can be expressed in any part of the system (Kerr, 1981).

All the elements of the definition above will have flesh-and-blood correlates in the family you are going to meet here. Unfortunately, Eleanor wouldn't tell me much about that family. I introduced the idea of making her genogram (Bowen, 1978), which is a chart of family members and events and dates, using a system of notation common in the family field. She agreed but without much enthusiasm. She came from plain and loving parents who were still alive and well in upstate New York. She was one of two children, and the only stressful event in her childhood was when her adored younger brother, Will, had a motorcycle accident that left him

439

hemiplegic. Things seemed all right in her marriage, and she described Frank as very supportive and loving. Her older daughter, Sue, was on the threshold of adolescence, and I noted with her that this is a stressful time for all families, demanding reorganization in the system. In addition, Frank's father had died in the last year, an event that often brings system change and rebalancing. However, she stressed that she just wanted to talk about her job.

As we talked about the job, I couldn't see anything that seemed so bad. What was I missing? Were there things in the system I knew nothing about? Did Frank not want her to work, so that she needed an excuse to quit? My wonderings were cut short when she came in one day and announced she had quit, felt better, knew she would have no more anxiety attacks, and would be stopping therapy next week.

After she left I occasionally thought of her, uneasily. Did I expect to hear from her again? Maybe. Eleanor was a member of a family, a part of a system. Up to then, all the parts had been functioning pretty well together. But now Eleanor had made a big change in her own role, just at a time when systemic change was demanded because of their children's moving into adolescence (Carter and McGoldrick, 1980) and Frank's father's death. Maybe her change was adaptive in a positive way, and the parts would all work together as well as or better than ever. But maybe her change was maladaptive? Sometimes a body reacts maladaptively to back strain by changing its gait, and a bunion develops. If Eleanor's quitting her job was maladaptive in that way, I would hear from her again. And if I did, the stress in the system could have shown up anywhere in that system. I might hear about individual problems with Eleanor or Frank, symptoms in a child, marital difficulty, or something else. The system, if you will, would have a symptom, would identify a patient. To keep my thinking clear, whatever Eleanor might call about, I would refer, in my own mind, to that person or unit not as patient but as "identified patient."

Prelude to Act Two

"Is this Dr. Taylor? Joan? Do you remember me? This is Eleanor Chapin."

"Eleanor, of course I remember you. How are you?"

"Pretty well. But we're having some trouble with our son, Ted, and I wonder if you could see him?"

"What's the problem, Eleanor?"

"Nothing serious. He got into a little trouble at school and is suspended, and he won't talk to us about it. I thought maybe he might talk to you."

"You know, Eleanor, I'd want to see all of you to talk about it. When I hear of a youngster having difficulty, that difficulty either affects the whole family or is affected by it, and I can't do a good job just seeing the young person alone. I might see him alone later, but to start, I'd want to see you and Frank and the other three kids."

Long pause. "Joan, Frank is so busy, and I don't want the other kids to know about this."

"Eleanor, I'm sorry. I'd be glad to give you the names of some colleagues who work individually. But remember what I said about the family emotional system? I can be most helpful to Ted—and to you and Frank—if I at least in the beginning have a chance to meet all of you."

"You really have a one-track mind, don't you?"

''No, that's exactly what I don't have, and what you're asking me to have by looking just at Ted. And I'm sorry, but I'm turning you down.''

If this situation were unknown to me, I might have relented and initially joined the system by meeting one member. But I was prepared for Eleanor's call, and I had a hypothesis I was following.

''OK, I'll talk to Frank.'' She did, and we set a time to meet.

Eleanor would meet, in the coming weeks, a more active therapist than she had known individually. So much goes on in family sessions that the therapist must operate from plans and take charge of the sessions. I would videotape the sessions and study them between meetings to help me begin to understand the complex relationships between the parts of the system I was about to meet (Haley, 1976).

Act Two: The Family

''Joan, this is Frank Chapin, my husband.''

Firm handshake, direct gaze—nice-looking. I was surprised, though, at Eleanor's appearance. She'd gained about fifteen pounds since I saw her last, which would have been OK, but she carried it poorly and looked much less attractive than before.

''Sue, our seventeen-year-old.''

Lovely, gentle, maybe a little shy, but a good handshake.

''Nell, twelve years.''

Looks like her sister.

''Will, ten.''

Ha, an imp!

''And Ted, sixteen.''

Nice-looking too, but sloppy—and mad. No nice handshake here for the doctor.

Pleasantries out of the way, video easily accepted—Will thought it was great, and the girls were used to it from school—the family sat and we got down to business.

Because family therapists often think of the shape of a family, what we call its structure, we pay a lot of attention to how people sit. The arrangement can provide data to form hypotheses about how they relate, where the coalitions are, who is an outsider, whether the parental alliance that ought to exist is split, and so on (Minuchin, 1974). I noted that Frank and Eleanor sat together, rather than with Ted, the ''identified patient,'' between them, and that Frank seemed unusually solicitous of Eleanor, folding her jacket, getting her an ashtray.

''Who'd like to begin?''

''Well, Joan—''

''No, Eleanor, you take a rest. Joan—can I call you Joan too? That's how Eleanor's always spoken of you. And call me Frank too. OK?''

And he went on to tell me about increasing trouble over the last year with Ted. Ted had gone from a pleasant, achieving kid, fun to be with at home, nice friends, to the sullen, messy boy who was slumped on my sofa. His grades had dropped, he had become rudely argumentative at school, had called his math teacher a ''dork,'' which had led to the suspension, and, after many breaks of increasingly strict curfews, had recently been grounded for two weeks. The call to my office had come after he had sneaked out of his bedroom window one night and had been picked up by the local police with a gang of boys who had taken two cases of beer to a school playground and proceeded to get noisily drunk and disorderly.

Frank stopped and looked at Ted and then at me, waiting.

"You've all really had a hard time! Sue, have you heard about all this before?"

The family therapist has to "join" the whole family, not a part of it. I must let Frank know I've heard him, yet not make Ted feel he is here to be dumped on.

"I—what—should I call you Joan too?" asked Sue.

"Well, Sue, maybe it's more comfortable if you and your sister and brothers call me Dr. Taylor."

Smoothly functioning families usually have a hierarchic relationship between adults and children. She is asking me to define our hierarchy here, and I do.

"I know *all* about it. Mom talks to me, and so does Ted." And she started to cry. So much for the other kids' being kept out of it.

The concept of boundary describes the regulation of how much emotion, relating, information, and so on flows between one person and another or one subsystem and another. If the boundary is too rigid, too impermeable, people and subsystems are isolated and cannot learn about or help one another. If it is too thin, too permeable, a kind of fusion can take place, and a person or subsystem has trouble developing individuality or may be overburdened by the troubles of others (Minuchin, Rosman, and Baker, 1978). Sue looked as though she was the confidant of two warring parties and was in danger of being overburdened.

"I hope your being here all together can help," I said softly.

"Nell, how about you?"

"Whenever I got up, when they were hollering, mom would say, 'Go back to bed!' and I did. But sometimes I talked to Sue."

"So you're probably hearing some new things today. I'm glad you're with us. Will, how about you?"

"I don't know what they're talking about." He wiggled and dropped his handkerchief—and snuggled against Sue, who hugged him. Sue, as oldest child, might have her hands full responding to perceived needs in the family. I would have to check up on that and see whether it was affecting her own life outside the family.

My strategy, and a usual one, is to address each family member early in the initial interview, getting from each some reaction to the opening statement of the problem. The constant question is when to go to the "identified patient." I'd try now.

"Ted, your father has told quite a story. I wonder if you'd like to tell me something of what's been happening, as you see it."

"No."

"You know, your input is important here. Parents and children don't always see eye to eye on things that happen—like parties and ground rules and stuff like that. Could you say a few words about how you see things at home?"

"Why should I? So you can dump on me too? Another nosy—"

"Ted," said Frank warningly.

"No—" I stopped him. Turning to Ted again, I said, "Please go on, Ted. I really want to hear what you have to say."

One of the things a family therapist does is to provide, by blocking, a boundary. I wanted to make a connection, of any kind, between Ted and me, as I had with the other family members, and Frank was stopping it. The therapy would see me again and again acting as a boundary regulator. Where people were separated, I would actively encourage their communication. When communication between two persons was stopped by the action of a third person, I would block that person. When decisions could not be made because too many people were speaking, I would direct who could speak, when, and to whom. This action in blocking Frank was the first of many in which I tried out my power to direct the flow of family communication. Would he accept, in this small way, my leadership?

"Sorry."

"Now, Ted, tell me again. It feels to you like I'm going to dump on you?"

"You heard my father. I'm no good. I'm dirty. I'm dumb. I'm a trouble-maker. Well, bullshit!" He looked up defiantly for a reaction.

Inside I was pleased. The angry, articulate kids are easier to deal with than the sullen, quiet ones, at least at the beginning. It's easier to change interaction than to get it going.

"Ted, you really feel like they think there's nothing good about you? How long's this been going on?"

"Like he said, a year. Just because I don't like sissy sports. I'm tired of Preppie Paradise—I'm old enough to do what I want. If we lived in the city, I'd have a job and could go to dances. Whose business is it who my friends are?"

"Ted—" This time it was Eleanor. I held up a hand to block her. She settled back.

"Ted, it sounds like you have some important concerns that have to do with growing up. I'm going to want to hear a lot more about them. Will you think about them, because I'm going to ask you about them later, OK?"

"Yeah, sure, big deal!" and he slumped back again. But it seemed OK. I think I'd succeeded, at least momentarily, in joining him and making him hope there might be something here for him other than criticism.

"Eleanor, you had something you wanted to say?" After blocking someone, it's important to come back to him or her.

"I listen to Ted, and I listen to Frank, and—I don't know, maybe all this is my fault. Since I stopped working, after I saw you, things have gone from bad to worse. I've been very involved with the kids, maybe too much so, and—well, Ted's a handful. He's always been active, into everything, but OK. But when he started playing football last year, and he's big, and he got a place on the team—well, I just couldn't take it. Every time he went out on the field, I was sure he'd be hurt. And then—I don't know if you knew there was a boy killed in our league. So every time he went out, that's all I could see. And he got knocked out once, and when he was down on the ground and didn't get up—" She started to cry.

"But, Mom—"

"Damn it, Ted, shut up."

"Ted, Mom's just—"

Frank put his arm around Eleanor to comfort her—and the second segment of the initial interview had begun.

In the first segment I make, as I said, a "joining maneuver" with each family member, in which I interact with him or her and protect that interaction from intrusion from other members. In the second segment, I direct them or allow them to interact with each other. I will observe the family as they interact in the problem area and see whether I can deduce from this interaction the meaning of the problem or symptom. I will try to see what possible use it serves for the entire system and for each individual and what family or individual maneuvers are making it continue. This is information that the family can't tell me, as many of the interactions take place out of awareness. I would now allow whatever would go on to happen and would later study it on the tape, to try to understand the sequences of behavior (Minuchin and Fishman, 1981).

Silence.

Eleanor wiped her eyes, Frank settled down and glared at Ted, and the boy slumped even lower on the sofa. Sue looked in pain, Nell looked anxiously from face to face, and Will giggled, his usual response to felt anxiety in the family.

"Eleanor," I said, "do you think you could go on?"

But Frank started to answer me. He took his role as Eleanor's protector very seriously.

"Frank, could I hear it from Eleanor?"

"No, listen," and he started to tell me about Eleanor's reaction to Ted's football playing. He would not accept my challenge to his role of protector, at least not now. This told me something about its importance to him.

"Frank, it's OK, hon. Let me." He took Eleanor's hand as she started to talk. She told me that after she left her job and stopped therapy, her anxiety attacks had abated for some weeks but then began recurring. They peaked about the time the football player was killed—and as Ted's high spirits were leading into one prank after another. His football injury, though not serious, had scared her intensely. After that, she and Frank had decided to tell Ted he could no longer play football.

"There's soccer, there's tennis—it's not as though we were telling him he couldn't have a sport."

"Yeah, sissy sports," Ted broke in. "What do you think the guys say to me—'Your mamma won't let you play football.' They think I'm a faggot!"

"Your father doesn't want you to—"

"Your mother can't stand—"

"Whoa. Let's back up a little!"

There's not much to be gained from the angry airing of feelings. I needed to help them get their reactivity under control so we could all figure out what was going on.

"Ted," I said, "it looks like a lot of what's been going on has to do with your not being allowed to play football. Frank, have you and Eleanor heard him out on this subject, and how he feels about it?"

"About fifty times!"

"Well, I wonder if you'd ask him to talk to you about it again, for the fifty-first?"

"He won't talk to us anymore."

"Maybe if you try it here?"

"All right. OK, Ted, what's all this nonsense about?"

"Frank—maybe when you start it off that way, he thinks you believe his reasons are nonsense, and that might make it hard for him to tell you?"

"Ted—I'm sorry—son, I really do care how you feel. Can you please tell me why this is so important to you?"

"Forget it! You had your chance!"

Frank looked at me. "See?"

"Ted, your father's trying. Could you?"

"What does it matter? They won't change their minds."

"You never know what'll happen when two people who care about each other try talking."

"Ted," Frank implored. "Please."

"Frank, let me," broke in Eleanor. "Ted, there are so many other sports you can do. And we don't keep you home from parties—"

"But, mom, listen—"

"Damn it, Ted, yes. I get feeling sorry for you about the football, and then I remember the beer and the staying out. What the hell—"

"Frank, stop it. He can play football, I don't care!"

"Like hell he can. If you think I intend to see you the mess you were about it. He will not be allowed to do that to you." And he pulled Eleanor to him in a clumsy embrace.

Who vetoed the football, mother or father? I was confused and made a mental note to myself that this warranted further inquiry. But before following up on that, there was something else that seemed to need investigation. What I saw in the previous interchange was that neither parent was effective in firmly establishing a dyadic interchange with Ted—that is, one in which each could make a statement and the other could hear it and then answer it effectively. We would need to practice this later until they could do it. What happened here is that they got in each other's way. Just as Frank finally really got going with Ted, Eleanor would intervene, and when Eleanor started making headway, Frank broke in. I decided to table the football topic and instead focus on the late hours, the beer, and what they'd done about these problems. As they talked together, I hoped I would be able to begin to work on their obstruction of each other.

"Ted, we're going to talk more later about the football. But before we do, could you fill me in a bit about the rules in your house—you know, like hours, and whether you're allowed to drink at home, and what happens when rules are broken? Sue, maybe you could help with this, for being a year older, you've probably run into some situations where your parents have had to hold the line on some things you've wanted to do."

"I just don't understand," blurted Sue. "Mom and dad have always been fair before this. They're good parents, but it seems they're lots harder on Ted than they are on me."

"I'll say," said Ted.

"Oh, big help, young lady," said Frank.

"Frank," I asked, "would you explore this with Sue? You and she talk about it a little."

"What do you mean, Sue?" he asked, accepting my orchestration.

"When I stayed out until four that night, after the prom, remember? You and Mom hollered—but you just hollered, or maybe just spoke to me—you didn't ground me. But when Ted does the same thing, even the first time, he gets grounded for a week. It seems like you act on him, but you talk to me. And you let mom handle it more with me, and you don't get physical."

"Boys need fathers when they start getting out of line."

"Well, I don't know if mom agrees. And if you ask me, I think this all has to do with Uncle Will, and that's not fair to Ted."

"Oh, Sue," said Eleanor, "that's not true."

"Eleanor, calm down, just calm down," said Frank. "Young lady, your mother gets upset when she thinks any of you children could be in danger. And boys get into more trouble than girls, that much I know. And I will not have your mother upset."

Was Frank making a self-fulfilling prophecy about boys being more troublesome than girls? Is that how he really expected Ted to be?

"Frank." Eleanor turned to me. "Joan, you remember my brother Will?"

I nodded.

"I do think of him when Ted's out carousing around, and it's true, it does remind me of my brother. But one thing Frank doesn't understand is that when I cry, it doesn't necessarily mean I can't handle something. He can't stand to see me cry, but sometimes crying helps"—she looked up at me—"as I seem to remember your telling me."

"Do you think there is a possibility you two *have* dealt differently with Sue and Ted? Because if you have, that might help to explain Ted's anger."

They looked at each other and shrugged.

"Maybe," said Frank.

"Well, look, we've run out of time for today. Could we meet on—this is Friday, how about Wednesday? We seem to be dealing at this time with teenage problems, so I'd say Nell and Will can be excused from the next session. (I saw no visible signs that they played a major role in the present issue.) All of you be thinking hard about this subject, and let's see what light we can cast on it next time. Agreed?" And I made a point to exchange farewells personally with each member.

Family therapists plan sessions. They operate from hypotheses, which they have formed in the previous sessions. Then they test those hypotheses in the following sessions (Haley, 1980).

I had several issues to track: (1) Teenage demands were stressing the system. When that happens, a hierarchy of authority should be maintained, and parental directions and responses should be clear and definite. Rules for and reactions to all teenagers should be relatively equal or at least fair and reasonably explained. Communication should take a form in which explanation is possible. Were things unequal between Ted and Sue? If so, why? (2) Why the football ban? And maybe even more important, who made it? Did the parents agree? (3) Could each parent sustain a dyad with Ted without the dysfunctional interference of the other? (4) Did this interference stem from and cover over some as yet unknown parental disagreement? (5) Where did the specter of Uncle Will's injury fit in? (6) What was the meaning of Frank's seeming overprotectiveness of Eleanor?

I would use the football topic as the content and then test out issues 3 and 4 as I directed the three to talk with one another.

But so much for well-laid plans. When I opened the door to the waiting room, Frank, Eleanor, and Sue got up to walk in. Frank turned to Ted.

"Get in here!"

"Forget it!"

Frank grabbed his arm and pulled him up out of the chair. Ted fought back, half shouting, half crying, "I won't—I hate you, jerk!"

Frank pushed him back in the chair, knocking the radio off the table.

"Oh, Joan, I'm sorry—Frank, stop it! Ted—"

"Hey, stop!" I shouted. I'm normally soft-spoken, and I usually get results when I do raise my voice.

"Frank, Eleanor, Sue—come on in. Ted, you stay out here and rest a bit. I want to find out what's going on, and there's no sense having a brawl." I counted on Ted's ambivalence. He didn't want to come in, but he had come to the office. I guessed he wanted, at least partly, some help in whatever was happening.

They walked in with me. "OK, everybody take a deep breath, and then let me in on what's going on."

Frank and Eleanor had been out Saturday night. They'd come home to find signs of a party with lots of kids—food on the carpet, beer cans in the trash, and a whisky bottle. Frank wanted Ted in the session so I could see—really see— what a problem he was. Sue was keeping a low profile. I wondered where she'd been while the party was going on. Eleanor was tired out from intervening all weekend between son and father. And Frank was onto his theme of "Ted is killing his mother, and I won't stand for it."

"Listen, we need Ted in here to try and figure this out," I said.

"All right. You want him in here, you'll have him in here," and Frank jumped to his feet.

"Wait, Frank," I said. "You're acting from your anger. When you get like this, it's as though you forget you even *like* Ted, and if you just force him to come in, he'll be mad and we won't get anywhere. And I'm confused by this, because I knew, even before I met you, because Eleanor told me, that you're a loving and caring father and you and Ted have always been good friends. What's going on?"

He looked at Eleanor, then back at me; took a deep breath and shook his head. "You're right, I don't know, I act like some kind of Neanderthal and treat him like he's a criminal. I don't know what gets into me. I've been under such pressure lately—my job has more responsibility, my mother busts my balls every chance she gets, Eleanor's problems—and now this. There was a little peace for a while, after she quit her—"

"Frank, tell her, not me."

"No, I—"

"Yes, tell *her*!"

"You know what I mean, El. After you quit, it was peaceful, quiet, you felt better, you took ma off my back, and it's like he's spoiling everything. I cannot stand it when you worry so about him!"

"But hon, worry comes with the territory, when you have teenagers. At least that's what my friends tell me. Sue just ushered us in easy."

"El, I could not bear looking at you when he was playing football!"

"Frank," softly, "is that it? Because even though it was hard, I could bear it."

"But you wanted him to stop."

"No, Frank, you wanted it. I went along with you, but I didn't really agree. I didn't think it was really right to stop him because I was scared. But after you said it, and he quit the team—well, it just didn't seem right, but I was relieved, and it seemed so wishy-washy to go back on it. But you know, somehow I think he knows I didn't really agree, that it was you, and I think that's why he's so mad at both of us."

"I knew, mom," said Sue softly.

"I thought you were just trying to be brave," Frank insisted. "I couldn't stand for you to be suffering bravely."

"But, Frank," and she leaned over to touch his hand, "let me be brave. If I give in to all my fears, I'll be worse for it, not better. I have to be a brave person, as much as I can be."

"Do you want him to play? Really?"

"Yes—even if I'm a basket case about it!"

Hypothesis: Frank has encouraged Eleanor to be weak, and she has accepted and given in. But concern about her son's welfare and the protest he raised have pushed her to a point where she no longer can do so. She is making a stand for her strength. But her last statement seems to throw a reassurance to him, that she won't be *too* strong. This points a direction for me. We will first work to resolve the issues around Ted's rebellious behavior, as it is the most pressing concern and the one that brought them to therapy. My longer-range goal will then be to explore what is going on between them. I sense that Ted's behavior may be only one area in which their personal struggle, whatever it is, is taking place.

"Look," I said, "how about talking out this football issue some more, and then we'll have Ted come in?"

"I don't think so," said Frank. "What more is there to say? Let's just let him play."

"Frank, this is so important to all of you. Please take five minutes more to explore whether there are any hitches in it. Maybe sometimes you and Eleanor come to conclusions too fast—and I think Eleanor agrees with you too fast. Would you explore with her here *all* the reservations she may have about the decision? Are you going to go to the games together? What kind of a basket case is she going to be? And what are you going to do when she is one?"

Eleanor does accommodate too fast to Frank's protective measures. They need to be encouraged and coached to talk longer about decisions, especially in that area, and to plan their reactions to stress. A good sign is that, after my encouragement, they do it well on their own, hearing and respecting each other's viewpoints and feelings and resolving minor differences. This interchange increases my belief that this has previously been a well-functioning parental unit. My thoughts wander back momentarily to my concerns and questions when Eleanor left her job.

"OK, which of you do you think can be more successful in getting Ted in?"

"I can," said Sue.

"No, Sue, this is a job for a parental voice." Boundary and hierarchy regulation remains my job.

"I'll do it," said Eleanor. "Sue thinks he knows I'm on his side, anyway." (Sue hadn't said exactly that, but I let it pass.)

Eleanor returned to the office, followed by a somber-looking Ted. They all sat silently for a few minutes.

"Ted," said Frank, "we're not going to talk about Saturday right now. Your mom and I have been talking about the football ban and—well, I guess that's been a disagreement. I thought your mom didn't want you to play, and—well, anyway, you can play."

Ted looked at his father, stunned. Then he erupted, "Big deal—after you wrecked me for the year!"

"Hey, hey, son—I know—" I could see Frank holding his temper. "We made a mistake, and we're sorry. And we'll do everything we can do to help you get back in."

"I can't get back in." He was half-crying now. "You jerk, you bully, you slug me, and now—"

"Oh, Ted, come on," said Sue.

"Ted," said Eleanor, "your father's not a bully. How can you—"

"Ted, damn it—"

"Hey, stop!" This family does it all the time. At moments of stress, everyone gets into the act, and chaos results. They don't talk enough when it's quiet, and they talk too much when it's tense. "Just everybody calm down." They did, everybody finally settling back.

"Ted has been truly hurt by this year's ban. And he'll probably have a lot of hard work and embarrassment in getting back on the team. You're going to have to give him time to deal with that."

"Ted," said Eleanor. "We are sorry, both of us. It's not the first mistake we've made, and it won't be the last."

"Yeah, so?" said Ted, in the infuriating way that only a teenager can manage.

"Look, again we've come to the end of our time. I'd suggest you put any discussions about this on hold at home. Ted knows your decision, and he heard you say you'd help him, if he needs you. He's been pretty good in the past about carrying the ball on his own problems. Let him figure out what he has to do. And, Ted, they'll keep out of it unless you ask them for help—but I think they'll be there for you if you ask. I know you've got a job to do figuring out how to get back your position."

"The next time we meet," I continued, "let's explore that business you brought up, Sue, about you and Ted being treated differently. Be thinking about it, will you, and you too, Ted. That's your assignment."

"How about one for us?" asked Frank.

"Why don't you take Eleanor out to dinner somewhere nice, just the two of you, and give her a rest." (I join with Frank the protector and also set a boundary.) "You plan it and surprise her."

I hoped, when they left, that this change by Frank and Eleanor concerning the football ban was going to make a miraculous change in the family.

What I'd learned about them so far was that in tense moments and crisis, when Eleanor and Frank were challenged to be effective leaders of their family, their particular anxieties about being separate persons, and thus at times disagreeing, led them to a degree of overprotectiveness and caution with each other that interfered with their being effective. Ted had been the victim of their fear of challenging each other. If they had learned in our work together to be even somewhat different with each other, then things might proceed much more effectively.

I was halfway satisfied. There was change but not as much as I'd hoped.

Ted couldn't get back into varsity play for the rest of the year, but he could play town ball, and he got a promise for the varsity for next year. He didn't tell anyone much about his troubles with his friends, if they existed, and I discouraged his parents from asking. Teenagers need increasing autonomy—thicker boundaries—from their parents as they grow up. But I asked them just to let him know they were there to help if he asked. He continued to get into occasional trouble, however, in spite of our working on important subjects. We discussed the fairness of the rules, the clarity of rewards and punishments, and—maybe most important—the basic agreement on issues between Frank and Eleanor. As things settled down a little, Sue stopped being quite so good and nervously helpful at home and seemed to get freed up to pay more attention to her own life and friends, something she'd stopped as the trouble at home had begun. I included Nell and Will in about half the sessions, and the family adapted well to my coaching them in changing some aspects of their communication. They stopped interrupting so much, and as a matter of fact, Will took over some of Sue's role and helped me by gleefully pointing a finger at anyone who broke into someone else's conversation. I didn't worry about him, though, or about Nell, for both of them were going on very well with the business of their lives.

But there were still problems. Why was Ted so erratic? He'd do fine in school, then mess up a major homework assignment. He'd come home on time three times out of four and then come home late, with beer on his breath. It was just the kind of intermittent reinforcement to keep Frank and Eleanor holding their breath, never quite able to relax. Frank would blow up, Eleanor would cry, she'd storm at Ted, he'd slump in despair, we'd work on it, Ted would promise, there'd be peace for three weeks or so—and then it would begin again. I spent several sessions alone with Ted to explore his intrapsychic system. What I discovered was nothing remarkable. He was just a very bright, normally muddled adolescent. We were stuck. There wasn't any more or better of what they were doing that I could help them to do. This was very much a point of therapist choice.

What were my choices? I could give up and say, "Well, you've just got an adolescent you have to live with—and it will pass." That was a serious option I considered. There was another course, however, and it was the one I chose. It was dictated by clues given to me by aspects of Frank's and Eleanor's behavior that I had not addressed in any organized fashion. These clues related to the meaning of his extreme protectiveness, her anxiety symptoms and the relinquishing of her job, and his remarks about both his job pressures and his mother. True, I'd tried to explore these, but both Frank and Eleanor had shown reluctance to get into the issues, and the kids had proved no help in entering these areas either. I had said to myself, one day, that Ted's actions couldn't have kept Eleanor and Frank off balance any better if they had been designed to do just that. I decided to take myself seriously and make this the subject of a paradoxical intervention (Stanton, 1981).

The idea of paradox takes seriously the belief that a symptom has a purpose in the system, and the therapist often prescribes the symptom, suggesting that the system needs it for its continued functioning. I planned carefully.

The next session all family members were present and were talking in a rather bored fashion. As time was running out, I broke in.

"I've been giving a lot of thought to what's been going on in your family lately, and I've realized that for some weeks I've been leading you down the wrong track. I've really been making a mistake."

Instant attention from everyone!

"It's clear your family has made important and good changes. You've all worked hard. You've shown your caring for one another. The way you can discuss things now is fantastic—and all you have left is this little problem of Ted messing up from time to time."

Frowns from Frank.

"You know, I think you have to look at Ted in a different way."

More frowns, this time from Frank and Eleanor both. I think that they believe I'm going to suggest termination of therapy, the "live with it" option, and they don't like it.

"—in a very different way. I think that instead of considering him your bad kid, you really have to think of him as your most altruistic family member" (Madanes, 1981).

Bewilderment!

"What's *altruistic*?" said Will and Nell almost simultaneously.

"*Altruistic* means sort of being not selfish—giving up yourself, or what you want, for someone else. See—," and I turned back to Frank and Eleanor, "I think Ted somehow knows that this family, for some reason, can't stand peace and quiet. He may not even know he's doing it, but I think he's afraid that when it gets too quiet, something bad will happen, so whenever there's any chance of that happening, he makes sure that he gets a warning notice or goes to a beer party or something."

Lots of response—chaos and consternation.

"Now, we're just about at the end of our time today." I had timed this deliberately, because I did not want them to have time to discuss with me the intervention I was about to make. I wanted them to take it home and let it sit—or, more specifically, to let it reverberate throughout the system.

"Ted, it's getting too quiet. Before we meet again, I want you to have at least one big mess. I don't care how, or when you do it, but do a good one. You're expert by now. Do the worst you've done, and even get Sue involved in it. Don't let your parents know what or when. Keep them guessing, so every time they go out or sit down to rest, they'll wonder if today's the day. Can you do it?"

He gave me the look that family therapists have come to recognize from their tapes as the characteristic befuddled stare of the person who is the subject of a paradoxical intervention. As he opened his mouth to answer, I interrupted.

"Good, I knew you could! Now, we're running out of time. I have a meeting next week, so I have to make it two weeks. See you all a week from Monday." And I almost rudely hustled them out of the office. I didn't have a meeting, but I wanted time for this intervention to bounce around.

At least two possible dramatic results could occur following this intervention, if my assumptions contained a degree of correctness. One was that Ted would refuse to perform on demand, he would gain a new degree of insight, and his symptomatic behavior would lessen. The other was that he would "mess up" again, and we all would gain new information about the meaning and purpose of the behavior. My prediction was that the latter would occur, and there would be an opportunity to deal with elements that this rather rigid family had not allowed to be matters for investigation, such as Frank's and Eleanor's marital relationship. It was with this attitude of watchful waiting that I met them two weeks later.

When I opened the door, I found three very angry persons. What had happened? Well, Ted had trod a narrow line. He'd come home drunk last Friday, but he'd done it just down the street, so no driving was involved. When he came in, he made enough noise so that he woke up both his parents. And all hell broke loose. Eleanor had started storming at him, Frank had stormed at Ted for upsetting Eleanor, and Eleanor had turned on both of them with a vengeance, which she continued here.

"I have had it! I don't care if he's doing it to save us or because he's a damn spoiled brat, either way it is going to stop. And Frank! You are going to stop treating me like some damn china doll who's going to have a breakdown if her poor feelings are upset. I'm sick of both of you. You can take your house, and your kids, and job, and your mother, and take care of them yourself. I'm going to get a job, and I'm going to cry if I want to, and if you need someone to go to school for you, your father can do it. I am not a baby, and I am not a neurotic, and I—"

"Eleanor—"

"Shut up!" and she started to cry. Frank leaned over to her—and she punched him!

"Mom," and Ted started to cry.

Frank got up.

"Stop it! Everybody leave everybody alone! Sit!" I said this strongly and with a lot more assurance than I felt. But I had a long relationship with this family, and they trusted me, so sit they did. Ted was sniffling, Frank sat slumped with his head in his hand, and Eleanor was crying torrents of tears, which finally subsided into gasps. I got up to give her a Kleenex. She blew her nose and finally looked up at me and said, "Oh, shit!" We both laughed.

"You gave Ted a pretty strong message."

"Yeah, and Frank too. Hey, Frank, I'm sorry."

"Hey, hey, time for that later. He knows you're sorry. How about telling it to Ted again?"

"Telling him what?"

"About stopping what he's doing."

"Well, Joan, I think you're way off base about him doing something for me [I had never said *her*], but it doesn't matter why he's doing it. I'm just not going to let it get to me like it has. Frank has acted like I'm a weakling, and maybe Ted got that impression too. But I'm not. He is—"

"Tell him."

"OK, Ted, you are to stop what you're doing, messing up your life, whether you're doing it to help me or drive me crazy or whatever. Because whatever happens, I can handle it. I'm going to live my life and be OK, and if you make trouble, you'll suffer for it, not me. And if I decide to get a job, I'll do it, whether you need me at home or not, and yes, whether you want me to or not, Frank."

"Eleanor, tell Ted again, and make sure he's heard you and understands."

She did. "Ted, did you hear me?"

"Yes."

"And do you understand? I love you, and I'll do anything I can for you, but I will not sit around waiting to worry about you!"

"Ted, your mom says you can resign from your role."

He gave me a look usually reserved for idiots. Then he turned to Frank.

"Dad, did you forbid mom to work?"

It was poor Frank's turn to look befuddled.

"I swear to God I don't know what this is all about. Eleanor, you wanted to quit. I always supported your working. I know how much your career meant to you."

"Oh, I don't know," she said. "I don't even know where that came from. Frank, I'm so sorry I hit you. I can't believe I did it!"

"No, no, it's OK. Are *you* OK? I've never seen you so angry."

"I'm so sorry, Ted, I never hit your father before."

"Mom, it's OK."

Big mutual protection society!

"Hon, get a job. We'll manage just fine!"

"You're sure?" She leaned over to kiss him, and he hugged her. They looked as if they were now going back to day one, two years before, to put the system back together just the way it was before therapy began. But I was going to prevent it if I could.

"I think it's really important for Ted to hear the messages you're giving him today—both of them."

They looked up questioningly.

"Is this what you mean, Joan, that the message is that his messing up is not needed or wanted by the family, that it should stop, and that if it continues, it will be dealt with differently, by both Frank and me?"

"That's right. Frank, are you in agreement and telling him that too?"

"Damn right. No more, Ted, hear me?"

"Aye-aye, sir. But what's the second message?"

"The second is that you two are going to be discussing seriously between yourselves whether or not Eleanor is going to return to work. This is a decision that affects, first of all, you two and, secondly, the whole family. You know, Frank, and you too, Eleanor, I see you doing again something we've talked about—namely, rushing into a major decision too quickly, just like you did on the football thing. What I'd like to offer, if you're up for it, is for you to come in together, just the two of you, for a while, and let me help sort out the pros and cons. It isn't a move that has to be made tomorrow, is it, Eleanor? I mean, there's not a big job offer?"

"No, and I couldn't rush into it anyway if there were. I mean, my life got turned around too, just like Ted's did when he had to quit football." She smiled at both Frank and me. "You're right, it's not so simple."

"I don't think it's simple at all," said Frank, "because I'm completely confused where you get the idea I didn't want you to work." He turned to me. "Joan, you know—I've never told anybody that we're in therapy. I didn't want to be here in the first place and wouldn't have come, except Eleanor knew you and trusted you, and I wanted to help her. But you know, it has helped us."

"Thank you, Frank. I'm glad for you."

I think that Frank knew we were talking here about a new kind of contract, one that included, much more than before, him individually and their marital relationship. In many ways I was in the dark here. If indeed peace and quiet was threatening to this couple, I was not sure why. Nor did I know for sure what elements went into the ineffective and confusing ways they responded to Ted's misbehavior. But I hypothesized that we were moving onto new ground. Their reticence and emotional privacy were going to be challenged in weeks to come, and I wanted both of them to make a personal commitment to the work ahead.

"You think there's something that needs talking out, huh?"

"I do."

"Eleanor?" He looked at her.

"I'm game."

"OK, let's do it."

"OK, the kids get a break for a while. Listen, everybody's tired today, me included. How about we stop for a while, you guys go get a soda or something—and the three of us will meet next Monday?"

So with a lot of smiles and some hugging, they got up and left. I was again affirming a boundary. What we would begin on next Monday was the business of Frank and Eleanor, the marital system, rather than of Frank and Eleanor, the parental system. At the moment, it was no concern of their children.

Act Three: The Couple

It has become rather standard procedure of systems therapists to look for unresolved and often unarticulated conflict between a couple when a child in a family is experiencing trouble. That conflict may be expressed in difficulties over parenting, with parents arguing over the child, choosing sides, one attacking and one defending, or uniting in their concern over a problem child to keep them so busy that they do not have time to address more fundamental marital issues. Children sometimes seem to sense this and keep the trouble going just enough to divert their parents from something that the children fear might be more disruptive to the family unit. I had seen enough of this in the past to make the assumption that this was happening with the Chapins.

Eleanor and Frank did not take easily to marital therapy. They were both products of families who did not value "talking out" problems—and although this characteristic might just be the styles of their own particular families, I didn't discount their ethnic backgrounds, Eleanor's German and Frank's English and Scottish. These groups, in general, are not big talkers about emotional issues. I confirmed, as I sat with them in the ensuing hours, that theirs was not the kind of marriage based on long hours of talk, exploring each other's feelings, but, rather, was based on shared interests and world view. Where Middle Europeans might sit and talk, the Chapins skied and played bridge. I would not try to change this pattern drastically—it had worked for them and should do so again. I would try, however, to alert them to their two tendencies. One we had already noted: everyone talked and interrupted when anxiety was high, at least when the whole family was present. The second, which I confirmed as I sat with them as a couple, was that when they were alone and anxious and a decision had to be made, they became even more laconic than usual. Here they had to learn to go beyond their boundary of what was impolite, or what "just wasn't done." They had to ask more questions of each other and had to struggle to put sometimes half-formed doubts and objections into voice. Separateness was a problem for them. As I had noted before, they were very protective of each other. Frank's protection was more overt, but Eleanor's, while more subtle, was as strong, if not stronger.

I took the lead in the early sessions. There was no need to rush the job decision, so I gently and as unobtrusively as possible expanded my questioning to learn about Frank's background. I kept the issues fairly factual, and when I introduced the idea of adding Frank's side of the family to the genogram, he found it an acceptable and even interesting idea.

He came from a family that, in contrast to Eleanor's, had suffered greatly from the Depression. His father had been a bond salesman who, in 1932, when Frank was two, lost his job. Frank and his sister, Ailene, three years older, remembered growing up with the complaints of their mother ringing in their ears. She went to work as a secretary in a real estate office, at a time when "women of good family" didn't do such a thing, and for a time she was the only breadwinner in the family. Although his father regained his job as times got better, his mother never let the family forget that "your father failed us." Ironically, his mother actually loved her job, he thought, and when real estate began to boom in the 1940s, she got her license and became very successful. She was, as he remembered it, charming with her business associates but bitter and angry with her husband and children. He saw his father belittled, and he ached as he saw him become increasingly isolated and withdrawn at home. His father began a series of affairs which no one ever talked about in the daytime but which he and Ailene knew about from the hissed arguments at night. He had little real contact with his father and remembered being torn by the contradictory messages his mother seemed to be giving him. The first was that he must be successful, and all her efforts went in this direction—right schools, right sports, right friends, and so on. The other message, however, was that he probably wouldn't make it, because he was a man, and "that's what men do—they fail their women" (Nagy and Spark, 1973).

The making of the genogram sneaked up on Frank, as it often does. We had started out with factual material, dates, places—and were now ending up with a flood of old memories. Frank became increasingly agitated in the hours and depressed at home. He had never spoken to Eleanor—or to anyone—about the pain and conflict he had experienced in growing up. To him, weakness and vulnerability were unacceptable. He would prove his mother wrong at all costs.

I tried several times to slow the rush of Frank's memories—and pain. But there was no stopping him. Talk about Eleanor's return to work was completely forgotten. Eleanor often sat in helpless anguish as her husband talked endlessly in our hours and paced the floor sleeplessly at night at home. I was beginning to worry.

They came in one Monday looking different. Frank was more composed than I'd seen him for a while. Eleanor this time looked tearful. I looked at her.

"I had one of my old anxiety attacks last night. Frank was up, so I got up with him, and we had some coffee and talked—and I started shaking, I started crying, and just couldn't stop—Frank held me, and—"

"Joan," Frank interrupted, "I just can't, I won't put Eleanor through this anymore. We both know she's vulnerable—and with the kids and all we've been through this year—I've got to stop this dwelling on the past and pull myself together for her sake."

What to do? How to point out, without hurting, that this loving, caring wife was acting now in the same way that her loving, caring son had in the past? The protective mechanism was so strong in this family that when one member was perceived as threatened beyond tolerance, another member would offer himself or herself up as troubled or weak so that the threatened member would gather up his or her own strength. Eleanor was, in effect, offering to be impaired so that Frank could be stronger and would have to take care of her.

"Now I know where Ted gets it."

Silence. "What do you mean?"

"Eleanor, I think you're very afraid that Frank cannot stand the pain of living through the hurts of his past. I think you're deciding to be sick, so he can feel strong and take care of you and not be threatened by you. And I think that's very disrespectful of you!"

Silence, just silence! They both sat and stared at me.

"If he really can't handle all these memories and pain and wants to stop, I think he has a right to make that decision by himself."

Silence again. Had I gone too far? If I had, I thought they would be able to discount, in some way, what I'd said. But if they could hear it, could accept it, this could be a major turning point for them.

Frank shook his head, like a man recovering from a blow. When he opened his mouth to speak, the words made no sense. But as I listened carefully, I realized he was saying yes, yes—it was so—he liked it. Eleanor stared at him and then at me.

"What are you saying? That Frank used my anxiety?"

"No, no." I started to clarify, but Frank broke in, still speaking in a broken and shaken way.

"I felt it—felt it." The risk he was taking was enormous, but I could see he had no choice. "When you started to shake, Sunday—I was happy. God help me, I was happy. I could stop—no more—strong for you. You'd stay home—I'd hurry home from work, do the shopping—all through my mind, like lightning—you'd be grateful—I'd be OK, never fail you—," and he burst into uncontrollable and wracking tears.

I felt tears come to my eyes as I watched him—and watched Eleanor just sit there, looking at him with a stony face. I didn't have to stop her from trying to stem his tears.

He finally stopped—looked up at her. She sat still, untouchable.

"I knew it too," she said in a harsh, choked voice, tears held back, coldly. "I knew it too," as awareness broke over her like a flood. "When I cried about Ted, you didn't let me cry. It's like you were saying I was too weak to even cry, to even handle anything. 'I won't let you upset your mother,' you used to scream at him, and we all knew you meant his poor fragile mother. And I was too weak to cope with Barbara and all the problems of that stupid office. Come home, be my baby, I'll take care of you. Oh, I know why I hit you—you were trying to destroy me!"

"El—"

"No, no, no, no—you wanted to cut off my legs, and my arms, and make me helpless. Damn you! Damn, damn, damn you! So I'd stay home and take care of you, and you'd bring your little problems to me at night—bring the big bad world into your little doll's house at night, and you could be the big strong man who'd solve it all. You did it all, and just so—" She stopped, and her face softened momentarily. "Just so I'd never do to you what your mother did to your father. Oh, God!" She burst into tears.

This time it was Frank's turn to sit, a look of unbearable hurt on his face. He started to touch her, but I shook my head.

In the following silence, I said softly, "Can you hear me if I say neither of you could have done it alone? You did it together, because you cared for each other. No one planned it. No one wanted to use the other. It came out of who you were, what you each needed, who you'd been before you even met each other."

No one answered me. The hurt, the anger, were palpable in the room. Could they stand this without breaking apart?

"Eleanor, Frank has been very open with you. He's trusted you with awarenesses about himself that he thinks are awful. He trusted you, as he could never trust his mother."

More silence. I let it build, then spoke again. "Maybe you need to look at whether there were fears of your own that Frank played into—if part of you was glad to be little and taken care of?'' I had some evidence to go on here, because I remembered how strong she'd had to be when her brother Will nearly died.

She shook her head silently.

"But you know, he didn't force you to accept his hovering. You didn't fight it" (Sluzki, 1978).

Still silence. There seemed no place to go.

"Are we talked out for today? Should we take a break and meet tomorrow? Can you manage that? Don't talk about this—save it for here. Frank, don't worry about Eleanor. Think about yourself, your mom and dad, and Ailene—I think that will help more than anything. Can you do that?''

"I'll try." He looked at her, but she got up without looking at either of us and went out ahead of him. As he walked out the door, I touched his shoulder, softly, just once, for reassurance.

When they returned the next day, the mood was just as heavy and as distant. I tried hard to move them beyond Frank's depressed apologies and Eleanor's somber withdrawal but with little success. I had to ride it out—this had been the uncovering of a major marital collusion, unknown heretofore to any of us, and they had to work it out in their own way. I wondered whether the caring and good history between them were strong enough to help them weather this storm. I made one attempt to lighten things but in a way that really was a serious intervention.

"Look, maybe we could get Ted to help us out?''

They both looked at me warily.

"Maybe we could get him to really foul up in some serious way, like vandalize the school or something. You two'd have to pull together to get him out of it.''

"That's silly," said Eleanor.

Old family patterns, of deflecting marital conflict through a child, were no longer an option.

There was no magic in the ensuing hours—no bright paradoxical interventions to get beyond the present crisis. There was only my support to be offered as they slowly came to terms with their new awareness of themselves and each other. Things were cold at home. Eleanor asked Frank to sleep in the guest room, and when he moved, the kids became agitated. They both reported handling it very well, telling the kids they were having a problem but it was theirs and they'd handle it. They offered the kids an opportunity to come in to talk to me, and all four wanted to. Before I saw the kids, I asked Frank and Eleanor what I should say if the kids asked whether their parents were going to get a divorce. They answered at the same time, Frank saying, "Tell them of course not," and Eleanor saying, "Tell them we don't know!" That brought on more anguished hours, and I put off seeing the kids for a while.

In the middle of this cold period, Frank's mother, who was living alone in the family home some twenty miles away, fell and broke her hip. Frank and Eleanor were most heavily engaged in the decision about helping her, although Ailene, Frank's sister, came out from California to stay with her mother for a week. Mrs. Chapin, Sr., had no doubts about how her problems would be solved. She told Frank in no uncertain terms that she was moving in with him and Eleanor. Her domineering and belittling ways, which had been held in check with him recently, were pouring out now that she was older.

"Frank, we can't do it. It would wreck us!''

I hadn't heard that "we" in weeks. As we've seen before, two points of a triangle can unite against, or for, or about, a third.

"And she's going to tell me all good sons take care of their mothers, but all men fail women eventually. I'm a weakling like my father, who, incidentally," and he looked up at me and laughed ruefully, "died only to spite her."

"Maybe he did?" and I grinned.

He looked up at me very seriously. "I don't think the old man had enough life left at the end to even do that. You know, I'm so sorry I never got to know him. Maybe that's where all this trouble started, with how awful, how guilty, how Goddamned depressed I felt when he died, and I knew I'd never get the chance."

"I think it's one of the places it started."

"I was—afraid to be friends with him. Afraid it would mean I was like him—I was weak. It was as though I had to join with the strong one. It was one or the other—and I only knew which one I didn't want to be."

"Frank." Eleanor, softer than I'd heard her in weeks. "Frank, my mom and dad were both strong, and so are Will and I, in our own ways. It doesn't have to be one strong and one weak." She started to cry.

And this time Frank didn't try to stop her.

The Chapins, Eleanor and Frank, worked with me for several more months. In the sessions, each of them, with the other listening, dealt with issues carried over from his or her family of origin. Eleanor learned that she indeed did have conflict about being a career woman, rather than a homemaker like her mother. Her old boss, Barbara, had stirred up this issue, as well as threatening her by seeking a more open and confrontive relationship than Eleanor was used to. The terror about something happening to one of their children, as it had happened to her brother Will, remained with her, but she learned to share it with Frank, rather than acting it out with the children, and he learned that allowing her to express it to him was actually the best help he could give her. If she cried, it didn't mean he was failing her. She finally decided, with his full agreement, that she would wait for a few years to work, but she knew she could change her mind any day.

Frank had even more work to do. In many ways his father's death *had* precipitated this crisis, and he spent many hours grieving and mourning lost opportunities. When his sister was there again, he asked her to come for several sessions, leaving Eleanor at home, and they started the process of establishing a new and closer relationship with each other. I coached him in ways of dealing with his mother, and he was able to be calm and direct to her when he told her that she could not live with them but that he would help her find a suitable home in a retirement complex. I had prepared him for her angry onslaught, and he found that when he did not respond with his own anger or withdrawal, she backed down and even occasionally gave him some grudging appreciation.

Gradually we seemed to have done our work together. They weren't problemfree—life never permits that—but they did seem to know how to handle what came up. Their relationship included that each one could be strong without threatening the other, and each one could be vulnerable and needy when the situation demanded.

Termination was uneventful. There was no resumption of symptoms of any kind, and one day Frank and Eleanor just said they thought it was time to stop—what did I think? I agreed and asked them to tell the kids they were stopping, and did the kids have any work left to do here at the office? They returned the next week, saying that the kids sent their farewells and that this would be their last visit.

"Take one more week. It's been a long process, and you know how quickly you make decisions."

"How quickly we used to," laughed Frank. "No, seriously, we've talked this over carefully, and we're ready. But we'll give it one more week, just for you. And listen, when we come in next week—could you make a copy of our genogram? It's a pretty special sort of family tree, and I'd like to keep it."

"I think that's a great idea."

28

Couples Group Therapy with Family-of-Origin Sessions

James L. Framo

After five years of working together in cotherapy in our evening practice, my wife and I should have arrived at the point that we could predict after the first few sessions which couples were going to make it in marital therapy. In all honesty, however, our predictions have turned out to be pretty lousy. Couples who looked hopeless in the beginning often ended up with a new, vital marriage with the same partner, and others who we were sure were going to put their marriage together got nowhere in therapy or later divorced. Considering that behavioral scientists have isolated only about fifty percent of the million or so dimensions of marriage, however, maybe we do not have to turn in our credentials.

In any event, we were most pessimistic initially that Fred and Lynn's marriage had much chance of lasting in any meaningful way. Lynn had a whiny, high-pitched, irritating voice with which she righteously harangued her husband, and Fred had that maddening, smiling passivity that drives people up walls. Although on one level we liked them, we both had fantasies of choking them; evidently they stimulated some aspect of our shared introjects. Lynn was highly motivated for therapy for her husband; she not only was defensively impervious to any point of view but her own but was incapable of looking at her part in any transaction. It was more difficult to get Fred to commit himself to therapy, because he had had a bad experience with a psychiatrist in which each had engaged in a contest over who could keep silent longer. Besides, Fred was weakly motivated to stay married, whereas Lynn desperately wanted to keep her husband. I do not know whether it was these challenges or the tangled relationship between Lynn and Fred's family, which intrigued me conceptually, that made me decide to continue with them.

An earlier version of this chapter, entitled ''In-Laws and Out-Laws: A Marital Case of Kinship Confusion,'' appeared in P. Papp (ed.), *Family Therapy: Full Length Case Studies* (New York: Gardner Press, 1978).

Furthermore, I planned to put them in a couples group, where a lot of help would be available in handling them (for a description of my method of conducting couples groups, see Framo, 1973).

Fred and Lynn's problems were rather interesting. Both in their thirties, physically attractive, and moneyed, they had been married three years and had a two-year-old girl and a baby boy. Fred, very successful with his own business, had recently left his wife and children and moved into his parents' house because "I wasn't sure I wanted to be married." After a few days he had decided he did not want to break up his family, and when he returned home, he agreed to come for therapy. When asked how she saw their problems, Lynn poured forth the following story, insinuating that once the therapists heard it, they would look at Fred in astonishment and start therapizing him forthwith. Lynn said they had married in another city, where her own family was, and moved here, where his family was. Although Fred's sister, Elaine, vehemently opposed his marrying Lynn, she and Fred's mother, Ann, actively tried to ingratiate themselves with Lynn by buying her gifts, inviting her daily to go shopping with them, and dropping in to see her every day. Lynn said that initially she was flattered and pleased to have another family to take the place of her own; she had not recognized that her acceptance was based on being adopted and absorbed into the old system. Lynn said, however, "All that togetherness got to be more than I could handle. We had no life of our own because his family members were always under our feet." But Lynn said she was less bothered by the overcloseness than by the unusual displays of affection between Fred and his mother and sister. She said that Fred kissed his mother and sister "full on the lips, and they sat on his lap often and he patted their rear ends and caressed their legs. It's positively disgusting the way they slobber over him; everybody notices it and comments on it, and when I mention their behavior to his mother and sister, they say, 'But we love him; we're a close, affectionate family.'" Lynn went on to say with intense feeling, "He knows I can't stand it; it eats me up alive. I told him to stop it for my sake. I want to fight for my husband and get him away from them." Lynn said she could not understand why Elaine's husband (Elaine had recently married) did not seem to be bothered by the near-incestuous relationship between his wife and brother-in-law. Lynn began withdrawing from his family, but she showed increasing preoccupation with them, becoming furious whenever Fred visited his family. She was giving contradictory messages, however; she felt spurned and hurt when Fred's sister did not invite her to be maid of honor at her wedding. Fred felt he was being forced to choose between his original family and his wife, and he was resentful over having to sneak around to see his mother and sister. I did not realize Fred even had a father until Lynn said, "Fred's dad is a nothing, a zero, completely dominated by his wife." The incident that precipitated the open rift occurred when Lynn approached her mother-in-law for help in handling her problems with Fred, and her mother-in-law asked to speak to Fred alone, at which point she advised her son to get a divorce. Lynn had not realized that not only is blood thicker than water but it is wise in this world to know who your friends and family really are. Fred's private conference with his mother made him leave Lynn, but after he told us some history of his family, we understood why he again left his parents' home to return to his wife.

Fred said that while he was growing up, he hardly knew his parents. Since his parents had a business in which they worked together eighteen hours a day, he and his sister, who was five years younger, spent a great deal of time together and were "very, very, very close." With the utterance of each "very" I got an image of one intertwined body of fused parts. He said, "She came to me for everything; I tucked her in bed and read her stories and gave her baths and listened to her; I guess I was like a father to her." Fred's mother was eighteen years older than Fred and his father was fifteen years older than his mother, age gaps that promoted the realness of being an oedipal victor. As a matter of fact, Fred's mother became openly involved with another man, and when Fred was fifteen years old, she asked him whether she should leave his father. Fred said he was flabbergasted at being placed in this position and finally asked mother to stay because of the younger sister. Mother's boyfriend became like a member of the family, and Fred said he felt closer to that man than to his own father. He was bewildered by his father's indifference about the situation and infuriated at him for doing nothing about mother's affair, but he said nothing. Although the other man had died some years earlier, to that day nobody had ever said anything about the affair, which went on for years; Fred said it was like an elephant in the living room, with everyone pretending it was not there. He and his father became so alienated in subsequent years that when one entered the room, the other would leave. In more recent years, Fred said, he and father had made some sort of peace with each other, and they were now partners in the business, although one got the impression, listening to Fred, that his father, in effect, worked for him.

Early in the therapy Fred said, longingly, "My father and I get along now, but I don't really know him, and I'd like to have a relationship with him before he dies." This kind of statement is always my cue to state that our therapy includes bringing in the family of origin of each partner for a session, usually toward the end of therapy, after the partners have changed and are ready to deal with their parents and siblings. (This method of involving adults in sessions with their families of origin is explicated in Framo, 1976.) Although most people fervidly rule out such sessions for themselves, invariably they encourage the spouse to bring in his or her original family, reasoning that all the stuff the partner had been dumping on them would be redirected to the original targets. In Lynn's case it was different: she strongly opposed Fred's bringing in his family. This position made us recognize that she had an investment in his family that went beyond her surface complaints. Her family background provided the clues for understanding her secret agenda of wanting to be the daughter in his family, something that could never be.

Lynn's parents divorced when she was two years old, and she was raised by her mother, grandparents, and mother's three sisters. She spoke glowingly of her relationship with her mother, saying they were very close and mother was "a perfect mother." Lynn was extremely bitter toward her father, saying that he had had nothing to do with her when she was small and that when she was a teenager, he would see her only every few years, when he went to her city for a convention. Their relationship was characterized primarily by conflict followed by long periods of hurt withdrawal on both sides. She knew little about the causes for the divorce because her mother did not want to talk about it; for years her father had been trying to tell "his side of the story, but I refused to listen to it because he'd tell a bunch of lies about my mother. I owe her a great deal and I owe him nothing." I initially got the impression that Lynn had had almost no contact with her father through the years, and it was only when pressed for more details that she reluctantly indicated that he sent her gifts, telephoned and wrote her frequently, and at one point had taken her to Europe with him and one of his daughters from his second marriage. Then Lynn added acidly, "He never came to my wedding or invited me to his, and he never introduced me as his daughter to his second wife, who threatened to leave him if he had much to do with me."

Lynn's mother remarried when Lynn was thirteen, and after that man was killed in an accident, her mother married for a third time, this present marriage being described as "disastrous." When we suggested that at some point we would have a session with Lynn and her parents, she said, as expected, "No way. If you insist on that, you'll never see me again. My father still hates my mother after all these years and feels I have sided with her, which I have because I have good reason to." Then, crying, she said, "Do you think I give a damn about that man who's supposed to be my father?" I indicated that if she could ever bring herself to deal with her parents, and if I could give a father back to her, she would be less hooked into her husband's family, and she and Fred might have a chance to have a real marriage. Her uncharacteristic silence for several minutes following that intervention gave us our first hope that maybe change was possible in this situation. Insofar as Lynn rejected her own yearning for a father, she attributed to her husband an attachment to his family that she endlessly complained about but envied. Fred was also the target of her displaced fury. The fact that Fred's primary loyalty was indeed to his original family does not negate the validity of her dynamic efforts. For me, the best way of resolving this problem was to take Lynn's problems back to where they began, to bring her and her father together and to strengthen that relationship. At this point in the therapy, however, she was nowhere near ready to do that.

When Fred and Lynn joined a couples group with two other couples, Lynn proceeded to impress them with the juicy details of Fred's sexy relationship with his mother and sister. She went on and on about Fred's family, expecting the other two couples to be sufficiently shocked to tell Fred he should renounce his original family. However, the other two couples had been in a group for some time and were too sophisticated to take Lynn's words at face value; as a matter of fact, one group member picked up quickly how obsessed she seemed to be about his family. No matter where a discussion started in the group, she referred the topic back to his family.

Mary (my cotherapist) and I and the group made valiant attempts to get Lynn off his family and onto herself. It did not work; we would get a flood of self-justifying words. I then used an intervention that had been quite effective in the past with people who were openly critical of their in-laws: I told Lynn that by carping about his family, she was doing herself a disservice and sabotaging her own goals. So long as she criticized his family, he, of course, had to defend them and never had to get in touch with his own anger toward them, because she was expressing it for him.

I had not reckoned with Lynn's formidable defense; that confrontation brought a change in her behavior for only two weeks, and when Fred still could not acknowledge any negative feelings about his family, she went back to her broken record. I began to feel helpless. I was supposed to be the expert; besides, all those assistant therapists in the group could not budge them either.

Now, to be sure, we knew that the sexual overtones in the behavior between Fred and his mother and sister would have given a psychoanalyst a field day; the oedipal interpretations were so obvious you could get them for half price. But we wanted to deal with this material on our terms and with our timing, not his wife's. Moreover, since this "sexual behavior" was so ego-syntonic for him, we had to discover another route to changing the order of Fred's priorities.

Luckily, Fred's family provided an incident that for the first time made Fred deal with them in a different way. They did something that really got him mad at them; these are the serendipitous things that sometimes help the therapy to go. Fred was much better off financially than his sister and brother-in-law, and his parents, feeling their two children should have equal material advantages, would buy things for Elaine and charge them to the business in which Fred and dad were "partners." On the occasion of this particular incident, while Fred and Lynn were out of town, his parents went into Fred's house and removed some valuable items to give to his sister. Fred said that not only had they violated the privacy of his home, but they had lied to him, saying they had taken the items for themselves rather than his sister. (It should be mentioned that in recent months, since Elaine and Lynn had had a falling out, there had been no contact between Fred and his sister. Fred's parents acted as the communicators between their two children.) On seeing Fred's anger toward his family, Lynn was triumphant, but we all had to sit on her to get her to keep her two cents out of it. When Fred hinted that he could get back at his family by cutting off their funds, we began to get some sense of the power he had in that original family, in contrast to the relative impotence he manifested in dealing with his wife. At this stage of therapy the most Fred could do vis-à-vis his original family was to ask his parents not to enter his house when he was not there. He was not yet ready to deal with his family about the real issues.

Because the sexual relationship is extremely sensitive to other difficulties in a marriage, it was no surprise to discover that this couple had sexual problems. In one session Fred said that one reason he left Lynn was his dissatisfaction with their sex life. This statement made Lynn very angry; she said she was the one who had to approach him for sex and, besides, how dare he bring this up in the group without first discussing it with her at home?

This interchange confirmed further Fred's reluctance to confront Lynn except in the sanctuary of the group; Lynn, too, often said she had to come to group to find out what Fred was thinking. I have seen this phenomenon many times and have come to believe that one of the reasons people go to conjoint marital therapy is to provide a safe setting to tell their mates what they really feel or think. Husbands and wives, I have learned, are often afraid of each other. When they can level with each other, on all levels, on their own, they are probably ready to terminate therapy or perhaps the marriage.

In any event, Fred related that in the past he had always been attracted by "showgirl, trashy broads," and one of the reasons he was uncertain about being married was that he was not sure he wanted to give up a swinging bachelor life. Lynn, he said, was more refined, like his sister, and, moreover, she had a habit of compulsively washing her genital area before and after sex, which turned him off. The material that Fred had given was rich. I wondered to myself whether Fred split the erotic introjects of mother and sister into the familiar whore/nun dichotomy that men fantasize about women, and I thought he was bound to have difficulty relating sexually to a wife who chastely washed away dirty sex. I could not resist the temptation to communicate a piece of this thinking to him by wondering aloud whether he had not felt unfaithful to his mother and sister when he married Lynn. At that observation, Fred started giggling and then went into paroxysms of laughter he could not stop. His uncontrollable laughter contagiously spread to the rest of the group, suggesting that a universal theme had been triggered off.

In addition to exploring the deeper cross-currents in the marriage, I also dealt with the more external manifestations of the disturbed relationship. From time to time I used such techniques as quid pro quo negotiations, paradoxical instructions, task assignments, clarifying of communication, and the feedback technique (wherein one partner must listen and repeat back the other's message until the content and emotional meaning are heard correctly). Fred and Lynn had to repeat a message many times before the partner agreed that it was right. Fred's withdrawal and inability to share opinions or feelings were based in part on his feeling of being overwhelmed by her barrages and his inability to match her clever use of words. Audiotape playback of Lynn's monologue sometimes helped her realize how she must sound to others and why people often closed their ears to her; Fred also came to see how silence can be more devastating than screaming.

Closely connected with Fred and Lynn's style of communication were their fight styles (Bach and Wyden, 1969) and their difficulty in reconciling the natural ambivalence of love and hate that exists in all intimate relationships (Charny, 1972). Compared with her howitzers, Fred felt he had a pop gun; besides, her belt line was so high and she was so sensitive to criticism that Fred had to be most circumspect in dealing with issues with her. However, Fred's dirty-fighting technique of avoiding fights and being Mr. Nice Guy did not change until he observed angry interchanges in other couples and came to learn that intimacy without conflict is impossible.

As the sessions progressed, Fred became more assertive and unwilling to tolerate Lynn's onslaughts. His anger grew to match hers, culminating in a fist fight between them at home, followed by Fred's again leaving her to live with his parents. I was discouraged anew by this turn of events, although the fist fight in their case was at least an indication that Fred was relying less on camouflaged and silent hostilities. Mary was more hopeful about them than I, and the group's impressions were mixed. I myself learned from this experience that sometimes physical violence can paradoxically communicate that important matters are at stake; it can show deep concern and can represent a desperate bid to be taken seriously.

Fred kept telling Lynn that she was too needy and demanding; he was alluding to what Martin (1976) has described as the "lovesick" wife. Lynn got very upset at this, saying, "I want to give him so much and he wants to give me so little." Group members kept telling her that she sounded as if she wanted to possess him 100 percent and that the hungrier she was, the more he moved away from her; they felt Fred could give more if she stopped pushing. With respect to her obsession with his family, she was repeatedly given feedback that it was his family, not hers.

Among the reasons I have come to believe that couples group therapy is the treatment of choice for premarital, marital, and separation and divorce problems is that the other couples provide not only models of how marital struggles can be worked out but also models of what to avoid. An event took place in the group that had the serendipitous effect of stimulating Fred and Lynn's movement in the therapy. Another couple in the group were planning to divorce, and the turmoil this couple were going through really shook up Fred and Lynn. For the first time they faced the real possibility of divorce, with its attendant pain. At this time another therapeutic dimension of couples groups emerged: certain events in a group can create a contagion of affect that reawakens in full force early, forgotten feelings. This phenomenon seems to have the same effect as Paul's (1976) cross-confrontation technique in reviving old suppressed or repressed feelings. The transactions of the other couple put Lynn in touch with her unremembered anguish surrounding the divorce of her parents, and Fred connected with the shock and anger about his parents' near divorce of many years ago. Both of them, like everyone else whose parents had had bad marriages, consciously wanted better marriages than their parents'. Furthermore, basically, neither partner wanted to lose the other. I myself became convinced again of the old adage about psychotherapy—that people do not change unless they have to, when they feel it in the gut, and when the consequences of not changing are unacceptable. Shortly after their fist fight, Fred moved back with his wife again, and they arranged to go away together for a few days to a resort area where they planned to "talk over our problems." Fred said he had wanted to tell Lynn how difficult it was for him to balance all his roles of son, father, brother, and husband, and Lynn had wanted to tell him she could better see how she was driving him away. "Instead of talking, however," Fred said, "we swam, had some great meals, slept late, made love, and then we didn't need to talk." (Remember the old advice of family doctors to "take a vacation"?) They were both, by now, strongly motivated to work on self, and the enormous resistance to bringing in original families had faded. Now I was ready to bring to bear that most powerful of therapy techniques, family-of-origin sessions.

I have become convinced, as have Bowen (Anonymous, 1972; Bowen, 1974), Boszormenyi-Nagy and Spark (1973), Haas (1968), and Whitaker (1976), that working things out directly, face to face, with the family of origin, rather than through the transference with a therapist, can have a powerful effect on the original problems for which people come to therapy. In fact, my experience with this method has convinced me that one session with the family of origin, conducted in a particular way, is usually far more potent and effective than numerous regular therapy sessions.

It needs to be kept in mind that this method does not just consist of bringing in the family of origin; clients need to be prepared to really deal with and confront their original family members in special kinds of ways (see Framo, 1976).[1] The clients' inordinate unwillingness and outright refusal to involve their parents and brothers and sisters in the treatment process testifies to the great power of this approach. Considerable experience is needed with the method before a marital or family therapist learns how to deal with the resistances. One of the reasons I integrate couples group therapy with family-of-origin work is that, in attempting to overcome the nearly instinctive aversion to bringing in original family, I will use whatever help I can get. I push in this direction forcefully because of my convictions

---

[1]In recent years I have had a number of requests from family therapists to have sessions with their families of origin. Although the preparation for these sessions has to be foreshortened, since these therapists are not regular clients in ongoing couple or family therapy, even these brief encounters, according to those who have had them, have proved worthwhile and productive. No other publication of mine has prompted so many letters from professional therapists as the family-of-origin paper, telling how it has affected not only their professional practice but their personal lives as well. There is, I believe, a universal longing to try at least to come to terms with parents before they die.

about what these sessions can do. An atmosphere develops in the groups whereby everybody is expected to bring in his or her original family. Bringing them in has become almost like a final exam before graduation, and the group members exercise considerable pressure on others to do it, even while they are frightened to do it themselves. When the reluctant members see the leaps in progress made by those who have had their sessions, they become more willing to consider it.

Although Lynn was now intellectually prepared to consider bringing in her parents, when we got right down to it, she was terrified of having her parents come in together. She said that her father would not sit in the same room with her mother. In addition, she was not sure her father would even come in with her alone. I told her that I had confidence in her and that when she herself really wanted him in, she would find a way. Late one night I got a call from Lynn: "Waddayaknow, my dad said he'd be glad to come in. I'm surprised."

Further preparation of Lynn for the session consisted in going over her family history again, this time in more detail. She was again resistive to the suggestion from all of us that she listen to her dad's side of the story, saying that she could not do that to her mother. I said that listening to him did not make her a disloyal traitor to her mother. Her fixed view of her father seemed so immutable that I wondered whether the session would accomplish much. Mixed in with her resentment and defensiveness, however, were the detectable signs of great foreboding that are prodromal for family-of-origin sessions. I have speculated that one basis for this intense fear may be that people must feel they were loved by their parents, and there always exists the risk that they will discover otherwise, and so they are afraid to expose themselves to this last chance to find out the truth. The group were supportive of Lynn around her anxiety about the session, and they helped her delineate the issues she would take up with her father. Lynn knew that she would be on her own in the session with dad, that even Fred would not be present.

Mr. T, Lynn's father, was a prominent research scientist in a nearby city, and when we met him, we were struck with his obvious interest in Lynn and her welfare, contrary to her statements about his lack of interest in her. In the early part of the session Lynn could not contain herself, and she told her father how she had felt rejected by him all her life, that he had abandoned her as a child and through the years had had little to do with her. She said the rejection was confirmed when he did not come to her wedding and did not invite her to his when he married again. Her father was taken aback by this onslaught, and, keeping in mind our belief that incoming parents need support, we cautioned Lynn to slow down and listen. Obviously relieved that finally Lynn was agreeing to listen to his version of past events, he told the following story. He said that his marriage to Lynn's mother had failed because his wife put her own family before him (sound familiar?). He said that they lived with his mother-in-law, and when his marriage relationship worsened, his wife and mother-in-law teamed up to get a court order evicting him from the house. Furthermore, they had the money to hire "tough" lawyers who managed to legally block all his efforts to see Lynn. Mr. T cried as he remembered not only the humiliation of the experience but the torment over being cut off from access to his little girl. Lynn was astonished at this story. She went through a period of great confusion, trying to reconcile her lifelong animosity toward her father with this new information that made the bitterness untenable and inappropriate. She had never seen her father cry before, and she did not know how to deal with it,

except to cry herself with a perplexity that seemed to say, "Damn it, I'm not supposed to care for you. You're my pet hate." They went on to talk about the misunderstandings and miscommunications that had occurred through the years, but Lynn
kept going back to that stunning realization: "You mean you didn't see me when
I was little because you were legally prevented from doing so? My God, do you
know what this means to me?" A number of other issues were discussed during
the session, but the foregoing interchange overshadowed everything else. However,
another issue came up that was important. Mr. T's present wife could not tolerate
any mention of his previous wife or child, and whenever Lynn visited him, she
could not stay at their house and instead had to stay with Mr. T's sister. Mr. T
decided at this session that he was no longer going to allow his present wife to determine the kind of relationship he was going to have with Lynn and that she would
be welcome in his home any time. Before he left the session, he asked me for the
name of a marital therapist in his home town because he wanted to work on his
problems with his present wife.

        After the session with her dad, Lynn had to face her mother with the truth;
and for the first time she got angry at her mother, not only for what her mother
and grandmother had done to keep her father from her but for concealing the facts
all these years. The rigid dichotomy of father-devil and mother-saint began to
dissolve, and this external shift was reflected in an inner rearrangement that, in
turn, created some new behaviors in Lynn. Her voice lost much of its stridency,
she began talking with her father for the first time about what was going on between her and Fred and his family, and everyone in the group noticed her lessening preoccupation with Fred's family.

        Since people fear not only change in themselves but also a change in their
intimate other, it was not surprising that Fred subtly began trying to nudge Lynn
back to some of her old ways. It became obvious that Lynn's behavior had served
a defensive function for him vis-à-vis his family, and when this time she did not
cooperate, he was forced to face his own conflicts about them. Fred, furthermore,
had progressed so much in therapy that only a few interpretive comments were
needed to block these efforts to use Lynn. There was now no escaping the need
for Fred to deal with his family. He handled his anxiety about the session by doing
a lot of preliminary work with each parent alone before the session. Although he
did not want to be met with any surprises in the session, the one person he did
not speak to was his sister, Elaine. He had not seen her for a long time because
of the hard feelings between his sister and his wife and also because, as he put it,
"Elaine's so damn spoiled I really didn't want to see her myself." Since his parents
were the go-betweens, his mother informed Elaine about the session. Some members
of the group developed hypotheses about what would happen during Fred's family
conference (for example, whether the family would discuss the other man in mom's
life), and Lynn said she was really looking forward to listening to the tape of the
session.

        Both of Fred's parents and his sister were present for the session. Elaine and
Fred were polite to each other, with the kind of controlled wariness that old lovers
display when they have not seen each other for a long time; they had to be careful
not to let the other know they still cared. Dad, looking like the grandfather of Fred,
said almost nothing, and mom, a handsome, well-dressed woman, did most of the
talking. It quickly became apparent that Fred called the shots in this family, however;

whenever he started to speak, everyone deferred to him. This was a Fred we had never seen before. Mom, early in the session, brought up the subject of her relationship with the other man. (Fred, it will be recalled, had prepared his mother to do so.) She attempted to justify it by saying that she came from a family where money was extremely important. She had married Fred's father, a much older man, because he had money, but shortly after they married, he lost his business, and in order to regain his wife's love he worked eighteen hours a day in a new business. She said, "My husband came from humble beginnings and would have been satisfied with less, but I spent the money faster than he could make it. So I don't blame him, in a way. Still, he was paying more attention to the business than to me, and finally I told him, 'You either stop being married to the business or I'm getting a divorce.'" It was apparently at that point that she asked Fred, at age fifteen, whether she should divorce, and also at that time she got involved with the other man, who had money.

The tension in the room began to rise at this point, and Fred confronted his father with how angry he had been for tolerating having this other man living in their house. Fred's father, paralyzed with feeling at that point, could not speak. Recognizing his inability to deal with this loaded area, we moved on to the relationship between Elaine and Fred. Elaine said that all she remembered about her childhood was being alone, except for Fred. She cried when she remembered the day Fred told her he was getting married. She was quite open about her jealousy, but we were startled when Fred said he had the same feelings of shock when she got married. At that point in the session Elaine switched from tears to intense anger, saying that Lynn was responsible for the alienation that existed in their family.

Other issues were discussed, such as the open display of affection between Fred and his sister and mother, the resentment over Fred's "ruling" them, and Fred's trying again, unsuccessfully, to reach his father. When the session ended, we knew there would have to be another one, the next time including Lynn and Elaine's husband. In addition to the unfinished business from this session, there was the issue of the parents' efforts to push Fred into taking Elaine's husband, Barry, into his business. We also knew that the two natural enemies, Elaine and Lynn, had to work out some rapprochement in order for their respective marriages to survive.

After Fred's family-of-origin session, Fred's mother got in touch with Lynn, and the two of them became friendly again. Lynn was very pleased by this development, but several members of the group cautioned her that perhaps her mother-in-law was using her in a tactical maneuver to gain favor with Fred. Besides, this alliance was an unstable one, since Elaine was now on the outside of the triangle and could not stay out. Lynn had changed considerably by this time and had more objectivity about the situation. Fred felt that although his session with his family had accomplished much, he was concerned about the rift between himself and his sister, as well as his inability to get through to his dad. When he mentioned that he hardly knew Elaine's husband, I suggested he have lunch with Barry to get to know him. The following week, coincidentally, Barry invited him to lunch, and Fred reported that when they got together, he realized for the first time Barry's resentment of him.

In preparation for the session to include Fred, his parents and sister, Lynn, and Barry, Lynn was warned to play it cool. She had a lot of feeling about being scapegoated but did manage to be less reactive. In this session several important things happened. Barry told Fred in no uncertain terms that Fred was arrogant and treated his parents badly. Barry said, "Everybody in this family is supposed to cater to you." He went on to say that Fred's worship of money indicated a distorted sense of values about life. Fred's dad, speaking up for the first time, noted that Fred had some of his mother's preoccupation with money. Fred said that before he would take Barry into the business, Barry would have to prove himself. Barry said, "Don't do me any favors." Mom kept deploring, in the background, the possible breakup of the family. Barry knew the history of the relationship between his wife and Fred; yet, he denied any feelings of jealousy. I then told him the story of a Sid Caesar skit I had once seen in which Sid Caesar comes into a room and catches Carl Reiner kissing Sid's wife. They all agree to handle this matter in a civilized manner and discuss it rationally, but a few minutes later Sid Caesar gets furious with Carl Reiner over the way the martinis were mixed. Barry got the point even if he could not respond to it.

The highlight of this session, however, was that Fred and his father were finally able to have a dialogue about the important things that had happened between them through the years. We had to exert some effort to keep mother out of that interchange. What really touched father was when Fred said he had longed for more closeness with him. Fred, like Lynn, was surprised that parents can feel rejected too. They broke through to each other when Fred told dad that he had never wanted to be passive like him and that he also, paradoxically, wanted to beat him out and be more successful. Although Fred felt he had turned out to be a better businessman, it was a hollow victory because he realized that he did not want to lose a father in the process. He also said he had come to admire many fine qualities in his dad, qualities that he himself did not have. The entire family then witnessed an event they had never thought they would see—a withdrawn, isolated father deeply sobbing about all the disappointments in his life. They were even more stunned when he pulled himself together and began, at long last, to take charge of all the squabbles in the family. He even mediated some agreements between Fred and Barry and between Elaine and Lynn.

Only a few more sessions were needed with Fred and Lynn after Fred's second family-of-origin session. Fred said that some pervasive, nameless dread that had always been present in his family of origin (a dread that other clients had reported in previous family-of-origin sessions) had disappeared. He felt he could love Lynn and his own family without feeling untrue to either. Fred said that he and dad had continued to talk personally ever since the family session. He was enormously pleased to have a relationship with his father at long last. Lynn recounted an event that had enormous significance to her. On her birthday, her parents were together with her for the first time since she was a little girl, and she took a picture of the two of them together. Her father's bitterness toward Lynn's mother had vanished after he felt Lynn had forgiven him. Lynn also reported that she and Elaine had gone shopping together for their children (Elaine was pregnant); Lynn's involvement with Fred's family appeared to be on a realistic basis. On their way to the last session Fred and Lynn had an argument, which I saw as the usual termination regression. When I called them six months later, they said they were doing "just great" and felt "truly married for the first time." I thought to myself: Considering where they started, not bad for twenty-five sessions.

Summary Evaluation

Although in some respects the marital problems that Fred and Lynn brought to therapy were of the garden variety, I selected this case to write about in order to illustrate the powerful effects that extended families have on a marital situation. We all know of the past dynamic forces that families of origin exert in shaping people and marriages (best exemplified in Dicks', 1967, work at Tavistock), but less widely realized are the current influences of both families and both sets of in-laws on the husband and wife. If you are treating a couple and you do not explicitly ask what is going on in their relationships with parents, brothers, sisters, aunts, uncles, and in-laws, they usually do not tell you. Individual therapists focus on their patients and tend to ignore the marital partners or the children. Family therapists and marriage counselors all too frequently ignore the families of origin, both from the standpoint of understanding the marital struggle and from that of utilizing extended family as a therapeutic resource.

It is possible that Fred and Lynn's marriage relationship would have improved just from marital or couples group therapy. (I do believe, however, that they would have had a destructive divorce without treatment.) Most of the marital cases I have seen, nevertheless, made their breakthroughs after the family-of-origin sessions. Through most of the therapy Lynn was not willing to bring in her father, and we had to clear away some other aspects of the troubled relationship before she could deal with that dimension. Once the more superficial aspects of their difficulties were handled, and under the threat of losing her loved/hated husband, her antipathy to dealing with her father was surmounted. When she got her father back, the force of her need to work out her intrapsychic conflicts through Fred nearly dissipated.

One aspect of Fred's role in his original family was the parentified one; his being an apparent winner resulted in a thin triumph, which exacted a high price. His exalted position in that family created a sense of confidence that enabled him to be successful in the outside world, but, like many prominent and socially successful people, he was severely damaged in dealing with intimate relationships. His emotional radar signaling system chose a mate who would fight the battle with his family that he could not; Lynn expressed his anger for him. His family-of-origin sessions had many aspects, but the critical event, like that of Lynn's, was getting the father he felt he never had. Lynn and Fred shared the introject of the longed-for father.

The couples group format provides many more therapeutic benefits than just serving as leverage to bring about family-of-origin sessions. In the group sessions, the partners learn by identification, get support and understanding, and profit from confrontations by the other group members. Marital interactions are often driven by strong, often too strong, emotions, and the group helps in tempering these, leading to more reality-based thinking. One part of my method of conducting couples group sessions consists in having every member of the group of three couples, in turn, give feedback to the couple who has just been focused on. By alternating in the ''patient'' and ''observer'' roles, the individuals often treat themselves through others, and they also gain a sense of adequacy and competence. Spouses, moreover, get to see how other people respond to their partners, and this helps loosen the fixed, distorted views that all people have about their mates. In Lynn's and Fred's case, the group did not see either partner as crazy and unreasonable, the way each saw the other.

Lynn's and Fred's therapy was an instance when the treatment worked the way it is supposed to, according to my conceptual outlook (Framo, 1965, 1970). It should go without saying that not all my cases do. Too often case reports in the literature make the treatment sound smooth and easy, as if therapy progressed evenly and barriers were easily overcome. Someday a book should be written on treatment failures, because I think we can learn a lot from them. I was glad to participate in this volume, which is a first in requesting contributors to describe the process of treatment as it really happens—like marriage, with its ups and downs, backsliding, treatment errors, despair, hope, times when nothing seems to be happening, and times when those occasional bursts of movement occur that make it all worthwhile.

⚒ 29 ⚒

Couples Therapy
with Marriage Contracts

Clifford J. Sager

What is surprising, since marriage is the most complex of human relationships, is that psychiatry and psychology have only recently begun to turn from studying and treating the individual to studying and treating the two mates within the context of their marriage. Marital therapy has advanced beyond the stage of mere advice and counseling only since about 1930 (Sager, 1966a, 1966b). The current status of this area of therapy has been summarized by Berman and Lief (1975), who indicate that conjoint treatment—working with the two partners together—has become the common modality for marital therapy but that there is still no comprehensive or generally acceptable diagnostic or theoretical system to describe and explain what factors contribute to establishing and maintaining good or poor marriages. Although there is an increasingly large literature on marriage and marital therapy, no unifying concepts have evolved. In a recent critical overview of marital and family therapy, Olson (1975) confirms the lack of a solid theoretical base.

As a step in developing a means of conceptualizing and making order out of the myriad intrapsychic and transactional factors that contribute to determining the quality of marital interaction, my colleagues and I several years ago developed the concept of marriage contracts (Sager and others, 1971).

Individual Marriage Contracts

In work with marital couples and families, the concept of individual marriage contracts has proved extremely useful as a model for elucidating interactions between marital partners. Specifically, we seek to understand these interactions in terms of the congruence, complementarity, or conflict of the partners' reciprocal expectations and obligations. These "contractual dynamics" are powerful deter-

This chapter was adapted from chaps. 1 and 5 of Clifford J. Sager, *Marriage Contracts and Couple Therapy* (New York: Brunner/Mazel, 1976).

minants of the individual's behavior within the marriage, as well as of the quality
of the marital relationship. It is, therefore, logical to assume that analysis of marital
transactions according to this model may clarify otherwise inexplicable behavior
and events within the marriage and also may provide a focus around which to
organize effective therapeutic intervention when an individual, a marriage, or a
family is in trouble.

The term *individual contract* refers to a person's concepts, expressed and unexpressed, conscious and beyond awareness, of his or her obligations within the marital
relationship and of the benefits that the person expects to derive from marriage
in general and from his or her spouse in particular. But what must be emphasized
above all is the reciprocal aspect of the contract: what each partner expects to give
and what he or she expects to receive from the spouse in exchange are crucial. Contracts deal with every conceivable aspect of family life: relationships with friends,
achievements, power, sex, leisure time, money, children, and so forth. The degree
to which a marriage can satisfy each partner's contractual expectations in these
areas is an important determinant of the quality of that marriage.

The terms of the individual contracts are determined by deep needs and wishes
that each individual expects the marital relationship will fulfill for him or her. These
will include healthy and realistically plausible, as well as neurotic and conflictual,
needs. It is most important to realize that although each spouse may be aware of
his own needs and wishes on some level of awareness, he does not usually realize
that his attempts to fulfill the partner's needs are based on the covert assumption
that his own wishes will thereby be fulfilled. Furthermore, although each spouse
is usually at least partly aware of the terms of his contract and some of the needs
from which these terms are derived, he may be only remotely aware, if at all, of
the implicit expectations of his spouse. Indeed, a partner may assume there is mutual
agreement on a contract when in fact this is not so; the individual then behaves
as if an actual contract existed and both spouses were equally obliged to fulfill its
terms. When significant aspects of the contract cannot be fulfilled, as is inevitable,
and especially when these lie beyond his own awareness, the disappointed partner
may react with rage, injury, depression, or withdrawal and provoke marital discord
by acting as though a real agreement had been broken. This response is particularly
likely to occur when one partner believes that he has fulfilled his obligations but
that his spouse has not.

In my practice the contents of the two individual marriage contracts are
developed by both the patients and the therapist in three categories of information,
or contractual terms: expectations of the marriage; intrapsychic or biological determinants of the individual's needs; and the external foci of marital problems, the
symptoms produced by problems in the first two categories. Each of these categories
contains material from three levels of awareness—conscious and verbalized, conscious but not verbalized, and beyond awareness. As a general rule, the therapist
is able to elicit contractual terms at the first and second levels of awareness from
the partners themselves. By the time couples come to therapy, they are usually
prepared to verbalize not only what has been expressed previously but what has
been conscious but unexpressed because of fear or anxiety. To discover the contractual material that lies beyond awareness, it is necessary to depend in part on
the therapist's interpretation of the patients' productions. In addition, spouses are
often helpful in shedding light on each other's terms in this area.

Applicability of the Contract Concept

Many techniques and approaches may be used in marital therapy, as long as they are consonant with the therapist's own theoretical views and preferences. The concept of the marriage contract can be adapted for use with most theoretical approaches. Specifically, the therapist who uses the contract approach assumes that contractual disappointments are a major source of marital discord. Accordingly, he or she tries to clarify the significant terms of the contracts, aware of the psychic determinants of most clauses, and if these are being violated, the therapist tries to help the couple renegotiate and develop more acceptable terms. Understanding and change may take place concurrently, but change may occur without understanding, and often understanding alone is not enough to produce change. Because we do not always know how to produce change most effectively, the therapist needs to have available a wide variety of theoretical and technical approaches.

It is useful to introduce the individual contract concept early in treatment and to emphasize the mutually satisfying elements of a couple's contracts at the outset. The concept may often be introduced in the first session. An emphasis early in treatment on positive contractual elements makes the couple aware of the valuable features of their marriage and helps to motivate them for the difficult therapeutic task that lies ahead. It is important that the therapist not lose sight of the positive elements in the relationship, including the positive complementarity that exists between the two persons.

Patients usually experience relief when they attain insight into the reasons for their smoldering rage and irritability, which may have been puzzling and disturbing. In contrast, confronting a spouse with the deep disappointments one has suffered in marriage can be upsetting, and therapists must be sensitive to the potentially disruptive effects of their interpretations on the relationship. The ultimate aim of treatment is to improve the marital relationship, family functioning, and the growth of the individuals. Since this may require open communication between the spouses on all levels, each spouse is encouraged to verbalize to the other the unspoken aspects of their contracts. Nevertheless, contractual material, especially when it reflects unconscious dynamics or an attempt to deal with an intrapsychic difficulty, requires the therapist's greatest sensitivity and skill both in eliciting it and in using it effectively. The interpretation of the unconscious contractual material can evoke intense reactions that may be highly constructive but may also have a negative effect on either spouse or the marital system. Such material has to be handled with respect, as in any other form of psychotherapy.

Advances in conceptualization and technique make it possible to deal with intrapsychic problems in conjoint therapy in ways not even developed fifteen years ago. Thus, the clarification of contractual transactions in therapy sheds light on intrapsychic factors and changes them, just as intrapsychic factors brought to light can help in clarifying and changing contractual terms. The therapist's efforts are guided by knowledge of both variables.

When a marriage is viable, clarifying the individual marriage contracts may lead to dramatic improvement in the couple's relationship and in the growth and development of each spouse. At some point in therapy each partner is confronted with realities that were previously beyond his awareness: "I can't get A in this relationship, but I do get B and C" or "My wishes are unrealistic, and no one can give me what I want." Such insights tend to lead to increasing commitment to the marriage and to the decision to accept its realistic limitations, which, in turn, facilitates the resolution of presenting problems.

Occasionally, however, exposure of the terms of the marriage contracts results in the discovery of serious disappointments and incompatibilities, which were previously denied and which may hasten dissolution of a marriage. One partner comes to the realization that "I can't get what I want from this marriage no matter what I give" or "I can satisfy him only if I am destructive to myself." A couple's decision to dissolve the marriage on the basis of realistic and comprehensive understanding that they cannot give each other what is wanted is not a treatment failure. Under such circumstances dissolution of an empty or painful marriage can be a constructive experience for both. Moreover, the agonizing and destructive experiences that often accompany divorce may be minimized.

The concept of individual marriage contracts helps to familiarize each marital partner with her own and her spouse's needs and willingness to give and to point out troublesome aspects of the relationship; couples are usually highly receptive to this way of structuring their problems. The technique is particularly valuable in conjoint sessions. Communication is facilitated, and spouses are better able to understand themselves, each other, and their relationship, when the terms of their contracts are revealed. The reasons for their unhappiness, apparently irrational behavior, and bickering or bitterness then become clear. Once they gain some understanding of the contractual disappointments each has suffered, marital partners often feel less helpless and are able to seek more realistic and effective solutions to their problems.

The couple's reciprocal expectations are powerful behavioral determinants. Psychodynamic insights and learning theory methods may be used, along with a system-transactional approach, as the therapist actively intervenes in the troubled marriage by trying to alter crucial aspects of the processes that result from these reciprocal interactional expectations. The individual contracts and the interactional contract provide an ongoing guide for setting therapeutic goals and for intervention.

The contract concept integrates the two parameters of behavioral determinants, the intrapsychic and the transactional. Individual contractual clauses derive from needs and conflicts that can best be understood in intrapsychic and culturally determined terms and are often adaptive attempts to resolve conflicts by means of specific interactions. The consequent interactional process, the interactional contract itself, then becomes a crucial determinant of the quality of the marriage or relationship.

The individual contracts provide us with a dynamic basis for improving our understanding of marital functioning. This concept provides indications for why, how, and under what circumstances marital disharmony smolders and becomes exacerbated. The dynamic diagnosis changes as therapy changes the marital system. As the separate contracts more clearly approach a single contract, whose terms are known to and agreed on by both partners, we can expect a healthier, more fulfilling give-and-take between the partners. Under these circumstances the individual contracts have become syntonic with the purposes of the marital system as well as with the needs of each partner.

The contract concept can be useful and valuable within the framework of almost any theoretical or technique system that allows for the interplay and validity of both transactional and intrapsychic aspects as determinants of the quality of a marriage. It provides a means of understanding these dual determinants and a way of using them therapeutically.

The Smiths' treatment not only shows how marriage contracts can be used in therapy but also illustrates the particular multifaceted, flexible, theoretically integrated approach that I try to use. The Smiths, their contracts, and their therapy will serve as a clinical application of the concepts discussed earlier.

My prime interest in this presentation is to illustrate the use of the marriage contracts as a conceptual and operational tool. Any number of treatment approaches, theories, or techniques could have been used instead of the ones described here. In fact, as the reader follows the case, I am sure he or she will see many instances in which particular transactions could have been handled differently, or he or she may disagree with the entire theoretical and technical approach. The point here is to judge how the marriage contracts can be used conceptually and as guidelines to therapeutic intervention within the framework of the reader's own convictions.

The Smiths: First Session

Susan Smith, aged thirty, and Jonathan, thirty-two, had been married seven years and had a son of five and a daughter of two when they came for treatment. The husband voiced their complaints first in the conjoint session: "Too much bitterness, not enough satisfaction, we fight about unimportant things." From Mrs. Smith: "I wanted a strong husband but not too strong or I would not be free. Once more it would be like it was and still is between me and my mother. Jon isn't free enough with me, and often he's more stubborn than strong. I can't play with him, he doesn't imagine enough. Sex is poor. It's not frequent and I don't have orgasms anymore. We don't have sex unless I start it."

Jon, an engineer, took a position a year ago at about two thirds of his former salary. He enjoys his new job because it allows him to be directly in command of a large number of employees in the field, rather than mostly doing paperwork, as in his previous job. Susan favored his taking this position because he would enjoy the work. She doesn't care if her husband doesn't wish to climb to the top of his profession, but she is concerned because they are committed to a high standard of living that necessitates that they once again accept money from her mother. Her mother, in turn, is insistent that Susan join her in her business. Susan does not want to, because her mother has a tough and domineering stance with her, especially at work: "You are not my daughter then—just another employee." Susan is a folksong writer and singer of moderate success who has also worked successfully and creatively in her mother's business. Her rage toward Jon is apparent as she looks at him and pointedly says that she does not mind accepting money from her mother but she will not accept her mother's control.

Jon had agreed to come to see me with his wife after they read a professional article (Sager and others, 1971) on marriage contracts that a friend had showed them. Hence, when they came in, they were already prepared to work on their contracts. I did not deal formally with the contracts at this first session because of the great pressure of their frustration and pain, but I partly did so when I elected to center first on their sexual relationship, which they had brought up as epitomizing much that was wrong in their marriage both as cause and effect. My decision to enter and to intervene in their system at this point was determined by the sharp difference in the terms of the sexual part of their contracts and by their agreement that improvement in this area was a high-priority goal. Each wanted a definite style of sex from the other, each thought it had been promised, and now both were disappointed and angry because each felt the other had not fulfilled his or her part of the contract. I believed that the sexual area epitomized their poor communication and misunderstandings about each other and therefore could provide an excellent field on which to begin work toward a single contract. I decided that in this case sex could lead us rapidly to the center of their differences.

Susan was a woman who had been uninhibited and assertive sexually; she had had sexual relationships with several men before her marriage. Her husband liked to hear stories from her of the details of these experiences and would become excited by them. Susan now felt that she wanted to be sexually desired by her husband and wanted him to excite her and not vice versa. This desire was consistent with her romantic image of having spontaneous sexual love in a forest glade, where she would feel one with all nature and with her mate. She felt that sex should not begin in bed but was part of a total loving, warm, and supportive relationship. Jon, who had also had considerable sexual experience before marrying, wanted to be sexually passive and expected her to be seductive and wanton and to initiate passionate sex with him. His wife felt guilty and repentant about her promiscuous past and felt she should be loved as a woman and mother, not just as a sex object.

Susan presented herself in the session as a sort of flower child, yet also very much in touch with reality. She had a beautiful fluid way of moving in and out of her ego boundaries. Jon was more pragmatic; he was set about his likes and dislikes and clearly passively aggressive in his adaptations. He had an honesty and bluntness that was very refreshing and was obviously devoted to his wife. He said that he wanted to be more giving to her but did not know how to do it her way. She wanted "to open him up more and then I will be more open," and as she said this, her smile made clear the intent of her double meaning.

He talked readily about his depressed, "morbid" moods and his preoccupation with violence. He was currently in charge of developing and overseeing the installation of the security aspects of a new prison. In this first session he was able to talk about his sadistic fantasies, the pleasure he received from the idea that "his" prison would really be secure and would keep the male inmates separated from society (and women) because they had injured innocent people. Susan, in contrast, expressed love for all humankind. She wanted to be true to herself and to be one spirit with the sky, sea, and earth. Their opposing views on crime and violence and his need to sequester "criminal forces" constituted the fodder for a running battle between them. He stated at one point that he enjoyed reading about violence and fantasized doing violence to those who hurt others. He recognized that this was his way of controlling his own inner violence and felt he was in good control of these feelings. The 1971 Attica prison revolt and its aftermath had left them at each other's throats as he sided with "law and order" and she saw the inmates as victims of the social ills that had spawned their crimes. As he put it, "I am more concerned for the victims of violence and she for the perpetrators."

I commented on their seemingly opposite views and feelings about violence and how they might be closer than they suspected, depending on whether they looked at their positions as points on an almost closed circle or as the extreme poles of a straight line. I did this not because I thought they would accept this almost-closed-circle idea but to illustrate how even the most apparently divergent viewpoints may be closer to achieving reconciliation than the protagonists realize, both philosophically and practically. He seemed to be in better touch with his primitive anger and the threat to his omnipotence than she. He freely sublimated his in his work and his fantasies about violence, whereas she used reaction formation as a major defense against her murderous impulses. Actually, each was coping differently with underlying feelings of infantile rage.

When I suggested the sexual area for initial work, I instructed them to take turns at home playing out each other's sexual desires. In this way neither would be capitulating to the other, an important issue to them. To avoid an argument over whose fantasy would be acted on first, I asked him to approach her the first time. In view of her more stubborn feelings of injury, it seemed that it would be easier for him to make the first move. She could then reciprocate more easily. This was the beginning of teaching the possibility of quid pro quo solutions to impasses.

Susan had fantasied how sensual and gratifying it would be for them to make love in a wooded area near their home. My task assignments to them were that within the next two days he should initiate and make love to her in the woods. Within two days after that she would initiate sex in the style he had fantasied, taking the initiative and being "wanton" and passionate while he remained passive. They both agreed and seemed delighted with these instructions. It was as if they had been waiting for someone to cut the Gordian knot of their power struggle. The tasks were designed to see whether they could accept what they claimed they wanted and whether they could give to each other. I was not concerned about their sexual functioning, since it was clear there were no sexual dysfunctions here. But how would they react to the opportunity to have what they claimed they wanted?

Second Session

I saw the Smiths again a week later. They had made love several times, taking turns playing out fantasies, and both had enjoyed each experience. It had been their most peaceful and gratifying week in a long time. However, all was not well, as indicated by Susan's dream the night before our second meeting. She had dreamed that her pubic hair was growing very long and that Jon stuffed it into her vagina so that her vagina was completely filled and blocked. She felt somewhat depressed in the dream because she could not have sex, although these feelings were not strong. Jon reported no dreams.

When asked about his reaction to her dream, Jon said he thought it showed that she believed he wanted her not to have sex. He said, "I don't want her to make love to other men, but I certainly want her to with me. Perhaps she thought stuffing the hair was like I was putting a chastity belt on her—we have kiddingly talked about that once or twice." Susan said there was something in what he said but she felt that he, or maybe she herself, wanted to turn off her sexuality. That idea bothered her because she had enjoyed sex this week. I pointed out that it was her dream. She had had her husband stuff her vagina. Perhaps she wanted to blame him if she turned off sexually. Was she upset in any way about enjoying sex this week? She said she had felt better when they had sex in the woods, rather than when he was passive. She had enjoyed his activity more. I suggested that in view of all they had been expressing about control and violence it was understandable that she might be on guard against trusting herself with her husband; yet, she seemed to prefer him to be assertive.

They both appeared to agree with my statement, but it made Jon somewhat defensive. He responded by stating that she had known how he was and she had seduced him by telling him about the other men she had been with and how sexually active she had been. They both knew that he was jealous but tried to control it. She said that she had been seductive at the start of their relationship but she had changed, and now, years later, she no longer wanted to talk about her previous sexual affairs, even when he pushed her to do so. She wanted their hearts to be open to each other and when that happened, sex would follow naturally and easily. He interpreted this to mean that she wanted to close up her vagina to him unless she had her way. At this point he reacted with mixed feelings, while she expressed adamantly that loving feelings and openness had to be evident for sex or she felt as if her vagina were closing up—"I can't even lubricate." I reminded them how good sex had been and suggested that the dream had brought to the surface her feelings of anxiety at their sexual success and that these feelings possibly reflected his anxiety as well. I told them that they need not agree fully but they should look at how much each had enjoyed implementing the other's fantasy.

Feeling that to pursue sex further at the moment would be counterproductive, I then drew them out about their expectations of each other's feelings toward their two children, the role assignments of the children, parenting responsibilities, and so on, thus getting more contractual material without trying to confront them too directly in sensitive areas so early in treatment. It was apparent that Susan enjoyed mothering but wanted greater participation from her husband with the children. She included the children as central in their unit. Jon kept them somewhat at a distance, to an extent resenting their existence as an intrusion into the mother/child symbiosis he wanted with Susan.

We then discussed the basic ideas of the marriage contract, using the concepts of the article they had read, which described the three levels of awareness: verbalized, conscious but not verbalized, and beyond awareness. This was done with emphasis on the exchange quality: I do for you and expect you to do for me in return. I asked them to write out their contracts separately at home, using the article as a model, and not to discuss them together until both had finished. If they wished to read or discuss the two contracts after that, it would be fine. If they made any changes or additions, they should leave in the original terms and clearly note any changes that had been added as a result of the discussion. I asked them to bring their contracts to the third session. I believed they were ready to write out their contracts and would use the opportunity constructively.

The Smiths left the second session with two sets of instructions: to write out their separate marriage contracts and to continue to take turns initiating sex and playing out each other's fantasies. The initiator would play out his or her own fantasy. I knew that genuine progress toward a single sexual contract would be achieved when each also used part of the other's fantasy on his or her own initiative, so that the leadership went back and forth in the same sexual encounter without thoughts of "What is for me and what is for my partner?"

Third Session

At the beginning of the third session, the couple reported that the first week's improvement in sexual activity and pleasure had not been sustained. Susan felt that her husband was merely following my instructions and did not feel the proper love for her, because he acted lovingly only when he wanted sex. She saw me as her mother pulling the marionette strings and her husband as her weak father. I used Susan's reaction to point out that many matters in their relationship had to be reevaluated but that good sex and love were ready for them when they both felt willing to give as well as receive, and that was not up to me or for me. I interpreted her transferential designation of me as strong mother and showed her how self-defeating that was for her in this situation. Sex would have to wait for further attention or would eventually take care of itself when suspiciousness, hostility, and the use of sex in their power struggle were no longer necessary.

The early focus on sex had illustrated the essence of their problems to them and indicated that remedy and satisfaction were possible if they wanted them but that their sex problem was a symptom, not a cause, of their more general marital difficulties.

I suggested that we look at the marriage contracts (Exhibits 1 and 2) together. They had not had time to discuss them together before the session but in response to my question said they did not mind the other's learning the contents now.

Exhibit 1. Susan Smith's Contract.

This is my summarizing miniscript: If you make it possible for me to be independent and need no one you provide me with stability and security. When responsibilities overwhelm me I stop giving love and sex. I will not give love if you do not provide status and security. In return I will be a loving wife. Hestian.

My obligations:	*My benefits:*
to be faithful.	to have children.
to enjoy giving pleasure (injunction from husband "Don't be close" interferes with my fulfilling my obligations).	to receive pleasure from husband and children.
Hestian—I will care for hearth and children.	Power—I will have power to do my own work and pursue my way of life.

The More Detailed Contract:

1. Verbalized

My expectations:	*What I will receive:*
He will give me financial and emotional security—to be a sane balance wheel for me. He will share my interests.	I will get deep satisfaction from our relationship—I will feel safe and protected. We will work toward a common end (we're after the same rainbow's end, my huckleberry friend).

2. Conscious but Not Verbalized

Give	*Receive—in exchange*
I want to be completely at his mercy, his victim. He will make me feel. Weak women feel. Strong women don't feel. I will put myself completely at his mercy. I will be his concubine, slave, victim.	He is powerful male. Womanly deep feelings—it is good to be dependent on this strong man; it is my realization of my deepest being as a woman. A strong man. So I will receive protection on an earthly level.

Exhibit 1. Susan Smith's Contract, Cont'd.

---

3. Beyond Awareness

YOU ARE A STRONG MALE unlike my father. I fear your strength and I
want to destroy it. I will not encourage your strengths because you may destroy me.
I need to be the strong and independent one.
I want you dependent and weak.

Exhibit 2. Jonathan Smith's Contract.

Conscious Verbalized

Give	*Take in exchange*
1. Support you monetarily to the best of my ability.	1. You will be a good wife and mother; carry the household.
2. Be your companion and escort socially.	2. You will be my companion and escort socially.
3. Be faithful sexually.	3. Be sexually faithful.
4. Assist you in solving day-to-day problems.	4. Share sharable experiences.
5. Do work around the house that is heavy or unusual and that I am capable of doing.	5. Help relax and ease tensions after the day of work.
6. Be a father figure for the children.	6. Be understanding of personal hang-ups and prejudices.
7. Share verbally and emotionally in sharable experiences.	
8. Accommodate your personal hang-ups and prejudices.	

Conscious Not Verbalized

Give	*Take in exchange*
1. Will allow you to engage in activities which I personally dislike—religious, spiritual, and the like.	1. Allow me to engage in activities you don't like.
2. Tolerate your moodiness.	2. Want you to be passionate and demanding of me sexually.
3. Will not impose on you sexually but will be available sexually on your demand.	3. Bear with my negative personality traits.
4. Prepared to admit I do not earn enough to properly support you.	4. Make do with my income without complaint.

Sub- or Unconscious

Give	*Take in exchange*
1. Prepared to ''forgive and forget'' past sexual experiences although I am jealous and feel insecure in comparison to (your) former sex partners.	1. Want a wild, passionate, and whorelike bedmate who will be verbal in lovemaking and accommodate my sexual fantasies.
2. Prepared to forgo demand that you don't take money from your mother because I realize it's absolutely necessary.	2. Want an adoring and verbally complimentary female who will be ego-massaging to me as both person and male.
3. Prepared not to pursue other women though attracted to the idea.	3. Want you to be attractive and teasing to other men but never to be available to them.

The crux of their struggle was clear. He needed reassurance, support, the
love of an adoring woman, sexually teasing to and desired by other men but letting
the world know she belonged to him. If she did not behave so as to reassure him

and quell his anxiety, he would withdraw punitively and not give her what she wanted. Her contract demanded that he be strong and weak at the same time, which presented him with an impossible double bind. Actually her sexual withdrawal and refusal to move toward him sexually gave her a potent weapon in her struggle for power. He could not satisfy her for long because of her contradictory needs: He was to be strong and she his slave, but to be enslaved was to be controlled by mother and required rebellion. She could be independent only if he was weak and her slave (as her father was her mother's), but if this happened, she would despise him as she did her father. She had endowed Jonathan with real and fantasied qualities of both parents. (This is an example of a spouse's being endowed by the beholder with both mother and father transferential reactions at the same time.) By using the marriage contracts in marital therapy, we are often in a better position to observe this phenomenon than we might be otherwise. Thus, with her husband's unwitting collaboration, Susan found it easy to evoke countertransferential (parataxic) reactions from her husband that readily supported her own distortions and negative expectations.

Each was acting the role of a childlike partner in their interactional contract. I classified them as childlike/childlike partners, or two children in search of a parent. This is in contradistinction to the child-like partnerships in which the spouses are playmates, the "sandbox marriage."

From the data gathered in the first three sessions I began to develop the Smiths' individual contracts more fully while the treatment continued. The marriage contracts as I formulated them more elaborately were developed after the fifth session, with the use of all the information available to me, including the contracts the couple had written; my evaluation of their productions, including the initial history; the dream material; and their statements about each other and their parents. How they interacted in sessions, how they reacted to and treated each other as they reported other events, how they carried out tasks, as well as their reactions to these— all contributed additional interactional information. The contracts as formulated at this point were working hypotheses constantly subject to change. They were to be a guide toward the goal of a single commonly agreed-on contract. Compromises would have to be made between the two individuals and within each person in regard to his or her own conflicts and ambivalence. Some new contract terms would have to be created. Compromise with acceptance is one method of arriving at a common contract; using newly created contractual terms or facets that develop during treatment of life experiences is another.

Such contracts are formulated in accordance with the three major classes of contractual terms: (1) what is expected from marriage, (2) those terms based on biological and intrapsychic factors, and (3) the parts of the contract that reflect derivative or externalized foci of marital problems rooted in the first two areas. In the formulation presented in Exhibit 3, the three levels of awareness of the terms of the contracts are merged, since these contracts are the therapist's statement. Because these two contracts are my working hypotheses, I find they are more useful when I pool the partners' information from their three levels of awareness and from all other sources. What I formulate is done within the limits of my best awareness and theoretical bias. I am able then to transmit my hypotheses, observations, and therapeutic maneuvers to the couple so that they can be used constructively to move toward our common therapeutic goals.

Exhibit 3. Projected Contracts.

Susan Smith   *Jonathan Smith*

Parameters Based on Expectations of the Marriage

1. Marriage means that the center of my life and Jon's is with each other and our children. We are a unit, self-sufficient and mutually supportive. My creative career is definitely secondary to the above; yet, I must have it too. I should not have to exclude one or the other if Jon will cooperate.

1. Sue and I are central; the children are secondary to us and are often an intrusion. Each of us has our work too, which is also an important center for me. I do not know which is more important to me. If pressed, I might choose my work over Sue and the children.

2. We are the family unit—Jon, me, and the children—not his original family or mine.

2. Same as Susan, but the children are secondary. The less we have to do with our original families, the better.

3. I want him to be gentle and understanding as well as firm as a father. He should be concerned and participate in caring for the children.

3. I will be a father image to my children. They must see me as strong, wise, and just. I do not want to be too close or involved in daily problems with them.

4. Family life will be run democratically, and decisions about what, when, and how we do things will be joint. I prefer that Jon make decisions about money and support—I don't want to know about these, just that it is all OK.

4. I will take care of money and my work decisions; Sue will be in charge of family and social matters as long as I can depend on her to do what I want.

5. Roles will be traditional. That approach makes me feel right and content. I will care for home and children; he will earn money and be my protector against outside forces I can't cope with.

5. Same as Susan. But she should not expect me to bail her out or fight her battles with some of her far-out friends.

6. In marriage two people should like the same things, think similarly, share their feelings and thoughts. I feel uneasy and troubled when Jon won't accept what to me is so important (nature, spiritualism, the concept of the essential goodness of human-

6. I am a private person; I share only what I want to. My likes and dislikes can differ from Sue's and do. I am a separate person and must remain so. Sue wants me to merge with her—I won't and can't. That is definite!

ity, and so on). If he can't do this, I don't know whether I want to try to meet him on what he wants.

7. In marriage we should be sexually available to each other. If he gives me security and love, I will then be a model wife to him. He must want me sexually and reassure me of my desirability if I am to give him what he wants.

8. I do not want to be controlled in my marriage as I was at home by my mother. If I am secure with my husband, I can flower and grow like a plant that gets the right nutrients, water, and sun. I can then be free to be creative. My husband will be richly rewarded for this—I want to and will take care of the house and children (with his help) and give to him sexually and make life exciting for him with my rich fantasy and imagination.

9. If I do not get what I need, I will not give him what he wants. He must be strong enough to give me what I want. I don't want to be allowed to take what I want just because he is weak. I don't want to have to be strong for us both.

10. I will compromise—he does not have to join me in most of my interests if he allows me to pursue them.

7. I expect my wife to always want me sexually and to show it. My wife will be my refuge, my supporter. She will cater to my ego needs and will demonstrate how much she loves me and how sexual a man I am by making passionate love to me while verbalizing how wonderful I am and how I turn her on.

8. My wife must understand my needs—I am special and should be catered to because I am a man and because I am me. I must control our life. I will allow her some freedom to pursue her silly friends, but this threatens me and makes me anxious.

9. If I do not get what I want, I will not give her what she wants. I must establish my authority so that it is not constantly contested.

10. I will not give her all she wants, because she would engulf and change me. If she gives me what I want, I will give her as much as I can. I know compromises must be made, as when I now agree to accept money from her mother.

11. I do not think much about sexual fidelity. It is not the important issue—being there for another when needed is. I would be upset if my husband could not give to me sexually but could give to someone else.

11. My wife must be sexually faithful to me—I feel insecure enough about myself as it is.

12. We should be able to let our fantasies go with each other.

12. Same as Sue. But our fantasies can be different. I cannot and will not have the same fantasies she has. That is not necessary in marriage. A couple do not have to be the same but should fit together properly.

Toward the Single Contract

After I had formulated the preceding contracts, with dynamic hypotheses (see Sager, 1976), the Smiths and I began in earnest to work toward a single contract.

They agreed to accept their differences on numerous issues and types of problems and worked out several quid pro quos with me present as well as on their own. I was concerned with teaching them the process of discovering and elucidating sore spots and then arriving at their own acceptable solution.

It was important for them to learn in their sessions that they wanted similar things—love, security, independence while being cared for too; that each could give to the other if assured he or she would not be taken over; that each wanted power to make sure his or her world held together but was also fearful of having power and was only too glad to hand it over to the other if assured of not being hurt. Some tasks were designed to break their impasses by developing trust, to overcome the watchful waiting and suspicious assessing and weighing of the "who did what for whom last" approach. A very useful task—one that helped with the passive/active area as well as power and trust—was instructing each to be in charge for three days at a time. The strong feelings engendered by this task were then discussed in the next session. With some ups and downs, trust began to improve. Jon became more active on his three days and then became dependent and asked Susan what to do or sometimes planned activities he knew she would not like. She reciprocated in kind in her turn. But they were beginning to change their interactions with each other.

Therapy had to be terminated (ten sessions had been planned for) before some of the changes hoped for could be realized. Treatment was stopped with the knowledge that all was far from perfect but that they had turned a corner and were now better equipped to identify and work on the problem areas of their contracts.

Follow-up Interview

At my initiative I saw the Smiths nine months later in a lengthy follow-up interview.

They had had some difficult times but had continued to review their contracts. Jon was now more accepting of her spiritualist friends and no longer so threatened by them; he realized that he had a solid relationship with his wife. They discussed some of their feelings and ideas together these days. At one point during the meeting I misunderstood something Jon had said, and Sue quickly informed me of my mistake, which had conveyed a negative connotation about Jon.

Sex was excellent when they had it, but some of the old problem of lack of assertion on Jonathan's part persisted.

The Single Contract

Six months after the follow-up visit I telephoned the Smiths to arrange another follow-up session and to ask them to write out together a single contract that would include what they agreed on as well as their differences. They had copies of the individual contracts they had written at the start of treatment and could refer to these if they wished to. They seemed to welcome the idea, and it was decided that when they had finished their single contract, they would mail it to me and call to make an appointment.

Three weeks later, not having heard from them, I called again. They sounded pleased to hear from me. Jonathan had looked at the reminder list, shown it to Susan, and put it in a drawer. They were glad I had called again because my call would help them overcome their inertia. It sounded as if Jonathan was less enthusiastic about the project than Susan, but within a week I received their single contract, which had obviously been carefully and thoughtfully worked on by both of them, and the next day they called and made an appointment.

The single contract indicated that both knew themselves better now and had fewer illusions about each other and themselves. They were very clear about where and what their problems were. They saw themselves as a couple and had made some advances in trusting each other, but sex, though better in general, still suffered from each one's being set in his or her fantasy of what he or she wanted to receive before giving.

They no longer accepted money from Susan's mother, so that financially they were in a crunch, but they felt united and pleased with themselves. However, Susan showed her resentment over the pressure on her (a large house, no help, caring for and chauffeuring the children, and so on) and what she felt was too little help from Jon. She resented what she described as his macho position. They agreed that they had many ideological and taste differences.

When they came in for the follow-up interview, I felt much better about them than when I had read their single contract. They looked well and happy and treated each other with affection and respect. I asked them how they felt about the single contract. They said it had been difficult for them to write out because it had confronted them with themselves and they felt negative when filling it out; however, they went on to say that they had felt much better about themselves since then. They had realized that they had focused on negative things in writing up the contract and there were actually many positive things going on between them.

In working with their written single contract, I did not go down the list item by item but stimulated discussion. In advance I had noted areas which needed to be covered or which I wished to interpret or reinforce.

I started by reading Susan's response: "I feel we both want terrific romance in our lives. . . . I feel hopeful, as though the marriage begins again after the first seven years—at a different plateau, with some trust."

At one point Sue reminded Jon of several good sexual experiences they had shared recently. He then reminded her of how close they had felt driving together at night through a heavy snowstorm: "We worked together like one person with four eyes." When they got home early that morning, they had the best sex they had had in a long time. As the session went on, more and more positive aspects of their behavior came through, not only in what they remembered but in their interaction and tenderness to each other.

Jon pointed out how Susan would accumulate frustration and bitterness toward him and then let it come out all at one time. He made a plea for her to be more open and spontaneous with him. She responded with an insight about why she got upset when praised or told how attractive she was—not because she feared sex or feared being only a sex object, but because as a child she had to be perfect. She felt imperfect and therefore inadequate. This was a whole new area for Jon; he was surprised because he had felt he was the flawed one.

Susan and Jon have moved closer together. They, with their children, have become more united as a family unit. They are struggling, making headway, and dealing more realistically with each other and their life situation. They are now less like two children in search of a parent and realize that neither will be parent to the other. They still want that, but more as if it has become a pro forma demand—a ritual that no longer has meaning or expectation of fulfillment.

In the last session I tried to focus on giving them the tools to continue to work on their own problems by means of the single contract. They are equipped and motivated to continue to try to make changes in their problem areas.

This is not the most dramatically successful case I have treated; yet, I am pleased with the results, especially in view of where Sue and Jon were when they began therapy. We have done very well to have reversed a deteriorating process in the marital and family systems and the two individuals. I believe Sue and Jon and their children now have a good chance for a better life together. Their work on themselves and their relationship will have to continue as they periodically review and update their single contract.

❧ 30 ❧

Strategic Psychotherapy

John J. O'Connor

Strategic therapy is a unique way of thinking about and doing psychotherapy. It differs from other therapy models in theory, premise, assumptions, focus, method, and criteria for success. Strategic therapy is not a set of techniques but a way of thinking about and solving people's dilemmas. There is not one strategic therapy but many. In this chapter I will outline some characteristics common to various strategic models. I will also sketch a brief description of three predominant approaches and their theory and treatment. Then I will describe four clinical treatment cases to illustrate some of the principles of strategic therapy: the cases of a bulimic woman, an obsessional boy, a problem of impotence in a couple, and a migrainous girl.

Strategic therapy can be traced to the development of general systems theory and cybernetics, which appeared in 1948 with the publication of Wiener's *Cybernetics*. This stimulated a circular, rather than linear, view of the formation and maintenance of problems. From general systems theory and the pioneering work of Gregory Bateson, a number of ways of thinking about problems and relationships were developed, which crystallized with the seminal publication of the theory of the "double bind" by Bateson, Haley, Jackson, and Weakland in 1956. The idea of the "double bind" influenced many therapists to begin thinking from a communicational, or relationship, perspective.

Haley's (1973) popularization of Milton Erickson's directive therapy provided the clinical complement to many of Bateson's theoretical concepts and provided the impetus to others to develop ideas about how problems develop and how people can change (Watzlawick, Weakland, and Fisch, 1974).

Definition and Characteristics

Rather than defining a problem intrapsychically, strategic therapists study the problem within the context in which it is occurring. This means that therapists define the problem or symptom in terms of interactions and behavioral sequences that embed the symptom and the ways these patterns are related to a family's overall system of behavior or organization. A therapist tracks the sequences of behaviors of different family members before and after a symptom has occurred, noting how different family members respond to others' responses. For example, a therapist may learn that after a daughter comes home late, mother yells and father is quiet. After the yelling, the daughter is sent to her room, and mother and father argue. During the argument, the daughter runs away and both parents alternately blame and console each other, and so forth. Tracking this sequence repeatedly over time gives information about the pattern of behavior that maintains the problem as well as information about relationships (for example, a marital conflict routed through the daughter, who runs away to unite the parents and distract them from their problems).

Rather than waiting for symptoms to vanish as intrapsychic problems are "worked through," a strategic therapist tries to solve problems by giving family members tasks to do outside the therapy session. The therapist designs these tasks to solve problems by changing how individuals and families relate to one another or to a symptom. This requires clear goals, and strategies are designed individually for each problem. In contrast to therapy that takes many months or years, with symptomatic relief as a by-product, strategic therapy is usually brief, and problem resolution is a sufficient goal of treatment. A general objective of treatment is to interrupt or supplant the sequential pattern of interactions of which the symptom is a part. Interventions are designed to block or strain the problem-maintaining matrix of behaviors of the client and family. Action directives increase the repertoire, complexity, and alternatives of families engaging in a rigidly choreographed, dysfunctional "game without end." Although insight and change in affect often accompany a successful therapy, clients are not encouraged to be introspective, and they need not understand either their system or the therapist's approach.

Circularity. Strategic therapists subscribe to a circular, rather than a linear, causality. This means that no one behavior is seen as causing another; each is related in a circular way to many other events or behaviors. These behaviors or sequences form redundant patterns over time that function to stabilize the family. A symptom is often seen as an unacceptable part of the pattern which helps to maintain a family's equilibrium. For example, a linear cause-and-effect explanation of a child's problem behavior may be that the child is acting out because he has a rejecting mother. A circular hypothesis would see the child's acting out as part of a larger set of relationships that serve to maintain the whole. This view might pose that "mother becomes critical of her son when father, who feels controlled by mother, undermines her authority by being overly permissive with the son. In response, the son supports the father against the mother, causing mother to become increasingly antagonistic toward the son" (Papp, 1983, p. 8). In a simple two-person system, a linear view would see that a wife nags her husband because he stays out late, while a circular view would see that the wife's nagging is a response to her husband's staying out, which he does because his wife nags, and so forth.

Unit of Focus. With the focus on relationships and patterns, problems or symptoms are seen to involve, usually, two or more persons. Haley (1976) has suggested that a problem is a type of behavior that is part of a sequence of acts among several persons. This two-or-more-person definition of a problem assumes that a problem or symptom is one way a person can metaphorically communicate with another. A man's being depressed, for example, may communicate sad feelings but also that his wife does not appreciate him. A man's headache may reflect pain in the head but may also be a way to decline sex or to deflect criticism. Haley (1976) might ask the man to pretend to have a pain in the head to achieve the same interactional result without the pain. Such a directive alters the meaning of pain to the relationship, and changes in structure, patterns, or perception become possible.

Paradox. Interventions that therapists make may be "straightforward" or deliberately paradoxical. Straightforward interventions are given when families are expected to comply and do what is suggested. These interventions include teaching parents how to control children, establish rules, regulate privacy, and so forth. Paradoxical directives are deliberately planned to have the client or family recoil into a healthier pattern of relating.

Thinking about paradox emerged from two sources. One source was the paradoxical, or bilevel, communication of schizophrenic families, noted by Bateson and others (1956). A communication is paradoxical when it expresses two orders of message and one order qualifies or denies the other at a different level of abstraction, which constitutes a metamessage. The messages "Be spontaneous" and "Don't be so obedient" are common paradoxes (Haley, 1963). They are paradoxical because if the receiver of the message complies with the request, he or she is not complying with the request. If a boy is disobedient in response to the injunction "Don't be so obedient," he is obeying the request, which he was told not to do. If he is obedient, he is disobeying the request to be less obedient. Human dilemmas are often characterized by such dual, incongruent levels of communication.

A second source of thinking about paradox emerged from clinicians struggling with the pervasive problem of resistance to change by individuals and families. One view of individuals or family systems is that these systems reflect two processes simultaneously: (1) the capacity to change and therefore grow and develop and (2) the capacity to stay the same and therefore maintain integrity and continuity, called homeostasis. Both processes are necessary for systems to thrive, and yet when a symptomatic family come to treatment, they are stuck in the paradox of requiring change of some sort while persisting in relationship patterns that prevent the type of change needed to evolve. The type of change needed is often felt to be threatening to the family's homeostasis, or long-practiced patterns of relating to one another. In systemic terms, the family's interactions are regulated by a series of error-correcting positive and negative feedback loops that serve a homeostatic function, while the family requires a different *order* of change.

Paradox: Reframing, Symptom Prescription, Pretend, and Ordeal. The symptom is felt in the family as alien and involuntary, and families need to change and yet feel incapable of changing. Strategic therapists counter this systemic impasse in a number of ways. One way is to provide directives that place the involuntary nature of the symptomatic behavior into a voluntary context and therefore free people to solve voluntarily that which was involuntary. A psychotic son or anorectic daughter over whom parents feel powerless is reframed as defiant or oppositional; parents can now exert control (Minuchin, Rosman, and Baker, 1978). A therapist asks a woman who compulsively washes her hands and feels powerless over her compulsion to deliberately and voluntarily increase her handwashing as a way to gain "control and mastery" over the symptom (Haley, 1976). The mother of a ten-year-old fire setter is asked to pretend to be burned so that her son can help her put the fire out (Madanes, 1981). Such interventions alter the nature of the relationship between the client and the symptom or between family members. Relationships shift from escalating, symmetrical "struggles without end" to complementary, hierarchally congruent exchanges (Bateson, 1972; Madanes, 1981), in which a person has control over a previously involuntary symptom or a parent is able to control the child.

A related way to solve the impasse is to prescribe an ordeal that will be more difficult to do than eliminating the symptom (Haley, 1984). Haley (1984) has provided a number of cases in which ordeals were quite effective in eliminating problems. For example, an overanxious woman is asked to get up at two o'clock each morning to wash and wax the floor until her "abnormal" anxiety is eliminated. She stops being anxious and instead is furious at her husband.

Paradox: Systemic. Still another way out of this systemic impasse is to alter the family's premise, perception, or world view that the symptom is alien. A symptom can be connected to the family system and be defined as serving a benign function to the family, such as protection. Symptoms or behaviors can then be prescribed by the therapist to occur voluntarily; the family is then in a therapeutic dilemma, or counterparadox (Palazzoli and others, 1978). In the context of therapy change is implied because of the benign intent of individuals, such as a child's acting out to protect a couple from separating, or because of the catastrophic consequences of change that would occur to the family system if a symptom were dropped (Papp, 1983), such as a couple's divorcing if their daughter stopped running away. Out of this therapeutic dilemma, which may be intensified by consultants or cotherapists beyond its usual point in equilibrium (Papp, 1980, 1983), researchers and clinicians have noted that individuals and families can transform themselves in discontinuous ways into more functional patterns of relating without the symptom. When therapists paradoxically take a no-change position in homeostatic relation to the family's wish to change, the family proves the therapist wrong by making the changes needed or forges a new relationship system that solves the problem.

Strategic Models

Currently, there are three predominant strategic models that have a number of the features noted above: the models of Haley (1976, 1980) and Madanes (1981, 1984), the model of the Mental Research Institute (MRI) (Watzlawick, Weakland, and Fisch, 1974; Fisch, Weakland, and Segal, 1982), and the "systemic" models of the Milan group (Palazzoli and others, 1978) and the Ackerman group (Papp, 1983).

Haley and Madanes view problems as results of hierarchal incongruities in relationships, and strategies are directed to realign the relationship hierarchy in functional ways. Hierarchies are ways to order recurring patterns of interaction—who does what, to whom, and how often—that speak to status and power variables in families or relationships. These researcher/clinicians also assume that a symptom analogically, or metaphorically, expresses a problem and is simultaneously a solution for the relationship problems that exist. For example, disturbed behavior in a child is often seen as a metaphor for a parent's difficulties, as well as an attempt to solve these difficulties by protectively distracting parents from their own problems. Within this organizational view, two incongruous hierarchies are defined. For example, in a couple relationship, a depressed man is in an inferior, or one-down, position in relation to his wife, who tries to help him be less depressed. The wife is in a superior position of helping her husband be less depressed. Yet, the depressed man is also simultaneously in a superior position in that he refuses or fails to be helped and to change, and the helper is in an inferior position in failing to influence her spouse or to solve the problem. If the man is no longer depressed, he loses his superior position to his wife, who will no longer try unsuccessfully to change him. If the wife is successful in influencing her symptomatic partner, she loses the superior position of being the nonsymptomatic member of the couple (Madanes, 1981, p. 30). Such malfunctioning hierarchies are usually present in symptomatic families. Approaches Haley and Madanes have used to solve problems include exaggerating the hierarchal incongruity beyond its usual point in equilibrium (for example, the wife increases her efforts to be helpful), reframing the reality presented (for example, the husband is defined as irresponsible, not depressed), creating a consequent ordeal that is worse than having the symptom (for example, each time the man is depressed, he must iron his wife's blouses as reparation for being so unavailable), and pretending (for example, the husband pretends to be depressed). Many of these approaches alter the meaning of the symptom to the interactional pattern. The wife, for example, may no longer know whether her husband is really depressed or is pretending to be, and the power of the symptom to organize a relationship is lost.

The model of the Mental Research Institute (Watzlawick, Weakland, and Fisch, 1974; Fisch, Weakland, and Segal, 1982) extends the view that the social or family context is the system in which a symptom is embedded. The sequential model of MRI also views the individual's own system of behaviors as creating, maintaining, and exacerbating a problem in a circular way. Specifically, this group believes that when solutions people develop to problem behaviors are rigidly applied and become entangled with the symptom they are attempting to eliminate, the solutions become part of the symptom-maintaining behaviors, and the person becomes symptomatic. For example, an individual who experiences temporary insomnia may increase his or her efforts to induce sleep. The energy expended and the behavior used to fall asleep further interfere with the conditions that allow sleep to occur naturally. The individual applies more of the same strategies, the solution becomes part of the symptom-maintaining system, and the individual develops a sleep disorder. A central therapeutic task is to break or interdict the problem-maintaining "solutions" by symptom prescription, by supplanting a symptomatic sequence with more functional behaviors with which the symptom cannot coexist, and by prescribing positive and negative ordeals or rituals, as well as other techniques. It is presumed that once dysfunctional, or "vicious," cycles have been eliminated, other, more functional, or "virtuous," patterns will naturally blossom.

As described above, the "systemic-strategic" models provided by the Milan group (Palazzoli and others, 1978) and researchers at Ackerman (Papp, 1980, 1983) use strategies to organize the entire family system to solve a problem. The symptom of one person is linked in a circular way to the patterns and sequences of other family members—that is, the system—and the systemic organization is prescribed as benevolent. Papp and her colleagues have used consultation teams (Papp, 1980) and cotherapists (Papp, 1983) to articulate and intensify the systemic impasse of a family struggling to change.

The following cases illustrate the application of some strategic principles as outlined above. The cases were formulated and treated mainly using concepts explicated by Haley, Madanes, and the MRI group.

A Bulimic Woman

Laura was a sophomore at college at the time she sought treatment. Her father had died when she was four, and her mother had died of cancer when Laura was seventeen. After her mother's death, Laura moved in with her aunt for four months until she left to begin college at a local school. She visited her new home on holidays and summers. By the end of her first summer there, she was binge-eating and vomiting every other night. Her bulimia diminished in frequency for the first two months of college, and then she began to overeat and vomit every other night until treatment began, in the spring of her sophomore year.

Laura overate at stressful times and showed a number of classic signs and symptoms of bulimia. Her weight fluctuated fifteen pounds during her freshman year, she was self-deprecating and self-critical after overeating, and she found herself obsessed not only with food but with her fear that she could not stop overeating or stop the bulimic cycle. She felt that her aunt pushed her to eat fattening foods and wanted her to be fat. Laura felt weak and inadequate with her aunt and with her own impulse to indulge, and she felt angry over her perceived flaws.

Laura, a psychology major, was quite insightful into the stresses and meta-issues of her life, as well as into the multileveled metaphorical meaning of food. Her aunt was overweight, and Laura's overeating was equated with her own continued dependence and lack of individuation. She viewed overeating and vomiting as symptomatic of the ambivalence she felt toward her aunt. Overeating was equated with her compliance, dependence, and connectedness to a parental substitute, and vomiting served her rebelliousness and her wish for autonomy and an independent identity. She wished for and feared a genuine relationship with her aunt/mother around which she could begin to negotiate these tasks of late adolescence. Food was reliably present and dependable in times of stress, unlike her parents. To make conflict overt and to reject food from her aunt was to reject her aunt, which then stimulated the pain of her earlier losses. This formulation helped Laura to understand her life issues and her bulimia but not to control or eliminate this cycle.

Early in treatment, Laura described her bulimic episodes and her obsession with food. A paradoxical symptom prescription to obsess daily for thirty minutes without distractions was given with a rationale regarding Laura's gaining increased control over the amount of time thoughts of food were consuming her life. Laura obsessed successfully four out of seven days but became too bored with the thoughts to continue. Although bulimic episodes continued at a rate of about six per month, her obsessions interfered less with her day.

In the fourth session, a series of directives were given to substitute several mutually exclusive, compulsive behaviors for the compulsion of eating, in order to increase her repertoire to handle anxiety and stress. Laura could identify chronic, stressful times, during which she was to call a friend and talk for twenty minutes, listen to music on headphones, or masturbate. Listening to music was given as an alternative to masturbation so that she had some control over which diversion to substitute for eating. Masturbation was chosen because some issues of sexuality and fear of being a woman with a healthy sexual "appetite" were discussed, it was related to the issue of indulging herself in a different way, it was naturally reinforcing, and Laura herself was eager to try.

In the sixth session, a positive ritual was introduced to help Laura resist temptation. She was told to write out all the food she was to eat before she ate. This was described as an inviolate self-rule, and she was then allowed to eat only what had been written down.

At this point, the interventions resulted in the frequency of bulimic episodes stabilizing at around two per week. By report, the instructions were carried out sometimes but not consistently.

During the ninth session, an aversive ritual, or ordeal, was formulated. At this point, vomiting was as troublesome to Laura as binge eating. I told Laura that I knew of a way that she could definitely master this problem, and what I was thinking for her to do would be very difficult but she was physically able to perform it. It was a way to stop these episodes that would allow her to worry about more important life issues which were scary but which I felt she was ready to undertake. I asked her not to agree or disagree right away, because this would be a difficult task, and that if she finally agreed to it, I knew she would definitely do even the most difficult task because she was a woman of her word and a woman of integrity (which she was). A directive was given in which Laura would overstuff herself with food immediately after each time she vomited. She might need to do it three times a day or not at all, but the rule had to be kept if she agreed to it. Laura agreed to the conditions.

There was only one bulimic episode following this directive. She did not follow this episode with overeating, and she said she had needed to use her old solution just once, when she felt the stress was overwhelming. I framed this episode as a temporary and common regression to a "dying" symptom and problem that was "leaving," used as a metaphor for her grief for her dead mother, as well as for her own psychological separation and "leaving home." I also told her that if the problem were to resurface, she would know how to stop if she wanted to and that she would need to decide whether she really wanted this symptom to end. During the two years after the ordeal was prescribed, Laura had only this single episode of compulsive eating and vomiting, and her food intake gradually became more moderate.

The four strategic interventions were all designed to stop the cycle of binge-eating followed by vomiting. The first, a prescription of the symptom to obsess about food, began the process of helping Laura gain control over her actions by gaining come control over her thoughts. She reported that she did indeed stop thinking about food as much as she had before. The effect on the number of vomiting incidents was not dramatic, but the obsession with food, which was part of the cycle, was helped, and this represents the first step.

The second set of directives, to substitute compulsions, was an effort to give the client mutually exclusive activities that would interfere with the binge-purge cycle. Again, the effect on the basic pattern was not remarkable, but it was the beginning of efforts to give Laura a larger range of behaviors with which to deal with stress. The third directive, to write down what was to be eaten, was a first attempt to develop a positive ritual with which Laura could resist temptation. Laura personally found this directive helpful, probably because it came at a time when she was experiencing an increasing sense of control.

The final intervention was an ordeal that was specifically designed to interdict the problem-maintaining solution. The pattern had been for Laura to lose control and go on a binge; afterward, out of self-disgust, she would vomit to regain control.

Binging was the behavior Laura wished to avoid and to control. In this intervention, she would binge-eat on purpose, which paradoxically reestablishes her control, since she would purposely lose control. The punishment was worse than the symptom, and so she was able to modulate her food intake willfully.

By report, Laura indicated that she found two parts of this directive helpful: the idea of indulging after she vomited was repulsive to her, and my view of her as a woman of her word resulted in her sense of her own strength to eat reasonably. In the strategic treatment of bulimic women, however, at least three systems must be considered. The systems include the one-person system of sequential behaviors the woman engages in, the family or social system where bulimia developed and/or is maintained, and the therapeutic system within which new coping strategies for stress are practiced.

One consideration to explore before a directive is given to specifically eliminate a symptom is whether more functional methods in responding to these conflicts are available to supplant the functions the symptom has served for so long. For Laura, bulimia was entangled within a social system at home, and she generalized this system of behavior to life at school. Consequently, a directive to eliminate the cycle had implications not only for the one-person system of behaviors but also for the other social or family systems where the symptom was occurring.

In the implications of this symptom and of a solution at home, the function of the symptom and its metaphorical significance to the family context and to hierarchal incongruities within the family were important considerations. Laura's binging/purging was a metaphor for both her helplessness and her power with regard to her aunt. This bulimic cycle allowed Laura to covertly reject her aunt's intrusiveness while maintaining the appearance of being a compliant "daughter" who avoids displeasing her aunt. Though not overtly interactional, the prescribed ritual had the effect of removing this symptom from the usual transactional field with her aunt so that Laura needed to explore in therapy different methods to deal with her aunt. Laura developed several alternative ways to solve this dilemma, including spending more time out of the home and asserting herself more directly with her aunt.

A major developmental issue for Laura was her confusion around her identity and a sense of being alone—not only the existential isolation of a late adolescent who is individuating but the isolation of being orphaned. In addition, since her mother was idealized and conflict was avoided during her illness and death, Laura's repertoire for dealing with conflict verbally with parent figures was quite limited.

In talking about her mother, Laura reexperienced her grief and the sense of loss in the newer context of her individuation. Her mother was not present for Laura to define herself in relation to her mother's characteristics. So her aunt was framed as a woman who was providing conflicts for Laura around which Laura could negotiate the developmental tasks of separation and providing a model against which Laura could discover what she was like and how she wanted her life to be.

Other strategies were developed to help Laura deal with conflict more overtly, and therapy was concluded after twelve sessions over six months. At a two-year follow-up, Laura had not engaged in the bulimic cycle and had transferred to a university away from home.

An Obsessional Boy

Michael was ten at the time of referral. He had been referred by his pediatrician because of his preoccupation with and fear of vomiting. The thought of vomiting or the word *vomit* would flood him with panic and fear. He would then experience an intense stomachache, headache, cold sweat, and incapacitation for one to three hours. These episodes occurred most frequently at school, where these feelings would "overtake" him. A typical sequential pattern involved Michael's ritualistically and repeatedly seeking reassurance in the morning from his mother and father that he would not vomit. Michael's request would result in the parents' escalating their comforting statements, and neither parent could use the word *vomit* in his or her encouragement. Father would call Michael from work, providing reassurance over the phone. Michael would state that if his father told him he would not vomit, he felt sure he would not.

Before referral, episodes of school refusal were common. At school, Michael was allowed to go to the school nurse and lie down, but despite the nurse's reassurance that he would not vomit, Michael's mother would invariably come to school and take him home. These episodes were occurring twice a week at the time of referral.

Michael would also obsess when his parents left the house. Efforts by his parents to get away to a movie, for example, were countered by Michael's vigorous protest and fear, and he would sit by the clock and cry, despite a sitter's presence. Michael feared they would never return or would die ("That's why I hate for you two to go out alone"), fears that reflected an obsessive child's typical preoccupation with death and decay. The parents did not allow themselves to be away for more than two hours because of Michael's distress, promising they would be back at the designated hour. Michael was an only child.

A history of extensive medical tests on his digestive system revealed no significant medical problem. In the past two years, Michael had actually vomited once during an illness and had not been particularly distressed or repulsed. His parents described him as a fragile child, plagued by allergies, always sick with a cold, a stomachache, or a headache. They saw him as an anxious child, always fidgeting, biting his nails, and spending most of his time indoors. He would build models and collect coins, but he did not participate in sports. He did well academically. He reported having a few friends and was apparently liked by his peers and teachers in school, but peer relationships were depicted as fairly superficial. During the summer before referral, he was allowed to cross the "big street" and visit his friends in their territory. Michael experienced a good summer with no complaints, and somatic difficulties were almost nonexistent.

The parents described Michael as always having had a fear of vomiting, but in the six months preceding referral, these fears had been especially vivid and overpowering. The mother reported that, as an infant, Michael was colicky and was happy only in their own house; he would scream and cry outside until brought back in.

Michael seemed overly attentive to inner feeling states and to environmental detail. For a brief time, he had a substitute teacher who was blind, and Michael began to obsess that his own body was falling apart or decaying—fearing he was losing his teeth, hair, and eyesight. The parents reported these events in a casual way, diminishing their importance to Michael and his pain. His speech and thought were diphasic and inclined toward contradictions, uncertainties, and unknowables—for example, "If I go to sleep, will I have a bad dream?" "If I go to school, will I vomit?"

On interview, Michael was initially quite anxious and fidgety but seemed somewhat more at ease over time. He reported feeling plagued by intruding thoughts of vomiting and related a subjective sense of these ideas' being forced and his being unable to stop them. Thus, he obsessed about his obsessions. He was rigid in bodily movements, and he appeared unhappy, serious, and tormented. There seemed to be a deliberateness and lack of spontaneity in thought, word, and action.

Michael was attentive and generally agreeable to all his mother said. Mother did most of the talking throughout the entire session. Michael and his father would nod in agreement, but periodically Michael would express a burst of hostility to his mother, to be undone or denied by Michael or his parents in the next sentence. For example, he said angrily that his grandmother had been the only one who could get him to walk as a toddler because his mother was so afraid to let him try. Mother smiled and agreed that she had been extremely overprotective when he was younger, and she assumed the blame for his current obsessional style. She indicated that she now wanted Michael to try to do more things on his own, but "now he doesn't want to." She said that she had not let him get dirty when he was younger and indicated she was afraid of "germs." When asked, she recognized a reciprocal shift in her and Michael's attitudes over the years.

Father was passive and yet close to Michael. During the interview, Michael hopped on his father's leg, and his father hugged, squeezed, and kissed him several times, the only occasion when the father displayed any zest. Father was described by mother as affectionate with Michael and perhaps "hugged and kissed him too much." There were no displays of affection between parents during the session.

Michael was seen by his parents as an overly compliant, polite child who never really "sassed back." He also had essentially no responsibilities at home, and his room was a mess. Father "never" exhibited anger, and all described a close, affectionate family. Michael said, "I hope you can help me because I want to have fun." When asked what bothered him most, he said, "Why does it have to come out of my mouth? Why can't I get hives or have it come out someplace else?"

Formulation. If Michael's problems are viewed from a strategic, problem-focused context (Fisch, Weakland, and Segal, 1982), the problems can be described as (1) Michael's obsessing, which indeed caused him much personal anguish and interfered with his schooling, home life, and personal development, and (2) his reporting of the obsessions to his parents, which engaged a dysfunctional, homeostatic cycle of family interactions. Because Michael psychologically equated thought and action, his obsessions can be viewed as two similar problems: his fear of vomiting and also, more centrally, his fear that he could not stop thinking about vomiting. His fears were self-perpetuating: by thinking about how much he thought about vomiting, he would become alarmed that these thoughts could occur during circumstances over which he would have no control—at school, at home if his parents were out, and so on. Michael was engaged in an elaborate but ineffective program to delay facing the fear by constantly preparing to face it. His solution was to prepare for thoughts of vomiting in such a way that these thoughts and his fear would be mastered in advance by seeking solicitations from his parents, avoiding certain words, and ritualizing the morning conversation. Attempts to distract himself and not think led to major and magical efforts at self-deception that were ineffectual.

Within this view of problem maintenance, Michael's reporting of his obsessions to his parents precipitated a circular, homeostatic parent/child loop of reassurances, complaints, reassurances, and so forth. Parental reassurances were never enough to dispel Michael's anxiety completely. The family was organized and regulated by Michael's descriptions of feeling states, which sequentially evoked a series of verbal reassurances by his parents. Michael would continue his visceral monitoring and report changes, and the parents would increase their reassurance. In this way, the parents' behaviors in finding a solution became part of the symptom-maintaining matrix.

Within this view, treatment strategies would be directed at interdicting Michael's problem-maintaining solutions—obsessing as preparation to master his fear of vomiting and engaging in a circular interaction of reassurances and complaints with parents.

Organizationally, it is easy to see the dual hierarchies at work here. Michael was in an inferior position by virtue of his symptom and complaints, and his parents were in the superior position of helping. Simultaneously, the parents were in the inferior position of failing to help Michael with his problem, and Michael was in the superior position of refusing or failing to be helped to change and regulating their lives. If Michael was no longer symptomatic, he would lose his superior position in relation to his parents, who would no longer try to help him with the symptom. The parents would lose the superior position of being the helpers to Michael and would perhaps confront the lack of vitality in their relationship.

Intervention. I met with the family five times over a three-month period. In the initial session, I stated that Michael was indeed in a great deal of personal pain, tormented by these thoughts over which he felt powerless. At this point, his parents' reassurances were not enough, and Michael needed to do some difficult tasks in order to master these fears and thoughts, as other children his age had. I told him that I knew how desperately he wanted to master the fears and thoughts and that although the tasks would be difficult, he had impressed me with his strong, age-appropriate wish to be competent and that I thought these tasks would help. I told him I was thinking of a way he could "borrow" and "use" the strength of his father, a man who had mastered many fears. I told Michael that the new ways I was thinking of would not involve his father's continually reassuring him, since the power of his father's words to help Michael lessened over the course of the morning.

I then told Michael that the first step in mastering his fear of vomiting was to take charge of when and where he would vomit or think about vomiting. I told him that now he worried most of the time about vomiting and that I wanted him to sit in a kitchen chair for one hour daily, to think hard about trying to vomit, and to mop it up if he did. At other times, if he began to think he would vomit, he should "give" those thoughts to the hour and chair in which he would sit. He should say to himself, "I'll think and worry about it then." This was framed as a way for Michael to begin to get control over his thoughts and feelings. At this point, Michael was cringing and anxious but attentive.

I then asked Michael's father to give me a button he had pinned on his sweater. I told Michael that this was his father's button and would represent his father's strength and reassurances. I wanted Michael to wear the button and told him that as long as he wore it or had it in his possession, his father's strength and reassurance were with him and he would not vomit. His father was not to verbally reassure him in the morning but could ask whether Michael had his button.

As part of Michael's learning to master these fears on his own, I stated that the parents should obtain a sitter and go out one evening during the week for at least three hours. The parents readily agreed, and Michael grudgingly stated he would try his tasks. I also indicated that, as part of Michael's developing age-appropriate skills and mastery over his body, he should be required to perform certain tasks around the house, as other ten-year-olds do, and that his parents were to agree on what responsibilities they would require of him.

In the second session, two weeks later, Michael had been in school every day until dismissed, his parents were not reassuring him verbally, and both parents had gone out on a "date." Michael had tried sitting in the chair, thinking and trying to vomit, but he could not sustain these thoughts. I told Michael that this was an important aspect of his learning to control and master these feelings, and I instructed him to try to think about vomiting and try to vomit during the rest of the session as I talked with his parents. He could not keep these thoughts in his mind and gave up trying. Michael was wearing the button, had worn it every day, and said it was helping him. I then asked Michael's father for a penny and gave it to Michael, saying that the penny was just like the button and represented his father's strength and reassurance. I asked the parents to continue to go on at least one "date" a week for more than three hours and for Michael to continue to perform those tasks around the house his parents agreed to and to do them as well as he had during the previous two weeks.

In the third session, Michael said that he had forgotten the coin on two days but had had a good week. His thoughts of vomiting were fleeting, and everyone reported feeling happier. Michael had gone to a friend's house and talked of spending the night there. I asked Michael's father for a nickel and gave it to Michael with the same description as before of the coin's power.

In the fourth session, Michael had stayed overnight at a friend's and had forgotten to take the nickel to school on a number of occasions. I said I was pleased that he had felt strong and reassured enough himself not to always need his father's coin. I added that he could always use coins that his father gave him in the ways described if he ever needed to. A follow-up session in one month found Michael asymptomatic, not complaining to his parents, visiting, and having friends over; there was no mention of his fear of vomiting. Behaviorally, he appeared more at ease and less tense. The parents remained disengaged from Michael's developmentally normal concerns and were maintaining a nurturing distance.

Discussion. The intervention consisted of three parts designed to interrupt Michael's circular obsessive style and the homeostatic interplay of parent and child as Michael reported his fears. The first part of the intervention addressed Michael's fear of vomiting and fear of thinking about vomiting. A paradoxical symptom prescription addressed both problems, and Michael was asked to deliberately obsess about vomiting and to try to vomit. As expected, when given a directive to deliberately bring on these usually involuntary cognitions and feeling states, Michael was unable to do so, gaining mastery by failing to force thoughts into consciousness. A symptom prescription to alter the frequency, time, and place of a symptom removed the behavior from an involuntary, passive context to a voluntary, mastering one over which Michael could exhibit control. It was unnecessary to differentiate the type of function of paradox—whether he would compliantly attempt to perform the directive, thereby fatiguing the obsessional style by habituation, or whether he would be unwilling to obsess about vomiting because of covert defiance. The effect was the same—diminution of obsessional thinking and reporting.

The second set of directives was aimed at interrupting the problem-maintaining solutions in which Michael and his parents were entangled. Asking the parents not to reassure Michael directly blocked their usual, ineffective solution of verbal reassurances. This created a vacuum in which more functional solutions and interactions could be tried. The introduction of a magical button capitalized on the perceived, magical potency of his father's words to prevent vomiting. Systemically, the effect of the directive was to remove the symptom from one transactional field and to place it in a field of Michael's developing autonomy and independence. This removal allowed other transactions to surface—for example, encouragement by the parents of Michael's own coping skills, his increased social contact and success, and a growing sense of his own personal competence. In Madanes's (1981) model, the meaning of the symptom was altered from one of increasing parental overinvolvement to one of a ten-year-old developing age-appropriate, autonomous coping skills. I also wanted these stimuli ultimately to be objects his father would naturally give Michael (coins), so that the potency of coins as father's reassurance would fade and be replaced by their conventional power to buy lunch, play games, and so forth. Coins allowed Michael the reassurance of common objects when needed, so that his fear was not allowed to build. These consequences allowed Michael greater independence and permitted his parents to disengage with grace.

The third set of directives—for parents to "date" and for Michael to experience age-appropriate responsibilities in the home—simply reinforced these newly emergent interactional sequences and allowed other transactions to surface. The parents' dating allowed them to engage each other in other than parental ways, reinforced their belief and expectation that Michael could solve his own problem, and disengaged them from their usual dysfunctional patterns of interaction. Michael's performing age-appropriate household tasks altered the family view of him as fragile and dependent and reinforced each family member's sense of Michael's developmental progress and differentiation.

In a two-year, follow-up phone call, mother indicated that Michael was "doing terrifically." He was achieving good grades in school, had a larger network of friends with whom he visited and spent overnights, and was not complaining about any obsessions or fears to his parents.

An Impotence Problem in a Couple

Bob called for an appointment, saying he felt as if it were the end of the world. Bob and Lois were planning to marry, and increasingly Bob had difficulty maintaining an erection. Intercourse was becoming infrequent and quite frustrating, mostly for him. He had been divorced six months before referral. His first wife was highly anxious when she and Bob had sex; she was reluctant, and penetration was always painful for her. They had been married for three years and, because of a number of other problems, had decided to separate.

When Bob met Lois, his dream came true. Lois was a lovely, warm, relaxed, and responsive woman who enjoyed sex, but increasingly Bob's ability to maintain an erection lessened. At best, intercourse was sporadic, and Bob's penis would be semierect throughout. Bob would become highly agitated, and Lois would try to comfort and console him, try to help him relax, which only increased his frustration and wish to will himself an erection. By our first session, they had not had intercourse in two months, and Bob's dreams for a happy life with this wonderful woman were fading, despite Lois's assurances that she was not planning to leave him. Urologic and physical examinations were negative.

Bob showed many of the signs of secondary impotence and was completely aware of the devastating effects of worrying how he would perform and of assuming a "spectator" role in which he focused on how well he was performing. But he could not help himself. Lois used to signal her openness for sex by placing a jar of lubricating jelly on the nightstand. Bob would get anxious, try to have sex, and fail.

Interventions. Bob had always felt more comfortable being active in lovemaking, and if he was passive, he felt anxious that he should be doing something or should be relaxing. I prescribed a number of traditional exercises in which each person would provide the other with erotic, nongenital contact through massage and gentle caressing as a way to focus on erotic sensations and to distract him from his obsessive worry. Intercourse was also prohibited as a way to ease the burden of "performing" intercourse instead of giving and receiving pleasure. We talked about his fantasies of Lois, the burden men place on themselves to perform, and abandonment of self to erotic feelings. I prescribed some tasks to make sexual contact as exciting and anxiety-free as possible, in gradual, nondemanding ways. I told him not to expect an erection and spoke metaphorically about the earth and about trees planted in the earth by their roots. At one point I asked him to talk to his penis, which he just wanted to beat up. None of the suggestions was particularly successful, and all seemed to increase Bob's frustration and rage at himself. He feared Lois would see this "impotence" as a measure of his not caring enough or not being attracted enough, and he feared he would never have an erect penis again. Lois remained supportive, sensitive, with "no inhibitions." I asked Bob to masturbate at home and the next week, he had some confidence that he would be able to attain an erection but perhaps not with a woman.

He woke up with erections and, with Lois's consent, attempted intercourse but failed. When asked, Lois and Bob indicated that Lois was very responsive to Bob's overtures and ministrations. She would move about and groan, which sensitized Bob to the coital performance in which he feared he would fail. When asked, Bob said he could bring Lois to orgasm without coitus and without much difficulty, and Lois confirmed that this was so.

In the fifth session, I said that I was going to suggest something which was unorthodox but which would be fun to do. I told Lois not to place any lubricating jelly on the nightstand. I told them that this whole business was so serious that they needed to play a game. At this point, the couple immediately lightened up. The game would be that Lois was to lie flat on the bed, with her hands at her sides, immobile and impassive. I then said that her job was to try not to be turned on or excited by Bob. I said that she was to try her best and resist his skillful hands and movement. I said this would be very difficult because Lois was so responsive and Bob was so skillful. She might find herself squirming and fidgeting, but she was to resist being aroused by Bob as hard as she could. I said it might be so difficult that she should try to fantasize about nonsexual matters such as work or knitting (which she did not know how to do) or baseball or football (which she knew nothing about). I told Bob that his job was to arouse Lois and that he should try to "penetrate" her resistance, which I thought was formidable, since Lois had such a good sense of herself. I also told Bob he was still prohibited from intercourse, Both laughed for one of the first times and agreed to do the task.

In the sixth session, two weeks later, both came in smiling. Bob said they had both failed—Lois had failed to avoid being aroused, and Bob had failed to restrain himself from having intercourse. Lois said she had really tried not to be aroused but couldn't help herself. Bob smiled sheepishly, and I seriously questioned Lois about whether she had tried hard enough and about her failure to do as I had asked. Bob said he felt more in control of their sexual encounters, which he liked. I sent them both home to try again, since they had failed this time to play by the rules of the game.

Bob canceled the next session as not needed, since both were feeling wonderful about their sexual relationship. Therapy had involved six sessions over three months. Follow-up at three months found them happy, and six months after treatment ended, I received a postcard from Hawaii, where Bob and Lois had gone to honeymoon, saying, "You can count us as one of your successes."

Discussion. From an interactional perspective, Bob's performance difficulties existed in relation to his will to do voluntarily that which was involuntary (that is, sexual arousal) and also in relation to Lois's openness prior to sex and her solicitations following coital failure. As the lubricating jelly was placed out, this sensitized Bob to a performance in which he feared he would fail. Mentally, he tried to distract himself and hurry the encounter, which further sensitized him to the issue of failure. As Lois increased her responsiveness, Bob was further intimidated by what he felt he must do to "be a man." As Bob began to fail to maintain an erection, Lois would increase her responsiveness or solicitations, which further sensitized Bob to this issue, and "failure" was inevitable.

The therapeutic goal was to change the context, meaning, and sequences of the sexual encounter within Bob and between the couple. The directive involving the game in which Lois was to try not to respond and Bob was to excite her shifted the problem from Bob's performance to Lois's performance. The directive shifted Bob's loss of control over his erection to control over Lois's arousal, which he could easily control. If Lois did not respond sexually to his overtures and movements, the problem would implicitly be her lack of responsiveness, not his adequacy. When the directive was given, Bob quickly knew he would succeed in arousing Lois. If she did respond, Bob's sense of mastery and masculinity would be confirmed and elevated, since she was responding despite her best efforts to resist. By responding, Lois failed to perform the task as I told her to, and her failure to not respond became the focus of the next therapy session. Either way, Bob would succeed, and of course, so would Lois, by her failure to not respond. Such a directive also altered the meaning of the sexual encounter from a test of masculine prowess to a game of gentle, erotic competition.

More formally, the directive simultaneously blocked Bob's obsessing about his penis and his performance and interdicted the couple's problem-maintaining sequence of behaviors of Bob trying harder to maintain an erection while Lois increased her arousal or solicitations in a circular response to his heightened frustration.

A Migrainous Girl

Diane was ten years old, the third of four children. She was referred by her pediatrician for two reasons: she appeared depressed and had threatened to stab herself because of migrainous pain. Her mother had found her measuring kitchen knives to ensure that one would be long enough to reach her heart.

Diane had a history of migraine from age four. The pain usually began in the temporal region and radiated to the top of her head. She was migrainous at various times of the day, and she experienced an aura and tinnitus. She reported no eye discomfort or nausea when migrainous. The diagnosis of migraine had been confirmed at age eight by Diane's positive response to a vasoconstricting medication. Diane re-presented sixteen months later with consistent migrainous complaints: she was nauseated and said her eyes hurt when she had a headache. Diane was hospitalized and was evaluated neurologically several times, with inconclusive results. Several medications were tried, with no alleviation of symptoms. Because of Diane's depressed presentation on examination, her current lack of responsiveness to medications, negative test results, and the regular pattern of her pain (onset approximately 8:00 P.M., relief by 10:00 A.M.)., her pediatrician properly diagnosed a psychogenic pain disorder and referred Diane to psychotherapy. At the time of referral, Diane had missed forty days of school because of the pain.

In my interview, a brief history revealed that Diane's parents had separated four months before her appearance in the health clinic. Diane had been very close to her father, and before sleep he used to read her stories and have long talks while mother prepared the youngest child for sleep. At the time of the interview, Diane saw her father three times a week for brief periods.

With me, Diane looked sad and depressed and once put her head on her arms on a table and cried softly as we talked about her father. She readily admitted missing her father. Diane's mother was ambivalent about her husband's return and did not know whether she would ask him to return. Diane told her mother that she was always worried about her father, especially his not coming back. Diane said that she had pain in the front of her head and that it happened most when she got mad. She felt sad and angry that her father might not return and added that she thought that if her father came back, he could help her with her headaches; mother agreed this was possible. When Diane complained of headaches, her mother became increasingly solicitous, asking questions about what troubled her, where it hurt, what could help, and so on. When Diane got headaches, she asked her mother to call her father. Diane added that if she went into a hospital, she was going to ask her father to come back home and that he probably would. Mother also appeared depressed. When asked about the family history of headaches, Diane's mother reported that Diane's father had headaches because of "high blood pressure." The night before the interview, Diane had asked her mother to kill her so her headaches would stop.

Formulation. For the child, the diagnosis was grief reaction and depression, secondary to the loss of her father and the emotional loss of her mother to her own depression. From this psychodynamic view, the symptom was a way for Diane physically to represent her father, who also experienced headache, much like a transitional object or experience. The traditional analytic view of a transitional object is that it is an object, ritual, or experience that a child uses to allay separation anxiety;

for example, a teddy bear at bedtime comes to represent the person who is lost. The child can then displace and project feelings onto this object that are often felt by the child to be unacceptable or not able to be expressed to the real person. For example, teddy bears can be clung to, beaten, loved, or thrown, which allows the child to express safely a range of feelings that are otherwise painful to tolerate.

Turning to a diagnosis of the family system, the symptom in Diane, though a response to stress and grief, represented also an attempt to reengage the father into the family. Interactionally, the complaint mobilized the family to respond in different ways: mother would call father, father was more involved when Diane had pain, mother expressed the belief that perhaps father's return would help Diane's pain, and so forth. There was a circular pattern of Diane's complaints, followed by parents' increased involvement, which, in turn, maintained the pattern of complaints. Speculatively, Diane's headaches were also probably an attempt to have her father return to help her mother feel less depressed.

Intervention. In this first interview, the intervention consisted of four parts. First, I asked mother whether Diane's pain would bring Diane's father back into the home or whether his return was a decision she and her husband would make on the basis of their relationship and whether they could live together. She said that the decision depended on her own relationship with her husband and that Diane's pain would not make her father return. I asked mother to tell Diane that even though her father and she loved Diane very much and wanted her pain to go away, her father would return only if the parents, the adults, were able to work it out and that she could not help them work out problems in their relationship. She told Diane this with elaboration.

Second, I asked mother to track the frequency, intensity, duration, and time of Diane's pain over the next three weeks.

Third, two suggestions were given to supplant the function of the migraine to Diane and to the family system. These suggestions were to create a "transitional" bedtime ritual that resembled the rituals she had developed with her father before the loss. In one directive, I suggested to mother that after Diane was in her pajamas and ready for bed, she be allowed to call her father and talk as they used to. In the second directive, I asked mother to increase the amount of time she usually spent with Diane at bedtime, from a few minutes to about twenty minutes. During this time, I asked her to talk to Diane as her father used to talk to her. She was to talk not as a problem solver or comforter, as mother usually did, but to tell stories and to listen to what Diane had to say without the need to help solve her problems.

Fourth, I spoke to Diane directly. I told her that I knew she wanted desperately to get rid of the headaches and that I knew of a way to help. I asked her to remember back when she was smaller, when she had a favorite toy or stuffed animal that she loved very much. She said she had a stuffed horse and she still slept with him. I asked her to remember what a strong horse this was, one who could take any feeling or action Diane could give him. This was a horse who could be squeezed very hard when Diane was full of love and who could be punched and thrown when Diane was angry or hateful. She said she did remember. I told her that her horse was still strong and could take any pain that Diane could give him. I asked her to notice when she was beginning to get a headache and to "give" her headache to her horse. She could even try to bring on a headache to give to the horse, because the horse was very strong. She could give the headache to the horse in any way she wanted to, by touching her head to the horse's head or maybe in some other way she could think of. I reminded her that the horse was strong and could take any pain Diane could give him. I told her that if she could give her pain to the horse, her pain would be gone. I then set an appointment for three weeks.

Results. In three weeks, mother reported that Diane had had only one headache, without the characteristics of migraine. Diane said that her mother "gave" her the headache after touching her forehead. All the directives were followed, except that Diane said that she didn't give her headache to the horse but to an ugly doll whose pain she didn't care about. Follow-up visits in six months and at one year found Diane asymptomatic. The parents had not reunited, but both parents were available and engaged with Diane around activities and time not organized by migraine.

Discussion. From an interactional formulation, Diane's headaches existed in relation to her mother's solicitude in a circular, homeostatic way. Their relationship was organized around Diane's migraine, which increased mother's solicitous remarks. Mother's solicitude, in turn, modified how Diane would relate to her, and mother would respond by calling father, talking about how father might help, and so forth. The migraine allowed mother to be closer to her daughter, since her depression made her less available at other times. The headaches also allowed mother and daughter to talk about Diane's father and to keep alive the myth that he would be returning. In solving the problem, the objective was to interrupt the cycle of interactions that helped to maintain the symptom, to identify the social function of the symptom, and to develop more functional ways to achieve the same interactional result.

With that information in mind, the directives were meant to facilitate changes in structure, patterns, and world views. Asking the mother to tell her daughter that the father would return only if the adult relationship were more workable and that she could not help with this problem served three purposes: structurally, to create a parental subsystem boundary within which adults would be the ones to make decisions; to block the child's attempts to solve a marital problem by becoming symptomatic; and to diminish or eliminate the myth, subtly reinforced, that this girl was powerful enough to reunite her parents. As a result, future interactions around migraines were not to be associated with her father's return.

Asking the mother to identify the frequency, intensity, time, and duration of headaches would provide data for evaluating the extent of the problem and the effects of interventions on the headaches. There is also a strategic effect on the problem when obtaining these data. One way to begin to interrupt interactional cycles that maintain a problem is to intensify one side of the system beyond its usual point in equilibrium—that is, for the girl to increase her headaches or for the mother to increase a type of involvement and vigilance. This type of directive can result in an unstable system that can lead to change in the symptom.

The next directives were aimed at creating new rituals for the girl and her family to compensate for the loss of the people and rituals that had organized the evening. Calling the father at bedtime simply identified for whom the child grieved and created a new experience with the father that allowed Diane to regain her father in familiar patterns of interaction. Asking the mother to talk in ways like the father at bedtime—to tell stories—interrupted and supplanted the mother/child interactions around migraine and allowed them to be close in different, more positive ways. In the past, much of mother's exchanges and intimate solicitousness with Diane had centered on a problem—do you have a headache, where is it, and so on. The directive interrupted this system of interaction and fostered an intimacy that was not based on the mother's usual style of relating to her daughter.

The last strategic directive is perhaps the most interesting. I asked the girl deliberately to displace pain to a previously used transitional object, as a preoperational, self-healing ritual. The origins of this kind of intervention can be traced to the belief systems and theories of preoperational children (ages one through eight) in our culture (Piaget, 1960), as well as to beliefs and practices of shamanic magic in other cultures (Frazer, 1959). Most children have experiences with a "transitional object," with highly similar interactions between object and self. Piaget described this magical reality of children as usually connected with strong feelings, wishes, and fears of the child's.

With Diane, I stimulated her memories of transitional objects and invited her to regress to these earlier, magical ways of diminishing pain from loss. Various literatures describe this regression in different ways—from the "trance logic" of hypnotic practices to the preoperational logic of cognitive-developmental theories. But the effect is the same: the use of a childlike reality in which inanimate objects can be treated as "pretend" people and in which beliefs and logic are not bound by the rules of formal operational thinking.

Strategically, asking Diane to do something deliberately that was previously involuntary changed the context of the symptom from a passive, involuntary arena to one in which she was exercising autonomy and self-help. The migrainous pain was placed in a "different universe" and set of interactions that altered the meaning of the pain to the system.

Lastly, the statement "If you can do this, your pain will be gone" simply reflects a hypnotic "truism." Obviously, if she could "transfer" the pain to the object, the pain would be gone. If the pain was not gone, she had not transferred the pain as I had told her to. In either case, the power of the therapist is enhanced for further interventions, if necessary.

Conclusions

This chapter has outlined some of the characteristics of strategic therapy. Most of the chapter was devoted to cases which illustrate these principles and which demonstrate how a strategic therapist might work with particular problems. Although many basic concepts were covered, the chapter was brief, omitting or only alluding to many topics in theory and practice. These include the nature and theory of paradox, the nature of change (homeostatic versus evolutionary models—Hoffman, 1981), the relation between hypnotic phenomena and strategic therapy, the therapist's use of self, the theory of triangles, circular questioning, the therapeutic use of a consultation team and live supervision, couples choreography, the nature of the supervisor-therapist-family system, the models of using a family's matrix of meaning, or world view, as the point of therapeutic entry, the various uses of ritual, and the new developments in cybernetics.

The chapter was meant to provide the reader with some basic strategic concepts and to show how these concepts can be applied to help individuals and families in distress. It is hoped that the reader will be stimulated to explore various sources further to appreciate the excitement, richness, and practical effectiveness of helping people in these ways.

References ❧

Addiego, F., and others. "Female Ejaculation: A Case Study." *Journal of Sex Research*, 1981, *17*, 13–21.

Adler, A. *Understanding Human Nature*. New York: Greenberg, 1927.

Adler, A. *The Science of Living*. New York: Greenberg, 1929.

Adler, A. *What Life Should Mean to You*. New York: Putnam, 1958.

Adler, A. *Problems of Neurosis*. New York: Harper & Row, 1964.

Akiskal, H. S., and McKinney, W. T. "Overview of Recent Research in Depression." *Archives of General Psychiatry*, 1975, *32*, 285–305.

Alexander, F. "Principles and Techniques of Brief Psychotherapeutic Procedures." *Proceedings of the Association for Research on Nervous and Mental Disease*, 1951, *31* (16).

Altschul, S., "Denial and Ego Arrest." *Journal of the American Psychoanalytic Association*, 1968, *16*, 301–318.

Anderson, M. *Joan of Lorraine*. In G. Freedley (ed.), *Three Plays by Maxwell Anderson*. New York: Washington Square Press, 1962.

Anonymous. "Toward the Differentiation of a Self in One's Own Family." In J. L. Framo (ed.), *Family Interaction: A Dialogue Between Family Researchers and Family Therapists*. New York: Springer, 1972.

Anzieu, D. *Le psychodrame analytique chez l'enfant*. Paris: Presses Universitaires de France, 1956.

Argyris, C. *Exploration and Issues in Laboratory Education*. National Training Laboratories/National Education Association, 1966.

Arlow, J. "The Genesis of Interpretation." *Journal of the American Psychoanalytic Association*, 1979, *27* (Suppl.), 193–206.

Atwood, G., and Stolorow, R. *Structures of Subjectivity: Explorations in Psychoanalytic Phenomenology*. Hillsdale, N.J.: Analytic Press, 1984.

Bach, G. R. "The Marathon Group: Intensive Practice of Intimate Interaction." *Psychological Reports*, 1966, *18*, 995–102.

Bach, G. R. "Marathon Group Dynamics." *Psychological Reports*, 1967, *20*, 1147–1158.

Bach, G. R., and Wyden, P. *The Intimate Enemy*. New York: Morrow, 1969.

Baker, A. A. "The Misfit Family: A Psychodramatic Technique Used in a Therapeutic Community." *British Journal of Medical Psychology*, 1952, *25*, 235–243.

Balint, M. *Psychotherapeutic Techniques in Medicine*. London: Tavistock, 1961.

Balint, M., and others. *Focal Psychotherapy: An Example of Applied Psychoanalysis.* London: Tavistock, 1972.

Bandler, R., and Grinder, J. *The Structure of Magic: A Book About Language and Therapy.* Vol. 1. Palo Alto, Calif.: Science & Behavior Books, 1975.

Bandura, A. *Principles of Behavior Modification.* New York: Holt, Rinehart & Winston, 1969.

Bandura, A. "Vicarious and Self-Reinforcement Processes." In R. Glaser (ed.), *The Nature of Reinforcement.* Orlando, Fla.: Academic Press, 1971.

Barber, T. X. (ed.). *Biofeedback and Self-Control: An Aldine Reader on the Regulation of Bodily Processes and Consciousness.* Hawthorne, N.Y.: Aldine, 1971.

Bard, J. *Rational-Emotive Therapy in Practice.* Champaign, Ill.: Research Press, 1980.

Basmajian, J. V. *Biofeedback: Principles and Practice for Clinicians.* Baltimore, Md.: Williams & Wilkins, 1983.

Basmajian, J. V., and Blumenstein, R. *Electrode Placement in EMG Biofeedback.* Baltimore, Md.: Williams & Wilkins, 1980.

Bateson, G. *Steps to an Ecology of Mind.* New York: Ballantine Books, 1972.

Bateson, G., and others. "Toward a Theory of Schizophrenia." *Behavioral Science,* 1956, *1* (4), 251–264.

Beatty, J., and Legewie, H. (eds.). *Biofeedback and Behavior.* New York: Plenum, 1977.

Beck, A. T. *Depression: Causes and Treatment.* Philadelphia: University of Pennsylvania Press, 1972.

Beck, A. T. *Cognitive Therapy of Depression: New Perspectives.* (P. Crayton, ed.) New York: Raven Press, 1983.

Beres, D., and Arlow, J. "Fantasy and Identification in Empathy." *Psychoanalysis Quarterly,* 1974, *43,* 26–50.

Berger, P. "Antidepressant Medications and the Treatment of Depression." In J. Barchas and others (eds.), *Psychopharmacology from Theory to Practice.* New York: Oxford University Press, 1977.

Bergler, E. "Frigidity in the Female: Misconceptions and Facts." *Marr. Hyg.,* 1947, *1,* 16–21.

Bergler, E. *Neurotic-Counterfeit Sex.* Orlando, Fla.: Grune & Stratton, 1951.

Bergmann, M., and Hartmann, F. *The Evolution of Psychoanalytic Technique.* New York: Basic Books, 1976.

Bergmann, M., and Jucovy, M. (eds.). *Generations of the Holocaust.* New York: Basic Books, 1982.

Berman, E. M., and Lief, H. I. "Marital Therapy from a Psychiatric Perspective: An Overview." *American Journal of Psychiatry,* 1975, *132* (6), 583–591.

Berne, E. *Games People Play.* New York: Grove Press, 1964.

Berne, E. *Principles of Group Treatment.* New York: Oxford University Press, 1966.

Berne, E. *What Do You Say After You Say Hello?* New York: Grove Press, 1972.

Bielski, R. J., and Friedel, R. O. "Prediction of Tricyclic Antidepressant Response: A Critical Review." *Archives of General Psychiatry,* 1976, *33,* 1479–1489.

Binswanger, L. "Über Ideinfluct." *Swiss Archives for Neurology and Psychiatry,* 1932–1933, *30.*

Binswanger, L. *Grundformen und Menschliches Erkenntnis.* Zurich: Max Niehaus, 1942.

Binswanger, L. *Being-in-the-World.* New York: Basic Books, 1963.

Bion, W. R. *Experiences in Groups.* New York: Basic Books, 1959.

Birbaumer, N., and Kimmel, H. D. (eds.). *Biofeedback and Self-Regulation.* Hillsdale, N.J.: Erlbaum, 1976.

Birk, L. *Behavior Therapy in Psychiatry*. Task Force Report no. 5. Washington, D.C.: American Psychiatric Association, 1973.

Birk, L. (ed.). *Biofeedback: Behavioral Medicine*. Orlando, Fla.: Grune & Stratton, 1976.

Bischof, L. J. *Interpreting Personality Theories*. (Rev. ed.) New York: Harper & Row, 1970.

Blanchard, E. B., and Epstein, L. H. *Biofeedback Primer*. New York: Random House, 1978.

Blanck, G., and Blanck, R. *Ego Psychology: Theory and Practice*. New York: Columbia University Press, 1974.

Blanck, G., and Blanck, R. *Ego Psychology II: Psychoanalytic Developmental Psychology*. New York: Columbia University Press, 1979.

Blatner, H. A. *Acting In: Practical Applications of Psychodramatic Methods*. New York: Springer, 1973.

Blum, H. "Acting Out, the Psychoanalytic Process and Interpretation." *Annual of Psychoanalysis*, 1976, *4*, 163–184.

Blum, H. "The Curative and Creative Aspects of Insight." *Journal of the American Psychoanalytic Association*, 1979, *27* (Suppl.), 41–70.

Blum, H. "The Value of Reconstruction in Adult Psychoanalysis." *International Journal of Psychoanalysis*, 1980, *61*, 39–54.

Boring, R. O., and Deabler, H. L. "A Simplified Psychodramatic Approach in Group Therapy." *Journal of Clinical Psychology*, 1951, *7*, 371–375.

Bornstein, B. "The Analysis of a Phobic Child: Some Problems of Theory and Technique in Child Analysis." In *The Psychoanalytic Study of the Child*. Vols. 3–4. New York: International Universities Press, 1945.

Boss, M. *Psychoanalysis and Daseinanalysis*. New York: Basic Books, 1963.

Boszormenyi-Nagy, I., and Spark, G. M. *Invisible Loyalties*. New York: Harper & Row, 1973.

Bounsaville, B. J., Klerman, G. L., and Weisman, M. M. "Do Psychotherapy and Pharmacotherapy for Depression Conflict?" *Archives of General Psychiatry*, 1981, *38*, 24–55.

Bowen, M. "Toward the Differentiation of Self in One's Family of Origin." In F. D. Andres and J. P. Lorio (eds.), *Georgetown Family Symposia*. Vol. 1: *1971–1972*. Washington, D.C.: Department of Psychiatry, Georgetown University Medical Center, 1974.

Bowen, M. *Family Therapy in Clinical Practice*. New York: Jason Aronson, 1978.

Boyer, B. "Provisional Evaluation of Psychoanalysis with Few Parameters Employed in the Treatment of Schizophrenia." *International Journal of Psychoanalysis*, 1961, *42*, 389–403.

Boyer, B. "Introduction." In B. Boyer and P. Giovacchini (eds.), *Psychoanalytic Treatment of Schizophrenic, Borderline and Characterological Disorders*. New York: Jason Aronson, 1980a.

Boyer, B. "Office Treatment of Schizophrenic Patients: The Use of Psychoanalytic Therapy with Few Parameters." In B. Boyer and P. Giovacchini (eds.), *Psychoanalytic Treatment of Schizophrenic, Borderline and Characterological Disorders*. New York: Jason Aronson, 1980b.

Boyer, B. "Analytic Experiences in Work with Regressed Patients." In P. Giovacchini and B. Boyer (eds.), *Technical Factors in Treatment of the Severely Disturbed Patient*. New York: Jason Aronson, 1982.

Brentano, F. *Psychology from an Empirical Point of View*. Leipzig: Meiner, 1974.

Breuer, J., and Freud, S. "On the Physical Mechanism of Hysterical Phenomena."

In J. Strachey (ed. and trans.), *The Standard Edition of the Complete Psychological Works of Sigmund Freud*. Vol. 3. London: Hogarth Press, 1962. (Originally published 1893.)

Bronfenbrenner, U. "The Mirror-Image in Soviet-American Relations." *Journal of Social Issues,* 1961, *17* (3), 45–56.

Bronfenbrenner, U., and Newcomb, T. M. "Improvisations—An Application of Psychodrama in Personality Diagnosis." *Sociatry*, 1948, *4*, 367–382.

Brown, B., and Selye, H. *Stress and the Art of Biofeedback*. New York: Harper & Row, 1977.

Brown, B. B., and Downs, H. *New Mind, New Body: Bio-Feedback—New Directions for the Mind*. New York: Harper & Row, 1977.

Bugental, E. K., and Bugental, J. F. T. "Dispiritedness: A New Perspective on a Familiar State." *Journal of Humanistic Psychology*, 1984, *24*, 49–67.

Bugental, J. F. T. *The Search for Existential Identity: Patient-Therapist Dialogue in Humanistic Psychotherapy*. San Francisco: Jossey-Bass, 1976.

Bugental, J. F. T. *Psychotherapy and Process: The Fundamentals of an Existential-Humanistic Approach*. Reading, Mass.: Addison-Wesley, 1978.

Bugental, J. F. T. *The Search for Authenticity: An Existential-Analytic Approach to Psychotherapy*. (Enl. ed.) New York: Irvington, 1981.

Bugental, J. F. T., and Bugental, E. K. "A Fate Worse than Death: The Fear of Changing." *Psychotherapy*, forthcoming.

Burns, D. D. *Feeling Good: The New Mood Therapy*. New York: William Morrow, 1980.

Butler, F. *Biofeedback: A Survey of the Literature*. New York: Plenum, 1978.

Capponi, A. "Origins and Evolution of the Borderline Patient." In J. Leboit and A. Capponi (eds.), *Advances in Psychotherapy of the Borderline Patient*. New York: Jason Aronson, 1979.

Capra, F. *The Turning Point*. New York: Simon & Schuster, 1982.

Carter, E. A., and McGoldrick, M. *The Family Life Cycle*. New York: Gardner Press, 1980.

Charny, I. *Marital Love and Hate*. New York: Macmillan, 1972.

Comfort, A. *The Joy of Sex*. New York: Crown, 1972.

Cooper, T. B., and others. *Lithium: Controversies and Unresolved Issues*. Amsterdam: Excerpta Medica, 1979.

Corsini, R. J. "Psychodramatic Group Therapy." In R. J. Corsini, *Methods of Group Psychotherapy*. New York: McGraw-Hill, 1957.

Corsini, R. J., and Putzey, L. J. "Bibliography of Group Psychotherapy." *Group Psychotherapy*, 1956, *9* (3), 178–249.

Culbertson, F. M. "Modification of an Emotionally Held Attitude Through Role Playing." *Journal of Abnormal and Social Psychology*, 1957, *54*, 230–233.

Danskin, D. G., and Crow, M. A. *Biofeedback: An Introduction and Guide*. Palo Alto, Calif.: Mayfield, 1981.

Danysh, J. *Stop Without Quitting*. San Francisco: International Society of General Semantics, 1974.

Davanloo, H. *Basic Principles and Techniques in Short-Term Dynamic Psychotherapy*. New York: Spectrum, 1978.

Davanloo, H. "Techniques of Short-Term Dynamic Psychotherapy." *Psychiatric Clinics of North America*, 1979, *2* (1), 11–22.

Davanloo, H. *Short-Term Dynamic Psychotherapy*. New York: Jason Aronson, 1980.

Davidson, D. *Inquiries into Truth and Interpretation.* New York: Oxford University Press, 1984.

Day, M. "Process in Classical Psychodynamic Groups." *International Journal of Group Psychotherapy,* 1981, *31,* 153–174.

DePascalis, V. *Biofeedback e autocontrollo.* Rome: Bulzoni, 1981.

Desoille, R. *The Directed Daydream.* New York: Psychosynthesis Research Foundation, 1965.

Deutsch, H. "On the Pathological Lie." *Journal of the American Academy of Psychoanalysis,* 1982, *10,* 369–386. (Originally published 1922.)

Dicks, H. V. *Marital Tensions.* New York: Basic Books, 1967.

DiMascio, A., and others. "Differential Symptom Reduction by Drugs and Psychotherapy in Acute Depression." *Archives of General Psychiatry,* 1979, *36,* 1450–1456.

Donlon, P., and Tupin, J. "Overview: Efficacy and Safety of Rapid Neuroleptization." *American Journal of Psychiatry,* 1979, *136,* 273–278.

Dreikurs, R. "Adlerian Psychotherapy." In F. Fromm-Reichmann and J. L. Moreno (eds.), *Progress in Psychotherapy.* Orlando, Fla.: Grune & Stratton, 1956.

Dreikurs, R. *Psychodynamics, Psychotherapy and Counseling.* Chicago: Alfred Adler Institute, 1967.

Dreikurs, R., and Mosak, H. H. "The Tasks of Life 1: Adler's Three Tasks." *Individual Psychologist,* 1966, *4,* 18–22.

Dreikurs, R., Mosak, H. H., and Shulman, B. H. "Patient-Therapist Relationship in Multiple Psychotherapy II: Its Advantages for the Patient." *Psychiatric Quarterly,* 1956, *26,* 590–596.

Dryden, W. *Rational-Emotive Therapy: Fundamentals and Innovations.* London: Croom Helm, 1984.

Durkin, J. (ed.). *Living Groups: Group Psychotherapy and General System Theory.* New York: Brunner/Mazel, 1981.

Dusay, J. "Egograms and the Constancy Hypothesis." *Transactional Analysis Journal,* 1972, *2,* 37–41.

Dusay, J. *Egograms.* New York: Harper & Row, 1977.

Dusay, J., and Dusay, K. "Transactional Analysis." In R. Corsini (ed.), *Current Psychotherapies.* (3rd ed.) Itasca, Ill.: Peacock, 1984.

Dusay, J., and Steiner, C. "Transactional Analysis in Groups." In H. Kaplan and B. Sadock (eds.), *Comprehensive Group Psychotherapy.* Baltimore, Md.: Williams & Wilkins, 1971.

Edwards, D. G. *Existential Psychotherapy: The Process of Caring.* New York: Gardner Press, 1982.

Eissler, K. R. "The Effect of the Structure of the Ego on Psychoanalytic Technique." *Journal of the American Psychoanalytic Association,* 1953, *1,* 104–143.

Ellis, A. "A Study of Trends in Recent Psychoanalytic Publications." *American Imago,* 1949a, *5,* 306–316.

Ellis, A. "Towards the Improvement of Psychoanalytic Research." *Psychoanalytic Review,* 1949b, *36,* 123–143.

Ellis, A. *An Introduction to the Scientific Principles of Psychoanalysis.* Provincetown, Mass.: Journal Press, 1950.

Ellis, A. "The Effectiveness of Psychotherapy with Individuals Who Have Severe Homosexual Problems." *Journal of Consulting Psychology,* 1956a, *20,* 191–195.

Ellis, A. "An Operational Reformulation of Some of the Basic Principles of Psychoanalysis." *Psychoanalytic Review*, 1956b, *43*, 163–180.

Ellis, A. *Reason and Emotion in Psychotherapy*. Secaucus, N.J.: Lyle Stuart/Citadel Press, 1962.

Ellis, A. "A Cognitive Approach to Behavior Therapy." *International Journal of Psychiatry*, 1969a, *8*, 896–900.

Ellis, A. "A Weekend of Rational Encounter." In A. Burton (ed.), *Encounter: The Theory and Practice of Encounter Groups*. San Francisco: Jossey-Bass, 1969b.

Ellis, A. *Growth Through Reason*. North Hollywood, Calif.: Wilshire Books, 1971.

Ellis, A. *Psychotherapy and the Value of a Human Being*. New York: Institute for Rational-Emotive Therapy, 1972.

Ellis, A. "Are Cognitive Behavior Therapy and Rational Therapy Synonymous?" *Rational Living*, 1973a, *8* (2), 8–11.

Ellis, A. *Humanistic Psychotherapy: The Rational-Emotive Approach*. New York: McGraw-Hill, 1973b.

Ellis, A. "RET Abolishes Most of the Human Ego." *Psychotherapy*, 1976, *13*, 343–348. Reprinted by Institute for Rational-Emotive Therapy, New York.

Ellis, A. "Discomfort Anxiety: A New Cognitive Behavioral Construct. Part 1." *Rational Living*, 1979a, *14* (2), 3–8.

Ellis, A. "The Issue of Force and Energy in Behavioral Change." *Journal of Contemporary Psychotherapy*, 1979b, *10*, 83–97.

Ellis, A. "Rational-Emotive Therapy: Research Data That Supports the Clinical and Personality Hypotheses of RET and Other Modes of Cognitive Behavior Therapy." In A. Ellis and J. M. Whiteley (Eds.), *Theoretical and Empirical Foundations of Rational-Emotive Therapy*. Monterey, Calif.: Brooks/Cole, 1979c.

Ellis, A. "Discomfort Anxiety: A New Cognitive Behavioral Construct. Part 2." *Rational Living*, 1980, *15* (1), 25–30.

Ellis, A. "The Use of Rational Humorous Songs in Psychotherapy." *Voices*, 1981, *16* (4), 29–36.

Ellis, A. "Rational-Emotive Group Therapy." In G. M. Gazda (ed.), *Basic Approaches to Group Psychotherapy and Group Counseling*. Springfield, Ill.: Thomas, 1982.

Ellis, A. "The Essence of RET—1984." *Journal of Rational-Emotive Therapy*, 1984a, *2* (1), 19–25.

Ellis, A. "Rational-Emotive Therapy." In R. J. Corsini (ed.), *Current Psychotherapies*. (3rd ed.) Itasca, Ill.: Peacock, 1984b.

Ellis, A. *Overcoming Resistance*. New York: Springer, 1985a.

Ellis, A. *Rational-Emotive Therapy and Cognitive Behavior Therapy*. New York: Springer, 1985b.

Ellis, A., and Abrahms, E. *Brief Psychotherapy in Medical and Health Practice*. New York: Springer, 1978.

Ellis, A., and Becker, I. *A Guide to Personal Happiness*. North Hollywood, Calif.: Wilshire Books, 1982.

Ellis, A., and Bernard, M. E. (eds.). *Rational-Emotive Approaches to the Problems of Childhood*. New York: Plenum, 1983.

Ellis, A., and Grieger, R. (eds.). *Handbook of Rational-Emotive Therapy*. New York: Springer, 1977.

Ellis, A., and Harper, R. A. *A Guide to Successful Marriage*. North Hollywood, Calif.: Wilshire Books, 1961.

Ellis, A., and Harper, R. A. *A New Guide to Rational Living.* North Hollywood, Calif.: Wilshire Books, 1975.

Ellis, A., and Whiteley, J. M. (eds.). *Theoretical and Empirical Foundations of Rational-Emotive Therapy.* Monterey, Calif.: Brooks/Cole, 1979.

Elms, A. C. "Influence of Fantasy Ability on Attitude Change Through Role Playing." *Journal of Personality and Social Psychology,* 1966, *4* (1), 36–43.

Elms, A. C., and Janis, I. L. "Counter-Norm Attitudes Induced by Consonant vs. Dissonant Conditions of Role-Playing." *Journal of Experimental Research in Personality,* 1965, *1* (1), 50–60.

Epstein, L. "The Therapeutic Use of Countertransference Data with Borderline Patients." *Contemporary Psychoanalysis,* 1979, *15,* 148–275.

Euripides. *The Bacchae.* (G. Murray, trans.) In W. J. Oates and E. O'Neill, Jr. (eds.), *The Complete Greek Drama.* Vol. 2. New York: Random House, 1938.

Euripides. *The Bacchae and Other Plays.* (P. Vellacott, trans.) Harmondsworth, England: Penguin Books, 1954.

Eysenck, H. J. *The Structure of Human Personality.* London: Methuen, 1953.

Eysenck, H. J. *Experiments in Behaviour Therapy.* New York: Macmillan, 1964.

Eysenck, H. J., and Beech, R. "Counterconditioning and Related Methods." In A. E. Bergin and S. L. Garfield (eds.), *Handbook of Psychotherapy and Behavior Change.* New York: Wiley, 1971.

Ezriel, H. "Notes on Psychoanalytic Therapy: II. Interpretation and Research." *Psychiatry,* 1952, *15,* 119–126.

Ezriel, H. "The Role of Transference in Psychoanalytic and Other Approaches to Group Treatment." 2nd International Congress on Group Psychotherapy, Zurich, 1957. *Acta Psychotherapy,* 1959, *7* (Suppl.), 101–116.

Ezriel, H. "Psychoanalytic Group Therapy." In L. R. Wolberg and E. K. Schwartz (eds.), *Group Therapy: 1973, an Overview.* New York: Intercontinental Medical Book Corp., 1973.

Fairbairn, W. R. D. *An Object-Relations Theory of the Personality.* New York: Basic Books, 1952.

Fantel, E. "Psychodrama in a Veterans Hospital." *Sociatry,* 1948, *2,* 47–64.

Fantel, E. "Report on Psychodramatic Therapy." *Group Psychotherapy,* 1950, *3,* 55–58.

Fenichel, O. "Conversion." In O. Fenichel, *The Psychoanalytic Theory of Neurosis.* New York: Norton, 1945.

Fenichel, O. "The Economics of Pseudologia Phantastica." In O. Fenichel, *Collected Papers, Second Series.* New York: Norton, 1954. (Originally published 1939.)

Ferenczi, S. "The Problem of the Termination of the Analysis." In *Final Contributions to the Problems and Methods of Psychoanalysis.* New York: Brunner/Mazel, 1980. (Originally published 1927.)

Ferenczi, S., and Rank, O. "Development of Psychoanalysis." (C. Newton, trans.) *Nervous and Mental Disease Monographs,* 1925, *40.*

Fisch, R., Weakland, J. H., and Segal, L. *The Tactics of Change: Doing Therapy Briefly.* San Francisco: Jossey-Bass, 1982.

Fordham, M. *Jungian Psychotherapy: A Study in Analytical Psychology.* New York: Wiley-Interscience, 1978.

Framo, J. L. "Rationale and Techniques of Intensive Family Therapy." In I. Boszormenyi-Nagy and J. L. Framo (eds.), *Intensive Family Therapy.* New York: Harper & Row, 1965.

Framo, J. L. "Symptoms from a Family Transactional Viewpoint." In N. W. Acker-man, J. Lieb, and J. K. Pearce (eds.), *Family Therapy in Transition*. Boston: Little, Brown, 1970.

Framo, J. L. "Marriage Therapy in a Couples Group." In D. A. Bloch (ed.), *Techniques of Family Psychotherapy: A Primer*. Orlando, Fla.: Grune & Stratton, 1973.

Framo, J. L. "Family of Origin as a Therapeutic Resource for Adults in Marital and Family Therapy: You Can and Should Go Home Again." *Family Process*, 1976, *15* (2), 193–209.

Frankl, V. E. *The Unheard Cry for Meaning*. New York: Simon & Schuster, 1978.

Frazer, J. *The New Golden Bough*. New York: Criterion, 1959.

French, T., and Alexander, F. *Psychoanalytic Theory*. New York: Ronald Press, 1946.

Freud, A. *The Ego and the Mechanisms of Defense*. New York: International Univer-sities Press, 1946. (Originally published 1936.)

Freud, A. *Normality and Pathology in Childhood*. New York: International Univer-sities Press, 1965.

Freud, S. *Project for a Scientific Psychology*. Vol. 1. London: Hogarth Press, 1961. (Originally published 1895.)

Freud, S. "The Interpretation of Dreams." In J. Strachey (ed. and trans.), *The Standard Edition of the Complete Psychological Works of Sigmund Freud*. Vols. 4 and 5. London: Hogarth Press, 1953. (Originally published 1900.)

Freud, S. "On Psychotherapy." *Standard Edition*, Vol. 7, 1953. (Originally published 1905.)

Freud, S. "Analysis of a Phobia in a Five-Year-Old Boy." *Standard Edition*, Vol. 10, 1955. (Originally published 1909.)

Freud, S. "Recommendations to Physicians Practising Psychoanalysis." *Standard Edition*, Vol. 12, 1958. (Originally published 1912.)

Freud, S. "On Beginning the Treatment." *Standard Edition*, Vol. 12, 1958. (Origi-nally published 1913a.)

Freud, S. "Two Lies Told by Children." *Standard Edition*, Vol. 12, 1958. (Originally published 1913b.)

Freud, S. "On Narcissism: An Introduction." *Standard Edition*, Vol. 14, 1961. (Originally published 1914.)

Freud, S. "Observations on Transference-Love." *Standard Edition*, Vol. 14, 1958. (Originally published 1915a.)

Freud, S. "Thoughts for the Times on War and Death." *Standard Edition*, Vol. 14, 1961. (Originally published 1915b.)

Freud, S. "Introductory Lectures on Psychoanalysis." *Standard Edition*, Vols. 15 and 16, 1963. (Originally published 1917a.)

Freud, S. "Mourning and Melancholia." *Standard Edition*, Vol. 14, 1957, 1961. (Originally published 1917b.)

Freud, S. *Group Psychology and the Analysis of the Ego*. (J. Strachey, trans.) New York: Bantam Books, 1960. (Originally published 1922.)

Freud, S. "The Ego and the Id." *Standard Edition*, Vol. 19, 1961. (Originally pub-lished 1923a.)

Freud, S. "Remarks on the Theory and Practice of Dream-Interpretation." *Stan-dard Edition*, Vol. 19, 1961. (Originally published 1923b.)

Freud, S. "Inhibitions, Symptoms and Anxiety." *Standard Edition*, Vol. 20, 1959. (Originally published 1926a.)

Freud, S. "The Question of Lay Analysis." *Standard Edition*, Vol. 20, 1959. (Originally published 1926b.)

Freud, S. "Analysis Terminable and Interminable." *Standard Edition,* Vol. 23, 1964. (Originally published 1937a.)

Freud, S. "Constructions Analysis." *Standard Edition*, Vol. 23, 1964. (Originally published 1937b.)

Freud, S. *The Basic Writings of Sigmund Freud.* (A. A. Brill, ed. and trans.) New York: Random House, 1938.

Freud, S. *Moses and Monotheism.* (K. Jones, trans.) New York: Random House, 1962. (Originally published 1939.)

Freud, S. "Splitting of the Ego in the Process of Defence." *Standard Edition*, Vol. 23, 1964. (Originally published 1940.)

Freud, S. *Psychoanalysis and Faith.* (E. L. Freud, ed.; H. Meng, trans.) New York: Basic Books, 1963.

Fromm, E. *Man for Himself.* New York: Holt, Rinehart & Winston, 1947.

Fromm, E. *Zen Buddhism and Psychoanalysis.* New York: Holt, Rinehart & Winston, 1960.

Fromm-Reichmann, F. *Principles of Intensive Psychotherapy.* Chicago: University of Chicago Press, 1950.

Fuller, G. D. *Biofeedback: Methods and Procedures in Clinical Practice.* San Francisco: Biofeed Press, 1978.

Fuller, G. D. *Behavioral Medicine, Stress Management and Biofeedback.* San Francisco: Biofeed Press, 1980.

Furman, E. *A Child's Parent Dies.* New Haven, Conn.: Yale University Press, 1974.

Gaarder, K., and Montgomery, P. S. *Clinical Biofeedback: A Procedural Manual for Behavioral Medicine.* Baltimore, Md.: Williams & Wilkins, 1981.

Gaby, N. S., and others. "Treatment of Lithium Tremor with Metoprolol." *American Journal of Psychiatry*, 1983, *140*, 593–595.

Gardos, C., and Cole, J. "The Prognosis of Tardive Dyskinesia." *Journal of Clinical Psychiatry*, 1983, *44*, 177–197.

Gatchel, R. J., and Price, K. P. (eds.). *Clinical Applications of Biofeedback: Appraisal and Status.* Elmsford, N.Y.: Pergamon Press, 1979.

Gendlin, E. T. *Experiencing and the Creation of Meaning.* New York: Macmillan, 1962.

Gerardin, L. *Le bio-feedback: Au service de la maitrise et de la connaissance de soi.* Paris: Retz, 1978.

Gill, M. M. *Analysis of Transference.* Vol. 1: *Theory and Technique.* New York: International Universities Press, 1982.

Giovacchini, P. "The Many Sides of Helplessness: The Borderline Patient." In J. Leboit and A. Capponi (eds.), *Advances in Psychotherapy of the Borderline Patient.* New York: Jason Aronson, 1979a.

Giovacchini, P. *Treatment of Primitive Mental States.* New York: Jason Aronson, 1979b.

Goulding, M., and Goulding, R. "Injunctions, Decisions, and Redecision." *Transactional Analysis Journal*, 1976, *6*, 1.

Goulding, R., and Goulding, M. *The Power Is in the Patient.* San Francisco: TA Press, 1978.

Goulding, R., and Goulding, M. *Changing Lives Through Redecision Therapy.* New York: Brunner/Mazel, 1979.

Green, E., and Green, A. *Beyond Biofeedback.* New York: Delacorte Press, 1977.

Greenberg, I. A. "Audience in Action Through Psychodrama." *Group Psychotherapy*, 1964, *17* (2–3), 104–122.

Greenberg, I. A. *Psychodrama and Audience Attitude Change.* Beverly Hills, Calif.: Behavioral Studies Press, 1968.

Greenberg, I. A. (ed.). *Psychodrama: Theory and Therapy.* New York: Behavioral Publications, 1974.

Greenberg, I. A. (ed.). *Group Hypnotherapy and Hypnodrama.* Chicago: Nelson-Hall, 1977. (Now available only through Behavioral Studies Press, Box 5323, Beverly Hills, Calif. 90210.)

Greenberg, I. A., and Bassin, A. "Reality Therapy and Psychodrama." In A. Bassin, E. Bratten, and R. L. Rachin, *The Reality Therapy Reader.* New York: Harper & Row, 1976.

Greenberg, J. C. "A Clinical Case Study of Maria." Paper presented to New Jersey Board of Psychological Examiners to fulfill New Jersey psychology licensing requirement, 1984.

Greenberg, J. R., and Mitchell, S. A. *Object Relations in Psychoanalytic Theory.* Cambridge, Mass.: Harvard University Press, 1983.

Greer, V. J., and Sacks, J. M. (eds.). *Bibliography of Psychodrama.* 1973. Available through Valerie J. Greer, 505 West End Ave., New York, N.Y.

Grieger, R., and Boyd, J. *Rational-Emotive Therapy: A Skills Based Approach.* New York: Van Nostrand Reinhold, 1980.

Guy, W. *Ecdell Assessment Manual for Psychopharmacology.* Department of Health, Education and Welfare publication no. ADM 76–338. Washington, D.C.: U.S. Department of Health, Education, and Welfare, 1976.

Haas, R. B., and Moreno, J. L. "Psychodrama as a Projective Technique." In H. H. Anderson and G. L. Anderson (eds.), *An Introduction to Projective Techniques.* Englewood Cliffs, N.J.: Prentice-Hall, 1961.

Haas, W. "The Intergenerational Encounter: A Method in Treatment." *Social Work,* 1968, *13* (3), 91–101.

Haley, J. *Strategies of Psychotherapy.* Orlando, Fla.: Grune & Stratton, 1963.

Haley, J. *Uncommon Therapy: The Psychiatric Techniques of Milton H. Erickson.* New York: Norton, 1973.

Haley, J. *Problem-Solving Therapy: New Strategies for Effective Family Therapy.* San Francisco: Jossey-Bass, 1976.

Haley, J. *Leaving Home: The Therapy of Disturbed Young People.* New York: McGraw-Hill, 1980.

Haley, J. *Ordeal Therapy: Unusual Ways to Change Behavior.* San Francisco: Jossey-Bass, 1984.

Hall, J. A., and Crasilneck. H. B. "Hypnosis." *Journal of the American Medical Association,* 1978, *239,* 760–761.

Hansen, B. "Sociodrama in a Small Community Therapy Program." *Sociatry,* 1947, *1,* 92–96.

Harrison, J. E. *Prolegomena to the Study of Greek Religion.* New York: Meridian Books, 1957. (Originally published 1903.)

Harrison, J. E. *Themis: A Study of the Social Origins of Greek Religion.* New Hyde Park, N.Y.: University Books, 1962. (Originally published 1912.)

Harrison, J. E. *Ancient Art and Ritual.* (5th rev. ed.) London: Oxford University Press, 1951. (Originally published 1913.)

Harrison, J. E. *Epilegomena to the Study of Greek Religion.* New Hyde Park, N.Y.: University Books, 1962. (Originally published 1927.)

Hartmann, H. *Ego Psychology and the Problem of Adaptation.* New York: International Universities Press, 1958a. (Originally published 1937.)

Hartmann, H. "Comments on the Scientific Aspects of Psychoanalysis." *Psychoanalytic Study of the Child,* 1958b, *13,* 127–146.

Hartmann, H. *Essays on Ego Psychology: Selected Problems in Psychoanalytic Theory.* New York: International Universities Press, 1964.

Hartmann, H., and Kris, E. "The Genetic Approach in Psychoanalysis." In *The Psychoanalytic Study of the Child.* Vol. 1. New York: International Universities Press, 1945.

Haskell, M. R. *An Introduction to Socioanalysis.* Long Beach: California Institute of Socioanalysis, 1967a.

Haskell, M. R. *The Psychodramatic Method.* Long Beach: California Institute of Socioanalysis, 1967b.

Hastings, D. W. *Impotence and Frigidity.* Boston: Little, Brown, 1963.

Hauck, P. *Overcoming Depression.* Philadelphia: Westminster, 1973.

Hilgard, E. R. "Pain: Its Reduction and Production Under Hypnosis." *Proceedings of the American Philosophical Society,* 1971, *115,* 470–476.

Hoffman, L. *Foundations of Family Therapy: A Conceptual Framework for Systems Change.* New York: Basic Books, 1981.

Hofmann, H. (ed.). *The Ministry and Mental Health.* New York: Association Press, 1960.

Hogarty, G. E., and Goldberg, S. C. "Drug and Sociotherapy in the Aftercare of Schizophrenic Patients." *Archives of General Psychiatry,* 1973, *28,* 54–64.

Holt, H. "The Three Stages of Being-in-the-World." *Transactions of New York Institute of Existential Analysis 1960,* pp. 1–15. (Expanded lecture given at the 4th International Congress of Psychotherapy, Barcelona, Spain, 1959.)

Holt, H. "The Problem of Interpretation from the Point of View of Existential Psychoanalysis." In E. F. Hammer (ed.), *The Use of Interpretation in Treatment.* Orlando, Fla.: Grune & Stratton, 1968.

Holt, H. "Existential Psychoanalysis." In A. M. Freedman (ed.), *Comprehensive Textbook of Psychiatry, II.* Baltimore, Md.: Williams & Wilkins, 1975.

Holt, H. *Free to Be Good or Bad.* New York: M. Evans, 1976.

Holt, H. "A Theory of the Life-World in Existential Group Therapy." *Modern Psychotherapy,* 1978, *3,* 3–25.

Holt, H. "An Existential View of Neurotic Conflict." *Modern Psychotherapy,* 1979, *2,* 1–7.

Holt, H. "Some Fundamental Ideas in Existential Analysis." *Modern Psychotherapy,* 1981, *3,* 1–26.

Holt, H. "Existential Psychoanalysis and Modern Psychoanalysis." *Journal of Modern Psychoanalysis,* 1985a, *9* (1).

Holt, H. "The Subjective Experience of the Self." *Modern Psychotherapy,* 1985b, *1,* 1–8.

Horner, A. J. *Object Relations and the Developing Ego in Therapy.* New York: Jason Aronson, 1979.

Horner, A. J. *Object Relations and the Developing Ego in Therapy.* (2nd ed.) New York: Jason Aronson, 1984.

Horney, K. *The Neurotic Personality of Our Time.* New York: Norton, 1937.

Horney, K. *New Ways in Psychoanalysis.* New York: Norton, 1939.

Horney, K. *Our Inner Conflicts.* New York: Norton, 1946.

Horney, K. *Neurosis and Human Growth.* New York: Norton, 1950.

Horney, K. "Lectures on Psychoanalytic Technique Presented to Candidates-in-Training of the American Institute for Psychoanalysis." Unpublished transcript, Association for the Advancement of Psychoanalysis, 1952.

Horney, K. "Constructive Forces in the Therapeutic Process." *American Journal of Psychoanalysis*, 1953, *13*, 4–19.

Horwitz, L. "Group-Centered Interventions in Therapy Groups." *Comprehensive Group Studies*, 1971, *2*, 311–331.

Horwitz, L. "A Group-Centered Approach to Group Psychotherapy." *International Journal of Group Psychotherapy*, 1977, *27*, 423–439.

Horwitz, L. "Projective Identification in Dyads and Groups." *International Journal of Group Psychotherapy*, 1983, *33*, 259–279.

Hume, W. *Biofeedback.* New York: Human Sciences Press, 1980.

Ingram, D. H. "Time and Timekeeping in Psychoanalysis and Psychotherapy." *American Journal of Psychoanalysis*, 1979, *39* (4), 319–329.

Ingram, D. H. "Discussion of 'Horneyan Developmental Psychoanalytic Theory and Its Application to the Treatment of the Young.'" *American Journal of Psychoanalysis*, 1984, *44* (1), 73–79.

Jackson, J. E., and Bressler, R. "Prescribing Tricyclic and Antidepressants. Part 1: General Considerations." *Drug Therapy*, 1981, *11*, 87.

Jacobi, J. *The Psychology of C. G. Jung.* (R. Mannheim, trans.) (6th rev. ed.) New Haven, Conn.: Yale University Press, 1973.

Jacobson, E. *The Self and the Object World.* New York: International Universities Press, 1964.

James, W. "What Pragmatism Means." In M. Konvitz and G. Kennedy (eds.), *The American Pragmatists.* New York: New American Library, 1960. (Originally published 1907.)

Janis, I. L., and Gilmore, J. B. "The influence of Role Playing on Opinion Change." *Journal of Abnormal and Social Psychology*, 1954, *49*, 211–218.

Jeste, D., and Wyatt, R. "Changing Epidemiology of Tardive Dyskinesia: An Overview." *American Journal of Psychiatry*, 1981, *138*, 297–309.

Jones, E. *The Life and Work of Sigmund Freud.* 3 vols. New York: Basic Books, 1962.

Jones, M. C. "Elimination of Children's Fears." *Journal of Experimental Psychology*, 1924a, *7*, 382–390.

Jones, M. C. "A Laboratory Fear: The Case of Peter." *Journal of General Psychology*, 1924b, *31*, 308–311.

Jourard, S. M. *The Transparent Self.* New York: Van Nostrand Reinhold, 1964.

Jung, C. G. "The Practice of Psychotherapy." In G. Adler (ed.), *The Collected Works of C. G. Jung.* (R. F. Hull, trans.) Vol. 16. Princeton, N.J.: Princeton University Press, 1966.

Jung, C. G. "Approaching the Unconscious." In C. G. Jung and M.-L. von Franz, *Man and His Symbols.* New York: Doubleday, 1969a.

Jung, C. G. *On the Nature of the Psyche.* Princeton, N.J.: Princeton University Press, 1969b.

Jung, C. G. *Analytical Psychology: Its Theory and Practice.* New York: Random House, 1970. (Also under title "The Tavistock Lectures" in G. Adler (ed.), *The Collected Works of C. G. Jung.* (R. F. Hull, trans.) Vol. 18: *The Symbolic Life: Miscellaneous Writings.* Princeton, N.J.: Princeton University Press, 1976.)

Jung, C. G. *Dreams.* Princeton, N.J.: Princeton University Press, 1974.

Kanfer, F., and Saslow, G. "Behavioral Diagnosis." In C. M. Franks (ed.), *Behavior Therapy: Appraisal and Status.* New York: McGraw-Hill, 1969.

Kanzer, M. "Writers and the Early Loss of Parents." *Journal of Hillside Hospital,* 1953, *2,* 148–151.

Kanzer, M. "Freud's 'Analytic Pact': The Standard Therapeutic Alliance." *Journal of the American Psychoanalytic Association,* 1981, *29,* 69–188.

Keefe, F. J., Kopel, S., and Gordon, S. *A Practical Guide to Behavioral Assessment.* New York: Springer, 1978.

Kegel, A. H. "Sexual Functions of the Pubococcygeus Muscle." *Western Journal of Obstetrics and Gynecology,* 1952, *60,* 521.

Kelly, G. A. *The Psychology of Personal Constructs.* New York: Norton, 1955.

Kelman, H. "A New Approach to Dream Interpretation." *American Journal of Psychoanalysis,* 1944, *4,* 89–107.

Kernberg, O. "Notes on Countertransference." *Journal of the American Psychoanalytic Association,* 1965, *13,* 38–56.

Kernberg, O. "Early Ego Integration and Object Relations." *Annals of the New York Academy of Science,* 1972, *193,* 233–247.

Kernberg, O. *Borderline Conditions and Pathological Narcissism.* New York: Jason Aronson, 1975.

Kernberg, O. "Technical Considerations in Treatment of Borderline Personality Organization." In J. Leboit and A. Capponi (eds.), *Advances in Psychotherapy of the Borderline Patient.* New York: Jason Aronson, 1979.

Kernberg, O. "The Theory of Psychoanalytic Psychotherapy." In S. Slipp (ed.), *Curative Factors in Dynamic Psychotherapy.* New York: McGraw-Hill, 1982.

Kernberg, O. *Object Relations Theory and Clinical Psycho-Analysis.* New York: Jason Aronson, 1984.

Kerr, M. E. "Family Systems Theory and Therapy." In A. S. Gurman and D. P. Kniskern (eds.), *Handbook of Family Therapy.* New York: Brunner/Mazel, 1981.

Kestenberg, J. "Psychoanalyses of Children of Survivors from the Holocaust." *Journal of the American Psychoanalytic Association,* 1980, *28,* 775–804.

Kibel, H. D., and Stein, D. "The Group as a Whole Approach: An Appraisal." *International Journal of Group Psychotherapy,* 1981, *31,* 409–427.

Kinsey, A. C., Pomeroy, W. B., and Martin, C. E. *Sexual Behavior in the Human Male.* Philadelphia: Saunders, 1948.

Kinsey, A. C., Pomeroy, W. B., Martin, C. E., and Gebhard, P. H. *Sexual Behavior in the Human Female.* Philadelphia: Saunders, 1952.

Klawans, J. L., Goetz, C. G., and Perlik, S. "Tardive Dyskinesia: Review and Update." *American Journal of Psychiatry,* 1980, *137,* 900.

Knight, R. "Borderline Patients." *Bulletin of the Menninger Clinic,* 1953a, *19,* 1–12.

Knight, R. "Management and Psychotherapy of the Borderline Patient." *Bulletin of the Menninger Clinic,* 1953b, *17,* 139–150.

Koch, S. "The Image of Man Implicit in Encounter Group Theory." *Journal of Humanistic Psychology,* 1971, *11* (2), 109–128.

Köhler, W. *The Mentality of Apes.* (E. Winter, trans.) New York: Vintage Books, 1959.

Kohut, H. "Introspection, Empathy and Psychoanalysis." *Journal of the American Psychoanalytic Association,* 1959, *7,* 459–483.

Kohut, H. *The Analysis of the Self.* New York: International Universities Press, 1971.

Kohut, H. *The Restoration of the Self.* New York: International Universities Press, 1977.

Kohut, H. *How Does Analysis Cure?* Chicago: University of Chicago Press, 1984.

Kohut, H., and Wolf, E. "The Disorders of the Self and Their Treatment." *International Journal of Psychoanalysis*, 1978, *59*, 413–425.

Korzybski, A. *Science and Sanity.* San Francisco: International Society for General Semantics, 1933.

Kris, E. "The Nature of Psychoanalytic Propositions and Their Validation." In S. Hook and M. Konvits (eds.), *Freedom and Experience.* New York: Cornell University Press, 1947.

Kris, E. *Psychoanalytic Explorations in Art.* New York: International Universities Press, 1952.

Kris, E. "The Recovery of Childhood Memories in Psychoanalysis." *Psychoanalytic Study of the Child*, 1956, *11*, 54–88.

Kutash, I. L. "Prevention and Equilibrium-Disequilibrium Theory." In I. L. Kutash and L. B. Schlesinger (eds.), *Handbook on Stress and Anxiety.* San Francisco: Jossey-Bass, 1980.

Kutash, I. L. "Psychoanalysis in Groups." Paper presented at meeting of the American Group Psychotherapy Association, 1984a.

Kutash, I. L. "Comments on 'Psychoanalysis in Groups: Creativity in Di-Ego-phrenia' and Treatment Methods with Case Material." *Group*, 1984b, *8* (1), 23–26.

Kutash, I. L., Schlesinger, L. B., and Associates. *Handbook on Stress and Anxiety: Contemporary Knowledge, Theory, and Treatment.* San Francisco: Jossey-Bass, 1980.

Kutash, I. L., and Wolf, A. "Recent Advances in Psychoanalysis in Groups." In H. I. Kaplan and B. J. Sadock (eds.), *Comprehensive Group Psychotherapy II.* Baltimore, Md.: Williams & Wilkins, 1983.

Kutash, I. L., and Wolf, A. "Psychoanalysis in Groups: The Primacy of the Individual." In H. S. Strean (ed.), *Inhibitions in Work and Love: Psychoanalytic Approaches to Problems in Creativity.* New York: Haworth Press, 1984.

LaBarre, W. *The Human Animal.* Chicago: University of Chicago Press, 1960.

Langs, R. *The Technique of Psychoanalytic Psychotherapy.* 2 vols. New York: Jason Aronson, 1973, 1974.

Langs, R. *The Bipersonal Field.* New York: Jason Aronson, 1976.

Lazarus, A. A. "The Treatment of a Sexually Inadequate Man." In L. P. Ullman and L. Krasner (eds.), *Case Studies in Behavior Modification.* New York: Holt, Rinehart & Winston, 1965.

Lazarus, A. A. "Behavior Rehearsal vs. Non-Directive Therapy vs. Advice in Affecting Behavior Change." *Behavioral Research and Therapy*, 1966, *4*, 209–212.

Lazarus, A. A. "Hypnosis as a Facilitator in Behavior Therapy." *International Journal of Clinical and Experimental Hypnosis*, 1973, *21*, 25–31.

Lazarus, R. *Psychological Stress and the Coping Process.* New York: McGraw-Hill, 1966.

Leboit, J. "The Technical Problem with the Borderline Patient." In J. Leboit and A. Capponi (eds.), *Advances in Psychotherapy of the Borderline Patient.* New York: Jason Aronson, 1979.

Leboit, J., and Capponi, A. *Advances in Psychotherapy of the Borderline Patient.* New York: Jason Aronson, 1979.

Lerner, J. A. "Horney Theory and Mother/Child Impact on Early Childhood." *American Journal of Psychoanalysis*, 1983, *43* (2), 149–157.

Leuner, H. *Initiated Symbol Projection.* New York: Psycho-Synthesis Research Foundation, 1965.

Levenson, E. *The Ambiguity of Change.* New York: Basic Books, 1983.

Liberman, R. P. "Behavior Therapy in Psychiatry." In J. P. Brady and H. K. Brodie (eds.), *Controversy in Psychiatry.* Philadelphia: Saunders, 1978.

Lieberman, M., Yalom, I., and Miles, M. *Encounter Groups: First Facts.* New York: Basic Books, 1973.

Lobitz, W. C., and LoPiccolo, J. "New Methods in the Behavioral Treatment of Sexual Dysfunction." *Journal of Behavioral Therapy and Experimental Psychiatry,* 1972, *3,* 265–271.

Locke, H. J., and Wallace, K. M. "Short Marital Adjustment and Prediction Tests: Their Reliability and Validity." *Marriage and Family Living,* 1959, *21,* 251–255.

LoPiccolo, J., and Lobitz, W. C. "The Role of Masturbation in the Treatment of Primary Orgasmic Dysfunction." *Archives of Sexual Behavior,* 1972, *2,* 163–171.

LoPiccolo, J., and Lobitz, W. C. "Behavior Therapy of Sexual Dysfunction." In L. A. Hamerlynck, L. C. Handy, and E. J. Mash (eds.), *Behavior Change: Methodology, Concepts and Practice.* Champaign, Ill.: Research Press, 1973.

LoPiccolo, J., and Steger, J. C. "The Oregon Sex Inventory: An Instrument for Assessment of Sexual Dysfunction." Unpublished manuscript, University of Houston, 1973.

LoPiccolo, J., Stewart, R., and Watkins, B. "Treatment of Erectile Failure and Ejaculatory Incompetence of Homosexual Etiology." *Journal of Behavioral Therapy and Experimental Psychiatry,* 1972, *3,* 233–236.

Lorand, S. "Contributions to the Problem of Vaginal Orgasm." *International Journal of Psychoanalysis,* 1939, *20,* 432–438.

MacLean, P. D. "Some Psychiatric Implications of Studies of the Limbic System." *Journal of Neurophysiology,* 1948, *4,* 18–22.

MacLean, P. D. "Man and His Animal Brain." *Modern Medicine,* 1964, *32,* 23–28.

Madanes, C. *Strategic Family Therapy.* San Francisco: Jossey-Bass, 1981.

Madanes, C. *Behind the One-Way Mirror: Advances in the Practice of Strategic Therapy.* San Francisco: Jossey-Bass, 1984.

Mahler, M. S. "On the Current Status of the Infantile Neurosis." *Journal of the American Psychoanalytic Association,* 1975, *23,* 327–333.

Mahler, M. S. "Notes on the Development of Basic Moods: The Depressive Affect." In M. S. Mahler, *The Selected Papers of Margaret S. Mahler.* Vol. 2. New York: Jason Aronson, 1979a.

Mahler, M. S. *The Selected Papers of Margaret S. Mahler.* 2 vols. New York: Jason Aronson, 1979b.

Mahler, M., Pine, F., and Bergmann, A. *The Psychological Birth of the Human Infant.* New York: Basic Books, 1975.

Malan, D. H. *A Study of Brief Psychotherapy.* New York: Plenum, 1963.

Malan, D. H. *The Frontier of Brief Psychotherapy.* New York: Plenum, 1975.

Malan, D. H., and others. "Group Psychotherapy: A Long-Term Follow-Up Study." *Archives of General Psychiatry,* 1976, *33,* 1303–1315.

Manning, M., and van der Veer, M. *Psychotronica: Kirlian- of aurafotografie, bio-feedback, electroslaap, luchtionisatie, plantgevoeligheidsmeting, piramidekracht, psychotronische energie, leugendetectie, voor en tegen, ifiltratie vanuit Rusland?* Deventer, Netherlands: Ankh-Hermes, 1976.

Mariella, N., and Sovine, A. L. *Textbook of Biological Feedback.* New York: Human Sciences Press, 1981.

Martin, P. *A Marital Therapy Manual.* New York: Brunner/Mazel, 1976.

Masters, W. H., and Johnson, V. *Human Sexual Inadequacy.* Boston: Little, Brown, 1970.

Masterson, J. F. *Psychotherapy of the Borderline Adult: A Developmental Approach.* New York: Brunner/Mazel, 1976.

Masterson, J. F. *The Narcissistic and Borderline Disorders: An Integrated Developmental Approach.* New York: Brunner/Mazel, 1981.

Mathew, R. J. (ed.). *Treatment of Migraine: Pharmacological and Biofeedback Considerations.* Jamaica, N.Y.: SP Medical & Scientific Books, 1981.

Mattoon, M. A. *Understanding Dreams.* Dallas: Spring Publications, 1978.

Mattoon, M. A. *Jungian Psychology in Perspective.* New York: Macmillan, 1981.

Mattoon, M. A. *Understanding Dreams.* (2nd ed.) Dallas: Spring Publications, 1984.

Maultsby, M. C., Jr. *Help Yourself to Happiness.* New York: Institute for Rational-Emotive Therapy, 1975.

Maultsby, M. C., Jr., and Ellis, A. *Techniques for Using Rational-Emotive Imagery.* New York: Institute for Rational-Emotive Therapy, 1974.

Maxissakalian, N. "Pharmacologic Treatment of Anxiety Disorders." *Journal of Clinical Psychiatry,* 1982, *43,* 487–491.

Medical Board, Karen Horney Clinic. "Guidelines for Identifying Therapeutic Modalities." *American Journal of Psychoanalysis,* 1981, *41* (3), 195–203.

Meichenbaum, D. *Cognitive-Behavior Modification.* New York: Plenum, 1977.

Meissner, W. W. *The Borderline Spectrum.* New York: Jason Aronson, 1984.

Melamed, S. *Behavioral Medicine Practical Applications in Health Care.* New York: Springer, 1980.

Melamed, S., and Shapiro, D. *Biofeedback and Behavioral Medicine.* New York: Aldine, 1973.

Miller, T. *So, You Secretly Suspect You're Worthless. Well, You're Not a Shit and I Can Prove It!* Manlius, N.Y.: Tom Miller, 1983.

Minear, V. "An Initial Venture in the Use of Television as a Medium for Psychodrama." *Group Psychotherapy,* 1953, *6,* 115–117.

Mintz, E. E. "Time-Extended Marathon Groups." *Psychotherapy: Theory, Research and Practice,* 1967, *2,* 65–70.

Mintz, E. E. "Marathon Groups: A Preliminary Investigation." *Journal of Contemporary Psychotherapy,* 1969, *2,* 91–94.

Mintz, E. E. *Marathon Groups: Reality and Symbol.* New York: Appleton-Century-Crofts, 1973.

Minuchin, S. *Families and Family Therapy.* Cambridge, Mass.: Harvard University Press, 1974.

Minuchin, S., and Fishman, H. C. *Family Therapy Techniques.* Cambridge, Mass.: Harvard University Press, 1981.

Minuchin, S., Rosman, B. L., and Baker, L. *Psychosomatic Families.* Cambridge, Mass.: Harvard University Press, 1978.

Modell, A. "The Ego and the Id: Fifty Years Later." *International Journal of Psychoanalysis,* 1975, *56,* 57–68.

Moore, B. E. "Frigidity in Women." *Journal of the American Psychoanalytic Association,* 1961, *9,* 571–584.

Moreno, F. B. "Psychodrama in the Neighborhood." *Sociatry,* 1947, *1,* 168–178.

Moreno, J. L. *Who Shall Survive?* Washington, D.C.: Nervous and Mental Disease Publishing Co., 1934.

Moreno, J. L. "Psychodramatic Shock Therapy." *Sociometry*, 1939, *2* (1).

Moreno, J. L. *Mental Catharsis and Psychodrama*. Psychodrama Monographs, no. 6. Beacon, N.Y.: Beacon House, 1940.

Moreno, J. L. "Spontaneity Procedures in Television Broadcasting." *Sociometry*, 1942, *5*, 7.

Moreno, J. L. "The Concept of Sociodrama: A New Approach to the Problem of Inter-Cultural Relations." *Sociometry*, 1943a, *6*, 434–449.

Moreno, J. L. "Sociometry and the Cultural Order." Sociometry Monographs, no. 2. Beacon, N.Y.: Beacon House, 1943b.

Moreno, J. L. "Psychodrama and Therapeutic Motion Pictures." *Sociometry*, 1944, *7*, 230–244.

Moreno, J. L. (ed.). *Group Psychotherapy: A Symposium*. Beacon, N.Y.: Beacon House, 1945.

Moreno, J. L. "Psychodrama and Group Psychotherapy." Paper presented at meeting of the American Psychiatric Association, Chicago, May 30, 1946.

Moreno, J. L. "Hypnodrama and Psychodrama." *Group Psychotherapy*, 1950, *3*, 1–10.

Moreno, J. L. *Sociometry, Experimental Method and the Science of Society*. Beacon, N.Y.: Beacon House, 1951.

Moreno, J. L. "Some Comments to the Trichotomy, Tele-Transference-Empathy." *Group Psychotherapy*, 1952, *5*, 87–90.

Moreno, J. L. *Who Shall Survive?* (Rev. and enl.) Beacon, N.Y.: Beacon House, 1953.

Moreno, J. L. (ed.). *Sociometry and the Science of Man*. Beacon, N.Y.: Beacon House, 1956.

Moreno, J. L. (ed.). *Psychodrama*. Vol. 2. Beacon, N.Y.: Beacon House, 1959.

Moreno, J. L. "Sociometric Choice Process in Personality and Group Formation." In J. L. Moreno (ed.), *The Sociometric Reader*. New York: Free Press, 1960.

Moreno, J. L. *Psychodrama*. Vol. 1. (Rev. ed.) Beacon, N.Y.: Beacon House, 1964.

Moreno, J. L. "Psychodrama." In S. Arieti (ed.), *American Handbook of Psychiatry*. Vol. 2. New York: Basic Books, 1965.

Moreno, J. L. *Psychodrama*. Vol. 3. Beacon, N.Y.: Beacon House, 1969.

Moreno, J. L., and Toeman, Z. "The Group Approach in Psychodrama." *Sociometry*, 1942, *5*, 191–194.

Moreno, Z. T. "A Survey of Psychodramatic Techniques." *Group Psychotherapy*, 1959, *12*, 5–14.

Mosak, H. H. "Adlerian Psychotherapy." In R. J. Corsini (ed.), *Current Psychotherapies*. (2nd ed.) Itasca, Ill.: Peacock, 1979.

Mosak, H. H., and Shulman, B. H. *Individual Psychotherapy I: A. Syllabus*. Chicago: Alfred Adler Institute, 1974.

Nagy, I. B., and Spark, G. *Invisible Loyalties*. New York: Harper & Row, 1973.

Nattland, C. Unpublished paper for Introduction to Group Psychotherapy course, Graduate School of Applied and Professional Psychology, Rutgers University, 1983.

Obler, M. "Systematic Desensitization in Sexual Disorders." *Journal of Behavioral Therapy and Experimental Psychology*, 1973, *4*, 92–102.

Office of Strategic Services Assessment Staff. *Assessment of Men*. New York: Holt, Rinehart and Winston, 1948.

Olson, D. H. "Marital and Family Therapy: A Critical Overview." In A. S. Gurman and D. G. Rice (eds.), *Couples in Conflict*. New York: Jason Aronson, 1975.

Olton, D., and Noonberg, A. *Biofeedback: Clinical Applications in Behavioral Medicine*. Englewood Cliffs, N.J.: Prentice-Hall, 1980.

Olton, N. *Clinical Applications in Behavioral Medicine*. Englewood Cliffs, N.J.: Prentice-Hall, 1980.

Ormont, J. "Analysis of the Analyst's Wife." *New York Times Magazine*, November 12, 1961.

Ormont, L. "The Resolution of Resistances by Conjoint Psychoanalysis." *Psychoanalytic Review*, 1964, *51* (3), 89–101.

Ormont, L. "Principles and Practice of Conjoint Psychoanalytic Treatment." *American Journal of Psychiatry*, 1981, *138*, 69–73.

Ormont, L., and Strean, H. *The Practice of Conjoint Treatment*. New York: Behavioral Sciences Press, 1978.

Orne, M. T. "Hypnosis, Motivation and the Ecological Validity of the Psychological Experiment." In W. J. Arnold and M. M. Page (eds.), *Nebraska Symposium on Motivation*. Vol. 18. Lincoln: University of Nebraska Press, 1970.

Ornstein, A. "The Dread to Repeat and the New Beginning." *Annual of Psychoanalysis*, 1974, *2*, 231–248.

Owen, S. M., Toomin, H., and Taylor, L. P. *Biofeedback in Neuromuscular Re-Education: History, Uses, Procedures*. Los Angeles: Biofeedback Research Institute, 1975.

Palazzoli, M. S., and others. *Paradox and Counter-Paradox*. New York: Jason Aronson, 1978.

Pancheri, P. *Biofeedback: tecniche di autocontrollo in psichiatria, psicosomatica e medicine*. Rome: Bulzoni, 1979.

Papp, P. "The Greek Chorus and Other Techniques of Family Therapy." *Family Process*, 1980, *19*, 45–57.

Papp, P. *The Process of Change*. New York: Guilford Press, 1983.

Paul, H. "Horneyan Developmental Psychoanalytic Theory and Its Application to the Treatment of the Young." *American Journal of Psychoanalysis*, 1984, *44* (1), 59–73.

Paul, N. "Cross-Confrontation." In P. J. Guerin (ed.), *Family Therapy*. New York: Gardner Press, 1976.

Paykel, E. S., and others. "Response to Phenelzine and Amitriptyline in Subtypes of Outpatient Depression." *Archives of General Psychiatry*, 1982, *39*, 1041–1049.

Peper, E., and others (eds.). *Mind-Body Integration: Essential Readings in Biofeedback*. New York: Plenum, 1978.

Peper, E., and Williams, E. A. *From the Inside Out: A Self-Teaching and Laboratory Manual for Biofeedback*. New York: Plenum, 1981.

Perkins, F. T., and Wheeler, R. H. "Configurational Learning in the Goldfish." *Comparative Psychology Monographs*, 1930, *7*, 1–50.

Phadke, K. "Some Innovations in RET Theory and Practice." *Rational Living*, 1980, *17* (2), 25–30.

Phelps, S., and Austin, N. *The Assertive Woman*. San Luis Obispo, Calif.: Impact, 1975.

Piaget, J. *The Child's Conception of the World*. Paterson, N.J.: Littlefield-Adams, 1960.

Pollock, G. "Mourning and Adaptation." *International Journal of Psychoanalysis*, 1961, *42*, 341–361.

Pomerleau, B. *Behavioral Medicine: Theory Practice.* Baltimore, Md.: Williams & Wilkins, 1979.

Racker, H. *Transference and Countertransference.* New York: International Universities Press, 1968.

Rangell, L. "The Nature of Conversion." *Journal of the American Psychoanalytic Association,* 1959, *7,* 632–662.

Rangell, L. "The Psychoanalytic Process." *International Journal of Psychoanalysis,* 1968, *49,* 19–26.

Rangell, L. "Contemporary Issues in the Theory of Therapy." *Journal of the American Psychoanalytic Association,* 1979, *27* (Suppl.), 81–112.

Rank, O. *Will Therapy* and *Truth and Reality.* New York: Knopf, 1945.

Rathus, S. A. "A Thirty-Item Schedule for Assessing Assertive Behavior." *Behavior Therapy,* 1973, *4,* 39–406.

Ray, W. J., and others. *Evaluation of Clinical Biofeedback.* New York: Plenum, 1979.

Redl, F. "Group Emotion and Leadership." *Psychiatry,* 1942, *5,* 573–596.

Reik, T. *Ritual: Four Psychoanalytic Studies.* (D. Bryan, trans.) New York: Grove Press, 1962.

Richter-Heinrich, E., and Miller, N. E. *Biofeedback: Basic Problems in Clinical Applications.* Amsterdam: Elsevier North-Holland, 1982.

Rickels, K. "Benzodiazepines in the Treatment of Anxiety." *American Journal of Psychotherapy,* 1982, *36,* 358–370.

Rickles, W. H., and others (eds.). *Biofeedback and Family Practice Medicine.* New York: Plenum, 1983.

Rinsley, D. B. *Treatment of the Severely Disturbed Adolescent.* New York: Jason Aronson, 1980.

Rogers, C. R. *Client-Centered Therapy.* Boston: Houghton Mifflin, 1951.

Rogers, C. R. "A Theory of Therapy, Personality and Interpersonal Relationships as Developed in the Client-Centered Framework." In S. Koch (ed.), *Psychology: A Study of a Science.* Vol. 3: *Formulations of the Person and the Social Context.* New York: McGraw-Hill, 1959.

Rogers, C. R. *On Becoming a Person.* Boston: Houghton Mifflin, 1961.

Rogers, C. R. *Carl Rogers on Encounter Groups.* New York: Harper & Row, 1970.

Rogers, C. R. "Client-Centered Psychotherapy." In H. I. Kaplan, B. J. Sadock, and A. M. Freedman (eds.), *The Comprehensive Textbook of Psychiatry III.* Baltimore, Md.: Williams & Wilkins, 1980.

Rokeach, M. *The Three Christs of Ypsilanti: A Narrative Study of Three Lost Men.* New York: Knopf, 1964.

Rosen, V. "The Reconstruction of a Traumatic Childhood Event in a Case of Derealization." *Journal of the American Psychoanalytic Association,* 1955, *3,* 211–221.

Rosenbaum, M. "Group Psychotherapy and Psychodrama." In B. B. Wolman (ed.), *Handbook of Clinical Psychology.* New York: McGraw-Hill, 1965.

Rosenbaum, M., Franks, C., and Jaffe, S. (eds.). *Perspectives on Behavior Therapy in the Eighties.* New York: Springer, 1983.

Rosenthal, H. M. "On Early Alienation from the Self." *American Journal of Psychoanalysis,* 1983, *43* (3), 231–241.

Rossi, E. (ed.). *Collected Papers of Milton H. Erickson.* New York: Halsted Press, 1980.

Rowan, J. "Encounter Group Research: No Joy?" *Journal of Humanistic Psychology,* 1975, *15,* 19–28.

Rubin, I. "Sex and Aging in Man and Woman." In C. E. Vincent (ed.), *Human*

Sexuality in Medical Education and Practice. Springfield, Ill.: Thomas, 1968.

Rudhyar, E. F., and Branham, B. "The Development of a Psychodrama Department in a Mental Hospital." *Group Psychotherapy*, 1953, *6*, 110–114.

Russell, E. "The Facts About Encounter Groups: First Facts." *Journal of Clinical Psychology*, 1978, *34* (1), 130–137.

Rutan, J. S., and Stone, E. *Psychodynamic Group Psychotherapy.* New York: Wiley, 1984.

Sager, C. J. "The Development of Marriage Therapy—an Historical Review." *American Journal of Orthopsychiatry*, 1966a, *36*, 458–466.

Sager, C. J. "The Treatment of Married Couples." In S. Arieti (ed.), *American Handbook of Psychiatry.* Vol. 3. New York: Basic Books, 1966b.

Sager, C. J., and others. "The Marriage Contract." *Family Process*, 1971, *10*, 311. Also in C. J. Sager and H. S. Kaplan (eds.), *Progress in Group and Family Therapy.* New York: Brunner/Mazel, 1972.

Sager, C. J. *Marriage Contracts and Couples Therapy.* New York: Brunner/Mazel, 1976.

Salter, A. *Conditioned Reflex Therapy.* New York: Creative Age, 1949.

Sandler, J., Dare, C., and Holder, A. *The Patient and the Analyst.* London: Allen & Unwin, 1973.

Sandler, J., and Sandler, A. "On the Development of Object Relationships and Affects." *International Journal of Psychoanalysis*, 1978, *59*, 285–296.

Schachter, S., and Singer, J. E. "Cognitive, Social and Physiological Determinants of Emotional State." *Psychological Review*, 1962, *69*, 379–399.

Schafer, R. *A New Language for Psychoanalysis.* New Haven, Conn.: Yale University Press, 1976.

Schauer, G. "The Function of an Audience Analyst in Psychodrama." *Group Psychotherapy*, 1952, *5* (4), 197–205.

Scheidlinger, S. "On Scapegoating in Group Psychotherapy." *International Journal of Group Psychotherapy*, 1985, *33*, 131–144.

Schutz, W. C. *Joy: Expanding Human Awareness.* New York: Grove Press, 1973.

Schutz, W. C. *Elements of Encounter.* New York: Irvington, 1982.

Schutz, W. *The Truth Option.* Berkeley, Calif.: Ten Speed Press, 1984.

Schwaber, E. "Narcissism, Self Psychology, and the Listening Perspective." *Annual of Psychoanalysis*, 1981, *9*, 115–132.

Schwartz, E. K., and Wolf, A. "On Countertransference in Group Psychotherapy." *Journal of Psychology*, 1963, *57*, 131.

Schwartz, G. E., and Beatty, J. (eds.). *Biofeedback, Theory and Research.* Orlando, Fla.: Academic Press, 1977.

Searles, H. F. "The Place of the Neutral Therapist Response in Psychotherapy with the Schizophrenic Patient." In H. F. Searles (ed.), *Collected Papers on Schizophrenia and Related Subjects.* New York: International Universities Press, 1965.

Searles, H. F. *Countertransference and Related Subjects.* New York: International Universities Press, 1979a.

Searles, H. F. "The Countertransference with the Borderline Patient." In J. Leboit and A. Capponi (eds.), *Advances in Psychotherapy of the Borderline Patient.* New York: Jason Aronson, 1979b.

Shapiro, D., and others (eds.). *Biofeedback and Behavioral Medicine: Therapeutic Applications and Experimental Foundations, 1979–1980.* Hawthorne, N.Y.: Aldine, 1981.

Shapiro, E. R. "The Psychodynamics and Developmental Psychology of the Borderline Patient: A Review of the Literature." *American Journal of Psychiatry*, 1978, *135*, 1305–1315.

Sheets, P. H. "Sociodrama as an Aid to Large Group Communication." *Sociatry*, 1948, *4*, 431–435.

Shneidman, E. S. *Voices of Death.* New York: Harper & Row, 1980.

Shulman, B. H. "The Adlerian Theory of Dreams." In M. Kramer and others (eds.), *Dream Psychology and the New Biology of Dreaming.* Springfield, Ill.: Thomas, 1969.

Sifneos, P. *Short-Term Psychotherapy and Emotional Crisis.* Cambridge, Mass.: Harvard University Press, 1972.

Sifneos, P. "Short-Term Anxiety-Provoking Psychotherapy." In H. Davanloo (ed.), *Basic Principles and Techniques in Short-Term Dynamic Psychotherapy.* New York: Spectrum, 1978.

Simkin, J. S. "Gestalt Psychotherapy." In D. Bannister (ed.), *Issues and Approaches in the Psychological Therapies.* London: Wiley, 1975a.

Simkin, J. S. "An Introduction to Gestalt Therapy." In F. D. Stephenson (ed.), *Gestalt Therapy Primer: Introductory Readings in Gestalt Therapy.* Springfield, Ill.: Thomas, 1975b.

Simkin, J. S. "The Development of Gestalt Therapy." In C. Hatcher and P. Himelstein (eds.), *The Handbook of Gestalt Therapy.* New York: Jason Aronson, 1976a.

Simkin, J. S. *Gestalt Therapy Mini-Lectures.* Millbrae, Calif.: Celestial Arts, 1976b.

Simkin, J. S. "Gestalt Therapy in Groups." In G. M. Gazda (ed.), *Basic Approaches to Group Psychotherapy and Group Counseling.* (3rd ed.) Springfield, Ill.: Thomas, 1982.

Simkin, J. S., and Yontef, G. M. "Gestalt Therapy." In J. C. Raymond and Contributors, *Current Psychotherapies.* (3rd ed.) Itasca, Ill.: Peacock, 1984.

Singer, J. *Boundaries of the Soul.* Garden City, N.Y.: Doubleday, 1972.

Skinner, B. F. *Science and Human Behavior.* New York: Macmillan, 1953.

Slowik, O. J. "Two Trials with Rehearsed Psychodrama." *International Journal of Social Psychiatry*, 1958, *3*, 286–298.

Sluzki, C. E. "Marital Therapy from a Systems Theory Perspective." In T. Paolino, Jr., and B. McCrady (eds.), *Marriage and Marital Therapy.* New York: Brunner/Mazel, 1978.

Smith, M. L., Glass, G. V., and Miller, T. *The Benefits of Psychotherapy.* Baltimore, Md.: Johns Hopkins University Press, 1980.

Socarides, D., and Stolorow, R. "Affects and Selfobjects." *Annual of Psychoanalysis*, 1984/1985, *12*, forthcoming.

Sovak, M., and Stiefvater, E. W. *Migrane-Therapie: Biofeedback Akupunktur.* Heidelberg: Haug, 1975.

Spiegel, H. "Is Symptom Removal Dangerous?" *American Journal of Psychiatry*, 1967, *123*, 1279–1283.

Spiegel, J. *Transactions.* New York: Jason Aronson, 1971.

Spitz, M. *The First Year of Life: A Psychoanalytic Study of Normal and Deviant Development of Object Relations.* New York: International Universities Press, 1965.

Spotnitz, H. *Psychotherapy of Preoedipal Conditions.* New York: Jason Aronson, 1976.

Stanton, M. D. "Strategic Approaches to Family Therapy." In A. S. Gurman and D. P. Kniskern (eds.), *Handbook of Family Therapy.* New York: Brunner/Mazel, 1981.

Starr, A. *Psychodrama.* Chicago: Nelson-Hall, 1977.

Stein, A., and Kibel, H. D. "A Group Dynamic-Peer Interaction Approach to Group Psychotherapy." *International Journal of Group Psychotherapy*, 1984, *34*, 315–333.

Stein, M. (ed.). *Jungian Analysis.* LaSalle, Ill.: Open Court, 1982.

Steiner, C. *Scripts People Live*. New York: Grove Press, 1974.

Steiner, C., and Cassidy, W. "Therapeutic Contracts in Group Treatment." *Transactional Analysis Bulletin*, 1969, *8*, 29.

Sterba, R. "The Fate of the Ego in Psychoanalytic Therapy." *International Journal of Psychoanalysis*, 1934, *15*, 117–126.

Stern, R. M., and Ray, W. J. *Biofeedback: Potential and Limits*. Lincoln: University of Nebraska Press, 1980.

Stolorow, R. "Self Psychology—a Structural Psychology." In J. Lichtenberg and S. Kaplan (eds.), *Reflections on Self Psychology*. Hillsdale, N.J.: Analytic Press, 1983.

Stolorow, R., and Lachmann, F. *Psychoanalysis of Developmental Arrests*. New York: International Universities Press, 1980.

Stolorow, R., and Lachmann, F. "Transference: The Future of an Illusion." *Annual of Psychoanalysis*, 1984/1985, *12*, forthcoming.

Stone, L. "Notes on the Noninterpretive Elements in the Psychoanalytic Situation and Process." *Journal of the American Psychoanalytic Association*, 1981, *29*, 89–118.

Stoyva, J. (ed.), *Biofeedback and Self-Control: An Aldine Annual on the Regulation of Bodily Processes and Consciousness*. Hawthorne, N.Y.: Aldine, 1972.

Strauss, E. W. *Psychiatry and Philosophy*. New York: Springer-Verlag, 1969.

Strean, H. *Resolving Resistances in Psychotherapy*. New York: Wiley, 1985.

Strupp, H., and Hadley, S. W. "Specific Versus Non-Specific Factors in Psychotherapy." *Archives of General Psychiatry*, 1979, *36*, 1125–1126.

Sullivan, H. S. *Conceptions of Modern Psychiatry*. New York: Norton, 1940.

Sullivan, H. S. *The Interpersonal Theory of Psychiatry*. New York: Norton, 1953.

Sullivan, H. S. *Clinical Studies in Psychiatry*. New York: Norton, 1956.

Sutherland, J. D. "Notes on Psychoanalytic Group Therapy: I. Therapy and Training." *Psychiatry*, 1952, *15*, 111–117.

Tauber, E., and Green, M. *Prelogical Experience*. New York: Basic Books, 1959.

Tillich, P. *Systematic Theology*. Vol. 1. Chicago: University of Chicago Press, 1951.

Tillich, P. *The Courage to Be*. New Haven, Conn.: Yale University Press, 1952.

Toeman, Z. "Role Analysis and Audience Structure." *Sociometry*, 1944, *7*, 204–221.

Toeman, Z. "Clinical Psychodrama: Auxiliary Ego, Double and Mirror Technique." *Sociometry*, 1946, *9*, 178–183.

Torrance, E. P. "Psychodramatic Methods in the College." In P. B. Haas (ed.), *Psychodrama and Sociodrama in American Education*. Beacon, N.Y.: Beacon House, 1949.

Torrance, E. P., and Mason, R. "The Indigenous Leader in Changing Attitudes and Behavior." *International Journal of Sociometry*, 1956, *1*, 23–28.

Turkle, S. *Psychoanalytic Politics*. New York: Basic Books, 1978.

Umansky, A. L. "Psychodrama and the Audience." *Sociometry*, 1944, *7*, 179–189.

van den Daele, L. "The Self-Psychologies of Heinz Kohut and Karen Horney: A Comparative Examination." *American Journal of Psychoanalysis*, 1981, *41* (4), 327–337.

Van Patten, T., May, P. R. A., and Marder, S. R. "Subjective Response to Antipsychotic Drugs." *Archives of General Psychiatry*, 1981, *38*, 187–190.

Vogeler, E. J., Jr., and Greenberg, I. A. "Psychodrama and Audience, with Emphasis on Closed-Circuit Television." *Group Psychotherapy*, 1968, *21* (1), 4–11.

Von Bozzay, G. D. *Projects in Biofeedback: A Text Workbook*. Dubuque, Iowa: Kendall/Hunt, 1984.

Waelder, R. "Psychoanalysis, Scientific Method, and Philosophy." *Journal of the American Psychoanalytic Association*, 1962, *10*, 617–637.

Walen, S., DiGiuseppe, R., and Wessler, R. *A Practitioner's Guide to Rational-Emotive Therapy*. New York: Oxford University Press, 1980.

Wallerstein, R. "Reconstruction and Mastery in the Transference Psychosis." *Journal of the American Psychoanalytic Association*, 1967, *15*, 551–583.

Wallerstein, R. "Psychoanalysis and Psychotherapy (the Relationships of Psychoanalysis to Psychotherapy: Current Issues)." *International Journal of Psychoanalysis*, 1969, *50*, 117–126.

Walsh, R. N. "Psychotherapy as Perceptual Training." *American Theosophist*, 1984, *72*, 171–175.

Warren, M. "Psychological Effects of Parental Suicide in Surviving Children." *Excerpta Medica*, 1966, Series 117, 433.

Watson, J. B., and Rayner, R. "Conditioned Emotional Reactions." *Journal of Experimental Psychology*, 1920, *3*, 1–9.

Watzlawick, P., Weakland, J., and Fisch, R. *Change*. New York: Norton, 1974.

Way, L. *Adler's Place in Psychology*. New York: Collier, 1962.

Weinberg, G. *The Heart of Psychotherapy*. New York: St. Martin's Press, 1984.

Weinshel, E. "Some Observations on Not Telling the Truth." *Journal of the American Psychoanalytic Association*, 1979, *27*, 503–531.

Weissman, M. M. "The Psychological Treatment of Depression: Evidence for the Efficacy of Psychotherapy Alone, in Comparison with, and in Combination with Pharmacotherapy." *Archives of General Psychiatry*, 1979, *36*, 1261–1269.

Weitzenhoffer, A. M. *General Techniques of Hypnotism*. Orlando, Fla.: Grune & Stratton, 1957.

Wentworth-Rohr, I. *Symptom Reduction Through Clinical Biofeedback*. New York: Human Sciences Press, 1984.

Wessler, R. A., and Wessler, R. L. *The Principles and Practice of Rational-Emotive Therapy*. San Francisco: Jossey-Bass, 1980.

Wexberg, E. *Individual Psychology*. New York: Cosmopolitan, 1929.

Whatmore, G. B., and Kohli, D. R. *The Physiopathology and Treatment of Functional Disorders*. Orlando, Fla.: Grune & Stratton, 1974.

Wheeler, B. I. *Dionysos and Immortality*. Boston: Houghton Mifflin, 1899.

Wheeler, R. H., and Perkins, F. T. *Principles of Mental Development*. New York: Crowell, 1932.

Whitaker, C. "A Family Is a Four Dimensional Relationship." In P. J. Guerin (ed.), *Family Therapy*. New York: Gardner Press, 1976.

White, L., and Tursky, B. (eds.). *Clinical Biofeedback: Efficacy and Mechanisms*. New York: Guilford Press, 1982.

Whitmont, E. C. *The Symbolic Quest: Basic Concepts of Jungian Psychology*. Princeton, N.J.: Princeton University Press, 1978.

Who's Who in America. Vol. 34, 1966–67. Chicago: Marquis, 1966.

Wickramasekera, I. (ed.). *Biofeedback, Behavior Therapy, and Hypnosis: Potentiating the Verbal Control of Behavior for Clinicians*. New York: Nelson-Hall, 1976.

Wildgruber, C. *Biofeedback und Angstbewaltigung: e. vergl. Studie zur Therapie sozialer Angste*. Frankfurt, Bern, Las Vegas: Lang, 1979.

Wing, J. W., Cooper, J. E., and Sartorius, N. *The Management and Classification of Psychiatric Symptoms*. London: Cambridge University Press, 1974.

Winnicott, D. "The Theory of the Parent-Infant Relationship." *International Journal of Psychoanalysis*, 1960, *41*, 585–595.

Winnicott, D. *The Maturational Processes and the Facilitating Environment*. New York: International Universities Press, 1965a.

Winnicott, D. "Ego Distortions in Terms of True and False Self." In D. Winnicott (ed.), *The Maturational Processes and the Facilitating Environment*. New York: International Universities Press, 1965b.

Winnicott, D. "The Mentally Ill in Your Case Load." In D. Winnicott (ed.), *The Maturational Processes and the Facilitating Environment*. New York: International Universities Press, 1965c.

Wolberg, L. R. *Medical Hypnosis*. Orlando, Fla.: Grune & Stratton, 1948.

Wolberg, L. R. *Hypnoanalysis*. (2nd ed.) Orlando, Fla.: Grune & Stratton, 1964.

Wolberg, L. R. "Hypnoanalysis." In B. B. Wolman (ed.), *Psychoanalytic Techniques*. New York: Basic Books, 1967.

Wolberg, L. R. *Handbook of Short-Term Psychotherapy*. New York: Thieme-Stratton, 1980.

Wolf, A. "The Psychoanalysis of Groups." *American Journal of Psychotherapy*, 1949, *3*, 525–558, and 1950, *4*, 16–50.

Wolf, A. "Discussion of 'Psychic Structure and Therapy of Latent Schizophrenia' by Gustave Byschowski." In A. Rifkin (ed.), *Psychoanalytic Office Practice*. Orlando, Fla.: Grune & Stratton, 1957.

Wolf, A. "Psychoanalysis in Groups." In H. I. Kaplan and B. J. Sadock (eds.), *Comprehensive Group Psychotherapy II*. Baltimore, Md.: Wiliams & Wilkins, 1980.

Wolf, A., and Kutash, I. L. "Book Review of 'Psychoanalytic Group Dynamics.'" *Journal of the American Academy of Psychoanalysis*, 1982, *10* (4), 632–635.

Wolf, A., and Kutash, I. L. "Psychoanalysis in Groups: Creativity in Di-Egophrenia." *Group*, 1984, *8* (1), 12–22.

Wolf, A., and Kutash, I. L. "Di-Egophrenia and Its Treatment Through Psychoanalysis in Groups." *International Journal of Group Psychotherapy*, 1985, *35* (4), 519–530.

Wolf, A., and Schwartz, E. K. *Psychoanalysis in Groups*. Orlando, Fla.: Grune & Stratton, 1962.

Wolf, A., and Schwartz, E. K. "Psychoanalysis in Groups." In H. I. Kaplan and B. J. Sadock (eds.), *Comprehensive Group Psychotherapy*. Baltimore, Md.: Williams & Wilkins, 1971.

Wolpe, J. *Psychotherapy by Reciprocal Inhibition*. Stanford, Calif.: Stanford University Press, 1958.

Wolpe, J. *The Practice of Behavior Therapy*. New York: Pergamon Press, 1969.

Wolpe, J., and Lazarus, A. A. *Behavior Therapy Techniques: A Guide to the Treatment of Neuroses*. New York: Pergamon Press, 1966.

Wolstein, B. *Theory of Psychoanalytic Therapy*. Orlando, Fla.: Grune & Stratton, 1967.

Yablonsky, L. *The Tunnel Back*. New York: Macmillan, 1965.

Yablonsky, L. *Psychodrama: Resolving Emotional Problems Through Role-Playing*. New York: Gardner Press, 1981.

Yablonsky, L., and Enneis, J. M. "Psychodrama Theory and Practice." In F. Fromm-Reichmann and J. L. Moreno (eds.), *Progress in Psychotherapy*. Vol. 1. Orlando, Fla.: Grune & Stratton, 1956.

Yalom, I. D. *The Theory and Practice of Group Psychotherapy*. New York: Basic Books, 1975.

Yalom, I. D. *Existential Psychotherapy.* New York: Basic Books, 1980.

Yates, A. J. *Biofeedback and the Modification of Behavior.* New York: Plenum, 1980.

Zetzel, E. R. "A Developmental Approach to the Borderline Patient." *American Journal of Psychiatry*, 1971, *127*, 867–871.

Zitrin, C. M., and others. "Treatment of Phobias. Part 1: Comparison of Imipramine Hydrochloride and Placebo." *Archives of General Psychiatry*, 1983, *40*, 125–138.

Name Index ✌

Subject Index 🙦

A

Ackerman group, 492, 493

Acting out: in conjoint therapy, 427; in diegophrenia, 33, 40; in psychoanalysis, 7; and psychoanalysis in groups, 342

Active Imagination, in Jungian analysis, 131, 140–141

Adaptation, in ego psychology, 56

Adlerian psychotherapy: approach of, 101–123; and changes, direction of, 113–114, 117–119, 123; dreams in, 108–109; family constellation in, 105–107; first months of, 103–109; and freedom from symptoms, 102, 103; goals of, 123; humor in, 109–111, 117, 118, 121, 122; initial interview in, 101–103; initial phase of, 107–108; interpretation in, 112, 120–121; one year after, 109–119; recollections in, 106, 113–114, 121; repetition compulsion in, 119–122; resistance in, 111, 114–117, 123; and social interest, 114, 123; structured interview technique in, 104–107; summary of, 122–123; therapeutic relationship in, 114, 122

Affect theory, and self psychology, 45–46

Alcoholics Anonymous, 150

Ambivalence, in psychoanalytic psychotherapy, 39–40

American Board of Examiners in Psychodrama, Sociometry and Group Psychotherapy, 412

American Society for Group Psychotherapy and Psychodrama, 412

Amoxapine (Ascendin), in psychopharmacology, 320–321, 322

Analyst: attention of, in Horney's technique, 145–146; as coexplorer, in Gestalt therapy, 209–210, 211, 217, 221; male and female, for group psychoanalysis, 351–352; pres-

ence of, 223; in self psychology, 44; transference and countertransference of, in psychoanalytic groups, 345–346

Analytic stance: in Adlerian psychotherapy, 123; in interpersonal psychoanalysis, 164; in psychoanalysis, 4; in psychoanalytic group, 335; in psychoanalytic psychotherapy, 34; in self psychology, 43–44

Animus/anima, in Jungian analysis, 127–128, 132, 134, 140

Antianxiety drugs, in psychopharmacology, 312, 316

Anticholinergic drugs, in psychopharmacology, 314–315, 318

Antidepressant drugs: and cognitive-behavioral sex therapy, 266; in psychopharmacology, 312, 319, 320, 322, 326

Antipsychotic drugs: and behavior modification, 261; in psychopharmacology, 312, 317–319, 322–323, 325, 326, 327

Anxiety: and cognitive-behavioral sex therapy, 264, 275; equilibrium-disequilibrium theory of, 333–334; in interpersonal psychoanalysis, 161–162, 163–164, 171–172, 175–176; in mother/infant dyad, 60–61; rational-emotive therapy for, 279–287

Aprazolam (Xanax), in psychopharmacology, 316

Archetypes, in Jungian analysis, 126, 130, 133, 138

Ascendin, in psychopharmacology, 320–321, 322

Aspirin, for Raynaud's disease, 293

Assertiveness, and behavior modification, 248, 249, 250, 252, 256–257

Assessment, for behavior modification, 243–244, 247, 254–255, 256–257, 261

Associations. *See* Free association

Awareness, in Gestalt therapy, 209–221

view in, 224–225; and presence, 222–223, 226–231, 233–235; summary of, 236; theoretical background of, 222–223

Existentialism, and Gestalt therapy, 219–221

Experience of feelings, in client-centered therapy, 200, 202, 203, 205–206, 208

Externalization, in Horney's technique, 153, 154, 156

Extroversion/introversion attitudes, in Jungian theory, 126–127

F

Family-of-origin sessions: and couples group, 466–470; and family therapy, 458; resistance to, 466–467

Family systems and marital therapies: approaches of, 437–507; in couples group with family-of-origin sessions, 460–472; family approach to, 439–459; with marriage contracts, 473–488; overview of, 437–438; principle of, 437; strategic psychotherapy as, 489–507

Family therapy: approach of, 439–459; boundary in, 442–443, 448, 449, 454; case materials for, 439–459; couple sessions in, 454–459; dyads in, 445, 446; and family-of-origin, 458; family sessions in, 441–454; hierarchy in, 439, 442, 446, 448; hypotheses in, 446, 448, 449, 453; identified patient in, 440–441, 442; individual sessions in, 439–440; initial interview in, 441–446; paradoxical intervention in, 450–452; segments in, 443–444; system concept in, 439; termination of, 458–459

Fantasy: in encounter groups, 374–376; in existential analysis, 193

Federation of Trainers and Training Programs in Psychodrama, 412

Feelings: experience of, in client-centered therapy, 200, 202, 203, 205–206, 208; in Horney's technique, 147, 151, 155–156

Fluphenazine decanoate (prolixin decanoate), in psychopharmacology, 323

Free association: in existential analysis, 188; in Horney's technique, 146–147, 150, 152–153, 154; and hypnoanalysis, 303–307, 309; and interpersonal psychoanalysis, 162–163; in psychoanalysis, 3–4, 10–11, 17; in psychoanalytic groups, 436

Functions, in Jungian analysis, 127, 132, 139

G

Galvanic skin response (GSR), and biofeedback, 289, 290, 291, 294, 296

Gestalt therapy: approach of, 209–221; awareness in, 209–221; case materials for, 209–

219; and change, 210, 216, 219, 220–221; commentary on, 217–221; congruence in, 217; theoretical background of, 219–221; therapist as coexplorer in, 209–210, 211, 217, 221

Goals: of Adlerian Psychotherapy, 123; of behavior modification, 244, 247–249, 250, 252, 255, 257–258; of ego psychology, 66; of Jungian analysis, 124; of psychoanalysis, 24

Group therapies: approaches of, 329–435; conjoint, 424–435; with couples, 460–472; encounter, 364–377; family-of-origin sessions in, 460–472; ingredients of, 332; integrated approach to, 353–363; marathon, 378–391; overview of, 329–331; psychoanalytic, 332–352; psychodrama as, 392–412; in rational-emotive therapy, 285; transactional analysis as, 413–423

Growth movements. *See* Marathon groups

Guilt, survivor, and psychoanalysis, 15–16

H

Haloperidol (Haldol), in psychopharmacology, 316, 322–323

Hamilton Depression Interview, 254

Headaches: biofeedback for, 291–292; and Jungian analysis, 131–134; migraine, strategic psychotherapy for, 504–507

Hierarchy: in family therapy, 439, 442, 446, 448; and strategic psychotherapy, 492–493, 496, 499; of values, in ego psychotherapy, 64

Homework, in biofeedback, 291, 292, 293, 295

Homosexual impulses: and ego psychology, 58; and interpersonal psychoanalysis, 165–170; and psychoanalysis, 9, 11, 12

Horney's psychoanalytic technique: approach of, 144–158; attention of analyst in, 145–146; case materials for, 148–158; dreams in, 147–148, 150–151, 153, 154, 156; externalization in, 153, 154, 156; feelings in, 147, 151, 155–156; free association in, 146–147, 150, 152–153, 154; interpretation in, 151–152; projection in, 151, 156; resistance in, 147; and termination, 157–158; theoretical background of, 144–148; therapeutic alliance in, 149, 151, 154; transference in, 148, 153, 155, 156

Humanistic psychology: approaches of, 195–236; client-centered, 197–208; existential, 222–236; Gestalt, 209–221; overview of, 195–196

Humor: in Adlerian psychotherapy, 109–111, 117, 118, 121, 122; in rational-emotive therapy, 283–284

L

Librium, in psychopharmacology, 316
Lies: function of, 10; in psychoanalysis, 5, 6–7, 8–10, 11, 12, 16, 17, 18–19
Lithium carbonate, in psychopharmacology, 312, 318, 319, 324–327
Locke-Wallace Marital Happiness Scale, 273, 274

M

Marathon groups: approach of, 378–391; encounter games in, 389–390; group stratagems in, 386–388; initial phase of, 381–382; intimacy in, 383–384; participant selection for, 379–381; and peak experiences, 390–391; phases of, 382–383; role-playing in, 385–386; socializing influence of, 384–386; termination of, 390; theoretical background of, 378–379; transference in, 384; values of, 391
Marital Adjustment Test, 254
Marital therapies. See Family systems and marital therapies
Marriage contracts: applicability of, 475–477; approach of, 473–488; case materials for, 477–488; and dissolution of marriage, 476; and dreams, 479–480; follow-up on, 486–487; individual, 473–474, 480–483; initial interview for, 477–479; interpretations in, 474, 475; middle phase of, 479–486; projected, 484–486; single, 486, 487–488; terms in, 474, 483
Maternal depression: and interpersonal psychoanalysis, 165, 166; and psychoanalysis, 8, 9, 12, 13–14; and self psychology, 48, 49–50, 53
Medical Board, Karen Horney Clinic, 145, 524
Mental Research Institute (MRI), 492, 493
Milan group, 492, 493
Monoamine oxidase inhibitors (MAOIs), in psychopharmacology, 312, 321, 327
Mother/infant dyad: anxiety in, 60–61; communication in, 61–62; and ego development, 57–58; frustration in, 59–60. See also Maternal depression

N

Narcissistic personality disorders, and self psychology, 44
Nardil, in psychopharmacology, 316, 321, 322
National Training Laboratories (NTL), 364, 365
Negative tranference reaction, and ego psychology, 59
Neo-Freudian and non-Freudian analytic therapies: Adlerian, 101–123; approaches of, 99–193; existential, 177–193; Horney's, 144–158; interpersonal, 159–176; Jungian, 124–143; overview of, 99–100
Neuroleptic drug, and behavior modification, 253, 256, 257, 258, 261
Neuroleptization, in psychopharmacology, 322, 323–324
Neurosis: as purposive, to Jungians, 125–126, 137; vicious cycles of, 145
Neurotic process, and short-term dynamic psychotherapy, 83–98
Neutrality: in psychoanalysis, 4; in psychoanalytic psychotherapy, 34, 35, 36, 38, 40, 41
Nomifensine, in psychopharmacology, 321, 322
Nontricyclic antidepressants, in psychopharmacology, 321, 322
Nonverbal behavior, in psychoanalysis, 6–7
Norpramin, in psychopharmacology, 314, 315–316, 320, 322

O

Object loss, and psychoanalysis, 6–17
Object relations, and psychoanalytic psychotherapy, 25
Obsessions, strategic psychotherapy for, 497–501
Oedipal issues: and psychoanalysis, 7, 10, 11–12, 13, 14, 19, 20; and short-term dynamic psychotherapy, 81. See also Preoedipal issues
Office of Strategic Services Assessment Staff, 525
Open encounter. See Encounter groups
Oregon Sex Inventory, 273, 274, 275

P

Panic attacks, psychopharmacology for, 315–316
Paradox: in family therapy, 450–452; in strategic psychotherapy, 491–492, 494, 502–503
Participant observer, in interpersonal psychoanalysis, 164, 171, 174
Pathogenesis: and psychoanalysis, 13–14, 19; and psychoanalysis in groups, 335
Person-centered therapy. See Client-centered therapy
Persona, in Jungian analysis, 126, 135
Personality: constructive, 145, 155; and culture, 144–145; in interpersonal psychoanalysis, 161–162, 166; in Jungian analysis, 125–128
Phenobarbital, for Raynaud's disease, 293
Phenylzene (Nardil), in psychopharmacology, 316, 321, 322

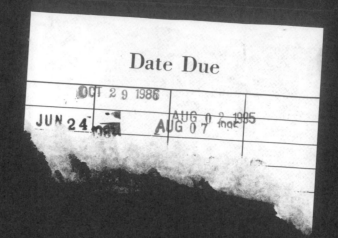